INSIDE SOUTH AMERICA

INSIDE

SOUTH

AMERICA

JOHN GUNTHER

HARPER & ROW, PUBLISHERS

NEW YORK, EVANSTON, AND LONDON

This book is dedicated to
HOBART LEWIS
with the broadest possible esteem
over many years

SOUTH AMERICA
— Author's Route

Those who make peaceful revolution impossible will make violent revolution inevitable.

—JOHN F. KENNEDY

There is absolutely no doubt in my mind that revolution is inevitable in Latin America . . . only the form it takes is uncertain.

—MILTON S. EISENHOWER

We have seen the light and it is not our desire to be thrust back into darkness.

—SIMÓN BOLÍVAR IN THE 1820'S

Contents

MAPS

Foreword

Our wine is bitter, but it is ours.
—JOSÉ MARTÍ

THIS, THE EIGHTH Inside book, joins its predecessors like *Inside U.S.A.* and *Inside Africa* in a series designed to describe the known political world of today continent by continent. I have written about Latin America before but this new book, *Inside South America*, is a totally fresh work following a long, arduous, and comprehensive recent trip through the ten South American republics. It is not in any sense a revision or updating of the old book, *Inside Latin America*, which was published as long ago as 1941, and bears no relation to its predecessor except that it necessarily deals with ten of the same countries. But, although this new *Inside South America* has been written altogether from scratch, I pick up passages here and there from the older book and paraphrase a paragraph or two. After all I still have to mention that Brazil is big.

The continent has changed vastly since my visit twenty-five years ago on the eve of American participation in World War II. In the early 1940's the principal preoccupation of hemisphere foreign policy was something that seems today as remote as Nebuchadnezzar—fear of Nazi invasion and Fascist overturn, actively directed by Germany. Today we have the threat of Communist agitation and the possibility of subversion and indigenous overturn, but Moscow is pursuing an official hands-off policy and China is far away. In the 1940's most of South America was frozen into a kind of derelict immobility in domestic affairs, punctuated by sporadic "revolutions" which meant little but temporary shifts in political power; today nearly the entire continent is in a state of active flux, grasping for a future, with fundamental, yeasty impulses for change apparent almost everywhere. The key word is advance.

Tempo is what counts, and the pace of South America is both fast and slow—a difficult paradox, and one of the factors that makes the continent so hard to write about. Contrasts are sharp as well as perplexing, and there are two—or more—sides to almost everything.

These are some of the basic questions we must face:

Is the United States finished in South America?
How well is the Alliance for Progress working?
Is Castro's influence on the decline? What about Communism?
Why do the South Americans change governments so often?
What about army, church, and the population explosion?
Is anything being done seriously to ameliorate one of the most vital and piercing of all South American problems, that of narrowing the gap between rich and poor?
Who or what runs each country, and what do they need most?

This book, unlike its predecessor, does not deal with Latin America at large, but restricts itself to the continent of *South* America, the ten mainland countries below the Panama Canal—field enough. I do not include Mexico, Central America, the Caribbean islands, or the Guianas.[1] But I will have to use the term "Latin America" frequently to indicate the context within which I am writing, or by way of general reference. The name "Cuba" will appear often enough in these pages, to say nothing of "Dominican Republic," with all its unhappy connotations.

The ten countries which I deal with in full form a remarkable constellation—Argentina, Bolivia, Brazil, Chile, Colombia, Ecuador, Paraguay (a long alphabetical gap there between "E" and "P"), Peru, Uruguay, and Venezuela. Although they form an obviously compact geographical unit, they differ widely from one another. The diversity within South America is spectacular, even if all ten republics have roughly the same historical origin, cultural development, and religion, and nine of the ten speak the same language. Consider Paraguay and Uruguay, which are neighboring buffer states between Argentina and Brazil. But Paraguay is a medieval backwater run by an anachronistic military dictator, whereas Uruguay, with its highly advanced social services and a free democratic development, resembles Switzerland or Denmark. Or take cities. São Paulo

[1] I did not visit the Guianas because I was limiting myself to independent states. British Guiana became free under the name Guyana in May, 1966, too late for inclusion in this work. French and Dutch Guiana (Surinam), are still linked to their mother nations.

in Brazil, the eighth-largest and the fastest-growing city in the world, with a population above 4,500,000 and more than that by the time you have finished reading this page, is as different from Quito, the remote jewel-box capital of Ecuador, as Chicago is from Marrakesh.

I have sought to give banisters to the reader by means of several maps and a chart. But statistics are not reliable in South America, and this difficulty is compounded by tricky pitfalls as between "Latin" and "South." In prewar Japan the person of the Emperor was considered too sacrosanct to be touched, even by his tailor, who had to estimate measurements while standing respectfully several yards away. The journalist today is often put to the same kind of comic inconvenience when he tries to obtain accurate figures on South America.

Some Elements in Ignorance

Somehow the people of the United States will do anything for Latin America except read about it.

—JAMES RESTON

South America lies close to us physically (but we should keep in mind that the eastern tip of Brazil is nearer Africa than it is to Miami or New York), but most North Americans do not know it well. It has prodigious importance to the United States in politics, strategy, trade, investment, what not, but it does not lie close to us emotionally. Many in the United States still think of South America as an alien continent; some view it with a vague—or even active—distaste. We do not, by and large, feel the same community of interest and affection that we have for Europe. And—let me add quickly—the distrust felt by North Americans toward South Americans is fully reciprocated by plenty of them in their attitude to *us.* They think that we are often juvenile, materialistic, crude in manners, uncultured, politically capricious, and overbearing.

Ignorance plays a large role in this on both sides. What we do know we are apt to know wrong. To many in the United States the concept "South America" still prominently includes generals in white sombreros on mangy horses picking their teeth and shooting peasants at random, love in the hot sun, polo ponies, a peculiar capacity for disorganization, the philosophy of *mañana,* llamas, cha-cha-cha, excessive edgy pride and sensitiveness, gigolos drenched in eau de cologne, the overemotionalism of personal contacts, Indians squatting over dark pots of beans, *gauchos,* and fragile young women in black lace dresses with large red roses in their hair leaning over grilled balconies within range of a serenading guitar.

South America is off the beaten track, still terra incognita. Timbuctoo is

more familiar to most Americans, if only as a symbol, than thriving
hemisphere cities like Medellín, Córdoba, or the new industrial complexes of
Venezuela. Such a distinguished and otherwise cosmopolitan man of letters
as Edmund Wilson makes a point of never having visited the continent or
read its literature. We have seen King Tutankhamen's tomb, but not
Pizarro's body still visible under glass in Lima, Peru, and looking rather like
yesterday's turkey with a few bones sticking through the cracked skin. South
America lies "on the margin of history." There are no more than eight
references to it in the index of the H. G. Wells *Outline of History*, first
published in 1920 and 1,288 pages long; a comparable contemporary book,
The Rise of the West by William H. McNeill, similarly has exactly eight
such entries for 829 large pages. Nor do we receive South American news adequately on a day-to-day basis. The *New York Times* and *Christian Science
Monitor* do their best, but it is by no means easy for a reader in the United
States to keep fully abreast of what is going on in the hemisphere, and vice
versa. More on this later.

Visitors to the continent below us should brace themselves for several
shocks—and not merely because there are still hotels in Chile that never
heard of an American Express check. Among the first overriding and in-
escapable characteristics are poverty, backwardness, and lack of development. The average per capita income is only $269 a year, compared to
$2,975 in the United States, and the whole area, including all ten coun-
tries, is statistically classified as being "underdeveloped"—the only continent *all* of which is underdeveloped even though it comprises half the
western hemisphere. What makes the impression sharper is a preposterous
and shameful inequality of means. Two percent of the people of Latin
America own 70 percent of the wealth. Rich men ship out hundreds of
millions of dollars a year to secret bank accounts in Switzerland and New
York, while peasants in the sterile hills or squatters in the shanty towns
have to live on 40 cents a day—or less.

In Brazil I talked about plans for this book with a friend, and he
exclaimed, "Give us a jab now and then!" I hope I am not overdoing it, but
listen—

In Bolivia prisoners in the public jails are not fed; their families feed
them, or they starve. In the continent as a whole 40 million people need
housing; the shortage of units is between 12 and 14 million. Only 43 percent
of the population of Montevideo, generally regarded as a progressive city, has
any access to a sewage system. Only three capitals out of ten have safe
drinking water, and literally millions of citizens in all ten countries are
drastically short of water. The town of Cuzco, Peru, up in the Andes, where

Indians still live in the Stone Age, has a 40 percent mortality rate up to the age of four, and 20 percent of *all* children in Brazil die in their first year, largely because of diseases spread by filth. Smallpox is still "entrenched" in Brazil, Peru, and Colombia. Doctors are in short supply.

Half the farmland of Brazil is in the hands of 1.6 percent of owners, and there are only 14,000 passenger automobiles in Bolivia, a huge country. Only 2 percent of the gross national product of South America as a whole goes to education, and the over-all illiteracy rate is close to 50 percent. Only 15 percent of adolescents of high school age attend school, as against 90 percent in the United States, and there are some 15 million children of primary school age who do not go to school at all because there are no schools available.

Take communications. Paraguay, which looks like a small blot on the map but which is the size of California, has not more than 450 miles of paved road. Par for the course for airmail delivery between Buenos Aires and Santiago, Chile, is around five days, although the two cities are only two hours apart by plane. One rail journey in Brazil between cities only a thousand miles apart takes a week—if the train is running. Or consider political stability. Argentina had till very recently 222 different political parties, believe it or not, and Venezuela has had more than 100 revolutions in a century and a half. Chile, although it is the most enlightened country on the continent, once had 8 presidents in 18 months. Bolivia has had 179 changes of government in 126 years, and Paraguay had 39 different heads of state between 1870 and 1954.

I have used the word "revolution" in the preceding paragraph and Latin America is, indeed, widely known for the bewildering frequency, variety, and raucous color of its so-called revolutions. *But in plain truth most of these revolutions are not revolutions at all.* They are no more than barracks revolts or capriciously forced substitutions in personnel, carrying no basic or permanent weight, and effecting none but superficial changes—outs replacing ins, or ins quarreling with other ins. Mexico, it is true, had a real revolution, resulting in a genuine transfer of power, in the years following 1911, but this is beyond the province of this book, as is Castro's revolution in Cuba, which was also genuine. The nearest to an authentic revolution in any republic on the South American continent itself came in Bolivia in the early 1950's, but it petered out.

Bloody tyrants have been cast down, and both Perón and Vargas made seminal changes in their respective countries, Argentina and Brazil. But most other of the innumerable changes in government that have afflicted South America in recent years were mere *Putsches* or coups d'état. So the question that now arises—are genuine revolutions in the offing?—has a special significance. Is South America in a true pre-revolutionary stage? We will explore.

On the Job

Of course I visited and saw at first hand intensively the ten countries I write about. The route my wife and I took included Venezuela, Brazil, a hop across the Andes, up the west coast, and over the Andes several times again until we reached Colombia at the top. I had the good luck in Chile of rounding Cape Horn in an American Navy DC-3, after a trip to Tierra del Fuego, a segment of the earth's surface not often seen, and we had the further good fortune of skimming the Amazon in a nautical craft like a dragonfly 2,300 miles upriver at Iquitos—and sliding over an alligator.

Of the ten presidents of the countries we visited I met and interviewed all. Altogether we took notes of conversations with 722 people, counting husband-and-wife teams as one,[2] and sometimes we had a moment or two off from politics. We had a glimpse of a voodoo ceremony in Brazil, and inspected its marvelous golden scimitars of beach. We went to night clubs, casinos, and the lowest of *boîtes* as well as palaces, and had fabulous things to eat and drink with enlivening hosts of every category. We studied trade union statistics in Buenos Aires, and managed to see as well the grave and compelling Inca uplands of Peru.

What I have sought to do, country by country, is to describe each and tell what it is really *like* in a series of national profiles, as well as outline the major problems that carry across the entire continent—revolution, politics, land reform, inflation, population pressure, urbanization, industrialization, hemisphere relationships, American policy, the Communist position, and changes in the status of oligarchy, church, and army. Most of these factors are touched on three times, (a) in reference to Brazil, because Brazil is a separate world of its own; (b) in general in Chapters 7 and 8; and (c) in relation specifically to each country aside from Brazil. No one can doubt that South America is in transition—the question is to what. I do not promise easy answers, but at least we can have a look—perhaps keeping in mind John F. Kennedy's emphatic remark that Latin America is more crucial to us than any region in the world.

So we plunge now into the broad and brilliant maelstrom of Brazil, and thus begin this circumnavigation of a continent.

[2] These 722 were divided as follows: United States 56, Venezuela 53, Brazil 117, Uruguay 31, Paraguay 21, Argentina 107, Chile 121, Peru 99, Bolivia 36, Ecuador 22, Colombia 59.

INSIDE SOUTH AMERICA

CHAPTER 1

Brazil, a Piebald Mastodon

Brazil is the land of the future—and always will be.
—CARIOCA PROVERB

We progress at night when the politicians sleep.
—BRAZILIAN SAYING

MULTIFORM, variegated, prodigious, Brazil is one of the most spectacular of countries, the fifth-largest nation in the world, bigger than the continental United States, packed with bizarre characteristics and luminous with color. But its president at the moment of writing, Marshal Castelo Branco, is a man totally without flamboyance, as is Marshal Artur da Costa e Silva, who is scheduled to succeed him in the spring of 1967. Both are as homely as darned socks, although Costa e Silva is a more emphatic personality—a King Canute in dark glasses.

Presently I will attempt to describe these two dominant characters, together with other Brazilian men of affairs, and I will deal with a sheaf of cities too—like Rio de Janeiro, the *Cidade Maravilhosa*, and São Paulo, a kind of Detroit rising in glass and steel on a bed of red dirt and orchids. But first we must draw a broad general picture of Brazil's size and limitations, its overpowering physical presence, its fascinating racial mix, its energy and profuse charm and challenge for the future.

And we must deal with urgent and immediate political affairs as well, the transformation now going on whereby Brazil, a reasonably free democratic republic until yesterday, is becoming rapidly a military dictatorship, largely because of an almost morbid fear, justified or not, of Communism. If present trends continue, free expression by the people will soon become impossible under a tawdry regime which will go to almost any length to impede the restoration of normal political procedures in order to avoid losing its own

1

powers—and which dresses itself to look better than it is and has the cordial support of the United States.

*

Brazil is unique on the continent from several points of view quite aside from its sheer bigness and brilliance. (1) It is, as everybody should know (but not everybody does), Portuguese-speaking, not Spanish. (2) Alone among South American countries it was a monarchy until late in the last century. (3) It has come nearer to solving the racial problem than any comparable nation, and most of its people, although of differing stock, live together in *convivência*, harmony. (4) It gained independence without warfare, and has never had a revolution marked by serious bloodshed. (5) It has never had overt dictatorial government in the modern period except during the regime of Getúlio Vargas, who first gained power in 1930 and was a special case, although the present government pushes this close today.[1]

Brazilian problems are many and several have compelling magnitude; the most important is development. The country has been nicely described as a continent with its colonies inside it, and its basic national need is to develop the interior. More than 70 percent of the people live in a narrow strip of territory along the coast, hugging the fringe of the Atlantic. The situation is roughly comparable to that in the United States when our frontier was steadily being pressed westward, except that the Brazilians haven't pressed so hard. The chief recent frontier development is the creation of the new capital, Brasília, which cost $600 million and looks like an incandescent dream out of science fiction, deep in the interior.

We might as well face at the outset some of the more devastating statistics. The country is not less than 50 percent illiterate, a fact which has interesting political consequences in that illiterates do not have the right to vote. Only about 5 percent of its total arable land is under cultivation; this is a nation suffering from underexploitation as well as the reverse. The gross national product is only about $14 billion,[2] and the average per capita income is less than $200 per year. The rate of infant mortality is appalling, about 16 percent of births. Life expectancy is 46 for women, 40 for men, compared to an average of 69.4 in the United States. Malnutrition is one of the gravest of national embarrassments.

And yet Brazil, with its twenty-two states, is fabulously rich—the first

[1] President Vargas ruled from 1930 to 1945 and again from 1951 to 1954. More on him below.

[2] The gross national product of the U.S. is above $600 billion.

nation in the world in the production of coffee, the second in corn, cane
sugar, and cocoa, the third in tobacco. Although predominantly agricultural,
it has thirty-two cities with 100,000 people or more. It contains one-third of
the total reserves of iron ore in the world, and is uncommonly well-stocked
with other minerals, all the way from gold to nickel.[3] It has 16 percent of
the world's forest, the world's greatest hydroelectric potential, the biggest
steel industry in South America, and fantastic wealth in semiprecious stones.
It is the eighth country in the world in automobile production, and the
second in volume of air traffic.

Why should a country so rich be so poor? One answer is bad government.

On an immediate level, aside from modernization at large, the principal Brazilian problems are—

1. Economic troubles, including a ravaging inflation. The shortage of
foreign exchange is acute, because the country's agricultural exports do not
bring enough revenue to pay for essential imports, like the petroleum necessary for industrialization. The climb in the price level, which rose by a
terrifying 87 percent in 1964, has led to important events. The present government, under the stimulus of Dr. Roberto Campos, one of the ablest men
in South America, is doing its best to be rigidly deflationary, and the inflation
rate fell to 45 percent in 1965. But, even though this improved the basic
financial situation, it made the government unpopular with many. Deflationary governments are seldom popular.

2. An extremely difficult political situation. Three different "elections" had
to be scheduled late in 1966 so that the government could the more readily
maintain itself in power. When Castelo Branco took office in 1964 after
a military coup d'état he earnestly hoped to be able to "reconstitutionalize"
the regime, i.e., restore democratic or quasi-democratic processes, but he
failed. A single government party now controls almost all political activity,
and nobody can easily run for office without government approval. Indirect
elections ensure the victory of "official candidates," and Congress appears to
be on the way to becoming a rubber stamp. Effective opposition has been ex-
tinguished, and may remain so for many years. People grumble, but are
helpless.

3. Breaking up feudal patterns and alleviating hardship in the northeast,
which depends on land reform, a situation in which United States aid and
technical assistance are playing a helpful role.

4. Such basic factors as poverty and illiteracy.

5. Corruption. I will allude to this in passages to follow.

---

[3] But coal is scant and of poor quality.

The Behemoth

Now let us explore further—still by way of introduction. The most important nation in South America, Brazil is bigger than any country in the world except the United States (with Alaska), the Soviet Union, Canada, and China; with more than 3,200,000 square miles, it covers roughly 6 percent of the surface of the globe. It is the biggest country in the world speaking a Latin language, and the biggest Roman Catholic country. It has "the most extensive river system and the greatest mileage of navigable waterways in the world,"[4] the world's biggest swamp area, the world's largest and densest rain forest, and, just to come down to earth, the largest per capita foreign debt in the world; it owes the United States alone more than a billion dollars.

The nonstop flight from New York to Rio, 8½ to 9 hours, is somewhat long—even to seasoned travelers on seasoned jets; if the flight goes by way of Belém *half* the total distance will be over Brazilian territory. Rio is closer to Madrid than to Chicago.[5] The country has three states larger than Texas—Amazonas, Mato Grosso, and Pará—which should startle those of us, like me, brought up to believe that nothing in the world was as big as Texas. Maranhão, which most North Americans have never heard of, is the size of Italy, and the territory of Amapá, which I do not think anybody has ever heard of, is as big as France. But population is astonishingly thin in these areas—Amapá has fewer than 60,000 people. Bananal on the great Araguaia River is the largest fluvial island in the world, and at the mouth of the Amazon is Marajó, an island as big as Switzerland or Belgium.

Consider too some comparisons to the rest of South America. Brazil covers roughly one-half of the total area of the continent, and is three times bigger than Argentina, the next country in size. The state of São Paulo alone is bigger than any other South American country, Argentina excepted. The state of Amazonas is as big as Mexico (but its population is less than that of Milwaukee). Moreover, the geographical position of Brazil is such that, with 14,000 miles of continuous land frontier, it impinges on every other South American country except Ecuador and Chile. Another reason for its intense strategic importance is that it has 4,600 miles of coastline, and its swollen eastern hump reaches out into the Atlantic to a point only 1,600 miles from

[4] Gilberto Freyre, *Brazil*, p. 69. Also see *South American Handbook*, an invaluable guide which I have used throughout the whole course of this book, p. 599.
[5] Cf. *An Atlas of American Affairs*, by Robert C. Kingsbury and Ronald M. Schneider.

Africa. Thousands of United States officers and G.I.'s in World War II will remember crossing the Atlantic en route to Africa or the Mediterranean front by way of Natal or other ports in Brazil, because this was the shortest and least dangerous practicable route. Natal enjoyed this process. I think it was the widest-open town I ever had the good luck to visit.

With its fabulous combination of plateau-jungle-coastline Brazil has several outstanding physical characteristics aside from its sheer bulk and size. Actually it is not as "tropical" as is generally assumed, except in the Amazon regions and along the coast in summer, and even the Amazon bush is not always particularly hot. Snow sometimes falls in the south. The seasons are, of course, inverted from the North American point of view; our summer is Brazil's winter, our autumn is its spring. One local saying is that the weather "comes from the south"; rain is plentiful up to the center of the country, but nothing is left over for the north, which suffers from periodic severe droughts—an economic and political factor of formidable consequence.

Then too, Brazilians like to say, their mountains are all in the wrong places. An escarpment hugs the coast, which means that there is no room for a true coastal plain—only a narrow shelf—and this, from the beginning of Brazilian history, has hampered communication and penetration into the interior. A vast plateau stretches inland, part of which is known as the *sertão*, backlands. Some areas in the deep interior, populated by primitive Indians, have never been explored even to this day; some are not yet adequately mapped. An aerial survey is going on. The chief natural wonder of Brazil at large is, of course, the Amazon, of which more hereafter. Something else impressive, far away from the Amazon in the deep south, is the Iguassú Falls, which Brazil shares with Argentina and Paraguay, and which are more familiar under their Spanish name, Iguazú. One of the great sights of the hemisphere, these are almost two miles wide, higher than Niagara, and, to some eyes, more beautiful.

Communications throughout most of Brazil, except by air, are like some fearful dream touched by comedy. The whole immense pachyderm of a country has only 23,000 miles of railroad,[6] and the trains puff and whistle on five different gauges. The trip between Rio and Bahia, over a distance roughly that between New York and Des Moines, which can be done in about two hours by plane, takes three *days* by train—if the train is running—with three changes of railroad. The mileage of paved roads is only 6,417, less than that in the environs of a big city in the United States. Unpaved roads are like the Verdun battlefield. The mail service is fantastically unreliable. Nobody seems to know what postal rates are, and mailboxes are few and

[6] The United States has 214,387, the Soviet Union about 76,000.

irregularly emptied. On Copacabana beach, in the heart of metropolitan Rio, we slipped a card into the top of an overstuffed box; we could still see it there three days later. Yet Brazilian irregularity, dash, and charm operate even in these realms. Writing to a friend in Rio from New York I made a mistake and did not give his full address. The letter duly came back from the Rio post office (after eleven weeks) with the envelope marked in a bold penciled hand, "What the street!"

And telegrams! The American Embassy in Rio cannot establish contact with its own consulate-general in Recife, a city of more than a million people, except by a device equivalent to ham radio. My wife and I sent five telegrams from Brasília, the new capital, via the national telegraph on a Tuesday morning to friends in Salvador, Bahia, and Recife announcing our impending arrival in these great cities. We reached Salvador on the Thursday and Recife the following Monday and beat all five.

*

Development is, of course, taking place in Brazil; indeed its pace is spectacular in some fields, particularly industrialization, although there are plenty of citizens who laugh it off or say, "Oh, wait a year or two." One factor making the country so difficult to understand—and so fascinating—is that physical development does not necessarily proceed in the order made familiar by the United States. We progressed from train to car to airplane. But in Brazil exactly the reverse is true—the progression is airplane-automobile-train. The local air services are swift, frequent, comprehensive, and, in general, admirably run, even if procedures are apt to be helter-skelter. Varig is the fifth-biggest airline in the world, and Brazil invented the shuttle with its Rio–São Paulo flights, which run every half hour. Another fruitful phenomenon is the growth of cities. Belo Horizonte, the capital of Minas Gerais state, did not exist sixty-five years ago, and is bigger than Denver today. Londrina in the state of Paraná was not to be found on a map a quarter of a century ago, but its current population is 150,000. And think of Brasília!

The People

With more than 80 million people—about half the population of all South America—Brazil is the eighth most populous country in the world. The rate of growth, 3.4 percent, is extravagantly high, and the population has quadrupled since 1900. Demographers predict, moreover, that this colossus will have one hundred million people by 1970, *two hundred million* by the year 2000. But nobody I met in Brazil appeared to be much troubled by statistics so staggering in their potential consequences—although the abortion rate is admittedly disturbing. There are an estimated 1.2 million illegal abortions a year, compared to 4.5 million live births.

The line generally taken is that a better distribution of population, not the velocity of its rise, is the basic demographic problem, but this is a dubious statement. Much of Brazil, the authorities say, is still empty, and could easily contain a population of 900 million or even more, but nobody seemed able to explain what they would get to eat. What is needed most urgently is to get people off the edge of the sea, where they cling like periwinkles, and settle them into the interior. But how?

Indeed the virginal emptiness of the Brazilian interior is startling. Anybody flying the direct overland route from Caracas to Rio will find that, for mile after mile, hour after hour, there is not a house to be seen: not a farm, not a road, not a fence, not a light at night—nothing but untracked bush or forest. But the mere fact that the country has room for expansion does not, of course, solve its fundamental problems, no matter what the Brazilians, so often blinded by euphoria, like to say. If I had just one generalization to make about Brazilians it would be that they are the most optimistic people on earth, a pleasant trait, but one known to lead to wishful thinking.

The most interesting characteristic about the population is its mixed racial nature. The country is, the best statistics have it (but statistics are not very finite in Brazil), 60 percent white, 15 percent Negro, and 25 percent half-caste. But "white" is an extremely loose and indeterminate term; there are all manner of varieties of white, ranging from cream and alabaster to deepest olive; actually a great many "whites" have a touch at least of Negro blood. There are also some half a million surviving Indians, the *pardos* or "browns"; of these about fifty thousand in the deep interior have never been reached by a census or other appurtenances of modern civilization. Then too, at the other end of the spectrum, there are prosperous, modern-minded colonies of Italians, Germans, Poles, and above all Japanese, who live mostly in the São Paulo district or in the south.

The original whites, the sixteenth-century settlers and traders, included Frenchmen and Spaniards, but were predominantly Portuguese; this is a Portuguese country *par excellence*, although it is Portuguese in a special Brazilian way. The original Negroes were imported from Africa as slaves to work the sugar plantations, as in the West Indies. They were Africans mostly of healthy stock, coming from the western Sudan and Angola, which is still part of the Portuguese domain and has been called the "black mother" of Brazil. The Negroes brought not only their color but their religious pantheon, their superstitions and complicated relation to the supernatural, their voodoo, their folkways and roll of drums, their dances and habits in food and drink, all of which have strongly tinted Brazil ever since. They even brought a certain amount of Muslim influence, as many Sudanese were Islamic converts.[7] Altogether some three and a half million African Negroes arrived in Brazil between 1500 and 1800, and the population became sharply polarized between white master and Negro slave.

But not for long. As Dr. Freyre tells the story, "miscegenation broke up the culture of the two extremes." The Portuguese had no aversion to physical contact with the African women, made attractive by their "hot and oleous air"; indeed the contrary was true, and a large mulatto population came promptly into being and has expanded ever since. One old saying is that "the Portuguese used white women for marriage, mulattoes for sex, Negroes for work." A variant of this is the description of seventeenth-century Brazil as "a hell for blacks, a purgatory for whites, and a paradise for mulattoes."[8]

Today Brazil is as mixed as a bag of marbles, with innumerable complicated crosses. The principal term used as the equivalent for the Spanish *mestizo* (half-caste) is *mameluco*. Aside from the mulattoes (black and white) there are those born of white and Indian (*caboclos*) and Negro and Indian (*curibocas*); many people blend all three strains. A quadroon is sometimes known as a *cabrocha*. Then too in one small area there are, as an example, *chulos*, with "crisp rolled hair and skin the color of burnt sugar or tobacco," and *cabo verdes*, black but with straight hair, together with three other different types of mixed people.[9] Color is deceptive. A man white as white will tell you that he has a Negro grandmother.

There have been two mulatto presidents in the modern period, including a man with the remarkable name João Café Filho (Junior), who succeeded Vargas in 1954; the other was Nilo Peçanha (1909–10). Both these were, however, vice presidents who succeeded to the presidential office when this was suddenly vacated. A good many other politicians and men of affairs have

---

[7] As a matter of fact Islamic influence in Brazil converges from double roots, because many of the early Portuguese had Moorish blood. Gilberto Freyre, the foremost Brazilian anthropologist-sociologist-historian, whose great book, *The Masters and the Slaves*, is one of the most germinal works of its kind ever written, makes a point of this. Brazil became "subject to the sensual mysticism of Islam." Freyre's book had the impact it did largely because it woke Brazil up to the reality of its own racial origins, and made citizens less sensitive about being members of a mixed society. It broke a taboo.

[8] Charles R. Boxer, *The Golden Age of Brazil*, p. 1.

[9] Charles Wagley, *An Introduction to Brazil*, p. 133, quoting Marvin Harris, *Town and Country in Brazil*.

been of mixed blood. The first Roman Catholic cardinal ever to be appointed in Latin America, by name Arcoverde, claimed descent from an Indian princess, like Pocahontas. The man who would be ranked by most of his countrymen as the most celebrated living Brazilian today, the soccer player Pelé (full name Edson Arantes do Nascimento), is a Negro. Going back into history there is the renowned sculptor Aleijadinho (Little Cripple), a mulatto. Having lost the use of his hands, he continued to create works of art by tying tools to his withered arms; his superb religious sculptures, still to be seen at Ouro Prêto, the old gold-rush town in Minas Gerais, are one of the glories of Brazil. The best-known Brazilian novelist of recent years, Machado de Assis, was the son of a Negro laundress; other eminent writers of mixed blood have been the poets Gonçalves Dias (partly Indian) and Cruz de Souza. Mario de Andrade, an essayist and novelist who cardinally stimulated contemporary Brazilian literature, was a half-caste.

Today Negroes live by and large in northern Brazil rather than in the south, and are most numerous in the rural areas originally devoted to sugar plantations, like Bahia and the northeast, though large numbers have drifted in recent years into the big cities. A physician in São Paulo told me that, in his youth, he had never once seen a Negro until he took a trip north to Salvador. But there are mulattoes almost everywhere.

In a word, Brazilian blandness and tolerance have served to produce what is probably the most successful society of its kind in the world, a melting pot that really melted, astonishingly free from racial prejudice. People are, in the words of Dr. Freyre, "hybrid, but harmonious." In anthropological jargon it is not a "plural" society, which means people of different races living amicably together, but not intermingling; it is a genuinely "mixed" society produced by miscegenation. Some authorities go so far as to say that, as a result, the Brazilians are a new type of "race," which serves to explain not merely their immense vitality but their "temperateness, sense of balance, and acceptance of reality."

Racial tension is at the minimum, and there has never been a race riot in Brazil.[10] A Brazilian family may have children by the same father and mother who range in color from dark amber to white. On Copacabana beach men and women of every conceivable shade of color mingle freely. Negro children go to school on equal terms with whites (if schools are available at all) and Negroes have perfect freedom to vote provided that they are literate. The literacy qualification applies to whites as well. Racial issues seldom, if ever, reach the political level, and the expression of political or economic

---

[10] Fodor's *Guide to South America*, which is particularly good on Brazil, p. 446.

discontent *on a color basis* is virtually unknown. Jorge Amado, the distinguished Bahia novelist, summed up the matter when he said to us, "There is no racial problem here for the simplest of reasons, namely that we are all mulattoes."

But—and it is a big but—discrimination does certainly exist, even if outright segregation doesn't. Comparatively few marriages take place these days between pure whites and blacks. Most slum dwellers are Negro or mixed. There are few Negroes in the best clubs, in the diplomatic service, or among officers of the armed forces. Negro surgeons and dentists, if any, serve their own communities. A honey-colored blonde will have a better chance than a mulatto of winning a beauty contest if the jury is white. *American* Negroes visiting Brazil often encounter unpleasant instances of discrimination in hotels and so on. The darker the skin, the worse the treatment. Economic bias against local Negroes is particularly severe, and want-ads ask pointedly for "light-skinned help." Negroes become relegated to the lowest class of work in the big cities—street sweepers, manual laborers, garbage collectors—and only an infinitesimal few become rich, whereupon these few may become "accepted." There is nothing like money to whiten the skin, as the Brazilian adage has it.

*

A word about the Indians. The Portuguese, unlike the Spaniards, were not martial conquerors; most of the early Indians melted away largely because of malnutrition and disease, notably syphilis, which European whites brought into the western hemisphere. Not remotely do the survivors resemble those in Peru, Ecuador, and Bolivia, where the inert, oppressed, and impoverished Indians form a huge unassimilated mass and are an indigestible problem.

Most Brazilian Indians today live in isolation in the upper reaches of the Amazon and its great tributaries, like the Xingú, and in the interior of states like Mato Grosso only partially explored. Many are as primitive as the Stone Age men in New Guinea, and some—wearing lip plates or tusks in their noses and devoted to cannibalism and ancestor worship—startlingly resemble Bantu or Negro tribesmen in Central Africa, except that they are brown in color.

There are 240 different Indian tribes in Brazil, and they speak more than 30 different languages, despite their small number. Serious efforts to protect and "renovate" them are a comparatively recent development. A pioneer in this was the anthropologist-mystic-explorer General Cândido Rondon, who was three-quarters Indian himself, and under whom the Indian Protective

Service was organized in 1910. It was Rondon, as a young man, who accompanied Theodore Roosevelt on his remarkable journey up the Amazon in
1913 during which the "River of Doubt" was discovered in the basin of the
Madeira. Rondon died in 1958 at the age of ninety-two, a legendary figure
and a hero to his countrymen.

Aspects of the National Character

The visitor to Brazil discovers soon that this is a country in which nothing
quite works or fits. The hotel stationery is too big for its matching envelope
by an eighth of an inch. Telephone service is such that on one occasion a
man in Rio, trying to reach a number six blocks away, is supposed to have
given up in despair at last—and routed the call via New York, whereupon it
came through. A favorite word is *bagunça*, which means "a mess," "confusion" or "disorder." "Brazil," Peter Fleming wrote once, "is a subcontinent
with imperfect self control."

The tempo of Rio is slow, except for automobile traffic—cars fairly chase
pedestrians down the street, and I do not think I have ever seen traffic jams
so convulsed. Disciplinary action against traffic offenders may take summary
and novel forms; for instance, if a car is improperly parked the cops may
simply let the air out of the tires. This does not allay congestion, but it
mightily impresses the errant driver. A popular slogan having to do with
traffic accidents is, "Don't go home dead—your wife may be disappointed."[11]

A principal constituent of Brazilian character is charm, and this in turn
depends to a degree on softness, on the gift of being easygoing. "We have
two thousand laws, but none to say we should obey the law," is a proverb.
Brazil compares to Argentina, with its harsh rigidities, as Austria compared
to prewar Germany. A Brazilian, hearing that some sort of coup is going on
in the streets, will telephone his wife, if he can find a telephone, "There's a
revolution—I may be late for dinner." And of course nobody would ever be
so vulgar or inept as to make a revolution during carnival or on the day of a
really big soccer game.

The connoisseur of social patterns in Rio will soon become aware of the
word *jeito*, which means a way out of a situation, or an unorthodox solution

[11] In the event of a traffic accident everybody concerned *runs away* from the
scene as quickly as possible, even a bus driver, who may leave his bus stranded.
This is because an offender caught "in flagrancy," or as a direct participant in an
act, is not, if arrested, allowed bail by Brazilian law. Of course the police find out
in time who the miscreant is, but by that time the offender will have a lawyer
and the case will probably be fixed.

to a problem—a fix. This symbolizes the national desire for accommodation and mild hypocrisy. The word also means favor. If you get an advantage but have to pay for it, it is not true *jeito*. Another universal phenomenon is *jôgo do bicho*, a kind of numbers game based on animals. I heard it solemnly averred that the real reason why telephones are so fantastically overloaded in Rio is that everybody is calling everybody else up all the time about this game, or lottery. *Jôgo do bicho*, I was assured, is the only completely honest institution in Brazil; nobody can corrupt it and anybody who tries will meet an evil end. Of course the joker involved in this is that the game is illegal!—and the police sometimes threaten to stamp it out. This is considered by the vast bulk of the population to be nothing more than laughable bad manners.

Brazilians are optimistic, pliable, full of panache, tolerant, jovial, generous, often melancholy, and the friendliest people on earth—also sloppy. A Peruvian once gave me an explanation of this: "Brazilians *have* to be good-humored in order to be able to bear the affronts and indignities imposed on them by their own politicians, to be able to endure their lot."

Threats of public disorder came after the Vargas suicide in 1954, and army tanks were dispatched to control the situation. These could not, however, manage to get through the traffic; photographs exist showing tanks hopelessly snarled up by civilian automobiles—a comedy performance. The tanks reached their destination eventually and, in front of the presidential palace, found that rival tanks had already arrived there. The enemy crews then proceeded to play football together, using their tanks to mark the goals. In September, 1963, an army unit received an order to break up a public meeting in the suburbs being addressed by Carlos Lacerda, the governor, and to arrest him forthwith on a political complaint. This unit was held up by the usual storm of traffic and reached the meeting after Lacerda had gone. Nobody bothered to follow him and he went scot-free. But a parachutist officer who leaked news of this episode to the press was disciplined by being sent to a remote garrison in the hinterland.

Brazilians seldom harbor grudges. They just don't give a damn. President Vargas once made an official visit to São Paulo in order to dedicate a street named for the occasion of one of his own big defeats. Nothing is ever last-ditch in Brazil. Like warlords in the old China, the politicians play for time, seldom take an unalterable line, always keep an avenue of escape open, maintain access, and buy each other off.

One pleasant characteristic is an extreme ease of relationship among social classes. Brazilians love children, pets, and even their wives and husbands. Nowhere are masters on better terms with servants, and vice versa; for a maid to call the lady of the household by her first name is a commonplace, although it may be preceded by "Dona" or "Senhora." Names are, in other realms, a source of much confusion, if only because family names are in extremely short supply. There are Oliveiras, da Silvas, Vianas, Cunhas, Costas, Andrades almost without number among the old families; Brazilian history is festooned from the earliest days with names still conspicuous today, like Peixoto, Teixeira, Vasconcelos, and Castro Alves. The confusion is such that official rosters in embassies often list people by their Christian names. Portuguese custom is, incidentally, to put the mother's name in the middle, not at the end as in Spanish. Politicians are almost always known popularly by their given names or diminutives.

Brazilian blandness, *Gemütlichkeit*, and dislike of being hurried do not mean a lack of spirit. Navy and air force once had a "battle," with gunfire and all, between rival pilots claiming jurisdiction over an aircraft carrier. Mass violence is rare, but personal violence common. In September, 1963, a state legislator in Santa Cruz was shot and killed by an inflamed opponent while he was making a speech on the radio. Later a federal senator was killed during an open session of the national parliament in Brasília, caught innocently in a fierce bout of shooting between two other excited senators.

Immigration Patterns, Youth, and Education

Along about 1880 a wave of European immigrants swept into Brazil, and about five million entrants have arrived from that date to this, mostly Italians or Portuguese. The Italians, as in Argentina, have given a strong coloration to the country, although no Brazilian city, not even São Paulo, is quite so Italianate today as Buenos Aires. Later came a surge of Germans and Slavs, who settled mostly in the southern states like Santa Catarina and Rio Grande do Sul, and many of whom became expert small farmers. By their skills and diligence the Germans have added greatly to the diversification and value of small industry as well. During the period preceding World War II the German minorities were the focus of a serious Nazi movement and threat, but this disappeared when Vargas unexpectedly brought Brazil into the war against the Axis.

In the past decade immigration has dropped to about 50,000 a year; most of these entrants are now Portuguese, with Japanese and Spaniards next. The Japanese, numbering about 500,000, form a distinctive, useful, and popular community; they maintain their own identity, but absorb Brazilian folkways easily; intermarriage is common, and there are thousands of Brazilian-Japanese "Nisei." The main Japanese locations are São Paulo and Paraná, where most Japanese go into specialized agriculture—chicken breeding, horticulture, fancy vegetables—but the number of shopkeepers in the towns is growing.

*

Brazil is, like most of the South American republics, a young country: not less than half its population is under the age of eighteen, which necessarily means acceleration of the birth rate even above its present dismaying level, and clearly affects problems steadily becoming more urgent in housing, education, and public health, also politics. But the Brazilian youth does not—perhaps this is a risky generalization—seem to be quite as politically involved and restive as the student class in, say, Chile or the Caribbean nations. Recently, however, the government closed down the leading students' union because of political activity called subversive.

University education in Brazil is in a shabby condition; the record here is probably worse than in any country on the continent except in backwater sheep states like Paraguay. Brazil never had any national university at all until, incredibly enough, 1924 (just as it had no printing press till the 1820's); compare this to San Marcos University in Lima, Peru, which was founded in 1551, or Mexico, which has had printing for three hundred years. Universities were not established—again these dates almost defy belief—at São Paulo till 1934, or in Bahia, Recife, or Paraná till 1946. Several universities still have no libraries or laboratories. In some an archaic system is in force whereby a professor, too lazy or too occupied with outside work to teach, can hire out his chair to an underling who may be totally unequipped for the job, and who may hire out *his* chair in turn.

But if the universities leave a lot to be desired the condition of the primary and secondary schools is even worse. The country in theory devotes 10 percent of the national budget to education, but at least half the population is, as we know, still illiterate, and illiteracy is actually growing as the population expands, not diminishing. Elementary education is, in theory, compulsory, but six million children between the ages of seven and fourteen (perhaps more) do not go to school at all for the simple but conclusive reason that no schools for them exist. Only about one-fifth of primary school students remain in school long enough to learn how to read and write. Figures like these can only be considered a national disgrace.

Portugal and Africa

Since Brazil is a child of Portugal and Africa its relations with both parents have interest. The situation has recently been complicated by the nationalist revolts in Angola and the other Portuguese territories in Africa. Brazil cannot easily have it both ways, much as it would like to. If it associates itself too closely to Portugal it sacrifices the sympathy of renascent nationalist Africa with its new profound influence on world affairs—also vice versa. To be pro-African is to be anti-Portuguese.

On the whole links between Brazil and Portugal have not been strong in recent years; few Brazilians have much feeling for Portugal nowadays except in a vestigial sentimental way. They have outgrown it. They are the dog, Portugal is the tail. Not a single city in Brazil has ever been named for Lisbon.[12] On the other hand nobody wants to affront the Portuguese need-lessly. The Salazar government in Lisbon, on its side, wants the best possible relations with Brazil, and tries to encourage Brazilian support for its African policy. Lisbon makes yearning pronouncements about a future "Lusitanian confederacy," consisting of Portugal, Brazil, Angola, and the other Portu-guese realms in Africa like Mozambique: this bloc would number more than a hundred million people, be "a world power in the South Atlantic," and would dramatically reinforce the Portuguese position in Africa where it has been so hard-pressed.

Portugal some years ago offered Brazil a treaty of friendship and consulta-tion which the Brazilians refused because it excluded Africa. Now the Salazar government has made Brazil a new offer of free ports in mainland Portugal and other considerations as a bait for joining a confederation, but with no result so far.

Brazil has, of course, been through the years a substantial contributor to Portugal—to Angola as well. Brazilians helped wrest both Angola and their own northeast from Dutch invaders, and, a little-known fact, the governors of Angola were Brazilian, not Portuguese, for a period in the seventeenth century. Not only did Africans come to Brazil: Brazilians went to Africa. But as of today it should be kept in mind that plenty of Brazilians do not like to be reminded of their African heritage or be committed by it.

Some Elements in Economics

1. Brazil lives on a vegetable, coffee, of which it is the world's largest exporter as well as producer. By far the largest element in the country's economy, coffee accounts for not less than 60 percent of its *total* exports, which makes it particularly vulnerable to world prices. For several centuries the nation's wealth was based on sugar; then came the rubber boom, which dramatically collapsed; coffee followed. A quasi-government agency buys

[12] Although there are eight Lisbons in the United States. *Brazil, the Infinite Country,* by William L. Schurz, p. 15.

most of the crop going to the internal market, stockpiles it, and releases it at heavily subsidized prices. Overproduction is a serious problem. The coffee planters were the major force running the country for many years, but this pattern is changing as the result of industrialization. A quarter of a century ago Brazil dealt with its glut of coffee by a lunatic system euphemistically called "valorization" or "stabilization," which should have been called "vaporization." The government bought up the surplus crop, and then destroyed it. In seven years in the late 1930's about 70 million sacks of coffee, worth at that time almost $350 million, were buried, hauled out to sea and dumped overboard, or burned. To *get rid* of the coffee, its prime crop, cost the country about a million dollars a year in warehousing, labor, and kerosene to feed the flames, because coffee, being 11 percent water, is hard to burn. All this occurred during a period of acute economic crisis over most of the world when people were thirsting for coffee. The Brazilian experiment was, of course, an effort to keep prices up. We in North America have done the same kind of thing.

2. The land. Brazil is such an extravagantly large country with so many local divergences that over-all simplifications are difficult. Coffee, a sensitive once-a-year crop, grows mostly on medium-sized *fazendas* (estates); ownership is mixed. Most workers are no more than rural laborers—pickers—who work for a wage, and a very small wage at that; but on some estates they own or are permitted to make use of small plots for growing their own food. Properties devoted to other commodities can be enormous, like the cattle ranches in the *gaucho* (cowboy) south and sugar plantations in the impoverished northeast. One owner in the eastern Amazon area has a holding, to be devoted to cattle, covering five thousand square *miles*—an area the size of Connecticut![13] Some large properties still have a purely feudal structure: the workers are sharecroppers—virtual serfs. A very large percent of persons engaged in agriculture—which provides almost 90 percent of the country's foreign exchange—are tenants who do not own the land they work on. Agriculture is still so badly organized that Brazil, one of the potentially richest lands on earth, is obliged to import food to live—particularly wheat. I have already mentioned that *one-half of all agricultural land in the nation is in the hands of 1.6 percent of the population.* This is a pattern we shall find almost everywhere in South America, although the comparative figures are not quite so inequitable in most other countries.

Abuses in landownership and distribution go back a long way in Brazil—at least four hundred years. Soon after the nation was discovered the king of

[13] Juan de Onis, *New York Times*, January 17, 1966. Also see "Brazil, Complex Giant," by Hilary O'Reilly Sternberg, *Foreign Affairs*, January, 1966.

Portugal "gave" large tracts of territory to twenty court favorites, and some of their descendants have held parts of these properties ever since.[14] Agitation for land reform has gone on for years; ninety-two different reform bills have been presented to Congress since 1945, but they were all knocked out by the powerful landowners' lobby.[15] A principal reason for the fall of President Goulart in 1964—see the chapter following—was his apparent intention to introduce the beginnings of land-reform legislation with teeth in it. The Castelo Branco government fostered a bill in November, 1965, called the Statute of Lands, opening the way to limited reform, and several emergency reform districts have been set up, but it is too early to estimate the real effect of this. Land reform, to be successful, means a good deal more than the mere cutting up and distribution of feudal estates. The gist of the problem is not merely emancipation of the peasant, no matter how miserably he is exploited, but the necessity to make agriculture more efficient in the large. Such factors as improved agrarian techniques, regional planning, credit, irrigation, building of access roads, rural housing, reform in marketing procedures, diversification of crops, electrification, all have to be considered, or the peasant will not be much better off than he is at present, even if he has his own land. But emancipation of the peasant must of necessity be part of this process, and should come first. Land is life.

3. Industrialization. Early in 1965 Brazil produced its millionth automobile; this is symbolic of a very substantial industrial effort centered on São Paulo, for which former President Kubitschek deserves full credit. Last year, in spite of the general recession, car production went up to 180,000. Volkswagen alone, one of ten principal automobile manufacturers, is producing some three hundred automobiles a day, a large number for South America; their retail cost is around $3,000—expensive. The largest company is Willys-Overland do Brasil, S.A. (trucks, cars, jeeps); Willys is a great name here. The company is more than 50 percent Brazilian-owned. The São Paulo automobile plants are not assembly plants but actual manufacturers that produce cars from scratch; parts may be imported (Brazil, however, not only produces most of the parts it needs but even exports them to the United States); import of complete cars is not forbidden, but the import tariff makes their price prohibitive. This pattern is now being followed by other hemisphere republics, notably Argentina and Venezuela, and it will soon be as difficult to buy a Cadillac anywhere in South America as a live brontosaurus.

[14] "Brazil's Land Reform Program," by Alvaro Carneiro, *Latin American Times*, August 25, 1965.
[15] Gerald Clark in *The Coming Explosion in Latin America*, a first-class book of contemporary reportage.

One reason for the brisk business in automobiles is that the local citizenry buy them as a hedge against inflation—expensive TV sets and refrigerators as well. Industrialization in Brazil is being paid for by several types of manipulatory device, but the basic fact remains that it could not exist on the scale it has reached except for the export of simple agricultural products, from rice to peanuts. Most of the gasoline which turns every wheel has to be imported, and the country is, in the long run, still at the mercy of the soil, water, and wind.

To repeat, coffee is the basic item. In no country in South America is the dependence of the national economy on a single crop more conspicuous. Early in 1966 Brazil had an unsold surplus of fifty million bags, "equal to a year's supply for the entire world."

4. Labor. No truly independent labor movement has existed since Vargas; the unions are government controlled, but they have substantial power. Also Brazil has, like practically all the South American republics, a strong and well-established social security system, to which employers, employees, and the state contribute alike in equal degree—8 percent of the wage. One Brazilian uniqueness is the so-called ten-year law; if an employee has served ten years in a post, he cannot be fired. This makes for profound and intricate confusions. Owners of factories, shops, and offices do a great deal of winnowing in the ninth year of an employee's service, and thousands of men and women are let out just before their tenure is established. This naturally causes hardship and instability, and is an example of a law originally designed to protect workers defeating its own end, like some of the welfare state legislation in Uruguay.

5. Public finance and taxes. The Brazilian government is bearing down hard on tax evaders, but evasion or plain cheating still goes on abundantly, as in every South American country. This is a hemisphere where people, especially the rich, simply will not pay income tax until this is literally wrested out of them. Only 150,000 tax returns were filed last year in Brazil, which has 80 million people; only 5,000 persons paid an individual tax higher than $1,000. Merchants alone are supposed to be bilking the government of more than a billion dollars a year, but tax evasion was not even made a penal offense until 1964. The only practicable way to check tax evaders was to refuse them bank loans until their debt was paid up, but this system was as full of holes as the net of a Bahia fisherman. Despite all this, tax collections rose from 450 billion cruzeiros in 1964 to 1,300 billion in 1965.

Brazil has, as already noted, the largest foreign debt of any comparable country in the world—about $3.5 billion, much of which is owed to the United States. The steep annual service on this sum—amortization and interest—is more than the country can afford. Twenty-nine percent of *all* outstanding loans in Latin America by the World Bank are, incidentally, to Brazil,[16] although these were suspended during the Goulart presidency, because he was thought to be "unreliable." Recently the World Bank resumed investment with a $49 million loan for electric power development in Minas Gerais. Meantime there came from the United States a $90 million Food-for-Peace contribution and a new $50 million loan to help support the currency in the summer of 1964. Washington did not want the new Castelo Branco government to drop dead.

6. Investment. A good many American private enterprises, like Sears, Roebuck (general stores and merchandising) and Anderson, Clayton (food-stuffs and much else), have huge investments in Brazil, and new capital is coming in but somewhat slowly. A word of warning was sounded on this topic by Professor Robert J. Alexander of Rutgers University, a widely admired Latin American expert, in the *New York Times* on February 4, 1966:

> At the moment Brazil is badly in need of new investment to get in motion again the process of economic development, virtually suspended for the last three or four years. The present regime is more than anxious to have foreign enterprises establish new industries in the country. . . . As yet, however, there is little indication of any wave of foreign capital coming here to establish new factories or other enterprises.
>
> However, there is a distressing tendency on the part of some foreign firms, and particularly some from the United States, to buy up going Brazilian enterprises. A few years ago a sizable bank was bought out by a large United States financial institution. A large oil company has announced its intention of taking over one of the largest Brazilian paint and chemical firms. The publishing and broadcasting industry of São Paulo has recently denounced the tendency of United States firms to buy radio stations, newspapers and magazines.
>
> All of this is much resented in Brazil. It is widely felt that powerful foreign firms are taking advantage of a weak moment in the Brazilian economy to obtain at relatively low prices enterprises which have been built up by Brazilians. Foreign companies which do this make no new contributions to the Brazilian economy—and such a contribution is, in the eyes of most thinking Brazilians, the only thing which justifies foreign investment here at all. . . .
>
> This unproductive type of foreign investment is helping to pave the

[16] Mexico has 21 percent, Colombia 12 percent. Brazil is similarly the largest Latin American borrower from the Export-Import Bank, with 38 percent of its total loans, followed by Argentina (16 percent) and Mexico (12 percent). See William Benton, *The Voice of Latin America*, p. 54.

way for a violent anti-Yankee and generally anti-foreign reaction in Brazil in the foreseeable future. When political considerations become such as to give room for the free expression of the Brazilian people's feelings on these matters, the firms which have "bought into" the Brazilian economy without really contributing anything to it will suffer severely.

Unfortunately so will a lot of enterprises which have given genuine assistance to the economic development of Brazil.

Nationalist Brazilians do, indeed, dislike it intensely that profits derived from enterprises within the country should flow out, even though the foreigners pay increasingly heavy taxes; on the other hand development, which is a basic need, cannot go forward without capital, and this can only be had by taking it out of the hide of the citizen, as was done in Russia, or by accepting foreign loans or investment. Fear of exploitation is, of course, no new thing. Back in 1941 I had a talk with President Roosevelt in Washington after a visit to Latin America. He reminisced about his experiences there and gossiped about the heads of state he had met. Among other things he told me that he had said to President Vargas that he, Roosevelt, would absolutely not stand for it if he were in his place, referring to the fact that "most Brazilian public utilities were owned outside Brazil," and stated there would be a "revolution" in the United States if American industry was "similarly controlled by foreigners."[17]

In 1961 Governor Leonel Brizola of Rio Grande do Sul, as if he were putting Mr. Roosevelt's words into belated effect, expropriated the state holdings of International Telephone and Telegraph; those of subsidiaries of the American & Foreign Power Company and the Canadian-owned Brazilian Traction, Light, and Power Company were threatened later. This produced a first-class row, and negotiations went on interminably for a settlement with adequate compensation to the foreign interests. IT & T was eventually reimbursed, and in October, 1964, Brazil agreed in the case of American & Foreign Power to purchase all its subsidiaries in Brazil, while the company on its side agreed to reinvest 75 percent of the proceeds in Electrobras, Brazil's electric power agency.[18]

The United States temporarily withdrew aid from Brazil during the early period of this quarrel as a result of action in the Senate, which passed what has come to be known as the Hickenlooper Amendment as a rider to the 1962 foreign aid bill; this makes it mandatory for the United States to withhold aid from any country which seizes American-owned property

[17] From my *Roosevelt in Retrospect*, p. 25.
[18] *Gallatin Annual of International Business*, 1965, p. 276.

without offering "adequate compensation" within six months. The Hicken-looper Amendment, which was named for the Iowa Senator and has also been invoked in cases having to do with petroleum in Argentina, makes it difficult for North Americans to argue with a straight face with their Latin American friends that the American government and private American business interests are not closely intertwined, although of course it is a major precept of international law that a country has the duty to protect its investors abroad. In fairness one should add that most sea-soned United States experts on Latin America thought—and still think—that the Hickenlooper rider was a deplorable mistake.

The blackmail or punitive power implicit in this amendment is, in any case, strongly resented by patriotic South Americans. On the other hand Brazil accepts United States financial and other aid with alacrity, when it can get it, and is by far the largest recipient of American aid on the conti-nent, despite several temporary interruptions. Total Alianza (Alliance for Progress) funds released to Brazil amounted to about $960 million between 1961 and 1965; in the latter year alone United States public aid came to more than $350 million. Assistance has also come from the International Bank for Reconstruction and Development (World Bank), as noted above, the International Monetary Fund, and from other sources including West Germany and, interestingly enough, Soviet satellites in eastern Europe. In August, 1966, the Soviet Union opened a $100 million credit to Brazil for buying industrial equipment.

To return to the private foreign investor. The American companies concerned deny vigorously that their profits are excessive. Sears, Roebuck, which contributes a good deal to Brazil, takes out no more than a modest dividend. The average profit of United States firms is put at 2.2 percent, and 80 percent of their total proceeds remain within Brazil, according to Professor William L. Schurz, in his authoritative *Brazil, an Infinite Coun-try*. But the fact remains that foreign investors control 60 percent of the automobile industry, 57 percent of automobile parts, 62 percent of pharma-ceuticals, 38 percent of machinery, and 37 percent of chemicals.[19] No wonder nationalist Brazilians feel bitterly that they are getting the short end of the stick.

Recent large and responsible United States investors in Brazil have been Gulf Oil (petrochemicals), Ford, Alcoa, and Corning Glass (television tubes). Union Carbide and Phillips Petroleum are undertaking projects in plastics and fertilizer, and the Hanna Mining Company of Cleveland, Ohio,

[19] *South American Handbook, op. cit.,* p. 613. For new investment see the *Brazilian Bulletin* throughout 1965–66.

has large interests. The Inter-American Development Bank is working with ADELA, a new international consortium to be described later, to establish a paper-and-pulp industry.

7. State monopolies. Statism as well as nationalism is a rallying cry. Petroleum was nationalized under Vargas, and a mixed agency, Petróleo Brasileiro, known universally as Petrobras, in which the government is the major stockholder and which is the largest single company in the whole of South America, controls and operates most of the oil industry. In spite of intensive efforts to increase domestic production, crude petroleum is still Brazil's largest import. No foreign oil companies are allowed to enter the country to explore or drill for oil, and extraction, refining, and transportation (but not distribution) are a strict Petrobras monopoly. The Brazilian government similarly owns and operates Volta Redonda, the country's largest steel mill, has a sizable stake in the airlines, owns 78 percent of the railways, and controls hydroelectric power and merchant shipping. In general this division between public and private enterprise conforms to the pattern elsewhere in South America, and Brazil's petroleum legislation closely follows that of Chile. One item is that foreign insurance companies are not allowed.

8. Inflation. Everybody but a handful of profiteers wants to stop the inflation, but no one wants to be hurt by the measures necessary, which is unfortunately the crux of the problem. The value of the cruzeiro fell from 310 to the dollar to 1,200 between 1962 and 1964, and dropped to 2,200 late in 1965, where it still is. Stabilization of the currency has thus been achieved. Stabilization of prices has not, but the figures today are a substantial improvement over the catastrophic 87 percent rise in 1964. This was cut to 45 percent the next year, as stated earlier in this chapter, but even such a level made living costs intolerable for citizens on fixed incomes. The main causes of inflation were lack of confidence, the cost of industrialization, and high spending by ex-Presidents Kubitschek and Goulart. To pay for his grandiose projects, like Brasília, Kubitschek started to print money, but he had definite objectives in view, and sought to keep the inflation under control; Goulart printed a great deal more just to keep going, and the currency dropped like buckshot in a bowl.

One minor concomitant of all this is that Brazil, when I was there, had the filthiest paper money I have ever seen outside the mangiest of Balkan countries before the war. There are no coins beyond 50 cruzeiros, and no denominations of paper beyond 5,000 cruzeiros, less than $5. The smallest paper money is a curiosity valued at a twentieth of an American cent, and not worth it.

Two other elements involved in this general picture are (a) a massive flight of capital and (b) fantastically high interest rates, running to 2–3 percent a month. Money is very, very expensive in Brazil. And the cost of living seemed to be going up again early in the summer of 1966.

Corruption Rampant

Corruption is a long and miserable story, and is blatant on almost every level. Everybody tolerates graft, and almost everybody expects it. Adhemar de Barros, former governor of São Paulo and a towering political figure, became a very rich man in his years of public office, and a remark attributed to him is widely quoted, "They say that I steal. It is true. I steal. But I also get things done." The picturesque Governor Barros was once found guilty of malfeasance, but was subsequently cleared by the Supreme Court. Former President Kubitschek was stripped of his civil rights in 1964 on a charge of "corruption" as well as for other reasons. One former governor is said to have appointed six hundred different men to the post of state taxidermist—"enough to stuff every man, woman, and child in his state"—and then collected their "salaries," as well as filching the entire appropriation for public highways ($6,400,000).[20]

But the man most talked about in this field is the engaging João ("Jango") Goulart, the president who was displaced in April, 1964. Charges against him are being assembled, but, since he lives in exile in Uruguay, it is difficult to press them. Stories about Goulart's acquisitions have acquired the quality of folklore. He was a very rich man when he assumed office, but his wealth grew by spectacular dimensions if stories about him are to be believed. Goulart is said by his enemies, who of course have an interest in discrediting him, to have bought up fantastic amounts of land during his presidency; his holdings in Goiás alone have been estimated at 494,200 acres, and one of his deals in Mato Grosso was supposed to be the largest transaction of its kind in Brazilian history. During this period Goulart's salary as president was $350 a month. Once this beguiling man is reputed to have run up expenses of $100,000 in two hotels in Brasília in a brief period—of course charged to the government.

Dummy corporations, phantom payrolls, rake-offs on construction projects are familiar devices not merely in politics but in "normal" commercial affairs. Business goes by pull. One airline will use "unnatural methods," i.e., bribery, to keep a competitor at a disadvantage. A favorite trick is the use of foreknowledge of the route of a new road, so that speculators can buy up

[20] *Time*, July 3, 1964.

the adjoining land. Such larcenous peccadillos are not, of course, unknown in other countries; Boss Pendergast once paved a riverbed in Kansas City. But the point is that a rich country like the United States can afford a modicum of corruption, unpleasant and immoral as this may be; undeveloped countries in South America cannot.

Not long ago citizens of São Paulo, indignant at the mishandling of their public and political affairs, put up a rhinoceros named Cacareco to run for alderman. This was meant to be an ironic gesture, but the animal got more votes than any other candidate. It died some years later, and, to keep up the sardonic joke, its supporters gave it a "state" funeral. Similarly in Recife a billygoat accustomed to nibbling grass outside the governor's palace was put up for state senator. Its name was Cheiroso (odorous).

*

But anybody who thinks that Brazil is a comedy country is dead wrong. This stupendous land is not merely vital in itself and the essential key to the rest of South America but it is the only country in the western hemisphere, not counting the United States, capable of becoming a great power. It has the basic geography necessary, the potential resources, and, in the tumultuous ebb and flow of the modern world, the priceless advantage of a mixed racial heritage. President Kennedy once called it the "India" of the western hemisphere if only because of the scope, variety, and positive grandeur of its problems, challenges, and hopes.

CHAPTER 2

From 1500 to 1966 in Twenty-One Pages

God is a Brazilian.
—LOCAL ADAGE

Voting does not fill anybody's belly.
—GETÚLIO VARGAS

BRAZIL, such a dazzling salmagundi of backwardness and advance, so volatile and various, was discovered by a Portuguese seaman, Pedro Alvares Cabral, on April 22, 1500, eight years after Columbus landed in the West Indies. Like Columbus, Admiral Cabral thought that he had found India. The new country has had several names; first it was called Vera Cruz, then the Island of Santa Cruz, then the Land of Santa Cruz, but eventually it became Brazil (literally "glowing coal") or "the Brazils" after the Indian name of a local species of hardwood. In 1815, having been a colony of Portugal for more than three hundred years, it was promoted to be a "realm"; subsequently it became an empire, and finally the republic—correctly, the United States of Brazil—which it is today. Locally the name is spelled with an "s"—Brasil.

The Tupí-Guaraní Indians encountered by the first settlers had no civilization, and were a feeble people who could not stand up to hard labor in the sugar fields; hence the Portuguese brought in Negro slaves from Africa. Their most productive characteristic was not, however, labor, but the "generative female belly."[1] One strong influence in the early days was that of the Jesuits, who, as in Paraguay,[2] were vigorous proseletizers, and also provided a modicum of education and development. The Dutch, who held Pernambuco on the bulge from 1630 to 1654, were other early arrivals on the scene, and

[1] Again I am paraphrasing Freyre, *The Masters and the Slaves*, p. 278.
[2] See Chapter 13 below.

26

so were French Huguenots, who established themselves in Rio. Also, little
known as the fact is, Brazil once had an interlude of being ruled by Spain as
well as Portugal, as a result of a dynastic crosspatch, but this did not modify
its essential Portuguese configuration.

Early in the nineteenth century came resounding events. Napoleon
threatened Lisbon in the course of his Peninsular Wars, and the Braganza
Court of Portugal, to escape capture by the French, fled bodily to Brazil, a
sensational thing to do. The cavalcade, which embarked in a sizable fleet,
numbered two thousand people, including Queen Maria I, who was insane;
her son Dom João (John), the Regent; his consort, the "wanton Carlotta,"
who was a sister of the King of Spain; and their children. Arriving in Rio in
January, 1808, they were greeted by an enthusiastic crowd, but sanitary
conditions were such that, among other things, "the beach was covered with
the offal of a huge city."[3] A prime element in this whole operation was
British. Napoleon had set about harassing Portugal in the first instance
because the Portuguese were British allies, and the hegira crossed the
Atlantic under British escort.

Thus Rio de Janeiro became the co-capital of a European empire, the only
city in the western hemisphere ever to have this distinction. The prince
regent became King João VI in 1816, ruling both Portugal and Brazil, but he
returned to Lisbon in 1821, when it appeared that his position there was
shaky. His pockets were, to put it mildly, well lined with gold. A period full
of paralyzingly difficult dynastic confusions followed.

At this time most of South America was being ignited by the independence movement, and Brazil was not immune to this. A rebel known as
Tiradentes, the Toothpuller, because he was a dentist, led a romantic
nationalist conspiracy against the crown; this failed, and he was brutally
executed. He has been a national hero ever since. An open revolt came in the
north in 1817 by rebels who sought to establish a secessionist republic, the
Confederation of the Equator, but was put down. However, the nationalist
movement in Brazil never had the punch and sting of those in Spanish
domains. There was no war of independence or revolution by the people;
Brazil had no Bolívars or San Martíns. In plain fact, the country was placidly
liberated by its own royal family, as we shall see.

Meanwhile other developments were fruitful. Efforts to open up the
country came early, even though the Portuguese are a coastline people, and
Brazil's "Wild West"—the region immediately inland from São Paulo—was
penetrated and partly tamed in circumstances roughly analogous to those in
the United States in frontier days. Adventurers, gold seekers, Indian fighters

[3] George Pendle, A *History of Latin America*, a useful small book.

pushed south and west; they were called *bandeirantes*, because each group fought under its own *bandeira*, or flag; most were *mestizos*. Gold and diamonds were discovered in Minas Gerais at an early date, and there came a gold rush startlingly like that in California later. The northeast, with its economy based on sugar, continued to be the principal source of the wealth of the country, but the tough frontiersmen of the south, continuing to expand during the nineteenth century, were largely responsible for shaping Brazil as it is today.

But to return to affairs of court. The Braganzas were a complicated lot. João VI, on returning to Europe, left his twenty-three-year-old son Pedro behind as regent of Brazil and in 1822 this young man, refusing an order to go back to Portugal—which wanted to reassert hegemony over Brazil—declared the independence of the country with himself as emperor. So Brazil became a free nation, although a monarchy. João VI died in Lisbon in 1826, and Pedro, now called the First, succeeded him, theoretically a double king with two thrones, one in America, one in Europe, where he was known as Pedro IV. His prime minister, José Bonifácio de Andrade e Silva, was a mineralogist and poet. The British played an indispensable role in all this, both officially and unofficially; Admiral Lord Cochrane, a stunning old sea-dog who had already tussled for South American independence in both Chile and Peru, helped the Brazilian Portuguese fight off the Portuguese Portuguese in romantic, if trifling, naval battles.

Pedro I kept getting into difficulties, and was presently forced to abdicate the throne of Portugal. The story becomes a mad extravaganza like the librettos of unplayable old operas. Pedro left the throne in Lisbon to his five-year-old daughter, provided that she marry one of her uncles, his brother. Then in 1831 he lost his Brazilian throne as well, following sinuous troubles with the military and an inflammatory series of love affairs; his son Pedro II became Emperor of Brazil at the age of six, under a regency. Pedro II did not accede to the actual throne until 1840, when he was fifteen, but then he reigned for almost half a century until 1889.

Pedro II was one of the most remarkable rulers of modern times. He stood six feet four, had a heavy square beard, and was temperate, sophisticated, and distinguished—also an "off ox," as the British say; he translated Hamlet, and encouraged his own people to demand more freedom. Though he was a good Catholic and a member of the Braganza family, he was an ardent freemason. As he grew older he became known as the "Good Grey Emperor," and was called "Queen Victoria in breeches." His queen was a daughter of the King of Naples; apparently he paid little attention to her. He loved books, philosophy, and languages; he translated Aeschylus, and studied Arabic, Hebrew, Sanskrit, Provençal, Tupí, and Guaraní; he could speak

Latin, Greek, English, German, and all the romance languages. He wrote verse constantly.

Pedro traveled widely, founded scientific societies, and maintained friendships with such men as Pasteur, Louis Agassiz, and Emerson; visiting the United States he made contact with poets and inventors, attended services in a Mormon tabernacle, and cultivated friendships in the Jewish religious community. His reign was progressive and humane as well as idiosyncratic, and there is no doubt that the monarchy performed a considerable service in holding the country together and giving it order and tranquillity. Brazil had no civil wars or military adventurers grasping for power in the ferocious manner of its neighbors. Pedro devoted himself to "purification" of the army, the creation of an elite civil service, and, like a Scandinavian monarch today, to the development of unity and national good will.[4]

He was, however, made to abdicate in 1889 for a variety of reasons, including the inevitable growth of republican sentiment under such formidable statesmen as Benjamin Constant and Marshal Deodoro da Fonseca. Another was the unpopularity of a French princeling who had married his daughter Isabel, called "The Redeemer," the heir to the throne; he affronted the people by refusing to learn Portuguese. An additional important factor was the abolition of slavery in 1888; Pedro strongly supported emancipation, but this alienated the powerful landlords, who turned against him, and he was finally forced out, despite his splendid record, after forty-nine years on the throne. He retreated to France and died there in 1891. The monarchy was finished.[5]

Immigration began on a large scale after the freeing of the slaves; the beginnings of industrialization came, and a middle class emerged. Politics were for the most part uneventful till 1930, and the pattern evolved whereby the presidency was held alternately by men from São Paulo and Minas Gerais under comparatively tranquil circumstances. Then in 1930 came Getúlio Vargas, and Brazil entered into modern times.

The Ineffable Getúlio, "Father of the Poor"

Getúlio Vargas ruled Brazil for almost eighteen years, from 1930 to 1945—the first ten years became known as the *Década Getuliana*—and again from 1951 to 1954. Born in 1883 in the cowboy area of Rio Grande do Sul, he grew up, as has been aptly said, with a lasso in his hands and a horse

---

[4] I have followed Hubert Herring, A *History of Latin America*, in some of the above, and am also indebted to "History of the Reign of Dom Pedro II," by Hector Lyra, in *The Green Continent*, a splendid anthology edited by Germán Arciniegas.

[5] There are, however, several Braganza princes surviving today who are pretenders to the throne.

between his knees. He never let go of the lasso, and the horse became Brazil. After taking a degree in law Vargas went into the army briefly and then entered politics, becoming a deputy from the cattle country; by 1926 he was minister of finance. Then in 1930 he ran for the presidency, and was beaten. But he claimed that he had been counted out by fraud, and proceeded to make himself president by means of a bloodless coup d'état, supported by the army. As is the case almost everywhere in Latin America, the president cannot legally succeed himself until an intervening term has passed—in some countries never—but Vargas went on holding office until 1945, becoming an outright—but amiable—dictator.

One story about the agile Getúlio is that he was the only man in history who could take off his socks without removing his shoes. He was industrious and had great political sense and loved to improvise. He cultivated relationships in all quarters, and the legend is that, during one period, the anteroom of his office was the only place in Brazil where one might see simultaneously the cardinal archbishop of Rio, an extreme reactionary; Prince Pedro, one of the Braganza pretenders, and the Communist leader Luís Carlos Prestes.

Vargas never talked much—he is supposed to have been able to be "silent in ten languages." Winning, unhurried, wary, he was devoid of any of the more complicated dignities. He liked to play golf—best score around 122. On one occasion several members of his club could not reach their lockers because the president, naked except for a towel around his middle, lay sound asleep on the metal bench in the locker room.

His principal historical significance is that, like Perón in Argentina, he sought to bring the man on the street, the workingman, into the fabric of political life and society. He did not go so far as Perón did, but he was the first Brazilian president to think broadly in terms of the basic needs of the people and, in particular, of the industrial working class. He did his utmost to modify the power of the big foreign enterprises in the country; he set up Petrobrás, the state oil monopoly, and laid the foundations for Volta Redonda and the Brazilian steel industry; he gave women the vote, improved the social security system, abolished child labor, wrote a new labor code with collective bargaining, and sought to break the feudal power of the great estates.

Politically he worked both sides of the street. He broke up the Integralistas, the chief local Fascist organization, and João Goulart, a convinced left-winger, was his minister of labor for a time. On the other hand, he modeled his Estado Novo on Mussolini's corporative system, and assiduously copied Fascist legislation from Portugal. In plain fact Vargas cared little for political ideas or the forms of political organization as such; he even believed in such a contradiction as "Democratic Caesarism." What he wanted was what would work—and, as he liked to put it, "to save Brazil for the Brazilians."

After fifteen years, Vargas was deposed in 1945 by a military coup, without violence. The pretext was that the president had appointed his brother Benjamin, who was violently disliked, to be chief of police—but the real reason was that the army, fed up with the dictatorship, wanted elections, strange as this may seem. Two months after being ejected as president Getúlio ran for the federal senate and won a seat, an astonishing thing to happen. Then, under normal constitutional procedures, he contested for president again in 1950 with the support of a powerful socialist-labor coalition—while being called a Fascist by the liberals! The analogy to Perón in Argentina is suggestive.

Vargas easily won these 1950 elections, which were legally conducted, and so became a constitutional president *after* having been an authoritarian dictator, something new to history. But he had made many enemies; one of these was the inflammatory Carlos Lacerda, editor of the sensationalist newspaper *Tribuna de Imprensa,* who had opened fire on the Vargas regime with a series of blistering editorials, charging corruption and nepotism in the presidential circle. Vargas, who appeared to be losing grip, did not seem to know what was going on in his own palace, which fairly boiled with graft, intrigue, and corruption. Presently one of Vargas's sons, Lutero, sued Lacerda for slander. Then in August, 1954, came a decisive event—Lacerda and one of his bodyguards were attacked by assassins; he was wounded, and the bodyguard, a popular young air force officer, killed. This made a passionate public storm. Lacerda accused Lutero Vargas of having instigated the attack, in collusion with Gregório Fortunato, a Negro nicknamed the Black Angel, who was chief of the presidential guard. Getúlio himself, it became clear later, had nothing to do with the plot. But air force men burst into Catête, the president's palace, to arrest Fortunato, and a group of senior officers called on Vargas to demand his resignation.[6] That night, August 24, 1954, Vargas killed himself rather than give up office. He left a suicide note saying, "To the hatred of my enemies I leave the legacy of my death."

I met Vargas twice and I would like to write about him extensively, but space forbids. He was one of the most attractive men of politics I ever knew. His enemies on the extreme right hate him today as relentlessly as when he was alive, much as the reactionaries in Argentina still hate Perón. They say that Vargas was a posturer, altogether insincere—false. The Communists

[6] The Black Angel, a veritable monster of corruption, was sentenced to prison for twenty years and subsequently murdered by a fellow prisoner.

hate him too. The fact remains that almost everything in Brazilian politics continues to stem from him, and it can hardly be gainsaid that, after Pedro II, he probably contributed more to his country than any figure in its history. He is the father of modern social legislation in Brazil.[7]

Three Presidents

We want to be on the side of the West, but we do not want to be the West's proletariat.
—JUSCELINO KUBITSCHEK

Between Vargas and Castelo Branco came three altogether remarkable presidents—Juscelino de Oliveira Kubitschek (1951–61), Jânio da Silva Quadros (January to August, 1961) and João Belchior Marques Goulart (1961–64). Two of the three had elements of freakishness; one has been called a nut; two have been accused of large corruptions; and one played closely with the Communists. They were intertangled politically, even if their personal relations were not good. Goulart was, for instance, vice president under both Kubitschek and Quadros, although not of the same political flavor; vice presidents in Brazil run independently of the president, and can belong to a different party.

The enterprising and brilliant Kubitschek was the most important of the three, and is the only one who still—conceivably—might reach power again. Two large monuments are to his credit: the creation of Brasília, the fantastic new capital out in the sticks in Goiás, and stimulus to industrialization in São Paulo, in particular the automobile industry.

Dr. Kubitschek had, indeed, vast dreams: "Fifty years' progress in five" was his motto. And indeed his government raised agriculture, steel, oil, and aluminum production, sought to improve communications and hydroelectric development, and laid out plans for the great new highway connecting Brasília with the Amazon. He had a lively and fertile imagination and was the father of a project known as Operation Pan America, which included many ideas subsequently embodied in the Alliance for Progress. But nothing came of it at that time because of United States opposition during the Eisenhower administration. Kubitschek did not resent this personally. He was a generous man. When President Eisenhower visited Rio Kubitschek presented him with a seventeenth-century candelabrum of such dimensions that Ike said that he would donate it to a museum, and gave Mrs. Eisenhower an aqua-

---

[7] On the other hand Lacerda told me that in eighteen years Vargas never built a single new school in Rio. Of course Lacerda is a hostile witness.

marine "an inch wide and three inches long."[8] Later, Kubitschek's budget deficits became unmanageable, and the United States cut down on credits to Brazil until it should put its financial house in order, a severe blow to the country's economy. The cost of living rose steeply, and Kubitschek began to print money. A nice euphemism for this was "currency emission financing of the federal budget deficit." Moreover, in the sober words of the Manchester *Guardian*, "every kind of graft was rampant, every economic skulduggery passed muster, every species of adventurer prospered."[9] Yet the income of the country rose.

A native of Minas Gerais, Dr. Kubitschek was born of Czechoslovak stock in the old diamond town appropriately named Diamantina in 1902; his parents were immigrants. He trained for the priesthood briefly and then turned to medicine (working his way through medical school as a telegraph operator), became an M.D., and studied urology in Europe. But politics gripped him early and, surrendering his practice, he served as mayor of Belo Horizonte, the capital of Minas Gerais, and then became governor of the state. He was—and still is—an original, persuasive, useful, and stimulating personality. By political affiliation he is a social democrat, but the Social Democratic party in Brazil is neither socialist nor particularly democratic; he stands much further left, and in fact what the conservatives disliked about him most was his seeming tolerance of Communism. But his leftist supporters stood by his side, and he rode out his full term as president, something rare in South America.

After the Castelo Branco coup in April, 1964—if I may get ahead of my story—Kubitschek retired to voluntary exile in Paris. He was not forced to leave the country, and no charges were prepared against him. He was, however, in June, 1964, deprived of his civil rights for ten years along with many other politicians whom the new military leaders disfavored. The principal effect of such a deprivation is to deny a man the right to vote and run for office. Sentences to this effect were imposed by an institution known as the National Security Council, which had the power of a drumhead court-martial; "suspects" were not necessarily informed of the charges against them, and the council met in secret without taking evidence from those accused or, for that matter, anybody else if it did not wish to do so. More on this later.

Kubitschek returned to Brazil from Europe in October, 1965, and received a warm popular welcome; there was no legal indictment against

[8] *New York Times*, February 26, 1960.
[9] James Morris, *South America*, a pamphlet reprinting a group of articles in the *Guardian*, p. 44. Kubitschek "promised to achieve 50 years' progress in 5, and . . . achieved 40 years inflation in 4."

him, and he did not indulge in any overt political activity, but his arrival
came at an awkward moment for the Castelo Branco regime because elections for governorships had just taken place in eleven states, and men allied
to Kubitschek had dramatically beaten Castelo Branco candidates in several
of these. The upshot was that various investigatory commissions subjected
Kubitschek to prolonged and severe questioning, and it became known that,
if he stayed in the country, he would be forced to stand trial for "subversion
and corruption" not in the civil courts but before a military tribunal. Rather
than submit to this procedure he left Brazil in November and took up
residence abroad again. No effort was made to hold him in the country, and
he received a certificate to the effect that he didn't owe any income tax.

If Dr. Kubitschek ever returns to Brazil and is permitted to run for
president again—or if circumstances otherwise change—most Brazilian observers think that he would win a thumping victory with strong left-wing
support. The mark he left on Brazil is ineffaceable, even if the cost was staggering.

*

Quadros, who was called "Jânio" by almost everybody, is a puzzle. He was
the greatest vote getter in Brazilian history, who threw his career away just as
it was getting under way. He was—and is—a São Paulo man, a former
mayor of the city and governor of the state. Quadros has never been touched
by any breath or hint of financial scandal. But his behavior was so weird in
other realms that it became difficult to take his views seriously. One wisecrack was that he was Marx all right, but not so much Karl as Groucho.

Quadros had big round glasses and a smudge of black mustache; he looked
awkward, and sometimes wore a kind of motorman's cap. A good speaker
and administrator, he gave São Paulo probably the best government
it ever had. His campaign sign was a broom, the symbolism being obvious. Quadros was born (1917) not in São Paulo but in the frontier state of
Mato Grosso, but he moved to the great industrial city as a youth, and
became a lawyer. His father was a doctor or pharmacist—stories vary. He has
always liked food, drink, and the other good things in life.

Early in his career Quadros came under the influence of Colonel Nasser in
Egypt, and he wanted to set Brazil off on a policy of "benevolent neu-
trality." But nobody ever knew quite how he defined this term. Arthur
Schlesinger, Jr., calls him "delphic," the creature of some mysterious and

unpredictable oracle. He himself declared that he was both Marxist and rightist, a believer in both public regulation and free enterprise. He conspicuously visited Castro's Cuba, gave an important decoration to Che Guevara when Che came to Brazil, opened the way to Brazilian resumption of diplomatic relations with the Soviet Union—which had been broken off in 1947—sent emissaries to China, and established trade treaties with the Communist satellites, although he was the candidate of Brazil's principal *conservative* party, the UDN.

Indeed, when he ran for the presidency in 1960, he was sneeringly called the "Esso" (Standard Oil) candidate by the Communist opposition. He had not wanted to run and was, in fact, taking a six months' holiday in Japan when he was nominated. Jânio liked trips. Politics in Brazil are inveterately helter-skelter. Men do not play the game like chess, seeking to close in on an antagonist, but like checkers, with jumps all over the board. Quadros's opponent in 1960 was a well-known military figure with the interesting name Henrique Baptista Duffles Teixeira Lott. He bore the highest military title the republic can bestow—Marshal. He had been minister of war several times, and helped to smooth the entry of Kubitschek into power. But nobody seemed to know what Marshal Lott represented, since he was supported by a bizarre mix including the extreme nationalist right *and* the Communists—by Kubitschek as well. In any case Quadros beat him by a thumping margin.

Quadros gave his side a good many headaches during the campaign; for instance, he resigned his candidacy halfway through, then resumed it. This was probably a device to test support and get agreement on his program. Then between his election and inauguration he took a leisurely trip to Europe, where his behavior was eccentric, to put it mildly. He refused invitations to meet Queen Elizabeth and President de Gaulle, saying that he was interested only in the "people." "Disappearing" for a time, he was eventually "discovered" studying art in Florence.

Taking over the presidency with Goulart as his vice president, Quadros set out to use the broom. Inflation was raging, and there was scarcely a cruzeiro in the till. Washington came to the rescue, if only because Jânio—even if he had adopted an independent foreign policy—seemed to be a better bet than Kubitschek, and Alianza and other funds began to enter Brazil again. Summarily Quadros countermanded some Kubitschek extravagances, even to the point of throwing out his $8,000 grand piano and firing the palace chef. He abolished cock fighting, reduced horse racing in Rio from seven days to one, and put a ban on beauty contests in bathing suits. But he had little chance to inaugurate more serious reforms, because, after seven months in office, he suddenly and dramatically quit his job. There was no revolt or coup. Without warning he threw up the presidency in a tantrum and walked out. Neuroticism could scarcely go further.

This is still a mysterious episode, although several reasons for it can be suggested. Carlos Lacerda, who had come to be nicknamed "the president killer," had been attacking Quadros fiercely, calling him "the most perfidious of all men ever to emerge in Brazil's public affairs," although they were members of the same party. Lacerda was a dangerous adversary; in fact he made serious threats against Quadros on TV the night before the resignation, "demanding" that he resign. The big *fazenda* operators and businessmen had berated him because of his plans for land and tax reform, but any Brazilian president should have known how to take such attacks in his stride. Probably the attitude of the army, which, in the words of one commentator, was still the decisive factor in "the uneasy balance of power between the wealthy landowners and the rising strength of labor," counted most. One story is that the minister of war of the time prepared a speech for the president to read at an Army Day celebration, which Quadros refused to accept because he thought it gave too much favor to the military; this provoked an angry scene. But a stronger man could probably have maneuvered himself out of a crisis based on such a comparatively minor incident. Anyway, Quadros quit. He simply gave up the job. Possibly he thought that the people would rise and demand him back. He had a prolonged sobbing fit as he boarded a boat to leave Brazil. The effect of all this on the country was positively traumatic. It was as if President Kennedy had unaccountably resigned office in his first months as president.

So João Goulart, the vice president, automatically became chief executive. He had been on an official visit to China, and the news caught him in Singapore. He hurried home.

*

Almost everybody referred to João Belchior Marques Goulart, who was forty-three when he became president, by his nickname Jango. He was born in Rio Grande do Sul, had substantial properties there, and entered politics as a Vargas protégé at twenty-eight. He was a lawyer by profession, a good Catholic, and a strong family man. His wife is exceptionally pretty. He himself has a healthy open manner, rough good looks, and an amiable personality. He has always been a reformer and man of the left.

On his visit to China immediately before his accession to the presidency in 1961, Goulart met Mao Tse-tung, and publicly called him an "outstanding poet, theoretician, and revolutionary strategist . . . a most important personage in the contemporary unstable world," and said that his memory would be "ineffaceable." Nobody paid much attention to this, but hackles began to rise in Rio—and Washington—when Goulart next aligned himself in public with the views of Ko Ching-shi, the mayor of Shanghai, when at a banquet Ko assailed "United States monopoly capitalism and imperialism as the common enemy of both Brazil and China." Assenting, Jango declared, "Our victory and those of the Brazilian government and people are in complete unanimity with those of the mayor. . . . Geographic distance can never separate the people of our two countries. . . . I would like to express my profound appreciation to the working people [of China] . . . their heroic and extraordinary participation in the building of a new, free, and powerful China."[10]

These remarks were carefully noted in Brazil, and, when Goulart arrived in Rio to take over after Quadros, the army quietly but effectively prevented him from assuming the presidency, and he had to cool his heels in Rio Grande for a week. The army's methods were strong-arm, illegal, and overt. During this interval Congress, which was also nervous, passed a hurried constitutional amendment installing a European-style parliamentary system in Brazil, which greatly reduced the power of the presidency. Goulart accepted this as the price of being inaugurated. An exacerbating factor in the bad feeling between Goulart and his opponents which now developed was the personality and activity of Leonel Brizola, the former governor of Rio Grande do Sul, who was his brother-in-law. It was Brizola who had expropriated American utilities interests in his state, thrown out the Peace Corps, and publicly assailed the Alianza. Brizola's nationalism increased when he became a deputy from Guanabara to the federal parliament in 1962, and Jango was thought to be heavily under his influence.[11]

There were at this time four or five principal political parties in Brazil out of a total of seventeen. Relations between them were largely decided by *politicagem*, intrigue, particularly since no single party had a majority in either the Senate or Chamber. Those leading were (1) the PTB or Brazilian Labor party, the strength of which was based largely on the trade unions; (2) the PSD or Social Democratic party, the leader of which

[10] *New York Times*, August 20, 1961.

[11] But Jango was capable of cracking down on Brizola on occasion. For instance, in 1963 he forbade him to broadcast over government-owned radio stations. Of course this and similar anti-leftist actions by Goulart, including a refusal to issue visas to Brazilian intellectuals planning a visit to Cuba, may have been motivated by a desire to appear publicly less of a fellow traveler than people thought he was. Also he desperately needed bailing out by the United States, and sent a financial mission to Washington which negotiated there for months.

was Kubitschek; (3) the Social Progressive party (PSP), dominated by Adhemar de Barros of São Paulo, on whom more later; and (4) the left-wing Brazilian Socialist party (PSB). The Communist party, led by Luís Carlos Prestes, had no official status, but it was powerful underground and it usually elected a number of deputies running under other labels. On the conservative side the principal party was the National Democratic Union (UDN), founded to oppose Vargas, and representing predominantly rightist interests, although it is difficult to draw the line. Lacerda was one of its leaders, as was Quadros, and so was General Juracy Magalhães, the governor of Bahia who subsequently became a hard-handed minister of justice and foreign affairs.[12] Finally, a Christian Democratic party (Catholic) had emerged; it supported Quadros, and gained control of the state of Paraná.

A further word of warning here about politics and parties. They must be thought of in the South American context, not ours. Allegiance in Brazil—as it is almost everywhere else in South America—is predominantly personal. Principles are seldom involved, and party labels mean little. Moreover, the politicians themselves continuously shift positions. Tags are interchangeable.

One persistent issue under Goulart was votes for illiterates, who, although they number at least 50 percent of the population, were—and are—excluded from voting. One effect of this is to make political campaigning easy; candidates do not have to go out into the hinterland to dig out the vote. Another is to make the city vote stronger, since most illiteracy is rural. Of course the ruling class seeks to perpetuate this device because it keeps the vote down.

Goulart, however, did very little about this in his two and a half years of power; in fact he scarcely made any reforms at all, in spite of copious promises. First, he kept pounding away at the constitutional issue—in order to restore the office of president to its original status—and in 1963 won a plebiscite which restored the former presidential system by a resounding five-to-one majority, which certainly proved that the people were behind him on this. But he gave little evidence of talent for administration or actually running a government. He was not evil; just incompetent. One healthy contribution was, however, his vigorous support of SUDENE (Superintendência do Desenvolvimento do Nordeste), the agency devoted to development of the northeast under a regional aid program. This had been set up late in 1959 under Kubitschek; its executive officer and living spirit was the brilliant young economist Celso Furtado. Subsequently Goulart promoted Furtado, who had strong left-wing views, and who believed in what he called "controlled social transformation," to be Director of

[12] Magalhães is the Portuguese rendition of Magellan.

National Planning.[13] When Furtado was purged in 1964 he was, incidentally, at once offered jobs by Harvard, Columbia, and Yale, and is now teaching at the Sorbonne.

Instability and financial crisis shook the Goulart regime in 1963–64. There were forty-four changes in cabinet personnel in two and a half years. The cost of living rose by 300 percent, and the currency went to pieces. I have already mentioned that Kubitschek, when he was forced to print currency, had genuine objectives in view and was gambling that they would pay off; Goulart just spent to keep afloat. A runaway flight of capital took hundreds of millions of dollars to the sanctuary of Swiss and North American banks. Once more the United States reduced aid to Brazil until the country should tidy up. A rash of strikes took place—in the banks, the railways, and the civil service—and the big unions kept pressing for higher wages. When the coup came which displaced Goulart it was nicknamed the "trillion cruzeiro revolt," since by that time the government deficit had reached the astronomical sum of 1,500,000,000 cruzeiros or $833 million.[14] Disorganization almost reached the point of chaos.

Now enters an important element—Communism. None of the above would alone have caused the blizzard that came. Finance was not what upset the country to the breaking point. What did was the widespread fear that Jango was becoming an overt instrument of the Communists, although he was not a Communist himself. But he was undeniably tolerant of the extreme left, and gave critical posts to left-wingers like Albina Silva and Evandro Lins e Silva, the military and civilian chiefs respectively in the presidential household.[15] The only *known* Communist close to Goulart was Raul Ryff, his press secretary.

Students, labor leaders, noncoms in the armed forces, made unceasing left-wing agitation. Brazil, it seemed, might be on the way to becoming another Cuba, and this, in the Washington view, might mean in turn that all the rest of South America could be influenced to follow suit. Absent in Europe on a brief trip, Carlos Prestes, the Communist leader, boasted that an actual takeover was unnecessary, since the substance of power belonged to the Communists already. This was not quite the case, because Goulart had no intention of letting himself be supplanted by a Communist regime; he thought that he could "handle" the Communists as they thought they could "handle" him. But Goulart was the man responsible for the basic situation.

[13] Albert O. Hirschman, *Journeys Toward Progress*, pp. 89–90.
[14] Barnard L. Collier in the New York *Herald Tribune*, April 15, 1964.
[15] *Newsweek*, March 11, 1963. Lins e Silva accompanied Goulart to China and later became foreign minister.

The wry jokes were heard that the government had not been undermined from the bottom but "overmined" from the top, and that the whole process was not one of "subversion" but "superversion."

In September, 1963, sergeants in the navy and air force made an attempt at revolution in Brasília, taking over military installations and arresting their officers, but this was a left-wing demonstration *against* Goulart because he had been so dilatory about land reform. The higher ranks of the army stayed loyal to Jango, and the revolt was put down. But Goulart, frightened, asked Congress for authority to impose a state of siege, i.e., modified martial law, which would serve to strengthen him, and this was refused. Then talk began to be heard that Goulart planned to circumvent Congress and make a popular front government, which would embody formal coalition with the Communists.

Various civilian groups particularly in São Paulo meantime worked out plans for saving the state in their image, and had established close contact with the military. The national disintegration almost reached the point of anarchy. I met in São Paulo one distinguished Brazilian, a doctor of medicine, who said that he had virtually decided to give up his life work and emigrate to the United States, because the local atmosphere was so unpredictably "horrible." People were sick of all the crooked politicians. Conspicuous in the São Paulo movement were publishers like Júlio de Mesquita Filho, owner of the important newspaper *O Estado de São Paulo* and such businessmen as Paulo Ayres Filho, a pharmaceutical manufacturer. An agency called IPES was set up to organize sentiment against Goulart, and this soon tied in with vigilante groups. Arms were distributed, and a youthful officer, Lieutenant Colonel Rubens Resstel, who played a considerable role in all this, said frankly later, "We decided to have them for lunch before they had us for supper."[16]

Meantime Carlos Lacerda, who hated Jango, was inflaming people in Rio against the regime by means of television speeches, and anti-Goulart sentiment began to be organized in Belo Horizonte as well. But, as was obvious, nothing much could happen unless the army took the lead, and this it was reluctant to do because its tradition was, and is, based firmly on the principle of *legalidade*, legitimacy. What this means in effect, a critical observer might well say, is that it never moved against a civilian regime unless it felt like it. But, although the army certainly exerts weight in civilian affairs on the rightist side, it dislikes taking a nonconstitutional position, because—as in

---

[16] See "The Country That Saved Itself," by Clarence W. Hall, *Reader's Digest*, and "When Executives Turned Revolutionaries," by Philip Siekman, *Fortune*, September, 1964.

most South American countries nowadays—it regards itself as the custodian of national continuity. So long as Goulart did nothing overtly unconstitutional it felt that it had no right to interfere.

The key to the situation now became General Castelo Branco. He did not, however, want so much to throw Goulart out as to check him. Castelo Branco had been commander of the Fourth Army, one of Brazil's four principal military commands, in Recife, where he had repeatedly come in conflict with the radical governor, Miguel Arraes, a Goulart man. Goulart eventually brought Castelo Branco back to Rio and made him chief of staff— ostensibly a promotion, but in reality a device to pull his teeth because, as chief of staff, he would no longer be in direct command of any troops. Castelo Branco then passed from passive to active opposition to Goulart. He decided that his constitutional duty was to the "structure" of the government, not to its occupants, and he circularized this view to fellow officers in a secret memorandum. Military action would be justified and in fact was necessary, Castelo Branco implied, if Goulart overstepped constitutional bounds; this gave a big lift to the would-be *Putschists*, because the general had unassailable prestige as a constitutionalist as well as military hero, and his integrity was believed to be beyond question.

On March 13, 1964, came the first climax. Goulart was now being forced into action by pressure from his own *left* wing. He convoked a spectacular mass meeting in Rio, attended by more than a hundred thousand people, and announced that he would ask Congress to stabilize rentals, legalize the Communist party and extend the vote to illiterates. This became known as the "Rally of Decisions," and it is generally believed that Carlos Prestes, the Communist leader, talked Goulart into holding it. Moreover, Jango dramatically signed two decrees on the spot, before the eyes of the great assembly, one of which nationalized the handful of petroleum refineries (Brazilian-owned, not foreign) still not in the embrace of Petrobras. One motive for this was probably to distract public attention from a previous ugly scandal involving Petrobras, which was now being run by a left-wing military man known as the "Marxist Marshal."

The other decree, more important, provided for "the expropriation of all unused land in large estates adjoining federal highways, railways, and other public works," to a distance of six miles.[17] This would have meant the beginnings of serious land reform in central Brazil, although it is doubtful if Goulart, even if he had stayed in office, would have had the power or funds to carry it out.

Both these decrees angered the conservatives, who were given additional

[17] Christopher George, "The Coup in Brazil," *World Today*, May, 1964.

cause for alarm by a speech by Leonel Brizola on the same platform to the effect that the government would dissolve Congress, call a plebiscite, and create a legislature of "soldiers and farm workers" if their proposals were not accepted.

Next came trouble in the navy, where conditions were already turbulent. Noncoms were openly contemptuous of their officers. The old Russian film *Potemkin*, which describes a naval mutiny, was pointedly shown at sailors' mass meetings. Then came a rally by some fourteen hundred noncoms and sailors at a trade union hall in Rio to air various grievances, held in defiance of their officers. This caused a furious row. The navy minister resigned because a subordinate commander refused to discipline the mutineers; Goulart veered from side to side and eventually fired the admiral originally responsible for *not* enforcing discipline.

This episode, minor as it was, had a profound effect, because the army now became convinced that, no matter what Goulart did, the rank and file of the forces would no longer respond to discipline. Next an unprecedented event occurred—a procession of several hundred thousand women in the streets of São Paulo, which was called "The March of God and Family," protesting against the Goulart regime and calling for change. Nothing so expressive of the power of women in politics had ever taken place in South America before, and a similar women's march was then organized in Belo Horizonte. Jango and Brizola laughed the matter off as a demonstration by a lot of "rosary carriers," but the public effect was impressive. The tide had turned for Goulart now. The army struck.

The Coup

Sociology is the art of saving Brazil quickly.
—MARIO DE ANDRADE

But it struck in a very mixed-up way, with leadership, coordination, and planning at the minimum. This was no swift, certain plunge of a Fascist dagger into the heart. The first outbreak occurred in Minas Gerais when the commander of the Fourth Army there, General Olimpio Mourão, proclaimed the small industrial city of Juiz de Fora to be "the revolutionary capital of Brazil," in order to forestall further Communist penetration of the government. Mourão seemingly acted on his own initiative, although Magalhães Pinto, the influential governor of Minas Gerais, was behind him. Brazil is, we should know by now, a country strongly marked by sectionalism, and the governors of the great states have authority almost on the level of the semi-independent rases in, let us say, prewar Ethiopia; moreover, the military has always had special strength on the provincial level. The Mourão pronunciamento occurred on March 30, two days after Easter. This is an important holiday in Brazil. Goulart, not believing that anything serious was afoot, had gone down to Rio Grande do Sul for a weekend's fishing. He rushed back to Rio and ordered government troops to confront the Minas Gerais rebels, but it soon became clear that the president had lost control of the armed forces.

Some of the military chieftains were, however, still reluctant to press forward hard enough to make their victory certain. During an agitated day everybody waited for everybody else to move. The state was falling to pieces, but nobody would act; men didn't want to risk their necks without orders. And who, as a matter of fact, was giving orders? The minister of war was ill in a hospital, and Castelo Branco, trying to hold to a moderate line, did not make his intentions altogether clear. One suggestion was to impeach Goulart constitutionally rather than depose him by force. The key question was what would São Paulo do. The commander of the Second Army there, the doughty General Amaury Kruel, delayed action for some hours. A point of interest was that Kruel had once been Goulart's own minister of war and had, it seemed, a long-standing feud with Castelo Branco. At the end Kruel, after talking on the telephone with Goulart in Rio, and pleading with him to get rid of the Communists, decided to act with the rebels, put his powerful army in motion, and announced, "I am going to Rio to depose the president."

This he did not do. Nor did anybody. Goulart saw that the end had come. Seeking to avoid bloodshed and finding it impossible to rally military support, he quit office and fled first to Brasília and then back to his home state, Rio Grande do Sul. Guerrilla resistance was feared, but did not materialize. By April 1 the coup was over. Fourteen out of Brazil's twenty-two states joined the revolt, and Goulart, whose own prestige had been eroded away, attracted no popular support whatever. He had hoped for decisive help in a pinch from the great unions which controlled transportation and communications, but these did not respond and an attempt at a general strike was a miserable failure. Instead, hundreds of thousands of men and women cavorted rapturously on the Rio streets to celebrate. Nobody against Goulart had dreamed that the turnover would be so easy. There was practically no bloodshed.

A man named Ranieri Mazzilli, a Social Democrat and the son of Italian immigrants, at once became acting president because, as president of the Chamber of Deputies, he was constitutionally next in line to the succession; there was no vice president, since Goulart himself had stepped up to the presidency from the vice presidency when Quadros resigned. Mazzilli had been acting president four different times before. He lasted for ten days. On April 11 Congress elected General Castelo Branco to be president to serve out the remainder of Goulart's term, and the revolution, or counterrevolution, was thus constitutionally confirmed.

A period of headhunting now began. Castelo Branco stated in his inaugural speech (April 15) that he "recognized the impossibility of fighting leftist subversion by encouraging rightist reaction,"[18] and he did his best to check excesses. Even so some seven thousand persons were arrested—most were soon released—and Goulart's last-minute land reform decree was annulled. Land reform is one thing the oligarchy will not tolerate. Forty members of Congress were expelled from their seats; two university rectors were discharged, thirty-three hundred civil servants fired, and half a dozen diplomats and governors removed from office; twenty-six out of eighty-two generals on the active list, eight out of sixty-eight admirals, were retired. Several left-wing governors were replaced by federally appointed "interventors," a familiar practice in South America; one, Miguel Arraes of Pernambuco, was arrested and held in confinement without trial for a long period. Provincial purges went on through most of 1964. Governor Plinio Coelho of Amazonas was suspended from office in June, and this was followed in November by the ousting—for alleged subversion—of one of the best-known administrators in Brazil, Governor Mauro Borges Teixeira of Goiás.

Immediately after the coup the army promulgated its celebrated "Institutional Act"; this gave authority for the star chamber proceedings under the National Security Council which I have already mentioned, whereby citizens could be deprived without trial of their political rights for ten years—meaning that they could not vote, run for office, or hold a government job, although they were still free to speak in public or edit newspapers. "The legality of this act was doubtful, and it was not signed by Acting President Mazzilli or any legislator," writes a British commentator. The three service chiefs simply claimed powers equivalent to those of Congress and the judiciary. The activity of the council administering the act was short lived, but, by the end of the year, 378 citizens had been proscribed, including former Presidents Kubitschek and Quadros as well as Goulart; also Celso Furtado, the former head of SUDENE, and Francisco Julião, the radical leader of the Peasant Leagues in the northeast. There were at least fifteen hundred political prisoners in the jails awaiting trial a year after the coup, and some of those tried got severe sentences. Hundreds of men and women fled the country. On the other hand, nobody was shot.

[18] *Ibid.*

The United States took a position on the April coup with unusual speed, largely on the advice of Lincoln Gordon, the American ambassador to Brazil, a former Harvard professor and one of the creators of the Alliance for Progress. President Johnson transmitted his "warmest wishes" to Acting President Mazzilli within twelve hours of his being sworn into office. The State Department held that there was no need to "recognize" the new regime because there had been no rupture in "continuity."[19] The quickness of this American response presently gave rise to the suspicion in some quarters that the Central Intelligence Agency might have been involved in the revolt. Following are excerpts from testimony by Ambassador Gordon before the Foreign Relations Committee of the United States Senate in March, 1966, when it was considering confirmation of his appointment as Assistant Secretary for Inter-American Affairs.

> Sen. GORE: I am particularly concerned with the part you may have played, if any, in encouraging, promoting or causing that overthrow [of Goulart in Brazil].
> Mr. Lincoln GORDON: The movement which overthrew President Goulart was a purely 100%—not 99.44%—but 100% purely Brazilian movement. Neither the American Embassy nor I personally [as Ambassador] played any part in the process whatsoever. . . . Neither I nor other officials of the U.S. Government, nor the Government in any way, shape or manner was involved. . . .
> Sen. GORE: Do you include the CIA in your answer?
> Mr. GORDON: Yes. In the Brazilian situation . . . there was no lack of coordination, and there is none, among the CIA personnel, the military attachés . . . and the Ambassador. This was and is all one team.[20]

Promptly after Castelo Branco's inauguration United States aid to Brazil, which had become a distinctly up-again-down-again process, was substantially resumed.

The assumption was almost universal during the first months following these events that Communism was the only issue, and that the Brazilian army had rendered great patriotic service and also served well the interests of the hemisphere as a whole by making a coup which aborted a genuine Communist conspiracy. Now the tendency is to adduce "demoralization" and "disintegration" as well as the threat of Communism as principal factors. Many fewer outright Communists held positions under Goulart than had been estimated, and the possibility of a Communist takeover was

---

[19] Several other American republics, including Venezuela, took a different view and at once broke off relations with Brazil.

[20] I. F. Stone's Weekly, March 7, 1966. Mr. Gordon was confirmed.

probably exaggerated. But this does not invalidate the point that, at the time, Communism was *thought* to be the issue and, patently, the Communists would have been in a good strategic position for seizing the country if disintegration had been allowed to go much further.

Brazilian wits are still busy with wisecracks about the coup; one is to the effect that it was a counter-*pre*-revolution. And the net result is that representative government has been virtually snuffed out.

*

Goulart escaped from Brazil a day or two after the coup and became an exile in Uruguay, where Brizola joined him. Criminal charges have been prepared against Jango, and he could not return to Rio without risking arrest and trial.

CHAPTER 3

Brazil: A Sheaf of Personalities

It's such a useless thing for a man to want to be: the p-p-president of Brazil.

—TRUMAN CAPOTE IN *Breakfast at Tiffany's*

MARSHAL (formerly General) Humberto de Alencar Castelo Branco, the president of Brazil, was nicknamed "the Jeep" by his fellow officers in World War II—because he was small, not pretty, and could not be stopped. He is five feet five, and his head seems to rise directly out of his powerful torso, with a minimum of neck. One old joke having to do with his size is that his mother, on giving him birth, did not know that he was not preshrunk, and made the error of plunging him into a bath. Photographs of the president are seldom seen publicly, at his own request: he says, "If *you* had a face like mine, would you like to have to stare at it everywhere?" His wife was, it happens, an exceptionally good-looking woman named Argentina; she died some years ago, and Castelo Branco has been a widower since her death. Once she told a friend, "What do I care if my husband is not handsome? He is beautiful within."

The president is prosaic, stubborn, dignified, and methodical. Talking to you on business he carefully ticks off items on an agenda pad, but his social demeanor, especially to women, is more flowery. He hates to be called a "dictator," and is not in the slightest degree a fire-eater of the conventional military type. Several years ago a group of politicians, meeting in private, agreed that he was the one officer in Brazil who had no political ambitions, and could not imaginably take part in a coup d'état. Indeed he did not join the *Revolução* until after a period of reluctant hesitation, as we have seen. Senhor Castelo Branco took off his uniform the day he became president, and has never worn it thereafter; he respects the civilian nature of the

47

presidential office, and likes to compare himself to General Dwight D. Eisenhower, who similarly gave up his uniform when he resigned from the army. The analogy to Eisenhower, a "peace general," is often stressed by members of Castelo Branco's entourage. The point is neglected that Ike was twice elected president of the United States by large majorities, whereas Castelo Branco has never been elected to anything at all.

General de Gaulle, in his quick-skimming tour of South America in 1964, the purpose of which still mystifies most South Americans, asked the president with some disdain why he, a military man, had given up his uniform. The Brazilian replied that he had replaced it with another robe of office, and added tartly, "I will wear my military uniform only once more, when I am in the coffin."

The president was born on September 20, 1900, of parents in modest circumstances in the northern state of Ceará; the house where he was born is now an ice cream parlor. His family, however, goes back a long way and a Castelo Branco (but the spelling is different) was a governor of Rio de Janeiro early in the eighteenth century. Young Castelo Branco decided to become a military man, went to officers' training school, studied for a time in Paris, and became one of the group of intellectually inclined officers who became known later as the "Sorbonne colonels." The turning point of his life came with the outbreak of World War II, when Getúlio Vargas, confounding the experts who thought that his sympathies were pro-Axis, brought Brazil into the war on the side of the Allies. This was, among other things, a triumph for Franklin D. Roosevelt's Good Neighbor Policy. Castelo Branco went to Fort Leavenworth, Kansas, and took advanced training there before going overseas. He has been inflexibly pro-American ever since. Brazil was, one might add, the only South American country ever to fire a shot in World War II, although the whole continent (except Chile) declared war on the Axis; twenty-five thousand men served in Italy, and the first surrender of a German division to an Allied unit was to the Brazilians.

One American officer discerning enough to catch Castelo Branco's quality early was General Vernon Walters, who, a brilliant linguist, was Eisenhower's principal interpreter for several years, and later became the American military attaché to Brazil. He met Castelo Branco at Leavenworth, where he was teaching, and then shared quarters with him on the Italian front. "He was the negation of the old idea that the only good officer was one who knew about close order drill," General Walters reminisces. "He knew all about everything, even the size of the crops. He reminded me of Al Gruenther."[1] Once Castelo Branco and Walters, sleeping on the roof, were interrupted by

[1] A high compliment—General Alfred M. Gruenther was Eisenhower's chief of staff for a long period.

BRAZIL: A SHEAF OF PERSONALITIES

a heavy German bombardment. Castelo Branco paid no attention. A man of the tropics, he did not appreciate the cold of the Italian mountains, and slept in an "envelope" or sleeping bag. Walters said that it was madness to remain on the exposed roof; the Brazilian said that he didn't want to get out of his bag because he would be too cold, and refused to budge.

Even today, the president cannot be pushed. If a minister is under fire this will tempt him to back the minister. A lone wolf, he has few friends—except for a handful of fellow officers who have been cronies since the Italian days. There is no *éminence grise* in the president's circle. When a journalist congratulated him on the success of the policies of Dr. Roberto Campos, the planning minister, he replied, "The policies are mine—Campos merely executes them." His regard for Campos is, nevertheless, extremely high, as is Campos's for him. Castelo Branco takes his job, which he defines as getting the country back on the tracks, with profound seriousness.

A man of painstaking honesty, with no false face, he made a public declaration of his wealth soon after becoming president, as did Eisenhower and Adlai E. Stevenson during the 1952 election campaign in the United States; this stipulation was called for by Brazilian law, but nobody had paid much attention to it before. His assets were a small apartment in Rio, a cemetery plot, a Willys compact, and $4,000. There is reason to believe that, at the beginning of his administration, his behind-the-scenes intervention saved a good many people from the military courts, and lightened several sentences; it worried him that so many congressmen had become *cassados*, the name given to citizens deprived of civil rights. Plenty of advisers thought that Castelo Branco was being too moderate, not the reverse, during this period when right-wingers were urging the outright abolition of Congress. He appointed a largely civilian cabinet, and leaned over backward to try to minimize the influence of the military. Later, as has been seen, this situation changed.

Mr. Castelo Branco received my wife and me for a half hour's talk in the presidential palace in Rio, a sumptuous building with painted ceilings and marble columns, festooned with old-style statuary; no air conditioning, but a lively breeze sailed in from windows open on all sides. This is known as the Palácio das Laranjeiras, orange groves. (The old presidential palace, Catête, is not used nowadays, since Vargas killed himself there.) Profuse courtesies took place before the interview—handshakings with members of the household and so on—and a troop of TV, radio, and other reporters, stationed downstairs, closed in on us when we emerged—a familiar aftermath to interviews with South American presidents. They wait and pounce like a pack of ferrets—as indeed they do in more developed countries.

Mr. Castelo Branco sat at the end of a long shiny table in a large conference room, and was abundantly polite. But I thought that, for all his glossy urbanity, he was defensive and hard to reach. He was smooth, careful, and told anecdotes to avoid questions. The two things he emphasized were the essential civilian nature of his government, and, in regard to foreign policy, that Brazil would not tolerate any "beards," meaning Castro. To indicate the usefulness of the April coup, he asked us how the United States would have liked it if Brazil, the largest and most important country in South America, had gone Communist. Now, he said, all danger of Fidelismo had disappeared. He made one puzzling off-the-cuff remark to the effect that Brazil "was a complex country, but not difficult," and said that its "colonialism" (in that it has regions both developed and undeveloped) must be ameliorated without exploitation.

General Artur da Costa e Silva

How to solve the "constitutional" problem was the great issue during 1965–66. Castelo Branco had vowed resolutely from the beginning that, once his term as president was concluded, he was out for keeps, and moreover that he would not turn his office over to anybody who was not a properly *elected* president. But an election would have posed "insuperable difficulties," i.e., the government might have lost it, and so Congress, after an angry debate in July, 1964, voted 205 to 93 to extend the president's term to March, 1967.[2]

Soon three military candidates announced their candidacy for the succession—General Artur da Costa e Silva, the minister of war; General Amaury Kruel, whom we have met as commander of the Second Army in São Paulo; and General Oswaldo Cordeiro de Faria, minister of the interior, who had been a leading officer in the Brazilian expeditionary force overseas in World War II. (That expeditionary force is still the alpha and omega of political power in Brazil.) General Kruel was talked about as "the Kubitschek candidate." Of the three the most powerful by far was General Costa e Silva, a taciturn, hard-bitten, somewhat sinister-looking officer of the old school, who was a tank commander in Italy. He wears dark glasses, has a ridge of mustache, and carries the style of the typical old-fashioned military man. But, far from being flamboyant, Costa e Silva keeps aloof from the public, and tries to be inconspicuous at official gatherings. He played a large

---

[2] The sardonic cry was heard on the left, "Why be a hypocrite?—Lincoln Gordon for president!" The implication was that Ambassador Gordon ran the country anyway, and so why bother to have an election at all.

role in the April coup, and believes that to take care of the country is the army's natural function.

General (now Marshal) Costa e Silva, sixty-four, born in Rio Grande do Sul, rose out of rough-and-tumble beginnings and was graduated from the Brazilian Military Academy in 1921. He and Castelo Branco were classmates, and have been friends ever since. His wife, Dona Yolada, is attractive, and their son, Alcina Barbusa, works in his father's secretariat. As a young officer Costa e Silva took part in the suppression of Paulista revolts in 1926, 1927, and 1932, studied at the U.S. Armor School at Fort Knox, Kentucky, during World War II, served with distinction in Italy, became military attaché in Argentina after the war, did a good deal of teaching, and eventually was named commander of one of the four regional commands in the Brazilian army (1956–58). But Goulart relieved him of this post, presumably because he would not yield to local left-wing pressure, and put him on the shelf in the war ministry.

On April 15, 1964, two weeks after the coup, he was appointed to be minister of war by Castelo Branco. In May, 1966, ARENA, the new hold-all government party, nominated him for the presidency. His program includes "restoring and consolidating democratic institutions," welcoming foreign investment that "wishes to cooperate in development," reduction of the cost of living, "encouragement to the youth," and friendship with Brazilian labor. Such clichés mean little, and it remains to be seen what kind of president this hard-headed, somewhat mysterious man will turn out to be. Liberals have little hope. In July, 1966, during the election campaign Costa e Silva even went so far as to state that citizens who were appealing for direct elections "just want to put the Communists back in power," which was an outrageous distortion of the truth. For one thing, as many citizens were quick to point out, the Communists never *have* been in power.

After the Coup

Now we must retrace steps a bit. The story is full of difficulties, but essential to an understanding of the present situation. After the 1964 *Putsch* conditions became stabilized for a time; there were two main reasons for this— confidence instilled by the person of the new president, Castelo Branco, and the sophisticated skill of his finance men steering a new deflationary course. The rate of inflation dropped, and the *cruzeiro* began to level off. The government put in new tax laws, overhauled the banking system, cut the budget by 30 percent and took other austerity measures. On the other hand this program necessarily brought unemployment, a drying up of industrial expansion, and screams and yells from taxpayers brought to book.

Lively debate was heard in Congress at this period, the opposition parties still made politics, the press was tolerably free, and the courts were functioning. But the country was divided between *linha dura,* hard-line, and soft-line elements. Castelo Branco continued to be considered far too "soft" by the extreme conservatives; they said that he had not "finished the job," and that the country was in danger of sliding back to chaos. One theory is that his so-called temperateness at the time was caused largely by respect for liberal opinion in the United States and western Europe and by the influence of the able, alert Lincoln Gordon, the American ambassador.

Behind all this was, as we know, the vexing constitutional problem of what would be the apparatus of succession when Castelo Branco's term ran out. The hard-line military, together with equally hard-line civilians, wanted the president to stay on, on the ground that the country was not yet ready for a return to normal parliamentary procedures, but he himself insisted that he would not continue in office beyond the stipulated date and would not under any circumstances run again.

Against this background came the gubernatorial elections of October, 1965. The hard-liners sought to cancel them, but Castelo Branco wanted them to take place as an essential step in the process of returning to constitutionalism. "Our government is not afraid of the ballot box," he proclaimed. But his regime went through every kind of connivance to ensure that candidates it feared or disliked could not run; for instance a "Law of Ineligibles" disqualified members of the Goulart government and other "undesirables" from being candidates. Nevertheless, free elections did take place, and their results were a profound shock to the government. The regime actually *lost* in five out of the eleven states contested, an astonishing thing to happen. It certainly proved that Castelo Branco was not a full-dress dictator at that time. Dictators do not lose elections. Setback to the regime was most spectacular in the great states of Minas Gerais and Guanabara (metropolitan Rio). In this latter the campaign was a wild, wacky shambles. Three different anti-government candidates, including the venerable Marshal Lott, were put forward in turn to oppose the man backed by Governor Carlos Lacerda, who could not constitutionally succeed himself as governor and naturally wanted one of his own kind to follow him. But one of his opponents won.

The party position was, to say the least, confusing. Five states were won by the PSD (Kubitschek), with assists in several from the PTB (Goulart), but, to make the situation even more complex, the PSD supported the

Castelo Branco government in several states, depending on local circumstances. Guanabara was a special case because of the enigmatic position of Lacerda. His man ran as a candidate of the UDN, the party generally identified with the government, but Lacerda was *anti*-government. In fact he had been vitriolically attacking the regime on a national level although it was, in effect, his ally at home in Rio. Lacerda wanted a harder line in national affairs. As a result of the defeat of his candidate in Guanabara, Lacerda withdrew from the forthcoming presidential race himself; this was a convenience to the regime because it removed the dangerous Lacerda from the *presidential* arena—at least for the time being—even though it was a setback on the provincial plane.

Now the hard-line military closed in on Castelo Branco, because the vote frightened them. Several officers demanded that the elections be annulled and measures taken to prevent the newly elected anti-regime governors from taking office. This the president refused to do, if only because, had he done so, any pretense that he was seeking to bring Brazil back to constitutionalism would have vanished.[3] But he soon yielded on practically everything else. He too had been piqued by the elections. So—a climax to all this—a shattering decree was issued on October 27, 1965, just before Congress was to assemble, putting a new Institutional Act into force, which was much more drastic than the one before. It abolished all political parties, packed the Supreme Court, provided that the president be elected by Congress rather than direct popular vote, and set up indirect elections for governors. The president was given the right to impose federal rule in areas he found to be "in internal commotion," to rule by decree for a period up to six months, and to "void the mandate of elected officials" if desirable, i.e., throw them out. Military courts were given the right to hear cases involving internal security, and, as in the first Institutional Act, which had expired, political rights of citizens were again made subject to suspension for ten years.

One deputy had courage enough to rise in Congress and declare that "the last shreds of democracy in Brazil have been destroyed." Congress was reduced to an "operetta status." On the other hand the provisions of the new act apply only until March, 1967, when Castelo Branco's successor is to be inaugurated. In theory at least it is a temporary act, but the general impulse toward full-scale authoritarianism became more emphatic day by day, and will be extremely difficult to reverse.

The president, still trying to hold to what he could call a middle line, but of course representing basic conservative interests, disciplined several army

[3] "Brazil Stops Pretending," by Emanuel de Kadt, *World Today*, December, 1965, is a discerning account of these perplexities.

hotheads, warned "anti-Communist military radicals" to give up a "creeping conspiracy" against his government, and dissolved an extreme right-wing political group called LIDER. On the other side his regime took measures against the left as well, and several intellectuals—among them two of the most distinguished writers in Brazil—were jailed briefly. This followed an anti-American demonstration, marked with banners saying, "Long Live Freedom," which took place against a meeting of the OAS (Organization of American States) in Rio.

Another crisis came early in 1966 with a laborious attempt to regularize the situation and rebuild the political structure by creating two national over-all parties, one to represent the government, one the opposition, to replace those abolished. The new government party is called ARENA (National Alliance for Renovation), and the other MODEBRAS (Brazilian Democratic Movement); it has been difficult so far to persuade men to join this new "opposition" group, for obvious reasons, one of which is that it is completely bogus. A similar attempt to create an artificial opposition came in Turkey under Kemal Atatürk in the 1930's. The idea was to build up something like "the loyal opposition" in England. It didn't work. And progression to full dictatorship continued by all manner of devices. For instance, government-controlled electoral courts have the right to eliminate candidates for Congress who are considered "subversive" or "enemies of the revolution," and the authorities themselves define these terms—which can be highly ambiguous under a dictatorship.

The Devastating Lacerda

Carlos Lacerda has one of the most priceless of all gifts—focused vitality. His drive, his energy, are boundless, and he gives himself with absolute fullness to whatever he may be doing at the moment. He has been called the most dangerous man in Brazil, the most relentless, and the most inflammatory. But beneath the heat there is a solid core of cold. Lacerda was a major instrument in the downfall of Vargas, and contributed substantially to the defeats of both Kubitschek and Quadros. I can think of no other person in contemporary history responsible for such a toppling of opponents under a parliamentary system except perhaps Andrew Bonar Law, the Conservative leader in England who played a critical role in unseating two prime ministers, Asquith and Lloyd George, and inhibited the selection of a third, Lord Curzon.

One sardonic joke of today defines the ideal Brazilian politician as a man as ethical as Adhémar de Barros, as incorruptible as Goulart, as stingy as

Kubitschek, as brilliant as Castelo Branco—and as laconic as Lacerda. Indeed Lacerda is given to words and speaks profusely. He is one of the most effective orators of the time; he wrote—and talked—his way to power. Sometimes a pointed blast reaches him in return. Not long ago he called Roberto Campos, one of his archenemies, "a mental weakling . . . leakier than a boardinghouse showerhead"; Campos replied that Lacerda "deliriously needs a climate of catastrophe so that he can present himself as the messianic savior." This interchange was provoked when Lacerda, opposing the Campos deflationary program, said that he would give more aid to agriculture and industry even if he had to print the money.

Brilliant, versatile, adroit, Lacerda is sometimes called "The Crow," because unfriendly caricaturists make him look like one. Another nickname is "beggar killer," which arose out of his campaign to clear beggars off the Rio streets: his enemies charged that the police, enforcing his orders, simply picked up a few sample beggars and tossed them into the bay.[4] Lacerda, who is almost crazily honest (even his most bitter antagonists concede that), gave Rio an excellent administration. His construction projects in Rio were considerably assisted by Alianza funds to the government.

About fifty, born in Rio, the temperamental Lacerda (one adjective commonly used about him is "unstable") was to politics born; his grandfather was a Supreme Court justice and his father a congressman. His father is often said to have been one of the founders of the Communist party in Brazil, but Lacerda told me that this was not true; his father was a Socialist. But two of his uncles, who strongly influenced him in his youth, were Communists; one moved to Moscow, became the Brazilian representative on the old Cominform, and died there; the other gave him a book on Communism by Nikolai Bukharin, one of the early Communist theoreticians, when he was eighteen, and this set him off as a youthful radical.

Lacerda in fact started political life as an outright Communist himself (like Betancourt in Venezuela) but left the party early. He did not, however, like Betancourt, evolve into a man of the moderate left, but became a violent reactionary. Such an evolution is by no means a uniquely Brazilian phenomenon. Now a *bon mot* about Lacerda is that he has gone so far to the right that he has almost become a Communist again.

He studied to be a lawyer, but left law school in his second year; he is one of the few Brazilian politicians with no university degree, who is not a doctor of something-or-other.

He considers himself today to be a writer by profession. As a young man

---

[4] A typically Brazilian happening was that, when word of this fable got around, irrepressible beggars appeared on the streets wearing life preservers.

he was arrested several times and spent brief periods in jail. Then, having veered to the right, he helped to organize the National Democratic Union as an attempt to build up a conservative counteraction to Vargas, who was president at the time. "I became a leader of the opposition," Lacerda reminisces now, "but nobody thought that I would get anywhere. I disagreed. I really knew intimately what the Communist danger was." Then: "People believe that administration is a by-product of politics. I don't. The art of politics is to know who is going to support whom for what price. Good administration is quite different."

Lunch with Lacerda when he was governor was a dashing experience. He led us briskly across a hot, steaming garden behind his headquarters in Rio, a splendid palace, to a small smart building, which he uses for entertainment. We saw a line of macaws, floriferous in scarlet and green, chained to tall posts, and the governor told us that, when he recently entertained Léopold Senghor, the president of Senegal, he was amazed to find out that the African had never seen birds like these before. Lacerda proceeded to send him two, and now he has just had word that Senghor, reciprocating the gift, is shipping him a pair of lion cubs. He wonders what to do with them.

Lacerda is an admirable host, and the lunch was one of the best I had in South America. We ate a lobster pilaf, côtelettes à la Kiev, pommes Anna, and a magnificently rich cake for dessert. Lacerda's talk was provocative. I asked him my favorite question on Brazil, why a country so rich should be so poor; his answers were colonial heritage, poverty of the soil, lack of education. In the old days all the wealth flowed back to Portugal and England. "The tram went the wrong way." I proceeded to ask what was going to happen now, reform or revolution. He did not give a direct answer. The principal force in the country is, he thinks, the little fellow, the common man, because all Brazilians are individualists, and the people are discovering that they have a *right* to be consumers; it is their *right* to own TV. The political left is, however, in his view immature and lacking in vitality; the leftists lie down like lambs, partly from remorse at having been "hoodwinked" by the Communists. As to the right, the danger is "lack of culture, lack of comprehension, among the elite." Castelo Branco? His chief source of power is his intense respectability, his conscientiousness. People lose their anxieties because they feel that he will not let them down. But is the government popular? No government is ever popular. "I hate political fiction as much as I hate science fiction." But the Castelo Branco regime is respected rather than hated. What is most necessary is to draw the young people in, and to make development cultural as well as economic. Castelo Branco cannot give up holding elections, because that would mean the end of hope. But he cannot hold them either because he knows that he will lose. A dilemma!

Brasília? No country should have a capital isolated on the frontier, because this makes for sterility, loneliness. Why are 400,000 Rio citizens on the waiting list for telephones, some of whom have waited for fourteen years? Because the government, for fear of alienating the consumer, will not allow the utilities company to charge "economic" rates. What about the church? Perhaps it is losing ground among the masses, and this is what is forcing it to become more liberal. What about the future in general? Answer: "How can anybody make changes *fast* enough in a country which is 52 percent illiterate?" What does Brazil need most? First, self-respect. Second, the need to give people a sense of *meaning* for their unrest.

For all his passionate intensity about politics Lacerda has room for other interests. He is a Sunday painter of distinction, and loves gardening. He learned English, of which his command is perfect, in jail; then studied French, Spanish, and Italian; during his governorship he took German lessons "for mental disclipine." When he has time these days Lacerda amuses himself by translating plays; he is at work on *Julius Caesar* now. Some years ago he translated the Broadway hit *Come Blow Your Horn;* it became a large success in Brazil, and his royalties amounted to half his salary, he told us with amused pride. Last year he translated another musical, *How to Succeed in Business Without Really Trying,* and hopes that it will do as well.

A man of utterly fixed and relentless antagonisms, Lacerda is well known for idiosyncratic behavior. For no readily understandable reason he refused to receive General de Gaulle when the French president came to Rio. On a different scale he happened to be at the airport one day and by chance saw the press officer of the American Embassy shake hands with a Rio publisher whom he detested. Outraged, though it was certainly none of his business, he promptly severed relations with the press department. He is not, however, particularly anti-American. Perhaps he tended to avoid too close association with the official Americans because these were so deeply committed to Castelo Branco, and he did not want to be bracketed with them. Lacerda was, of course, ravenous to become president himself, but even then the wiseacres were saying that he did not have a chance because "they" (i.e., the army) would not have him. And this is probably still the case.[5]

---

[5] Lacerda withdrew from politics—temporarily, one assumes—when the Castelo Branco government became more rigid during 1965. In August, 1966, however, when the new presidential campaign, if it may be called such, got under way, he issued a public statement as follows: "What has to be done in Brazil must be done with [the] support of the army, but without the army in [a] position as the head of the

The Grand Tetrarch of São Paulo

If Carlos Lacerda is the d'Artagnan of Brazil and Castelo Branco a kind of Aramis, then Governor Adhemar de Barros, governor of the master state São Paulo, is Porthos—a true swashbuckler. Rough, large-hewn, capacious, he dominates by bluff, bluster, and sheer weight of personality.

We met him in Rio, which he happened to be visiting for a weekend, in mildly peculiar circumstances. We had been lunching that day in Petrópolis, the suburb well known as the favorite habitat of the last emperor, when an urgent summons came from Governor Barros giving us an appointment in the evening. We said that this was impossible, because we couldn't get there in time, and a voice said explosively, "Come any time!" We arrived at his apartment about 9:30 after a trip through violent rain, and the governor, together with his secretary, an attractive young woman, received us with exuberant good will and determination. He wanted very much to be sure we would visit São Paulo.

After lively talk for half an hour we rose to go. Obviously the governor was busy. "Wait!" he commanded. Two men entered, of the type one sees hanging about county courthouses, but I could not tell if they were retainers, journalists, or officials receiving instructions. Barros disappeared with them, returned presently, and announced that we were to stay for dinner. "However," he went on, "there is only enough food for three. But my secretary is a clever woman and will work something out." Again the governor retired to speak to the mysterious retainers and we did not sit down to dinner till 11:30; then seven of us had fish roasted in coconut sauce, curry of chicken, rice, escalopes of veal, the usual attendant vegetables, salad, large quantities of cold sausage, and two desserts. Indeed the secretary was a clever woman.

Barros, who insisted on speaking English although his knowledge of this language is not exactly copious, said that a Brazilian politician, to become a success, must be able to do two things, gulp down a live frog and peel an *abacaxí* (pineapple) with a spoon, meaning that he had to be able to swallow things unpleasant and manipulate difficult problems. A Brazilian

---

government. . . . Unless there is rehabilitation of the revolution by democratic ways, there will be Communism." (*New York Times*, August 18, 1966.) And here the governor touches on a sensitive point because it is indeed true—not merely in Brazil but in other South American republics—that if citizens are totally denied an opportunity to express themselves in democratic terms they have no recourse in the end but to turn to the left. One unfortunate effect of military dictatorship, as practiced in several countries, is that it may tend in the long run to encourage just what it most deplores.

will say, "What an *abacaxí!*" or "Throw that fellow an *abacaxí!*" in the way that we say, "Catch a fast one!"

The governor went on to describe how, to impress one group of guests, he had served a wine supposedly French but actually Brazilian; he had simply pasted French labels on the bottles, which gave the wine a great name and vintage, to see if anybody would know the difference—then boasted about how good Brazilian wine was. Once, on a different level, he refused contemptuously to receive Marshal Tito of Yugoslavia in São Paulo, and even refused to let him enter his state, because Tito was a "murderer" and had "insulted the church." His analysis of the political situation in Brazil at the time of our talk was brisk. If the government did not hold elections soon there would be "spilling of bloods" on the streets. He himself had determined to become president. He was *bound* to become president. "This time the race is mine." (He ran a bad third in 1960.) Governor Barros was one of the true fathers of the 1964 revolution; he really put his neck out, and his potential importance was considerable because São Paulo has its own well-trained state militia, with some sixty thousand men. Barros said that nobody thought, at the time of the coup, that Castelo Branco was a politician, "but he became one very quickly." About another president he said that he drank so much Scotch that this upset the national trade balance. Mentioning Goulart briefly, he called him totally "irresponsible" but said that he had a certain sympathy for him because he, like Barros himself, was "a middle-class man, a man of the people." "As to the present situation there is danger from the right, and the left is still with us." A boom of laughter. "Now I stop, I talk it too much." Then he added that he was very rich, could live anywhere he pleased, and needed nothing for his own advancement.

Of course the worthy Adhémar talked glowingly of São Paulo. The *Paulistas* make what Rio spends. "Rio was built by God, but São Paulo by man." He added shrewdly that nobody should make the mistake of thinking that *Brazil* was industrialized because São Paulo is. Then he talked briefly about his own life.

In his middle fifties, the governor is a doctor of medicine—a surgeon—by profession, having received his medical degree in Germany. He left surgery for politics because, he told us, he could handle only half a dozen cases a day as a doctor, but as a political figure he could give aid to thousands. A singular man. But I do not think he will ever be president of Brazil.[6]

[6] Barros was deposed as governor of São Paulo and deprived of his civil rights for ten years in the early summer of 1966 while this book was in press. The regime charged that, preparing to fight new elections, he had handed out 13,000 state jobs in five days and was offering up to $27,000 a head for support from assemblymen.

Dr. Roberto de Oliveira Campos

If I may pursue the *Three Musketeers* analogy, Dr. Roberto Campos, the minister of national planning, is Athos—a man of impeccable principles, modest, neither an adventurer nor a buffoon, easy in manner, humorous, and becomingly grave as well. One of his best qualities is a subtle sense of timing.

Every Sunday morning, having worked a hard week, Dr. Campos takes a boatful of friends on a cruise in the Rio de Janeiro harbor, one of the supreme sights of the earth, with its incomparable view combining blue water, pincushions of dark island, and long blond beaches. Seen from a distance the roof line on Copacabana, with chalk-white buildings all of the same height, looks like the white cliffs of Dover, but in the form of a long scallop. First a swim from the deck of the cruiser; ham sandwiches and beer; then lunch at a bivouac along the shore. The boat is, incidentally, not his, but one lent him by friends—Campos is a civil servant, not a millionaire.

He was born in 1917 in Cuiabá, a town in Mato Grosso which was an outpost then, but has a population of sixty thousand now; his father, a professor, died when he was five. His mother took him to a village near Belo Horizonte, where he grew up; she had to work for a living, and became a seamstress. Young Campos studied for the priesthood for ten years—he still speaks Latin fluently—and then, because of "intellectual restlessness," as he put it to me, gave up this vocation. He went into the commercial department of the foreign office, boned up on economics at night, and was appointed third secretary of the Brazilian Embassy in Washington during World War II. While in the United States he did advanced work at several universities, and served briefly with the UN. He returned to Brazil to become president of the National Bank of Development (1956–59), resigned from this post because of disagreements with Kubitschek, went to Los Angeles as consul, and, under Quadros, served in Europe as ambassador for economic negotiations. He became ambassador to the United States in 1961 under Goulart, but resigned in 1964 because he was "tired of being the interpreter of a nonexistent policy." Castelo Branco made him minister of economic planning and coordination, his first cabinet post, and, along with Dr. Otávio Bulhões, the minister of finance, he became a dominating figure in the new government.

Dr. Campos had us to tea one day after the boat ride, and talked vividly about his problems while we sipped brandy made of oranges. What makes a country rich or poor? Denmark is small and totally dependent on specialized agriculture, yet rich; India is enormous, possessed of almost every natural resource, but miserably poor. Development, education are the keys. But which should come first? Ah, Campos smiled enigmatically, that *is* the question. As to Brazil several historical elements have to be considered. The pattern of colonization defrauded the country of enormous wealth. It was bypassed by the industrial revolution, and as a result had no technology to build on. Portugal—Spain too—had become "obsolete" by the end of the nineteenth century. Local disadvantages were many, chiefly the shortage in "energizing" factors, coal and oil. Then too a climate largely tropical made the country torpid. Can *any* tropical country become a truly successful modern power? Finally there is the lack of competent personnel. It has been fantastically difficult to provide an adequate staff for administration.

Campos has been vigorously attacked for his deflationary program, but he has managed to reduce substantially the shrieking rise in living costs, and, by introduction of the "strong" cruzeiro, to check further disintegration of the currency. He cut imports in order to build up reserves of foreign exchange, and cracked down on wage increases, which made him unpopular. But Brazil is by no means out of the financial woods as yet.

Dr. Campos went to Moscow in the summer of 1965 to negotiate an agreement with the Soviets. This was not a step in any new trend; Petrobrás made a $21 million deal with the Soviets back in 1963. One little-known development is that Communist satellites in Eastern Europe have advanced roughly $183 million in aid to Brazil, and trade with the U.S.S.R. has reached an impressive 3.7 percent of all Brazilian trade. Recently the Soviets were reported to have offered Brazil a $200 million credit to assist a huge dam and hydroelectric project at Urubu-Punga on the Paraná. Italian capital is also involved in this.

Americans in Brazil call Campos "Bob Field," which is indeed the equivalent of his name. There are few more attractive men of affairs in any country; the range of his intelligence, acumen, and good judgment are alike remarkable. He wrote an essay on American-Latin American relations in *Latin America, Revolution or Explosion*, edited by Mildred Adams, which really talks hard sense, and should be scrutinized attentively by every United States official entering the Latin field.

What Runs Brazil?

The big independent politicians played a certain role until the dictatorship became entrenched in 1965-6—even Congress; so did the provincial governors in the key states, some of whom operated like medieval thanes; so does the church, but in diminishing degree; so does a phenomenon that might be called "cliquism," small personal groups buried deep in the establishment which can have disproportionate power in any country so huge and lacking in organization. But what really runs Brazil, now as before, is the army.

Being a conscript army, it pretty well represents a cross-section of the nation as a whole in its rank and file. It is not a caste army, not the agent of a special class, not a monolithic army. What it stands for is *legalidade* or continuity in what it conceives to be its own and the country's interest, and of course this tends to make its orientation much more conservative than radical. Virtually all high officers are on the right, even if they are not "feudal" types.

Roughly 100,000 conscripts out of 2,500,000 available are inducted every year at the age of eighteen; half are illiterate, and roughly 40 percent of those called up have to be rejected on grounds of ill-health, caused principally by malnutrition. A fair proportion of conscripts will have been taught to read and write by the time they have finished their terms of service, and many will have learned the rudiments of a trade as well. The total personnel of the armed forces is around 200,000, of whom 120,000 are in the army; there are 13,000 officers.

One reason why officers, no matter how conservative they are, do not normally represent the feudal oligarchy as such is curious, and derives from the Emperor Pedro II. Eager to build up an integrated national state eighty or more years ago, Pedro saw to it that the officers' training schools became open to every kind of aspirant, not just the rich. Hence the aristocracy of the day snubbed these schools because they were not exclusive enough!—and did not encourage the young generation to pursue an army career. The navy is much more aristocratic, as it is in most South American countries. Another relevant point is that about 80 percent of Brazilian officers in the air force, about 40 percent in the other services, receive training in the United States, which affects their orientation. Incidentally the military budget consumes only about 17 percent of the national budget, a small figure for South America. A general gets about $300 a month, a private 75 cents a day.

Is the army truly moderate? This depends on circumstances; many senior officers are decided reactionaries, and it is the officers who count in a pinch. Who runs the army? The presumptive new president, Marshal Costa e Silva, is more important than the service chiefs; this is because he has the confidence of the younger officers, dating from the time he was minister of war and earlier. Why is the army so important as an arbiter? *Because it has arms.*

*

Late in 1965 the commander in chief of the Argentine army, Lieutenant General Juan Carlos Onganía, who is now president of the country, made a ceremonial visit to Rio for consultations with the Brazilian service chiefs. The story then leaked out that proposals had been put forward for a secret agreement between the two countries to pool their forces for joint action against any outbreak of Communism in either, under the aegis of an "Inter-American Peace Force." Whether the United States was behind this suggestion is unknown, but it probably was; nor is it clear whether it ever reached discussion on a formal governmental level either in Brazil or Argentina, although it had important political repercussions in Buenos Aires later. Anyway it died soon because two other South American countries, Chile and Uruguay, with a heavy distrust of the military, made their opposition known.[7] Nobody should ever assume that the ten South American states are one, but they still have a pointed capacity to influence one another.

*

The other great power factor in Brazil is the propertied class. In close analysis Brazil is run, the government and army aside, by industrial and financial interests in the cities, represented by urban politicians, together with the *caciques* (bosses) on the land representing the feudal landlords. The business community has—naturally—very large influence political and otherwise, and the industrialists and other financial groups maintain a potent lobby in Brasília.

But if a division of interest occurs between industrialists and the land-owners the latter are almost certain to win, if only because they have deeper roots. The land counts most, as it does almost everywhere in South America. The government will, if pressed hard enough, enact almost any form of reformist legislation having to do with the urban communities, but not the land. In fact the landed interests sometimes actively encourage urban measures supported by labor and the great unions, as a price for being untouched themselves.

---

[7] Juan de Onis in the *New York Times*, September 7, 1965, and the *Latin American Times*, August 26 and 30, 1965.

CHAPTER 4

Brazil: A Sheaf of Cities

God made the rest of the world in six days and saved the seventh for Rio de Janeiro.

—LOCAL PROVERB

> . . . The ocean was the old Atlantic still,
> always the swell greened in, rushed white, and fell,
> now warmer than the air; however, there
> red flags forbade our swimming.
>   No one swam.
> A lawless gentleness. The Latin blonde,
> two strips of ribbon, ripened in the sun,
> sleeping alone and pillowed on one arm.
> No competition. Only rings of boys
> butted a ball to keep it up in air,
> while inland, people starved, and struck, and died—
> unhappy Americas, ah triste tropique!
> and nightly in the gouges by the tide,
> the candle flaring for Macumba wooed the sea,
> black goddess, virgin of fertility. . . .

—ROBERT LOWELL

ALMOST ANYBODY who has seen Rio under a soap-bubble moon—or even without one—will agree that this is one of the most sensuously beautiful cities in the world, like a glorious toy in a misty veil of spun sugar. But it has squalid notes as well. Most of its romantic quality rises from its unique combination of ocean, beach, and mountain, but hills rising immediately behind the harbor contain some of the most revolting slums on earth—the *favelas*, which hold a quarter of its population. There are patches of higgledy-piggledy jungle a quarter of a mile away from the incomparable harbor, and much of the population is squeezed between sea and hillside. The city, for all its air of being a celestial fairyland, has had to expand lengthwise like a worm under pressure, which imposes throttling problems in traffic control, housing, and the like.

The roughness of the neighboring terrain contributes to the city's beauty, but it also makes for other difficulties. An airline pilot told me, "The clouds around Rio are full of rocks."

Two of the city's "mountains"—stubby hills in reality—are Sugar Loaf, which rises to twelve hundred feet and has probably decorated as many postcards as Niagara Falls, and Corcovado, on top of which stands a celebrated tall figure of Christ in concrete illuminated at night. I don't know if the Brazilians invented this type of religious monument, but it is astoundingly effective; capitals like Santiago and Bogotá have them too. But the beaches are what give Rio its most spectacular and seductive quality. Sixteen of these stretch, with interruptions, for five or six miles along the portcullis of apartment buildings on the shore, and, in the proper season, they fairly pullulate with happy Cariocas; youngsters play all kinds of ball games and children of every shade of color fly marvelous kites. None but the brave, however, actually go into the water except when the sea is at its most dulcet. Much of the time the breakers roll in as if they had been gathering momentum all the way from Africa; the surf booms, and the foam is so thick that you can hold it in your hand, like a cupful of milk. It is considered very bad form on the part of a visitor to get drowned actually on the beach in front of his own hotel—something like committing suicide in the gardens of the Casino at Monte Carlo, instead of a few steps away.

The whole city is beach-crazy. The Copacabana section looks like St. Tropez, with people in bikinis dodging traffic; swarms of cars prowl through bare flesh. Nobody with experience goes to the beach alone, because there are no cabañas or places to change clothes and it is unsafe, plunging into the water, to leave anything untended on the sand, even a pair of sunglasses or a pack of cigarettes. There are plenty of light-fingered souvenir hunters in Brazil, as there are in Coney Island or the Lido. Nor are the beaches always as clean as they might be; in fact the way they were described when the Portuguese royal court arrived in 1808, as being spread with offal, comes to mind on occasion.

Rio de Janeiro ("River of January") has an estimated 3,800,000 people in its metropolitan area, and is thus bigger than Chicago, Berlin, or Leningrad. Its correct name is São Sebastião do Rio de Janeiro. The legend says that it was discovered quite by accident, when a mariner named Gonçalvo Coelho, blown off course, made a landfall at the mouth of Guanabara Bay on

January 1, 1502. Then French Huguenots established primitive settlements which were eventually taken over by the Portuguese. For a long time little more than a sleepy tropical outpost, Rio came to life when gold and diamonds were discovered in Minas Gerais; then it developed into a flourishing port and was the federal capital of Brazil from 1763, succeeding Bahia, until 1960 when it gave way to Brasília—at least in theory. Nowadays it has been demoted technically to be the mere capital of Guanabara state, which consists largely of itself, but important elements of the federal administration still remain in Rio. A separate *state* of Rio de Janeiro also exists, with its own capital at Niterói across the bay.[1]

Rio has some admirable modern buildings, like the new Museum of Modern Art—which rises on land reclaimed from water, as on the Chicago lake front—and the Ministry of National Education designed by the great Swiss-French architect Le Corbusier.[2] The contemporary style of architecture now commonly known as "Brazilian" was given its first impetus by this Le Corbusier masterpiece, but Rio, in contrast to Brasília, has not carried on with this mode; it does not look like a modern city. Many pavements, on the pattern of Lisbon, are tesselated in black-and-white scrolled designs. These are popularly supposed to symbolize racial harmony between black and white, but the origin of the practice was quite different; it derives from the great earthquake and tidal wave that smote Lisbon in 1755. The ripples on the pavement are supposed to represent wavelets of water.[3]

Traffic congestion, as mentioned in a previous chapter, is appalling, if only because different sections of the city are separated by tunnels which are solidly plugged by cars much of the time. Overloaded trucks emit jets of dense black smoke and taxis, of a vintage and state of deterioration that would not be tolerated in Cawnpore or Rustchuk, pursue you down the streets uproariously like missiles set on an inflexible and deadly course. Pedestrians are expendable.

I didn't see many bookshops, but there are a fantastic number of beauty parlors.[4] Pharmacies also seem to be abnormally numerous, and a familiar story is that seventy-nine million out of eighty million Brazilians are doctors, meaning that practically everybody practices self-medication or goes to the

---

[1] The name "Guanabara" comes from an Indian phrase "Bay like the Sea"; "Carioca," the name for a citizen of Rio, means "White Man's Home."

[2] Le Corbusier first came to Brazil on the invitation of President Vargas and arrived in a Zeppelin. Pendle, *op. cit.*, p. 199.

[3] *Brazil*, by Elizabeth Bishop, Life World Library, p. 99. Landscape architects use different-colored grass in gardens to achieve the same pretty effect.

[4] As a matter of blunt fact, cosmetics are the biggest manufacturing industry in Brazil.

back room of a drug store for an injection. There are some good shops specializing in the semiprecious stones characteristic of the country, and occasional cable offices where you will find, to your consternation, that a brief message to New York costs $20. Imposing sights are the municipal theater, which, patterned on the Paris Opéra, is the equivalent of the opera in other South American cities, and the sumptuous Botanical Gardens, 156 years old, which have a famous avenue of royal palms, and are a similarly typical hemisphere phenomenon. The race track, owned by the Jockey Club, proves, if nothing else, that no capital in South America can get along without one.

One breathtaking sight is Gávea (Crow's Nest), which has what is probably the most spectacular golf course in the world; membership in the club here costs about $2,100 (the high cost of clubs is another characteristic phenomenon), and it looks down on *favelas* where a family of twelve may be living on $10 a month. One convenience is that the Santos-Dumont airport, named for the Brazilian aeronaut who was the first man ever to fly a fuel-engined airship, is located almost in the center of the city (like Aeroparque in Buenos Aires), an exercise in modernity which I wish North American cities could copy.[5]

Another item in folkways is that the siesta in urban communities is not nearly as conspicuous an institution as in former years. One thing that killed it is the new regime of office hours based on United States business habits, and air conditioning probably makes it less necessary than it was before.[6] Still another is that girls of good family in their late teens or early twenties get jobs as salesgirls or secretaries and have their own careers until they marry and even if they don't—an astonishing development for South America. I met one young girl, working on a newspaper, who had her own car—a neat white convertible—at eighteen.

Brazilian taste in food is rich, the menu opulent, and there are any number of good restaurants in Rio, like the Bec Fin. The national dish, if any country so large can be said to have one, is *feijoada*, a concoction of dark beans cooked with nuggets of meat, sausage, and bacon, and seasoned with onions and tomatoes—sometimes with a dusting of manioc on the top and slices of orange on the side. Several restaurants serve specialties from Bahia and the north, like *vatapá*, made of *dendê* (palm) oil, shrimp, and coconut milk. From the barbecue country in the south come standard dishes like *churrasco*, charcoal-broiled beef. A good provincial dish from Minas Gerais is

[5] The big international airport is however located outside the city.
[6] "Siesta" means literally "sixth hour." A siesta *before* lunch is known as the "siesta of the sheep." One nice Brazilian apothegm is that a man who takes a siesta has two mornings. *Atlas*, August, 1963.

picadinho, scraped meat with okra and pimento. A favorite soft drink is a variant of *yerba maté*, the herb tea deriving from holly which is known everywhere in South America, and which is sometimes served in a gourd hollowed out, dried, and trimmed with silver. *Cafèzinhos*, or tiny cups of very hot sweet coffee, are, of course, available everywhere. In Rio almost everybody has a sweet tooth, and we went to one extravagant lunch in Petrópolis where four different desserts were served: (1) a Minas Gerais specialty, *baba de moça*, which, literally translated, means "saliva of a young girl," and which is made of sugar, eggs, and coconut, and tastes of honey—a concoction extremely difficult to make; (2) purée of *mayo*, a custard mashed with bits of orange; (3) *dolce de leite*, a caramel-flavored purée; (4) a paste made of pumpkin, oranges, and coconut.

Brazilian fruit is incomparable. The country has all the tropical fruits well known in the north, like mangos and papaya, and no fewer than twenty-one different varieties of banana—and also such exoticisms as *carambola*, a waxy yellow fruit eaten raw; *fruta de conde*, custard apples; orange peppers; *jaca* or jack fruit, a large green object shaped like a football which grows on tree trunks; the *pítanga* or Surinam cherry; the *jaboticaba*, a purplish fruit which grows directly on the tree trunk but is picked like a single grape; a potato-like fruit called *sapota*; the *cajú*, a kind of apple which is poisonous if eaten unripe but safe enough roasted; and the *jenipapo* which has a powdery brown skin and belongs to the coffee family. Indians blacken themselves with its juice.

Then too the vegetables have an exotic range, all the way from *maxixé*, a kind of small fragrant cucumber eaten boiled, to tubers like *inpame* and *xuxú*, a pale green squash. *Jiló* is a delicate variety of eggplant and *baroa* is a cream-colored relative of the carrot.[7]

The national drink is *cachaça*, a colorless alcohol similar to drinks like pisco in Peru and tequila in Mexico, or, for that matter, vodka and slivovitz in eastern Europe, but made of rum. Almost every South American country has its own brand of this sinister but enlivening fluid. *Cachaça*, which runs from 94 to 100 proof, and costs about 30 cents a bottle, is often served in an iced mixture with lemon juice and sugar. Such blended or beaten drinks are called *batidas*. Two or three will make almost any dinner party bearable. Brazilian wines are first class, the best on the continent except Chilean, and the beer is as a rule very good, as it is indeed almost everywhere in South America. Draft beer is called *chopp*, and is consumed in herculean quantities. Scotch whiskey has recently become difficult to obtain because of import restrictions, but the Brazilians make a tolerable Scotch of their own;

[7] These names are from a fascinating pamphlet, *Feira Fare*, by Eileen Spence, Anna Lopez and Cathy Levinson, published in Rio.

Orson Welles is reputed to have said that it was the best non-Scotch Scotch he ever drank.

Rio has some giant names in recent culture, like Heitor Villa-Lobos (1884–1959) among musicians, and Cândido Portinari (1903–1962) and Emiliano di Cavalcanti, born in 1897, among painters, but there seem to be comparatively few younger men coming up. Eminent writers are on the oldish side too, like Erico Verissimo, Jorge Amado, and the novelist José Lins do Rego, who died in 1957. The great architects such as Lúcio Costa and Oscar Niemeyer, who created Brasília, lead a stunning group, and Roberto Berle Marx is one of the foremost landscape architects and creators of gardens in the western world. Niemeyer, a follower of Le Corbusier, built the Brazilian Pavilion at the recent New York World's Fair, and helped design the UN building; Costa is director of the National School of Fine Arts, and the story is that he won the competition for doing Brasília by scribbling a design on a postcard and mailing it in.

On a popular level the most conspicuous Brazilian contributions to culture are, of course, the samba, which has clouded roots in Africa, and bossa nova, which represents a "new look" in music. A normal samba is not taken seriously by jazz buffs, unlike bossa nova, with its intricate dark rhythms. The origin of bossa nova is obscure—it may have stemmed from the maxixe, and is clearly related to the mambo and cha-cha, but is more flowing, more melodic and relaxed—harder to dance to as well. The first Brazilian composer of bossa nova is supposed to have been Antonio Carlos Jobím, and it was famously introduced to the United States by Stan Getz.

One good place to hear bossa nova in Rio is the Café Zum-Zum, where Vinícius de Morais reads his poems in a remarkable act with four singers from Bahia, all sisters. Mr. de Morais, a professional diplomat and a well-known man of letters as well, wrote the book out of which the movie *Black Orpheus* was made, and he performs at the Zum-Zum with a delightful muted but lyrical quality. Don't go to the Zum-Zum early and don't worry if Mr. de Morais is going to be late for work the next morning.

Carnival and Voodoo

All we are good for is carnival,
football, and making love.
—PELÉ, THE GREAT SOCCER STAR

The playtime epitome of Rio, its gala apotheosis, is carnival, which has been called everything from "the greatest folk spectacle in the world" to "collective dementia." It lasts from the Saturday preceding Ash Wednesday until Wednesday evening, and for that interval everything else in the city is tightly shut; shops, businesses, government offices close down, and all ordinary activity stops. During this berserk joyride the lights have to be dimmed in São Paulo 250 miles away even though that city is having a carnival of its own, because Rio draws off so much electric power.

Both rich and poor share in the Rio carnival, with its ninety-six-hour nonstop festivities; most of the city never seems to go to sleep at all. A practice of the past—youngsters playfully and indiscriminately using squirt guns to spray ether on passers-by—was forbidden this year, but there was exuberance enough. Some fun lovers always manage to get arrested in spite of the lightheartedness of the whole proceeding and the tradition is that any such are held till carnival ends; then thousands of onlookers mass around the jails and cheer wildly as those so unfortunate as to have been locked up are dramatically released en masse. The first commanding event on Saturday night is on the high social level, a masked costume ball at the Hotel Copacabana Palace, which is a shimmering debauch full of pearls and sweat and as crowded as the Oktoberfest in Munich, although tickets can cost as much as $100 each, and are hard to get. The temperature was around a hundred and ten degrees in the ballrooms when I was there last year. The costumes, fabulously elaborate, risqué, and dashing, soon wilted. On Sunday night comes the parade of the samba "schools," that is clubs, down a broad avenue cleared of all traffic and before thousands of dripping spectators— it happened to be raining—in temporary open grandstands. Club members, the performers, are practically all Negro; the spectators are largely white. The participants practice all year for this event, spend fantastically disproportionate sums on their costumes, and perform complicated dances and present artfully contrived tableaux as they march; some of the more elaborate exhibitions, always in movement, take as much as half an hour to pass a given point. There are some fifty clubs in all. Naturally, nobody goes to bed.

Carnival is more than mere prankishness or exhibitionism. It is a circus for the masses put on by the masses themselves, a ritualistic festival expressing their own most remote, atavistic, and magical desires. One thing is certainly true—if Brazil put into everything the amount of money, energy, talent, spirit, and organizing skill that goes into carnival every year it would be the most successful country in the world.

*

A few nights after carnival we went to see a voodoo ceremony, called *macumba* here.[8] This exotic and sinister performance, which goes far back

[8] In Bahia the term is *candomblé*; in Recife *xangô*, a word also used for the Afro-Brazilian god of lightning and thunder.

into the darkness of African superstition, took place in a patch of clearing—completely isolated by wild bush on all sides—not more than a mile from the chic modernity of Copacabana beach. You can reach it only by leaving your automobile on a highway below, and climbing steeply up a path hewn through dense hillside vegetation. In the clearing a large white tablecloth lies on the ground before a primitive altar lit by candles: bits of colored paper, mystically endowed, hang from the edge of a shed, and along the sides of the enclosure are glasses of *cachaça* and similar offerings—libations for the voodoo gods. As a matter of fact small nests of ritualistic foodstuffs, lit by candles, may be found almost every night lying out unattended in dozens of places in Rio, along the beaches and in the hills; they are the one thing *never* stolen in Brazil. People are too frightened of Oxalá, Zâmbi (= zombie), and other gods who invisibly guard these supplicatory gifts.

The tall witch doctor, black and gnarled of face and smothered in a long white robe, advances to the center of the clearing and his supplicants approach him; they lament their woes and plead for cures for diseases which have stricken them or their kin. Then come hand clapping and a roll of drums, and a chorus of young women all in purest white, with petticoats fluttering, performs a febrile, vibrating dance around the witch doctor. Suddenly one woman, going into a trance, begins to shake violently, sobs, and then, becoming rigid, falls flat on the hard ground as unconscious as if she had been hit on the head with a mallet. The pitch of the dance rises, fetishes are offered, and the women career in higher tempo; crash! down goes another mothlike figure, twirling like a dervish as she falls, and as the others wail.

The drums stop, and the witch doctor revives the prostrated ones with a snap of the finger. They rise out of their hypnosis like automata, and a long wavering moan gushes out of the audience. Then the doctor holds more consultations and gives advice. This kind of proud, primitive, and garish display goes on a dozen times a month in Rio and elsewhere in Brazil. I have never seen ceremonies so full of hobgoblins even in the most remote divisions of Africa. The roots of Brazil lie deep but they continue to sprout to the surface naked and unabashed.

The Favelas

All over South America, not least in Brazil, the "new slums" are an urgent and menacing phenomenon. Great cities have become literally surrounded—encrusted—by these shanty towns, which are not only pestholes in themselves but which bring up difficult problems in police protection, water supply, sewage, education, communications, public health, juvenile delinquency. Millions of people live in circumstances which Adlai E. Stevenson, on seeing the *favelas* for the first time, called "subhuman squalor." The shanty towns have different names in different countries—*ranchos* in Venezuela, *villas misérias* in Argentina, *barriadas* in Peru—but the reasons for their mushrooming, such as population pressure, lack of housing, the desire to live in a city, and the fundamental natural impulse of people to improve their lot, are the same in most. The precipitousness of this evolution is almost beyond belief, and the number of persons involved enormous. For instance, to touch on other countries, both Caracas, the capital of Venezuela, and Bogotá, the capital of Colombia, have quadrupled in population since 1940, rising from roughly 400,000 to 1,500,000 and 1,700,000 respectively, and a great many of these are necessarily slum dwellers. Or consider Lima, where almost one-*third* of the total population lives in shanty towns, the most vicious on the continent, which surround two-thirds of the entire city.

As to Rio de Janeiro, about 800,000 citizens out of nearly 4,000,000 live in *favelas*, the peculiar distinction of which is that, as has been aptly said, they are "vertical," being built on hillsides. This came about partly because much of the land in Rio is too steep for normal building purposes and, when urbanization began on a serious scale, speculators let the hills alone. So the squatters, divided about equally among whites, Negroes, and mulattoes, swarmed to the cliffs, scraped off plots from jungle shrubbery, and built their miserable huts out of tin cans, hunks of stone, and cardboard, on the sharpest slopes. The irony is that they now have the best views in the city. But there are no amenities whatever, not even water or a postal service. Filth and flies are everywhere. Dogs howl, and children drip with slime. I have seen nothing worse even in Johannesburg or prewar China.

Why do peasants from the interior plateau, or workers in the sugar fields or elsewhere, move into Rio with such a rush? The answer could not be simpler. They think that—eventually at least—they will get a better deal in the city, a better standard of life. Conditions may be frightful in the squatter towns but they may well have been even worse in the *sertão*, backlands, where the serfs lived like animals, barely managing to survive even on a subsistence level. Once in the towns they have at least a fighting chance to get some kind of job and thus enter a money economy, earn wages, and perhaps see movies, read newspapers if they are literate, and above all have the possibility of education for their children and partake of other social benefits provided city dwellers by the state.

Nowhere in South America is the contrast between rich and poor more dramatic than in Rio, where slum dwellers live in such close proximity to the well-to-do. And nothing could have made this contrast more tragically pointed than a storm which smothered Rio in rain in January, 1966, and washed out thousands of shanty dwellings on the hillsides. Mud and rubble cascaded into the town almost directly on the heads of residents of glossily rich hotels and apartment buildings. About fifty thousand people became homeless; no fewer than four hundred were killed, some drowned in fetid mud.

The Locomotive

> . . . Several immense Madrids breaking half the horizon.
> —RUDYARD KIPLING IN 1927

SÃO PAULO, called by its proud citizens "the locomotive which pulls the rest of Brazil," is the biggest city in the western hemisphere after New York, the biggest in Latin America, and the eighth-biggest in the world, with a population close to 4.5 million—almost 5 million, taking in the metropolitan area as a whole. It covers four times more ground than Paris, and is more widely spread out than Los Angeles. The approach by air is a unique experience; the surrounding terrain, made of earth known as *terra roxa*, is so brilliant a red that it seems almost crimson, and this is punctured by splotches of luminous bright green; then, on this ornately tropical bed, a compact galaxy of skyscrapers rises as solidly concentrated as those in lower Manhattan, with serrated shelves, battlements, and towers.

Not only is the bigness of São Paulo spectacular; so is its rate of growth. It had around 250,000 people in 1900, half a million in 1919, a million in 1929, three million in 1955; then it passed Rio. It thrusts outward all the time, and the "ABC" complex of satellite cities—Santo André, São Bernardo, and São Caetano—has grown up around it together with other smaller industrial suburbs. Of the total population roughly two million are Italians or are of Italian decent, giving it a complexion like Buenos Aires, or, for that matter, Turin or Milan.

São Paulo, which was founded as a Jesuit outpost in 1553, is the contemporary heart of Brazilian industrialization. This is what counts. It was built on two things, wealth from coffee and hydroelectric power, and it represents the largest agglutination of industrial and financial power in the western hemisphere outside the United States.

The rest of Brazil likes to make jokes about São Paulo—also vice versa. The non-Paulistas say, "The minute a Paulista has tucked away his fortune he moves to Rio." The rivalry between the two cities is almost like that between St. Paul and Minneapolis in the old days or Leningrad and

Moscow. One standing joke is that nobody else in Brazil can understand the São Paulo variety of Portuguese because this has been subject to so many polyglot strains—Polish, Ukrainian, Japanese, Greek, German, and Arabic, to say nothing of Italian.

There are any number of sights, but the great sight is the city itself, as several observers have pointed out, with its cosmopolitanism, vibrating tempo, and atmosphere of success, stress and power. São Paulo has—just to pick up a few facts—8,000 restaurants and a new house is built every eight minutes. The tallest skyscraper in South America, 45 stories, is here, and the city uses more electricity per capita than Chicago to feed its 37,000 industrial establishments. It is certainly the most "American" city on the continent and the United States colony is large; about 6,500 United States citizens live here, of whom no fewer than 900 are members of the local (North) American Chamber of Commerce, a fantastic number.

São Paulo has what is reputed to be the biggest zoo in the world, and one park has been deliberately left in its original jungle state, to show what the city came from. The botanical gardens contain, believe it or not, 32,000 varieties of orchid. There are homely touches in this dynamo of a city; for instance pumpkins are cut in half and used as traffic dividers. One contrast with Rio is that the traffic cops are white, not Negro. Near a movie showing *From Russia with Love*, which has been a wild success, I saw youngsters squatting on the pavements eating a kind of watermelon with bright orange flesh. There are many more bookshops than in Rio. The center for atomic research is the biggest on the continent, and the São Paulo State Bank owns VASP, a flourishing and well-run airline.

Restaurants of practically every nationality make a considerable pretense of sophistication; in one I saw waiters pick coffee cups out of bowls of scalding water—with tongs—before filling them, so that the coffee would surely be both clean and hot. On one menu I saw "Poulet Great Mother" (languages do get mixed up) and had a chateaubriand covered not merely with a slice of pâté but of ham as well. Richness is the mode—not just in food. The city has a number of citizens called "Sears millionaires," meaning that they have made fortunes out of newly established manufacturing industries which sell their products to the Sears stores in Brazil; 90 percent or more of Sears retail products are Brazilian-made. But São Paulo has 700,000 people in *favelas* too who, to understate the case, have not made fortunes through Sears or otherwise.

One well-known institution is the Butantan snake farm, which, like its prototype in Bangkok, Thailand, prepares vaccines for use all over the continent; it has ten thousand snakes of twenty-five hundred different species.[9] The public library, twenty stories high, is the largest in South America, and three universities are now functioning—none, however, very big. One called Mackenzie University, a private school founded some years ago by an American Protestant, which particularly attracts foreign students, is probably the most important center for scientific research in Brazil. Also in São Paulo are two good museums of modern art, one donated to the city by Assis Chateaubriand, the great newspaper tycoon, and it has a well-known *bienel*, or biennial exhibition, which makes it the art center of South America. Here, as in the Biennale in Venice, painters from all over the world show their wares. More than fifty countries were represented by five thousand works of art in 1965, and a Hungarian-born op artist shared first prize with an Italian who paints on burlap, wood, and metal. Finally a São Paulo Philharmonic has just been established, the first privately financed symphony orchestra on the continent.

Francisco de Assis Chateaubriand Bandeira de Mello, the Beaverbrook-Hearst of Brazil as well as a diplomat, philanthropist, and political mentor ("Mr. Brazil"), is a very old man now. But Chateaubriand created modern journalism in Brazil, and his large chain of newspapers still exerts signal influence. The country would not be what it is today without him.

The city's most prominent citizen today, after Chateaubriand, is probably Francisco Matarazzo, Jr., reputed to be the richest man in Brazil, possibly in all South America, who is head of the largest industrial nexus on the continent. His father, an Italian immigrant, began at the bottom as a lard peddler and, before he died at eighty-three some years ago, had set up more than three hundred enterprises, covering almost the whole spectrum of modern business. "Feed and clothe them," was a Matarazzo motto, and a huge vertical complex was built up specializing in foodstuffs on the one side, textiles on the other, as well as cement, chemicals, and much else, with the result that the family enterprises are supposed to produce today not less than one percent of the gross national product of the whole of Brazil, an astounding figure. The present Matarazzo was the twelfth of his father's fourteen children. A papal count, he once gave what was called "the most resplendent wedding in history" for a daughter.

São Paulo stays up all night—one of the hallmarks of a true megalopolis. It throbs and hums with wheels within wheels, and it has justly been called the "world's most diversified industrial complex." It houses more than 800,000 industrial workers, and its automobile production, founded by Kubitschek less than ten years ago, is greater today than that of the entire Soviet Union. Just the same São Paulo is still a small town. Most of the

[9] *Brazil*, by Pierre Joffroy, in the Vista Travel Series, p. 58, a brilliant essay-guide.

streets are paved with medieval cobbles and there are some 200,000 people on the waiting list for telephones; the nearest airport capable of handling big jets is an hour and a half away, and you can't trust the drinking water.

*

São Paulo state, almost as big as Yugoslavia, has a population greater than any other *country* in South America except Argentina—about fifteen million. It has the greatest agricultural as well as industrial wealth of any Brazilian state, pays 43 percent of the country's income taxes, and contributes about a third of its total national revenue. The Paulistas have a fierce local pride and patriotism, and fly their own flag above the national flag; they fought a civil war (largely bloodless, however) against Vargas, and have made at least one serious attempt at secession from the rest of Brazil. One distinction is that São Paulo, the state, is the largest Roman Catholic archdiocese in the world.

SANTOS, a lively city on the Atlantic with around 350,000 population, is São Paulo's port and the greatest coffee center in the world; it handles more than half of all Brazilian imports. As far back as 1910 it was exporting coffee to the value of almost $100 million a year. Once half a century ago forty-seven British ships lay simultaneously in its harbor with their crews dead or dying—yellow fever.[10] Now it sparkles with healthy beaches.

Below São Paulo, cutting across the thick southerly appendix of Brazil, is the interesting state Paraná, with its capital at CURITIBA (pop. 380,000). Here are a temperate climate, open hilly country, and diverse agricultural development. Coffee has moved into Paraná in a big way, and made it the fastest-growing state in Brazil; the former governor, Nei Braga, is one of the most enterprising administrators in the country.[11] The people are heavily underlaid with German and Slav stock. Next in line to the south is Santa Catarina, a small state also partly German in complexion; FLORIANÓPOLIS, a charming city, is its capital. Nearby are Joinville, which is supposed to have more bicycles per capita than any other city in the world, and Blumenau, with its obviously German name, prosperous dairy farms, and rising industrial development.

At the end of the line in the south is Rio Grande do Sol, one of the key states, which I have mentioned often, alluding to its *gaucho* quality, cattle culture and solid, stolid atmosphere. The capital, PÔRTO ALEGRE (pop. 740,000), from which Vargas and Goulart came, has the highest literacy

---

[10] James Bryce, *South America, Impressions and Observations*, p. 372.
[11] He was recently appointed minister of agriculture in the national government.

rate in Brazil, the most progressive outlook, and probably the most up-to-date administration. Here—aside from beef—are cotton, applejack, and beer. Pôrto Alegre makes it difficult to believe that the Rio *favelas* can be in the same country. The taste of Africa is left far behind. Large numbers of Italians and Germans live here on well-tended family-size farms; one nearby town, Novo Hamburgo, has no fewer than 300 small shoe factories,[12] and is as German as *Lebkuchen*.

Fabulous Brasília

BRASÍLIA, which became the federal capital on April 21, 1960, is the third in the country's history, the others having been Salvador (Bahia) and Rio de Janeiro.[13] A spectacular city like none elsewhere in the world, it lies out in the blue about six hundred miles northwest of Rio and was, of course, an artificial creation—not a capital which grew naturally but one put together from scratch, like Washington, New Delhi, Canberra, and Ankara, Turkey. Perhaps the analogy to Ankara is the closest. Kemal Atatürk built Ankara in the 1920's to make his new Turkish republic impregnable, to minimize the European and Byzantine influence of Constantinople, and to develop the interior. Similarly Kubitschek created Brasília to dim the obsessive national focus on Rio, get away from the sea, and symbolize the largely unappreciated greatness of the country as a whole. Even so, fierce controversy has attended Brasília since it was born.

Brasília and Kubitschek are synonymous; generally speaking, if you are for one you are for the other. But, in actual fact, the idea of building a new capital deep in the hinterland predates Kubitschek by many years. When I first visited Brazil a quarter of a century ago the concept was talked about in connection with the *Marcha Para O Oeste*, the March to the West, which was a major Vargas dream, but nobody thought in terms of an imminent date or site. Long before this the first suggestion for moving the capital into the interior came in 1808, and José Bonifácio, one of the principal statesmen of the early imperial period, brought it up as a serious proposition in the 1820 's. The motive then was mostly military—to build a fortress capital out of the reach of any invader—but the idea of keeping the coastal strip from being overpopulated also played a role.

Anyway work started at last under Kubitschek. In 1956 the area of what is now the Federal District, covering 5,814 square miles, had exactly three

12 *South American Handbook*, p. 584.
13 The United States has had four capitals since 1776—New York, Philadelphia, York (Pennsylvania) and Washington, D.C.

settled inhabitants except Indians; today the population is around 200,000—
nobody knows exactly—including some 90,000 civil servants. The maximim
population expected in the future is 750,000, but nobody thinks that this
figure is ever likely to be reached, because funds are short for further building. The site might well have been better chosen, many people think.[14]
Roberto Campos told us that a spot sixty miles to the south, where the land
is more fertile, would have been better. But any location in this harsh area of
planalto, the interior plateau, would have presented similar problems in
transport and communications. All the first building materials for Brasília,
even cement and steel, had to be brought in by air.

Communications are still difficult, except by plane. The nearest railhead,
Anápolis, is about forty miles away, and the trip by road to Rio takes
around fourteen hours, to São Paulo the same. Roads—mostly dirt tracks—
are few. The whole area is, in fact, still a frontier; even today there are occasional strikes of precious or semiprecious minerals out in the sertão, and
gold-rush episodes are seen again.

One fascinating spectacle is the road, BR-14, that has been hewn from
Brasília through unending jungle to Belém on the Atlantic 1,582 miles due
north. Still a track mostly for adventurers, largely unpaved, it does, however,
have a bus service; the trip takes a week if weather permits. Brazilian technicians performed heroic feats to make this highway. First the air force dropped
napalm bombs to burn out a route; then parachutists jumped in; jeeps and
equipment followed, also dropped by parachute. During long spells of rain
workers had to be provisioned from the air, and cannibals with poisoned
arrows lurked in the adjacent bush. Some villages had no names; some are
still known only by numerals denoting the distance in kilometers from Brasília; one hamlet, 759 miles from the capital, is called "Cidade President
Kennedy." The magic of the Kennedy name penetrates almost everywhere in
South America.

But to return to Brasília itself. The men mainly responsible for its unique
and bizarre beauty are, as mentioned above, Lúcio Costa and Oscar
Niemeyer; Costa is largely responsible for the plan as a whole, Niemeyer for
most of the actual buildings. The city is laid out in the shape of an airplane—or locust—a brilliantly imaginative concept. Surrounding it is a lake
made by damming three rivers, which meet here; the lake consists of mud,
but is blue on top.

Everything has a note of the fantastic, and in general the town resembles
some marvelous creation out of science fiction; a city on the far side of the
moon, dreamed up in the movies, might well look like this. The basic design

---

[14] A team of specialists from Cornell University helped choose it.

provides for uninterrupted traffic by means of special channels, loops and whorls; one decorative motif is a frieze of toothlike protuberances which local wits call "Niemeyer cardiograms," because they look like the patterns in electrocardiogram tape.

The presidential palace, or Palácio da Alvorada (Dawn), is the most unusual of buildings. Broad shining flagstones lie between flat rectangular pools of water leading to a reception hall in gilded brick lined with mirrors. A scarlet ramp leads to a maroon and gray open staircase, and then to rooms where chairs of the most modern design recline like fawns on great tawny circular rugs. It is difficult, depending on the light, to determine what is indoors, what outdoors—where reality begins. But the visitor is quickly brought to earth by a large double sculpture rising from one of the pools which depicts two heroic nude women washing their hair—also by squat little sentries (alive) patrolling the grounds attentively with tommy guns.

Congress is a towering twin block built in the shape of a letter H with a huge flat white bowl on either side, one right side up, one inverted; these are the legislative chambers. Nearby—I don't suppose this has any symbolic significance—are twin metal statues of what appear to be a pair of robots. The great ministries—War, Navy, Education, and so on—rise in a series of high glass rectangular blocks. And the hospital is by all odds the most imposing building of its kind in South America; it is, however, not yet in full use, because of lack of staff. A TV tower is to be erected nearby higher than the Eiffel Tower. Perhaps the most controversial building of all is the cathedral, which, built underground, symbolizes the catacombs. All that one sees exposed on top is a huge crown of metal thorns. But this cathedral has not been consecrated as yet, because local elements in the church disapprove hotly of the leftward views of Oscar Niemeyer, its creator.

The main commercial and shopping street, Avenue W3, is five miles long; near one end is Brasília's shanty town, known as the "Free City." About forty to fifty thousand workers, called *candangos,* live here or in temporary dormitories without water, garbage disposal, or a sewage system. Even in a brand-new city, it seems, *favelas* cannot be avoided. During the whole length of Avenue W3 I saw only one restaurant, one movie. But we visited one shiny supermarket where actual Scotch whiskey ($16 a bottle) and actual American cigarettes (75 cents a pack) could be obtained. Taxis are orange-colored Volkswagens. The circumstances of life in Brasília are such that it is still officially considered a "hardship post" for American diplomatic personnel, and its newness such that so far only one American child has been born here out of the staff in residence.

Brasília is still violently attacked for a good many reasons, but it is here to stay. It cost far too much money, but the fact that the Castelo Branco government accepted it means that it will not be given up. I have heard it called "a crazy dream by Kafka," "a Daliesque nightmare," a "theoretical city not for human beings," "a robot capital," and "the billion-dollar flop." Since it has only a small percentage of the administrative cadre necessary to make it a city fit to work in, many citizens suffer from a disease which is wrily called Brasíliaitis, a form of neurotic depression caused by the stark landscape and the sameness of the giant *super-quadrases* (tenements) where officials are housed. The streets have been built so that it is difficult to walk freely, but this may be because the work is not yet completed, and there are too few parks, schools, and amenities for sports. But it would be all but impossible to turn the clock back on Brasília now. Airplanes fly 140,000 round trips to the coast every year, as against 33,000 a few years ago. Moreover, it is no longer predominantly a commuter town. About a quarter of the Congress now live here permanently, and the cabinet and foreign embassies will presumably have to follow soon.

I even met citizens who said that they liked Brasília, and it symbolizes hope to many. One reason adduced for liking it was that husbands cannot stray very far, wives see more of them than in Rio, and family life is healthier.

*

The Federal District was hacked out of the state of Goiás, but this has a different capital—GOIÂNIA (pop. 165,000), a true frontier town. Westward lies the enormous state Mato Grosso, much of which is still a wilderness. The capital, CUIABÁ (pop. 57,000) is difficult to reach, and nothing much happens when you get there.

Between Brasília and the sea is Minas Gerais, the great state of the central plateau which is almost as vital to the country as São Paulo; it has as many people as the whole country of Chile, and its capital, BELO HORIZONTE (Beautiful Horizon), is a spic-and-span lively modern metropolis with a population of 800,000. Built in 1897, on the site of an older city, it is, like Brasília, an artificial creation; the streets are laid out like spokes in a wheel, and its aggressive architecture seems to be pointing out proudly that this city, "with its heart of gold and bust of iron," is the focus of the country's mineral wealth. Niemeyer did several of its best buildings, including a spectacular church, reminiscent of a serpent or a moth in flight, which he designed with the painter Portinari. Nearby are towns favored by tourists like Ouro Prêto, the old gold city once called Vila Rica, and Diamantina, the biggest diamond center in the world until Kimberley was discovered in South Africa. Also nearby is something more important nowadays, the $250 million Usiminas Steel Mill, 40 percent of which is controlled by Japanese investors, 35 percent by the Brazilian government, and 25 percent by the state of Minas Gerais—one of the largest industrial enterprises on the continent. In a step one moves from the sixteenth century to modern industrial Brazil at its most strident and complex.

Salvador, Bahia, or Primocap

About twenty minutes after arriving in Bahia I sat cozily in a bar with Jorge Amado, the writer, and I put a question to him: "If Brasília is Novocap, Rio is Belacap, and São Paulo Supercap, what is Bahia?" Amado, an original and gusty character, the author of several classic novels like *Gabriela, Clove and Cinnamon*, replied immediately, "Primocap." And indeed Bahia, which was discovered by Amerigo Vespucci in 1501, was, as I have already mentioned, the first capital of Brazil. Mr. Amado, who is modest, did not add that Bahia is sometimes called "Amadoville," because he is its most distinguished citizen, universally known and loved from one end of the community to the other even though conservatives may deplore his extreme left wing politics.

This, the fourth-biggest city in Brazil, is a bustling Atlantic port misty with a romantic tradition and luminous with ancient color as well. Correctly its name is Salvador, or, even more correctly, São Salvador da Bahia de Todos os Santos ("Holy Savior of the Bay of all the Saints"), but it is usually known merely as "Bahia," from the state of which it is the capital. Bahia the state is as big as France. Bahia the city has about 900,000 people, and, like everything else in Brazil, grows voluminously day by day. Local pride is vivid. A skeptical visitor once asked a Bahiano whether Brazil was really a nation, and received the reply, "I don't know, but Bahia is."

Communications are hesitant, except by air. The rail trip to Rio, 1,200 miles away, takes 70 hours according to the timetable, but often lasts much longer. By road 35 hours is par for the course if the weather is good and your car muscular. Some 270 miles northeast of Bahia is Aracajú, the capital of the adjoining small state of Sergipe. This is 28 hours away by train, 7 hours by car, and 35 minutes by jet. There are dimensions in which Brazil *does* advance.

BAHIA, founded in 1549, represents Portuguese colonial architecture at its most winning, and is studded with churches—one for every day in the year, according to proud local figures. Several are spectacularly ornate and gilt-encrusted, like those in Quito, Ecuador, with jacaranda (rosewood) altars, and the whole town gives out the flavor of a religious museum, antique, unspoiled, eternal. But what chiefly distinguishes Bahia is not so much its old Christian ornaments as its aura of Africa. This city, despite its station in our hemisphere, resembles Accra or Dakar much more than it does Boston. Here we enter fully the world of *African* Brazil; this is the only place in all South America where I felt that I was not in the western hemisphere at all.

At least 70 percent of the population is Negro or mulatto; one of the great beaches is called "The Beach of the Arrival of the Negroes." If there are 365 Christian churches there are at least 1,000 voodoo places of worship. Several of the local deities are formidable, like Yemanja, the Goddess of the Sea, who is also well known in Yoruba (Nigerian) mythology. Christian and African forms of worship seem to merge in Bahia, and African influence extends to all manner of other fields.

A good luck charm, used by almost everybody, is the *figa*, shaped like a hand, which wards off the evil eye and brings good luck, but only if you get it as a gift. Buying one is no good. Another curiosity is the *berimbau*, a musical instrument African in origin, consisting of a bow with an iron string, a hollow gourd, and a coin with which the bow is stroked. Still another is the duel dance known as the *capoeira*. Slaves were forbidden to fight with their fists in the early days, and invented this form of combat as a substitute; kicking and butting are permitted, but not striking with a hand. Now it has developed into a formalized kind of calisthenic dance, at which almost all youthful—and many adult—Bahians are adept.

The sights, smells, noises of Bahia seem to have crossed directly from the bulge of one continent to that of another. Cakes fried in palm oil on tin stoves in the open streets; women wearing multiple, multicolored long skirts with fantastically opulent looped beads around stout necks, the status symbol being the number of separate petticoats; a tiny bright silver coffin containing the corpse of a baby being led to burial; marmosets and turtles in cages in the market near a noseless leper; stark-naked children mottled with disease, their eyes staring; serious sweating gamblers standing in line before the lottery bureau with its large tin safe; *candomblê* priests; burros carrying "querosene" tanks—these are familiar street scenes near the market.

Bahia lives on sugar, cocoa, sisal, rubber, and petroleum. This is the home of Petrobras among other industrial establishments. Prices are high, because of bad distribution and, in the case of foodstuffs, lack of refrigeration. The minimum wage is 51,600 cruzeiros a month (roughly $26 at the time of our visit), and a cook is lucky to get $1.75 a week. But nobody seems to mind much, at least on the surface, because this is a town saturated above all with *je m'en fichism*. The citizenry will queue up two hours for a bus without a murmur, nothing ever gets done on time, and a favorite toast is, "To the Bahian virtues of which there are none." Strangely, most residents of the town seem to dislike the sea. Windows opening on an ocean view are often kept shut, and are sometimes even blacked out; servants' quarters are generally on the sea side of the house. Bahia is full of art and artists, but nobody would ever dream of painting a marine landscape, although the coastline is extravagantly picturesque. Among interesting artists are Genaro de Carvalho, who paints in the form of closely woven tapestries; the well-known sculptor in metal, Mario Cravo, who has a growing reputation in the United States; and a distinguished caricaturist and artist at large, Argentine in origin, who goes by the name Carybé.[15]

The governor, of Italian descent, is a dentist by profession, and the local archbishop is one of the best-known liberal churchmen in Brazil. But the man I will always remember is Jorge Amado, who, with his wife, warmly opened up this city of treasure to us, gave us unstintingly of his own civilized devotion to its sights and institutions, and enriched us with his robust, humorous, and discriminating delight in the good things of life.

*

North of Bahia is an interesting constellation of provinces and cities. The capital of Rio Grande do Norte, an aggressive small state on the tip of the bulge, is NATAL, (pop. 180,000), a vigorous port. Here a paved road exactly 9.8 miles long, built by the United States in the 1950's, leads to the airport; this is the *only* all-weather road in the whole state—area 53,000 square miles, bigger than Czechoslovakia. The capital of nearby Ceará, often called the "best" state in the north, because it is the most developed, is FORTALEZA, which has tripled in size in twenty years, has on occasion two hundred successive days of rain although it is situated in the heart of a drought area, and produces, among other things, extraordinarily delicate lace.

Big Fresh Water

The white sap of rubber—from the udders of the jungle . . .
—GERMÁN ARCINIEGAS

The Amazonian city MANAUS, like Samarkand in Central Asia, is steeped in myth, and is the capital of the state of Amazonas, as big as Mexico. It lies deep in the interior of northwestern Brazil on the Rio Negro, named

[15] Carybé did the murals in the American Airlines terminal at Kennedy Airport in New York.

for its black water, a few miles from its confluence with the Amazon; with some 160,000 people, it is a ghost town trying to come to life again.

In the closing years of the last century Manaus was the pivot of Brazil's rubber boom and, as such, achieved picturesque renown. Buried in steaming jungle as it was, this was the first city in South America to have a streetcar line; Pavlova danced in its celebrated rococo opera house, which was built in 1896 and still survives, although in a dilapidated state. No roads lead to Manaus, even today, and it is accessible only by river or by air.

Why should a city as remote as this have had an opera at all, let alone one as imposing—relatively speaking—as that in Paris? Because opera symbolized opulence in older days, and the roughnecks, gamblers, and overnight millionaires of the epoch thought that to have one was the *dernier cri*. Similarly opera houses were built in boom towns, now ghost towns, in the American West in frontier times, as may be seen today in Nevada and the interior of Colorado.

Large fortunes were carved out of the Manaus jungles when rubber ruled Brazil in the late nineteenth century; then the boom dramatically collapsed, for at least three reasons. First, the Amazon regions were heavily marked by malaria and other tropical diseases and relatively inaccessible to world markets. Second, Brazilian production was both extravagant and inefficient, and the world price of rubber dropped. Third and most important, British agents stole some Amazon seedlings, smuggled them out of the country, grew them experimentally in Kew Gardens near London, and transported these to Malaya, where they set up a rival rubber industry which has been flourishing ever since.

In the 1930's Henry Ford, in order to be self-sufficient in rubber, bought an enormous Amazon tract, more than 3½ million acres, near Manaus, and named it Fordlândia; here seven thousand workers cleared the jungle, planted trees, and set out to produce rubber. But a fungus struck the new trees just as they were beginning to produce, and the project was abandoned. Then Ford made a second attempt at a location called Belterra, where more than three million trees were planted, but this too turned out to be a failure and was given up. Incidentally an outpost called Santerém exists in this neighborhood that still contains the descendants of American Confederate soldiers who refused to accept General Lee's surrender in the Civil War, and migrated to Brazil. A similar community, called Vila Americana, is an enclave near São Paulo.

Much of Amazonas and the other great Amazon state, Pará, is still *terra incognita*, but large plans for their development are being advanced. Sturdy work in public health and public works is going on. An organization called

SPVEA, the Superintendency of the Plan for Economic Valorization of the Amazon Region, has been set up, and is eager for investment; breweries, cement, power projects, paint, and meat industries are a-building. The Amazonian shores hold natural wonders all the way from eight thousand different kinds of tree—this is the world's densest rain forest, with enough lumber to build every person in the world a house[16]–to a tribe of aborigines, the Curupira, who walk with their feet turned backward. If you do not believe this or want to know how it is done, consult Professor Freyre.

PÔRTO VELHO (pop. 51,000), the capital of Rondônia territory, lies isolated in the bush on the Bolivian frontier. Here the legendary Madeira-Mamoré railroad, 228 miles long, to build which is said to have cost a life a tie, still runs—from nowhere to nowhere.

*

This chapter is about cities, but it is convenient to include here a word about the Amazon itself, the most phenomenal river in the world. True Brazilian superlatives must be hauled out of the bag to describe it. The Nile is a shade longer, but the Amazon is more powerful; its average flow, 17,500,000 cubic feet a second, is enough to flood Texas to a depth of one inch in a day. When it reaches Belém, after starting life within a hundred miles of the Pacific in Peru and having traversed almost the entire width of the continent, its volume is still twelve times that of the Mississippi, and its energy is such that it discharges fresh water one hundred miles or more out into the Atlantic.

Peru, Bolivia, Ecuador, Colombia, Venezuela, and the Guianas—as well as Brazil itself—feel its mighty and invigorating touch. No wonder it has been called "the world's greatest body of fresh water," and indeed it contains, according to one authority, one-fifth of all the fresh water in the world. The Brazilians call it the River-Sea, and I have seen ocean vessels, coming straight from London, discharge their cargo at Iquitos, Peru, 2,300 miles upriver.[17] In 3,900 miles not a single bridge or dam crosses it or interrupts its stupendous flow, and it has no fewer than 1,110 tributaries, 18 of which are major rivers themselves; one, the Madeira, is 3,000 miles long, with 90 tributaries of its own; 6 others are longer than 1,000 miles.

One tributary, the Araguaia, became famous for a cause célèbre in the 1920's—the disappearance without trace of an eccentric British explorer,

[16] Juan de Onis in the New York Times, January 17, 1966.
[17] See Chapter 20.

Colonel Percy Fawcett. Anybody still interested in adventure might try to find his bones. Search for his person produced a considerable literature for a period, including one high-hearted book, *Brazilian Adventure*, by Peter Fleming. As an introduction to the Amazon itself nobody could do better than read *The Sea and the Jungle*, by H. M. Tomlinson, a classic.

*

BELÉM, sometimes called Pará, lies at the mouth of the Amazon, on the equator, has half a million people, and is the capital of the state of Pará. The United States consular district here is our second-largest in the world, Moscow being first. Belém is among other things famous for its colonial architecture (it was founded in 1616), its massive religious processions, the ornate dolls it sells, and its execrable climate. It has been called the "Paris of the Equator," than which no description could be less apt. Half of its people live in *favelas*, and it is one of the least attractive communities on earth.

*

We turn now to Recife, Pernambuco, the last city in this Brazilian journey, and the problems with which it bristles.

CHAPTER 5

The Northeast Plus Other Brazilian Headaches

> . . . *Unfortunately the rich in Latin America talk too much about reform and label as Communists all those who would enforce it. This is easy to understand: the rich in Latin America go on holding 80 percent of the land on the continent. Often they control parliament and have the intensity of their idealism and hope in the future gauged by the bank deposits kept in their names in the United States and in Europe.*
>
> —DOM HELDER CÂMARA, ARCHBISHOP OF PERNAMBUCO

BRAZIL BEGAN here on its northeastern bulge with sugar plantations worked by the "Guinea Pieces," Negro slaves. When people say today that there are "two" Brazils what they mean is that the northeast still has such a special homogeneity and file of unique characteristics as to be sharply differentiated from the rest of the country. This is the area par excellence of feudalism, poverty almost to the starvation point, and incipient unrest—probably the touchiest rural area not merely in Brazil but in all South America except the Inca highlands.

Defined in the round, the northeast consists of nine states on the edge of the continent facing the Atlantic, with parts of others inland; the whole region, three times the size of Texas, has twenty-five million people, almost a third of the nation, and is sometimes called the "Polygon of Drought." Infant mortality in some districts goes as high as 80 percent; life expectancy among the *flagelados*, "beaten ones," is under forty years; the average income is probably not more than $70 a year; 50 percent of the urban labor force is

87

unemployed.[1] The landowners on the great *fazendas* have overweening economic power and the local *patrão* still controls most political activity, because he can teach a peasant to sign his name, thus claim that he is literate, and take him to the polls, where he votes for—guess whom—the boss.

The northeast is—an odd paradox—also the intellectual fountainhead of Brazil. *Nordestinos* comprise at least half the membership of the Brazilian Academy of Arts and Letters, and the country is thickly sprinkled with its teachers, artists, and men of letters. It supplies other human resources as well, including labor. Workers from the northeast made the building of Brasília possible, and form important elements in the highly trained labor force in São Paulo and elsewhere. Industrial development is now becoming important in the northeast itself; the area throbs with projects. "Know anybody who wants to be a millionaire? Get him started canning northeast fruit," a man in Recife told me. New roads, new water systems, new power plants are in the works. Finally the region has intense local patriotism. One word I heard was, "Half the people of São Paulo are foreign born. Up here we're all Brazilians."

RECIFE (the word means "reef"), the capital of Pernambuco and metropolis for the area, with about 1,060,000 people, has literally doubled in population in fifteen years. It has the oldest daily newspaper in Brazil, founded in 1825, and no fewer than forty *thousand* registered prostitutes. Recife is not what you would call an advanced metropolis. Only about a quarter of the streets are paved and none but a few are served by any public transportation; water reaches less than half the people, and only 20 percent have access to any sewage system. About five hundred United States citizens live in Recife, clustered mostly along the beach; left-wing students call this district "the American *favela*," with a heavy irony that is understandable when it is learned that at least 70 percent of the people of Recife live in real *favelas*—the filthy *mucambos* or cavelike slums. The city is sometimes called the "Venice" of South America. Do not believe that it is. Take a trip instead to the mud flats on the edge of the city and watch the crab hunters, one of the most appalling sights in the western hemisphere. Men and women slowly prod along in deep mud and, with their hands, dig out slimy crabs and other shellfish which, to avoid starvation, they sell or eat.

Recife's most distinguished citizen is the sociologist Dr. Gilberto Freyre. A man with a compelling joy in life, as well as commanding intellect, he lives in a house with a brilliant garden landscaped in a typically Brazilian manner.

[1] In two villages taken at random in 1960 in the state of Piauí not a single baby survived the first year. Tad Szulc in the *New York Times*, October 31, 1960.

Dr. Freyre served us two enticing nonalcoholic local drinks, *pitanga*, pale rose-amber in color, with a subtle taste of orange, and *maracuja*, luminous but frothy, with a mysterious flavor of pineapple, which is not quite pineapple. His language is distinguished. He talks of the "sectarian exaltation" of Brazil, the cult of *sertãoejismo* or worship of the backlands, and the "idealization" of Brasília as a symbol of "interior quest." Dr. Freyre thinks that the Castelo Branco revolution was an absolute necessity, that it might well not have happened except for the women's marches in São Paulo and Belo Horizonte, and that the army, far from wanting to intervene, had hoped against hope that Goulart would command enough stability to finish out his term.

Factory and Farm

One hot, blustery morning we drove out of Recife to visit a $30,000,000 synthetic rubber factory newly set up in the countryside. This was the first industrial plant I saw in South America. It rose out of isolated bushy scrub as if the earth itself had spontaneously belched forth a cluster of pipes, tubes, and machinery; its aim is to produce 27,500 tons of artificial rubber a year to help meet the country's 100,000-ton annual demand. Even though Brazil is one of the few countries in the world to produce natural rubber it needs more. Of the seven hundred men employed here, 60 percent are illiterate and others read and write only with difficulty, but they seemed to be doing well jobs which demanded considerable technical capacity. When I asked if the labor force was unionized and had the right to strike, answers were ambiguous. The state of Pernambuco is 90 percent owner of this plant, and it has been helped by $3.4 million from the Alianza; the French have also put some money in, and Firestone and Union Carbide have lent technical assistance under contract.[2] This represents the basic Brazilian pattern in new industrial developments—national (or state) ownership together with capital contributions and technical assistance from abroad. The managing director is a Negro, and the average wage for a forty-eight-hour week about $25 a month.

Our road cut through frowzy villages along the sugar estates, *fazendas*. Here is poverty at its rawest. About half of all the tillable land in the vicinity is owned by a handful of feudal landlords, many of them absentee, who have their property worked for them by managers. There seem to be an abnor-

[2] Barnard L. Collier in the New York *Herald-Tribune*, September 6, 1963.

mally large number of animals, mostly burros and goats; the burro is, like a dog in the United States, man's best friend. Most peasants are share-croppers, and about 40-50 percent of the crop goes to the landowner; the farmer gets a crude shack, a vegetable patch, and a cash return which may be as low as 12 cents a day. "Sometimes the landlord's wishes are enforced by his private police force," says one recent American visitor to this realm, and another reports, "The people are merely vegetables." In some cases the peasant is "shackled by the medieval obligation to work ninety days a year for five cruzeiros (less than 1¢) a day."[3]

Education in the Recife neighborhood is a lugubrious subject. Fewer than half the children of school age actually go to school—for the simple but shocking reason that there are no schools. Many teachers are only marginally literate, and the curriculum is based on the French system, which means that if a child fails in one subject he fails for the whole year. Ninety-one percent of the students are dropouts before the fourth grade, the last grade in primary school, and fewer than 5 percent are graduated. As to secondary schools conditions are even more deplorable. The fact is hard to believe, but there are only *two* public secondary schools in the entire city of Recife, which is as big as Baltimore or Kiev. Public libraries scarcely exist; one near our hotel circulated a total of exactly 603 books in a month. Universities are not true universities in our sense, but ramshackle collections of schools, which are as a rule miserably equipped and have substandard faculties. Most professors have to hold other jobs outside in order to earn a living, but this is accepted as being part of the system.

Salaries in Recife? An economist at SUDENE will start at the equivalent of $185 a month, and a young man going into a government bureau as a career officer may earn $120; a bus driver gets $33, a domestic servant about $9.35, and a schoolteacher, believe it or not, $5.10. Of course she has to have another job to live. But a schoolteacher, protected by social security, may retire on full salary for life after twenty years; if he or she works twenty-five years, full salary plus 25 percent.

So we have here a gamut running from a new sparkling factory out in the parched wilderness which pays tolerable wages considering its milieu to peasants on the brink of starvation and grossly underpaid workers in the towns. Speaking broadly it would seem that in the interest of the nation as a whole southern Brazil will have to give up something to help support the north. The situation is the reverse of that in Italy, as an example, where the industrial north has had to make substantial contributions to the *mezzo-*

[3] "Brazil's Big Dust Bowl," by Kathleen Walker Seegers, *Reader's Digest*, July 1963.

giorno, or impoverished south. Another obvious analogy is the American South. The best solution for Brazil would be more industrialization all around.

Three Men of God

An unusual man is Dom Helder Câmara, the Archbishop of Pernambuco and one of the highest-ranking churchmen in South America, who, in spite of his ecclesiastical position, stands strongly on the left. He is president of Catholic Action, and a prelate on particularly good terms with Pope Paul VI, whose works he has translated into Portuguese. Dom Helder has been nicknamed—without irreverence—"the electric mosquito"; he is small in stature, wiry, magnetic, with tousled hair and burning eyes, and positively buzzes with radiant energy. I have given a brief indication of his intellectual point of view by the quotation at the head of this chapter. Dom Helder is a great humanist as well as Christian. He believes not merely in God but in man. He is a passionate advocate of the common man's basic human rights. He wants a better world. He said recently, "Liberty is only a name, a sound, for two-thirds of mankind, without clothes, without houses, without food, without a minimum of education and above all without human conditions for working." Many Roman Catholic churchmen, in particular young priests, are coming to share this view all over South America although few are so courageously outspoken. During the Castelo Branco coup the military police raided and searched Dom Helder's palace in Recife, apparently looking for hidden subversives. Furious, the archbishop got in touch with the local army commander, and the police were promptly withdrawn. Dom Helder and sixteen of his bishops then issued a manifesto asking clemency for political prisoners who had been seized in the first heat of the fracas.

Helder Câmara was born in the northerly state of Ceará and, as a boy, wanted to change his name because an army post nearby was called "Helder" and he hotly disliked any association with the military, no matter how accidental. Later, learning that the word also meant "clear air" in an Indian language, he decided to keep it. He rose rapidly in the priesthood and became in time the auxiliary bishop of Rio. Here his articulate radicalism incensed the cardinal archbishop of Rio, his superior, an antediluvian conservative, and he was kicked upstairs to exile in Recife. Then eventually he became archbishop of Pernambuco, and is probably the most-respected and best-loved man in the whole northeast.

Dom Helder received us one afternoon in a bone-bare room in the Archbishopric Palace, talking halting English; he wore a simple black robe and looked like an ordinary priest. His brown eyes, large and luminous, carry a glow; when he makes gestures, with long, slim, supple fingers, he seems physically to be weaving a spell. We mentioned racial tolerance in Brazil; the archbishop replied that the situation was much more complicated than it appeared on the surface, and that to think that discrimination, intolerance, and hatred do not still exist would be to make a grave error. To the question, "Why is the United States unpopular in some Brazilian circles?" his reply was, "Because you control our money."

As he turned to other themes the archbishop's voice bubbled with irony. "If I hand out food and teach children to read, then I'm a saint. But if I concern myself with underlying problems of reform, then I am a Communist." Communism, he went on, is oppressive and, people say, will crush the free human spirit, but the dilemma is that most residents of northeastern Brazil have never known anything but oppression, and are crushed already. He does not think that Communism was the major problem at the time of the April, 1964, overthrow of Goulart. The problem was development. Development must come even before education. "My father told me when I was a boy that as a priest I would have to lead a 'terrible' life. But the priest loves both God and man and must leave the world a better place. An artist lives for his creation. A priest lives for the happiness of man in the life of God."

I asked about birth control—the first time I ever had a talk on this ticklish subject with a Roman Catholic leader of such rank. Dom Helder's reply was cautious. He cannot approve of planned parenthood, but he said that it was a moral problem, one in the heart of man itself, which demanded personal solution, particularly because so many people in Brazil live on a "subhuman level." "There are men who live as if they were not men."

In April, 1966, this indomitable archbishop refused to celebrate a mass for the second anniversary of the Castelo Branco coup as part of the official local ceremonies. Catholic students supporting him were thrown in jail. Later came other tribulations.

*

Father Antonio de Melo Costa and Father Paulo Crespo, much younger men, form a team. They are the Catholic organizers of SORPE (Serviço de Organização Rural de Pernambuco), the collection of rural syndicates which, all over this area, has its own way of seeking to promote the peasants' welfare. Their basic line, which borrowed much from Pope John XXIII, was that the agrarian workers were poor not because they were designed to be poor but because there was something wrong in the system at large. Less leftist than Dom Helder Câmara, they are fiercely anti-Communist. Brazil— to say it once again—has an intricate variety of cross patterns. Dom Helder had to appeal to the regular army to save himself from the secret police; Father Melo once had to go into hiding to avoid harassment by the *leftist* government of Pernambuco.

Father Melo introduced us to the phenomenon—or call it ritual—of the hammock. In Brazil a hammock is at once a throne, a podium, and a bed. We went out to a village called Cabo where Melo has his church, which is whitewashed and scraped clean of all adornment; the altar is a stone table covered by a plain green piece of cloth; behind is a harsh, inexpensive litho-graph of Christ. No gilt, no adornment. Father Melo who has a school in his church, holds court from six until ten every morning, sitting in a yellow-and-red-striped hammock. Women make coffee in a sordid little kitchen, cats crawl limply over the floor, supplicants come and go. One we met was a member of the local gentry dressed in shining whites with sleekly polished long black boots and spurs; others looked like objects picked out of a gutter.

As he talked, Father Melo squatted in his hammock, bounced, rolled, reclined, jerked, sat, and all but stood, while making emphatic gestures with his hands. He never once left it while we were there, an hour or longer.

Melo, thirty-two, was born in nearby Sergipe. This is his first parish. He has a black crew cut, a throbbing voice, and warnings of hellfire in his eye. He said that there had never been a truly representative government in Brazil, and that "nothing ever gets done, even if the government does well." What causes Communism? "Lack of opportunity." Communists should be welcomed into the community as individuals but they should not be per-mitted to take part in any government based on an "opening to the left," as in Italy, because this will only encourage them, not make them more amenable to conversion. "If the Communist problem was what it is thought to be by stupid reactionaries, it would not be a problem at all but something that could be solved by simple police methods."

Land reform is, Father Melo thinks, the first Brazilian essential, and he told us that he and his colleagues have so far organized more than 150,000 agrarian workers in thirty-six large unions, to work for rural betterment. "Solution to problems lies within the problem itself, not outside." Poverty itself is not a problem, but a symptom. What you have to do is fight poverty by fighting that which brings it. "Suppose you have a bottle with a hole in it, which oozes. The answer is not to wipe or lick the fluid off the floor or to pour more water in from the top, but to plug the hole."

The other member of the team, Father Crespo, somewhat stout, is a mulatto, given to speaking slowly. Melo is the orator, Crespo the man of action. Like Melo, he is thirty-two. Born in a town near Recife, he found that no school existed which would carry him beyond the fourth grade, and so, at the age of twelve, he left home to make his way. He studied at a seminary in Olinda, and the church, seeing his promise, sent him to Paris to finish his education; here he was strongly influenced by the French worker-priests. Returning to Brazil, he became vicar of a parish in an industrial community heavily Communist. Young Father Crespo got the idea of preaching by radio; this made him a public figure. His collaboration with Melo and his work as co-director of SORPE followed. What can the government do? we asked him. Enforce the minimum wage law. This has been passed, but the mill owners still won't pay. Second, change the basic structure of the sugar properties by breaking up the big estates into family-size farms run by cooperatives. But powerful "economic groups" will oppose this to the death, and so incessant organization and agitation must continue. Third, encourage small industry and build up handicrafts—radios, shoes, bakeries, tile. Fourth, avoid external aid. "We do not wish to become beggars."

We asked Father Crespo what, in view of the 3.7 percent birth rate prevalent in the area, one of the highest in the world, he thought of the population explosion. He replied that it was a "blessing," and said that Brazil needed "as many people as it could get." He did not think that overpopulation made an economic problem. He was sure that Brazil was so potentially rich, with such enormous possibilities for development, that there would never be any question of having to support a "surplus" population.[4]

The Present Situation, SUDENE, and USAID

In 1958–59, when Kubitschek was president, a condition close to chaos came to northeast Brazil. Peasants rose and burned landowners' houses, agitators were killed by the police, bombs were thrown in the cities, shortages of food became crippling, and a serious threat developed of a general Castro-like revolt. A country lawyer, Francisco Julião, became leader of a peasants' *jacquerie*. The peasants came to him, not the reverse. Sharecroppers in a small town, Vitória de Santo Antão, some thirty miles from Recife, organized a cooperative for protection of their interests, and desperately needed a

---

[4] That same day I heard that the governor of Pernambuco has thirteen children. Indeed, Brazilians of all strata are a progenitive people and Father Crespo's remark reflects a widespread—but uninformed—local attitude.

lawyer who could give them advice and defend them in court. Julião, a Socialist deputy to the state legislature, about forty-five, was their choice. Promptly he showed marked qualities of leadership, and, under his stimulus, the celebrated Ligas Camponesas, or Peasant Leagues, were formed. Soon they had thirty thousand members in Pernambuco and spread into the north and west with their watchword, "Land to those who till it."

Julião's precise ideological line was difficult to define. After visiting Castro in Cuba he declared that he was a "Communist," but he was never an outright Kremlin man, and, so far as is known, never had any connection with the Soviet hierarchy, although he took one trip to Moscow—also Peking. The official Communists, on the scene in Brazil, fought him bitterly because he was so "undisciplined," and set up several organizations of their own to draw his teeth. But his relations with Castro remained cordial, and he was generally regarded as being a convinced and faithful Fidelista, whose main effort would be to introduce "Castroism" (Marxist-Leninism) to Brazil.

Meantime a new Catholic group, under the leadership of the liberal bishop of Natal, Dom Eugenio Salas, rose to compete with the Peasant Leagues and draw off Julião's supporters, in addition to the Melo-Crespo organization. Politics at their most internecine entered this abstruse picture. In 1961 the mayor of Recife, an outspoken radical named Miguel Arraes de Alencar, was elected governor of Pernambuco; his administration, reflecting that of Goulart on the national plane, was strongly leftist, and he appointed a number of Communists to various jobs. A year later came an important event—a federal statute was passed making it legal to unionize rural workers. So several political leaders, including Arraes, promptly sought to take advantage of this by setting up unions of their own, or gaining control of underground organizations. Then Goulart and Arraes split. Goulart, who did not want any local satrap to have too much power, set up his own union in the northeast. Both he and Arraes competed hotly for the favor of the Communists. Presently, by 1963, there were eight different groups, all representing the peasants in theory and asking for their support, in Pernambuco and the surrounding states—the Julião Peasant Leagues (Fidelista), the two Catholic organizations, the Arraes union, the Goulart union, and no fewer than three different Communist unions—Chinese, Trotskyist, and Kremlin. This led to a raw power fight in which every kind of line was crossed. One consequence was that Arraes managed to gain control of the local police. They were no longer automatically an arm of the landowning class but were forced to give their first allegiance to the state itself, where it should have been all along.

Soon came the 1964 coup d'état. Both Arraes and Julião were arrested, and the Peasant Leagues and the other leftist groups dissolved. Arraes, charged with various delinquencies, was interned on Fernando de Noronha, an island which is incidentally the site of an American missile tracking station, and then jailed in the headquarters of the fire department in Recife. After fifty-four weeks of confinement he was released without trial. Julião had become a federal deputy by the time of the revolution; when the army struck he ducked out of Brasília and spent several months in its outskirts disguised as a bricklayer. Caught in the end, he too was jailed in the Recife fire house, never tried, and eventually released in September, 1965. While in prison he wrote a book, smuggling it out page by page in the lid of a container in which his wife sent him milk every day. Some of it is supposed to have been written on toilet paper. Published and hawked on the streets while he was still imprisoned, it was a sellout. After his release Julião went to Mexico, where he still is.

Once the army took over in 1964, peasant agitation died down, and whether land reform will be pushed or not remains to be seen. It is the chief point of issue between the local Brazilian authorities and the American Aid mission. The Americans want land reform—serious structural change—as an essential first step in relief for the whole area.

Plenty of political prisoners still remain in Recife, and there are many exiles. Some offenders were punished after the coup by being stripped down to their shorts and made to parade publicly through the streets with bells around their necks, which did not leave a pleasant impression. Father Melo was offered a job as state Secretary of Labor, but the church authorities would not allow him to accept.

*

Relief for this distressed and turbulent area is an old story. Back in 1883 a drought caused no fewer than 300,000 deaths, and the government has been studying the problem ever since. Dams were built and watercourses surveyed, but the work was badly planned and speculators got the best land—plots with water holes. Nobody seemed to catch on to the fact that this was, or should have been, treated as a national problem. Obviously the big industrialists in São Paulo would benefit just as much from economic improvement of the northeast as the local citizenry, because their markets would expand, but south and central Brazil showed little interest. They seemed to be taking the line that the northeast was "expendable."

At last a new federal entity—SUDENE—was set up in 1959, but it did not begin to function fully until two years later. Its first director was Celso

Furtado, mentioned in a preceding chapter and one of the most promising men in his field in the Americas. The over-all concept was rather like that of TVA in the United States, with the emphasis on long-range development on a broad regional scale, rather than anything hand-to-mouth, and the Brazilian government put up the equivalent of $145 million to establish it. This was to be genuine reform, not mere relief.

In July, 1961, the United States began to take part in these seminal developments. Furtado, who came under bitter attack for being left-wingish, too doctrinaire, and too much addicted to abstract planning, called on President Kennedy in Washington, who listened sympathetically to his exposition. Actually Furtado, far from being a "Communist," as was loosely charged, wanted to make SUDENE an instrument to woo the inflamed peasantry *away* from Julião's leagues. He was succeeded in time at SUDENE by João Gonçalves de Sousa, an economist, lawyer, and sociologist, who had been an official of the OAS with long experience in the United States. His job has been called the hardest in Brazil. One reason is that SUDENE is a federal institution and yet must maintain the most intimate of contacts with something like ten Brazilian state governments. The other is a congeries of points at issue with the United States.

For, following the Kennedy-Furtado conversations, Washington decided to go into northeastern Brazil on a major level, and the U.S. Aid Mission Northeast Brazil was set up in Recife in April, 1962, under the Alliance for Progress, with funds of $131,000,000 in a four-year program. This is by far the largest American aid project in Latin America. What our men do, under the leadership of Donor M. Lion, director of the project, is to give implementation to the SUDENE plan. Development is proceeding on education, water supply, roads, power generation, public health, and increased agricultural production. "It's a spectrum flight," Mr. Lion says. The difficulties are vast, and the prospective cost enormous; for instance, to get every child of school age into a school by 1971, as the plan provides, will cost $100,000,000. But both Mr. de Sousa and Mr. Lion seem to be optimistic within reason, and they confront their onerous task with cooperative good will.[5]

* * *

The United States is helping to ameliorate social unrest in northeastern Brazil by several other means. One is a program by which surplus milk and

[5] By early in 1966 SUDENE had built 2,000 kilometers of roads, begun work on a major hydroelectric installation, installed 400 water wells, built schools for 63,000 children, and planted 500,000 experimental fruit trees. *Visión Letter*, May 4, 1966.

other food are distributed in substantial quantities to students in adult literacy classes newly established in Recife. Another has to do with the price of sugar. We buy 340,000 tons of sugar a year from Brazil at what is euphemistically called a "preferred" price, about 4 cents higher than the world price. This bonus gives about $26,000,000 in extra income to the sugar industry in Pernambuco, and without it the whole area might well collapse. All this means, of course, that it is the United States taxpayer who is helping to finance relief in northeastern Brazil, but the process is part of an essential contemporary pattern. Rich nations have to give to poor nations no matter what the cost because all are interbound.

Back to the National Scene: The Communist Position

Leader of the official Communists in Brazil is still Luís Carlos Prestes, the "Cavalier of Hope." In a country of romance Prestes, who is in his sixties now, has always been a romantic figure. The son of a republican revolutionist in the last days of the empire, he responded to this tradition, went into the army, and became a professional officer. With strong people's sympathies he joined a conspiracy of young lieutenants fed up with the government of the day, and took part in what were called the *"tenentes"* revolts. With him were several men who later became powerful servants of the state under Vargas. In 1924 he organized and led an armed rebellion in Rio Grande do Sul—more than forty years ago. This was duly crushed, but Prestes himself was not.

A kind of Robin Hood, he became a creature of folklore. With a small intrepid band of men, about eight hundred, resisting capture by government forces, he performed a feat something like that of the Communists on their Long March in China years later, although he did not, of course, succeed in founding a regime out in the wilderness as did Mao Tse-tung. In fact he was not yet a full-fledged Communist—only a radical minded officer and adventurer. Prestes fought fifty-six battles; he made treaties with Indian tribes; he set up shadow "states"; he marched from the extreme south of Brazil—always through back country, always eluding stubborn army pursuers—to Bahia in the north, and then down the Amazon and across to the Bolivian border, a stupendous adventure. Finally, after three years, the Prestes column disbanded, and he and the remnant of his men crossed into Bolivia, where they were interned. He was never beaten in the field or caught.

Vargas came to power in 1930, and eventually permitted Prestes to return to Brazil, where he organized the National Liberation Alliance, a Popular

Front group. Then Prestes went to Moscow, became fully converted to Communism, and, returning to Rio, was arrested in 1935 after fomenting a so-called revolt. Accused of sedition, he was sentenced to seventeen years in jail—a monstrous sentence for easygoing Brazil. This was later extended by an additional *thirty* years when Prestes, although he had the alibi of being in jail at the time, was accused of complicity in the murder of a young woman Communist who had been the mistress of the party secretary. She had been strangled by members who thought that she had betrayed them.

After a time Vargas gave Prestes a presidential pardon; a free man and now the acknowledged leader of the Communist party, he became its secretary general and vigorously re-entered politics. The Communists were still legal at this time, and in the 1945 elections, following Getúlio's first fall, they won 10 percent of the popular vote. Fifteen Communist deputies gained seats in the Chamber; Prestes became a federal senator. Then in 1947 the party was outlawed, and he was forced to go underground.

But, unquenchable, he emerged again in the second Vargas administration, and gained the president's favor once more, although the party itself remained suppressed. After Vargas he contributed substantially to Kubitschek's election to the presidency by delivering the underground Communist vote, and, in 1960, campaigned openly for Marshal Lott, even sharing a platform with him. After the Castelo Branco coup in 1964 he lost his civil rights, and is believed to be in hiding. He has not been found or arrested.

During the entire period from 1947 to 1964 the official Communist party, although dissolved in theory, contrived to operate on almost an open level. But, partly because of Castro in Cuba, partly because of the conflict between Russia and China, it split apart in the 1960's. Prestes was a soft-line man, who wanted to reconstitute the party through legal methods, remaining close to Moscow, whereas others were interested in a more radical route to revolution. The dissidents thereupon seceded from the official party (PCB—Brazilian Communist party), and established an independent Communist party of Brazil (CPB) of their own, claiming that *it* was the legitimate party. This group is solidly pro-Chinese, and, at the moment, probably has more punch and influence than the Prestes-Moscow wing, but is much less strong numerically. A Trotskyist party exists as well, and there are several other varieties of splinter deviationists, which, in a crisis, would probably coalesce. Finally, since the downfall of Khrushchev, the PCB itself is divided between "Kremlinists" and "Khrushchevists." Altogether the party numbers about thirty thousand.

The chances of a Communist coup d'état in Brazil are minuscule. The only possibility would be the sudden seizure of key posts, after prolonged infiltration, which is why infiltration is so much feared in Brazil. But the possibility of a Communist revolution continues to be a gnawing preoccupation to many citizens, particularly those who thought that Goulart almost made one. As to the Communists the central committee of the official party still continues to make a show of being what it once was, occasionally issuing manifestoes from clandestine headquarters urging "guerrilla war" against the government; also it acrimoniously engages in "auto-criticism" because of the failure of the left to have produced any counteraction to the coup in 1964. But actually the extreme left had lost most of its vitality before this date.

Relations with the United States

Brazil's present government is probably the most pro-American on the continent. Obviously the two nations share common interests, and each is important, if not vital, to the other. A definitely anti-American regime in Brazil would be a disaster for American hemisphere policy and Brazil, as is only too clear, would have a hard time keeping afloat without American support. Moreover, 70 percent of all Brazilian exports go to the United States.

Brazil contributed to the military forces sent into the Dominican Republic in April, 1965, and the commander-in-chief of the OAS forces there is, in fact, a Brazilian. The United States has the use of Brazilian facilities on the island of Fernando de Noronha off Recife, where, as noted above, we operate an important missile station. On the other side of the fence, we assist Brazil militarily in several ways, for instance by maintaining training missions for all three branches of the Brazilian armed services—army, navy, and air force.[6] As to financial aid, we contribute more to Brazil than to any other country in the world except India. After a period of ups and downs already noted, total American aid to Brazil rose steeply to $513 million between April 1, 1964, the date of the Castelo Branco coup, when the country became "respectable" again, and June 30, 1965, much more than went to any other South American country. Plenty of Brazilians think that this is too much—that we are overdoing it. But the country takes the money.

The overwhelming preponderance of United States power in Brazil, no matter how tactfully it is exercised, produces embarrassment. V. K. Krishna Menon, the Peck's Bad Boy of India, called Brazil "a colony" recently in the New Delhi parliament; such remarks are bitterly resented in Brazil—

---

[6] Before World War II foreign military missions in Brazil were split three ways—the Germans trained the air force, the French the army, and the United States the navy.

and not merely by the left. Carlos Lacerda, resuming political activity, gets his biggest response when he attacks the government for being a "satellite" of the United States.

Brazilians dislike intensely the assumption that they are a nation on apron strings; they want to be on their own—so much so that they habitually tend to separate themselves even from the rest of South America. "We must work out our own destiny" is a watchword. One minister told me, "We have our own tempo here. Don't disturb it." This is a nationalist world—and not least in countries below the Panama Canal.

Neutralism, sometimes called Nasserism, sometimes "nativism," could be a powerful potential force in Brazil, although it does not reach the surface or play much of a concrete role at present. But Quadros and Goulart both supported a quasi-neutralist position, thought vaguely of a "third force" which Brazil might come to represent, and did not enjoy being part of the defense system of the United States. Meantime, American policy planners in Washington should not assume that Castelo Branco and his putative successor, General Costa e Silva, will last forever or that Brazil will continue to look on every aspect of American policy with an indefinitely friendly eye.

The best, the most fruitful American contribution to Brazil today is the Peace Corps, which is the case elsewhere in South America as well. One reason for this is that no taste of money, a curse to most of our inter-American relationships, is connected with this enterprise; another is that it symbolizes youth. Peace Corps activities in Brazil are numerous, running all the way from school lunch programs to X-ray techniques in the hospitals, from community development to agricultural reform. I shall describe Peace Corps activity in detail in relation to several countries in chapters below. Brazil has 545 Peace Corps volunteers.

*

Brazilian relations with the United Nations are and always have been close and cordial. A Brazilian contingent is included in the UN force patrolling the Gaza strip. On the scene in Brazil itself is the work of the UN Development Programme, formerly known as the Special Fund, the director of which is the calmly pertinacious and indefatigable American administrator, Paul G. Hoffman. The Development Programme is an agency to assist practicable projects all over the world in cooperation with governments. It has no fewer than thirteen projects in Brazil, being variously executed by the FAO, the World Health Organization, and UNESCO, at a total cost of about $36 million, of which sum Brazil contributes a part. This may seem small potatoes compared to Alianza funds, but the UN programs are pinpointed with a very close focus and a maximum regard for concrete worthy results. Brazil gets more development assistance from the UN than any country except India. Among the projects are a survey of the San Francisco River basin, tropical food research, sanitary engineering in Guanabara, a plan for power development in South Central Brazil, fisheries, and the teaching of technology at the University of Brasília.

Brazil—to Sum Up

So now we finish with Brazil. Such a spectacular country, so copious and various, with such multicolored and dramatic contrasts, it exists in several dimensions which I have sought to explore. The struggles for power are several—between the federal government and the states, between the army and civilian interests, between the landlords and the peasants, between conservative industrialists and the experimentalist technocrats, between the plutocrats and labor, between stand-pat forces in general and impulses toward reform, development, and renovation.

The major theme is development, and against formidable obstacles this has been prodigious. But a great deal more needs to be done.

Brazil needs democratization, honesty, education, clarity, vision, better organization, and a redistribution of economic power—in a word, to get all the way into the twentieth century. The most depressing factor today is that no readily foreseeable alternative to the present military government exists, and this becomes more drearily repressive and reactionary day by day. The army won't let the people in, but the people cannot possibly throw the army out. Even so Brazil has as full and brilliant a promise as any nation in the world.

Brazilian Miscellany

Brazil has more potentially arable land than all of Europe, the biggest football stadium in the world (Maracanha in Rio, which seats 155,000), and remarkable dances like the *frevo*. I never tasted juice made of passion fruit until I had it on a Brazilian airliner, and I never knew before that Brazil grows no fewer than nine hundred varieties of palm. Even Brazilian toothpicks are magnificently oversized.

The state of Guanabara has more civil servants than New York, and Brazil exports more than thirty million litres of wine every year to France. Its prodigious output of coffee, sugar, corn, cocoa, and tobacco are well known, and it is also among the first ten countries in the world in the production of oranges, sisal, cotton, jute, tomatoes, sweet potatoes, peanuts, soybeans, and rice. But I never saw a Brazil nut in Brazil.

Brazil invented the idea of the shuttle air service, and has fifty thousand different vegetable species, eighteen hundred different kinds of edible fish, and five hundred species of ant. Coat hangers are, for some mysterious reason, rare items in Brazilian hotels, and soap is often in short supply. At the bar in the Bahia airport I wondered what a *blum mery* was until it dawned on me that this was the local spelling of Bloody Mary.

CHAPTER 6

The Spanish-Speaking Half
of the Continent

*I will not give rest to my arm or my soul till I have broken
the chains that bind my fatherland to Spain.*
—SIMÓN BOLÍVAR IN HIS YOUTH

*America is ungovernable. Those who served the revolution
ploughed the sea.*
—SIMÓN BOLÍVAR IN RETIREMENT
AND DISILLUSION

So NOW we confront the rest of South America. In this and the following
two chapters I hope to survey the continent as a whole, hanging down as it
does formidably from the twig of Panama like a huge lopsided pear or
bunch of grapes. Of course it is a cliché to say that no such thing as South
America exists, and indeed a continental approach is difficult because the ten
independent states (eleven including Guyana) of the continent differ so
widely from one another. What does exist is a complex of ten strikingly
different countries.

Latin America, with twenty-three countries, is even more diversified.
Mexico is a world of its own; Haiti speaks French and Creole; Jamaica and
Trinidad-Tobago are former British colonies; several West Indian islands are
still administered by the French, the Dutch, and the Americans. And of
course Cuba is different because it is Communist—it brought the Communist
frontier within ninety miles of Florida.

South America is more coherent, more homogeneous. Its constituent
republics may differ, but the continent is a true entity; just look at a map
and inspect again that swollen, distorted pear. All its countries arose out of
the same historical process, have the same religion, share a common culture,

104

and face similar gravid political, economic, and social problems. All speak Spanish or Portuguese officially. There are, however, millions of Indians who still communicate in their native languages, like Quechua, Aymará, and Guaraní, and one estimate is that at least half the population of Bolivia, Peru, and Ecuador still do not understand Spanish, remarkable as this fact may be.

"South America" is a perfectly good geographical expression, but many specialists are dissatisfied with it. Some would even prefer "Indo-Europe" as a name for the continent, inasmuch as most educated Latin Americans consider themselves to be more European than American, and the Indian strain is obvious. Lord Bryce, author of *The American Commonwealth,* one of the greatest books of political science ever written, suggested back in 1912 that the hemisphere should be divided terminologically between "Teutonic America," that is, the United States and Canada, and "Hispanic America."[1] But Brazil is not Hispanic. "Ibero-America" is an alternative. No doubt "Indo-Afro-Mediterranean-America" would be considered too prolix, even by the pedants. Incidentally most Latin Americans dislike being called "Latin Americans" and in particular hate the term "Latino."

In spite of its geographical unity, South America is not fully integrated. Surprisingly few residents of one country visit their neighbors, even though communications, at least by air, are better than they have ever been before. Few South American universities or similar institutions have a continental point of view. Newspapers rely most on dispatches from New York for news of their neighbors, and political figures who speak for the hemisphere as a unit are few and far between; there are no statesmen even remotely comparable to men in Europe who have a continental reputation, like General de Gaulle, and who are rightly called "European." Attitudes are made provincial by limited horizons.

South Americans themselves are well aware of their divided tendencies, "resent being lumped together," and engage in ceaseless and sometimes anguishing intellectual debate on whether they represent a continent *in toto,* their separate nationalisms, or both.[2] One suggestive point is that no single country is the leader. "The feeling of a common Hispano-American brotherhood is weak," Lord Bryce pointed out fifty years ago.

The continent has several frictions within itself even on the direct political level. Bolivia and Chile do not have diplomatic relations, and Ecuador is not on good terms with Peru as a result of a long-standing frontier dispute

[1] James Bryce, *South America, Observations and Impressions,* still an illuminating book half a century after it was written.
[2] *An Atlas of American Affairs,* p. 1.

which, in Ecuadorian eyes, ranks with the prewar quarrel between France and Germany over Alsace-Lorraine. The long-drawn-out Tacna-Arica quarrel between Chile and Peru in the 1920's will be remembered by those familiar with the old League of Nations. Venezuela broke off diplomatic relations with Brazil after the April, 1964, *Putsch* in Rio, because of its disapproval of military coups d'état upsetting civilian governments, and similarly with the Argentine later. There have been five major wars in South America since liberation—a conflict between Argentina and Brazil in the 1820's; another some years later involving Argentina and Uruguay against Brazil; the War of the Triple Alliance, 1865–70 (Brazil, Argentina, Uruguay against Paraguay, which resulted in the extermination of a considerable proportion of the Paraguayan nation); the War of the Pacific, 1879–83 (between Chile and Peru, which still leaves a heritage of atavistic bad feeling in Peru); and the Chaco War in the 1930's between Paraguay and Bolivia.[3] A troublesome little scrape took place between Colombia and Ecuador over a disputed frontier (Ecuador has intermittently been eaten away by its big neighbors) in the early 1930's, as did one between Colombia and Peru, and Argentina and Chile had a minor military scuffle as recently as 1965.

On the other hand there are several forces making for unity and cohesion in South America, quite aside from those arising out of similarity in geography, history, and temperament. The Organization of American States, ECLA (Economic Commission for Latin America, a UN organization), and the Inter-American Development Bank are among these. ECLA has been a stimulating success. Another, potentially the most fruitful, is LAFTA (Latin American Free Trade Association), which was established in 1960–61 and is seeking to set up a common market for the continent on the model of the European Common Market and which follows a notably successful organization of the same kind recently put into operation by the Central American republics. Membership in LAFTA now includes seven South American nations plus Mexico. The object is to reduce hemisphere tariffs, and thus stimulate intra-American trade and promote development.

Another centripetal element on a different level is the principle of asylum. South America is interlaced with a miscellany of refugees and exiles living in countries not their own, usually because they have been deposed from office, been ejected from their home republics for other reasons, or have fled for safety or out of principle. Examples of the privilege of asylum, which is almost universally recognized, are numerous. Former President Goulart of Brazil is, as we know, living in Uruguay; members of the junta (ruling group) which governed Ecuador until early 1966 have been received by

[3] Pendle, *op. cit.*, p. 115.

neighboring states; Bolivian labor leaders were deported recently to Uruguay and elsewhere; former President Paz Estenssoro of Bolivia lives in Lima; Rómulo Betancourt of Venezuela, one of the great men of the continent, spent long years in Costa Rica and elsewhere, as did most of his early revolutionist collaborators; Brazilian liberals lived all over the continent during the Vargas regime; so did assorted Argentines during Perón; and Haya de la Torre, the Aprista leader in Peru, was forced to spend five years in the haven of the Colombian Embassy in Lima, his own city, in circumstances resembling to a degree those of Cardinal Mindszenty in the American Embassy in Budapest.

To sum up, South America may not be a cohesive political unit, any more than Europe is, but it certainly exists.

A General Statement to Begin With

South America, as has been nicely pointed out, begins with an isthmus and ends with a strait, which is one reason for its isolation. Most of its great cities lie on or close to the coast, like Buenos Aires, Santiago, Guayaquil, Rio de Janeiro, Montevideo, Caracas, as is the case with most nations with colonial roots. Brazil is not the only country where an overriding problem is conquest of the interior, expansion of the frontier. Most (but not all) are one-city countries, in that a single huge megalopolis dwarfs the rest. But, in spite of the large recent growth of the great cities, this is still predominantly a rural continent, with at least 60 percent of the total population dependent on agriculture. And, although it has notoriously one of the highest rates of population growth in the world, most of it still looks empty.

South America—not Latin America but just South—covers about one-eighth of the earth's surface, and is about half again the size of China. It has 6,800,000 square miles as against 8,646,000 for the Soviet Union and 3,620,000 for the United States. Chile alone, set on its side, would stretch from San Francisco to Bermuda. There are three principal river systems aside from the Amazon—Orinoco, La Plata, and Magdalena. The Orinoco and Amazon rise in the western highlands within a few hundred miles of one another, and I have read—but I don't believe it—that it is possible to cross the entire continent by boat. The principle physical feature of the continent as a whole is the giant cordillera of the Andes, which is the major fact of life in six countries. Stretching in an uninterrupted granite flow for forty-five hundred miles from the Caribbean to Cape Horn, the Andes are the most stupendous mountains in the world; nothing can rival their solid and continuous immensity. There are single peaks in the Himalayas that are higher, but the Andes include no fewer than forty-nine over twenty thousand feet, much higher than anything in the continental United States, Switzerland, or the Caucasus. Mount Aconcagua in Argentina and nine other giants are at least a mile higher than Mont Blanc or Mount Whitney.

The population of the continent is around 170,000,000, less than that of the United States (195,000,000), but it will catch up soon because of the population explosion. About half the present population is under the age of eighteen, and, an incredible statistic, about *half* of all births are illegitimate. Three quarters of the population live under the duress of unremitting severe poverty.

Most of the South American republics are one-crop countries, if copper as an example can be called a crop. They live largely by the export of a single commodity or small group of commodities grown on the soil, hewn from the mines, or sucked out of the earth—like Colombia (coffee), Ecuador (bananas), Bolivia (tin), Chile (copper), Venezuela (oil)—making their economies particularly sensitive to forces beyond their own control. We have seen this phenomenon in Brazil, and will see it elsewhere. The result is debt, poverty, and inflation.

Impulses toward industrialization are plentiful, as shall be noted in the next chapter, but every country except Venezuela and the three western ore-bearing states lives by the export of agricultural raw materials. For several reasons agriculture is in a bad way. First, the land itself is not productive. Only 6.7 percent of its total area is under cultivation, as against 30 percent in the United States. Second, agricultural methods are in most cases still hopelessly primitive. Third, discrepancies in land ownership, the chief cause of the tragic gap between rich and poor on the continent, are such that roughly 90 percent of all arable land is owned by 10 percent of the population, and the oligarchy is bull-necked in resisting land reform. One reason for the great contemporary migration into the towns is hunger in the countryside. South America cannot feed itself.

The importance of South America to the United States is so obvious that it scarcely needs to be stressed—not only in politics and diplomacy but as a source of raw materials: not merely copper, sugar, coffee, but strategic substances as well. About one-fifth of all United States exports go to South America, and not less than one-third of our total imports come from there. Our investments are widespread, and our financial stake (say $10 billion) is considerable, though less than what it is in, as an example, Canada.[4] The Latin American bloc controls about a quarter of the vote of the General Assembly of the UN, and has two seats permanently on the Security

[4] United States direct investment in Canada is above $13 billion.

Council. We think of it practically as a matter of principle to have South America on our side, with our prestige at stake. But the South Americans do not always automatically vote with us, as we shall see.

No South American country has ever waged an aggressive war outside the hemisphere, although all but one (Chile) declared war on the Axis in World War II, and one (Colombia) sent a detachment to Korea.

A Difficulty About Nomenclature

The Hispanic custom is for a man to bear three names—the given name, his father's, and his mother's—in that order, but it is the *middle* name, not the last, that he is generally known by. For instance, Fernando Belaúnde Terry, the president of Peru, is known not as "Terry," but as "Belaúnde." In introducing a person I have thought it wise to follow Spanish custom and give as a rule all three names, although this may confuse the reader. There are certain exceptions to the rule which make for more confusions. The president of Colombia at the moment of writing is Guillermo León Valencia, but, contrary to general usage, he is called "Valencia," not "León." Some politicians have altogether dropped the mother's name, or use one surname only—like Arturo Frondizi, the former president of Argentina, or Rómulo Betancourt, former president of Venezuela. But most stick to triple names. One reason for this is that surnames are in short supply, and the use of the mother's name is necessary to differentiate among people. There are said to be only about one thousand surnames in all South America. Sometimes the two last names are identical, which means that both father and mother happened to have the same name, as in Gonzalez Martínez Martínez, and there have been cases in which all three names are the same. Some men cut the maternal surname to an initial, so that names like Carlos Pérez G. are encountered. A wife is, of course, known by her husband's name.[5]

The guide which I am citing adds that if you send a letter to a married couple you do not use the equivalent of our "Mr. and Mrs.," but say, "Sr. Don Tomás Martínez Sánchez y Sra." Nicknames, which are widely used in South America, can be confusing too. Francisco is Pancho or Paco, José is Pepe, Jesús is Chuchu, Concepción is Concha, Dolores is Lola, *und so weiter.*

Accents and diacritical marks are a nuisance, particularly in Brazil. They indicate stress in pronunciation. I omit them on some well-known place

[5] Cf. *A is for Abrazo*, by Mary George, pp. 125–26, a lively little book about Venezuela which has a passage on these matters.

names where their use in English seems to be sheer pedantry, as in Peru or Panama, which are correctly Perú and Panamá.

News and the Times

I have already mentioned the difficulties which confront readers in the United States attempting to keep up with South American news. The reverse is also true. It is by no means easy for the average South American to keep abreast of *North* American news and opinion. The biggest-selling magazine on the continent by far is *Reader's Digest*, which has both Spanish and Portuguese editions, but these do not specialize in news. The Latin American edition of *Time* has a circulation of 92,000 (out of a total of 4,150,000), but this appears in English.

It occurred to me after several months of travel in South America that I had not once seen a copy of the *New York Times* on sale, whereas this can be had almost everywhere in Europe. Only once in my whole trip did I ever see a copy of the New York *Herald Tribune* on a newsstand; this was in Bogotá, and it cost 75 cents a copy. A friend in Brazil told me that he had subscribed for a time to the European edition of the *Times*, published in Paris, but had given it up because airmail made it cost too much, about $190 per year. Checking on all this when I returned to New York I found that the *total* circulation of the *Times*, both newsstand and subscription, in South American countries was the following—Argentina, 17 daily, 2 Sunday; Bolivia, 7 (Sunday only); Chile, 29 daily, 5 Sunday; Peru, 100 daily, 50 Sunday. The figures for Venezuela and Colombia were slightly higher. But there are no *New York Timeses* for sale at all in the Guianas, Uruguay, Paraguay, Ecuador, or Brazil.

I do not mean to sound provincial about this. Of course I can add that such a great newspaper as *La Prensa* of Buenos Aires is not generally available in the United States, and that South Americans have plenty of opportunity to read about the United States in their own newspapers. But the point remains that there are extremely few South Americans who, even if they want to, are able to keep up with United States news and opinion on the *New York Times* level, and this reflects the intellectual separateness of the continent. The paper is simply not there to buy. The obstacle is mostly exchange restrictions.

Americans traveling in South America who do not read Spanish have daily tabloids in English at their disposal in three countries—the Buenos Aires *Herald*, the *Brazil Herald* published in Rio, and the *Daily Journal* in Caracas. A weekly exists in Lima.

The Americans, North and South

I came for gold, not to till soil like a peasant.
—HERNÁN CORTÉS

North and South America present some remarkable physical similarities as well as contrasts. Each has a tremendous range of mountains on its western side, great rivers, and seacoasts on both cheeks. Both were populated by largely primitive Indians, penetrated and conquered by invaders from Europe, and liberated from European control by patriotic nationalist revolutions made by descendants of the European settlers themselves, as Bryce wrote in an effective passage. George Washington and Simón Bolívar were, despite their manifest differences, historical twins. Both North and South America derive essentially from European immigration, and are indissolubly part of the same western society.

But large differences are clear as well; Anglo-America has only two countries, the United States and Canada, but South America has eleven and the rest of Latin America twelve more. Other contrasts are too obvious for detailed mention, all the way from climate, an important factor, and altitude, to religion and political evolution. Why should political development have been so divergent in North and South? Why do North and South America differ so profoundly in social structure although they have the same origins? Why is there no United States of South America?

First, South America was, it happened, colonized by two countries, Spain and Portugal, which never experienced the Protestant Reformation, and which were absolutist monarchies. The Roman Catholic Church controlled education, became by far the biggest landowner on the continent, which it still is, influenced folkways in every direction, and exerted almost unlimited secular power in the service of absolutism, not democracy. The men who made South America had little, if any, previous experience of self-government.

Second, the motive for colonization was altogether different. The pioneers who came to North America came to stay; they had left Europe behind them for good; their aim was to carve out new lives in the wilderness, free of European bondage, under a new form of government. But the early Latins came to despoil, exploit, get rich, and return home again, although many stayed. They were not seeking a new world of religious freedom and representative government. They were plunderers, not colonists. The essential principle was different.

Third, Virginia did not become one with Massachusetts without a struggle, as we well know, but elements of cohesion were embedded in North America from the beginning that did not exist in South. The Americans in the north worked with their own hands with pick and plough. They represented the middle class, created their own small farms, and had craggy Puritan ideals of thrift and saving, at least in New England. The United States moved westward to expand the frontier in what was an essentially unitary manner. But partly for reasons of geography and the divisions of power imposed by Spain, South America grew up piecemeal.

Fourth, the early English and northern European settlers in North America *brought their wives with them.*

*

Race is a touchy subject to most South Americans outside Brazil (and to many Brazilians too), but the fact remains that South America is a mixed continent with a very large *mestizo* population—and this is what differentiates it above all from the United States and, indeed, from any other continent. We North Americans butchered our Indians—killed them off mercilessly—and then more or less ignored those who remained. The South Americans killed off their Indians too in great number, but, partly because they had arrived on the new continent womanless, they promptly interbred with the survivors. Crosses between white and Amerindian are, speaking broadly, seldom encountered in the United States today, but South America has them by the million.

Negroes too became part of the South American amalgam, as we have seen in Brazil. Of course there are millions of Negroes and mulattoes in North America as well, but they did not become integrated into the national pattern as they did in Brazil and elsewhere in South America.

The Latin American republic nearest to being pure white today is Uruguay; after that Argentina and Costa Rica. Another element in mixedness—not racial, but national—is profuse immigration mostly of Italians, Germans, and Slavs into most of the American republics in the modern period. I have mentioned this in connection with Brazil, and will soon discuss it again when we reach Argentina, where one of every two citizens is Italian born or has Italian blood; the European entrants are so important partly because they augment and strengthen the middle class. Immigration from Japan has also been substantial recently in several countries, particularly Peru.

A Word on History

Out of the chasm of time rose the Indians. We do not know for certain where they came from—probably from across the Bering Strait. Most anthropologists see a close relationship between both North and South American Indians and the primitive Mongoloid hunters of eastern Asia, and indeed this is not merely a plausible historical thesis but a phenomenon still obvious to the eye. The contemporary Peruvian highlander today often bears a startling physical resemblance to Mongol peasants from the neighborhood of Ulan Bator.

The aborigines, beginning with the trickle that presumably slid over the ice from Siberia or crossed the Pacific by frail rafts or other seacraft, settled most firmly in the Andean countries and along the west coast, although they spread out elsewhere too. Ecuador is still 40 percent Indian, Peru 45.9 percent; Bolivia has an Indian majority. Millions of Indians still adhesively survive in South America, in spite of depredations, hardships and exploitations beyond measure throughout centuries. And, of course, nobody will forget that the early Indians built three extraordinary civilizations long before any white face was seen in the western hemisphere—the Aztec, Maya, and Inca. Other Indian semi-civilizations, like the Chibcha, long predated these. An example of history repeating itself, though with a stutter, is that the Inca system was collective under a dictator, as may be seen in large parts of the world today.

Christopher Columbus, having duly discovered the Americas in 1492, made a landfall on the actual South American continent on his third voyage in 1498. The name "America" derives, as everybody knows, from Amerigo Vespucci, the Florentine mariner who did not discover the continent at all but who explored the mouths of both the Amazon and the Río de la Plata somewhat aimlessly. "Amerigo" is an Italian variant of the name "Amalrich," which had been borne by, among others, two Latin kings of Jerusalem in the twelfth century. In French and German it is "Amaury" and "Emmerich" respectively.[6]

After Columbus and men who were primarily explorers and discoverers, like Balboa, came the onrush of the *conquistadores*, conquerors. It did not take them long to get in motion. Cortés (who set an example of large consequence by taking an Indian princess, Malinche, as his mistress) subjugated Mexico in 1521 and Pizarro, a ratlike grasping little man who conquered Peru with 183 men, betrayed and destroyed the Inca king in

[6] Bryce, *op. cit.*, pp. 484–6.

1533. In speed, bite, and comprehensiveness the Spanish advance was unprecedented. There has been nothing like it. With minuscule handfuls of troops the *conquistadores* established the rule of Spain over almost an eighth of the earth's surface in a quarter of a century. They ravaged, prayed, and governed. They built monasteries, palaces, universities; cities like Quito (founded 1534) and Lima (1535) preceded the establishment of the first North American outposts by almost a hundred years; the University of San Marcos in Peru was founded almost a century before Harvard, in 1551 as against 1636. Resistance by the Indians, who of course did not have firearms, and who were peaceably inclined, was hopeless, and about 200,000 Spaniards conquered between twenty-five and thirty million of them. Not less than 20,000,000 Indians were killed according to one estimate. It was the greatest blitz in history after Genghis Khan.

The Colonial Period, that is the rule of South America (except Brazil) by Spain, lasted for almost exactly three hundred years, from the 1520's to the 1820's. The new territories were not colonies or dependencies but parts of the kingdom of Spain itself, belonging to the crown of Castile. No practice of the art of government was permitted, beyond that exercised in a meager way by the *cabildos*, town councils. The major power factors were the *conquistadores*, the entrepreneurs and landed class that promptly emerged, officials representing the crown, and, of course, the clergy.[7] Populations were estimated not in persons, but in "souls." The Spanish dominion was not merely dogmatic but absolute. This concentration of authority produced embarrassing problems for independent-minded underlings. The watchword of local officials, seeking to evade viceregal power, became, "I obey, but I do not do it." That the Spaniards considered their properties to be in effect integral parts of Spain itself has an interesting contemporary parallel in that the Portuguese have adopted the same theory today to justify the withholding of self-determination from their colonial dependencies.

The prodigious Spanish domains in Latin America, not to mention those in North, were at first divided into two hold-all viceroyalties, New Spain (pivoting on Mexico) and Peru. Both subsequently split within themselves. New Granada broke off from New Spain in 1718 and took in Colombia, Venezuela, and Ecuador, later to be known as the three "Bolívar countries"; and the Viceroyalty of La Plata, largely composed of what is Argentina today, broke off from Peru in 1776. Each viceroyalty was divided into districts called captaincies-general, like Chile, which are more or less the basis of national frontiers today. Since the early frontiers were often ambiguously drawn, several have been many times contested.

[7] *The Church and the Latin American Revolution*, by François Houtart and Emile Pin, p. 8.

During the colonial period the Spanish ruling class sucked power, wealth, prestige, out of the dependencies, exploiting them endlessly. The Spaniards on the continent came to be divided into two classes, those born in Spain, who journeyed to the new world temporarily as officials, administrators, army officers, and the like; and the Creoles, pure-blooded Spaniards who were *born* in South America in subsequent generations and who stayed there. The Creoles became merchants, landowners, intellectuals, and were at first much looked down upon. Today a pure Creole is the top of the heap. The *mestizo* class was growing up at the same time, but Indians and half-castes were mostly reduced to working on the land—virtual serfs, as many still are today—in feudal circumstances. The contrast to the growth of free institutions and open political and social procedures in the North American colonies during the same period is striking.

Much contemporary stultification derives from Spanish economic policies of the time. Land came to be held by individuals in enormous tracts, and society was polarized between lord and peasant. Independent farmers and small businessmen were few. Above all, among deleterious factors, Spain did not permit any colony to trade with the others (except under special circumstances), and this erected bars to intercourse which exist to this day; trade was exclusively the privilege of the mother country, to loot its subjects better. Such a fatuity arose as that Buenos Aires, on an estuary leading immediately to the Atlantic, and facing Spain across the ocean without any intervening obstacles, was forced to conduct all its trade *via* Lima, the viceregal capital of Peru, so that Lima would derive the exclusive benefit; this meant that goods had to be shipped by mule across the Andes to Lima, all the way from the Atlantic to the Pacific and in the precisely wrong direction, then up the Pacific coast by sea to Panama, then across the isthmus by land, then by sea once more to Spain. It was as if—today—Chicago had to trade with New York via San Francisco and Alaska.

In the early 1800's revolutions blazed like torches all over South America, the Spanish dominion collapsed, and ten new free nations arose. Reasons for the timing of these events were the fermentations caused by the French Revolution and the attainment of independence by the United States; another was Napoleon. His invasion of Spain in 1808 weakened it and promoted nationalist feeling in the colonies. Moreover it brought the British into the picture; it was good strategy for them to encourage colonial revolt. Another potent factor was the intolerable stupidity and backwardness of the old Spanish rule, which made the rise of dissent inevitable. Most of the great revolutionaries, like Bolívar, were Creoles, who, being American born, had an ingrown nationalist bent.

The bold and brilliant chieftains who set South America free from top to

bottom in twenty years—Miranda, Bolívar, San Martín, Sucre, O'Higgins—
had continental rather than merely nationalist vision. Bolívar himself liberated six nations (including Panama), and San Martín two beside his own.
But, a most extraordinary point, these conquerors did not work together
except briefly; the wars of independence took place in north and south at the
same time but, even if simultaneous, they were not interconnected; both
Bolívar in the Caribbean and San Martín on the west coast rose spontaneously; there was no "master plan" or "unified command."[8] Even so every
hemisphere state (except Cuba and Panama) was free by 1825. The strain
of sudden release brought explosive fission like that in today's liberated
Africa. Dizzy, shaken, uplifted, but lamed by internal fractures, the continent set out to walk on its own. It has not had an easy time.

*

The Venezuelan *libertador*, Bolívar, born in Caracas in 1783, came of a
wealthy Creole family that had lived in South America for two hundred
years; he had some Basque blood, and also a touch of local Indian. From his
childhood he was passionate, disharmonious, and elevated. One of his
biographers says that his poetry and eloquence always soared highest when
"he was kneeling at the foot of a volcano or a woman." He fought no fewer
than two hundred battles, winning most, although his ragamuffin forces were
usually inferior to those of the royalist Spanish enemy, and he had to
perform feats, like repeated crossings of the Andes, that are comparable to
the exploits of Hannibal. He is supposed to have had the same number of
mistresses as battles—two hundred. He had no racial prejudice whatever,
and married one of his sisters to a Negro general.

Bolívar was virile, handsome, and black of eye. He had superlative dash
and style. He incarnated the early nineteenth-century revolutionary age. His
life, like those of most great men, was utterly dominated by one idea—to
free South America from Spain. But Bolívar was a good deal more than a
brilliant revolutionary nationalist; he saw far into the future, with dreams a
long way ahead of his time. From Bolívar stem most of our contemporary
concepts of hemisphere solidarity, good neighborliness, and joint defense.
What he hoped for was the creation of a single continental state in South
America; more than this, he dreamed of a league of all nations, and of establishing Panama as the capital of a peaceful, united world. He convoked the
first Pan-American conference in history, left political writings which have
been compared to those of Thomas Jefferson, and set up the first locally
chosen junta in the history of the continent.

[8] Pendle, *op. cit.*

In 1810, after education largely in Europe and a visit to the United States, Bolívar set out on his first campaigns. There were fantastic periods of vicissitude. He flitted from supreme leadership to episodes of forced humiliating exile. Ferocious cruelties, like those of the Spanish Civil War a century and a quarter later, attended his campaigns on both sides. Bolívar had formidable energy, and formidable recuperative powers. In 1813 his men took Caracas; in 1819, with the help of his accomplished general Antonio José de Sucre, he crossed the Andes to beat the Spaniards at Boyacá; this battle freed both Colombia and Venezuela, and in effect signaled the end of Spanish power in the north of the continent. Proceeding southwestward Bolívar liberated Ecuador. Meantime San Martín, the Argentine, having freed Chile, was operating in Peru. Cooperation between the two conquerors did not proceed without hot spasms of jealousy on the part of Bolívar, and a conference at Guayaquil, Ecuador, in July, 1822, did little to improve their relations; extraordinarily enough, what went on at Guayaquil is not fully known to this day.

San Martín, hurt and humbled, gave way to Bolívar and, to serve the best interests of all, patriotically withdrew. Bolívar completed the liberation of Peru and set up a new civil administration for the country. In December, 1824, came the great battle of Ayacucho, won for Bolívar by Sucre, which finished Spanish rule on the continent. Bolívar proceeded to liberate Bolivia, which was named in his honor. The *libertador* created a government for the new country, distributed land to the Indians, and devoted himself to civic projects. Back in Peru, he refused a state gift of a million dollars, and went on to Panama. But severe troubles were mounting behind his back in New Granada, the amalgam he had made of Colombia, Venezuela, and Ecuador, and of which he had been president for fourteen years. Colombia, one of the most intemperate of countries, began to explode, and Ecuador and Venezuela seceded from the union. Bolívar was bitterly disillusioned. After a dramatic attack on his life, he left public office in 1830, turning over the presidency of Colombia to Sucre. Since Sucre had previously been president of Bolivia he takes rank as one of the few men in history ever to have been a chief executive of two countries. Bolívar, now a broken man but still capable of histrionics, retired to a haven near Santa Marta, Colombia, intending to put his memoirs in order—and, of course, to return to the political scene if possible. But he died there that same year, aged forty-seven, worn out.

José de San Martín (1778–1850) was a hero too, but less tempestuous, less spectacular. He came of a good Creole family; his father was governor of the upriver Argentine province, Misiones, where he was born. Sent to Spain for his education at the age of seven he adopted the army as a career, became an officer, and fought with detachments of Moorish troops against

Napoleon in both North Africa and France. Then, returning to Argentina, he became a revolutionary and joined the junta which had set up an anti-Spanish government in Buenos Aires. Already he had a dream, like Bolívar's, for liberation of the entire continent. To this end he made a foray into Peru in 1814 to look over the situation, returning with the conviction that no campaign of liberation could be successful without an external base; to conquer Peru he had to conquer Chile first, after securing his position in Argentina. San Martín applied to the military chiefs in Buenos Aires for permission to raise a cavalry regiment. This was the modest beginning of one of the most phenomenal campaigns in military history. At Mendoza, in the western Argentine, San Martín raised and trained a small army of Chilean and Argentine volunteers, which he turned into an expert fighting force. He presently crossed the Andes (1817), an almost superhuman feat, catching the royalists in Chile by surprise. Consolidating his position, he refused to accept the governorship of Chile on the ground that he was nothing but a simple soldier, cooperated closely with the British Admiral Cochrane, sailed up to Peru, and took Lima in 1821, proclaiming the independence of Peru and becoming its "Protector." There followed the confrontation with Bolívar at Guayaquil. Three years later San Martín retired from public life, exiled himself to Europe, and lived in poverty in Boulogne-sur-Mer, France, until his death in 1850. He is Argentina's Washington-Lincoln, incomparably the country's greatest national hero.

San Martín was, unlike Bolívar, modest, painstaking, and disinterested. He cared nothing for pomp or personal aggrandizement. He was a Freemason, that is, anticlerical in politics. A tall fiery-eyed man, martial in bearing, he had a magnificent bushy black beard and dark olive skin. Speaking to a group of Indians he said once, "I too am an Indian," although it is unknown whether he did have Indian blood. On his campaigns, he "smelled of horse," one contemporary chronicler says. Unlike Bolívar, who became a widower at an early age, he had a happy married life; when his wife, Doña Remedios, died, he had the words "Wife and Friend" put on her tombstone. She embroidered a flag for him when he set out for Chile, and this never left his side. San Martín traveled widely before and after his campaigns, and knew some English; he liked to make small philosophical apothegms like, "It is the storm which brings us to port." He was a religious person, which Bolívar (who never knew when to kneel during a church service) was not. His rank in history would probably be higher if he had cared more for politics. One well-known comment is that "Bolívar was an eagle, San Martín was a fox."

CHAPTER 7

"More Changes, More Chances"

The alternative is not between the status quo and violent revolution. It is between peaceful and violent revolution.
—TEODORO MOSCOSO, FIRST ADMINISTRATOR
OF THE ALLIANCE FOR PROGRESS

FOLLOWING are some of the changes I noticed in South America compared to twenty-five years ago. But it is well to keep in mind the old French proverb which annoyingly reminds us that the more things change the more they remain the same.[1]

Influence of the United States. This is on the rise everywhere, and can be seen in phenomena all the way from credit cards to comic strips, from Coca-Cola to supermarkets like those that the Rockefellers have implanted in Venezuela. The situation has altogether changed from the days when the British ran South America's economic affairs, the French its culture. Paris is still the spiritual home of any number of South Americans but, on examination, most of these will be found to be old people or members of the social elite. Few middle citizens look up to France nowadays. Medicine in South America was for many years dominated by French influence, which was perhaps one reason why it was so bad, but today young doctors tend to go to the United States for their training, if they can, particularly orthopedists, dentists, and neurosurgeons. The military missions are American nowadays, not French, British or German, and New York has replaced London as the principal financial center. I asked a Jesuit professor of sociology, born in Belgium and now resident in Chile, if he had ever visited the United States and he replied blandly, "Thirty-seven times."

French was the universal second language of the upper classes a quarter of a century ago, but it has been substantially replaced by English now. I met a

[1] See Chapter 29 for a similar list of generalizations.

splendid old aristocratic lady in Buenos Aires who said, "All my friends over fifty speak French; most of my friends under fifty do not."

Communications. These are still fantastically backward, and I have made a hard point of this in several passages in this book before. But the advance in a quarter of a century has been immeasurable. In 1940 taking an airplane almost anywhere in South America was an adventure. The continent was like Africa—planes ran on Tuesday, maybe. There was a lot of romance to South American aviation yesterday. Nobody could descend from a Pan American DC-3 until the captain himself strode down the aisle and left the plane; a mariner's bell was sounded on the apron of the airport at the time of takeoff; no smoking was permitted. Nowadays jet travel is almost as standard as it is in the United States, and the continent is interlaced with airlines—although freakish things still happen and a few companies continue to use planes as antiquated as the old Scandias, which sometimes spit fire when they take off, or even the unwieldy C-46 which preceded the DC-3 in the United States.

Every South American country has, of course, an airline of its own. It could not call itself a country without one. An airline is like the steel industry—an essential badge of independence. Several of the South American companies are first rate, like Faucett in Peru, limited as its operations are, and Avianca in Colombia. The immense contribution of United States lines like Pan American World Airways and its west coast partner, Panagra, to Latin American development as a whole should be cordially noted; Pan American has been a vital pioneer, and is still an indispensable adjunct to both the external and internal workings of the continent.

Not everybody realizes how great distances are in South America. From Buenos Aires to La Paz (you have to fly by way of Lima) is almost as long as from New York to London. There are still plenty of airports (e.g., Quito, Ecuador) where landings after dark are not permitted, and many still lack modern equipment. But almost the entire continent has been opened up—more than that, interconnected. When I first visited Peru there was no way at all to get from Lima, the capital, to Iquitos on the Amazon except by ship through the Straits of Magellan or the Panama Canal, a journey which took several weeks; today the flight averages around two hours. In the old days it took sixteen *days* to get from Bogotá, the capital of Colombia, to Barranquilla on the Caribbean by a laborious river trip interrupted with passages by rail or road; today you can fly it in an hour and a half. No cities in Colombia are more than two hours apart by air today.

Population Pressure. This was a subject unheard of in the 1940's; it is hot news now. The population of South America (170 million) at its present growth rate will double in twenty years and reach around 350 million by the year 2000, well within the lifetime of some of us and of our children. *Latin America* is expected to have 600 million people by 2000, as against a projected United States total of 300 million, a staggering prospect.[2] Figures for several individual countries exhaust the imagination. Colombia, which has 17 million people today, grows by about 150,000 a year; if this rate is maintained it will have a population of 55 million by the year 2000, 325 million a century from now, and 6 *billion* a hundred years later in 2166.

Yet premonitions of alarm are scant on the local governmental level, and many persons minimize the implications of the population explosion. In Venezuela, with a population increase of 3.4 percent, one of the highest in the world,[3] citizens assert proudly that this is a good thing for the country, not bad, because Venezuela needs all the people it can get. Four points are made: (a) The rate of industrial growth exceeds that of births, so that economic advance is not put back; (b) the country is empty and could easily support additional millions; (c) to talk about such a concept as planned parenthood is ludicrous where 54 percent of births are illegitimate; (d) immigration, not natural growth, has been largely responsible for the recent increase.

Points (a) and (b) are, in the minds of practically all modern sociologists and economists, clearly fallacious. A country may be "empty" in that it can have large areas still untapped and unsettled, but this does not take away from the basic point that, as population increases, there are more mouths to feed day by day, more children to educate, more jobs to find, than is possible in the settled areas. It is not growth that counts, but *rate* of growth. A country may be empty, but this can make feeding its citizens more rather than less difficult. More people enter the urban labor market than can possibly secure jobs, as the movement of population toward the cities becomes intensified. Uneven distribution of population severely aggravates the problem; for instance four-fifths of the people of Venezuela live on one-fifth of its area. Point (c) is irrelevant, since birth control can or should be applied to unmarried mothers as well as wives. As to (d) it is a manifest distortion of the truth.

Roman Catholicism plays a vital role in this whole issue, because of its traditional taboo on birth control, but Catholic moods are changing and the

---

[2] Some authorities give the projected figure for Latin America as 700 million.
[3] The United States figure is 1.6 percent.

church is loosening up to a remarkable extent.[4] Officially it has not relaxed its position, but the point has been reached where *discussion* of the subject is no longer forbidden—a significant opening of the door—and we even met churchmen, mostly Jesuits, who were actively working with groups devoted to population studies. There are several reasons for this, one being that the population explosion, augmenting poverty, may also encourage Communism, and after all restriction of births is better than that in the Catholic view. Another is the shocking rise of abortions, which are illegal.[5] Still another is that church liberals have come to concede that a person who produces a family too large to be supported is an economic drag and thus deleterious to true Catholic interests—and South American families with eight, ten, twelve, or even more children are notoriously abundant.

Church or no church, women of childbearing age are, in several countries which we shall soon inspect, beginning to absorb the first rudiments of education on planned parenthood, and even to take matters into their own hands. For instance about 5 percent of women between fifteen and forty-five in Colombia, roughly 250,000, are now regularly making use of contraceptive pills, an extraordinary development. The issue has several political ramifications. Some Yanqui haters assert vociferously that the United States interest in population control is based on our nationalist desire to keep Latin America weak, by preventing its natural growth, and even that North American drug manufacturers, ravenous for profits and eager to expand their markets, are responsible for the whole commotion.

We should have a word too about *machismo*, the cult of virility so conspicuous among South American males. This is a continent with an extremely lively sexual content, and many husbands like to have large families because this proves their *macho* and for economic reasons as well. Big families are an economic asset, because children are put to work to help support the family. Of course *machismo* rises from complicated sources. Professor J. Mayone Stycos of Cornell University wrote recently, "My inquiries show that the typical Latin American lacks confidence in his potency, but is eager to prove it on every possible occasion."[6] An ancillary but suggestive point that may conceivably tend to keep births down has to do with the siesta, which is usually regarded as the favorite love-making period of the day. But the siesta is gradually going out. However, most South

[4] See hereunder in this chapter.
[5] Reliable figures on abortion are hard to come by, but one demographer I have consulted says that in South America as a whole there is now at least one abortion for every three births.
[6] "Sex and the Argentine Man," translated from *Primera Plana*, Buenos Aires, *Atlas*, March, 1964.

Americans, like most inhabitants of the earth's surface, are prepared to make love at almost any hour.

Incidentally the United States nowadays maintains "population attachés" in every important AID mission in Latin America, mainly to report on population problems but also to assist local agencies engaged in the field, a somewhat hush-hush operation. Meantime the countries where family planning activities exist are Argentina, Brazil, Colombia, Peru, Ecuador, and Venezuela, and in particular Uruguay and Chile.

Urbanization and Industrialization. Brazil has given us an introduction to these topics. As to the rest of the continent, Bogotá, Caracas, Santiago have tripled or even quadrupled their population in a quarter of a century. Lima had 470,000 people when I first visited it; today, 1,700,000, an almost unbelievably steep rise. This is particularly interesting in that during an equivalent period several important North American cities have shown a decline in population, not a growth. St. Louis fell from 816,048 in 1940 to an estimated 768,777 in 1965; Boston from 770,816 to 683,253; Pittsburgh from 671,659 to 570,489. Between 1950 and 1960, Chicago, Detroit, Baltimore, and Cleveland all dropped slightly.[7]

As to industrialization, most South American countries lived mostly by the export of raw materials twenty-five years ago; their economies were colonial and depended largely on American and British markets. This dependence continues and still dominates much of the economy, but industrial advance and diversification have been spectacular. Venezuela is building up an important steel industry and much else; Argentina has a variety of new small industries. New raw materials have been developed, like fish meal in Peru, which, as a result, has now passed Japan to be the first fisheries nation in the world.

Industrialization is, however, still a subject of considerable controversy. Critics say that South America has no "right" to industrialize when it still cannot feed its own people. And the cost is high. Most South American businessmen will not touch an investment unless it pays off at what their counterparts in the United States would think is an abnormal rate—20 percent or more. Foreign investors coming in are also expensive, because they want to insure their risks, compounded by the fear of political instability, and ask for a quick and high return. But as a matter of fact foreign investment is falling off compared to the lush 1940's. I met a Chicago industrialist who said recently, "I wouldn't touch South America with a ten-foot pole. They squeeze you dry, then chuck you out."

Urbanization and industrialization are both profoundly associated with

[7] *Look,* September 21, 1965.

other factors making for change. Both usually produce a trend to smaller families and a drop in the birth rate; the best antidote to overpopulation is industrialization.[8] Agriculture is bound to be affected too, since it will probably be impossible to feed the great new mass of workers in the towns without agrarian reform. Politics are influenced because both urbanization and industrialization promote more political consciousness on the part of workers, and add vitality to the labor movement. Even today a political leader has to carry the new slums in most of the great cities to win an election.

The squatter towns are another new and sensational development. Their size is as staggering as their ghastliness. Just *one* of several in Lima has 200,000 people; just one in Chile is the size of a large municipality itself.

Politics. 1. Personalist rule in the old *caudillo* style has pretty well gone out. Only two countries are unmodified dictatorships today—Paraguay and Argentina, with Brazil running them close. Dictators who have lost power or who have been pitched out of office or otherwise eliminated in the last quarter century include Vargas, Perón, Pérez Jiménez in Venezuela, Rojas Pinilla in Colombia, and many others, to say nothing of venal monsters like Somoza in Nicaragua and Trujillo in the Dominican Republic.

This brings up large public issues. American business tended conspicuously to support the old-style dictators (Perón excepted), and the American government did likewise, partly because they were thought of as a defense against Communism. Things began to change with President Kennedy, which is one reason why he is so passionately idolized in South America by the rank and file of people. The Alliance for Progress, no matter how it has stumbled, set a different mode.

2. The extreme right has lost parliamentary power almost everywhere and the moderate (non-Communist) left has become respectable. Impulses toward paternalism, collectivism, social security, and the intervention of the state in economic matters, which scarcely existed twenty-five years ago except in Uruguay, are growing with vigor. Trade unions have expanded. State programs for social improvement, like Cooperación Popular in Peru, are in effect. Moreover, labor has risen phenomenally as a direct political force through the unions and otherwise.

3. It would be risky to predict that democracy *per se* is on the advance. Several reasons for this are clear. For one thing most Latin Americans are bored with the way democracy has been abused. "Who cares about votes— we want to build!" is a familiar remark from younger people. For another,

[8] John J. Johnson, *Continuity and Change in Latin America*, p. 7.

democracy has lost much prestige because of the outrages conducted in its name by the propertied class. It was the oligarchy, not the left, which most conspicuously made use of nominally democratic procedures in several countries; they organized the parties, chose the leaders, and ran parliaments under a bogus "democratic" façade. This was the easiest way to retain control, and took the onus off their own position. Again, several South American countries are not yet educated enough to be able to understand the sophistication of the democratic process or indulge in its luxuries. A word of warning should, however, attend this statement, because it is the excuse normally given by the oligarchs as a reason for delaying democratic reforms.

Still again, among elements making the practice of democracy difficult, there is the fact that no true electorate exists in most countries, and few real parties are in operation; most are little more than indiscriminate groupings or personalized cliques. On the other hand the rise of the Christian Democrats in Chile and, on a different level, of Acción Democrática in Venezuela, are encouraging developments.

4. Presidential power is still the acme of the political process, and most South American presidents have the power to declare a state of siege, which means nullifying civil rights, at will, or to replace refractory governors in the provinces by personally named "interventors," or proconsuls. This can obviously make a *reductio ad absurdum* of democratic government. One of the most prickly of all political problems is how to bring about effective change in the policies of an unpopular president by nonviolent means. Suppose a president happens to be a drunkard, as happened recently in Ecuador. The only way to get rid of him is to make a *golpe* (coup).

5. One dilemma making for political instability has been stated by Walter Lippmann: "If the governments come from the progressive left, they are threatened constantly, whenever their reforms begin to bite, by military dictatorships. If the soldiers control the government, they are constantly threatened by proletarian and peasant uprisings."[9]

Social fluidity, the middle class, and the position of women. Here there have been advances all along the line. Because of education, meager as this may be, more people are emerging out of the lower and entering the middle class, and the middle classers, if they become rich enough, soon become uppers. The position is gradually being reached where a man's position in society depends on his achievement, not merely on family and social status. The middle class is even more important in South America than in other underdeveloped areas because without it there is no buffer between an upper that doesn't work and a lower prostrated by poverty. Another important

[9] *Newsweek*, January 3, 1966.

factor is the steady growth of a technical elite, something almost unknown twenty-five years ago. This makes for intercommunication between countries, something badly needed, and diminishes as well the intellectual isolation of the continent, which most South Americans—who yearn to "belong"—deplore.

Women are advancing too—but not fast enough. I met in one country the wife of a surgeon. He runs the household, handles the accounts, and pays the bills. She has to ask for spending money every day—not merely for clothes and the like but for routine shopping. The husband never refuses, but every day she has to ask. Several times she has brought up the subject of their financial position, and what would happen to her and their children if the husband should die. He tells her nothing, pats her on the shoulder, and says, "It's all written down here in an envelope in the desk drawer." But the drawer is locked.

Twenty-five years ago this would have been typical, but it is less so now. Women are on the march almost everywhere, especially women of the middle class, though their emancipation is very far from being complete. Even at sophisticated dinner parties South American women tend to sit silent and abashed, like pretty, well-taught pets, or are plumply maternal and isolated. But one may encounter a sprinkling of women lawyers these days, women doctors and bankers, even women engineers. Women in Argentina now comprise a third of the total work force, and the universities are full of girl students everywhere. Women ask for answers; they want to know what's going on; they demand an end of their miseries and want to be direct beneficiaries of the revolution of rising expectations, not mere retainers who get leftover slops.

Economic Factors Aside from Industrialization. 1. I don't need to labor the point that a principal hallmark of the continent is still its excruciating poverty. I have already described the plight of peasants in northeastern Brazil, and I talked to a woman in Bogotá, Colombia, whose husband, a chauffeur, had to support a family of twelve on $22.40 a month. "The average Latin American is a starving man with a gold mine under his feet," wrote Tad Szulc in the New York Times not long ago. Much of life is still a monumental struggle against environment, to get *at* the wealth that should be available to all, and that ought to be equitably distributed.

2. Public finance is a dismal subject. In 1940 the national debts of most countries stood at a manageable level; today the opposite is true, and full payment of amortization and interest on loans has become impossible. Six of the ten countries have budgets out of balance; seven out of ten have adverse trade balances. The local currencies are at a discount almost everywhere.

3. Economic nationalism is vigorously on the rise. This applies particu-

larly to the extractive industries and utilities. It would have been almost unthinkable ten years ago for Brazil, as an example, to have expropriated American utility holdings; the marines might have marched in. The atmosphere is altogether different today. Bolivia has nationalized tin, and at least three nations—Argentina, Chile, Peru—are involved in abrasive negotiations to modify the terms of old contracts and concessions concerning minerals and petroleum.

4. In several countries tax collections are tightening up, and tax receipts are incomparably higher than in the 1940's. But much remains to be done. At the end of 1965 fewer than thirty thousand of the eighty thousand businesses in Bogotá—as an example—had even bothered to register with the tax authorities. When I was in Chile the first case ever recorded in the history of South America occurred in which a business person was actually jailed for nonpayment of income tax, partly as a result of the stimulus of the Alianza, a major plank of which is tax reform. In most countries tax fraud is not yet a penal offense.

The big tax dodgers are, of course, the rich, because workers in the lower categories have their taxes deducted at source. Tax dodging has profound effects in several fields not merely financial. Talk of democracy is idle if the wealthy are so lacking in public spirit that they will not even pay taxes. Most types of reform, which the continent needs desperately, will be impossible if tax collections are so short that there is no money in the till. Some oligarchs possibly avoid tax payments as a direct means of preventing reform. One reason why Latin America has been smothered by a surfeit of expensive foreign investment is that so little capital has been available at home.

A British critic, discussing these problems, warned me not to stress tax dodging as a major element in South American lack of development, by adducing the example of the United States, where our national expansion and conquest of the frontier were achieved long before the income tax. But circumstances in North America, a rich and united land, were altogether different. People say too that "You cannot make Latins pay taxes." But Frenchmen and Italians now do—through the nose.

5. South Americans have little, if any, spirit of philanthropy to compare with that in North America. The wealthy seldom leave their fortunes to foundations, donate libraries or museums to the community, or endow hospitals and the like. (An honorable exception is Assis Chateaubriand in Brazil.) One reason may be that, because their tax obligations are light, they do not feel the need to give to philanthropic organizations as a means of tax relief.

6. Not only do the rich seldom indulge in good works at home; they export vast amounts of their own earnings and capital to banks abroad. This

phenomenon was not nearly as conspicuous twenty-five years ago as it is today. Figures are hard to get, but the evacuation of capital from South America almost certainly exceeds $500 million a year, and may reach a billion. One responsible estimate is that a total of almost $15 *billion* is held by Latin American persons or institutions abroad, of which $4 billion is in the United States. Some of this is revenue from exports, which the South Americans prefer to keep in dollars in New York, but this does not modify the inherent deleteriousness of a practice whereby stupendous amounts of capital are systematically withdrawn from a notably poor continent by its own citizens. It is a paramount reason why the continent is so poor and why development is so difficult. The basic cause is lack of confidence, but this doesn't excuse its stupidity, because it is likely to produce in the long run just what its promoters seek most to avoid in the short—Communism, disintegration, revolution.

7. The gap between rich and poor, like the yawn of an alligator, is probably greater today than a quarter of a century ago, if only because many of the rich are richer, and the poor, partly because of population pressure, are poorer. The pity is that there is no real reason for this except greed, fright, and lack of development. South America should be able to produce enough for all if population growth can be slowed down. Meantime it has become clear that the poor will not accept "their status quo of misery" forever.

8. Twenty-five years ago American assistance to South America came largely in the form of private loans and investment; aid today is mainly public. The new factor of U.S. aid through the Alianza and similar instrumentalities can be an immeasurably important element for advance even though the Alianza itself is full of troubles.

Army, Church, Oligarchy

A Latin American once remarked of his own people: "The rich do not think. . . . They are not really bad . . . they simply do not think. . . . They have not been trained to think."
—WILLIAM V. D'ANTONIO AND FREDERICK B. PIKE

We now reach the three major elements in the power picture in South America—army, church, oligarchy—and here too profound changes are taking place. These three forces have controlled the continent since colonial days, and it still rests in large part on the tripod they form. But the structure is not what it once was.

I said in reference to Brazil that the reason the armies were so powerful all over South America was obviously that they had the arms. Since democratic procedures are not fully developed the only practical method of changing government has been by coup d'état in which the armed forces necessarily played the decisive role. This is still the case, but the complexion of the armies themselves is changing.

First, most South American armies today are created by conscription, which means that the recruits rise out of the broad body of the nation and are not as likely as before to be mere unwitting tools of *caudillos* or capricious adventurers. Many come from impoverished urban slums or rural areas, and, far from being slaves of the right, have no particular love for feudal landlords. Many are radical. Officers for the most part are middle-class boys who go through military academies like our West Point, and graduate on merit. Some have advanced education, become technical experts, and swerve to the left. They want reform. Second, the armies have come to take on a mystique strictly of their own, based on the concept that they represent constitutionalism and continuity and are the watchdog of the nation, guarding its collective soul.

It is they, however, who decide what "continuity," "constitutionalism," and "collective soul" mean at a given moment. The paradox is clear that, to preserve constitutionalism, they must take it on themselves to decide when it is justifiable to break the law. Then too it would be foolish to deny that plenty of officers are still extreme reactionaries, altogether outside the main stream of contemporary social thinking, who are still capable of making irresponsible revolts. Moreover, they count.

Several countries, like Peru and Bolivia, use their armies nowadays in "civil action," a suggestive evolution. Recruits are put to work on public works and are given technical training in various crafts, with the result that they resemble a kind of uniformed WPA, and learn a trade. Another phenomenon is the rise of "Creole Nasserism," which means a new socio-political orientation on the part of youthful officers who have absorbed neutralist ideas. The movement is intensely nationalist, and has a strong left-wing base. It embraces neutrality in foreign policy, which in effect means anti-Americanism, domestic reform, and above all technical training for citizens. I heard a priest in Chile say, "The army technocrats are a much more potentially dangerous force than the Communists, because they are better able to seize power. They are the new menace from the left."

Generally speaking the navy tends to be more conservative than the army in most of South America, because naval officers come mostly from the upper class and are seldom stirred (except in Chile) by intellectual pursuits. Air force officers are usually pro-American because most have been trained in the United States.

South American armies are, like armies everywhere, not exactly cheap to maintain. Argentina, Bolivia, and Peru all spend about 25 percent of the national budget on their armed forces, a steep price to pay for organizations which, in the last analysis, have no function except to provide prestige and be a dubious guarantor of constitutionality. Latin America as a whole spends not less than a *billion and a half* dollars a year on arms, but seldom, if ever, fights a war. Costa Rica, if I may venture upward to Central America for a sentence, has, incidentally, no army or navy at all, but no other country is willing to follow this sensible example.

*

The Roman Catholic Church too is in the full throes of change. As President Frei of Chile, a devout Catholic himself, said recently, "The church knows that the continent is alive with revolution, and cannot remain indifferent to this fact." The Mexican novelist Carlos Fuentes, one of the best-known left-wing writers in the hemisphere, writes, "In the final analysis one of the true barometers of change in Latin America will be the trans-formation of the Catholic church . . . in order to maintain its influence." He mentions the church's "liberal elite" and concedes that the reforms it espouses are "forcefully real."[10]

Here, once more, we need a word of background. The Catholicism that dominated South America for generations was peculiarly undiluted and all-embracing. The early *conquistadores* fought in the name of the cross and baptized Indians by the tens of thousands. The great archbishops admitted allegiance only to the king of Spain, and ruled like princes; the clergy were their troops, and the Inquisition their Gestapo. The church had no competi-tion, since no other religion but Catholicism was permitted. It grew fabulously rich and fabulously decadent. So, after independence was won from Spain, anticlericalism began to rise, if only because the church was indissolubly associated with the stagnation of the old order; anticlericalism was a protest against the abuses of churchly power. In most countries two political parties eventually grew up, both Catholic, but separated by anti-clericalism. The conservatives stood behind the church unreservedly, the liberals did not, even if they remained good Catholics. This cleavage has dominated much political development in South America to this day.

At present the country where the church is strongest is probably Colom-bia; after that Ecuador, then Peru. The most anticlerical state is Uruguay. The church is still what is known as "established" in Argentina, Bolivia,

[10] *Book Week*, April 24, 1966.

Paraguay, Peru, and Venezuela; it is "disestablished," that is church and state are separated, in Brazil, Chile, Uruguay.

Reformist trends are conspicuous in several countries, and there are Catholic intellectuals scattered through the continent almost as leftist as Dom Helder Câmara in Brazil—socialist teachers and even priests who have given up their robes to become guerrilla leaders. Much of this general evolution dates from *Mater et Magistra*, the liberalizing encyclical issued by Pope John XXIII in 1961. The principal public manifestation of this new bent is that the church is much more relaxed on birth control, as noted above. In several countries priests have publicly joined study groups on population problems. The church has little to lose by reform, and much to gain by a higher standard of living. After all, its income comes from the masses.

It would be an overstatement to say that the Latin American church has gone left, but, on the other hand, it is equally true that "Catholicism no longer equates automatically with conservatism." The truth is that there is a split in the church, just as there is a split in several of the armies. There are plenty of Latin American prelates who think that Pope John was a heretic, and the upper clergy is still almost immovably conservative. One reason is that most of the men of the rank of bishop or above in South America come out of the orders, and do not rise from the secular priesthood; they have little pastoral experience, and have not worked with people in the parishes.

Not less than one-third of all Roman Catholics in the world live in Latin America, with more to come. But the church is losing membership at the rate of several million nominal members a year; most of these are Indians being reabsorbed by their pagan religions. One worry on the part of the church is a serious shortage of priests. The number of Catholics per priest in a typical South American country can be 11,000 to one; in the United States it is 7,700 to one. Fewer than 20 percent of the Roman Catholics in South America are, according to responsible figures, *practicing* Catholics; only a small proportion of believers regularly go to mass. Protestantism is strongly on the rise. There were only about 107,000 Protestants on the continent in 1920; today, 4,500,000.

*

Finally, the oligarchy, which is the third leg of the tripod. Here too the scene is changing, but not so fast. To transform feudalism into modern society is not an overnight matter. But heat is beginning to blow up from the countryside, the best proof of this being that the great landowners themselves feeling its blast have become defensive—scared. One reason for this is that the Alliance for Progress made land reform "respectable" by listing it as a major necessity. The wealth of the oligarchs is based, of course, on their land, and what they fear most is the prospect of losing it.

Many oligarchs live almost in the absolutist manner of the old aristocracy in prewar Hungary or Poland, on great estates called haciendas. "The *hacendado*—" I am quoting a Catholic source—"owns lock, stock and barrel all he surveys—crops, huts, and in a sense the people. This feudal power is the essence of his prestige and the source of his wealth. In economic terms the hacienda is practically self-sustaining. With almost no investment it produces everything from its own furniture to food, and the little that can not be made or grown the *hacendado* buys or bargains for surplus crops. . . . The hacienda is a way of life. It is a closed, family-operated society, a political entity unto itself."[11]

Peasants on many haciendas are virtual serfs, "part and parcel of the hacienda." They can quit their miserable huts and move—and many do, as witness the migrations into the towns—"but great numbers are still so indebted to the landlord, their only source of credit, that leaving the land is difficult." South America today has two-thirds as many serfs as did Russia before the revolution, according to one estimate. Senator Robert F. Kennedy pointed out in one of his eye-opening twin speeches to Congress in May, 1966, that "serdom in Peru" is an "evil" equivalent to *apartheid* in South Africa and outrages even more overt elsewhere in the world.

In country after country the disproportion in land ownership is almost too gross to be believed.[12] In Colombia 3 percent of the population owns 60 percent of the arable land; in Venezuela 1.7 percent owns 74.5 percent. Figures for Peru and Ecuador are even more lopsided. Or consider Chile, where 2.2 percent of owners control three-quarters of the cultivated area. The extreme concentration of economic power represented by such figures is out of fashion these days in North America, where defenders of the free enterprise system strive to dissociate the capitalist structure in general from such abuse. "Capitalism in Latin America has not evolved into modern forms," it is said, or, "The South American style of free enterprise is not *our* style." The countries where the landed oligarchy is still most vigorously conspicuous are Argentina, Peru, Chile, and Colombia. Brazil is a middle case, if only because it is so varied, and so is Ecuador for a different reason.

---

[11] *Latin America, Fact Sheet No. 3,* published by the National Council of Catholic Women, Washington, D.C. This closely follows an eloquent passage in Frank Tannenbaum, *Ten Keys to Latin America.*

[12] *Latin American Issues,* edited by Albert O. Hirschman, p. 164.

The countries freest of landlordism are Venezuela, Bolivia, and Uruguay. But even in the states where the oligarchy is strongest changes and stirrings are apparent. The great *estancia* (ranch) owners in Argentina will never have the power they had before Perón, who irremediably changed the social structure of the nation. Chile has some fantastically rich landowners, but they do not control President Frei. Peru may still be feudal to a large degree, but President Belaúnde, close as he is to the landowning class through family and other associations, is certainly not a puppet of feudal interests.

The frustrations, archaicisms, imbalances caused by bad agriculture in South America derive largely from feudalism. Land reform is, however, a difficult subject. The mere confiscation and division of land is not going to produce more food, in the opinion of most serious experts on the subject. The problem is how to make agriculture as a whole more productive, as in Brazil, and this brings in all manner of ancillary factors. Nevertheless the alpha and omega of the issue, if only as a psychological factor, is to get land to the people so that peasants, as a minimum, will have property of their own to till. This means taking it away from the big landowner, which makes the problem. If any political scientist could ever work out a method for making the poor richer without making the rich poorer, without revolution, South America would be an easier continent to live in.

Land reform projects are being pressed at varying rates of speed today in Bolivia, Peru, Venezuela, Colombia, several states in Brazil, and, above all, Chile. Much of this, however, still exists only on paper.

What South America Needs Most

First, education, which should induce more consciousness by citizens of the needs of the nation as a whole.

Second, development and modernization.

Third, political stability. But political stability is impossible under present social conditions. Governments change, as Walter Lippmann recently pointed out, because problems are insoluble; moreover, citizens steadily demand a better break.

Fourth, reform and modernization, particularly land reform. (In contemporary jargon "reform" is called "institutional modernization.")

*

Chief problems? I have mentioned several, like the necessity to give a fairer share of income and economic as well as political power to the people at large. Another, perhaps the most critical of all, is the possibility that population pressure, the population explosion, will become unmanageable and, by its mere weight, stifle social advance.

South America is still in several areas a hundred years behind Western Europe, the Soviet Union, or the United States—despite the changes and ameliorations outlined above.

Some Generalizations at Large

Among characteristic South American traits is an acute sensitiveness, both personal and in regard to national dignity. Of course this is a hallmark of dozens of other nations. Any number of instances of Latin sensitiveness may be cited on almost any level. I happened to be in Caracas when the announcement came that Jack Hood Vaughn, now the head of the Peace Corps, had been named to succeed Thomas C. Mann as Assistant Secretary of State for Inter-American Affairs. "But the man was a prize fighter!" my Venezuelan friends protested in horror. Indeed Mr. Vaughn had been a professional boxer in his younger days, but this had nothing to do with his ability or fitness for the job. Nationalism is a vivid concomitant of sensitiveness. In Lima we learned that patriotic Peruvians deplored the term "pre-Columbian" or "pre-Hispanic" for their incomparable Inca works of art, and insisted on saying "ancient Peruvian" art instead.

Another dominant and admirable South American characteristic is respect for culture even in the noneducated classes. As to those educated, one little story has it that an eminent Chilean dignitary was tremendously impressed by President Kennedy not because of his youth, intellectual acumen, or other qualities, but because he spoke a few words of French. The Chilean, a cultivated man, had never dreamed that any president of such an "uncultured" country as the United States could know a foreign language. Intellect is admired. Four South American presidents today are military men; the other six are intellectuals—lawyers, doctors, professors. Not one is a professional politician.

South American patterns of thought differ substantially from ours, it would seem. Most thinking is short term; citizens do not see beyond the next election (as is indeed the case with most of us), which is one reason why the work of the new technocrats and planners is hindered so frequently. Most South Americans tend to be dogmatists rather than, like most North Americans, pragmatists. They like to evolve doctrines whether or not these have a close relation to the facts. Moreover, once a thing is on paper it is apt to be considered real and that is the end of the matter. Some of the South American constitutions are among the most beautifully progressive documents on earth, but no one ever thinks of enforcing their provisions; this is also true of civil rights legislation in several countries.

Power went from the top to the bottom under the Spaniards, not from the bottom to the top, which has produced lasting effects. For instance most South Americans still tend to prefer monopoly to competition in business affairs; nepotism is taken for granted in politics and other spheres; form is often given greater rank than substance.

A predisposition to violence lies close to the surface in many Latin Americans, as is well known. The *abrazo*, the comfortable and appealing hug with which South Americans greet each other, is said to have its origin in frisking: the friend was trying to find out if his so-called friend was carrying a gun. But we in North America should not make too much of this, or be smug about it. There has never been a Dillinger or Al Capone in South America. Four United States presidents have been assassinated in a century, more than in any single country below Panama.

Corruption needs a further word. Here too the United States has no copyright on virtue; think back to Frank Hague ("I am the Law!") in Jersey City or glance at contemporary Boston. But it is undeniable that graft, corruption, bribery exist on almost every plane in most of Latin America; of one country it is said that no president ever left office in recent years without becoming a millionaire. A familiar phrase is, "He bathed well, and splashed a little," meaning that a man not only takes loot for himself, but gives leftovers to friends. Former President Cárdenas of Mexico, one of the great men of the continent, told me mournfully when I met him many years ago, "Every time I put my hand in the basket, I pull out a thief." The most spectacular cases of corruption have to do with dictators who, on being deposed, managed to escape with large fortunes; Perón in Argentina is supposed to have made away with something between $50 and $500 million; Pérez Jiménez in Venezuela with even more, improbably fantastic as these figures seem.

Finally, the simple but major point should be made that so many South Americans are such delightful people. Their warmth, joy in life, volatility, optimism, spontaneity, uninhibitedness make most North Americans seem sterile and pallid by comparision. Few South Americans have ulcers.

The Universities and Education

The universities vary in South America almost as they do in the United States, but there are similarities within the common frame. We shall visit several. They are massively entrenched, have great prestige, and play a considerable political role in several countries. Most are—and have to be—altogether state supported, because private endowment is, as noted above, all but unknown; this means that most are poor.

Two dominating aspects of the South American national universities are the immunity principle and student expressiveness. We in the North have lately had some lively experience of this last, particularly at Berkeley, and we should not be too superior or supercilious when we read about student strikes or riots below the Rio Grande. Our youngsters too are learning not to conform.

South American universities differ markedly from ours in many respects. Professors operate on a kind of cash-and-carry basis; most are miserably underpaid, and many work in several institutions at the same time, holding outside jobs as well. Students in some schools have such freedom that they do not even have to attend classes, and scholastic discipline is lax. (Of course this is true in England and much of Western Europe too.) There are few fixed entrance requirements. Tuition is generally free, as in our state universities. Students have little campus life in our sense of the term; such ornamentalia as fraternities, proms, the veneration of alma mater, sentimental alumni influence, and so on are all but unknown. Education is a serious matter. A student is apt to take himself much more seriously than ours do; to be a student is practically to be a member of a profession. Most students are passionately political, and many are Communists or Communist-inspired. Student councils are powerful, and actively assist in the running of most hemisphere universities; this may seem unusual, but Yale late in 1965 took the first step toward adopting a system whereby students will have an official voice in appointing faculty members to positions of tenure. This has been a rule for a long time in several South American institutions.

Autonomy means that the national university is theoretically exempt from search or seizure by army, police, or other government authorities; students have, in a word, immunity from arrest. In actual practice autonomy is something of a fiction because the universities are supported by the federal budget and the government could, if it dared to, exercise pressure by withholding funds. But it would be a rash government which would ever instruct the military or police to penetrate a campus. Such an event might well cause a revolution—and almost did in Colombia some months ago.

This immunity system grew up following a student revolt at the University of Córdoba in Argentina just after World War I, and its primary impulse came not so much out of fear of government as out of resentment at interference by the church. With an almost unbreakable hold on primary and secondary education, the church wanted to extend its influence to control the universities as well. This it did not succeed in doing.

Encouraged by the victorious strike at Córdoba, students felt liberated all over the continent. Their political self-consciousness and assurance have increased ever since. Having the right of refuge, they had more temptation to defy authority. Moreover the universities became convenient asylums for bogus students, semi-students, and the like.

Students make demonstrations, cripple the continuity of teaching by prolonged strikes, and take political sides, but so, *mutatis mutandis*, do students in other countries; it is part of the profession of being a student. As to Communism it is undeniable that there are strong Communist or extreme left-wing elements today in almost all the national universities, both in the faculties and student bodies, as we shall see in several countries, but this is inevitable in view of local conditions.

Student violence should be taken with a certain perspective. The circumstances are almost like those in pre-revolutionary Russia. When a student throws a rock at a window this is not an example of mere hooliganism, but part of an essential revolutionary mood and mentality. The student has no other way of expressing immediate effective protest.

Another variety of institution has grown up in South America recently, the specifically Catholic universities run by the church: Latin America had thirteen of these ten years ago, thirty-one today. They rose mostly because so many of the national universities were, in the church view, rowdy, inadequate, and leftist. The Catholic universities are smaller than the national; they charge tuition, which means that their students come by and large from better-off families; their teaching standards are probably higher; their discipline is more severe, and their professors are better paid. Interestingly enough they accept Protestant and Jewish students, and have, if necessary, non-Catholic teachers. But the basic orientation is parochial.[13]

Why are students so important in South America? The answer is so obvious that it may be missed—because they *are* literate in a continent more than half illiterate. Why is education the *sine qua non* almost everywhere? Just look at the difference between Juan Vicente Gómez, the late dictator of Venezuela, and Rómulo Betancourt, a recent president; the gamut between them proves how much progress can be made in a generation.

Coda

Americans returning home from a trip to South America generally find that they are asked two questions above any. First, why do the "Latins" have all those "revolutions"? Second, are they all going broke and will we have to bail them out? But there is much more to the continent than that.

[13] *Time*, November 26, 1963.

CHAPTER 8

Big Neighbor, Communism, and the Alianza

> I helped make Mexico safe for American oil interests in 1914.
> I helped make Haiti and Cuba a decent place for the National
> City Bank boys to collect revenues in. I helped purify Nica-
> ragua for the international banking house of Brown Brothers.
> . . . I helped make Honduras "right" for American fruit
> companies. . . . Looking back on it, I might have given Al
> Capone a few hints.
>
> —GENERAL SMEDLEY D. BUTLER, UNITED STATES
> MARINES, IN 1931
>
> The freedom of the New World is the hope of the universe.
>
> —SIMÓN BOLÍVAR

IN SIX out of the ten capitals we visited we ran into anti-United States
demonstrations, most of them petty but unpleasant just the same—a bomb
scare here, rocks thrown at an embassy there. The conclusion was in-
escapable that our stance in South America, just where it should be best, was
not altogether good. Americans generally assume that, in spite of minor
irritations and dissatisfactions, the whole of South America stands solidly on
our side, but this is not quite the case. Take some votes in the UN and the
Organization of American States (OAS) as examples.

Back in December, 1957, on a UN resolution calling for self-determination for Cyprus, six Latin American republics abstained, as did the United
States. But eight (Bolivia, Costa Rica, Ecuador, El Salvador, Haiti, Guatemala, Panama, Uruguay) voted with the Soviet Union in favor of the
resolution. In October, 1959, seven Latin American countries (Argentina,

Brazil, Mexico, Venezuela, Cuba, Panama, Ecuador) voted for Poland, backed by the Soviet Union, instead of Turkey, backed by the United States, to fill a vacant seat on the Security Council.

In April, 1961, ten Latin American nations voted in the first instance against a resolution, strongly supported by the United States, to provide financing for the UN operations in the Congo. In one recent year, four (Mexico, Guatemala, Haiti, Bolivia) withheld support from the United States in the UN more than half the time. We won at the Punta del Este conference in Uruguay in January, 1962, but not without a fierce struggle. Haiti, run then as now by one of the most offensive of dictatorships, had the deciding vote, and this was only cast after we had promised it some $30 million in economic aid. Even so—in the crucial vote to expel Cuba from the OAS—six Latin American countries abstained, including four of the most important—Mexico, Brazil, Argentina, Chile.

I should add in qualification the important fact that, confronted with a really supreme crisis in October, 1962, when John F. Kennedy forced Nikita Khrushchev to withdraw Soviet missiles from Cuba, the Latin American countries did solidly close ranks behind the United States. Before this several republics had been on the fence about Cuba, partly because they felt that it was necessary to placate their own agitated left wings, partly to gain bargaining power vis-à-vis the United States, and partly out of resentment at American domination of South American affairs. They felt that Cuba's right to an independent policy should be defended, but the acknowledged fact that Soviet missile bases had been installed on the island, capable of offensive action against both North and South America, acutely shocked them, and they acted accordingly and deserted Castro. Three countries went on record, however, to the effect that they would not take part in any actual invasion of Cuba. These were Brazil, Mexico, and Bolivia.

In 1964 Venezuela, charging that Castro had used sabotage and terrorism in an attempt to overthrow its government, asked OAS members to sever diplomatic relations with Cuba, which the United States had previously done in January, 1961. Fourteen out of eighteen countries agreed to do so, but Mexico, Chile, Uruguay, and Bolivia refused. Three of these, responding to heavy United States pressure, have, however, subsequently broken off relations; Mexico is the exception. As of today Mexico and Canada are the only two hemisphere countries maintaining relations with Cuba. Canada is not a member of the OAS.

The United States was naturally pleased to see Castro thus isolated, and the hemisphere front became solider. But then in April, 1965, another portentous event occurred in the Caribbean. President Lyndon B. Johnson sent the marines into the Dominican Republic—the first time we have intervened militarily in any Latin American country since the 1920's. Some 21,000 United States troops occupied Santo Domingo on the grounds that a Communist takeover was imminent. This has not yet been proved to the satisfaction of everybody, although factors making for disorder were certainly present; in any case the decision to intervene was taken in agitated haste. South America doesn't like Communism, but it doesn't like United States military intervention either, and so impulses of protest and alarm swept through the continent, not merely from left-wing elements. I had direct experience of this in four capitals, when I ran into demonstrations against American embassies. People at large seemed to feel that the State Department was up to its old tricks again, and that we were wielding the "Big Stick" once more.

Senator Fulbright said in Washington that the administration, on the basis of "inadequate evidence," had "intervened against social revolution and in support, at least temporarily, of a corrupt, reactionary, military oligarchy." Several experts predicted that our intervention, far from checking Communism in Latin America, would serve to stimulate it. Some criticism of the administration undoubtedly went too far. It was not understood how sensitive we were to the possibility of the Dominican Republic's becoming another Cuba. Somewhat belatedly the United States applied to the OAS for cooperation in creating an inter-American military force "to help restore peace and constitutional government in the Dominican Republic," thus giving us a cover. Then, on May 6, five countries voted against this crucial resolution—Mexico, Uruguay, Peru, Chile, and Ecuador. Venezuela abstained. A two-thirds vote is necessary to carry OAS resolutions, and the United States, although we went to unprecedented lengths to beg, borrow, or buy support, came close to being beaten.

Then, while the Dominican crisis was being resolved, American proposals were launched to change procedures in the OAS and make it "a more effective body for mobilizing inter-American action when an emergency rises in the hemisphere," i.e., when we deem intervention to be desirable or necessary. We have pushed these proposals hard, but without success, at several conferences, in Panama, Lima, and Rio de Janeiro. The OAS may not amount to much, but we need it as a device, a screen. So far Brazil, Chile, and Peru have refused to go along with us in these new proposals, and the net result is a blank. A considerable amount of bad feeling and recrimination followed.

In 1965 came an odd fiasco, Operation Camelot. This was a $6 million project fostered by the Pentagon for "research" in certain South American countries. The idea was to find out how susceptible they were to revolution, what their position was in regard to "the potential for internal war," and how effective they would be at "counter-insurgency," i.e., beating down Communists. The countries included were Chile, Colombia, Peru, Vene-zuela, and Argentina. The research was to have been conducted by military and other specialists under academic cover. When news of this leaked out it caused furious indignation throughout South America, particularly in Chile, on the ground that it was an unwarranted intrusion. United States officials on the spot protested vigorously as well, and the project was withdrawn. Then other United States "study groups," designed to explore "behavioral patterns" in Latin America, had to be dissolved. In January, 1966, came a similar crisis over Operación Simpático, a Pentagon research project set up by American University in Washington, D.C., to investigate the effective-ness of "military and civic" action in disturbed rural areas in Colombia. Legislators in Bogotá angrily called this an example of "Pentagon espio-nage," saying that it constituted "a new type of disguised political-military intervention by the United States that repudiates our national dignity." Simpático was not, however, suspended, because it had the backing of the Colombian government, and opposition to it in Bogotá, mostly inspired by domestic politics, presently died down.

Now came another crisis to prove that American relations with the con-tinent leave much to be desired. A United States congressman, Armistead I. Selden, Jr. (D., Ala.) introduced a resolution in the House of Representatives asserting the right of the United States or any other American republic to intervene (if necessary with armed force) to forestall or combat Communist subversion or aggression whenever it occurred in the western hemisphere. A key word here was "forestall," because this left the door wide open to possible armed intervention on what might prove later to be an ambiguous or flimsy pretext; Mr. Selden wanted a blanket authority for unilateral inter-vention. This Congressman had previously been distinguished in the realm of domestic affairs by sponsoring a resolution which would have barred federal authorities from entering any state unless invited to do so by the governor or legislature. When the Selden resolution passed in the House by 312 to 52 the repercussion in South America was immediate. The legislatures of Peru and Colombia, although their governments do not like Communism any more than Mr. Selden, went to the unprecedented length of taking public votes to deplore the resolution. The Colombian vote was unanimous, the first time in history it ever voted unanimously on anything,[1] even though Colombia is one of the most pro-American countries on the continent. In

[1] According to Senator Wayne Morse of Oregon.

Washington Senator Morse, holding that the resolution was "legally, morally, and politically iniquitous," dug up the fact that Mr. Selden had consulted the State Department before introducing his bill, and that the department had suggested changes in the text but had apparently approved it otherwise. A final touch came when the congressman was included in the United States delegation to the OAS conference in Rio; this may have seemed an odd appointment considering South American feeling about him, but it was made necessary by his rank on the Foreign Affairs Committee of the House.

Senator Robert F. Kennedy, preparing for his trip to South America early in 1966, was told in a State Department briefing that Castro would be an incessant preoccupation everywhere he went. As a matter of fact Mr. Kennedy scarcely ever heard Castro mentioned, but Selden, whom most North Americans have never heard of, was flung in his ear at every step. Now we should inspect this fracas with a sense of balance. Few citizens, here or there, want Communism in South America, and all the Selden resolution did was to give crystallization to an attitude widely prevalent in Washington. It did little more than express a view already held by many in the State Department, the Pentagon, Congress, the CIA, and elsewhere. Why then did it come as such a surprise and provoke such revulsion in Latin America? Why should such intensely conservative and pro-American newspapers as *La Prensa* in Lima and the great Brazilian daily, *O Estado de São Paulo*, attack it with such angry venom? Why did the leading political parties in Venezuela and Mexico, which detest Communism, make public protests? Even Argentina found the resolution "baffling." The answer is the word "intervention." To almost any South American this is a red flag to a bull.

*

From all this it becomes clear, if anybody needed to know, that South America does not cling to North exactly as happy spouse to spouse. Relations are, however, quite good at present. There has been no serious blowup since a convulsion in Panama in 1964. Moreover, in any really vital crisis South America is almost categorically bound to take the side of the North, no matter what the pinpricks are, because there is no alternative. The power of the United States comes close to being absolute, even though Castro has defied it. But, talking in the most brutal terms, if we wanted to blow Castro off the face of the map we could do so in half an hour. The fact that South America is, indeed, utterly at the mercy of the United States, if any unfortunate eventuality should put the relationship to a test, is one of the most powerful of factors making for distress, irritation, and resentment in the hemisphere. Proud and sensitive people do not like to be vassals. It may be argued that Canada is also at the absolute mercy of the United States, and, on a serious level, does not mind a bit. But South America is not Canada. Of course Canada has ties to the Commonwealth and Europe which South America lacks. To repeat, South Americans resent it that they have no power of choice.

Organization of American States

The OAS is a wind tunnel, open at both ends and full of chinks, through which words whir. It does little but give face to decisions largely taken elsewhere, and has no inherent power of itself. In this it resembles the old League of Nations, which was only useful if its principal members agreed on a policy, useless if they did not. Another complaint by South Americans is that the OAS is so much dominated by Washington that it no longer represents the continent as a whole but is, in effect, nothing but an instrument of United States foreign policy.

Even so the OAS is an important body because, as noted above, it provides a structure for hemisphere decisions, and membership in it gives the South American republics a voice. They like it for the prestige it brings. We, on our side, find it essential because of its convenience as a cover. A negative OAS vote would probably not, in any real emergency, impede unilateral American action, but it would be highly embarrassing in view of our concept of the unity and solidarity of the hemisphere, Cuba excepted.

Roots of the OAS go back to Bolívar, who worked out a so-called Treaty of Union among eight Latin American countries in Panama in 1826; the OAS calls itself the oldest functioning international organization in the world, and asserts that "it wrote a declaration of human rights before the UN and organized a regional defense pact two years ahead of NATO."

To explain this we must go back a bit. In 1890 came the organization of an International Union of American Republics, rising out of the Bolívar concept after a long intermission; this in turn evolved into the Pan American Union. This did effective work in matters of technical and cultural exchange for many years. Then, after another long gap, a vital development occurred in 1947, the signature of the Pact of Rio, which was a kind of hemisphere nonaggression treaty—in effect a military pact. This was followed in the next year, 1948, by a conference at Bogotá which set up the OAS as an organization to implement the Rio pact. The Pan American Union became its secretariat.

But then the OAS languished, and became almost a dead letter politically—its highest body never even met between 1954 and 1964—because of a familiar insoluble problem, that no country was willing to give it teeth if this interfered with or weakened its own national sovereignty. But presently it revived under the stimulus of hemisphere developments. Countries such as Venezuela found it useful in seeking to isolate Castro. At present the OAS operates mostly through a standing council of ambassadors in Washington. Several South American republics have three ambassadors resident in the United States—one at the UN, one at the OAS, and one accredited in the normal manner to the United States government. The United States also maintains an ambassador accredited to the OAS.

Some Gripes and Complaints

There is a full range of these on the part of hemisphere citizens vis-à-vis the United States. South Americans scoff at us for maintaining such enormous, unwieldy embassies stuffed to the thresholds with personnel and intersected laboriously by childish-looking iron grilles and other devices to ensure security. Many think that we are Nervous Nellies about Communism, and laugh scornfully at our visa policy, which makes it difficult, if not impossible, for anybody ever accused of association with Communism, even in the most remote way, to gain entrance to the United States. Some point incredulously to such phenomena as that seventeen out of twenty desk officers in the State Department, responsible for seventeen countries, had (as of recent date) never served in the republics over which they have authority, and that we have had no fewer than five assistant secretaries of state for inter-American affairs in five years. Intellectuals deplore our so-called imperialism, liberals decry our backwardness on racial problems, and practically everybody thinks of the CIA as a hidden, sinister force almost everywhere.

The principal grievances go beyond all this, however. Dr. Roberto Campos of Brazil, as firm a friend as the United States has in South America, summarized them as follows in a recent essay outlining South American "reactive tensions." An honest man, Dr. Campos knows how to use words with candor. He thinks the chief "deep seated resentments" of the continent against the U.S. derive from:

(a) Geographic mutilation like that "imposed on Mexico by the annexation of California and Texas, or in Colombia through the fostered secession of Panama to facilitate the building of the canal."

(b) Armed intervention and occupation. Dr. Campos cites the examples of Nicaragua, Mexico, Haiti, the Dominican Republic, and Costa Rica.

(c) Political intervention, as exemplified by the Platt amendment enacted in 1901 and abrogated only in 1934. A rider to an appropriations bill, this authorized American intervention in Cuba and enabled us to transform that country into a virtual protectorate.

(d) Economic domination, expressed by the "overwhelming influence exercised in the past by American private interests." Dr. Campos cites the oil companies in Venezuela, the sugar interests of Cuba, and the United Fruit Company.

Even when United States policy is modified, Dr. Campos goes on, tensions remain beneath the surface. "This explains the morbid sensitiveness of Latin America to United States intervention even when, in individual cases, there may be basic sympathy with its objectives, such as . . . the containment of the communist threat in Cuba." Finally, he mentions the use of armed pressure to "affect political systems," as well as economic pressure to "enforce canons of monetary stability and fiscal discipline."[2]

Walter Lippmann, writing in the New York *Herald Tribune* on January 20, 1966, outlines several reasons for anti-American feeling and "general distrust and suspicion of the Johnson administration," including:

1. "Fear among people of the Center and Left that President Johnson . . . will use United States military force and United States economic power to thwart or suppress radical social changes.
2. "Anger on the Right that the United States is inciting the masses to expect radical improvements in their way of living."

Looking at the problem from a slightly different angle I would say that South Americans are troubled most by factors such as these:

First, the sheer, overwhelming physical, economic, and emotional weight of United States power. The extent of our wealth, our influence, our prestige, is suffocating. Not only do many South Americans resent this, but they envy it as well and have to make use of it in addition, because advance is impossible without United States aid. This makes for a complicated psychological pattern. With one hand South Americans welcome United States loans, investments, and political support; with the other they scrawl "Yanqui Go Home" on billboards—of course not the same South Americans. Billboard scrawlers don't get the loans.

The problem is made more difficult by the fact that the United States is the only great power in the western hemisphere, and an almost universal tendency exists among smaller nations to fear *one* big neighbor. Moreover, the world is stretched taut between the United States and the Soviet Union, the second great power, with countries like Great Britain and France,

---

[2] "Relations Between the United States and Latin America," by Roberto de Oliveira Campos in the Mildred Adams anthology, already cited, p. 33.

which were once so important to South America, relegated to the sidelines. Perhaps this helps to 'explain the relatively uncritical attitude toward the Soviet Union held by many South Americans, as one hemisphere expert has recently pointed out. It does not displease some of them that the USSR is a counterpoise to the stupendous stifling weight of the U.S.A.

It should be reiterated that, even if South Americans resent our power, it plays a role in almost every calculation. We did not make the 1964 coup d'état in Brazil, but its authors were certain that we would take their side, and they counted on this as an indispensable adjunct to their authority. General Onganía in the Argentine was much discomfited when the United States withheld recognition from him even for such a short period as a fortnight after his counterrevolution in 1966. Not merely does our power count: so does our presumptive power.

As to anti-Americanism in general we should, of course, point out that this, no matter how pervasive, seldom influences concrete policy in South America, if only because of the mere fact that United States power is so weighty and voluminous. Another reason is that the oligarchs and landowners who, in the last analysis, control policy in most hemisphere countries are as a rule closely intermeshed with North American business interests, and do not want to disturb this relationship.

Second, inconsistencies in American foreign policy. South Americans look to the United States for guidance, and find this to be confused or contradictory. Not only do we exercise power; we exercise it capriciously. We have no single doctrine. Whom are they to believe, Senator Fulbright or, until yesterday, Assistant Secretary of State Tom Mann? Is our policy hard, soft, or both? How can we seemingly back General Onganía with one hand, and President Frei of Chile, an enlightened liberal, with the other? The South American forces on the right think that we coddle leftist elements; those on the left say that we support reaction. President Eisenhower gave one of the highest American decorations to Dictator Pérez Jiménez of Venezuela; a few years later, after the dictator had been thrown out and was living in exile in Miami, we deported him back to Caracas to face trial as a criminal.

Moreover, we seesaw all over the place on the vexing question of recognition. In July, 1962, we withdrew recognition from Peru—and suspended aid as well—when a military government was established by coup d'état, which is exactly what we had not done in similar circumstances in Argentina a few months previously. The surprising result in Peru—whether we anticipated this or not—was the subsequent installation of a constitutional civilian government, which still rules, whereas Argentina continued to disintegrate, and now lives under a repressive, retrograde dictatorship. The lesson from this should be obvious.

The largest criticism from most Latin Americans themselves is that, in general, we tend to support the status quo or even the status quo ante too much, which means identifying ourselves with older, standpat forces, instead of aligning with or actively supporting movements for popular reform. We think in terms of governments, not people. But this is a dilemma because governments are the only instruments available for official contact. We cannot go over—or under—their heads. Even so, liberals in South America contend that, with some exceptions such as in Bolivia and Chile, we continue to be anti-change, hence anti-progress, although the Alliance for Progress was supposed to have reversed this attitude.

Exactly what is the Johnson Doctrine, the name given to a potpourri of options and choices after the Dominican crisis in 1965? Nobody seems to know exactly. Presumably its gist is that, as in the case of the Dominican Republic, we will intervene to prevent any country we suspect of going Communist from doing so. But Mr. Johnson also stated recently that the United States stands unequivocally for democracy and social justice, and that "we will not be deterred [from our objectives] by those who tenaciously or selfishly cling to special privileges from the past, and we will not be deterred by those who say that to risk change is to risk communism." He has also stated that Communism cannot be beaten merely by force. What then does the doctrine mean?

In April, 1966, Senator Jacob K. Javits of New York proposed that the United States should recast its policies "of recognizing de facto regimes in Latin America as a deterrent against military turnover," suggesting that we refuse to recognize any new government emerging as a result of a military coup d'état unless the OAS approves. Mr. Javits has great hope of the efficacy of "collective consultation" in the OAS. He went on, "I am convinced that potential organizers of military coups will think twice if they are confronted with the possibility of ostracism from the inter-American organization."[3] Incidentally, Venezuela long ago adopted the policy of automatically breaking off diplomatic relations with any country suffering a military *Putsch*.

Third, the United States plays politics with AID. For years, long before the Alianza, our financial assistance helped keep General Trujillo and other dictators in power. As of today we have withheld—or pared down—aid to Brazil, Argentina, Peru, and Panama for various reasons on various occasions. The Hickenlooper amendment to the 1962 foreign aid bill makes this mandatory under certain circumstances, as I have mentioned in a previous chapter. Even so South Americans resent it bitterly that we use aid as an instrument for punishment or intimidation. In November, 1964, we drasti-

[3] Henry Raymont in the *New York Times*, April 2, 1966.

cally cut down on aid to Bolivia for purely political reasons, when a government we favored (it happened to be a quite good government) was deposed. Withdrawal of aid also occurs for overt financial reasons—we do not want to throw good money after bad, and, justifiably enough, refuse further assistance to countries until they put their financial houses in order. But in September, 1965, President León Valencia of Colombia stated publicly that the United States had suspended financial aid to his country "unjustly and inopportunely."[4]

During the negotiations with Haiti at the second Punta del Este conference, Dean Rusk announced frankly that, "While the United States as a matter of policy did not associate economic aid and political performance, now that Haiti itself had made the link it had to understand that any future aid would be scrutinized in the light of its role at Punta del Este."[5] Clearly in this case we were using aid as a potential political instrument. Of course the United States plays politics with aid in other regions of the world, although this may be glossed over. Ceylon, India, and particularly Pakistan are cases in point. President Nasser of Egypt charged in July, 1965, that the United States had made "astonishing demands on the Egyptian government in return for aid."

Fourth, intervention, the bugaboo of bugaboos. This is largely a problem involving the Caribbean and Central America, since the United States has never intervened militarily in the body of the continent, but Caribbean events cast their shadows southward, forming an indissoluble part of the whole picture. Altogether we intervened in Caribbean countries twenty-one times between 1898 and 1924; United States Marines were stationed in the Dominican Republic from 1916 to 1924, and in Nicaragua almost continuously from 1912 to 1933. Those were the days when the Caribbean area was conveniently regarded as our "back yard," which it still is although, in these public relations conscious times, such terms are avoided. A more recent event was the 1954 coup fostered by the CIA in Guatemala when President Jacobo Arbenz Guzmán was squeezed out because he was soft on Communism and had initiated a land reform which offended the United Fruit Company. This was not formal military intervention, but it amounted to the same thing. Direct intervention—on the mainland—would certainly have occurred in Venezuela in 1955 had Vice President Nixon come to actual harm when he was assaulted by a mob in Caracas. The marines, put on the alert by President Eisenhower, were ready to move in.

[4] *Latin American Times*, September 29, 1965, a UPI dispatch.
[5] Arthur Schlesinger, Jr., *A Thousand Days*, p. 782.

As of today the United States position on intervention is somewhat ambiguous. We are caught in a quandary, and the fact is that the government—including the State Department—is divided on the issue. Nonintervention has been the official American policy for many years, and is a root element in our hemisphere relationships, but it was manifestly contravened by both Presidents Kennedy (Bay of Pigs) and Johnson (Dominican Republic). One school of thought holds that the entire doctrine of nonintervention is obsolete because of the rise of Communism. The question is not merely whether or not we will intervene militarily to put down future Castros or rescue future Dominican governments in our own vicinity for vital reasons of security, but what we would do on the continent as a whole in the light of the Cold War and other factors. What would happen if, as an example, a successful internal Communist coup took place in such a country as Uruguay or Ecuador? Failure to intervene might not only make another Cuba, but would be an international embarrassment. But, equally, intervention would almost certainly produce unpleasant consequences for us throughout the hemisphere.

Remarkably, there has been one recent instance when a threat of intervention by the United States produced good results, not bad. This came in 1961 shortly after the assassination of Trujillo in the Dominican Republic, when, in a confused situation, a military coup seemed to be impending which would restore members of his family to power. President Kennedy decided, after careful deliberation, to send eight American ships with eighteen hundred marines on board to cruise just outside the three-mile limit in Santo Domingo waters, as a kind of demonstration. This produced an electrifying result. The plotters were frightened off, and relieved citizens "danced with joy" on the streets. Mr. Kennedy was taking an obvious chance, but it worked. The Dominicans may have disliked gunboat diplomacy, but they disliked Trujilloism more. And, as Arthur Schlesinger, Jr., points out, this was a happy episode in that, for once, "Yankee intervention took place to sustain a democratic movement, rather than destroy it."[6]

Fifth and finally, the point above all points, economic exploitation. This embraces a large field, aspects of which I have touched on in Brazil and which I will allude to in connection with other countries below. The issue goes far back. Exploitation of South America began, after all, with the Spanish freebooters. The veteran philosopher Salvador de Madariaga has pointed out that Bolívar granted concessions to foreigners for the extraction of mineral wealth in order to help pay for the wars of liberation, and that after independence South Americans were forced to give harbor to capital

[6] *Ibid.*, p. 771.

investment from outside because they lacked the technical education necessary to develop their resources by themselves.[7]

Exploitation is, in one way or the other, the rock-hard cause of almost every grievance, real or fancied, against the United States, as the South Americans see it. It was exploitation which provoked intervention in the old days, since we took military action in order to protect our economic investment, and, similarly, it was the basic reason for our standpat policy that followed, because of our fear that social reform would prejudice the safety of American investments. Almost all investors have tended, until recently at least, to support conservative governments, even reactionary dictatorships, and they have often powerfully influenced American public policy.

The total United States investment in Latin America, not just South, probably runs close to $10 billion. Again let me make a comparison with Canada, where the equivalent figure is $13 billion plus. The United States controls something like 60 percent of Canadian petroleum, more than 50 percent of mining, 30 percent of paper and pulp, and almost all of automobiles and rubber. But most Canadians do not complain that theirs is a "colonial" economy, whereas South Americans urgently do. Canadians do not say that we "own" them, or at least they are quieter about it. This is largely because Canada remains master in its own house, which many South Americans think they are not. Senator Robert Kennedy made an effective point of this in his recent Senate speech. What Latin America fears is North American *control*.

Figures are difficult to obtain, but United States investors probably control 40 percent of South American production. Of course a distinction must be made between legitimate investment and outright exploitation. Comparatively few South Americans resent the Rockefeller supermarkets in Venezula or the Sears, Roebuck stores in Brazil and elsewhere, because these are not exploitative even if profits go north. They have brought modern mercantile methods to the continent, stimulated local industry, given work to thousands, helped train a technical class, and improved living standards for the small consumer. What South Americans do resent is American or other foreign ownership and control of the great extractive industries—petroleum and minerals—on unreasonable terms. Utilities are a sore point too.[8] We have in effect a stranglehold on the nation concerned by dominat-

---

[7] *Latin America Between the Eagle and the Bear*, pp. 5 and 16.

[8] Thirty-seven percent of the total United States investment in Latin America is in petroleum, 13 percent in mining, and 8.5 percent in transportation, communications, and power. Ronald M. Schneider, *Current History*, January, 1965.

ing its chief source of wealth. Their most priceless indigenous resources are in pawn.

Of course the United States and other foreign powers are not the only elements involved in taking profits, i.e., capital, out of South America. Plenty of South Americans are exploiters of their own people, as has been frequently pointed out in these pages. Dean Rusk in recent testimony to Congress estimated that the amount of Latin American funds held in the United States is between $3 and $5 billion. Of course many South American plutocrats became rich partly because the United States supported their companies and interests.

A Glimpse Back

We are the good; you are the neighbor.
—SOUTH AMERICAN QUIP

Now to go back a bit. United States policy toward South America starts with the Monroe Doctrine, which asserts that "the American continents . . . are henceforth not to be considered as subjects for future colonization by any European powers. . . . We owe it to candor . . . to declare that we should consider any attempt on their part to extend their system to any portion of this hemisphere as dangerous to our peace and safety." The doctrine was enunciated in 1823, just at the period when most of the hemisphere republics were being born.

Indirectly the Monroe Doctrine was suggested to Washington by the British, who were playing balance-of-power politics against the Holy Alliance after Napoleon; frightened that the French and Spanish—even the Russians —might attempt to make trouble in Hispano-America, they sought our cooperation. But, as issued, the doctrine was a unilateral expression of policy by the United States. None of the Latin American republics was consulted, and several, particularly Argentina, have resented this ever since on nationalist grounds. The doctrine has been called a device to assure "defensive imperialism." Yet, had it not been for the doctrine and the power of the United States behind it, more than one hemisphere country might have lost its political independence.

Of course we interpreted the doctrine as the case demanded. Being very close to the British, we did not protest when they took the Falkland Islands from Argentina or Belize from Honduras. We did, however, invoke it when the French installed Maximilian as emperor of Mexico—not that this had any effect—and against Great Britain in 1895, over a boundary dispute in Venezuela. Secretary of State Cordell Hull enunciated the doctrine in July,

1940, in order to warn the Axis powers that we would not tolerate any changes in the status quo in the Caribbean, one of the last times it has been formally cited.

In the 1840's the United States took Texas and California from Mexico—almost half its territory. South Americans began to look at us with a certain trepidation when, soon after this, prominent Americans talked about our "manifest destiny" in the hemisphere. We became the "Colossus of the North."

In 1895, following some marvelously old-fashioned diplomatic exchanges with the British, Secretary of State Richard Olney stated in regard to our intervention in the British-Venezuelan boundary dispute, "Today the United States is practically sovereign on this continent, and its fiat is law upon the subjects to which it confines its interposition." Words could scarcely be more imperialist.

In 1898, during the Spanish-American War, we invaded Cuba, and this unhappy island became virtually an American protectorate. We annexed Puerto Rico, and, on the other side of the world, occupied the Philippines. By terms of the Platt Amendment, now defunct, we assumed the right to intervene in Cuba and set up a naval base at Guantánamo which, despite Castro or anybody else, is still there.

In 1903 Theodore Roosevelt, waving the big stick, "took" Panama from Colombia so that we could build a canal across the isthmus. When Colombia refused to cede us the necessary territory, the United States fomented a Panamanian "separatist" revolution, recognized the new government, and started digging. T.R. said forthrightly, "I took the Canal Zone and . . . while the debate goes on, the canal does also." Presently Mr. Roosevelt announced a "Corollary" to the Monroe Doctrine claiming for the United States the right to "international police power" in the western hemisphere in the event of "flagrant cases of wrongdoing"—by any of the American republics—or an "impotence which results in the general loosening of the ties of civilized society."

The grim era of "dollar diplomacy" followed. American banks poured money into Central and South America, and then looked to the State Department to protect them and help collect their debts. In 1914 the United States Navy bombarded and seized Veracruz, Mexico, to this end, and in 1916 we crossed the Mexican frontier from Texas to chase Pancho Villa, whom we never caught.

Woodrow Wilson is generally thought of as an idealist devoted to peace, but four different incursions into Latin America were made during his presidency. To help maintain the status quo, and thus protect American interests,

Wilson also developed the policy of nonrecognition of governments taking power by revolutionary means. This of course served to freeze dictatorships in many countries, since, at that time, no revolution could possibly succeed without our favor. Thus in effect we came to dominate domestic politics in several countries, to say nothing of those over which we had established quasi-protectorates.

Most of the above was reversed by Franklin D. Roosevelt and the Good Neighbor Policy, beginning in 1933. This was a sensational development and advance. FDR completely repudiated his distant cousin T.R. He annulled the Platt Amendment, swept the Roosevelt (T.R.) Corollary into the discard, and set up the office of Coordinator of Inter–American Affairs which, under Nelson Rockefeller, gave an altogether new and different tone to our relations with the hemisphere. South American loans were defaulted in profusion, but FDR did not send in the marines to collect them. All in all the Good Neighbor Policy was a deliberate, systematic, and integrated attempt to improve North American relations with South.

Secretary of State Hull announced at a conference in Montevideo that "no government need fear any intervention on the part of the United States under the Roosevelt administration," and Sumner Welles, the under secretary, worked indefatigably for better relations country by country. Mr. Roosevelt himself attended a conference at Buenos Aires in 1936, designed to convert the Monroe Doctrine into a collective pact. In 1938 came the eighth Pan-American conference in Lima, which, under our stimulus, produced the Declaration of Lima, a landmark establishing the principle that an attack on any Latin American republic would be regarded as an attack against them all. All this paid off. Hemisphere solidarity became a workable proposition. The best proof of this is the united support given to the United States by all but one of the twenty American republics during World War II in spite of spectacular Nazi efforts to subvert the continent.

But Mr. Roosevelt made no attempt to extend the principles of the New Deal to the hemisphere. That had to await John F. Kennedy and the Alianza a generation later.

Communism, with a Line on Castro

But before the Alianza came Castro, and, although Cuba is geographically outside the province of this book, there should be a word about it because events there have had a large psychological effect throughout the continent. As to Communism in general I have already dealt with some aspects of the Communist position in relation to Brazil in Chapter 5, and I hope to do the same for each ensuing country. Meantime a few observations at large are in order.

Little possibility exists, most good observers think, of any direct Communist revolution or overt takeover in any hemisphere republic in the discernible future. Disintegration may come; chaos may come; but Communism itself is unlikely in the *short* run, even though several countries would seem to be vulnerable. Ecuador is wildly unstable, and Uruguay riven; Bolivia is explosive, and Marxists control more than a third of the vote in Chile. (The *long* run is a different matter.)

There are two basic reasons for the general feeling that a direct Communist coup is unlikely even in these countries at present, as well as the rest of the continent—external and internal. Presumably, to make a successful coup d'état, local Communists would have to be supported either by Cuba, China, or the Soviet Union. But Cuba is fully engaged in its own onerous problems; China is busy elsewhere; and the Soviet Union has a policy of discouraging South American revolution at the moment, although propaganda and agitation may go on. There are two reasons for the Soviet lack of serious interest. First, the Russians do not want to risk a confrontation with the United States; second, they can't afford it. Castro has been an extremely expensive item.

Internally, no local Communist party in South America is even remotely in a position to make a revolution by itself under present circumstances, except through a fluke. They are too weak in numbers and otherwise. To succeed they would have to subvert the armies, an unlikely possibility, and risk intervention by the United States.

Yet Castro managed it. He fooled everybody. His takeover in Cuba was an astounding feat. His play was triple—he won a nationalist revolution, established a revolutionary social order, and thumbed his nose at the United States the while. He satisfied left-wing South American grievances on three scores at once, which is why his symbolic power remains significant. He represents much more than romantic chauvinism. In the very shadow of the United States, ninety miles from Florida, he made the first real revolution in the hemisphere since that in Mexico half a century ago.

One result is that American attention became fixed on the hemisphere republics as never before: we had grossly neglected Latin America after World War II, but Castro brought us back to it with a loud, emphatic bang. Castro may, in fact, strangely enough be called an indirect father of the Alianza. South American republics receiving aid from the United States today have Castro to thank for this in part, ironic as this may be, because he made us fearful of our southern fences and determined to strengthen them.

He has, however, become gravely discredited. Things have not gone well in Cuba. Had Castro been an unqualified success and had the revolution accomplished fully his ambitions, then indeed he would have been a more serious problem, because there would have been large temptations to imitate him elsewhere in South America. But a more important factor damaging his charisma was, as everybody knows, the Kennedy-Khrushchev confrontation in October, 1962. He lost ground to a devastating extent because he became an impotent pawn in a struggle between the United States and the Soviet Union, and the United States won against the Russians. Moreover, Castro's adoption of Marxist Leninism alienated his early liberal sympathizers elsewhere in the continent. When he became forced into the Russian sphere, clearly with no freedom of action on his own, what remained of his prestige outside Cuba diminished. What is more, the Kennedy-Khrushchev crisis demonstrated that the Soviet Union was willing, if necessary, to sacrifice a satellite. "Since Castro sold himself to the Kremlin, we are no longer interested," one South American head of state told me. All this being said it is wise to remember that Castro, commanding one of the smallest of nations, has managed so far to defy the United States in spite of the weightiest of political and economic sanctions, and has succeeded in doing so. He even won a pledge from President Kennedy not to invade Cuba.

To return now to our broader theme. There was a Communist problem in South America before Castro, and a Communist problem will remain no matter what happens to him. I have said that overt revolution is unlikely. But who can tell? Even Argentina might blow up if the army should, by some extraordinary chance, become disaffected with the way Onganía is running their dictatorship. The chief problem to American interests in most countries is that Communists or other extreme leftists might be able to take advantage of a chaotic situation and seize power by stages in a country where the government is disintegrating. Meantime, Communist propaganda continues to be active almost everywhere, leftist infiltration into the labor movement is conspicuous, thousands of Communist students are vociferous, and guerrillas have gravely damaged public order in Venezuela, Colombia, and, more recently, Peru. All this refers to the immediate present. The Communist potential in the future is much more serious.

The Communist party is legal in five South American countries today, although the legality may be masked by a different nomenclature—Colombia, Uruguay, Chile, Bolivia (in a dubious sort of way), and Peru. Six countries (Mexico as well) recognize the Soviet Union—Brazil, Argentina, Chile, Uruguay, Venezuela, Bolivia. No South American country has diplomatic relations with Cuba (Mexico does, however) or has recognized China as yet. This is because the United States has asked them not to. Chile has, however, permitted the Chinese to send in a trade mission. Relations with Soviet satellites in Eastern Europe are closer; most of these have trade missions stationed in the various hemisphere capitals. Colombia does not recognize the Soviet Union itself, but has diplomatic relations with Czecho-slovakia and East Germany. Brazil recognizes six satellites, Argentina five.

South Americans, except on the extreme right fringe, do not quite share the perfervid hatred and fear of Communism that is characteristic of a large body of opinion in the United States. Communism means a different thing to many South Americans. People think of it as a means of change, a holding out of hope, false as such hope may turn out to be. Moreover, many South American Communists are distinguished men, and, in a continent where culture and the intellect command more respect than with us, are respected for their attainments; nobody cares much whether they are Com-munists or not. The most distinguished painter in Ecuador is a Communist or extreme left-winger. So is the most distinguished novelist in Brazil, the most distinguished poet in Chile, the most distinguished social anthropolo-gist in Peru, and the most distinguished atomic scientist and one of the most distinguished architects in Brazil. The worlds of art, music, and the sciences reflect strong left-wing influences in several republics, and, as is well known, a principal focus of Communist zeal and success is in the universities, among professors as well as students.

But something else impressed me more than this, namely that most of the Communists I met, even those in the high intelligentsia, did not seem to realize fully all that Communism entails. Most have never been to Moscow or Peking, and have little concrete knowledge of what Communist systems mean. They were, it seemed, unrealistic—dilettantes, Bohemians, frustrated intellectuals and artists not seriously political—as indeed youthful radicals and idealists who call themselves "Communist" may be in many other countries of the world. Their picture of Russia and China was sentimentally uncritical—rosy, like that of liberals in western Europe toward the Soviet Union during the Popular Front period before the war. As is only too obvious, this could have serious consequences in South America, because the Com-munists, a tiny minority, are prepared to foster revolutions or deliver their countries to Moscow or Peking without adequate realization of what this would mean in the extinction of civil liberties, the throttling of expression, and the political slavery of a people. Only in Chile, Bolivia, and Venezuela did I meet Communists who were hard-line professionals. The Communist party in Chile boasts, as a matter of fact, that it is the oldest Communist party in the world, older than the Russian. (Of course I may have missed the veteran, Kremlin-trained *cadre* in other countries.)

Another point is that Communism in South America today is closely associated with anti-Americanism. We are the villains not merely as "capitalists" or "exploiters" but on the simplest nationalist grounds, and this is a valuable instrument in propaganda because the Communists are able to cash in, so to speak, on the latent anti-Americanism that exists almost everywhere. They are not merely Marxists but patriots rescuing the population from the North American ogre.

But the Communist movement in South America is sharply divided. One reason for this is Cuba, which destroyed the unity of the left. Part of the movement deserted Moscow for Peking because Moscow "lost" or "betrayed" Cuba; moreover, Moscow has steadily become more conservative, more stand-pat, which drives the extremists and youthful zealots to Peking, as well as some older professionals. The Kremlin is still being forced to spend about a million dollars a day in Cuba to fulfill its commitments to Castro and keep him going, which is one factor discouraging it from new adventures. But the Peking wing is overtly revolutionary no matter what the cost.

Division in Communist ranks in the hemisphere seems to be becoming accentuated day by day. There are not merely Russian, Chinese, and Fidelista elements but a number of splinters, some so small that they are called "taxi" parties. Chile has at least seven different Communist factions including Titoists and Trotskyists, and Bolivia has no fewer than four different *Trotskyist* parties as well as other toothpick groups. But Moscow and Peking are the influences that count. In general the Peking parties are the more active and extremist, but Moscow is far stronger numerically and controls the organization in every country. The Fidelistas generally take the Peking line.

Small and ineffectual as most Communist units in South America are, their impact can be sharply felt and their propaganda is often brilliantly effective because it addresses itself to the *primary* needs of the people, like land, food, education, shelter. In Montevideo I met a university professor who pointed out sardonically that the United States spends millions of dollars a year on various aid projects, but that the streets of the continent are plastered with signs "Yanqui Go Home." The Russians have never built a mile of road or given away a quart of milk, but local Communists elect senators and deputies to several parliaments largely because they promise real changes in the order of society. The principal problem is, I heard on every side, that the South Americans may go Communist in the long run by default. The people are not being given enough. They suffer abominable privation. Their governments are slothful, incompetent, and corrupt. Citizens say that they have nothing to lose by Communism because nothing could be worse than the conditions under which they live today.

The only eventual alternative to Communism—except military dictator-ship—is reform, reform, reform. But this is difficult to achieve because the propertied classes are immeasurably well entrenched, and, in some countries, will resist progress and improvement to the uttermost, no matter at what cost. But reform has to be pushed whether the plutocrats like it or not because the phenomena that really do induce Communism in South America are such, to pick two at random, as that the average per capita income on the continent is $269 per year, which means that a person has 75 cents a day to live on, and that the death rate of Indians in Bolivia, who comprise 70 percent of the population, is 75 percent before the age of two.

I asked the president of an important South American republic what he would like to say most to the people of the United States. His reply was, "Don't think that 'Communism' and 'change' are synonymous. Don't assume that men of good will who want to improve the existing order are Communists. If we try to improve the condition of the masses you call it Communism, but it isn't."

Alianza Para el Progreso

There can be no preservation of the status quo in Latin America.
—SENATOR ROBERT F. KENNEDY

The basic barrier to advance in Latin America is a regressive social structure.
—JOHN KENNETH GALBRAITH

I don't think that one North or South American out of a hundred thousand knows accurately what the Alliance for Progress is. I have mentioned this ambitions concept before and will touch on it again country by country as this book proceeds, but, as in the case of Communism, it may be useful to include here a brief survey of the subject in the large.

Indeed the Alianza, together with what goes with it, is difficult to define. You cannot look it up in the telephone book in Washington, D.C. It does not exist as such in the usual organizational charts showing the operations of the United States or other governments. It has no office under the name "Alianza," no headquarters, no chief executive or governing council in the normal sense of those terms. It has no "structural body" of its own, and its head is no more than a "deputy administrator" in the Agency for International Development (AID), a dependency of the State Department created in 1961.

Strictly speaking the Alliance is not even a "project." What is it then? The best answer is that it is a program or holdall growing out of a concept, an idea. The kernel of this idea, promoted by President Kennedy, was to stimulate the social and economic life of Latin America by a huge multinational hemisphere spending program under rigorous planning. It receives large financial and other assistance from USAID, one of the principal instruments in its armory, but it was not meant to be a bilateral aid program, not an organization dealing in short-term direct relief. The stress is, in theory, on self help; South America is supposed to give it more than we do. But without USAID the program would collapse. One critic describes it as a $20 billion bribe by the United States to stimulate the privileged classes in South America to make reforms.

Let us define terms further. The Alliance is a ten-year cooperative development program on the part of the United States and all the hemisphere republics (except Cuba) deriving from the Punta del Este conference of August, 1961, which wrote its charter.[9] This envisaged expenditure of not less than $100 billion in the decade to come, $80 billion of which was to come from Latin America itself, the rest from the United States and elsewhere. No such grandiose program has ever been known before. The Marshall Plan, which paved the way for the reconstruction of Europe after the war, spent only about $17 billion.

Our Alianza pledge amounts consequently to some $2 billion a year for ten years, five of which have now passed. Of this sum roughly $1.1 billion a year comes directly out of United States public funds, administered by AID, and including such other agencies as the Social Progress Trust Fund, the Export-Import Bank, and Food for Peace. The rest of the $2 billion is made up in principle by international lending agencies (Inter-American Development Bank, World Bank, International Monetary Fund), to which we contribute, and private American investment, which was set at $300 million a year by the Punta del Este formula. Every effort was made to give the program a mixed coloration with both public and private money involved, and to entice cooperation from Europe and Japan. How successful this effort has been is dubious.

But it was the vision that counted more than the figures, large as these were. The dream was wide, not merely aimed at "democratic modernization" of the continent but at making twenty countries effective partners. In an enormous variegated area, bound by centuries of inertia, the Alianza gave the promise of radical social change, the creation of new prolific instruments of wealth, technical advance, and copious plans for development at large. The concept was accepted (in theory at least) that economic advance, as envisaged in the charter, would be impossible without reform, which brought up sensitive issues, since obviously South America could not contribute its

[9] Not to be confused with the subsequent Punta del Este conference in January, 1962, which excommunicated Castro. There were two conferences at Punta del Este.

share of the program without collecting taxes. The entire socio-economic structure of the continent was to be subject to drastic change.

Seldom has a conception been so all-embracing as well as detailed. The economic growth rate for Latin America was set at 2.5 percent a year.[10] The necessity for land as well as tax reform was stressed—even the desirability of making the distribution of national income "more equitable." Each republic pledged itself to produce a master development plan (some were years late in being delivered). The charter promised "unequivocal support to democracy" and opposition to dictatorship—here idealism ran wild—and suggested an arms control program for the hemisphere. Ambassadors would be appointed who "understood and cared for the problems of Latin America," and the OAS was to be strengthened. Such problems as housing, wages, illiteracy, public health, and the stabilization of export prices were to be vigorously tackled. One index of the character of the Alianza concept is that all Communists and groups on the radical left without exception loathe and condemn it fiercely, because they stand to lose by stabilization, modernization, and reform in South America unless it is effected by them, and, of course, because they dislike and fear growing influence by the United States. Similarly, the Alianza is opposed and attacked by the extreme right.

From its inception the Alliance has lacked drive and centralized direction. It is amorphous. There is no independent executive authority. For several years its chief body of advisers was a panel of experts from several nations (including Great Britain) known as "the nine wise men," but this fell apart. The major complaint of the nine (which had become eight by the withdrawal of one member) in presenting their resignation was that the United States, in violation of the original spirit of the charter, was tending more and more to promote "program aid" on a country-by-country basis, instead of dealing in larger terms. Then a new committee known as CIAP (Inter-American Committee for the Alliance for Progress) was created in the hope of giving a push to administration and improving coordination. Another development, taken on American initiative, was colorful—the association of specific American states with individual Latin countries, to assist partnership. Thus Idaho has "adopted" Ecuador, and Texas has taken on Peru. Ohio has one state in Brazil—Paraná. So far twenty-two American states are assisting in this device.

The origins of the Alliance, which was formally launched in March, 1961, are a fascinating study, but are not part of our story here. Its creator was John F. Kennedy. His first speeches contributing to the idea were partly the work of Richard Goodwin, a leading member of his White House secre-

[10] Growth rate in the United States was 5.3 percent in 1965.

tariat. It was Goodwin who conceived the phrase "Alliance for Progress"; among other reasons he liked this because "progress" has the same meaning in both English and Spanish. Originally there was no "el" after "para" in the Spanish title, but linguistic purists in the State Department put this in. President Kennedy's death was a severe, almost mortal, blow to the Alliance. It took the magic out—courage and conscience too. It should also be mentioned that, long before Kennedy, an almost identical idea, called Operation Pan America, had been broached in July, 1958, by President Kubitschek of Brazil, acting under the stimulus of one of his economic advisers, Professor Augusto Federico Schmidt. But this was brutally rejected by the Eisenhower administration, mostly on the advice of George Humphrey and other extreme conservatives. The Eisenhower team took the line that private investment would amply solve South American problems of development, although it was perfectly clear that this was an outmoded concept. A large motivating force to creation of the Alianza by the Kennedy administration was reaction against the Eisenhower orthodoxy. Our South American relations were failing, the continent felt snubbed, and Kennedy determined to do something about it.

One remarkable irony is that Fidel Castro, no less, was an early progenitor of the Alliance idea. Castro visited the United States early in 1959, where he was coldly greeted, and then went to Buenos Aires to attend a meeting of an OAS committee. Here, according to Gerald Clark, he astonished everybody by suggesting that "the United States should advance to Latin American countries fifty million dollars over a ten-year period to finance the economic and social development of the continent."[11] This was before Castro's program became overtly Marxist. The Eisenhower administration presumably thought that he was crazy. Later, when it became clear that Cuba was a serious threat to democratic institutions in the hemisphere, Castro became a "father" to the Alliance in quite a different way, as noted above; apprehension about him stirred the Kennedy administration to turn the Alianza on full speed ahead, on the hypothesis that this would counteract his influence.

Every known brickbat has been hurled at the Alliance since its inception, and several criticisms are quite valid. Probably the organization should have been made autonomous, a department of its own, like the Peace Corps, and it might have worked better if its headquarters, such as they are, had been set up in a South American capital rather than in Washington. Many South Americans are still convinced that the Alliance is a kind of "plot" to put something over on them, and that it isn't truly "theirs." One grievance is,

[11] *The Coming Explosion in Latin America*, pp. 313–314.

indeed, that aid is "tied," meaning that goods and equipment have to be bought in the United States if they come under the category of "dollar aid," and then be transported to South America in none but American ships. Then too the original Alianza concepts were too ambitious; a 2.5 percent target for annual economic growth was probably too high, although several hemisphere countries reached it in 1965. Finally, the Alliance does not pay enough attention to human values. Not enough aid gets down to the people, as Senator Robert F. Kennedy pointed out with pith in his brilliant double-speech on the Alianza. Aid goes primarily to governments, and often these do not represent the governed.

The Alianza has not been an unqualified success, but it cannot be written off as a failure either. People became bored with it after the John F. Kennedy spark was gone. But its influence will, it is hoped, prove germinal in at least three quarters; it made the concept of land reform "respectable" in much of South America, although this is not to say that land reform is going forward fast enough; tax reform has been stimulated too; and it introduced long-range technical planning as a substitute for stop-gap "programming." In the four years up to 1965, President Johnson stated recently, the United States has more than met its obligation by contributing $4.5 billion to the system; the Latin American republics have contributed more than $22 billion. As to miscellaneous good works they can be cited by the hundred. In half a dozen countries I saw roads, dams, tunnels, hydraulic plants, irrigation projects, normal schools, agricultural laboratories, constructed or installed by the Alianza. The project has built new schoolrooms for a million children, put up more than 220,000 homes, improved 7,000 miles of road, irrigated 136,000 acres of farmland, helped finance 5,000 industrial firms, and assisted 36 universities.

*

Military aid, which comes from the Pentagon, lies in a different category. It derives from the Rio Treaty of 1947, the quasi-military alliance pledging the hemisphere republics to reciprocal assistance. Up to 1965 the total American military expenditure for Latin America since the 1940's came to $925 million (about one-tenth of economic aid for the same period). Brazil got $270 million, Argentina $68 million, Chile $110 million, Peru $126 million, Ecuador $42 million. And for what purpose? A frank answer is seldom given. Governments want arms to help put down revolution. That is the simple gist of the matter.

United States activity takes place in several adjacent fields. First, we maintain military missions in most hemisphere capitals—fourteen army missions, eleven navy, and fifteen air force in all—with a total American personnel of five to six hundred officers and men. The purpose of these missions is, among other things, to coordinate policy and train the local forces. Second, we bring a large number of South American cadets and officers to the United States every year for specialized training in various installations, all the way up to the General Staff College at Fort Leavenworth. Third, we sell arms and equipment to a dozen countries, and superintend their use through MAAGS, our Military Assistance Advisory Groups, which work closely with the military mission in each capital.

Special training is also available for counter-insurgency (i.e., antiguerrilla fighting) and antisubmarine warfare. We also lend warships to nations. One odd detail is that, during the Kennedy-Khrushchev crisis, the Pentagon made it known to various hemisphere governments that riot-control equipment would be on the way if necessary. As to MAAGS the recipient country takes a pledge to use United States–supplied arms and equipment only for hemisphere defense, but it would be foolish to take this at face value. In general South America gets none but *obsolescent* arms. The best are good enough for us, but too good for them.

As a result of recent agitation in Congress, arms sales have been reduced from around $100 million to a global total of $55 million per year for all the countries south of the Rio Grande, "including private sales of planes, tanks, and guns." Several senators, including Fulbright, Kennedy, and Morse, take the line that arms sales to South America are not only deleterious but dangerous, because they encourage reactionary forces. MAAGS actually stimulates Communism, in Senator Morse's opinion, by increasing the revolutionary potential. The reactionary plutocracies, in alliance with the armies, are in a better position to suppress disorder by reason of American arms, which in turn makes the peasantry more resentful.

Three Questions

Do we own South America?
No, but we often behave as if we did.

Do we take more out of South America than we give?
Probably.

Are we finished in South America?
No, but we should watch our step.

CHAPTER 9

Backdrop to Argentina

Argentina is more like Australia than it is like Peru.
—J. H. FERGUSON

IN JUNE, 1966, Argentina became an outright military dictatorship under Lieutenant General Juan Carlos Onganía (pronounced On-ghan-*ee*-a) and a military junta took power after complex vicissitudes. An energetic and determined man, the general announced that he intended to stay in power for ten years, during which he will presumably pull the country together under authoritarian rule, renovate it, and, at the least, maintain political stability no matter what the cost. This is what he offers in exchange for democracy, which vanishes. But almost at once he found himself inundated in angry troubles—perhaps beyond his depth.

Argentina has been in a bad way, although this does not justify the Onganía coup d'état, any more than the collapse of Italy in the 1920's justified Mussolini. By accepting Onganía the country has, in a sense, done no more than revert to type. Eight out of ten Argentine presidents between 1930 and 1958 were generals, and Onganía had better intentions than most. There should, however, be no blinking of the fact that this new regime is absolutist and totalitarian beyond qualification. Congress, the Supreme Court, and all the political parties have been brutally dissolved, the provincial governors have been ousted, and there has been no promise whatever to restore constitutional government at any time.

So Argentina reverts to tyranny, which is almost certain to throttle progress if only because rightist dictatorship in South America, even with the most patriotic motive, gives no future alternative except a swing to the extreme left. Granted that circumstances may have been difficult, or even intolerable, the intercession by General Onganía may well turn out to be a

164

gross tragedy for the country. At home the general was apparently astounded by the expression of opinion which quickly rose against him from both left and right. International reaction was mixed. Senator Jacob K. Javits of New York announced significantly enough that he would ask for action on an amendment to the foreign aid bill in Congress prohibiting Alianza aid to Latin American countries in which democratic governments are thrown out by military revolts.

*

First let us survey the permanent Argentine realities. The main preliminary point to make is that this is a truly important nation, the best-developed and strongest in South America—no Balkan pepper pot or intermontane backyard. We enter an equivalent to Europe here. Argentina, "the silver king," is powerful, fixed, and serious. It was the first Latin American country to win independence, and, with its conspicuous master-servant complex, has always sought to be the leader of the continent. Five times bigger than France, it has vast agricultural resources and the highest standard of living of any South American country (although it is not so rich as Venezuela), and, along with Uruguay, is the best educated and healthiest; it is one of the most important trading nations in the world, and is the only country in the southern hemisphere with an army—and navy—to be taken seriously. Buenos Aires is the biggest port in the Americas except New York, and is the ninth most populous city in the world.

Forty percent of the total railway mileage of South America lies in Argentina, and it has more than half the telephones. Buenos Aires, a thoroughly sophisticated capital, has two of the best-edited and most-responsible newspapers in the world, and the country has produced two Nobel prize winners in recent years, with a third—Jorge Luis Borges—a likely possibility soon. It has the most mature labor movement in Latin America, except possibly that in Mexico, and has produced political leaders of outstanding consequence.

But—

Its railways, which were nationalized by Juan Domingo Perón, of whom more later, are in appalling shape, and cost the nation fantastic sums; their deficit amounted to the equivalent of $350 *million* in 1964. Antiquated equipment (except on a few crack trains), featherbedding, fares so cheap (about one-sixth those in England) as to be utterly uneconomic, and outworn routes—these are characteristics. The lines (three different gauges) spread out from Buenos Aires like spokes without a rim—a spider's web leading nowhere.

Such a simple and indispensable commodity as water makes a grave problem. Less than 45 percent of the urban population has access to sewage disposal, and only 1.3 percent of the rural population has any regular water supply at all.

The country produces immense quantities of beef, wool, grain, but it is short on such basic sinews as iron, coal, and electric power.

The economy is stagnant. The GNP, around $10 billion, increased by only 4 percent between 1960 and 1964. Equivalent figures are for Bolivia 31 percent, Chile 14 percent, Brazil 16 percent, Peru 29 percent.

As to men and politics, Argentina had five ministers of the interior, three foreign ministers, four defense ministers, three ministers of economics, five army secretaries, four naval secretaries, three air secretaries, and five treasury secretaries in thirteen months in 1962–63.[1] Talk about political stability!

*

The second main point is that Argentina, for all its basic wealth, prestige, homogeneity, intense national pride, and degree of civilization, has been rent in recent years by severe intellectual, moral, and spiritual crisis. The country gives a sense not merely of lack of direction but of outright lostness; it seems spiritless, bereft, forlorn. Society is disoriented; people live from day to day, awaiting—what? It was disturbing to hear citizens say that they are "stifled" or "baffled" because they do not know what has happened to the nation, why it is that they were once great and are great no more. National purpose, faith, and a sense of mission seem to have disappeared.

This is the more striking because Argentina is, at bottom, sound. The climate is temperate, the people healthy, and opportunities plentiful. The country has no ethnic minorities, no racial problem, no Communist influence of consequence, no serious problems in foreign policy. "The Argentines have everything but themselves," is a remark that sums the matter up.

Another factor in the tormenting upheaval that afflicts contemporary Argentina is the national sensitiveness, which, like most sensitiveness, is based on a mixture of superiority and inferiority. "The Argentines are so superior that they even hate themselves for being so," was one remark I heard. Their chip-on-the-shoulderism expresses itself in the public sphere in at least three dimensions: (a) Extreme parochialism at home. An Argentine oligarch has been known to say "I am going to South America" when he

[1] *Time*, May 17, 1963.

NORTHERN ARGENTINA,
PARAGUAY AND URUGUAY

0 · · · 100 · · · 200 · · · 300

Miles

HS

was about to take off for a trip to Chile or Brazil. The "savages" of Ecuador and Paraguay are held in contempt. (b) Intense nationalism, plus a feeling of stewardship on behalf of the rest of the continent. (c) Offensive-defensive attitudes toward the United States. This is probably the most anti-American country in South America.

No Argentine likes to lose face; as a consequence he hesitates to take risks. A pretty young girl told me that, going out with an Argentine, she never had much fear of an unwelcome amatory advance, because her escort would be burdened with such a latent fear of rejection. But no doubt this generalization has often been proved wrong.

Argentina does not permit the Peace Corps, the best of all United States experiments in international good will, to operate in the country. I asked an eminent Argentine why, and he looked amiably stunned. "Why should *Argentina* have a Peace Corps? Do you send one to France?"

Some More Preliminary Points

What brought about Argentina's recent stagnation, maladjustment, and desperate lack of faith?

For one thing, World War II cut the traditional ties to Europe. For generations Argentina had been closely bound to British economy, French culture, and, to a degree, German military tradition. Now these links have disappeared or have been modified, so that the country feels set adrift.

For at least a hundred years Argentina's emotional capital was Paris; every educated Argentine as a matter of course learned French as a second language, and indeed many children of the aristocracy were taught French before Spanish. French was not merely the sine qua non of social, professional, and intellectual advance but a necessity for routine living in the upper class. The present trend is all toward English as a second language, as it is elsewhere in South America, and New York has supplanted Paris as a magnet. One hostess told me that her grandchildren know English now as "automatically" as her children knew French. When I first visited Argentina many years ago it astonished me to discover that many leading citizens had never been to the United States, although they knew Europe like the palms of their hands, and had no intention of ever coming. Now they flock to the fleshpots of New York.

Second, economic factors. The budget deficit is enormous ($860 million); unemployment is up to 800,000, almost 10 percent of the labor force; government salaries are heavily in arrears; tax collections are short, and wages cannot keep up with prices; the black market is active; the cost of living went up 25.5 percent in 1964; strikes are frequent; foreign investment has been scared off; interest rates are 30 percent or more; capital flees and inflation climbs.

Third, the prodigious political undertow left by Perón, the former dictator, and the division of the country between Peronists and anti-Peronists. This, as we shall see below, was the principal underlying reason for the Onganía coup.

Fourth, a change in basic patterns, which has put the country in a state of flux. Agriculture and livestock, the principal factors in the economy for generations, have given way to industry as the chief source of domestic income, although the country still depends on agricultural exports for foreign exchange. Urbanization has produced a large transfer of peoples, and the labor movement has become a vital component of the public life, largely as a result of Perón. An elaborate social security system—almost as intricate and expensive as that in Uruguay, which we shall inspect soon—has been set up. Patterns of education are changing; the church is not so monolithic as before, although still a mighty power; the landowning oligarchy is stretching at the seams. This is no longer a country altogether dominated by the wealthy "cattle aristocracy," but one increasingly based on manufacturing and the middle class.

A new world is, in a word, replacing the old in Argentina, and this is the essential reason for its apprehension, unsettlement, lack of joy, and loss of balance. Change should be a challenge; but not all people see it so. Not only is the old world breaking up, but nothing solid has arisen to replace it.

How Argentina Differs from Brazil

1. Argentina is almost exclusively a white man's country, whereas Brazil, as we know, is a melting pot. In some respects the former doesn't give the impression of being a South American nation at all, but a slice of Europe that happens to be situated in South America by geographical accident. But Brazil derives in large part from Africa, and its Portuguese origin gives it special characteristics.

2. Argentina is less charming, less colorful, less spontaneous, less abundantly romantic and flamboyant.

3. Brazil functions largely by means of compromises. The Argentines are stiffer in their political attitudes, less easygoing, not so fluid.

4. Argentina has more impressive statistics in relation to practically everything from literacy to public health. It is more fully developed, more

homogeneous. It has a stronger and more articulate labor movement, with more than 2.6 million unionized workers.

5. Argentina is more puritanical than Brazil, more religious, and more conservative in the social sphere.

6. Argentina is (as of today) a good deal less pro-American.

Argentina, Its Beam and Bulk

The extent of the pampas is so prodigious that they are bounded on the north by groves of palm trees and on the south by eternal snows.

—DOMINGO F. SARMIENTO

Superimposed lengthwise on a map of the United States Argentina would stretch from San Francisco to Cleveland; in girth, at its widest point, from Madison, Wisconsin, to New Orleans. Covering more than a million square miles, it is the second-largest country in South America, and the eighth in the world.[2] The province of Buenos Aires alone is as big as Italy. Temptation exists to assume that, because Argentina lies in the western hemisphere, it is "near" the United States. But put a string on a globe: from New York to Buenos Aires is as far as to Cairo.

The country has several conspicuous natural wonders, like the Uguazú Falls, which it shares with Paraguay and Brazil, the southern lake region, and above all the line of unbelievably spectacular Andean peaks on the frontier with Chile; no fewer than twenty-one of these rise above 20,400 feet, and are thus higher than Mount McKinley in Alaska, the loftiest peak in the United States. The formidable Mount Aconcagua, or Rocky Sentinel, (22,834 feet) is the highest point in the western hemisphere. Geographers generally recognize four divisions in Argentina: (1) the Andean highlands; (2) the hot, swampy lowlands to the north, including the Chaco spreading over from Paraguay; (3) the *pampa*; (4) the dry wastes of Patagonia to the south.

The *pampa*, covering about one-fifth of the country, is its heartland—a flat semicircle south and west of Buenos Aires which, magically fertile, holds 80 percent of the population to say nothing of 40 million cattle. Literally *pampa* means space, which its endless expanses do indeed provide. Here the solid black earth lies seven to eleven feet deep, without rocks or stones, not

---

[2] Exceeded only by Brazil, Canada, China, India, the Soviet Union, Australia, and the U.S. If you add the frozen wastes of Argentine Antarctica (477,000 square miles) to the Argentina total its area rises to 1,549,000 square miles, bigger than India, and it becomes the sixth-largest country in the world.

even pebbles, a factor which made road building difficult. The soil is so rich that fertilizers are seldom used. There are no trees except those imported by the *estancieros*, landowners. The typical local "tree," the *ombú*, is, technically speaking, not a tree but a bush.

This incomparable expanse of land has never been better described than by Archibald MacLeish, writing anonymously in *Fortune* in 1938. He mentions the country where the railway stations "come every twenty minutes as though laid out not by geography but by clocks." And—

> Argentina of the pampas, Argentina of the enormous plains, Argentina flowing out into the morning beyond the hills like a sea beyond capes . . . Argentina without towns, with few roads, with fences straight and wide apart as meridians on a map . . . It is a country in which the distances from house to house are too great for the barking of dogs even on the stillest night, a country in which the cocks crow only twice because there is no answer. It is a country so level that even time has no hold upon it and one century is like another; a country so empty that the watchers at night put their eyes along the ground to see the circle of the horizon; a country in which the sky is so huge that men plant islands of eucalyptus over their houses to be covered from the blue . . . It is . . . the country in which the green goes on and on like water, and the gulls follow the plows as seagulls follow ships—the country in which the women are always together under the dark trees in the evening, their faces fading into loneliness with the night.[3]

Patagonia, a wool-and-mutton factory, comprises the vast southern wing of the country east of the Andean cordillera. For Argentina's 20 million sheep graze on the thin, dry Patagonian plains, and are the source of the country's prodigious meat and wool production; Patagonia also holds the nation's oil deposits, and perhaps has iron as well. It covers about a quarter of the total area, but has only 500,000 people. The name derives from *patagones*, or big feet, a nickname given the aboriginal Indians by early explorers. Many settlers and ranch owners after the colonial period were British, Welsh, and Scottish: several communities are still predominantly Welsh, and I have even heard that one town has a daily newspaper published in Welsh. Sophisticates in Buenos Aires think of Patagonia and its austere steppes as a kind of Siberia, but it is capable of development almost in the way the Russians are developing their Siberia, different as theirs is. Patagonia ends at the Straits of Magellan, but below this is the Argentine wedge of Tierra del Fuego and still further south lies Antarctica. The capital of Argentine Tierra del Fuego (the major part of the island belongs to Chile,

---

[3] Quoted in *Inside Latin America*, p. 296.

and will be described in Chapter 16 below) is Ushuaia, the southernmost community in the world, except for one small settlement in Chile. Until recently it was the site of the country's most remote and forbidding prison, the last stop for criminals of various categories—among them white slavers, pimps, and prostitutes who trod the "Road to Buenos Aires," the old route of the white slave traffic which systematically brought women from Europe to the brothels of the great cities of South America.

In population Argentina, with 22 million people, is about the size of three Michigans. The ethnic pattern is 98 percent white, about 2 percent *mestizo*.[4] Probably there are not more than 15,000 surviving pure Indians, who live mostly in the deep south and in the province fittingly known as Mesopotamia between the Paraná ("Father of Waters") and Uruguay rivers. The country has some 700,000 Lebanese and 450,000 Jews. An estimated 60,000 Germans, of whom the late Captain Eichmann was an example, took refuge in Argentina after the war. The two dominant foreign-descended groups are, however, the Spaniards and Italians; Argentina has also received a considerable inflex of British, Poles, Russians, and French. The Spaniards go back ten or more generations, the Italians two. The Creole community contains today everything from exquisitely cultivated men of affairs to bricklayers and concierges. Some with "Spanish" ancestry may not, of course, be descended from true Spaniards at all, since many "Spaniards" were Moors; moreover, such peoples as the Maltese, Dutch, Flamands, and Venetians often took Spanish citizenship in colonial days or adopted Spanish names when they emigrated. As to the Italians, I have already mentioned that one-half of all Argentines have Italian blood.

More than a third of the entire population—say eight million people—lives in Buenos Aires or within commuting distance of this gigantic agglutinative capital. About 28 percent of wage earners work in industry, about 26 percent on the land. Literacy is put at 91 percent, but this is a statistic to be taken with a grain of salt. What does "literacy" mean? Many who rank as "literate" never got beyond the second grade of primary school, and countless others are literate only in the most primitive sense of the term. Life expectancy is the highest in South America, and infant mortality the lowest.

The annual rate of increase of population is 1.8 percent, which represents a falling off from 2.5 percent thirty years ago; there is no "baby boom," as the Buenos Aires papers put it, or population explosion here. Indeed, large

---

[4] One story no doubt apocryphal is that little intercourse took place between early Spaniard and Indian because the Indian women here were notoriously ugly. In Paraguay by contrast girls were extremely pretty, as they still are, and a large *mestizo* population rapidly grew up.

areas of the country are severely underpopulated, and it could easily support a population of fifty million or more. Big families today are encountered mostly in the aristocracy, not the middle class. I had lunch with one patrician who has twenty-seven grandchildren; seventeen children were living in his house. Emigration—among the non-aristocrats—has become a serious problem in recent years. Teachers, doctors, engineers, architects—even skilled workers—leave the country at the rate of about eighteen hundred a year, to earn better livings or fulfill their ambitions for careers in Europe, Israel, other places in Asia, and the United States.[5]

A Line of History

The land which we call Argentina today was taken by Spain from both east and west, from both Atlantic and Pacific, in a double thrust. The first wing of invaders from Europe penetrated the Plata estuary in 1516 and founded a river settlement called Puerto de Santa María del Buen Aire in 1536—today's Buenos Aires. The *conquistadores* named the estuary and its great river "Plata," meaning "silver," and the name "Argentina" also derives from silver although, oddly enough, this metal does not exist in the country.[6]

The other wing came overland from Peru beginning about 1543. The Spaniards crossed the Andes, a strenuous feat, descended on the old Inca road built by the Indians, and founded cities like Córdoba and Tucumán. Buenos Aires did not amount to much in the early days. The whole immense Argentine area was ruled by the Viceroyalty of Peru, which had Lima as its resplendent capital and which downgraded Buenos Aires to increase its own political and economic power, with the approval of the Spanish overlords. As we have seen, all Argentine trade to Europe had to be carried on via Peru, cumbersome as this route was.

Together with Uruguay, Paraguay, and parts of Bolivia, Argentina was no more or less than a colony of Peru, under Spain in turn, for more than two hundred years, from 1563 to 1776. Buenos Aires managed to live largely by trade based on smuggling. The Argentines resented Peruvian domination, and a powerful anti-Lima separatist movement grew up, which presently became nationalist as well. To control this situation Madrid liberated Argentina from Peru and established it as a new viceroyalty on its own. This was called the Viceroyalty of Río de la Plata, and Argentina, as part of it, became known as the United Provinces of the River Plata. Spain did not, it

[5] *Latin American Times*, August 2, 1965.
[6] Perhaps "silver" came from the glistening color of the river; perhaps it symbolized the silver mines in Bolivia which the conquerors hoped to reach.

might be added, do this primarily for the sake of the Argentines, but to make the Spanish position stronger vis-à-vis the Portuguese and British, both of whom were looking hungrily on the Plata regions.[7]

But the new Viceroyalty of the Plata did not last long—scarcely more than a generation. Argentine nationalism was mounting and could not be contained. Like every other region of Spanish America, the country yearned for freedom. There were two nationalist revolutions against the Spanish rulers during a chaotic period. The viceroy was pitched out in 1810 and national independence was declared at Tucumán in 1816. The intrepid Creole patriot José de San Martín, the greatest of Argentine heroes, organized his Army of the Andes, overthrew Spanish rule in Chile, and proceeded to invade Peru and liberate it as well, as has been described in Chapter 6.

After independence Argentina began to have astringent troubles. In one year, 1820, Buenos Aires had twenty-four governors. The rest of the country was fought over furiously by rival *caudillos*, most of them *gauchos* off the land. Not till the middle of the century did the new republic take on the contours of a coherent, integrated state. Developments proceeded in several realms concurrently; they overlap and I am not relating them in strict chronological order:

1. Political growth. The basic struggle in the early years was that between the *federalistas*, who represented the "camp" or *pampa* and who sought national unity under a federal system, and the *unitarios* who strove to perpetuate the special hegemony of Buenos Aires, which was both a city and a province. In 1835 began the dictatorship of Juan Manuel de Rosas which lasted for seventeen years till 1852. He ruled by terror, and his regime was one of the bloodiest, most tyrannical, and most obnoxious in the history of South America, but he brought order of a kind and ended the savage *federalista-unitario* feud. Federalism won, but Buenos Aires remained overweeningly powerful. For one thing it collected the entire customs revenue of the country and gave nothing as of right to the rest; for another both city and province were the same entity, which gave it practically the status of an independent dukedom. Not till 1880 was the city separated from the province,[8] and a fair division of the national revenue made possible.

Several presidents give luster to the history of Argentina in the middle of the nineteenth century. They were not *gaucho* monsters like Rosas. One, Bartolomé Mitre, was a journalist,[9] poet, historian, and soldier of fortune

[7] George Pendle, *Argentina*, p. 15. I have followed this admirable book closely for historical details.

[8] The province got a new capital, La Plata, which soon became a flourishing city on its own.

[9] Mitre was the founder of the great Buenos Aires newspaper *La Nación*.

He spent years of exile (during the Rosas dictatorship) fighting in Uruguay, Bolivia, and elsewhere, and was president from 1862 to 1868. He put down a bizarre secessionist rebellion by Buenos Aires, and became the country's first effective constitutional ruler. His successor, Domingo Faustino Sarmiento (1868–74), a mason, also spent years in exile, hated the *gauchos*, passionately believed in European culture, and was an eminent man of letters, educator, and philosopher. His nickname was Don Yo—"Mister I." He has been called "the greatest journalist the Americas have ever produced," "the schoolmaster president," and "the Argentine Thomas Jefferson."[10]

After the turn of the century there developed two main political groupings. On one side stood the conservatives (Partido Demócrata Nacional). mostly of Creole origin, representing the inheritance of colonial Spain, and based on the land, foreign investment, and big business—the oligarchs. On the other rose the radicals (Unión Cívica Radical, or UCR) who were mostly immigrants, townsmen, workers, and intellectuals. In a word the cleavage was conventional—between right and left—but it acquired some baffling Argentine characteristics. As time went on and industrialization progressed, the radical left became stronger in numbers, the right weaker. Therefore, to maintain power, the rightist minority had to suppress the leftist majority by force or stratagem. This was the root problem of Argentina politics until Perón.

2. Conquest of the frontier. The course of events resembles that in the United States during roughly the same period, the necessary allowances being made. Argentina did not finally pacify Patagonia or subjugate the last Indians in remote enclaves in the shadow of the Andes until 1878–83. A major Indian fighter was General Julio A. Roca, who served two terms as president (1880–86 and 1898–1904). Officers in his command were rewarded by being given immense tracts of land on the *pampa* and elsewhere, which assisted the formation of a dominant landowning class.

3. Immigration. The great period of European immigration into Argentina was 1880–1930. The country was a vacuum; it had to be filled. The analogy to mass immigration to the United States during the same half-century is striking, but whereas the United States attracted enormous masses of men and women from almost every European country, immigration into Argentina was largely confined to two national sources, Italy and Spain. Another difference is that immigrants into the United States tended for the most part to settle in cities and work in industry; in Argentina they tended to favor the land.

Nevertheless, plenty of immigrants stayed in Buenos Aires; 80 percent of

[10] Herring, *op. cit.*, p. 651, and Germán Arciniegas, *The Green Continent*.

the adult male population of the city was foreign born by the early 1900's. Some 700,000 more immigrants entered the country after World War II, but nowadays the figures have sharply tapered down.[11] Immigration not only ineffaceably changed the texture of the nation, but, old-school Argentines say, "wrecked its tradition." The original culture of the United States survived immigration, partly as a result of quotas which favored Anglo-Saxon stock and also because of such institutions as free compulsory primary education; the original colonial culture of Argentina did not, and became diluted. The country (I quote an oligarch) was "mongrelized."

4. The British. British economic power became paramount in Argentina in the last century, at about the same time when French culture first took hold. What caused British predominance was, in a word, beef. In 1870 refrigerated ships were invented (the first was a French vessel called the *Frigorifique*), and the export of fresh Argentine beef to British markets became practicable. British interests, multiplying rapidly, proceeded to invest in Argentine shipping, banks, insurance, and the railways; the British had their own station masters, clubs, shops, churches, and social structure throughout the country, as in India, and they "civilized" the *pampa*. Argentina was known (before World War II) as the "Sixth Dominion"; it was the largest British "colony" outside the empire.

Sir David Kelly, a former British ambassador to Argentina, once wrote the following:

> The British horse was followed in 1826 by the all-British "Racing Club." In 1827 John Miller imported the first shorthorn—Miller's Estancia is still British owned. In 1844 Richard Newton set up the first wire-fence—a typical feature of the Argentine landscape. The first steamship to arrive at Buenos Aires was the Royal Mail *Esk* in 1851. In 1874 a British *estancia*, Mr. Sherman's El Negrete, saw the first sheep-dip and the first game of polo. The first Aberdeen-Angus was imported by Mr. Grant in 1876. It sounds incredible, but it is true that all the following were started by British capital and engineers: gas, electric light, the meat packing industry, agricultural and industrial machinery, insurance, banks, tramways, telephones, telegraphs, wireless; and so, incidentally, were football, rugby, rowing, tennis, golf, polo, and boxing. I have left to the last the most important of all, the railways, on which the whole modern development depended. At the very end, out of 26,800 miles of railways, 20,000 were British owned.[12]

All told, British investments in Argentina, much greater than American, came close to half a billion pounds sterling in the 1940's; they have declined

[11] *South American Handbook*, p. 89.
[12] *Ibid.*, p. 93.

since. Italy replaced Britain to become Argentina's best customer in 1963, with West Germany close behind. As to imports Argentina's principal suppliers are the United States, West Germany, Italy, and the United Kingdom in that order.

*

In 1916 came a seminal event, the election to the Argentine presidency of an extraordinary character named Hipólito Irigoyen (pronounced Eari-go-jen), who had Indian blood. This was the first election ever held in Argentina under the secret ballot, and followed a reform in the electoral law pushed through by Roque Sáenz Peña, an able conservative president. Irígoyen, a radical, was the first people's man ever to be elected to the presidency of a South American republic. His first term ended a long conservative hegemony, and he served twice (1916–22 and 1928–30). A masterful politician as well as reformer, Irigoyen was called the *peludo* because he looked like a mole, and his followers were known as *peludistas* or *genuflexos*, knee benders. In his decline he became an intolerably befuddled and uncouth old man, a prisoner of his henchmen. One story is that his secretaries charged outsiders 1,000 pesos for an interview with him. But in his prime he was a character to be reckoned with, and when he died in 1933 his funeral produced a public display almost equivalent to Lenin's in Moscow in 1924.

In 1930 a conservative coup d'état ousted Irigoyen, and the country reverted to a ramshackle series of governments under a mélange of inept presidents mostly dominated by the military. Conservative rule lasted thirteen years. Then, in June, 1943, a vital date, came a revolution made by a clique of youthful reformist colonels bound in a secret society called the GOU—Grupo de Oficiales Unidos. One of these conspirators was Juan Domingo Perón. He took hold of the new government, and Argentina would never be the same again.

CHAPTER 10

From the Colonel to the General

Free America will triumph unless God is a reactionary.
But God is not a reactionary.
—PARAPHRASED FROM GENERAL JOSÉ DE SAN MARTÍN

PERÓN WAS—and still is—a remarkable person, probably the most interesting South American of his times. Until the Onganía *golpe* in June, 1966, which completely transforms the situation, it could fairly be said that Argentina, in all its vastness and complexity, was dominated by a man who had not set foot in it for eleven years—Juan Domingo Perón. This astonishing paradox needs explanation. Perón ruled from June, 1946, until September, 1955, when he was unceremoniously ejected. But for years thereafter it was virtually impossible to have five minutes of political talk with any Argentine without his name coming up as a fiercely vital and immediate issue. Today, seventy-one years old, Perón still lives in exile in Spain, with little hope of ever returning to his homeland, but it was his command of a large segment of Argentine opinion which forced Onganía to make his coup.

How? Why?

Perón was a charlatan, an opportunist, something of a clown, and an outright villain, in the view of his enemies. He also had grace, charm, and magnetism. He was passionately loved by the masses even though he left the country almost bankrupt, because he gave hope and promise. He amassed a vast illicit fortune, but he probably did more for the rank and file of people than any man in Argentine history. There were two Peróns. He was a combination of idealism and trickery. Many will say that he wrecked the country—but he brought the workingman into the fabric of society, and, like Vargas in Brazil, gave the underpossessed a voice. He was corrupt, but he represented the new world.

178

Thus the Perón legend persisted long after he himself was ousted, and Argentina became split like a butchered steer between two apparently irreconcilable divisions—the Peronistas and non-Peronistas. The overriding problem of the country, how to heal this breach, fill this yawning chasm, steadily became more painful, more difficult of solution. The Peronistas by 1965 grew to represent not less than 37 percent of the electorate—ten years after the Leader himself had been pitched out. Clearly they had to be brought back into the body of the state somehow, if the state itself was to survive. But how? For one thing the intransigent Peronistas resisted absorption except on their own terms. For another they faced implacable opposition from the dominant wing of the army, which rules the roost. The army never forgave Colonel Perón, one of its own, for his independent-mindedness and affiliation with labor during his dictatorship. It was determined at all cost to keep the Peronistas from a return to power. Thus, when it appeared in 1966 that the government of the day was shilly-shallying on the issue, and that certain elements in the army itself might be involved in this, General Onganía and his companions struck.

But first let me try to describe Perón and the years between the colonel and the general. Understanding of Argentina is impossible without this background and chronology.

A Bizarre Decade

Perón was born near Buenos Aires in 1895, coming of second-generation Sardinian stock; the original family name seems to have been Peroni and his father was a small farmer. He joined the army for a career, rose fast, and was always distinguished by vitality and charisma; he was an outstanding athlete and fencing champion. Dr. Milton Eisenhower once called him "the most attractive man" he ever met—also the most ruthless. Even today, exiled in his old age, he has flash, dash, and a compelling bravura quality.

All his life Perón has been entangled with women. His first wife, a schoolteacher named Aurelia Tizón, died in 1938; his second was the renowned Evita. After Evita's death in 1952 he lived with a girl, Nelida Rivas, who was only fourteen—perhaps thirteen—at the time. When it was brought to public attention that she was only thirteen Perón laughed the matter off with the remark, "I'm not superstitious."

He was, however, charged with statutory rape—long after the event—as a result of this affair. Nothing came of the matter although an attempt was made to extradite him and bring him back to Buenos Aires for trial. Today Perón lives happily in Madrid with a third wife, a pretty and sensitive-

looking girl thirty-six years his junior, named Isabel Martínez, who had been
a dancer in Panama. She provoked much commotion when she visited
Buenos Aires briefly in 1965, ostensibly to attend a rally to celebrate the
twentieth anniversary of Perón's accession to power, but she was also
supposed to have acted as an emissary to harmonize the activities of various
Peronist groups. She came again in 1966.

Perón adored money as well as power because money was an avenue to
power, but he liked it for its own sake as well. *Time* has quoted an apparently authoritative source to the effect that he acquired $500 million in
"loot" in his 9½ years of office.[1] The *New York Times*, more conservatively,
says that "there were rumors that he had $50 million to $100 million salted
away when he was deposed."[2]

Perón, as people talk about him in Buenos Aires today, is called "both
God and devil." He was an inspired mass leader, a demagogue, but a bad
administrator. He put on a bold front but, like Hitler, often seemed empty.
He was shallow, coarse, and grandiose all at once. He was both true and
false. The person he reminds me of most is, oddly enough, Huey Long,
although he was sleeker than Long, less bumptious. But one can well
imagine Perón saying, like Huey, "I was born into politics, a wedded man,
with a storm for my bride."

He seldom defined policy, and said once, "If I define, I exclude." He
never had a No. 2 man or seemingly paid any attention whatever to choosing
a successor. He was vehemently pro-Hitler, and thought till the last that the
Axis would win the war.

After being graduated from the National Military Academy Perón served
for a period as Argentine military attaché to Italy. He sucked deeply on the
Fascist breast. Mussolini's histrionics fascinated him, as did the Corporative
State. He absorbed the concept of passionate, rapacious nationalism associated with domestic regeneration. Returning to South America and while
still pursuing a military career he devoted himself to the study of political
theory, wrote several books, lectured, served as a professor of military history,
and never ceased whetting his knife for politics.

By the early 1940's he was convinced that he and his fellow colonels in
the conspiratorial Grupo must strike if the nation was to be saved. It seems
that Argentina always has to be "saved" by someone or other. Work, obedi-
ence, sacrifice, reform were his watchwords.

Came the historic coup of June 4, 1943, and Perón and his associates took
the government over with easy precision. He served successively as chief of

[1] June 3, 1957.
[2] December 13, 1963.

the secretariat of the ministry of war, war minister, and vice president, but what interested him most was labor. He became president of the National Department of Labor, and at once put through an astonishing series of reforms. He raised wages, established collective bargaining, set up housing projects, renovated the social security system, reorganized the General Confederation of Labor (CGT) which soon became the most powerful instrumentality in the country after the army, and, in the words of a responsible British historian, "did more for the working man in two years than the Socialist Party had done in a generation."

Thus Perón became a hero to the *Descamisados*, shirtless ones or working class. The European Fascists were symbolized by shirts black or brown; Perón's men by having, metaphorically speaking, no shirts at all. Perón called himself the disciple of Irigoyen, and, indeed, just as Irigoyen brought the middle class into the body of the state, he brought in the proletariat. But his colleagues grew alarmed both by his increasing radicalism and his immense popularity with the masses, and they decided to get rid of him. He was dimissed from his posts in October 1945, arrested, and deposited on an island in the Plata. But the *Descamisados* rose, and made mass demonstrations demanding his release. A leader in this protest was a youthful blond radio performer, Eva Duarte, with whom Perón had formed a close association. It was Eva who brought the mob out into the streets, and brought about his release by a *coup de main*.

Out of confinement, victorious, and owing much to Eva, Perón now prepared for the elections of February, 1946. Like Hitler, he wanted to be voted into power. He won the election hands down, in spite of intense overt opposition by the United States, and took over the presidency in June, 1946. So the years of formal power began.

Eva (= Evita) Duarte was about twenty-five when Perón became president. She rose from tawdry origins, and little about her youth is known. She found a job in radio and met Perón by a cleverly contrived interview when he was attending a labor meeting.[3] He fell in love with her and discovered her usefulness as well. Discretion had to be observed, because Argentina, contrary to most thought, is an excessively puritanical country, and Perón could not risk an open scandal; one story is that he was driven to secret meetings with Evita while lying flat in an ambulance. Eventually they married, and became the most celebrated husband-wife combination in contemporary history with the possible exception of the Chiang Kai-sheks. Eva greatly assisted her husband's career. She had guts and vision. Her instinct

[3] Fleur Cowles, *Bloody Precedent*, p. 150.

for political organization was advanced, and her lust for power insatiable. Though an uncommonly avaricious woman, she had style, dignity, and appeal. She organized Buenos Aires the way a Brooklyn wardheeler might coordinate a single district. She knew thousands of tenement dwellers, down to the children, by name, and she saw to it that those for Perón were rewarded. The major source of her power was the Social Aid Foundation, an organization she set up for disbursing favors to the poor; it was also a phenomenally convenient mechanism for feathering political nests. In effect Eva operated as secretary of labor for a considerable period and helped run the newly created Ministry of Health as well. She died of cancer in 1952, aged 33. Many think that if she had lived Perón would never have been ousted from power.[4]

To return to El Líder himself. Immediately on becoming president for the first time he set up a Five Year Plan. Fascists always borrow from Communists. His program, known as *Peronismo* or *justicialismo*, included a large public works program, industrialization, and continuing social reform. Workers received a forty-eight-hour week, thirteen months' pay for a twelve-month year, a minimum wage, and other substantial benefits. But industrialization was a knotty problem. It had to be paid for and this could be done only by exporting the agricultural products which provided 94 percent of the country's foreign exchange. Perón never knew quite what to do about agriculture. He was wary of attacking the great *estancieros*, landowners, directly and he never instituted a land reform, but he put the sale and export of both wheat and beef under government control.

Meantime reforms poured out in a variety of other fields. Perón initiated votes for women, gave status to illegitimate children (thus annoying the church, which felt that the sanctity of the family was attacked), closed the brothels, legalized divorce (this was rescinded later), whittled down the privileges of religious schools, and sought to reform the universities. His preoccupation with economic nationalism remained incessant. He expropriated the British-owned railways at a cost of £150 million, bought out the American telephone interests for $100 million, and nationalized the airlines, shipping, and local transportation. At the other end of the string there were ridiculous measures *à la* Mussolini like one which obliged all night clubs to play Argentine music half the time.

Steadily the regime became more repressive. Dictators have to keep on dictating. Perón packed the Supreme Court, a device not unknown in

[4] Enormous mobs at her funeral lost all control and eight people were trampled to death. Herring, *op. cit.*, p. 689. Also see Pendle, *op. cit.*, p. 122 and following.

nondictatorships, and instituted severe legislation against treason, i.e., against anything with which he disagreed. Hundreds of citizens went to jail for political "offenses," and the behavior of the police was barbarous. A favorite Argentine torture was an electric needle applied to the more sensitive areas of a man's body. On the other hand nothing remotely comparable to the atrocities committed by Hitler and Stalin—or Gómez in Venezuela for that matter—ever occurred in Perón's Argentina.

Now the Perón system had to be paid for. Dictatorship can be very, very expensive. The treasury had approximately $1,200 million in reserves when El Líder attained the presidency; this dropped to $450 million during his tenure. He piled up a billion-dollar debt as well. At the beginning of his regime Perón had had a good deal of support from nonlabor sources, including important elements in the oligarchy, business, and the church, particularly among citizens who, in the familiar pre-Fascist way, yearned for "order." But gradually he became more isolated. He was, however, easily re-elected president in 1951, though he did not feel strong enough to have Eva run at his side as a candidate for vice president, as he had planned; he won by a popular vote of 4.6 to 2.3 million, which certainly indicated continuing support from the rank and file. But then came rumblings from the army, which he had considered to be his very own. To forestall a mutiny he had to purge the entire high command.

In 1951 the government lost irrecoverable prestige by seizing *La Prensa*, the great Buenos Aires daily, ousting its directorate, shutting it down for some months, and then turning it over to the unions. This outraged and alienated liberal opinion all over the world, because *La Prensa* had won an international reputation as an irrefragably independent newspaper. Perón became nervous. The reaction to the seizure of *La Prensa* was an ugly omen for him. He knew that he was headed for serious trouble. In 1953 conspirators bombed a Peronist meeting; in return a mob of *Descamisados* burned down the Jockey Club, the holy of holies of the oligarchy. Finally a relentless day-by-day struggle with the Catholic Church developed. His temper worn down, Perón hustled two bishops out of the country, and in retaliation the Vatican excommunicated him. (Several years later the excommunication was rescinded.)

This was the beginning of the end. Perón needed Evita's hand; but she was dead. In June, 1955, came a major attempt to unseat him by military force. Argentine naval planes bombed the Casa Rosada, or presidential residence, while army troops attacked it from the streets. The circumstances were dramatic in the extreme, but the coup failed. Some three hundred citizens were killed, but Perón himself had left his study—which was demolished—a few minutes before the attack began, and escaped injury. That night Peronist mobs, seeking vengeance, swept through the streets and a number of churches were looted and burned. The leader sought to prevent this, but could not handle his own men. By this time he had lost face everywhere. He disintegrated. The last act came in September, 1955. Naval forces moved down the river against him, and he surrendered office without a fight. He fled first to a Paraguayan gunboat (so shaken that he slipped and fell into the water) and made his way abroad.[5] Thus his long years of exile began.

To sum up, Perón's enemies say that he was totally insincere, capricious, and irresponsible—a destroyer. But if this is so it is difficult to explain why, ten years later, he still commands the allegiance of millions. He could not have duped everybody. Argentines are civilized people. They do not worship thugs. The long and short of it is that Perón made the people people. He gave the country pride and glow. He gave political status to the weak, the despairing, the nonprivileged. "Perón" became a kind of semantic symbol for "modern world" and "better times." Who built that hospital? Who gave us that school and road? Who put shoes on our children? Perón, Perón, Perón! Perhaps this is to overstate the case, but the fact remains that the Peronistas, after a decade without him, still worship him, and more than this, control more than a third of the electorate.

Sometimes a person may be judged by the intensity with which he is feared or hated. One Buenos Aires newspaper never once printed Perón's name from 1955 to 1964 out of sheer hatred. No matter what news he made, he was always referred to by some such epithet as "the profligate" or "the tyrant." And, to this day, nobody knows where Evita lies buried. Her body was removed from its grave and hidden by the clerical-military government that followed Perón, and its whereabouts are still secret for fear that, if known, the site would become a shrine.

A well-known conservative editor who suffered much from Perón and has good reason to detest him told me, "After ten years we no longer have the right to say that all our present ills are the result of Perón. What produced him was our own failure as a class." A younger man, also an editor, put it this way: "He was the greatest Argentine since San Martín. But two things can never be forgiven him. He created class hatred in a country that had never had it, and he ruined agriculture by siphoning off labor into the towns."

---

[5] The man who hauled him out of the water and saved his life was an official in the Foreign Office who later became Argentine ambassador to the UN.

The Epigones

After Perón's fall in September, 1955, came a provisional military government under General Eduardo Lonardi. The country was understandably nervous, and he lasted only two months. His successor, General Pedro Aramburu, a complicated man of Basque extraction, was of sterner stuff and held office until 1958. Whereas Lonardi, hoping to establish national conciliation, had been somewhat soft on Peronism, the energetic Aramburu was not, and actively sought to suppress the Peronist agitation which still ruptured the country. In June, 1956, forty Perón leaders were arrested and shot. This was an unusual event for Argentina, where most upsets and overturns are bloodless.

But Aramburu, a man of basic good will (except toward Peronists) distinguished himself by preparing the way for a return to constitutional rule. Thus the next large step was an election which put a left-wing intellectual and radical leader, Dr. Arturo Frondizi, into the presidency in February, 1958. Why did General Aramburu and the military permit this election to be held, since they knew that it would mean the end of their regime? First, the general considered it to be his patriotic duty to reinstall civilian government. Second, the country might well have exploded had it not been given some outlet. Dr. Frondizi won an overwhelming victory against a rival radical candidate largely because the Peronists, forbidden to run a ticket of their own, supported him instead. So did the Communists, who had been rising in strength concurrently with the urbanization and industrialization that accompanied Perón, and who could turn out a sizable vote.

In March, 1962, came congressional-gubernatorial elections in which the Peronists—for the first time since their leader's downfall in 1955—were allowed to vote. Frondizi took this decision partly to pay them off, partly because he had a good deal of sympathy with them, partly because he thought this was essential to the country's welfare, and most of all to get their votes. The Peronists made a terrific showing, winning 34 percent of the popular vote, 42 seats in the chamber numbering 192, and 11 out of 16 provincial governorships. Clearly *Peronismo* was still a force to be reckoned with. The army, which now became absolutely determined to squelch any Peronist element in the nation, did not act against the Peronists directly but took the counter-step of incontinently throwing *Frondizi* out instead; he was deposed, arrested, and detained. Thus he served only four years (1958–62) of his six-year term.

Although Dr. Frondizi is out of power today he still ranks as a major political figure. About fifty, he is skillful, articulate, friendly, with a deft orderly mind; his remarks give a sense of structure, and he makes his points one, two, three, with immaculate precision. His capacity to organize his thoughts, even those most casual, into a logical sequence reminded me of the late Dr. Beneš of the late Czechoslovakia. But Frondizi would never sell out his country as the unfortunate Beneš was compelled to do.

The youngest of a family of fourteen, Frondizi came up from the bottom, rising like a bright bubble. He derives from humble Italian stock, which goes to show that Argentine society is not so closed as some people still think it is. Frondizi told me that his first ambition was to be a professor of law or economics, but politics seized him early. He entered the political arena as a red-hot radical, and has always been an acutely controversial figure. While he was still a student at Buenos Aires University, where he did a six-year course in three years, he was arrested for leading student demonstrations, and, in consequence, was refused the degree he had amply earned; he felt this snub so keenly that he has never returned to the university to accept it, although one of his brothers, another strong left-winger, was its rector for a time.

This first arrest came in 1931; Frondizi was protesting against the reactionary government put in power by the coup d'état of September, 1930. He has served several other terms in jail—in 1944–45, 1954, 1955, and again in 1962, when, as just mentioned, he was forcibly deposed from the presidency. On this last occasion he was detained for part of the time in a luxurious hotel at Bariloche, the best-known tourist resort in Argentina, where a floor was reserved for him and his entourage. But, even though nicely treated, he was not released till late in 1963. Few politicians anywhere in the world in recent times have had more experience of confinement than Frondizi; like Jawaharlal Nehru, he occupied himself in jail by writing books. One is a history of Patagonia.

Frondizi, semibald, with a sharp nose and big glasses, is swift, supple, and a brilliant negotiator. He slides in and out. During four years as president he had to deal with no fewer than thirty-five different crises, five of them serious, before the army finally unhorsed him. His relations with Perón were complex. A legend is that they lunched together every week during one period of the Perón regime, but Frondizi told me that in actual fact he and the ex-dictator never met at all. But there is no doubt that Frondizi became president in 1958 largely because of Peronist support. The Peronists took the line that they could affort to wait, and that Frondizi would be a good "front." But Frondizi wasn't anybody's front. He was the first freely-elected president Argentina had had in many years, and his record as chief executive was exemplary, although his enemies accused him of "chicanery" and of being a "juggler."

*

Dr. José Maria Guido, the president of the Senate, succeeded Frondizi as president. Like his predecessor, he was a son of Italian immigrants, arising out of the middle class. The Guido government dissolved the political parties while the Peronists lay low, and Congress recessed for a year. Guido, a much less forceful and enterprising man than Frondizi, lasted for a year and a half. Then came a major event, the elections of 1963, which resulted in the surprising victory of Dr. Arturo Illía, a radical leader hitherto unobtrusive and inconspicuous, as president. He too had Italian antecedents. The days of Creole (= Spanish) supremacy seemed finished. Illía was the third "Italian" president in a row.

Why did Guido hold this 1963 election which ended his own term as chief executive? He had to. He was no more than a stop-gap president, at best, and the army, which was the power behind him, again decided that it was time to return to constitutional procedures. This was a repetition of the Aramburu pattern. The poll was fairly conducted, and the military abided dutifully by the result—to the surprise of almost everybody. The Peronists participated but in a peculiar way; the details are too abstruse to go into here. They had been both legalized and delegalized. Perón issued an order from Madrid instructing his followers to vote "blank," thus expressing his disapproval of the election but also giving his adherents a voice. The blanks came to 21 percent of the electorate, which was a sharp drop from the 34 percent Peronist vote in March, 1962, the previous election.[6]

Next, in March, 1965, came highly important congressional and gubernatorial elections. Their principal significance was that the Peronists were allowed to run (but not under the name Peronist) for the first time since Frondizi; they rose dramatically from their drop in 1963 and became numerically the first party in the country, winning their highest vote in history with not less than 37 percent of the electorate. But—an important but—the Peronists had by this time split into two groups, Peronists and neo-Peronists. The former are those who, in theory, want El Líder back in person; the latter stand by his *mystique* but do not consider his physical return necessary or even desirable—they are "Peronists Without Perón." This 1965 election was *contested by no fewer than 222 different political*

[6] "Background to the 1965 Argentine Elections," by Peter Ranis, World Today, May, 1965, an illuminating account.

parties, counting splinter groups all over the country; fifty-three different parties participated on the national level. Personality factors are the chief divisive elements.

A word now about the Communists. They were declared illegal by a decree in May, 1963 (under Guido), but this ban was later modified. As of 1965 they were permitted to hold political meetings, maintain a headquarters, and publish literature, but they are not allowed to run candidates in a national election under their own label. Everything is false face. Probably the Communist party has 60–70,000 members, which makes it the biggest in South America, with another 150,000 sympathizers. The Communists dominate several major unions. The leadership is solidly Kremlinist, but a Chinese-oriented minority has been vociferous, and splinter groups of Trotskyists and other dissidents are active. The main point to grasp is that the Communist membership, since it cannot vote for itself, *votes Peronist* as a rule under one name or other, although—just to make things simple!—Perón himself is of course vigorously anti-Communist. What the Communists hope is that the Peronist movement will slide left. They await this and seek to filter into the solid body of sixty-two great unions controlled by the Peronists. Meantime the Peronists are, in a sense, Argentina's best defense *against* Communism, because they have captured most of the revolutionary élan of the country. Were it not for them the Communists might be much stronger than they are. Other parties and totals including neo-Peronists:

Union Popular (Perón)	2,848,000 votes
People's Radical Union (UCRO), the Illía wing of the radicals	2,600,000
Movement of Integration and Development (MID), the Frondizi wing	587,000
Intransigent Radicals (UCRI), led by Dr. Oscar Alende	411,000
Progressive Democrats (PDP), led by Horacio Thedy, a middle-road party	288,000
Christian Democrats (PDC), (former leader Horacio Sueldo), a party comparable to the Christian Democrats in Chile, Venezuela, etc.	248,000
UDELPA, the Aramburu party	183,000
Argentina Socialists (PSA), a radical left socialist party	181,000
Democratic Socialists (PSD), led by Américo Ghioldi, the orthodox socialist party (anti-Perón)	172,000

Tres Bandeiras, provincial Peronist	146,000
Popular Movement Mendoza (Neo-Peronist in Mendoza)	100,000
Acción Provinciana (Provincial Neo-Peronist)	100,000
Eloquista, a Perón party restricted to San Juan province	74,000
Popular Conservatives (anti-Perón)	68,000
Reconstrucción Nacional (conservative)	51,000
Social Justice (Peronist, then Neo-Peronist)	44,000
Autonomists (Peronists in Corrientes Province)	35,000
Las Flores Lujan (neo-Peronist faction in Buenos Aires province)	36,000
Liberal Revolutionists (called "Gorilas," violently anti-Perón)	5,491[7]

Despite their participation in the 1965 elections the Peronists contend that they are still "outside" the framework of the state. A final bizarre curiosity is that Peronists and neo-Peronists ran *against* one another in various constituencies.

The Unfortunate Dr. Illía

There are few experiences in South America—or elsewhere for that matter—to rival a formal visit to the presidential palace in Buenos Aires, the Casa Rosada or Pink House. I saw it for the first time many years ago, when a dry little sparrow of a man named Ramón Castillo was president. The building, erected on the ruins of a fort, commands one side of the magnificent Plaza de Mayo in the heart of the city, and the ensemble is superlatively ornate. It makes our White House look virtually like a chicken coop. Sentries at the Casa Rosada carry bold swords, and wear yellow-striped helmets with golden edges; their uniforms are a blue tunic and red-striped trousers, with bright red, blue, and golden epaulettes. The elevator which lifted us to the presidential quarters is as big as a small room, with a velvet-covered bench, a baroque mirror, and a chandelier.

Dr. Arturo Umberto Illía, who was president at the time of my second visit, is a lanky man with a long narrow face, deeply set dark eyes, and silver hair, who, I thought, was instantly recognizable as being of Italian blood. He might have been a factory manager in Turin—a realist, guarded, small-town-ish, with emphatic gestures. He wore a deceptively casual blue shirt. He

[7] Buenos Aires *Herald*, March 17, 1965.

was attentive. He was obviously a serious man. It was hard to make him smile.

One of his nicknames is the "Turtle," another is "Mr. Slowly." Indeed he may seem passive, but it was his chief contribution at the time to have relaxed the country, lowered its temperature, exactly by his technique of dealing with a crisis by pretending that none existed. His principal aim was to be conciliatory, and he was accused of being too soft with both the Communists and Peronists. But he brought Argentina closer to genuine democratic government than any president in years. The trouble was his extreme ineffectuality. Nothing got done, which was a basic reason for the Onganía coup.

By profession Dr. Illía is a physician, a doctor of internal medicine. He was born in western Argentina in 1900. His grandfather was an Italian immigrant; his father ran a brick factory in a small town, Pergamino. Illía had a hard youth. He fought for an education, and, after getting a medical degree at twenty-seven, found a job as a medical officer on the railways. He told me he resented stories that he did the rounds of patients in his neighborhood "on a donkey." He has dignity. No donkeys.

Nor, as is sometimes inaccurately said, was he any newcomer to politics. Though not particularly well known when he was picked by the party bosses, like Ricardo Balbin, to run for president in 1963, he did not come from the bottom of the barrel. The radicals chose him as a "sacrificial" candidate because they did not think they could win; he was dispensable. Politics have occupied him all his life. He mentioned in our talk how, as a boy of ten, he was fascinated by watching the electoral process; there was no secret ballot then, and voters wrote down a name on a slip of paper and handed it in as the village watched. He became a provincial senator as far back as 1936, a deputy to the national Congress in 1948, and governor of the great province of Córdoba in 1958. He has been called "an upstate Tammany Hall."

My wife and I spent most of an hour with Dr. Illía. He did not hurry us. On his desk were two telephones and a small switchboard plugged into eight or ten lines, but the lights did not flash more than once or twice. When they did, Dr. Illía paid no attention. I mention such a minor detail only because it is evidence of the seriousness with which most South Americans (like Russians) take political interviews. When a South American dignitary receives you he is almost certain to give you his full, private, and uninterrupted attention for the stipulated period. In the United States an interview with a governor or senator is likely to be interrupted any number of times and may turn into a circus. But in South America the proprieties are rigorously observed, although the interviewer may be interviewed himself on TV or the radio immediately following his reception by the head of state.

The talk with Dr. Illía centered on two topics, relations with the United States and Communism. At one point the president reached for an atlas, opened it to a big map of the United States, and kept jabbing at it with a long forefinger. He wanted to illustrate the breadth of development in North America in contrast to Argentina. The essential difficulty between the two countries is, he thought, lack of understanding. "You cannot treat us as if we were a business. We are a nation of human beings." As to Communist influence or takeover Dr. Illía minimized any possibility of danger. Perhaps some Communists vote Peronist but the Peronists are basically anti-Communist. No leftist coup could, he indicated, possibly succeed because the Communists do not have the opportunity to gain key positions in the government, which is the only way they could conceivably reach power since their numerical strength is small. Moreover, they have support only in the cities, not in the countryside.

My last question was, "What does Argentina need most?" Reply: "Faith."

*

Perón attempted to return to Argentina in December, 1964, after Illía had been in office about a year. The venture failed. Perón's preparations were cloak-and-daggerish, but bungled. He seriously miscalculated the acumen of his enemies. In circumstances of the utmost secrecy he left his Madrid villa late at night, and, hidden in the trunk of his car, was driven to the airport. One story is that he had planned to disguise himself as a nun. He boarded a Spanish airliner about to take off for Buenos Aires, with a stop at Rio, and then surprisingly dropped all the elaborate precautions he had been taking, perhaps out of bravado or sheer megalomania, perhaps because he thought that, once in the plane, he was safe. As a result, his identity became promptly known. Perón's basic intention is not fully understood to this day; apparently he thought that his mere arrival in Buenos Aires would set off a nationwide revolt, ensuring his return to power.

The Argentine government acted with precision and dispatch. It had already alerted the authorities in Brazil, Chile, and Uruguay to the possibility that the ex-dictator might appear, and asked their cooperation to keep him out, which they agreed to do. Now, with the news that he was actually in the air, events moved fast. Action must be taken before dawn. The Argentine security authorities got through to Rio, and when Perón arrived at the airport there he was met by Brazilian police, declared persona non grata, taken off the plane, and shipped back to Spain that night. Perón protested, "I know international law well. I am aboard a plane under the Spanish flag and under the protection of the Spanish government and you cannot interrupt my trip." The Brazilians paid no attention, and that was that. So Perón's adventure reached an inglorious end, and he found himself back in Madrid thirty-six hours after leaving it.

Workers in Argentina, representing the Peronist unions, started a general strike in protest, but it failed. As for the imperturbable Dr. Illía he took a characteristic stand. He said nothing for or against Perón but limited himself to the bland comment, "Perón's return is up to Perón."

*

Dr. Illía was the man who nationalized the American oil interests in Argentina, and this sensational story demands a word. Early in the 1900's prospectors exploring for water in Patagonia struck petroleum through a fluke. Aware that oil might become an extremely lucrative element in the economy and out of a natural desire to protect its own natural resources, the government passed a law reserving all subsoil rights to the state; no private citizen may own a mine or well in Argentina. These may, however, be developed and operated by private capital under contracts or concessions given by the government, and several American companies entered the field. The Argentines meantime set up a state monopoly known as YPF, or Yacimientos Petrolíferos Fiscales, to conduct exploration, drill wells, market oil, and otherwise handle their interests and supervise the industry, which flourished for a time. But YPF lacked capital, technicians, and facilities, and soon the foreigners had the larger share of the market.

As a result of this and other factors sentiment rose steeply in Argentina to throw the concessionaires out. This was not a new development. For some years the expropriation of the American oil companies had been a leading motif in local politics. It grew stronger when, for various reasons, production began to fall and the country found itself obliged to import large quantities of oil, an expensive process. Two sides rose: those who thought that full nationalization would solve the problem, and those who favored further cooperation with the foreigners, because they feared that a serious oil shortage, which would cripple industrialization, might follow if the foreigners were evacuated all the way.

President Frondizi (1958–62) took the side of cooperation with the foreign interests when the cost of importing oil rose to the prohibitive total of some $300 million a year. His line was that Argentina's first desideratum must be self-sufficiency, in order to cut down on imports; this clearly meant that production at home must be increased, and YPF could not do the job alone. So, daring to set himself against most public sentiment, he renegotiated the old contracts to give the American companies better terms, and even granted important new concessions. Exploration and drilling were stepped up, production tripled, and Argentina, reaching an output of 98 million barrels in 1962, came close to reaching Frondizi's goal of self-sufficiency.

But Frondizi was ousted from the presidency by the military, and in 1963 came the election won by Illía. Illía's principal campaign pledge was to reverse the Frondizi policy, throw out the foreigners, and nationalize petroleum. He was not taken altogether seriously because nobody thought he would win. He did win, however, and, on assuming office, proceeded at once to fulfill his pledge. Scarcely a month after becoming president he annulled the Frondizi and other contracts, claiming as an excuse that they had been unconstitutional or based on fraud. Thus oil in Argentina became nationalized.

Thirteen companies were involved, nine of them American.[8] The uproar was ear-shattering. The companies claimed that the value of their properties was $397 million (later reduced to $279 million): the Argentine figure was $70 million. Averell Harriman, the most experienced of United States negotiators, flew to Buenos Aires to try to make a settlement, but failed. Illía had, however, not gone the whole way. His caution is well known. He did indeed cancel the government's exploration and drilling contracts with most of the companies, and duly turned their concessions over to the YPF, but several continued to produce oil at the request of the government, as well as distribute it. The matter of compensation went to the courts. So far six American companies have settled their annulled contracts at a total cost to Argentina of $120 million. Meantime production has fallen off and at the moment the country is again having to import oil in large quantities—at a cost of $125 million a year. But freedom is worth this price, the Argentine nationalists insist.

The State Department during the early period of this dispute attempted to crack down on the Argentines, punish them, and bring them to heel, by the device of cutting down or withholding American aid, according to the Argentines. The Americans deny this, stating that we continued to honor

[8] Standard of New Jersey, Cities Service, Continental, Marathon Petroleum, Standard of Indiana (PanAmerican Argentina), Tennessee Argentina, Union Oil of California, Southwestern Drilling Company, and Kerr-McGhee Oil Industries (Transworld Drilling Company).

obligations made before the quarrel, but that "legislative restrictions" made the negotiation of new loans "difficult" until the conflict was resolved.

As a matter of fact, American aid has never been a particularly vital element in the Argentine economy, and its amounts have been comparatively small—only $74 million in a recent year. Most Argentines dislike receiving direct financial aid from the United States. By and large they oppose the Alianza, and think that Washington is full of old-fashioned oafs who cannot quite catch on to the idea that the national wealth of a country belongs to its own people. On the other hand they welcome foreign investment, which has fallen off, and would like to see it resumed intensively. Advertisements have appeared recently in the New York press "clarifying" the "positive position" made by new Argentine investment laws, and inviting investment in petrochemicals, pulp and paper, steel, and fisheries. The total United States private investment in Argentina today is between $700 million and $1 billion, with 260 American firms represented. About 7,000 Americans live in Argentina.

General Onganía and His Coup

Trouble began to stir between President Illía and General Onganía, who was commander-in-chief of the army, late in 1965. The upshot was that the general became the leader—or agent—of the conspiracy that unseated Illía, and, as we know, he succeeded him in the Casa Rosada on June 29, 1966, and was inaugurated as the thirty-first president of the Argentine Republic after a silkily smooth bloodless coup. Behind Onganía is a junta of three men, known as the "High Command"—Lieutenant General Pascual Angel Pistarini, the army chief; Admiral Beningo Ignacio Varela, head of the navy; and Brigadier General Adolfo Teodoro Alvarez, chief of the air force. The military lineup is complete, representing all three service chiefs.

That a blowup was coming had been sensed by almost everybody. Government under Illía had become too flaccid, too pallid and inept, to endure, despite his decency. He had held only three cabinet meetings in thirty-two months. Many observers did not, however, believe that General Onganía himself would be a party to any illegal attempt to seize power. He had always stood vigorously for constitutionalism. He was not an adventurer, not a Bonapartist. His proudest boast was that he had taken the army out of politics. Twice, in fact, after being named commander-in-chief in 1962, he had carried out the will of the civilian government and directed the armed forces to put down, not assist, attempts at *coups de main*. He saved the Guido government in March, 1963, when this was threatened by a revolt of navy units, and it was he who smoothed the way for Dr. Illía himself to become president. He wanted the army to be an impartial arbiter.

The Argentine army has been split for some years into two factions, the Reds and Blues. This came about in the period of confusion following Frondizi. The Red officers[9] wanted an outright military takeover; the Blues stood for constitutionalism. Onganía was a Blue, and won. He held that the army was not "co-governing," and that its function was to defend the constitution, not suborn it, under the authority of civilian government. How, then, is one to explain Onganía's sudden change of face? How did it happen that this officer, of all officers, felt compelled to make a *golpe* and unhorse an elected president, seizing power without the faintest pretense of constitutional authority? The answer from Onganía's side is that the general became convinced that such drastic and dangerous action was necessary to save the state.

It is true that he had had serious disagreements with Illía on a personal basis. In fact in November, 1965, Onganía suddenly and strangely resigned as commander-in-chief because the president had appointed a brigadier general named Castro Sánchez to be minister of war. Onganía apparently considered this to be an affront because Castro Sánchez, an officer of inferior rank, was put over his head without his having been consulted. He felt that this meant that Illía was withdrawing confidence from him, and that he had no recourse except to quit. The country was stunned, and waited breathlessly for action. It seemed almost inconceivable that the diffident Illía could have dared to pull the teeth of the tough soldier. The crisis between President Truman and General MacArthur is analogous up to a point. Apparently Illía and Onganía had been at loggerheads for some time on matters of basic policy as well. The army wanted to assist the United States forces in the Dominican Republic with a contingent of troops but the Illía government demurred. Onganía strongly supported a proposal for an inter-American peace force and hoped for a military alliance with Brazil to oppose Communism, but the cabinet would not agree.

More important was the perennial, insoluble issue of the Peronists. Onganía, out of office, felt that the government was not merely being lax with these, but was actively flirting with them. They seemed to be on top of the wave. They had won elections in three provinces and were almost certain to carry Buenos Aires province by a triumphant margin in elections soon to come. The army wanted to abort these elections. Events leading immediately to the June coup are the following. It was discovered that Major General

[9] Of course not "Red" in the Communist sense.

Carlos A. Caro, commander of the II Army stationed at Rosario, one of the three or four top generals in the country and a loyal Illía man, had met secretly with Peronist leaders in June. This produced such indignation among other officers that Lieutenant General Pistarini, one of Onganía's closest associates and his successor as commander-in-chief, arrested Caro and forced the resignation of the minister of war. President Illía at once fired Pistarini. But it was too late, and Pistarini's troops closed in on vital sectors of the capital. Preparations for the *golpe* had been made long before.

On Monday night, June 27, Dr. Illía was entertaining a group of visiting scientists at the Casa Rosada. He was informed at about 10 P.M. that a coup was in progress. Promptly he summoned an emergency meeting of the cabinet and party leaders. After two hours he signed a decree charging General Pistarini with insubordination, and assumed the post of commander-in-chief himself. This was a vain gesture, because the Casa Rosada was now cut off and surrounded by junta troops. At 3:30 A.M. (the 28th) police entered and arrested a group of Illía's political supporters. These made no resistance. What happened then is vividly described by H. J. Maidenberg of the *New York Times*, from whom I quote:

> This news reached Dr. Illía a half hour later and he ordered his aides to bring out a stack of photographs of himself, which he began autographing and handing out to his aides.
>
> As he was signing the last photo shortly before 5 A.M. for his office runner, the door of his office was flung open. In walked the commander of the Presidential honor guard, Brigadier Rodolfo Otero, and other officers.
>
> President Illía did not look up as Maj. Gen. Julio Alsogaray, commander of the First Army, moved to his desk and declared: "Dr. Illía, sir, you must leave this office in the name of the armed forces."
>
> The chief executive asked the 23-year-old office runner, "What is your first name, son?"
>
> "Miguel Angel López, señor Presidente," he replied.
>
> When General Alsogaray began to speak again, Dr. Illía again asked, "Now what is your first name, son? Miguel?"
>
> As the office runner repeated his answer, General Alsogaray angrily began to speak again, only to be put off by Dr. Illía, who said sharply without looking up: "Don't interrupt. I am speaking to a citizen."
>
> Then he handed the photo to the young man, stood up slowly and asked, "Who are you?"
>
> "I come to carry out an order from the commander-in-chief . . ." General Alsogaray said.
>
> Dr. Illía cut him off by shouting: "I am the commander-in-chief of the armed forces and you are a common mutineer who uses his guns and disloyal soldiers to violate the law. You are a midnight highway-

man. I repeat that I am the commander-in-chief and I order you to leave."

General Alsogaray angrily replied, "If you insist, we shall be obliged to use violence."

"You have already used it and continue to use it," Dr. Illía said. "I am here not to defend personal interests, but have been elected by the people to defend the law and the Constitution."

As General Alsogaray and his party turned to leave, Brigadier Otero momentarily seized his arm. General Alsogaray looked at the tearful chief of the honor guard and then said softly, "I understand."

The members of the honor guard are sworn to defend the President during their tours of duty. The night guard changes at 7 A.M.

At 7 A.M. 16 policemen, armed with machine guns and tear gas equipment, arrived at the President's office. One unarmed police official walked in and told Dr. Illía that he would personally guarantee his safety but could not do so for his aides and others in the room. He spoke softly and seemed uneasy. . . .

Dr. Illía nodded to his aides, who began leaving.

As they filed out, Dr. Illía, leaning on the arm of his former Foreign Minister, Miguel Angel Zavala, left Government House at 7:25 A.M.

About 70 people were at the street entrance and as he was led to his car for the 30-minute drive to the suburban home of his brother, Ricardo, they screamed, "Long live democracy and liberty!" as they tried to shake his hand.[10]

General Onganía was inaugurated president the next day.

*

Onganía is fifty-two, and was born of a middle-class family of Basque extraction near Buenos Aires. When I saw him he was still commander-in-chief. Outside his headquarters members of the guard wore uniforms which are a replica of those of San Martín—top hats, red sashes, white pants. The general has lively appraising brown eyes, a heavy divided mustache, not a gray hair, and a florid complexion—he flushes easily. There were four telephones on his desk; none rang during our hour with him. He told me, a pleasant compliment, that he had found my *Inside U.S.A.* too heavy to handle comfortably and had consequently torn it into segments which he read one at a time. I might have mentioned that Carl Sandburg and one other friend of mine had preceded him as inventors of this process, but did not do so. I cannot quote anything Onganía said because our conversation was strictly off the record. He was—and still is—extremely shy of journalists, and the off-the-record stipulation was made with pointed emphasis, though not by him. The general talked freely—even indiscreetly—and was courtesy

[10] July 3, 1966.

itself. My principal impression was that this was an exceptionally cool customer—alert, somewhat sharp, resolute, a marked conservative, intractable, and vigorous.

General Onganía attended the public schools, passed through the military academy, and went into the armored cavalry. He has the style and figure of an old-type cavalry officer. Since boyhood he had wanted to be an officer and has never had any other ambition. He likes to ride, hunt, play polo, and stick pigs, and is devoted to his five children. He fought a sabre duel in 1947 with a person described as "a scion of an aristocratic family," but nobody was hurt.

*

On assuming power, with the three-officer junta behind him, Onganía acted swiftly. He dissolved Congress, the provincial legislatures, the Supreme Court, and all the multifarious political parties—a clean sweep. He made no speech at the inaugural ceremonies. What seemed to be Fascist touches became apparent at once. There were a number of political arrests, and Communist headquarters were raided. Several Jewish shops were closed down, and the very large Jewish community in Buenos Aires became understandably nervous. The police were given the right of search and seizure without warrants. What is most surprising is that there was no immediate crackdown on the Peronists. In fact the secretary general of the Confederation of Labor, the heart of Peronism, was a conspicuous guest at the inauguration. Onganía came to power to keep the Peronists out, but it is just possible that negotiations may evolve to heal the breach with them.

According to the *New York Times* several Illía men called at the United States Embassy during the weekend of the coup seeking a statement of support, as had been given them before. "The Embassy was closed and Ambassador [Edwin M.] Martin was visiting in the United States."

During the ensuing summer (1966) things did not go well for the junta. General Onganía, who acted like a man somewhat bewildered by his new responsibilities, had difficulty in assembling a workmanlike cabinet, and seemed to be vastly puzzled and perturbed by the fact that he was not taken at face value everywhere as a simple patriot, savior, and soldier. He veered to the extreme right, became associated with violent reactionary forces, and found himself in acrid trouble with big business (which had expected "miracles") and even with the church hierarchy as well as labor, liberals and intellectuals. He attempted to crack down on the universities, which produced a blistering crisis still unresolved as these pages go to press.

CHAPTER 11

B. A.

They [the Argentines] have ceased to be Spaniards without becoming something new of their own. They seem to be a nation in the making, not yet made.
—LORD BRYCE IN 1912

AT ONCE, entering Buenos Aires, the visitor will perceive that this is a true *city*, a real contemporary megalopolis. It is not, like Rio, a series of villages strewn on a mountain, or, like Caracas, beads on a string. With 3,800,000 people, Buenos Aires is the ninth-largest city in the world, the second in the southern hemisphere, and the third in the western. It is bigger than any city in the Americas except New York and, by a narrow margin, São Paulo. Including the whole metropolitan area the population is above six million. If population and power were distributed in the United States on the pattern of Argentina, Washington D.C.—as the equivalent of Buenos Aires—would have 80 million people and control 70 percent of the nation's commerce.

Once more we must digest a few facts and figures in order to deal with Buenos Aires, so spacious, rich, and solid. It has 150 parks, 5 subway lines, and miles of sweeping boulevard. I thought it had more tennis courts than any city I have ever seen except Johannesburg. The Avenida Nueve de Julio, 460 feet wide, is the broadest street in the world—also one of the shortest because, the legend has it, the Ministry of Works put it in the wrong place and it had to be cut off when it interfered with new public buildings already planned. Underneath the Nueve de Julio is a huge garage. Another great street, the Avenue Libertador General San Martín, will hold twenty cars abreast, reminding me of the girth of streets in Salisbury, Rhodesia. On one side of San Martín, which is bounded by a park four miles long, are grounds for polo, on the other a race track, right in the middle of the city. A smaller famous street is Florida (originally Stone Pavement Street), the fashionable shopping center. Automobile traffic—anarchic in Buenos Aires—is forbidden on Florida after 11 A.M. every day, so that shoppers and viewers can move along without being murderously run down. Florida is narrow, without room for cars and shoppers both.

Then one must mention such details as that the National Stadium holds 100,000 people, that the zoological and botanical gardens are magnificent, and that the Recoleta Cemetery is probably the most elaborate in the world next to Forest Lawn in California. The adage is that "it is cheaper to live extravagantly all your life than to be buried in Recoleta."[1]

The conventional impression of Buenos Aires, with its luminous views, rounded plazas, iron-gray mansard roofs, and spiky iron fences, is that it resembles Paris. And so it does—including the diagonal layout of streets intersecting at sharp angles, the sound of iron shutters banging down over shop fronts at noon, impeccably dressed and well-behaved children, high ceilings over French windows in stately houses, feeble electric light bulbs in hotel rooms, and bathtubs shaped like narrow troughs with slippery rounded bottoms, so that taking a shower demands the sure-footedness of a mountaineer. But on closer inspection the analogy to Paris fades. Buenos Aires resembles more a Mediterranean city, a magnified Barcelona or Marseilles.

There are two airports. One, Aeroparque, lies in the middle of the city, ten minutes from the great banks and hotels, like Santos Dumont in Rio. It is well run but I noticed that three large clocks all told a different time. One curiosity is that Argentina demands no papers of any kind, except a passport, from the foreign visitor—not even the conventional air landing card. On the other hand, as an example of red tape, you have to show your passport in order to send telegrams to several countries. The flavor of the city may be gathered readily on a drive from Ezeiza, the international airport outside the town, along a splendid four-lane highway—of which there are only *two* in all Argentina, a country bigger than the United States east of the Mississippi. Neither of these runs for more than fifty miles. The trees are nicely pruned, as in France. The railroad tracks, seen from viaducts, are shiny—clearly the trains actually run. Gone are the exuberance and wild irresponsibility of Brazil. Signs scrawled on walls suggest some preoccupations of those who like to put up signs—*Contra la Oligarquia, Yanqui Go Home,* and *Abajo el Imperialismo.*

Those who think of Buenos Aires in terms of gracious *hôtels particulières* and glossy horses with straw hats to protect them from summer heat should visit the *villas misérias,* slums or squatter towns, the equivalent of the *favelas*

[1] *Buenos Aires Through Bifocals,* p. 43.

in Brazil, which surround and penetrate several quarters of the city. Here some 400,000 citizens live in the most degrading poverty and squalor. There are 55 different *villas misérias*, and they are among the worst sights on the continent. Yet citizens are probably better off in these wretched slums than in the hinterland they came from.

The Porteños, residents of Buenos Aires, have some puzzling characteristics. It is more difficult to define one than a New Yorker. Spiritual malaise is a keynote, yes; so is laziness. Only among the more raucous youth and in the chauvinist fringe is much tension evident. People consume large quantities of *caña* (a colorless spirit) and wine (the true national drink), eat meat, and do not change their habits easily. You have to prove to a shopkeeper that air conditioning, let us say, really works before he will install it. Citizens are cautious politically. They do not stick their necks out, as citizens of Córdoba may do. I have in the two preceding chapters mentioned a history peppered with coups d'état, but even during the embroilments over Perón men of Buenos Aires were extremely reluctant to mount the barricades and fight. One attitude, particularly in the upper reaches of society, is still, "Oh-if-only-God-would-save-our-country!" I met in New York recently a rich Argentine expatriate. He grabbed me howling with anguish—"What's going on in my country—it's being ruined!" But he hasn't gone back to see things for himself in twenty years.

One characteristic is the local accent, called Rio Platense. The Porteños thicken their vowels and pronounce "y" and "ll" like "j." This phonetic phenomenon is known as the yeismo. *Calle*, the word for street, comes out *caja*, and there are other dissonances revolting to the Castilian ear. "Yo" is "jo." A friend asked me to meet him at a restaurant which he called the "Gojo"; I could not find it for a time because it never occurred to me to look for the "Goya."

Strongly evident is an atmosphere of corruption, although this is not so flamboyant as in Brazil. The institution of *coima*, the bribe, is encountered by most citizens from their childhood; a tip to the schoolteacher from a parent can get a youngster better marks. Give a present to the nurse, and treatment will be better in a hospital; a small *douceur* will help expedite a telegram. Citizens at large cynically put politicians into two categories: those who take bribes, but deliver something in return, and those who take and do not deliver. On the highest level, however, Argentine politics are quite clean compared to several other South American countries. No one would dream of trying to bribe General Onganía, nor would he ever conceivably use his office to collect loot. Dr. Illía was an absolutely honest man, and, out of office now and bereft of salary, he is near to destitution.

Why do not superior members of the government crack down on those corrupt in the middle ranges? (1) They don't want to; (2) they wouldn't know how to do so even if they did.

Another unsavoriness is sporadic anti-Semitic gangsterism. One reactionary group is the Tacuara, which aims to become the "military arm" of a "national popular movement" against the Jews. One of Eichmann's sons, Horst, has been active in Nazi demonstrations, and ostentatiously flaunts a swastika armband. Deputies have risen in parliament to speak against Zionism and "international Jewry" and to ask investigation of the links between "local Jewish organizations and Israel." Responsible Argentines deplore such activity, and in fact the country has a high and honorable record for hospitality to Jews dating back to 1891, when a proposal was made to establish Jewish colonization in the country. Nothing came of this in a formal way, but large numbers of Jews from eastern Europe and elsewhere took up residence in Argentina, as in Uruguay next door. The Jewish community today numbers above 450,000, and is said to be the fourth largest in the world outside Israel. Anti-Semitism on the irresponsible fringes was stimulated by postwar *German* immigration. Dr. Frondizi told us that it could not be taken seriously as a force unless its propaganda took root in the Peronist movement or within the armed forces; Dr. Illía dismissed the hooligans on the streets as a factor beneath contempt and of no significance whatever. But a certain amount of swastika daubing and similar infantilism still goes on, and has led to more violent outrages in the recent past.

The Silver Queen

Buenos Aires is the most advanced city in South America from the point of view of culture, but this does not mean that it is the liveliest. It does not have the creative flash of Rio or Santiago, except in painting. There are, however, much wider opportunities for enjoyment of intellectual life and the arts. Buenos Aires is the biggest publishing center in South America and has any number of good bookshops; one of these, the Ateneo, rising seven stories on Florida, is supposed to be the largest in the world. I asked my Spanish publisher for a list of contemporary American authors translated into Spanish and available in Buenos Aires, and received eighty-six names, ranging from Irwin Shaw to Gore Vidal, from Harper Lee to Joseph Heller. The literary tradition, dating back to President Sarmiento in the 1870's, continues to be vital. Any list of the most distinguished living Argentines would be bound to include Victoria Ocampo, the poet, critic, and founder and editor of the literary journal *Sur*. Other Argentine writers of interest, aside from veterans like the novelists Eduardo Mallea and Jorge Luis Borges, are newcomers such as Julio Cortázar, whose *Hopscotch* was a recent *succès d'estime* in English; Ivan Goyanarte, not yet translated, and in particular Ernesto Sábato, far on the left, whose recent book *The Outsider* made a lively local splash.

Two newspapers are world famous, *La Prensa* and *La Nación,* and the proprietor of the former, Dr. Alberto Gainza Paz, like Miss Ocampo, incontestably ranks as one of the leading citizens of the nation. Both *La Prensa* and *La Nación* are much respected by journalists everywhere for their extensive coverage of foreign news, which rivals that of the *New York Times.* *La Prensa* was for many years inextricably associated with the rise of the great American news agency the United Press, which it used for the vast amounts of cabled news it printed. Buenos Aires has sixteen major dailies, including two in French, two German, one Italian, one Yiddish, and one English, the tabloid Buenos Aires *Herald,* as well as papers in twenty-one other languages. This is a polyglot city. There are eight TV channels in the country, of which four are in Buenos Aires. The magazine with the biggest circulation is the local edition—in Spanish of course—of *Reader's Digest.*

The Colón Theater, the municipal theater devoted to opera and the ballet, is the biggest and one of the most elaborate in the world. Modeled on the Paris Opéra, it covers most of a city block and has a stage which can hold six hundred, as well as its own orchestra, chorus, and corps de ballet. Five other symphony orchestras play regularly. A composer of outstanding merit and reputation is Alberto Ginastera. The theater in general, like theaters almost everywhere, is having troubles, and the younger generation considers it ossified beyond repair. But Buenos Aires has forty-five functioning theaters, more than London or New York, and an aggressive and experimental movie industry. One important director is Jorge Nielssen. The hit of the stage season when I was there was *Who's Afraid of Virginia Woolf?*, closely followed by *Becket;* the repertories, somewhat egghead-ish, resemble those in Moscow, with works by Shakespeare, Shaw, Bertolt Brecht, and Pirandello.

There are no fewer than seven *hundred* art galleries in Buenos Aires, though not more than a dozen of these count. Abstract art is, of course, the rage.[2] Argentine painting has, authorities in New York tell me, more vitality, originality, and excitement than any other in Latin America, even Mexico. Among outstanding contemporaries are Sarah Grilo, who is well known in North America, her husband Antonio Fernandez Muro, Luis Felipe Noé,

[2] In one museum I saw a contraption altogether new to me, although I have been told subsequently that these exist in the United States as well. A large recessed illuminated screen is set before a work of art, for instance a mobile, on which lights flash; a paddle, set with crystals, rotates slowly giving the sculpture extravagantly fanciful changing patterns.

Rómulo Maccio, Jorge Luis de la Vega, and Ernesto Deira. Several of these form a school, and all have growing international reputations. Julio Le Parc, born in Mendoza in 1928, won last year a first prize at the Venice Biennale; he does optical, kinetic constructions.

Argentina has six universities, of which the chief, with no fewer than 75,000 students (full or part time), is in Buenos Aires. Its strongest faculties are law and medicine, and, like most South American universities, it is autonomous. Both Peronist and Communist influences are marked in the student body, but it is not quite the hotbed that universities in Santiago, Lima, or Caracas are. Dropouts are a problem. Youngsters can't afford to stay the full term. On the other hand, as is the case in other universities on the continent, there are considerable numbers of "professional" students— "permanents" who stay on and on until they reach their forties or later.

I was astonished in Buenos Aires to discover that Monday and Tuesday were meatless days. This in Argentina, the land sacred to beef! Of course there is a catch here in that the Porteños do not consider pork, veal, mutton, or lamb to be "meat," and the visitor can gorge on these to the limit of his capacity; only beef is limited. Argentine steaks are reputed to be the finest in the world, and the fable is that you can eat a filet mignon with a spoon. My own experience, based on two visits, is that tough or sinewy beef is not uncommon, and the visitor is well advised to bring along a kit of dental floss. Meat is cheap. The national dish is the *asado*, beef roasted on a spit. The reason for the imposition of meatless days by the government is double. First, the great cattle herds were depleted by a recent severe drought. Cattle here eat green grass, and silos are all but unknown; when the grass dried up large numbers of livestock died. Second, domestic consumption is being deliberately cut to stimulate exports. Normally beef earns not less than half the country's total foreign exchange, and the authorities do not want this figure to slip. "Meat police" are on the job controlling packing plants and restaurants, and it is estimated that it will take two or three years before the depleted herds are brought back to normal.

Restaurants are great fun in Buenos Aires; one of the best-known meat places is the Cabaña, where a grilled sausage called *chorizos especiales* is a notable creation. Other items on the Cabaña menu, as I wrote them down, are:

> Thick intestine
> Roast lung
> Bloed [sic] sausages
> Sole-fish with salt-wort, spinnach, or pepers [sic]

One Spanish restaurant, built out of an old stable, has, of all things, a performing horse for the amusement of guests, and on the menu I saw "Coffee Made with Glass Filter" and the mystifying "Prices Without Any Charge." Several sound bourgeois restaurants are still primitively equipped; I ran into one with a Turkish seat in the men's room. Palermo beer—excellent—comes from one of the largest breweries in the world, and a dry martini bears the nice name *Clarito*, a little clear one. All over town are small bars called "whiskerias," and the service charge on hotel and restaurant bills is a shattering 24 percent, with a voluntary *laudo*, tip, expected in addition.

Porteños dine late—though dinner hours are not so late as in Chile—and Buenos Aires becomes a different city after 10 P.M. The dead of night transforms it into something paradoxically alive. Bars are packed, cafés thronged, till 3 A.M. or later. In a night club like "676" patrons listen to the "electronic" or "cool" tango, drinking champagne at 5,000 pesos ($25) a bottle—or good local wine at 300, $1.50. Also to be heard are *milonga*, or "happy" tango, a traditional dance of the Creoles in the Plata country, and *candombe*, which has Afro-Brazilian touches. The tango was, incidentally, at one period considered so "indecent" that it was not allowed to be played in Buenos Aires. Even today curious puritanical elements survive. I was thrust back at the door of one well-known night club because I was alone! Apparently the management thought that a lone man might disturb the harmony of decorous family parties. A final point in these realms is that Argentine taxis, mostly heavy American cars of the 1938–40 vintage with a high hunched look, are probably the cheapest in the world.

A Handful of Other Cities

The second city in the country, ROSARIO, has 620,000 people, and is the chief city of Santa Fé—sometimes called the "Gringo" province because it was settled largely by foreigners—Basques and Swiss. It lies on the Paraná about two hundred miles north of Buenos Aires, and is an industrial nexus and major river port. South of Buenos Aires across the edge of the pampa is MAR DEL PLATA (pop. 160,000), the "Pearl of the Atlantic," of an entirely different genre. Like Punta del Este in Uruguay this is a resort town par excellence, which has five miles of glowing beach and the largest casino in the world, with the possible exception of a new one in the Lebanon; it has sixty-five gaming tables, and can hold twenty thousand people. Here is some of the best salt-water fishing in the hemisphere—for shark, *pejerrly*, *corbina*, and *merluza*. Another celebrated resort in a different part of the country is

SAN CARLOS DE BARILOCHE, in the Andean region; it was first developed by Swiss, and commands some spectacularly beautiful terrain protected by a national park near a superb lake, Nahuel Huapi. The writer Guillermo Estrella describes it thus: "If the Argentine has a garden in the north, it has a park in this . . . hallucinatory lake region of the south, which emerges from the most dismal desert in the world, as though it had been created for the purpose of giving plastic form in rock, plant, and water to the totality of Dante's vision: Hell at one end, Paradise at the other."[3]

SALTA (altitude 3,895 feet, pop. 120,000) and JUJUY (4,127 feet, 52,000 people) in the northwest were posts on the old stone-paved Inca trail, the Camino de los Incas, which led down the Andes from Peru. They were settled early in the colonial period and are extraordinarily rich in churches. Salta was an early pivot of trade across the continent. Here mules (60,000 in an average year) brought goods from the eastern lowlands to be exchanged for silver from the Andes; then the muleteers sold their animals at a great annual fair, and trekked home.[4] Further south, and still on the eastern slope of the cordillera, is the important city TUCUMÁN (pop. 290,000), situated in "The Garden of Argentina" and the center of the country's flourishing sugar industry; more than a million acres are planted to cane. Founded in 1565, Tucumán marks the southerly end of the Inca road; Argentine independence from Spain was declared here in 1816. Another historic city, MENDOZA (altitude 2,480 feet, pop. 140,000), was built in 1562, and is famous for its fruit and wine. Viticulture is a highly important national industry. General San Martín built up his Army of the Andes here, and used it as the jumping-off place for his campaigns to liberate Chile and Peru. A hundred miles west is the Uspallata Pass, where a well-known monument, Christ of the Andes, marks the frontier between Argentina and Chile and pledges peace between them; the Trans-Andean Railway crosses the cordillera here, under the icy lip of Mount Aconcagua, through a two-mile international tunnel at 10,500 feet.

Finally, CÓRDOBA (altitude 1,440 feet, pop. 600,000), the third city in the nation. It lies 430 miles northwest of Buenos Aires in the Andean foothills, facing the mountains to the west, the *pampa* to the east, and has great emotional significance to most Argentines. Assisted by its mild climate, strategic location, and other geographical advantages it is one of the fastest-growing cities in South America; industrialization is swiftly modifying its old forms. Founded in 1573 by Spanish invaders from Peru, Córdoba has, culturally and otherwise, an emphatic Jesuit background; it is sometimes

[3] Arciniegas, *op. cit.*
[4] *South American Handbook*, p. 120.

called the "Rome of Argentina." The university dates back to 1613, the cathedral to 1678. Contemporary Córdoba is a powerful focus of clerical—and political—reaction. It was the principal anti-Perón stronghold in the country, and the revolution of September, 1955, which displaced the dictator, was organized by the Córdoban military.

Two Roundtables

A young man telephoned me in Buenos Aires one morning, identifying himself only as a student and saying that he had read in the newspapers that I was "studying" Argentina and had been interviewing statesmen, diplomats, and men of affairs: but I would get nowhere, he went on, if I did not talk to young people as well. This was exactly what I wanted and my caller set up an informal conference with a group of his friends. We met in the bar of my hotel.

I thought that these young men—and one girl—would be Communists, because the boy who called had been so conspiratorial in manner and would not give his name. But all, it turned out, were children of the middle class, and had a bourgeois point of view. I went around the group of eight or nine asking what they majored in; seven were studying law, one medicine. I criticized them, saying that South America in general and Argentina in particular had far too many lawyers and doctors and why were they not setting out to be something more concretely useful—agronomists or engineers? The girl responded perkily, "Because mathematics bores us."

This made for a lively beginning.

I asked these attractive young people how they had voted,[5] and they seemed to be evenly divided between Christian Democrats and non-Illía radicals. They despised Illía, who was at this time still in office. "A front for army colonels." They despised Frondizi. "He cannot be trusted." Above all they despised Perón. "He was all things to all people. He told the people that he would rule like a benevolent Roman emperor but all he wanted was to make himself a millionaire." They resented the possibility of soon having to make a choice between Peronists and anti-Peronists for leadership of the country. "That was our fathers' problem. It should not still occupy us." Then as to politics in general: "This country is lost. No communication exists between government and people."

The Communists? Probably they number 20 percent of the student body of the university, but are less strong on the faculty. "The Soviet Embassy finances student elections." "The party is stronger in the intelligentsia than

[5] Argentines vote at age eighteen.

in the working class." "The Communists are no longer revolutionary." "They hope to come to power through elections under the guise of Peronism." "We do not want to be frightened of Communists like you in North America." This sally produced much laughter.

I went around the table again asking each youngster what he thought Argentina needed most, and the answers were well put. (1) To think in the future, not live in the past. (2) A sense of national objective. (3) To know where we are going. (4) Honesty in politics. (5) Moral education. (6) Confidence in our mission as a nation. "We were once a great country, but now we are nothing." (7) To realize that tomorrow is already today. (8) Honest politicians, political stability, and a will to solve their problems within the South American context, from a Latin American point of view.

I asked why so many Argentines disliked the United States. The reply came with a rush—"Envy!" But then these students were quick to add that, in their opinion, Argentines were not as anti-American as was often supposed. Every country has "anti" feelings about some other country and it just happens that, in Argentina, the United States has always been an object of suspicion largely because of our "imperialism." Argentina's resentment at American power and interference goes back a long way, my friends pointed out. The Argentines rejected our Point Four program in the 1950's just as they refuse to accept the Peace Corps today. We argued cheerfully. This round table was an experience refreshing in the extreme.

The next day an American banker set up a lunch for me. Among the guests were a former Argentine ambassador to the UN, a distinguished army general, several business executives, and a publisher who doubles as a TV commentator. Both the general and the TV man reminisced with good humor about periods they had spent in jail. All talked of Perón with hostility, but with a certain grudging affection as well. "He distributed wealth that did not belong to him." "He created a fool's paradise." Ever since Perón there has been a power "vacuum." The country is rapidly going to pot economically. Nobody can buy or build a house because it costs too much to borrow money. I put the same question I had asked the students, what did the country need most, and received a suggestively similar group of answers, like "Faith," "A sense of mission," and "Political stability and order— getting together, making a consensus."

The Communists and Foreign Policy

Perón gave recognition to the Soviet Union and, for all its fright of Communism, relations between Argentina and the USSR are normal. Argentina also recognizes several Communist satellite states in Eastern

Europe or gives hospitality to their trade missions. One little-known fact is that the Soviets extended a recent $100 million credit to Argentina during a phase of the petroleum crisis, to provide equipment and bolster the drilling program when Argentine production was falling down.[6] But this should not be too surprising. The United States gives aid to Communist countries like Poland and Yugoslavia. The world, though riven, is still round.

In August, 1965, the sale was announced of 40.4 million bushels of Argentine wheat to the Soviet Union for $54 million cash. A previous shipment of 36 million bushels was exchanged for Soviet crude oil. A few months later Czechoslovak emissaries arrived in Buenos Aires to arrange a swap of industrial equipment for agricultural products. In November, 1965, Argentina sold 1.5 million tons of wheat to China for $80 million, the largest transaction of this kind on record. Peking has been Argentina's biggest wheat buyer for two years running.

But the Argentine authorities continue to be severely on their guard against political infiltration or subversion by the Communists. Castroism is closely watched.

I have mentioned above that the Communist party in Argentina is legal and is the biggest in South America, but badly split. There are at least five splinter groups known as "telephone booth parties" because their membership is so small. I had the feeling that Communists in Argentina are less amateur and dilettantist than those I met in Brazil, but that they were still handicapped by allegiance to a system of which they had little first-hand knowledge or experience. Their clichés were spongy and rang back to phrases familiar in Europe in the 1930's, although Russia itself has changed vastly. But they have potential importance in Argentina for two main reasons, their power in the labor movement and their hope to absorb left-wing Peronists.

Following is a quotation from the Buenos Aires *Criterio*, a liberal Catholic magazine, as reproduced in *Atlas*, after United States intervention in the Dominican Republic in 1965:

> The Big Northern Power now claims for itself the right to judge and classify Latin American governments and to act upon its judgment, as it did in the Dominican Republic. The U.S. behavior pattern closely resembles that of the Soviet Union, the difference being that the leaders of the U.S. lack the ideological background the Russians possess and therefore fall into confusion. In addition, unilateral intervention by the U.S. can serve only to consolidate injustice and create new revolutionary situations.

As to relations with the United States in general the Argentines bear two main grudges—the conviction that we have long exploited Argentina, and

[6] *New York Times*, August 12 and November 20, 1965.

that Americans think that they can buy anybody or anything. A particular irritant—from days long past—is, of all things, the hoof-and-mouth disease. The United States forbids the import of *fresh* (not processed) beef on the ground that a large proportion of Argentine cattle is subject to the ravages of this disease, which, if let loose in America, could produce a disastrous epidemic. The United States does not discriminate against Argentina alone in this, but vis-à-vis all countries where hoof-and-mouth exists. The Argentines consider, however, that the exclusion of their beef is a national insult, and assert bitterly that America uses a sanitary pretext to effect an economic boycott. And indeed the powerful cattle lobby in Washington is eager to keep fresh Argentine beef out of the United States.

One issue in Argentine foreign policy has to do with the Falkland Islands, locally called the Malvinas. These are a windswept, treeless group in the South Atlantic, sparsely populated and devoted almost exclusively to sheep raising, which are a British possession and which Argentina claims. The British have had suzerainty over the Falklands since 1833, when they threw out an Argentine administration by a naval action. Continued British rule is, the Argentines say, arrant colonialism, and year by year the Buenos Aires government seeks to bring pressure—at the UN and elsewhere—to regain the islands, or at least open the subject to negotiation. Argentine nationalism is inflammatory on the issue. One little story goes back to Perón when all schools in Argentina, no matter of what nationality, had to have their instruction given in Spanish by Argentine teachers half the day. Perón visited St. George's, the smart Anglo-American boys' school in Buenos Aires, and, entering a history class, asked a boy, "To whom do the Islas Malvinas belong?"

"To England in the morning and to Argentina in the afternoon," the boy replied. Even Perón smiled.

Lords of the Land and Other Power Groups

Until recently the Argentine landed aristocracy held a position comparable to that of the feudal class in prewar Hungary or Poland. The *estancieros*, with their wealth based on cattle, were the heart of what is still called "the oligarchy," consisting of some two hundred families closely interlocked by matrimonial ties and mutual interest and bound by several generations of social primacy and aristocratic tradition. It was the chief source of the country's wealth, and no class in the western world ever quite matched it for haughty exclusiveness.

The great estates were fiefdoms. Many of their owners were—and are—

perfectly responsible and decent men. They do not resemble story-book villains. But it was the *system* which produced inequality and injustice. I visited once an Argentine estate that covered 120,000 acres; it had 40,000 sheep, 30,000 cattle, and around 6,500 horses, with its own railway station, churches, hospitals, telegraph, shops, and a police post, for a handful of people. The peons were serfs. Yet this was, as *estancias* went in those days, one of medium size, not really big. Moreover, the economic power of the senior oligarchs was augmented because most were—and still are—closely allied to financial and commercial interests in the towns. They were powerful in banks and industry and intimately tied in with foreign investment.

Today the rural patricians still own a large percentage of the best land, concentrated in large estates, although many properties have been fragmented by inheritance or amalgamated into companies on account of taxes. One estimate is that 17 percent of *all* land in Buenos Aires province, the "Queen Province," belongs to 82 family groups, 17 cattle- and crop-raising companies, and 20 smaller individual owners; one estate still covers 260,000 acres. The family relationships among *estancieros* are inordinately complex. There are 24 different branches of the Alzaga family. I met one man who had 37 first cousins. The most "traditional" families, most of them of Creole origin, are reckoned to number twenty, and include such formidable names as Anchorena, Elizalde, Guerrero, Pueyrredón, Peralta Ramos, Sáenz Rozas, Uribelarrea, and Martínez de Hoz.[7]

Several great families operate through companies:

Leloir	Cabaña Santa Sergia (and three others)
Santamarina	Santamarina e Hijos
Herrera Vegas-Pereira Iraola	Pampas y Hacienda (and 5 other companies)
Sánchez Elía	El Bagual
Duggan	Bernardo L. Duggan, S.A.
Jamieson	Estancia Moy Aiké (and 2 other companies)
Braun Menéndez	La Ganadera Argentina LTDA (and 7 other companies)
Harriet	Juan Alberto

The Argentine men of landed wealth still carry considerable weight in public affairs, but their political influence is not what it once was. The two factors that have principally weakened their position are political change and industrialization. Until about 1930 the *estancieros* completely dominated the Conservative party, and the army was their plaything. Dr. Frondizi told me

[7] José Luis de Imaz, *Los Que Mandan*, pp. 106–111, Buenos Aires, 1964.

that "nothing" counted in Argentina except the oligarchy until industrialization unalterably changed social and economic patterns. Then came the rise of a middle class, the increasing power of the radical party based on Italianate strength in the towns, the unionization of labor, Perón, and the entry of the proletariat into political society. A fundamental "change occurred in the country's sources of wealth,"[8] and this inevitably diluted and diminished the *estancieros*' power.

Evidences of change are suggestive. In 1936 eight out of the twelve leading politicians of the country, including the speaker of the House and the governor of Buenos Aires province, were members of the Círculo de Armas, an exclusivísimo club. In 1941 this number dropped to four; since then virtually none. In 1936 sixty-six percent of members of the national executive belonged to the *distinguido* families; today the percentage is infinitesimal. In 1936 only one cabinet minister and two provincial governors were sons of immigrants; by 1951 these had become a majority. Before 1930 most government appointments were made on the basis of family connections, with no damned nonsense about merit involved; but not a single member of Illía's administration had any social status. Up to Perón, government was based largely on birth, nepotism, money, and social prestige: today these criteria have virtually disappeared.

Not until Perón had a labor man ever been a cabinet minister or governor, and no Jew ever attained cabinet rank until 1951. Frondizi contributed a new element in social mobility by giving important posts to the managerial class—bankers, engineers, and advisors to foreign businesses. In the Guido government (1962–63) the secretaries of war, navy, and air force were all, curiously enough, sons of German immigrants. Another comparatively new influence is intellectual—that of the law faculty of the University of Buenos Aires, members of which now take part in almost every government.[9]

*

Also among power factors we must mention the Roman Catholic Church, which is extremely conservative in Argentina and which for many years operated hand in glove with the army and oligarchy. Both president and vice president of the republic must be Roman Catholics by terms of the constitution, and the church is supported by the state. Evidences of the extent of its entrenched power are many. The broadcasting of Protestant religious services

[8] Pendle, *Argentina*, p. 88.
[9] *Los Que Mandan, op. cit.*, is my source for most of the above.

is forbidden, and the ban on divorce is now absolute. Uruguayan and Mexican divorces are not recognized in Argentina.

On the other hand, there has never been an official church party, and the Christian Democrats did not win a single seat in the last elections. Practicing Catholics are probably a minority in the country at large. As of today the church does its utmost to keep out of politics, and dislikes having to take sides. The Perón wounds are largely healed.

The old churchly hierarchy is still, in a word, strong, but, as is true almost everywhere in Latin America, forces for change work from within. A dramatic instance of this came in January, 1966, when Antonio Cardinal Caggiano, archbishop of Buenos Aires, took a strong public line in support of a dissident labor group during a strike of municipal workers, as a result of which he was accused by other labor leaders of being Peronist. The cardinal replied that he was following the new spirit of the Vatican. He proceeded to rebuke one of the great diocesan archbishops for being laggard in matters of reform. Such events would have been impossible in Argentina even five years ago.

*

The third great power group is, of course, the army. An outright military junta rules the country under Onganía, although the pretense is carefully maintained that the armed forces are merely an "arbiter." The army is expensive to Argentina—just to speak in financial terms—and gets about a quarter of the budget, although it has not fought a war since the 1870's. Social services only get 8 percent, which is perhaps one reason why Argentina suffers from frustration and imbalance. A considerable proportion of the military budget goes to the support of *retired* officers, of whom there are thousands and who constitute a special bloc of their own. Some thirty thousand get full pay.

Another Powerful Force—Labor

José Alonso, the secretary general of the CGT or General Confederation of Labor, is a handsome articulate man in his early fifties, tough, earnest, modest, with a touch of the flamboyant as well. A garment worker for twenty-seven years, he rose in the labor movement stitch by stitch, like David Dubinsky in New York, and is today probably the most powerful labor leader in Argentina, or, for that matter, all South America. The CGT, which comprises about ninety principal unions and has a membership of more than two and a half million, is one of the largest organizations of its kind in the world, and represents something like 85 percent of the total organized Argentine labor force.

During the course of a long afternoon Alonso told us that Peronists control about 70 percent of his membership—the well-known "sixty-two unions." The Communists have 15 percent and the Socialists 5 percent, with the remaining 10 independent or undefined. The chief Communist unions, bound in an organization called MUCS (Movement of Unity and Syndicalist Coordination), are chemicals, printing, delicatessen workers, matches, and newsboys. But the Communists play little role in the three governing bodies of the CGT—the Director's Council (no Communists), the Federated Central Committee (five Communists out of eighteen) and the General Assembly (25 out of 600). Alonso himself, a leading Peronist, is vigorously anti-Communist.

Italian syndicalism has had a certain influence on the Argentine labor movement; also the CGT was colored for a time by Italian labor leaders who fled Mussolini's Fascism. There are vestigial anarchist traces as well. One point Alonso made was that labor got 30 percent of the country's economic product before Perón; 53 percent under him; 46 percent today.

I have written in these pages something about Argentine wealth. There is also such a thing as Argentine poverty, which can be as miserable as anything in the western world. Shortage in housing is severe. The minimum wage has lost all meaning as a result of inflation and devaluation of the currency, and now amounts to about 9,800 pesos a month, or $49 at the present rate of exchange. "Can a man live on that?" I asked. Alonso replied, "He has to." But, as a matter of fact, many do not, because there are thousands of two-earner families. In 1955, Alonso told us, a worker with two children could buy enough food for his family by three hours and forty-three minutes of work a day, and the rest of his wages could go to other essentials; today, six hours and fourteen minutes are necessary. A chronic crisis in transportation aggravates this pinch. Buenos Aires continually spreads out, conveyances deteriorate, and traffic becomes more congested; a worker may spend as long as 3½ hours a day getting to his job and back, sharply cutting down his earning hours.[10]

*

Two other Peronist leaders in the labor movement are Augusto Timoteo Vandor, an ex-marine corporal and head of the powerful metal workers union,

[10] Alonso was ousted as secretary general of the CGT as these pages went to press.

which has 260,000 members, and Andrés Framini, a former textile worker who once won the governorship of Buenos Aires province by 400,000 votes but had his victory annulled by the military. Their unions are rich almost on the scale of American unions. Both men are members of a five-man "Committee for the Return" which is supposed to coordinate Peronist activity in the country, and Perón is supposed to be in steady contact with them. Sometimes emissaries arrive from Madrid carrying instructions in his actual voice recorded on tape.

Vandor's strength lies in the hard-line unions, "the sixty-two," whereas Framini is more openly political, also older and more emotional. Vandor still has a nickname dating from his days in the marines—"the Wolf." About forty-five, he is of mixed Spanish and Dutch descent, and spent many years as a metallurgical worker. He is not an effective orator, but is shrewd, personable, and ambitious; if Peronismo survives the leader's eventual death he is generally expected to become head of the movement. His influence began to fade, however, in recent months because of a seeming conflict with Perón's wife Isabel, who returned to Argentina for a prolonged visit in 1966 to oversee the local faithful. A new wing, the "Isabelistas," has consequently come into being.

In 1964 the sixty-two unions which are in effect the Peronist party announced a *plan de lucha* (combat plan) for a straight-out test of strength with the government, to be featured by "occupation" of the factories. Some 150,000 members of the CGT did indeed "seize" several thousand factories and take them over for periods ranging from a few hours to a few days, in a manner reminiscent of prewar Italy. Illía rolled with this punch, and did not attempt to intervene by police or military means; there was no bloodshed, and the strikers soon withdrew. What would happen under the Onganía regime would be different. Probably no such demonstration would be permitted at all, although the general realizes full well the necessity to get along with labor.

Argentina—a Recapitulation

1. Argentina is the most powerful and advanced republic in South America, but is riven by a formidable crisis. This is the "sick man" of the continent.

2. Since the assumption of power by General Onganía in June, 1966, the country has been an outright and overt military dictatorship, with democracy and civil liberties suppressed.

3. The cause of this coup was largely national disintegration caused in

turn by the 65–35 percent split in the country between anti-Peronists and Peronists.

4. The old entrenched powers of the church and landed oligarchy have been attenuated. Organized labor is an important force, more so than in any other South American country.

5. Some modus vivendi between Onganía and the Peronists may be worked out, despite their traditional antipathy.

6. Danger from Communism is minimal at present.

7. The heart of the country is being eaten away by inflation, but, even so, 1966 turned out to be a better year than most observers dared hope.

8. Relations with the United States are correct, but Argentina is the most anti-American country on the continent.

The World of Jorge Luis Borges

Long after the names of most political characters in this book are forgotten that of Jorge Luis Borges is likely to be remembered. A remarkable poet, essayist, scholar, story writer, and specialist in the abstruse, Borges is one of the most provocative writers South America has ever produced, with a reputation gradually spreading outside his native Argentina and the Spanish-speaking world. Four of his books are available in English, *Dreamtigers*, *Fictions*, *Labyrinths*, and *Other Inquisitions*. In 1962 he reached the world stage for the first time by sharing the Formentor International Publishers' Prize with Samuel Beckett.

Born in 1899, Borges has lectured and taught in the United States, and is at present director of the Argentine National Library and professor of English literature at the University of Buenos Aires. Even so several supposedly literate Americans in Buenos Aires had never heard of him when I asked his whereabouts. But I tracked him down, reached him on the telephone, and asked if we could meet. He said that he would pick me up in my hotel one afternoon that week. I was not sure of the quality of his English, and I invited a bilingual friend to stand by and serve as an interpreter, if necessary. I need not have worried. Borges's English is better than mine, and he speaks with no trace of accent. It impressed me that he had suggested meeting in my hotel, because I had been told by Argentine acquaintances that it was difficult for him to get around.

Borges has a wonderful face—seared, humorous, questing, faery. His voice has a light puckish tone, and he loves to talk, making gestures as if he were juggling invisible small balloons. We drove to the National Library, which he described gaily as being of the "Turkish bath school of architecture," and proceeded then to the headquarters of the Argentine Writers' Club, a building at once haughty and ramshackle which, of all things, reminded me of the Tolstoyan headquarters of the Writers' Union in Moscow. Here Borges pointed out literary souvenirs precious to him—various portraits and manuscripts, a ravishing portrait of Victoria Ocampo, and an impressive line drawing of himself. "I look like an archbishop. I was fat then." Maybe so, but the picture didn't *look* fat, and I remembered stories I had heard about him in his youth, when he was one of the most romantic *beaux* of his time.

Some members of the Argentine avant-garde tend to dismiss Borges as little more than "a venerable showpiece of Hispanic culture," but he is an extremely modern writer by any reasonable definition of the term. His dark, haunting, infinitely subtle stories resemble those of De Quincey, Poe, G. K. Chesterton, Kafka, the contemporary German existentialists, and, above all, Joseph Conrad. He is a difficult writer to grasp, if only because he combines melodrama with elaborate intellectualization. He thinks of life, he told me, as a "maze without a center." One of his most celebrated stories, "Funes the Memorious," which appeared in the *Paris Review* in 1962, has been explained as being a cryptic study of insomnia, but its metaphorical quality is such that this theme is not easily visible. One subject that appealed to him—so at least I have heard—was suggested by the early H. G. Wells, dealing with a flower that devoured a man. A recent critic in *Holiday* calls him "arcane," "defiant," "ornately mannerist," "outrageous," "metaphysical," and "hallucinatory." John Updike, dealing with him at appreciative length in *The New Yorker*,[11] talks about his inveterate bookishness, his preoccupation with the "hidden pivots" of history, and a basic concern for "the gravity of the human condition." He is a narrow writer, but one of tempestuous intensity.

This is a Borges poem which reflects one aspect of his disposition. He wrote it in English:

> What can I hold you with?
> I offer you lean streets.
> I offer you the bitterness of a man who has looked long at the lonely
>   moon.
> I offer you my ancestors.
> I can give you my loneliness, my darkness, the hunger of my heart; I
>   am trying to bribe
> you with uncertainty, with danger, with defeat.[12]

[11] October 30, 1965.
[12] From *Obras Completas Poemas*, 1925–1953, Emece Editores, S. A., Buenos Aires.

Borges is blind. He told me that he could not see my face or tell the color of my tie. Yet, with a stick, he walked with perfect security and grace in the surroundings with which he is familiar. His great great-grandfather, great-grandfather, grandfather, and father all slowly went blind; he himself began to lose his sight about a decade ago. I urged him to travel to the United States to see some ophthalmological specialists there, but he replied with a sigh that he had tried everything and that his condition—he didn't define it exactly—was incurable. His sister, a painter, is going blind as well.

Borges lives with his mother, a spry old lady of eighty-eight; his background is continental Spanish crossed with English and Portuguese. One of his grandparents came from Northumberland; another was a Portuguese ship's captain; still another forebear was an army officer who led a cavalry charge in an Argentine civil war, an event which still seizes his imagination. "Argentines are the best fighters in South America: after that, Venezuelans and Colombians."

He was born, he told me, in an old house in what is now the commercial center of Buenos Aires; it has long since disappeared, but it had a patio, iron gates, creepers, birds. He learned English as soon as Spanish; French came later. I asked him about the derivation of the name "Borges," and he sailed off at once into a far-traveling survey of its etymology; the name not only connotes "city" (Pittsburgh, Burgos, Edinburgh), but "mountain," "citizen" (burgher) and "bourgeois." I could not get him off the subject of proper names. Did I know that Kierkegaard meant "churchyard" in Danish, and could this have any symbolic significance? Where did the word "Zen" come from? (He fairly rolled in delight when I mentioned something that happened to be new to him, that a favorite Zen Buddhist riddle asks what is the noise of one hand clapping.) Did I know that the Russian word for bread, *khleb*, had a close relation to "loaf" in Middle English?

Borges is positively mad about early English, and conducts a postgraduate class in Anglo-Saxon. He will have to retire from the university this year, having passed sixty-five. "But I feel younger now than when I was forty. At that age I was miserable, but I enjoyed the misery." He loves to make literary pilgrimages, and, visiting the graves of English poets or pausing at their tombstones, recites long sections of their verse by heart. He was once so moved by a church in the Cotswolds that, I was told, he fell on his knees and recited the Lord's Prayer in Middle English. Not only is his memory for verse striking; so is his universal capacity for literary allusion. During our afternoon he broke into recitations from Chesterton, Valéry, Edgar Lee Masters ("Anne Rutledge"), and several other poets, and mentioned a wide miscellany of writers. One paradox, if it can be believed, is that he cannot memorize his *own* verse, although he knows countless other poets by heart; thus it is very difficult for him to put down his own work on tape since he cannot see to read.

It was difficult to persuade him to talk about Argentina, about which I was eager to have his opinion. "Argentina *was* a quite important country." Now, "All is disintegration—we stagnate." The Argentines have pride, humor, and "intellectual but not moral conscience." He listened with delight to an off-color joke about Evita Perón, and called her husband an abomination, a laughingstock and coward. "We were taken in, bamboozled. Both my mother and sister were arrested. I lost my job because I had sympathized with the allies during the war. . . . Perón sent *firemen* to burn the churches. . . . Nobody had the guts to fight."

Then his talk fluttered and floated back to Middle English, the Stoic philosophers, Greek texts, and the "wonderful nightmares" of Conrad, Wells, and Chesterton. "You will think I am an old fogy to talk about Chesterton." I asked him if he knew a small book by Chesterton on Robert Browning and, remarkably enough, he quoted from it the very sentence I had in mind—a passage explaining Browning's ambiguity on the grounds that he was always in such a hurry. Borges's talk, in spite of its range, is not in the least heavy. He is airy, colloquial, full of "don't-you-knows," quaintness, nuances, small jokes and quips. Late in the day, when I had to go, he told me how he had come to take up writing short stories, after decades devoted solely to verse and essays. He had never tackled fiction. Then he had a severe fall, and was ill for months; he showed me the bumps still visible on his head. He did not write a word for months, and did not dare to return to verse because he feared that he might have altogether lost his powers. So he said to himself cheerfully, "But if I try fiction that will be something new and readers will not be able to compare my old self with the new and hold the new against me." Thus began the stream of stories that have made him famous in his old age.

Borges took me to the door with a light resonant laugh. This was the best afternoon I had in South America.

CHAPTER 12

Uruguay on the Rocks

I have worked to prepare a plan of social reforms all designed to look after and to liberate the working classes.
　　　　　　　　　　　—JOSÉ BATLLE Y ORDÓÑEZ

A child is born a little Blanco or a little Colorado, and rarely deserts his color.
　　　　　　　　　　　—LORD BRYCE IN 1912

THIS small agrarian republic is the purest democracy in South America and one of its most progressive states. It takes its own somewhat ornery line on foreign affairs. Until recently it was one of the most prosperous countries in the hemisphere, and its people are middle class, independent-minded, homogeneous, and modest. On a map Uruguay may seem to be little more than a northeasterly projection of Argentina, but a local epigram says that there is one infallible way to tell the two countries apart. "If you ask a man from Buenos Aires how much he has he'll say ten million, when the truth is that he has one. Ask a Uruguayan, and he'll tell you one when he has twenty."

Uruguay is emancipated, civilized, and enlightened, yes, but its peculiar bureaucratic procedures are such that it has become almost a parody of democracy. There are abrasions and paradoxes without number. As for instance—

Item: It has the most advanced social security system in the Americas, and is a welfare state par excellence like Denmark or New Zealand. A man can retire on full pay for life at fifty-five or even earlier. It is also much given to bad management, inefficiency, and abuse of its good intentions. Its idealism has got it into a mess.

Item: There is no single head of state; it has nine presidents, not merely

220

one. The presidency, based on the example of Switzerland, is plural or collegial, and is vested in a council of nine with one man serving as chairman a year at a time. Three out of the nine "presidents" must be members of the opposition, which seems crazy and, as a matter of fact, is.

Item: Most Uruguayans are nominally Catholic, but the country is the most anticlerical in South America. This leads to such strangenesses as that Christmas is known officially as "Family Day," Epiphany (January 6) as "Children's Day," and Easter Week as "Tourist Week." One newspaper refused for many years to capitalize "God" and even called the Pope "Mister," using his non-papal name. Several leading families are overtly atheist—something very rare on the continent—and do not even have religious services at funerals. The Vatican has, for these and other reasons, often seemed to be cool to Uruguay, and the country never had a cardinal till the reign of John XXIII.

Uruguay, it would seem, is blessed with fabulous advantages:

A homogeneous population largely of white European stock. The country is the "whitest" in South America.

No population explosion. The rate of expansion is only 1.4 percent, the lowest on the continent.

A temperate climate.

No large uninhabited or undeveloped areas.

The highest literacy rate (91 percent) on the continent, along with Argentina.

The best public health record on the continent.

A strong middle class, with no pronounced extremes between rich and poor.

High living standards on South American terms—the average per capita income is $550 per year.

A sound tradition of political democracy and stability. There has been only one brief period of dictatorship (1933–38) since 1904. Violence is deplored. The last coup d'état was made by, of all things, the fire department back in 1942.

No domination by the army. Only 8 percent of the budget goes to the armed forces, and this is what enabled the country to spend so much on social reform for so many years.

Uruguay (unlike Brazil and Paraguay) never permitted slavery. Since independence it has never fought other than a defensive war. It abolished the death penalty long ago. It was the first country in Latin America to legalize divorce,[1] the first to grant status to illegitimate children, the first to introduce woman suffrage, and the first to make voting obligatory. Far in advance of the time, it adopted many years ago such measures as the eight-

[1] But divorce is possible only if the wife gives consent.

hour day, free medical care for the poor, free tuition at universities, thirteen months' pay for a twelve-month year, ownership of all subsoil rights by the state, and the separation of church and state.

In spite of all this and much else in the realm of the progressive, Uruguay faces grave difficulties today, and is the nearest to bankruptcy of any South American country, except perhaps Colombia. Its political institutions are shaky, and the possibility of a Communist coup is not excluded. A joke has it that only two things could cause a revolution in Uruguay—persistent defeat in football or tinkering with the welfare state. But today's crisis is beyond the joking stage. Why has Uruguay fallen into its present condition of muddle, stalemate, and abuse of its own institutions? Why can't it make both ends meet? Let us explore.

Countryside and Capital

Uruguay looks insignificant on the map, and indeed it is the smallest country in South America in area, but it is bigger than it seems—more than six times the size of Belgium. The word "Uruguay" derives from an old Indian term meaning "River of Painted Birds"; the official name is República Oriental del Uruguay. Locally it is sometimes known as the *Banda Oriental*, or Eastern Shore (of the Uruguay River) and its citizens are called Uruguayos, pronounced "Urugajos." The people speak a Río Platense argot even thicker than that of Argentina, but strongly resent it if anybody says so.

Uruguay has an estimated 2,800,000 people, 7,300,000 cattle, and 24,000,000 sheep. It is shaped like the end of a big toe, and has about 200 miles of Atlantic coastline. The countryside is composed mostly of rolling prairie and grasslands, and produces wheat, meat, and wool. The classic British writer W. H. Hudson called it *The Purple Land* in his book of that name many years ago, because its billowing pastures are covered every summer with violet-colored verbena and other flowers. Rural Uruguay closely resembles Argentina; here are unending miles of cattle country, and the *gaucho* is a true old-fashioned lord of the herds.

I quote from the *South American Handbook*, 1965 edition, pages 422–23:

> The great pastoral figure is the gaucho, or cowboy, usually stocky and wearing a broad brimmed black hat, tight fitting shirt, hand embroidered bolero-style jacket, knotted scarf, baggy trousers, a silver decorated belt and short leather boots. When it is cold he wears a *ruana*—a square of wool with a slit in the centre to slip his head through. He carries a silver handled rawhide whip, and a silver handled short knife at the belt. . . . His saddle is usually hand tooled and decorated with silver; and the bridle is elegant. He carries with him his

silver-edged gourd and silver straw for sipping his yerba mate. He is not easily separated from his horse, and sits astride it when talking to friends or even fishing.

Land is still cheap in Uruguay; a hectare (2.47 acres) costs about as much as a steer. There are no estates as enormous as many in Brazil or Argentina, though several are quite big; about 1 percent of the population still owns roughly 33.5 percent of the land, but the landowners do not form an oligarchical *class*. Agriculture is not nearly as productive as it should be; the yield has scarcely advanced in a quarter of a century, largely because techniques have not been modernized. A man with a biggish ranch earns enough to get along, and stubbornly resists technical change; his tendency will be to buy more land rather than improve what he has, partly because this is cheaper and also because land gives prestige and is a hedge against inflation. It is less expensive to buy than to improve. (We shall encounter this same phenomenon in Chile.) Most farms are, in American opinion, "miserably" operated. Cattle and sheep are raised side by side, which is unusual in grazing communities, and would have been unheard of in the American west in pioneer days; the pasture here is rich enough to support both.[2] One product out of the ordinary is *nonato*, the skin of an unborn lamb used in leather crafts; another is nutria, the fur of an animal resembling a beaver—Uruguayans boast that theirs is the finest in the world.

Why is Uruguay so underpopulated? The country could easily support twice its present population. One answer I heard was, "Because we are so civilized," meaning that almost everybody is advanced enough to practice contraception. But the rate of abortions is disturbingly high in relation to the total population, about 150,000 a year. Clinics giving advice on birth control and the like are hard at work.

Concrete population figures are, oddly enough, hard to get. For all its addiction to rationality, Uruguay does not seem to be rational about statistics, vital and otherwise: no census was taken from 1908 to 1963, and it is still all but impossible to get accurate figures even on such details as the gross national product, as an example. The country is, as noted above, predominantly white, like Argentina. The Indians—Charrúas—were quickly killed off by the Spanish invaders, and few pure Indians survive; only a small proportion of the population, mostly up-country *gauchos*, have enough Indian blood to be classified as *mestizos*. There are practically no Negroes. Much of the European white stock entering the country since the colonial period is (as in Argentina) Italian; there are also substantial numbers of

[2] *Gauchos* do not eat beef as much as lamb, although they crave it. This is because refrigeration facilities are scant and a whole steer, if butchered, would spoil before it could be eaten.

Spaniards, Basques, Portuguese, and, in the past two generations, eastern European Jews. The Jews have been well assimilated, and, in sharp contrast to Argentina, very little anti-Semitism exists. Recently a project was announced for opening the country to ten thousand Chinese emigrant families from Taiwan.[3]

Uruguayan society is remarkably homogeneous and, in the towns, almost solidly middle-class. A few rich families exist, but these are not ostentatious and do not even remotely resemble the gigolo aristocracy in Lima or Buenos Aires. There is no elite if only because everybody knows everybody else. The Uruguayos are serious bourgeois people, and do not go in for social effervescence. I don't think I have ever met a Uruguayan playboy.

MONTEVIDEO, the capital, has a bit over a million people, more than a third of the country's population. There are no other cities of consequence. The name Montevideo is supposed to have come from the cry of a Portuguese sailor on a ship of Magellan's, who, peering along the estuary, saw a knoll called El Cerro, and shouted, *"Monte vid eu"* (I see a mountain). But El Cerro was—and is—a very small mountain indeed, and the story is probably apocryphal. A colloquial name today is "Town of Roses"; no fewer than 850 varieties of rose are to be found in its gardens. Montevideo is probably the pleasantest city in all South America for a foreigner to live in from the point of view of the amenities, although it has dull corners and lacks veneer. There are no slums or *favelas*, the public services are well maintained, and the streets are clean—or used to be. Buses (fare 3 cents) provide excellent transportation everywhere, and taxis are plentiful and cheap. You can even drink the water.

But what really counts is the sea view and the incomparable beaches. The Plata estuary is a hundred miles wide here, and gives out a tang like the ocean. The beaches extend all the way up the coast to the Brazilian border with scarcely a break. PUNTA DEL ESTE, the resort town (pop. 16,000) where the Alliance for Progress was put into motion, is famous for its beaches. Those in Montevideo itself (like those in Chicago in older days) lie directly in front of the towers of the city, and are lined by an avenue known as the Rambla, one of the most comely boulevards in the world. Part of it is named for Woodrow Wilson, and the visitor will notice Franklin D. Roosevelt Park and the Plaza Winston Churchill. The wide strips of beach are an important economic factor in the life of Uruguay, because they attract tourists,

---

[3] Citizens of largely Italian blood today are called Gringos or Tanos; the Spaniards are known as Gallegos, although few come from Galicia. Old-generation Jews are nicknamed Rusos—Russians—whether they came from actual Russian territory or not. "Gringo" is also used to mean foreigners generally.

particularly from Argentina. About a hundred thousand Argentines a year escape the shrill rigors of Buenos Aires to take holidays in the blander atmosphere of Montevideo, much as South Africans leave Johannesburg for vacations in Mozambique. Second, the beaches are lungs for the people. Nobody is allowed to own beach property in Uruguay except the government, and no private building is allowed; the beaches are put at the disposal of the citizenry for their relaxation and enjoyment. Their use is free, and you can rent a mat and umbrella for half a cent a day.

The principal square in Montevideo is Independence Plaza, dominated by the twenty-six story Palacio Salvo, which I think is the ugliest office building I have ever seen. Here too is the colonnaded presidential palace where the country's nine presidents have nine neat little offices side by side. The tone of Montevideo is somewhat hard to define. It is frugal, yet open. There are two large gambling casinos on the Rambla, both operated by the municipality, and they bring in a handsome revenue;[4] stakes are low and the tables absolutely honest. Their atmosphere is, however, somewhat grubby, except during carnival. Montevideo takes carnival almost as seriously—and floriferously—as Rio does. Night life in Montevideo is not altogether easy to find, but uninhibited when you find it; the Uruguayans may be square, but they are not hypocrites or puritans. Girls in the strip joints peel down to literally nothing a couple of yards away from the visitor, and I was told that the price of a sexual encounter "of the first class" was $6.

Montevideo has several excellent newspapers and what is probably the most outspoken liberal—or call it radical—weekly in South America, *Marcha*. Anyway it is radical enough to be forbidden entrance into Argentina. It resembles the *New Statesman* of London to some extent. There are no fewer than 60 radio stations, several of them owned by the government, and four TV channels, one government-owned, three commercial. Other elements in communication are primitive and eccentric in the familiar South American manner. You have a better chance of reaching New York by telephone quickly than Buenos Aires next door. Or send a telegram to Paraguay!—it may take days to get there.

One intellectual influence that can still be felt is that of José Enrique Rodó (1872–1917), whose celebrated essay *Ariel* is a kind of lampoon on the United States. Latin America is the youthful, idealistic, and heroic Ariel, while the United States is Caliban with its "vulgarity, utilitarianism, and egalitarian mediocrity."[5] We are also castigated for our "material aggran-

---

[4] The similar casino at Punta del Este is state-operated.

[5] *Encounter*, September, 1965. See also Arthur Schlesinger, Jr., *A Thousand Days*, p. 793.

dizement, insufficiency, and emptiness." One large contemporary influence is that of the university. This has eighteen thousand students and is strongly under left-wing influence, but is not Communist controlled. One professor told me, "The students are in revolt for revolt."

The Montevideans love two things above all—*fútbol* (soccer) and meat. Almost all South Americans are football-mad, but none are madder than the stout citizens of Uruguay. The country has two first-rate teams, Peñarol and Nacional, and has won the Olympic and world's championships twice each. Wild scenes attend the important games—and not merely in the stadium. In a restaurant one evening I saw middle-aged citizens rise suddenly and smash glasses and chairs and hurl beefsteaks at each other in sheer frenzied delight when they heard over the radio that Uruguay had scored a point to break a tie, even though this was in a minor game.

Uruguayos are formidably carnivorous, and are the fourth-largest consumers of meat per capita in the world; consumption averages 176 pounds a year a head. Workers in the packing houses get five pounds of meat free per day to take home.[6] This is the heart of *parrillada* territory. A *parrillada* is an indoor barbecue grill, plainly furnished as a rule, inexpensive, and displaying what seem to be abnormal quantities of raw meat on giant trays waiting to be fed into the grill—and then into the guests. A typical dinner consists of three courses, all meat. I had one which began with pork spareribs, proceeded to portions of a whole baby lamb butchered in a manner unknown in North America and rather resembling the *meshoui* of Morocco, and ended with a triumphant *lomo*, or tenderloin of beef. This was considered to be a simple dinner. We did not go in for exoticisms like roast udder or testicles *en gelée*. It was also one of the best dinners I have ever had outside the great restaurants of France.

The obligatory service charge on restaurant and hotel bills is a stiff 22 percent, and you are supposed to add a voluntary tip as well.

Uruguay: *Its How and Why*

> *I am convinced that the remedy for all our ills lies in electoral freedom, in honest elections.*
>
> —JOSÉ BATLLE Y ORDÓÑEZ

The essence of Uruguay lies in a fundamental double concept—love of freedom and fear of losing it. This explains why political leadership is deliberately made diffuse, so that the risk of rule by an individual dictator is

[6] Howard Kershner, *Human Events*, December 14, 1963.

minimized, and why the entire social structure of the state is bent toward the *protection of the citizen*. It also helps to explain the country's cautious independent foreign policy.

A *conquistador* named Juan Díaz de Solís discovered Uruguay in 1516; he was captured by Indian cannibals and eaten.[7] The country was settled late, and its colonial history is meager. The Spaniards did not build a permanent settlement at Montevideo until 1624, when Asunción, up the river in Paraguay, had been in existence for eighty years and was already a flourishing community. Spain did not export much to Uruguay in the way of art or culture, and the area had little—if any—national or subnational identity. Then it rose to importance as a kind of pawn because of its position between the two emerging giants Argentina and Brazil. Each sought it as a buffer strip. European politics naturally entered into this rivalry and the British, operating against Spain in the Napoleonic Wars, took Montevideo for a brief period in 1806. Uruguay is thus one of the few South American republics ever to have its capital occupied by a European power other than Spain or Portugal.[8]

Argentina then became dominant. I am heavily condensing a story of great complexity. In 1821 Brazil annexed Uruguay outright, and held it for five years under the name Cisplatine Province. Meantime Uruguayan nationalists, craving independence, had organized a strong revolutionary movement. Under the leadership of the patriot José Gervasio Artigas, the George Washington of the country, "Father of Uruguay" and "Protector of the Free People," and a former cattle rustler, the patriots fought both Brazil and Argentina. In 1825 a band of thirty-three Uruguayan adventurers, known today as the "thirty-three immortals" led forays against Brazil. The upshot was the creation of an independent Uruguay in 1828, largely because the British, fearing further Brazilian penetration into the Plata region, put pressure on Argentina to permit the new state to be born.

Long before this the Spaniards had sent one hundred head of cattle into the country, which were the origin of its economy. In the early days of independence "Montevideo . . . ate a mixture of marrow and beef suet as a substitute for butter, and used bones and hoofs for fuel."[9]

After independence politics became chaotic. Argentina supported one local faction, Brazil another. Two political parties rose, the Blancos (whites) and Colorados (reds). The old story is that the Whites were

[7] Alive, some chroniclers say.

[8] Buenos Aires was also occupied by the British briefly during the Napoleonic period.

[9] Pendle, *op. cit.*, p. 152. Incidentally, Uruguay's first constitution was patterned on that of Massachusetts.

originally Blues but the blue badges on their uniforms faded to white; they represented the original Spanish stock and rural and commercial interests; the Reds were more radical, men of the towns, who drew increasingly on Italian immigration as a source of power. Civil war ("La Guerra Grande") broke out in 1843, and continued intermittently for a generation; one episode was a siege of Montevideo which lasted eight whole years. A detail little remembered is that Garibaldi, the great Italian patriot, came to Uruguay and fought valiantly with the Colorados. In 1880 one would-be *caudillo* gave up the struggle to tranquilize the country with the words, "These people are ungovernable."

However, political turmoil did at last die down. The Colorados held power uninterruptedly from 1865 until 1958—an unprecedented ninety-three years. The country pulled itself together. Largely this was due to the reformatory zeal of a man named José Batlle y Ordóñez, whose career is without parallel in the history of South America. Today—to jump to the present—Colorados and Blancos are still the only significant political parties. The divergences between them are not as marked as in former days. Colorados are left of center, Blancos right of center, but there are individual Colorados more conservative than the average Blanco, and vice versa. What makes a man join either party is largely a matter of inheritance—affiliation based on blood more than conviction. People are Colorado or Blanco much in the way that youthful Britons once went to either Oxford or Cambridge, under the influence of family tradition.

José Batlle (pronounced "Batje") y Ordóñez was president of Uruguay twice, from 1903 to 1907 and again from 1911 to 1915; his father had also been a Colorado president. Batlle's influence lasted long after his second presidency and continued until his death in 1929. He was a prodigious figure—also idiosyncratic. The father of both Uruguay's noncentralized political system and the welfare state, he was a journalist by profession, and lived in Europe for some years studying political systems and techniques. He was a man of action as well as an intellectual, and in his youth killed in a duel the father of the present chairman of the presidential council. (Dueling is still, oddly enough, legal in Uruguay, and duels between politicians still occasionally take place.) Batlle was universally known as Don Pepe. Very stout, he had a bland, agreeable look and wore a large, tumbling mustache.

Reaching the presidency for the first time in 1903, after a hot election, Batlle managed to negotiate an end to a new civil war that had broken out between Colorados and Blancos, and Uruguay has never had any civil strife of consequence from that date to this. His central concept was that dictatorial means are not necessary for the reformation of society. Clichés that became fashionable many years later—such as that Mussolini's Fascism was "justified" because "he made the trains run on time"—would only have made him snort. He believed in justice, democratic methods, and reform. He was a decided anti-Communist, and felt that fair and free social development would eliminate the class struggle more effectively than Marxism. His thinking was far ahead of its time. "His life objective was to make a paternalistic state whereby everyone would be employed in his productive years, and supported by the state thereafter."[10] And Batlle's germinal ideas worked—for a time. Uruguay became not merely the best run and stablest but the most prosperous country on the continent.

Batlle worked out his theories about the plural executive as early as 1917, but they did not become fully effective until years later. They were embodied in the constitution in full in 1951. The objective was to curtail irresponsible personal rule, which had been the curse of the country, by means of a rigid set of checks and balances to dilute presidential power. Get rid of the man on horseback by eliminating—or rather multiplying—the horse: that was the idea.

This is the way the system works today. Voters elect a nine-man presidential council for a four-year term; six of the nine members represent the majority party, the other three the opposition. Those four of the majority who won the most votes then act as chairmen of the council in turn, each for a year. Presidential decisions are taken by a free vote of all nine, which makes government cumbersome, dilutes executive power, and sometimes makes any effective decision impossible. The electoral system is inordinately complex because of the original concept that the rights of every voter to a free choice among candidates must be safeguarded to the utmost. The Blancos have split into seven factions, called *sublemas*, the Colorados into three. All these may run candidates in a presidential election, so that the voter is faced not merely with a choice between Blanco and Colorado but among candidates *within* each party. Thus the general election is also a kind of primary. It is as if, in the United States, a voter had had to decide not between Johnson and Goldwater in 1964, but among Johnson, Goldwater, Humphrey, Bobby Kennedy, Rockefeller, Nixon, and a hundred others. In a recent Uruguayan election candidates appeared representing no fewer than 123 party groups, or "lists." The paradox rises that people vote for nameless numbers; democracy becomes a *reductio ad absurdum*.

Other details are even more anarchic. Uruguay has a cabinet as well as the National Council, but cabinet members are subject to dismissal if they are

10 *Inside Latin America*, p. 336.

censored by parliament—again we see the country's demoniac zeal for limiting authority and thereby inadvertently suffocating it. While the presidential election is direct, the Senate is chosen by proportional representation and the lower chamber on a geographical basis. So anomalies are frequent. The party with six of the nine presidents may have less than a third of the Congress. How do laws get passed? Sometimes they don't. Legislative as well as executive authority is hamstrung or confused.

Still another seemingly wild eccentricity is that the government, i.e., the taxpayer, finances the campaigns of *all* candidates, even the Communists. This too derives from the national obsession with "pure" democracy, and is designed to prevent the capture of any party or subparty by private money. *Every* party is reimbursed by the national treasury for its expenses during a campaign on the basis of the number of votes received. Another point is that government salaries may not be raised in an election year. Patronage, very important in a bureaucratic state like Uruguay, is given out to members of *all* parties after an election in accordance with their voting strength, so that the civil service is riven with factionalism.

All the foregoing—and more to come—arises out of this extraordinary personage José Batlle y Ordóñez. He died a generation ago, but his wing of the Colorados, the Batllistas, still plays a large role in national affairs. A "dynasty" has carried on. One of José's sons, César, became an important political figure in his own right, as did a nephew, Luis Batlle Berres, who died in 1964. César and Luis were bitter rivals. Luis was president of the republic in 1947–50, the third man in three generations of his family to hold this post, an unexampled record. Like his uncle, he was a tempestuous character, and fought several duels; the last took place when he was sixty-one, and his opponent, a former minister of war, was sixty-eight; both men were wounded. The most interesting member of the family today is Jorge Batlle Ibañez, thirty-eight, the son of Luis and grandnephew of José; he is a deputy, the editor of one of the family newspapers, owner of the radio station "Ariel," and an exceptionally gifted young man devoted to the public service.[11]

The Colorados lost power, as noted above, in 1958, and the Blancos took office after ninety-three years in the wilderness. They won again in 1962. Most Blancos today stand firmly for the repeal of the plural presidential system, although they have gained greatly from it. Their more conservative members oppose the welfare state as well but they cannot make an open

---

[11] The Batlles own *El Día*, the country's most influential daily, and *Acción*, an evening paper. Jorge's brother is the country's leading pianist.

issue of this because to do so would cost votes. The other parties are minor. The Christian Democrats ran for the first time in 1962, and got 35,000 votes. The Socialist vote fell from 35,000 in 1958 to 27,000 in 1962. The Communists I shall mention later.

Chairman of the National Council and thus, for purposes of protocol, president of the republic when I visited Montevideo was a fifty-one-year-old publisher-lawyer named Washington Beltrán. Handsome, articulate, he looks like a TV actor. And indeed he is a powerful orator in a nation of orators both on TV and radio and in the flesh. The atmosphere of Uruguay's presidential headquarters is quite different from that in the splendid ancestral palaces in Caracas, Rio, or Buenos Aires. There is little glow or glitter.

Dr. Beltrán was named for George Washington, as was his father, but he doesn't use the "George." He mentioned that he was six when his father was killed in a duel by Batlle y Ordóñez. This was a painful experience, but the families have maintained a normal relationship. Beltrán has been up to his neck in politics since the age of sixteen, he told me. He first became a deputy in 1946, at thirty-two. His personality is winning, and his manner vigorous.

Much was worrying Dr. Beltrán when I talked to him, and no wonder. He faced harassing problems. Both management and labor demanded more income, but nobody would do more work. Citizens thought more of their rights than of their obligations, he said. They wanted to get something for nothing. The country's vast web of social legislation redistributed wealth, but did not create it. Nobody had the vision to see that what Uruguay needed was production. The president talked about two other elements in the national scene, Communism and the army. He did not think that a Communist take-over could occur in Uruguay, but he granted that the "emotional" appeal of the Communists was considerable. As to the army Dr. Beltrán ascribed to it no political role whatever, now or in the future. Uruguay is unique in South America in that its armed forces are totally apolitical, he insisted. Why, I asked him, since Uruguay was unlikely ever to be engaged in a foreign war, did the country bother to have an army at all—why not abolish it, as Costa Rica did? This question seemed to take the president aback. He replied after a pause, "The army symbolizes civil spirit and it is useful for public works such as flood control."

Dr. Beltrán was succeeded by Alberto Heber, another Blanco who similarly had a stormy term of office. Pressure became heavy to change the nine-man presidential system and revert to a more conventional type of executive power. Some 800,000 citizens signed petitions to this end, and a plebiscite on the issue is to take place soon. In August, 1966, came a curious episode—President Huber struck against himself. Irritated to the breaking point by the

impossibility of conducting affairs under the present system he simply closed
his desk one morning and walked out of the palace, "resigning" the presidency. But he returned some days later.

Welfare State Gone Wild

We should have a further word now about Uruguay's social security system,
which is probably the most comprehensive in the world and which is a direct
inheritance from Batlle y Ordóñez. Advanced it certainly is, self-defeating
too in some respects, and so badly administered by a top-heavy bureaucracy
that it has become abnormally expensive to maintain. President Beltrán said
recently, "It may sound amazing, but we are a country without any real
economic or social problems and yet we are in a state of crisis created solely
by our institutions."[12]

Regulations in force include the forty-four-hour week (thirty hours for
civil servants and bank employees), mandatory severance pay, twenty days'
paid vacation, family allowances, a minimum wage, workmen's compensation, unemployment insurance, free compulsory education, low-cost housing,
milk cooperatives, and disability and old-age pensions of excessive generosity.
Some government departments work only half a day in summer (our winter)
so that employees can spend the afternoons on the beaches. Employers are
obliged to provide seats for all working women ("the law of the chair,"
going all the way back to the first Batlle administration sixty years ago),
which has given rise to the joke that women in Montevideo go to work early
in order to get a seat. Quips and jibes arise because the atmosphere of
paternalism is so all-embracing and because the system is too cumbersome to
support. The bureaucracy has become so lopsided that government simply
doesn't work.

A government employee even of the lowest category, say a switchman on
the railways, has the right to demand a public inquiry if he is fired, and this
inquiry may be carried all the way up to Congress. The *Senate*, no less, must
approve a dismissal in a contested case. Uruguay has a work force of about a
million which has to support some 340,000 pensionaires; and there are at
least 250,000 civil servants. Bank employees are conspicuous and powerful.
The country is loaded with banks—4 government banks and 63 private with
500 branches—and it is virtually impossible for an employer to fire a bank
employee once he is hired and has served a few years.

Pensions and retirement make a fascinating story. A man is eligible for a
pension at *full pay for life* after thirty years of service. In general this means

[12] To Henry Raymont of the *New York Times*, June 13, 1965.

that retirement is possible at fifty-five, but it comes earlier in some cases. A woman retires at full pay for life at forty-seven (or after twenty-five years' service, whichever comes sooner) if she is childless; a woman with a child is eligible for retirement on one-third of her pay for life at age *twenty-eight*, if she has worked for ten years. Pension rates, in theory at least, slide upward to correspond with living costs, and a person on pension may get more income than when he or she worked for a salary, because no social security has to be deducted on pension income. Furthermore several different social security organizations exist, for government employees, domestic servants, bank workers (the best), and so on, and in certain circumstances a person may quit his job, accept a pension, and then find another job covered by a different pension fund, thereby collecting a pension and salary both! And it is quite possible to become eligible for two pensions. This is Utopia gone wild. The welfare state is coasting toward the rocks.

This system is financed by payroll deductions ranging from 14–17 percent from employee and employer alike. Actually the employer may find himself paying out as much as 80 percent of his total wage bill in addition to wages, because of other enforced contributions—unemployment insurance, medical benefits, and the "thirteenth month" holiday. Employers often cheat. They are nominally subject to a fine of 2 percent a month (a whopping 24 percent a year) of the sum due if they do not make their correct contributions to social security, but many deliberately fail to pay, accept the fines, and then lend out the money they have illegally withheld to private business at 3 or 4 percent a month, a tidy way to profit. Other abuses attend the system. The worst is administrative confusion and delay. Many payments are long in arrears, and few pensionaires get their money on time. It may take ten years—literally—for a person's papers to be processed, and complaints are frequent that some will never be processed at all if the applicant does not pay off, i.e., bribe, the right bureaucrat. Social security has become social insecurity.

Corruption in Uruguay is like a tricycle compared to a locomotive as against that in Brazil or Mexico. Even so, it exists to an extent that must make Batlle and the old-time idealists quiver in their graves.

A man meets a friend, and reports that Mr. X has just been appointed to a big job in a ministry.

"Is he honest?"

"Yes."

"What a pity. If he were even a small thief he would be watchful and not let the big thieves get bigger."

The upshot of all this is that Uruguay, once proudly called "the Denmark of Latin America," is on the brink of disaster. The peso has had to be devalued twice; inflation is eating up the middle class; unemployment is on the rise; the poor cannot live on their crops or wages; the foreign debt has reached $515 million, an astronomical sum for a state so small. The government sent a mission to New York in August, 1965, hoping to be bailed out by "resettlement" of $50 million of its debt, but this was only a drop in the bucket. Meantime strikes and labor disputes became serious. Bank workers struck in the winter of 1965 demanding a 48 percent wage increase, and 500,000 workers in other fields joined them. The government had to institute a state of siege (modified martial law) before a compromise was reached. Several banks were closed, and their officers were investigated on charges of corruption; on the other side of the fence numerous left-wingers and student agitators were arrested. Then some 200,000 state employees went on strike demanding raises up to 60 percent. This may seem excessive but one must keep in mind how intolerably low most Uruguayan wages are (although higher than in most South American countries), and how inflation has made a joke of the currency. A schoolteacher gets at present about 4,000 pesos a month; this was worth about $205 two years ago but only $68 today. The cost of living rose 85.6 percent in 1965. In general the strikes were settled with wage increases averaging 25–35 percent.

Social security alone did not bring Uruguay to the edge of bankruptcy, and it is important to point this out. Administration has been botched and the system abused, but social welfare payments do not take up a disproportionate share of the budget. It was the collapse of the economy that made the welfare system unworkable, not the welfare state that caused the collapse of the economy. Almost all good observers, foreign and Uruguayan alike, in Montevideo agree on this. What was responsible was mismanagement—plain simple bungling, a fault that has been known to afflict other countries—atop such other factors as an increasing trade deficit, decline in the price of wool, lack of raw materials, slipshod agriculture, a wasteful attempt at industrialization, technological backwardness, inflation, and a crazily archaic tax system. Agriculture did not produce enough to support industry. As to taxes the country had no income tax at all until 1961 (because the Batlle tradition held that an income tax tends to damage the poor), and even today there is no income tax for anybody earning less than $1,400 a year, which includes a large proportion of the population.[13]

How Socialist is Uruguay? This is a difficult question because private and

[13] The national dilapidation has other effects. Several international commercial airlines have threatened to boycott Uruguay unless the Montevideo airport is put in better condition. *Latin American Times*, August 24, 1965.

public sectors are so intermixed. The country has sought to have the best of both possible worlds. As to Socialist tendencies Uruguay has nationalized the railways, street cars, telephone, telegraph, electricity, the waterworks, the beaches, the subsoil, and all forms of insurance—life, fire, marine, industrial, accident. The government also plays a potent role in banking, TV, radio, gambling, and public entertainment like the opera, ballet, and theater. Still in the free-enterprise realm are the basic constituents of the economy—agriculture, industry, commerce. But a very large role is played by mixed agencies, which are vital in Uruguay; these are the *entes autónomos*, or autonomous administrations, which control various monopolies. One such giant is ANCAP (Administración Nacional de Combustibles, Alcoholes, y Portland) which refines all the country's import of petroleum and has a monopoly on cement, alcohol, and other fuels, as well as *caña*, the local firewater. A similar administration controls the fisheries, and another handles hydroelectric development and electric power. The National Ports Administration supervises all port and river facilities, and meat packing is similarly administered. The autonomy of several of these organizations is so complete that they levy their own taxes. A new national planning agency is CIDA, which operates more or less like CORDIPLAN in Venezuela.[14]

In the realm of these autonomous public administrations the Uruguayan passion for divided control, decentralization, and the diffusion of authority is particularly emphatic. Each is run, like the government itself, not by a man but by a committee; each has a board of five, with three men representing the majority political party, two the minority. Members are chosen not necessarily for their technical experience in the field but sheerly out of political considerations. Hence decisions are often slow, contentious, or the result of weak compromises. Bureaucracy could go no further, even if the original motive was to create the purest of democracies and extend this to the economy. Decentralization has defeated its own end.

Questions as Usual

What does Uruguay need most?
1. More Uruguayans.
2. One economist.

---

[14] But it has typically Uruguayan complications. The plan extends for ten years but this includes an "introductory" three-year plan "which in turn kicks off with a one-year plan." The entire plan, which took four years to prepare and cost $700,000, was assembled by a staff of three hundred Uruguayans and ninety foreign experts. It fills six volumes which weigh twenty-five pounds. These details are from a recent issue of the *Visión Letter*.

3. Vitality.

What runs Uruguay?

1. Anybody close enough to a minister to be able to ask a favor of his secretary on the telephone.

Communism, Foreign Affairs, and the U.S.

The Communist party is legal in Uruguay, and gets as a rule about 3½ percent of the total popular vote. One Communist senator and three deputies sit in a parliament of 130. In the last (1962) election the Communists went to the polls as part of a coalition called the Frente Izquierdista de Liberación (Left Liberation Front) and their vote went up. The initials of the new group spell "Fidel" and this is what it is commonly called, but it has nothing to do with Castro. The Uruguayan Communist leadership is stand pat and stoutly pro-Moscow, but a small China-oriented wing is active and a dissident Trotskyist element exists. The strength of the orthodox party lies not merely among youthful radicals and students, but in the labor movement, and the Communists dominate several important unions, as in Argentina.

Uruguay has full diplomatic relations with the Soviet Union and all the European satellites except pro-Chinese Albania. It does not recognize China. Trade between Uruguay and the European Communist states is brisk. The Soviets maintain an exceptionally large and active embassy in Montevideo, presumed to be a reception point for propaganda and other material which is retransmitted from Uruguay to other locations on the continent. Uruguay is, in short, Moscow's "window" for most of South America.[15] Meantime commercial relations with the USSR continue to be good, and the Soviets are, as a matter of fact, the country's third-best customer.

The whole angry issue of Communism and alleged Soviet influence came to a head in December, 1965, following serious new strikes and threats of strikes made by Communist-controlled unions. Communist impetus from outside was blamed for much of this turmoil, which all but paralyzed the government, and a Blanco member of the presidential council announced that Uruguayan relations with the Soviet Union would be severed and the Soviet embassy in Montevideo shut down. A Colorado member of the presidency replied by calling the threat to break off relations a "Blanco smokescreen" to hide Blanco failures, and no rupture occurred.

To sum up: Uruguay hoped to take the teeth out of the basic Communist

[15] Cf. Alphonse Max, *Latin American Times*, September 27, 1965, and Hal Hendrix, *Miami News*, January 2, 1963.

threat by social reform, as in Scandinavia. But the well-organized and shrewdly directed Communists have managed to achieve a considerable degree of penetration.

Uruguayan relations with its two big neighbors, Brazil and Argentina, are what might be called close but not affectionate. One sore point vis-à-vis Brazil is, as we know, the presence in Uruguay of two celebrated Brazilian exiles, former president João Goulart and his brother-in-law, Leonel Brizola. What exactly Uruguay fears from these two men is not clear, but agitation is intermittent to throw them out, even though this would violate the country's long-vested tradition of hospitality to exiles. And Brazil exerts pressure to get them back, so that they can be brought to trial. As to Argentina the Uruguayans disagree with it about practically everything, but even so they remain a chip off the old block and the two countries are bound by a large community of natural associations.

Like Argentina, Uruguay has always had close emotional ties to Europe; President Beltrán told me that the greatest popular demonstration ever seen in Montevideo occurred when Paris was liberated in World War II. The death of President John F. Kennedy also provoked profound response.

Uruguay has always been passionately anticolonial, and "intervention," whether by Washington or anything else, is still the dirtiest of words. The country's attitude toward the United States is generally cordial, but this small, stubborn, somewhat cranky country does not like to be pushed around. Uruguay was the last South American country to break off diplomatic and trade relations with Castro's Cuba in 1964, and finally agreed to do so only after strenuous cajoling by the United States. Then in the spring of 1965 Uruguay was one of the six Latin American countries which refused to go along with the United States on intervention in the Dominican Republic, and voted against the OAS resolution authorizing joint military action there. Here again we see a glint of the Uruguayan national character.

*

The United States private investment in Uruguay is about $65 million. Aid under the Alianza program has amounted to roughly $38 million since 1962, the smallest amount given to any South American country except Paraguay. British economic influence is still important.

The Peace Corps has been fruitfully active in Uruguay with projects ranging from instruction in sanitation to chicken culling, from rural development to basketball. The Development Programme of the UN has devoted about $2 million to Uruguayan projects, with more to come.

CHAPTER 13

A Semi-Affectionate Look at Paraguay

"So you have already been to Paraguay?" said Candide. "Indeed I have," replied Cacambo. . . . It's a wonderful system they have. . . . The people own nothing."
—VOLTAIRE IN 1758

This landlocked shoebox of a country has the most resonantly martial history in South America, a passionate patriotism, no TV, no stock exchange, and no income tax. Paraguay is one of the least-known nations in the world, far off the beaten track, derelict and remote. Few travelers penetrate to this Ruritanian wilderness, and news about it is scarce in the extreme. In one recent year the *New York Times* printed exactly two dispatches from Paraguay.

After returning from a trip to Latin America twenty-five years ago I had a talk in Washington with President Roosevelt, and to gain his attention mentioned that I had visited all twenty of the Latin American republics, an unusual thing to do at that time.

Mr. Roosevelt cocked a wary eye at me. "What!" he exclaimed. "Even Paraguay?"

But nowadays the big intercontinental jets stop regularly at Asunción, the capital, several times a week, and more and more visitors have opportunity to taste the paradoxical and primitive wonders of this forlorn, peculiar land. Many call it a "mad" little country—batty. Actually it is not little at all, but covers 157,000 square miles—the size of California. But, imprisoned between its two giant neighbors, Brazil and Argentina, it looks insignificant on a map.

238

Paraguay is one of the two nations in South America without access to the sea, the other being Bolivia, and is the only officially bilingual country on the continent; the two languages are Spanish and Guaraní, the original Indian language. It is the poorest country in the hemisphere, except Haiti, the least developed, and, in some respects, the most grubbily forlorn, but it has a genuine national character, and gives forth an exotic atmosphere. Paraguay has charm.

The country is ruled by the last[1] full-dress dictator on the continent, President Don Alfredo Stroessner. A dictatorship so blatant and unitary runs counter to the current political mood in both North and most of South America, and thus serves to isolate the country. At present this complicated general is loosening the reins a bit, but the mass of the citizenry still obeys his every whim and whisper, although—another paradox—ferocious political opposition continues to exist.

"Nothing ever happens in Paraguay—it just rolls along." This was a remark made to me in the course of my recent trip by a kindly, but not well-informed, United States official. Actually a good deal is going on, and it might even be that Paraguay, after a long autumnal doze, is beginning to wake up to the embrace of modern times.

*

It certainly is high time. Paraguay is, to repeat, as big as California, but it has only *three* roads worthy of the name; only 2 percent of its roads are paved, and the total mileage of all-weather roads is only about 450.[2] The total railway mileage is 309 as against California's 13,836. To get from Asunción to Buenos Aires by rail, a distance of 938 miles, takes almost 56 hours: the locomotives are woodburning, and the train runs once a week. There are only five cities with a population higher than 35,000; no city except Asunción is bigger than 70,000. Nobody is very rich, but even so the lopsided discrepancy between well-off and poor—the standard headache of South America—is marked; eleven huge farms cover not less than 35 percent of eastern Paraguay, the heart of the country.[3] Only 1.3 percent of the land is arable, and the average per capita income is $201, one of the lowest in the western world. Smugglers (this is a great country for smuggling) widen their pockets in Asunción; peasants in the "green hell" of the Chaco starve.

The population is around 1,990,000, but some 500,000 Paraguayans are

[1] Except for General Onganía in Argentina since 1966.
[2] California has about 120,000 miles of road.
[3] Tad Szulc, *The Winds of Revolution*, p. 55.

estimated to live in exile abroad, principally in Argentina—a percentage of more than one in four! The authorities assert blandly that most of these could safely return, but, even though they are fervently patriotic, the exiles prudently prefer not to do so; they have chosen to be expatriates because they did not like the military rule of General Stroessner—or were pitched out by his regime—and do not want to take the risk of coming back.

The Person of General Stroessner

Intensely proud, intensely sensitive, General Stroessner has been the dominating force in Paraguay since 1954. His sources of power are three: (1) his own personal qualities, which are considerable; (2) the army; (3) political identification with a confused mélange known as the Colorado or Red party. Of course this use of the word "red," traditional in several of the La Plata countries, has no connection with Russian red or Chinese red. Dictator Stroessner does not like Communists, to put it mildly, and the Communist party has been illegal in Paraguay since 1936.

The general, reflecting the fierce medievalism of the country, is not easy to see. He has three pet hates—first, journalists at large; second, foreign journalists; third, North American foreign journalists, because Paraguay usually gets a bad press, if any at all. I obviously qualified on all three of these counts, and labored under a specific disadvantage as well—namely that I had included a brief account of Paraguay in my old *Inside Latin America*, published twenty-five years ago, in which I said that the president of the republic at the time, General Higinio Morínigo, had "black eyes which shone like marbles and black hair which starts an inch above his brows." I had completely forgotten this passage but now I discovered that it had been considered to be an insult to the Paraguayan nation, and was still bitterly resented. But I was forgiven eventually and President Stroessner agreed at the last moment to receive me; the time was set for 7:15 A.M. on the morning I was leaving the country.

After half an hour the dictator was still talking hard and I took the liberty of interrupting to say that I must be getting on to the airport or miss my plane, due to leave at 8:30. The president waved me down with a calm but authoritative gesture, saying, "The plane will wait!"

*

As a matter of fact 7:15 in the morning is not an unusual hour for an appointment in Asunción, an early town. Normal office hours are from 7:30

A.M. till 11 or 12; banks *close* for the day at 10:30. After lunch comes a prolonged siesta, as befits a subtropical climate. Stroessner outdoes his fellow citizens in his preference for an early start to the day, as several anecdotes attest. Recently he telephoned his foreign minister at home at 5 A.M., to say that the minister's office phone did not answer, and why not. Once he called an associate at about six. The man answered instantly, "Good morning, Mr. President," whereupon Stroessner asked, "How did you know it was I?" Reply: "Who else would be calling me at six A.M.?"

I surveyed the presidential palace, an imposing but somewhat rundown structure, near the river, as I walked in for my interview. Not far away is the Colegio Militar, where Stroessner received his training as a cadet, and which has bright sulphur yellow walls. I could not believe my eyes when I saw the presidential guard doing the goose step in the palace courtyard. I had thought that this particular method of military ambulation had disappeared from the world along with Hitler. (Later I saw it again in Peru.) The uniforms were melodramatically colorful. Nearby a fat bare-footed Indian woman, with long braids, clad in a blanket, pushed a burro across the square while puffing leisurely on a stout cigar.

The dictator is a tallish, solidly built man who (I mean no offense) looks like a Bavarian butcher. He has thinning dark hair slicked back, a thin smear of almost colorless mustache, sharp steely blue eyes (they really do pierce you, like the eyes of the late Dr. Albert Schweitzer), and very large red hard hands. He is methodical, vigorous, devoid of imagination, and fanatic in his feelings about Paraguay—clearly a man of force.

Photographs all over Asunción show Stroessner in full uniform, weighted down with decorations, including a bejeweled star the size of a plate on his lower chest; it looks like a pinwheel about to whir. But, in office dress, he gives a somewhat plain, businesslike impression. This is not a man on horseback. If he rides anything it is a typewriter or blueprint paper.

Stroessner talks a streak like a phonograph record played at excessive speed, right over any question; he pays little heed to his interlocutor, and it was difficult to ask a question, get a word in, or pin him down. He had read my old chapter on Paraguay carefully and said that he thought I was wrong about several details. He repeatedly mentioned, with fervent pride, the recent visit to Paraguay of General de Gaulle, adding that the French president was the first foreign head of state *ever* to visit Asunción in its 440 years of history.

Two themes underlay everything Stroessner said. First, his love for Paraguay, his pertinacious joy in Paraguay. How "sweet" the Guaraní language is! How beautiful the countryside! How noble the peasants! There may well be poverty in the country, but it is a "dignified" poverty—not misery. People here taste the glory of their history every day of their lives, and exist in "peace, harmony, and liberty." He raced across the room, showed me dog-eared photographs of the presidential palace in the old days to give a taste of its historical associations, and picking up an *Almanach de Gotha* for 1865, tapped the pages and barked out figures to demonstrate that in that year, a century ago, Paraguay had more people than either Uruguay or Argentina. "Then we were massacred!" Second, Communism. The general pointed to a row of flags representing all the countries of the western hemisphere except Cuba. "No beards here!" The Communists, he stated, always play the same game—working within the guise of a democratic framework, then ending up by shooting people against the *paredón*, wall. And he stated firmly that Paraguay would never succumb to Communism under *his* administration. "No beards allowed!"

Another object of his fury was former president Betancourt of Venezuela. He thinks that Betancourt encouraged Castro with arms and money, then reneged.

*

Stroessner was born in 1912, the son of a German immigrant. He will not admit to knowing German and nobody has ever heard him use it, but his sister speaks it fluently. Probably he has a touch of Guaraní blood on his mother's side. Winning his commission in the army in 1932 he rose rank by rank to become a full general by 1951, when he became commander-in-chief as well. He was well regarded for his constitutionalism. In fact he had been invited to lead rebel forces in a revolution that took place in 1948, when he was commander of an artillery regiment at the garrison town of Paraguarí: this he refused to do, on the ground that the army must refrain from political activity.

Then circumstances changed. One decrepit government gave way to another, as the political situation degenerated. Stroessner became minister of defense as a result of a bloodless coup in 1954, whereupon elections took place for a new president. There are two principal political parties in Paraguay—Colorados and Liberals. It is a moot point today whether Stroessner captured the Colorados or the Colorados captured him. At any rate he ran for president as the Colorado candidate and won. Winning was not exactly difficult because the Liberals were not allowed to run and he was the only candidate! His mission was to restore stability out of chaos. Stroessner has been the dictator of Paraguay ever since, having been re-elected president in 1958 (again without opposition) and once more in 1963.

But 1963 was a different story, as a word of background will attest. A man of ruthless practicality, Stroessner still rules the coop, and Paraguay is still under a state of siege or modified martial law (as it indeed has been almost uninterruptedly since 1940, long before his regime began). But he was well aware in the late 1950's that the country was full of tensions, and he thought it would serve his purpose to provide escape valves and thus lighten the pressure. So in 1958 he allowed the Liberals to hold their first public meeting in a decade, and in 1959 he announced plans for "institutional normalization," declared an amnesty, and lifted the state of siege. But this gesture was followed by an outburst of rioting, and the state of siege was quickly reimposed. The legislature was dissolved even though it consisted entirely of Colorados, and the Liberal leaders—also a handful of dissident Colorados—were unceremoniously tossed in jail.

Then came 1963. Stroessner felt secure enough to loosen up, and, to improve his image, he invited the Liberals and two other opposition parties to participate in the elections. They agreed to do so but only on the condition that Stroessner, on his side, would promise to lift the state of siege, release any remaining political prisoners, and declare a general amnesty. When the dictator refused, the three principal elements of the opposition boycotted the election. Of course they knew that he was bound to win anyway. But the Liberals split, and a splinter wing, known as the "Revolutionary Directorate" and colloquially called the "In-Liberals" or "Stroessner stooges," agreed to fight the election on Stroessner's terms. In other words, he managed to get somebody to run against *himself*—but only after the most convoluted difficulties. So an "opposition" came into being, and it is one of the principal paradoxes of the country that, within limits, this is permitted to express itself, if only so that Stroessner can claim that his regime is *not* a full dictatorship, although it is.

To sum up, the president's main object in 1963 was to set up as respectable an opposition candidate as possible and then beat him. The In-Liberal chosen for the sacrifice was Dr. Ernesto Gavilán, and he received 45,000 votes as against 470,000 for the government. Dr. Gavilán was then rewarded by being appointed ambassador to London. Alice-in-Wonderlandish as all this may seem, the fact remains that this was the first Paraguayan election in thirty-one years in which two candidates participated, and an "opposition," which dares to become vehement at times, now sits in the legislature for the first time since 1928.[4]

*

General Stroessner finishes his office day at noon, then goes home to lunch. His house, the Casa Presidencial, lies on one of the most remarkable streets in the hemisphere, the Avenida Mariscal López, which is the local equivalent of Massachusetts Avenue in Washington, D.C. The French, Spanish, Argentine, Italian, and American embassies (appropriately No. 1776), the Argentine military mission, and several other institutions of a similar type are located here in a brief row, and at a curve stand four buildings within a hundred yards of each other which form the central ganglion of military power in the country—the barracks of the Escort Battalion, an elite guard; the officers' club; the Ministry of Defense; and the headquarters of the general staff. General Stroessner's house stands two blocks from the American Embassy between a pension and the headquarters of the 6th police precinct. A large establishment, his home is bounded by a silver-painted iron fence atop a six-foot wall. Armed police stand ten feet apart in a cordon along the walk, twenty-four hours a day; they wear field-green uniforms six days of the week, and smart whites on Sundays.

In other respects the Avenida Mariscal López does not resemble Massachusetts Avenue. Tropical vegetation festoons it, and in season it is lined with magnificently profuse scarlet flamboyants. In the gardens behind stout walls are jacaranda, the color of violets, jasmine, yellow and blue *lapacho*, a variety of cassia known as shower of gold, and the *palo borracho* or drunken tree, with blossoms of pink and cream. Another variation from Washington, D.C., is that the *avenida* does not have much traffic. There are only ten thousand automobiles in all of this somewhat sinister fairyland.[5] Driving toward the American Embassy at dusk one night my car almost hit a riderless wild horse. Once I saw an Indian under a black umbrella selling bows and arrows and an odd collection of other objects pulled out of a blanket, including horses' hooves for good luck and chunks of raw liver.

The dictator arrives home in a big car followed by a jeepful of armed guards, but he is more casual in other public appearances. He likes to go around town on inspection trips in the late afternoon, driving an old

---

[4] Another novelty is that women voted in this election for the first time in Paraguayan history. The total vote was, incidentally, less than the number of expatriates.

[5] Movie theaters number thirty-seven and newspapers four.

Chevrolet himself, with nobody but one of his two sons accompanying him.[6] Occasionally he goes to the dentist without escort, sits around the waiting room with other sufferers, and bows politely to the ladies present. The dentist is a graduate of the University of Michigan.

One of Stroessner's hobbies is fishing; he told me that he catches trout, salmon, and *surubí*, which can weigh up to 175 pounds, in nearby rivers. Another is to drive out to the "Aeropuerto Pte Gral Stroessner" (as the sign has it) in the evening and watch the silver jets ride in. His only ambition is to become a marshal. But of course he could promote himself to marshal at any time.

General Stroessner is a rich man, but lives simply. He is a Catholic, as indeed he has to be, by terms of the Paraguayan constitution; it is mandatory for the president to be Catholic in several South American countries. His intellectual tastes are limited; he studied English for a time, but is not comfortable with it. As a youthful officer he once visited the United States, and has made brief trips to other South American countries, including Brazil; he has never been to Europe. Nothing much interests him except his work, at which he is indefatigable.

Stroessner, to conclude, is neither a tawdry on-the-make adventurer nor a capricious parvenu, but a straight out old-fashioned despot who is convinced that nobody but himself can give order, stability, and progress to his country, and who rules by method, no matter how brutal or what the cost. No doubt there will be sighs of relief everywhere from the State Department to the streets of Asunción when he is gone, but it is just possible that he will leave something behind him, which has never happened in Paraguay before.

Dr. Ynsfrán, Politics, and Civil Liberties

The second most important man in Paraguay, Edgar Ynsfrán, minister of the interior, is forty-four and has occupied this critical post for ten years; no other man has ever held it for more than five. A quality of the Stroessner regime is cabinet stability; there has been only one change in the last three years. Ynsfrán, who comes of Basque stock, with a touch of Catalan, is the son of a distinguished former Paraguayan minister who studied at the University of London, and who gave his sons English names, Edgar and Walter. Edgar studied engineering and then turned to law and politics: he spent several years of exile in Argentina after an anarchic crisis in the Colorado party in the 1940's. He was married in New Rochelle, New York.

[6] His children are Gustavo Adolfo, a pilot; Alfredo Junius, an officer in the air force reserve, and a daughter, Graciela Concepción, a teacher.

This is a hard-hitting, accomplished, and brilliantly good-looking man. Ynsfrán is commonly called Stroessner's protégé and favorite, but one of the dictator's principal sources of authority is his secrecy about such matters; he likes to keep everybody guessing and waiting, as Churchill kept Eden waiting. In the end the army will probably decide.

Nothing is too small or transient to escape Dr. Ynsfrán's vigilant eye. The night I arrived in Asunción I registered at the Guaraní Hotel, of which more later, and was given a pleasant small room. At about one in the morning the manager knocked on the door, apologetically woke me up, and said that I was being moved into a suite. I protested. I didn't want to move. We argued. The hotel man was patient, but implacable. "It does not matter what you say or I say, Mr. Gunther. Orders have come from Minister Dr. Ynsfrán that you are to be moved at once into a suite." I was moved.

When I talked to the minister the next day, he had before him a Spanish translation of my old *Inside Latin America*, from which he proceeded to read. Among other things he noted that I had mentioned twenty-five years ago the need for a road and bridge to connect Paraguay with Brazil. This road and bridge have now been built, he said. In fact the bridge was opened ceremoniously by General Stroessner and President Castelo Branco of Brazil, in March, 1965. The road, 196 miles long, penetrates through the bush to a new town on the River Paraná named Puerto Presidente Stroessner, and was built with substantial help from USAID. This and the bridge, known as the Friendship International Bridge, will serve to give Paraguay a new and useful—if somewhat circuitous—outlet to the sea.

The building housing Ynsfrán's Ministry of the Interior is modest, but has one unusual characteristic at night—rows of red, white and blue electric bulbs which outline each floor. These convey a festive note and give the structure the atmosphere of a colorful toy, which it is not.

*

The principal political parties in Paraguay are, we know, the ruling Colorados (reds) and the opposition Liberals (blues). The Liberals are now split between the "Traditional" or "Authentic" Liberals who remain in opposition, and the splinter group of "In-Liberals" who seceded from the parent group to become an authorized "opposition." Paraguay had no political parties at all until 1874, when the Colorados, who originally represented the landed oligarchy, were founded. The Liberals, who rose to oppose them, were established in 1887, and soon became as conservative as the conservative Colorados, if not more so. The Colorados ruled uninterruptedly until 1904, when they were replaced by the Liberals, who remained in power for thirty-six unbroken years, until 1940, except during one brief period after the Chaco War.

One of the most interesting sights in Asunción today is the headquarters of the Colorado party, a handsome modern structure. This was financed and is maintained by a forced levy on all government employees, who are, of course, mostly Colorados. Members of Congress are obliged to return half their salaries to their parties. The dictatorship bites deep.

The limited political activity now permitted in Paraguay is, of course, held firmly in check by the fact that the Stroessner regime can, if it wants, turn back to absolutism at any moment. But as a matter of fact political discussion is surprisingly outspoken. Politicians are free to talk—on some levels—although not to act. Debates take place in parliament, and several newspapers berate the government—an unusual thing in a dictatorship. Two opposition "parties" exist in addition to the dissident Liberals—first, the Christian Democrats, who were permitted to form an organization in 1960; second, the Febreristas, originally an extreme left-wing group which dates back to revolutionary activity in the 1930's. Recently the Febreristas were given official recognition after long years underground, and even permitted to publish a newspaper, *El Pueblo*. As to the "In-Liberals" they are allowed to hold meetings in Congress, print a weekly newspaper, and give talks on the radio.

Anybody who rose in a public square and denounced Stroessner would, of course, get the shortest of shrifts; moreover, fear of reprisal serves to keep most citizens subdued. There is always the possibility of a rap on the door at midnight from the *pyragues*, or political police.[7] Labor organization is at the minimum, and strikes are dealt with in what I heard described cautiously by a Paraguayan as a "nondemocratic" manner. On the other hand Asunción does not at all give out the atmosphere of a police state, and citizens by and large have less to apprehend than many in Liberia, the Ukraine, or Mississippi.

The total number of political prisoners today is impossible to check—probably not more than a hundred, but several have been in confinement for a long time and have been brutally treated. The police, if they lay hands on a Communist or somebody suspected of being a Communist, are not gentle. Several Communists were imprisoned recently when pro-Castro Paraguayans living in Brazil made an abortive guerrilla "raid" on

---

[7] This is an Indian word meaning "people with hairy feet." *Gallatin, op. cit.,* p. 836.

their home country, and were routed after skirmishing, then captured. Dr. Ynsfrán led the government forces in this fray.

I heard talk of concentration camps up in the "Green Hell" in the north, and of torture chambers at police headquarters in the towns. It seems that student demonstrators and minor political offenders are not, as a rule, tried or sentenced to jail, but instead are "dropped across the river," that is, deported to exile in Argentina without any legal process. I met one boy in this category in Buenos Aires. He had been picked up by the police in Asunción for alleged subversive activity and interrogated sharply, but not tortured; he was then advised to leave the country promptly, which he did.

What liberal Paraguayans seem to resent most is not so much the day-by-day operation of the regime but the secret total power of Stroessner's political agents and underlings, particularly his finance men, and the army, which, untouchable, is beyond any popular criticism or control. The people of Asunción have artful ways of demonstrating opposition without sticking their necks out, but this does them little good.

Stroessner has been responsible for unfortunate events but he himself is not evil in the sense that Hitler, Gómez of Venezuela, or the white rulers of South Africa were or are evil. He is not a bloodthirsty monster or murderer. Paraguay has never had a democratic government, and Stroessner's excuse for dictatorship is that political stability is the first essential if the country is to survive at all, and that he is doing his best to assist development. He has had to move slowly because otherwise *he* might be deposed. Stability has reached the point where municipal elections could be held in 152 localities in October, 1965, an encouraging sign. The state of siege was lifted, and the Colorados, both groups of Liberals, and the Febreristas were allowed to vote. Of course the dictator won, but something approximating a true election did take place.

Paraguay: Its Base and Beam

Paraguay, a creation of rivers, is lined on the south and east by the Paraná, and on the west by the Pilcomayo and the Paraguay, which bisects the country north of Asunción. The rivers, with ill-defined banks and swampy margins, wander all over the place, and give rise to almost as much *confusionismo* as politics. The country has never been adequately surveyed, and the Inter-American Geodetic Survey, operating out of Panama, is now mapping it scientifically for the first time. East of the Paraguay River is the "civilized" area, where most of the population lives. To the north and west is the Chaco (= great swamp), a vast, hot plain-*cum*-jungle swollen by lagoons and waterways, where the density of population is less than two per square mile, and which spreads out into both Argentina and Brazil. Here jaguars flourish and Indians catch crocodiles with forked poles.[8]

Almost all citizens are partially of Indian descent except recent immigrants. Perhaps 3 percent of the population still claim pure Spanish blood, and, far out in the Chaco, some thirty thousand pure Indians survive; these have long black hair, hunt by bow and arrow, and are savages, but harmless. The rate of population increase is average by Latin American standards—about 2.4 percent. One Paraguayan uniqueness is, as mentioned above, the survival and permanent vitality of a second language, Guaraní, which is spoken alongside Spanish by virtually the entire population. Guaraní is not a sign of race or interior social status, nor is it the language of a subjugated or unassimilated people like Quechua in Peru; on the contrary, it is a national language, and is a major source of Paraguayan exclusiveness and pride even to those who speak Spanish as well. Conversation in Spanish often breaks out into Guaraní. Paraguay is, in a word, bilingual.

Comparatively few people, however, are able to *read* Guaraní, an exceptionally difficult language. There is no daily Guaraní newspaper, but the Spanish papers print columns in it and occasionally advertisements appear in it, for instance by Braniff and other North American companies prominent in Asunción. The radio uses it widely, as do poets and other artists seeking nourishment from the national tradition, and it has strongly influenced local Spanish; for instance Paraguayans are the only people in South America who pronounce "h" as a straight "h," instead of tending to keep it silent. One reason why Guaraní has maintained its hold is that comparatively few Spaniards entered the country in the early days except Jesuits, and the aboriginal Guaranís retained their identity. The Indians absorbed the Spaniards rather than vice versa.

Mennonite colonists originally from Russia, Germany, and Canada are the only significant non-indigenous group; many Indians upcountry speak a smattering of German as a result of long contact with the Mennonites. Since World War II some thirty thousand Japanese and Okinawans have moved in. There are virtually no Negroes, in strict contrast to Brazil next door. One odd place name is Filadelfia, a Mennonite village in the Chaco not far from Asunción; another is Villa Hayes, which was named for President Rutherford B. Hayes. Few North Americans know much about him but he is

---

[8] The name "jaguar" comes, oddly enough, from the Guaraní word for dog, *jagua,* although jaguars are cats. Locally they are known as tigers or *yaguaretés,* but there is much confusion about this terminology.

widely celebrated in Paraguay because he once settled a frontier dispute—naturally in its favor.

Paraguayan history coruscates, and has black periods of masochistic tragedy. These are extremely *simpático* people, but they remind me of King Lear. The national anthem begins, fittingly enough, with the words, "Paraguayans, republic or death."[9]

The country was discovered, in a manner of speaking, by none other than Sebastian Cabot in 1527, when he was searching for a westward route to the Pacific; ten years later a Spanish *conquistador* Juan de Salazar reached the junction of the Paraguay and Pilcomayo rivers, built a fort there, and named it Nuestra Señora Santa María de la Asunción. This became the Asunción of today, "the oldest European city on the continent which still survives." Pioneers from Asunción, working downriver, were the founders of Buenos Aires two hundred years later.[10] Paraguay long preceded Argentina as an entity, and is its mother.

The story of the early Jesuit (also Dominican and Franciscan) missionaries is unique. They entered the country to convert the heathen, and, to further this conventional end, established remarkably unconventional communities known as *reduccións*—communal settlements where the Indians, with whom relations had always been amicable, were taught trades, skills, and agricultural methods, while being converted. About thirty *reduccións*, with a total of 100,000 Indians, mostly Guaranís, were set up; Spanish goldseekers, colonizers, and explorers were rigorously kept out. There was no butchering of Indians in Paraguay, no ruthless search for wealth by hop-skip-and-jump adventurers. This fruitful development went on till 1767, when the Jesuit order, accused of attempting to set up "a state within a state," was expelled from Paraguay, as well as from the other Spanish colonies in South America by King Charles III. The reductions died.

Paraguay won its independence from Spain in 1811 after bitter squabbles with Argentina. Then came the rule uninterruptedly from 1814 to 1840 of a fantastic creature, José Gaspar Tomás Rodríguez Francia, known as El Supremo. He was a dictator in the grandest old-style manner—also an extreme isolationist. Partly to protect the country from Argentina he converted it into a walled-off, self-sealed, pressure-proof preserve, in which only the barest of contact with the outside world was permitted—almost like Japan before the Meiji restoration. A *"lapacho* curtain" rose; foreigners were

[9] Incidentally the Paraguayan flag is the only one in the world with a different pattern on each side; one carries the treasury seal, the other the national coat of arms.

[10] This statement may be disputed. Buenos Aires was "founded" several times. The details of Paraguayan-Argentine relations at this time are inordinately complex.

forbidden entrance to the country. El Supremo even went so far as to cut off relations with the Vatican, and Paraguay became strongly anticlerical for a period. The next ruler, equally formidable, was Francia's nephew, Carlos Antonio López, who ruled from 1844 to 1862. This López is called the first "constitutional" president of Paraguay, but he was as iron-handed a dictator as his uncle. He reversed El Supremo's policy and opened the country up to Europeanization. Then came a third absolutist ruler, Francisco Solano López, the son of the first López, who was dictator from 1862 till his death in battle in 1870. Pages might be written about each of these "romantic" figures. Solano López had an Irish mistress, Madame Eliza Lynch, whom he met in Paris, a woman in the authentic Pompadour tradition who really ran the country—and led troops on horseback.

The younger López came close to destroying Paraguay because, egged on by Madame Lynch, he picked quarrels with his neighbors and declared an insane war against them in 1865, which lasted for five years and is called the War of the Triple Alliance. Paraguay, the David, fought simultaneously against two Goliaths—Brazil and Argentina—plus Uruguay for good measure. And Paraguay, although hopelessly outweighed, almost won. The cost was dreadful. Women and even children fought as well as men, and the total population was reduced by more than half. Virtually the entire male population was killed off, so that, incredibly enough, only 28,000 men in the country remained alive at the end. As a result Paraguay was, in effect, ruled by women for some years. This was the bloodiest war in the history of South America, and it is still talked about in Asunción as if it had happened yesterday.

Another vicious and totally unnecessary war came in 1932–35 between Paraguay and Bolivia, the Chaco War. The known dead of both sides came to 135,000; both countries were set back years in development, and results were nil, except exhaustion. Observers flying over one battlefield saw ten thousand skeletons shining under them. Paraguayans, short on modern arms, fought with machetes. Bolivian troops from the *altiplano*, unused to the torrid lowlands, could not stand the change in altitude and died wholesale.

The origin of this sordid, sanguinary, and useless struggle was a frontier dispute; each side built forts on contested territory, until there came an explosion. Slipshod draughtmanship by Spaniards in the sixteenth century never properly defined the frontiers of the *audiencias* that later became Bolivia and Paraguay. The war was, among other things, a kind of test for competing European military systems; the Paraguayans were French-trained, the Bolivians German-trained. Also involved was a chase for oil by competing foreign companies. Paraguay won the war, but by the narrowest of squeaks. It took three *years* to work out negotiations for peace, a longer period than that of the war itself, and this contributed heavily to the country's subsequent political disintegration.

*

Paraguay is so poor because it lacks production. It lives on the land—cattle, tobacco, cotton, and such forest products as *quebracho*, a species of hardwood (the name means "ax breaker") from which tannin, used for curing leather, is derived.[11] The predominant economic influence is Argentina, but the country is no longer a virtual Argentine colony as it once was. For years it was altogether dominated by Argentina, which had a strangling hold on its communications and otherwise.

About two-thirds of the forest area is still virgin, and grazing land costs no more than 40 cents an acre. But a man needs a lot of cattle to support a ranch, because most of the soil, like that of West Texas in older days, is marginal. Some big ranches are now owned by companies, but for the most part they are still run by settlers who live close to the land, as in Uruguay, lead vigorous lives, and know full well how to master a horse or brand a calf.

United States aid, administered through the Alianza, amounted to about $37 million through 1965. The World Bank, the Inter-American Development Bank, the Export-Import Bank, and other agencies have also assisted in projects all the way from roads and public health to medical education and, above all, to SANOS, the National Potable Water Authority. Asunción has safe drinking water today for the first time in its history; the new waterworks plant looks as spic-and-span as the engine room of the *Queen Mary*. This program is presently being expanded to include safe water for every village in the country with a population over two thousand.

The Development Programme of the UN, working on parallel lines with USAID, has four projects in Paraguay—to improve the navigability of the River Paraguay, do research on telecommunications, set up an organization equivalent to the American Bureau of Standards, and survey a new road network in the "triangle" below Asunción. One curiosity in regard to things American is that the Peace Corps does not operate in Paraguay. Coca-Cola was not allowed in until last year.

What does Paraguay need most? Some marvelous, if impudent, answers to

---

[11] Another sizable export is *yerba maté*, the tea made of holly berries. Paraguay also produces three-quarters of the world's supply of petitgrain, an essence of wild orange used in perfumes.

this question may be heard locally, like "The ocean!"—also "Everything" and "Lots of time." Indeed the country, with its insufferable poverty and lack of momentum, does certainly need a great deal in several dimensions. But a certain up-beat note has begun to be discernible. The currency is stable and inflation has been checked; the export balance has lately become favorable; an oil refinery is about to open; light industry—like plastics, cottonseed oil, molasses—are beginning; and a modest land reform, the essential above all essentials, is at last in motion.[12]

Nuestra Señora Santa María de la Asunción

ASUNCIÓN (pop. 305,000), founded in 1537—which means that it is almost thirty years older than St. Augustine, Florida, seventy-two years older than Jamestown—has a special double-edged quality, as has almost everything in Paraguay. It is both a mudhole and a charming small metropolis. Paraguayans, even those in the upper level of society, seldom go out when it rains, because of the juicy red mud apt to be underfoot; the mere fact of rain is an acceptable excuse for not showing up at a party; no other explanation is considered necessary. On the other hand Asunción is a remarkably neat little city, and its atmosphere is pleasant as well as sturdy. There are no slums, no *favelas*. Courtyards look scrubbed, and I never saw a beggar. A man may wear a shirt full of holes, but it will be clean.

Nothing illustrates the contrasts and paradoxes of Paraguay better than Asunción's new de luxe hotel, inevitably named the Guaraní. (An equivalent name in the United States would be the Hotel Iroquois-Dollar, since the Guaraní, usually called a "G," is also the national currency.) Out of the forlorn remote primitiveness of Paraguay the Guaraní rises like a shimmering vision, an Aladdin's dream. To walk into it in Asunción is like confronting suddenly a super-Ritz in the parched wastes of Somaliland.

The Guaraní was built as an investment from funds of the social security administration of the country, and rises twelve stories in a sharply cut triangle—designed by Brazilian architects of the modern school, and crackling with the most contemporary gadgets. From the standpoint of comfort as well as style it is one of the two or three best hotels in South America. But the style—in derelict Paraguay!—is what takes the breath away. Triangular stone pilasters, lifting the building off the ground; big aluminum louvers on checkerboard windows; recessed lights bound in brass, like portholes; elegant bidets colored black and olive; trays set into bed tables; aluminum-

---

[12] Forty thousand plots of unused government land were recently distributed to landless peasants. *Time*, May 8, 1964. See also *Visión Letter*, October 27, 1965.

and-plastic chairs like those in a luxury airliner; lights in the form of clusters of white chrysanthemums manipulated by cords; telephones streamlined to the limit; in a word, the *dernier cri*. The chambermaids are obviously chosen for their winsome good looks. The night club on the roof is open only one night a week.

The people of Asunción represent typical elements in the national character. They are violently chauvinist, but not xenophobic; foreigners are liked. They have a stolid inflexibility like Finns or Turks, but are capable of fierce excesses of sudden wrath. Almost all are decent, frugal, humble, honest, clean; motorists seldom bother to lock their cars. No racial problem exists at all; nobody thinks anybody is inferior because his skin is dark. Problems may be difficult, but not insoluble as they are in the Andean countries, packed with vacant-staring Indians utterly excluded from society.

And Asunción citizens are fresh—unexpected.

Very early one morning, about 5:30, the telephone rang in my bedroom at the Guaraní, awakening me. I thought I must be dreaming when I heard the night porter say, "The colonel is here with your airplane!" Of course I did not have an airplane. The explanation was that I had been offered a trip by air over the nearby countryside which I had had to decline because of other engagements, but my message to this effect must have been misunderstood and an officer had now arrived to take me to the airport. I explained all this to the night porter. He broke off our talk and returned to the telephone. "Ah, never mind," he purred. "The colonel was looking for a different Mr. Gunther." Thus was disappointment assuaged and Paraguayan face adroitly saved.

Food and drink are hearty, honest, and colorful in Asunción. One renowned dish is *sopa paraguaya,* made of cornmeal, onion, baking powder, eggs, and oil. Cheeses (from the Mennonite colonies) are admirable, and so is the local honey. The beer is good, and a *rosé* wine grown by German colonists resembles the Alsatian vin *gris.* There is no service charge on bills in hotels or restaurants, and tipping is up to you—a refreshing difference from the obligatory 22–24 percent tip in Uruguay and Argentina. The citizens of Asunción are great party goers, and if a well-known person is leaving the country there may be a *despedida,* farewell party, every day literally for weeks. Paraguayans are pronounced music lovers, and one specialty is the *conjunto* of guitar and harp (a small harp placed on a chair) which provides music for the polka—no resemblance to the Polish polka—and flower and bottle dances, picturesquely marked by handkerchiefs held aloft.

People talk about art—for instance the abstract sculpture of Hermann Guggiari, who recently did a "portrait" of John F. Kennedy in the form of an iron spike struck by lightning. They compare notes out of the Latin American edition of *Time* every Thursday, wonder what Stroessner will do next, and ask if it can be true that Martin Bormann, the last of the principal Nazi war criminals, is still alive and hiding in Paraguay, as is often alleged. The Paraguayan authorities—a black mark—have steadily refused to cooperate in any search for Nazi fugitives, and, during one investigation, declined to allow foreign detectives to compare Bormann's fingerprints with those on file in the local immigration office.[13]

One preoccupation almost universal is smuggling. American cigarettes and Scotch whiskey are cheaper in Asunción than New York, because these and multitudinous other products are smuggled in duty free. Lines of bright little shops selling contraband—perfumes, nylons, cameras, watches, and transistor radios—make the airport look, *mutatis mutandis*, like the vitrines of the Paris Ritz. Smuggling is winked at—or even encouraged—by elements in the army or government, although it would practically be worth one's life to say so openly in Asunción. There are two types of "official" smuggling. Old C-46's and other planes fly in regularly from Miami, choked to the ceiling with contraband, which finds its way to local manipulators. Nobody gets cheated in the first instance but the country, which of course loses the revenue that would normally come from the duty. Second, smuggled goods arrive for transshipment to Argentina. It is impossible to condone this vicious system as it applies to Paraguay. An old axiom says that "contraband humanizes the law" but the average citizen of Asunción is not being humanized when he has to pay three times the normal price for textiles and the equivalent of $10 for streptomycin that should cost 60 cents, because of the smuggling racket.

One day I took a brief automobile trip outside Asunción with two Americans who, like most members of the foreign community, are madly in love with Paraguay in spite of its Balkanesque corruptions, irritations, and complexities. Their emotion reminded me of that of British enthusiasts for remote small countries, like Albania, before the war. We drove on the only paved road leading out of Asunción (a fork comes later, making a second road) to Itauguá, a village devoted to making lace, and then to San Bernardino, a resort on Lake Ypacaraí. This is a standard tour, and the only one feasible if time is short.

Dogs that looked like pigs covered the highway, as well as pigs that looked like dogs. Scarlet termite hills, resembling those in Africa, rise amidst curtains of bright flowers, and women walk with large bundles poised on

[13] "World's Most Wanted Criminal," by Blake Clark, *Reader's Digest*, March, 1965.

their heads. Most of the wayfarers and townsmen wear shoes nowadays, a new development; twenty years ago even the army went barefoot and workers mixed cement with their toes. Now the favorite footgear is a Japanese sandal, known everywhere in the world, which is nicknamed the *japonesa* here. They cost 40 cents a pair and their use cuts down hookworm. Again it was pleasant to see the exceptional cleanliness of the people, their generosity, simplicity, and pride. They work dawn to dusk, but they have a tough and upstanding dignity.

We stopped to buy *chipas* from a roadside vendor; these are heavy rolls flavored with cheese and baked with oil, a national dish; they cannot be prepared in an ordinary oven (so the folklore has it) but only in an authentic Paraguayan round oven burning hardwood. For tea at the lakeside hotel, which looked like something in the South Pacific, we had candied mangoes and strange tough little limes with crimson flesh.

There should be another word about the local lace, known as *ñanduti*, which is Paraguay's distinctive handicraft. By terms of an old legend the women of Itauguá started making lace in memory of a young girl whose husband-to-be was killed on her wedding day; his body was found that night, "covered by a shimmering mantle of spider webs."[14] So she made a lace shroud to perpetuate his memory, and this gave rise to the industry.

Paraguay is a mad little country, yes, but this means merely that it is still a frontier state going through concurrent evolutions on different planes at the same time. There are plenty of demerits. But in spite of Stroessner the country has a wild vitality which, even if this is mostly suppressed today, gives hope for a vivid future. I returned to my hotel one evening after midnight and ran into a demonstration in the plaza. Boys and girls marched singing a triumphant chant, which began "Pa-ra-*guay*, PARAGUAY," and ended in an explosion of exhortation. The marching went faster; flags waved; youngsters leaned into parked cars and tooted horns; the reverberating words "Paraguay, Para-GUAY" kept rippling and booming confidently through the darkness of the square.

I thought somebody had made a revolution. No. Paraguay had won a football game that afternoon.

---

[14] *Land of Lace and Legend, an Informal Guide to Paraguay*, p. 98. Jasmine, sugar cane, the guava, grains of rice, herons, owls' bills, ostrich feathers, the footprints of oxen, and the drapery of the cross are among standard designs for *ñanduti* today. Much of the work is of exceptional fragile delicacy.

CHAPTER 14

A Good Man in Chile

Chile . . . the pilot country of Latin America.
—GENERAL CHARLES DE GAULLE

EDUARDO FREI MONTALVA, the president of Chile, is a man far superior to the ordinary, just as Chile itself is superior. We have come a long way now from the brutal provincialisms of Argentina, the romantic extravagances of Brazil. President Frei (pronounced "fray") resembles the pug-dog dictators about as much as the Archbishop of Canterbury resembles Batman. His passion is civic responsibility, and Chile is one of the few hemisphere republics civilized enough to face up to the major problems afflicting South America as a whole on a serious adult level.

Chile came close to voting itself Communist in 1964, the only hemisphere republic ever to do so. But Frei, who calls himself a Christian humanist, averted this by winning the presidency against a Marxist candidate after a vigorously contested free election. Leading a semi-leftist democratic coalition, he became the principal exponent in South America of the hypothesis that reform by the moderate left is the best means of forestalling extremist revolution.

Chile seems somewhat run-down at the edges, dispirited by inflation, and, in a peculiar way, short on vitality, but it has a keen intellectual urbanity and sophistication. The electorate is educated and responsible. The army plays no role whatever in political life. There has been no revolution since the early 1930's. The country has, however, an extraordinarily powerful and deeply entrenched landowner class, which blocks reform, and the disparity between oligarch and *roto* ("ragged one") is probably as salient as in any South American republic. Then too there are statistics of a type only too miserably familiar. Schools for 200,000 children are lacking, and the death rate for infants in some rural areas is 129 per 1,000. The country needs

257

400,000 housing units, and half of all citizens are classified as suffering from malnutrition.

Copper, mostly foreign owned, dominates the economy. This and land reform are the two principal national issues, and Frei is having a hard time coping with them. But trying to cope he is, and this is what makes him significant. Chile is really trying to *do* something about social and economic change.

Corruption on a serious level is unknown. There may be petty graft in the lower bureaucracy—Chile is almost as bureaucratized as Uruguay—but not in the upper. No minister involved in even the faintest hint of financial scandal could last a day.

Eduardo Frei, who came into power under the slogan "Revolution in Liberty," is a tall grave man, long faced, with a big anchor of a nose, high arching cheekbones, emphatic black eyebrows, and thinning dark hair. He has large expressive eyes, an orderly mind, and magnetism to a marked degree. I thought when I met him that he looked like an El Greco saint, but not so tortured.

His approach to life is uncompromisingly ethical, but he believes in action too. Probably his two principal qualities are kindness and intellectual vigor. One of his secrets is that he is a man of the mind, but appeals through the heart. He has a remarkable intuitive comprehension of affairs, and he knows how to clarify as well. A defect is rigidity—perhaps a certain naïveté.

The president, a Catholic, is an extremely modest man, and his manner of life is simple to the point of austerity. He does not live in the Casa de la Moneda, the presidential palace, but in the small middle-class house in a residential suburb which he bought at the time of his marriage almost thirty years ago, and which he and his wife have never left. A proposal was heard some months ago to name a children's playground in his honor, but he rejected it politely, saying, "That sort of thing can come later, if necessary." He refuses to accept any public honors.

Mr. Frei has traveled widely, having visited the Soviet Union once and the United States several times. He has found time to write five books, one of which, a volume of essays, won a national literary prize a few years ago. One of his steadiest interests is intra-American affairs. Recently he attended a conference on the presidential level in Bogotá designed to promote economic cooperation throughout the hemisphere, and he is a warm—if discriminating—believer in LAFTA, the Latin American Free Trade Association.

His wife, the former María Ruiz Tagle, to whom he is devoted, was a schoolteacher when they married, and still works a full day in a Santiago public school. They met for the first time at a social occasion in the house of a priest. The president's wife is shy, and keeps totally out of the public scene. The Freis have seven children; one daughter is a nun. The president's sister, Señora Irena Frei de Cid, a professional social worker, was killed in an automobile accident two years ago, returning from a public meeting where she had spoken on behalf of her brother. He had relied greatly on her advice and stimulus, and her death was a stunning blow.

The president has no hobbies, except books. When tired out he reads Dickens; at other times works on history, philosophy, and economics. He passionately loves the profession of politics, and is very good at it. His workday at the Moneda is unusual in that, except in an emergency, he never gives appointments in the morning. Until noon every day he reads reports, works out his plans, and assigns duties to his staff. When I saw him I asked him what he did to relax. In his youth he played tennis and football, and liked to swim. Now he walks a mile or two every day, getting out of his car and hiking part of the way to his house. Then too he sometimes strolls around the city alone late in the afternoon. People who see him are very "distinguished" about this, he said; nobody ever accosts him, and if passers-by recognize him they do nothing but pass him "a smiled greeting" or doff their hats. I asked if he had any bodyguard, and he replied, "No, I walk alone, and it is the tradition of Chile that the president walks freely among the people; this has always been so."

*

The hour we had with the president was rewarding. I looked around the Moneda. It was built for use, not display; originally the mint, its stone walls are four feet thick, and it houses three ministries as well as the presidential establishment, including foreign affairs and interior. (Chile has no vice-president; the minister of the interior is the ranking officer of the cabinet.) This is an informal country; people wander at will in the two courtyards of the Moneda, and the square it faces, the Plaza de la Constitución, in the center of the city, is a parking lot. Here the celebrated band of the *carabineros*, national police, play at the changing of the guard, one of the most picturesque ceremonies in South America.

When President Frei rises behind his desk to greet you he looks lanky, but somewhat dumpy too; the over-all impression is a tall, skinny man who is strangely a bit pear-shaped as well, yet he is not at all fat. His manner is calm, but there is a sense of formidable energy in his movements. At once the visitor grasps the reality behind the election posters still on the streets: Frei IS Patriotism; Frei IS Liberty; Frei IS Work; Frei IS Chile.

The president is a burningly devout Catholic, and he leads the Christian Democratic party, sometimes called the "Demo-Christians." As we have noted this exists in several South American republics as well as Chile, but here is where it is strongest and most indigenous. It is a Catholic party, but not "confessional," not a direct organ of the church, although the church may influence his policies. A good many citizens manage to be good Christian Democrats and bad Catholics at the same time.

I asked Mr. Frei what had been the chief intellectual forces in his youth, and he replied "the Christian concept," in which he included elements all the way from the medieval philosophers to Jacques Maritain. He went on to say that, to his mind, the basic Christian philosophy and Roman Catholicism as an organized religion were two quite different things, and should not be confused.

When I asked what the fundamental sources of power in Chile today are, the president indicated that these are changing. The great landowners, the industrialists, and the church hierarchy had ruled the country for years, but now the base was widening, partly as the result of the growth of a middle class and of the labor movement. What ran Chile now was, he insisted, the great mass of voters; the country has an extremely alert electorate, voting is obligatory, and the people really demand to be part of what is going on.

Mr. Frei seemed to be naturally convinced that his regime was the country's best defense against Communism and he added that, if his reforms did not go through, there was no doubt that FRAP (Frente de Acción Popular), the Socialist-Communist coalition, would win the next election. Yet the extreme right continues to be obstructionist. "They even call *me* a Communist!" he snorted. He was then careful to point out that his own party, now that the recent elections are over, does not attack the Communists. It is poor policy to be anti-anything, he thinks. The Christian Democrats are a positive party, convinced that the fulfillment of their own program will satisfy the electorate. But he admitted, with a kind of reluctant admiration, that the Communists had an effective "mystique," were well organized, were not afraid of sacrifice, and had an unshakable nucleus in part of the working class.

The president made a passing reference to tax reform; it was extremely difficult to check on tax evasion by the rich, he said. The little man paid his taxes, but numerous wealthy individuals exported millions of tax-free dollars to banks in the United States.

I asked what Chile needed most, and he wagged a warning finger. Education, industrialization, agricultural reform—the obvious factors—are not, he said, enough of an answer, because if you give education without the possibility of economic advance the result is dissatisfaction, not progress. Similarly, economic improvement without education is self-defeating. So what Chile has to have is a plan, a plan for intermeshed development involving all these elements, particularly land reform. "I must start to give material and educational development under an organized plan which the people believe in and have faith in, and in the time I have at my disposal I can only make a beginning. And this is very difficult because the people may think that they are not getting enough. Yet I must make this plan and give the people some understanding of the ideal we seek to achieve."

It happens that I had met Mr. Frei in Santiago a quarter of a century before, when he was a young politician at the beginning of his career; I asked him now if it had ever occurred to him at that time that he would be president. He laughed, but made no other reply. Presidents of Chile may not be re-elected until an intervening term has passed; hence, when Frei's present term expires in 1970 he will have to wait until 1976 before being able to run again, and after that, if he wins, 1988. I asked him if he expected to be a candidate in both these years. He replied quite seriously, "One lives from day to day."

Lifeline of the President

Eduardo Frei was born in Santiago on January 16, 1911, of Swiss stock; his father, an immigrant from Switzerland, was an accountant on the railways. Young Frei grew up in a middle-class neighborhood, and rubbed shoulders with both rich and poor; he attended the public schools, became gripped by a passion for social justice, and was already a reformer by the time he entered Catholic University in Santiago.

Working his way by tutoring, he obtained a degree in law in 1933, and then, in a familiar South American pattern, went into journalism and became a teacher. He edited the newspaper *Tarapacá* in the northern town of Iquique for a time, and presently returned to Catholic University as a professor of labor relations. He was astoundingly precocious. His interest in action—political action—came early. He started as a Conservative, then broke away, and, with a group of friends, founded in 1935 an organization known as the National Falange. This, however, had nothing to do with the Fascist party of the same name which was emerging in Spain at about the same time. It was a reformist party, both Christian and on the moderate left.

Out of this came the Christian Democrats, or, as the official name is in Chile, the Partido Demócrata Cristiano (PDC). The movement spread out all over South America, and, indeed, the world; three hundred delegates attended a Christian Democratic conference in Lima in April, 1966, representing nineteen nations in Latin America and ten in western Europe. As of today in South America the Christian Democrats have participated in the government coalition in Venezuela, had a number of deputies in Brazil before the purges, and play a substantial role in Peru.

Obviously then the Christian Democrats have something—what? Their own spokesmen, like Frei, talk about the stimulus of reformist papal encyclicals and the "Judeo-Christian ethics" of the western world with their strong association with social problems. Pope John XXIII is one of their heroes; so is John F. Kennedy.

In a nutshell Christian Democracy offers an alternative in the world struggle between extreme right and left, a third force between reactionary capitalism, with all its wanton abuses in South America, and Socialism-Communism, with its threats to the established order. What Frei wants is to reform society without wrecking it. But he is more to the left—the democratic left—than to the right.

As a senator Mr. Frei voted in 1958 to restore legality to the Communist party, which had been outlawed in Chile for a decade, and on becoming president in 1964, he immediately gave diplomatic recognition to the Soviet Union. This is probably one reason why the State Department looked on him with a cold eye at the beginning. Probably a handful of former extreme left-wingers and ex-Communists have joined the Christian Democrats, but they do not exert any influence. Any forward-looking mass movement is bound to pick up extremists who view it in their own image, take refuge in it, or seek to make use of it. The same thing happened under Roosevelt in the early New Deal.

To return. Frei, working hard at politics, became a cabinet minister by 1945, and was elected to the senate later. He ran for the presidency unsuccessfully in 1958. Then the Christian Democrats began to grow with rapidity, and, in municipal elections in 1963, they emerged suddenly as the strongest party in the country. In 1964 Frei ran for the presidency again, and won with a thumping 56 percent of the total vote. Supporting him, aside from his own Christian Democrats, were Conservatives, Liberals, a leftist splinter group, and independents. The opposition was FRAP, the Socialist-Communist coalition, as well as a third contestant to be mentioned later. Frei won by 1,410,000 popular votes to 980,000, but FRAP made an impressive fight and received 39 percent of the total poll.

This election was, then, basically a struggle between moderate left and extreme left, and the moderates won. Frei was inaugurated president of

Chile on November 3, 1964, for a six-year term. "I am responsible now," he told Adlai E. Stevenson, who led the American delegation to the inaugural ceremonies. He looked determined, serene, and confident. That night he welcomed in the Moneda several thousand peasants and workers with their wives, who wandered through the palace. Saying good night to a friend, Dr. José Mayobre, the head of ECLA, the UN Economic Commission for Latin America, he murmured, "No one can ask me to do more than I promised, but neither can anybody ask me to do less."

Frei had won an amazing personal triumph—the largest plurality of any presidential candidate in Chilean history—but a lame duck congress frustrated him at every turn. The Christian Democrats had only 23 out of 147 seats in the house of representatives and an even smaller representation in the senate, and it was impossible to push through an effective legislative program.

Then came congressional elections in March, 1965, and Frei won a broader victory. His number of seats in the house rose by 55, and he found himself with an absolute majority there, the first time this had happened in Chile since 1851. He did not, however, carry the senate, although his representation more than doubled, and this failure has pursued him grievously ever since.

*

Chilean politics are as intricate as any in the world. I have said that voting is obligatory. Actually it is registration that is obligatory, but this amounts to the same thing. Voting is a legal duty for all citizens qualified to vote, which means everybody literate twenty-one or over. Every voter has a card with a serial number, so that votes cannot be "delivered," as they are in Brazil, by the local boss. These cards are like social security identifications in the United States, but have an even more widespread use; it is impossible to cash a check without a card, register a birth, or transact any public business. An eligible voter is subject to a prison term up to sixty days, commutable to a fine, if he fails to register.[1] And registration—particularly by women—may entail long and tedious waiting with a baby at the hip.

Another consequential factor is the extraordinary power of women since they won suffrage in 1949. Most have a stern sense of public duty, and help to keep politics pure; most take a somewhat conservative line, under the influence of the church, but, even so, they helped to a large degree to elect Frei to the presidency. Women are more emancipated in Chile than in any other South American country; many, entering the professions, insist on

[1] *Chile Election Factbook*, September 4, 1964, a valuable pamphlet, p. 14.

keeping their maiden names after marriage.[2] I met women even in the shantytowns who voted enthusiastically for Frei although their husbands voted for FRAP. The women's vote is totaled separately, and so accurate figures are available. In Santiago 345,000 women voted for Frei, as against 288,000 men. All told, 673,678 men voted for Frei, 606,356 for his FRAP opponent; but the women voted for Frei 744,423 to 375,766.

Then there are several unusual pressure groups, one of which is, of all things, the fire departments in the cities. Firemen are volunteers in Chile, even providing their own uniforms, and it has been a tradition for many years for elite young men to serve in this capacity, much as well-born youngsters in New York City in the old days joined fashionable regiments. They form an important cohesive group.

Other factors making political power are more conventional, and we shall deal with them in pages following. Most important are the landowners.

Interlude

For a hundred years after liberation, roughly from 1818 to 1920, Chile developed placidly but within a somewhat rigid frame. Mr. Frei told us—to illustrate the country's political maturity—that the principal political parties date back to 1833 or thereabouts, and have changed little since.

These were the Conservatives and the Liberals, who were just as conservative as the Conservatives. Both basically represented the landed oligarchy; the difference—in the familiar South American manner—being the degree of association with the Catholic church. The Conservatives were more churchly. A third major party, rising in the 1880's, was the Radicals; it represented the growing middle class and was strongly Masonic and anticlerical.

Chile had few forced changes of government and little internal strife. The record is not remotely like that of Venezuela, Colombia, or even Argentina. The country was the stablest in the hemisphere. Elections were held on schedule and constitutional procedures strictly observed under ostensibly democratic but in fact autocratic presidential rule.

Nobody had a chance of rising in political life without the approval of the landowners (one historian goes so far as to say that every president was a "landowner's nominee") and the peasants and *inquilinos*, sharecroppers, had practically no representation at all, a factor which is still the bare root of many Chilean troubles today.

Meantime, in relation to its neighbors, Chile took a surprisingly nation-

[2] There are an astounding number of women dentists.

alist line; it fought—and won—three wars in the nineteenth century, including a brief naval war against Spain, in which the British were involved. In 1833–39 came a war against a Peruvian-Bolivian combination, and this was repeated in 1879–83, the so-called "War of the Pacific"—a serious affair; the Chilenos occupied Lima, which Peru has resented ever since, and grabbed off large quantities of Peruvian and Bolivian territory in the north. This was an acquisition of the utmost value, because it included the great nitrate fields which for many years were the country's principal source of wealth.

Along about 1920 came explosive disintegration on the domestic side. The people could no longer be contained. The basic struggle for power, which still epitomizes so much of South America, was conventional enough, but acute—that between a rich privileged minority on the top and the under-possessed millions below, the slum-dwellers in the towns, the peons on the great estates. The easiest way to describe this conflict in Chile is by way of personality. I have been tempted to make a list of presidents, but this would be too long; Chile had six presidents in 1924–25, and eight between July, 1931, and December, 1932. The cork leapt out of the bottle.

But let us begin with a great and bizarre man, Arturo Alessandri Palma, the "Lion of Tarapacá," who was president for the first time from 1920 to 1924. A radical, he ended ninety years of uninterrupted domination by the right. He separated church and state, established the first income tax in Chilean history, wrote a labor code, and pushed through far-reaching social reforms. A man of enormous physical force, Alessandri once dragged a wounded policeman out of a mob single-handed, and once used a stick on an opposition deputy and threw him over a fence. He liked to lean over the balcony of the Moneda and address crowds of thousands, which gathered spontaneously, for hour after hour; he was the greatest orator of his time, but rough-tongued.

Putschists threw Alessandri out in 1924, and he fled the country. It was impossible for him to admit that Chile had another president, and he came back to power briefly in 1925. His prestige as a people's man was such that a crowd of a hundred thousand met him on his return; several men and women were trampled to death, and the mob tore bricks out of his own house as souvenirs. Presently he was forced out of office again, and a period of wild confusion followed until General Carlos Ibáñez del Campo, a semi-Fascist dictator, seized the presidency by means of a coup d'état in 1927.

Ibáñez lasted till 1931. He is remembered chiefly as a wildly lavish spender. During this period American banks lent Chile $208,000,000, which made it one of the most heavily overborrowed countries in the world. The

Ibáñez loans were among the most famous of the "sucker loans" that drained money out of small investors in the United States in the twenties; most have long since been defaulted, but, even today, the Chilean government is saddled with a very large indebtedness to the United States; one of the first items on Frei's agenda was, indeed, negotiations with Washington to refinance, i.e., postpone or reapportion payment of the long-standing national debt. As to Ibáñez he was much criticized for borrowing so much; his answer was that American bankers, with charming optimism, tossed the money at him, and that he would have been a blockhead to have turned it down.

Soon Ibáñez was overthrown; he fled to Argentina. A factor in his ousting was a remarkable "general strike of intellectuals," in which doctors, lawyers, engineers participated. In 1931 an army colonel with the memorable name Marmaduque Grove became president for twelve days, leading a left-wing junta which ruled as the "Socialist Republic of Chile." He was then pitched out, to be succeeded by a man who lasted three months, whereupon the great Alessandri assumed the presidency once more, and stuck out a new full term from 1932 to 1938.

There should be another word about Marmaduque Grove. He was a character almost incredibly picturesque. He called his brand of socialism Grovismo, and indeed it was like no other ever heard of. He was the son of an Irish doctor, and thought of himself as a victim of the oligarchy. Grove was an officer in *both* army and navy concurrently, and then joined the air force too, rising to be chief of staff. Previously he had gone to Europe and served in the *German* army. In 1925 he partook in the Ibáñez coup against Alessandri, and then joined Alessandri against Ibáñez. To get rid of him Grove was sent abroad to be military attaché in London, and on his return he was dismissed from the military service; promptly he went to Buenos Aires, and talked a newspaper there into backing him on a wild adventure by which he would fly back to Santiago, alone, and make a revolution. This exploit failed, and the Ibáñez government exiled him for ten years to Easter Island, the Chilean outpost 2,400 miles out in the Pacific, unreachable by air (in those days) and where a boat called once every six months or so.

This did not daunt Marmaduque Grove. Friends chartered a schooner, and soon rescued him. Now, returning to Chile, he was greeted as a hero and became minister of national defense. There came other energetic vicissitudes. In 1931 Grove revolted against the government of which he was a leading member. By this time he was a fanatical people's man. Later in one unbelievable week he threw out a president named Dávila, and then Dávila threw him out. Again he was arrested and shipped off to Easter Island. His partisans made a public collection for funds to procure a boat and fetch him back, to which the *government* contributed, although it insisted that it did not know where Grove was. Then, delivered from Easter Island once more, he announced his candidacy for the presidency of the republic. But his boat could only do eight knots, and he arrived in Santiago too late to run. Eventually this indomitable man became head of the Popular Front.

This story gives a hint of the marvelous passionate wildness which is still typical of South America. But, to proceed, Alessandri, whose career had been built on services to the left, confounded all observers by switching to the right during his new term. Probably this was caused by the influence of his finance minister, an ice-eyed conservative named Gustavo Ross. The left, outraged at Alessandri's apostasy and indignant at his harsh putting-down of strikes, set out to fight him vigorously. The Alessandri candidate for the 1938 elections was Ross, a formidable opponent. The left realized that their only possibility of success was unity, and so, at long last, a Popular Front was formed, consisting (like the Popular Front in France at about the same time) of radicals, Socialists, and Communists. Grove was nominally its chairman, but the candidate chosen to fight Ross was Pedro Aguirre Cerda, a radical. Nobody thought that he had the slimmest chance of winning, but he did—although by the narrowest of margins, some 4,000 out of 400,000 votes.

Ross scooted off to exile in Argentina, and Chile found itself with the first Popular Front government ever known in the Americas. In those days politicians skimmed back and forth across the Andes between Santiago and Buenos Aires like torn eagles.

This Aguirre Cerda (1938–44) regime was well-meaning, but muddled and ineffective. The Communists, preferring to exert power from the background, did not take ministerial posts. A nuisance was the local Nazi movement, powerfully fed by the large German element in the Chilean population. There were at least three Nazi parties. The Nazis disclaimed any association with the Reich's Embassy in Santiago but, naturally, when World War II came, took the German side. Interestingly enough Chile was the only South American country which never declared war against the Axis in Europe. It broke off relations, but did not go to war. It did, however, declare war on Japan—very late, in the spring of 1945—on the ground that it was a Pacific power and in order to gain a seat at the San Francisco Conference which set up the UN.

The Popular Front broke up, after which the Radicals held power alone until 1952. One president, Gabriel González Videla, gave cabinet posts to three Communists—marking the first time Communists had ever formally entered a South American government—presumably to strengthen his position with the left. Then, a few months later, González did a complete turnabout, dismissed the three, packed them off to a concentration camp, and outlawed the Communist party, because this was now showing *too* much electoral strength. Dictator Carlos Ibáñez returned to power in 1952, although he was now in his mid-seventies. He had become a kind of Peronista, and was now, strangely enough, being backed by *leftist* groups. Then in 1958, the last presidential election before that which Frei won in 1964, Jorge Alessandri Rodríguez, the son of the great Alessandri, won the presidency and set out to carry on his father's tradition. A wealthy industrialist in his sixties, he ran as an independent, but had Liberal, Radical, and Conservative support.

Alessandri Rodríguez was cool, decent, and uninspired. The most interesting development during his term (1958–64) was the rise of new political forms. The incohesion of years became crystallized. The Christian Democrats, rising hard, turned into a serious force; Frei, running against Alessandri in 1958, won 20.7 percent of the total vote, a consequential showing. FRAP was also on the rise. Born in 1956, it was a kind of successor to the old Popular Front, comprising Communist, Socialist, and other leftist elements; its leader was Dr. Salvador Allende Gossens, a left-wing Socialist. He had run for president back in 1952, coming out a bad loser with only 5.5 percent of the votes; but when he ran again in 1958 Alessandri barely beat him, and he got a larger percentage of the vote than Frei.

Before Alessandri's term was half finished it became clear that the next election (in 1964) would be out and out between Frei, representing the Christian Democrats, and Allende, running for FRAP. Oddly enough the two men had been close friends for many years.

Frei's Victory in 1964

We must mention this critical election once more. It would seem that Frei was bound to win at a walk, since he had behind him the church, a majority of women, and his own party, plus a good sprinkling of conservatives, non-Communist workers and farmers, and miscellaneous voters. Yet the fight was closely contested. Frei won, but, as noted above, FRAP got 39 percent of the poll. (Frei got 56 percent.)

This election, in the words of one Freísta observer, marked the first collision of the two fastest-growing forces in South America—"revolutionary" Christianity and Communism. Actually the picture was not quite so simple as that. Nothing in Chile is ever simple. There were, as a matter of fact, three contestants, but the third, Julio Durán Newman, a senator and former speaker of the house, was badly beaten, getting only 5 percent of the vote. His story is worth telling, however, if only because it is one more demonstration—not that we need any more—of the maniacal complexities of politics in South America.

Durán was (and is) an able and popular figure. He ran as the candidate of what was called the Democratic Front, a loose grouping of right-center forces (Conservatives, Liberals, Radicals) which had elected Alessandri in 1958 and was the government party. But Alessandri could not succeed himself, and so Durán took on the candidature, thinking that he could beat both Frei and FRAP. There came, however, a by-election in Curicó, a province near Santiago, in March, 1964, six months before the presidential election in September, and Durán's candidate finished a bad third. Humiliated, Durán himself then withdrew from the race, and the Democratic Front fell to pieces. But then Durán changed his mind, deciding to continue the fight in spite of the shattering defeat at Curicó, but he ran as a straight Radical, not as a candidate of the Democratic Front. This left the Conservatives and Liberals without a candidate. So, even though these represent the extreme right, they voted—albeit grudgingly—for Frei because, after all, he was preferable to the Marxist FRAP, and they did not want to support Durán. Frei would have won anyway, but hard-crust reactionaries helped him. This is one reason why the extreme left, even today, denounces Frei as a cat's-paw of the right, its "new face," which he is not.

The fact remains that a principal reason for his victory was that many rightists voted for him not because of his positive program—which they indeed deplored—but to keep FRAP out.

As to the right itself, it was all but obliterated as a parliamentary force in this extraordinary election. Clearly the people thought that Communism could be best beaten by measures of liberal reform taken by the non-Communist left, as represented by Frei, rather than by reactionaries on the right.

Other reasons for Frei's victory were these:

1. His obvious personal qualities. For one thing he is an extremely good family man. Honest, serious, clean, he was respected as a good husband, a good father, a factor much appreciated by women voters. He projected a moral image.

2. He was fresh, a new face—after years of monotonous confusion and mediocrity. Voters wanted change.

3. He held control of the strategic center.

4. He benefited from an electoral reform made by Alessandri, which greatly extended the electorate.

5. Not merely a party leader, he was a man with a doctrine—something that people could hang on to. He offered concrete solutions to deep and adhesive dissatisfactions.

6. The Christian Democrats, evolving into a mass party, made a brilliant campaign in strictly political terms. Frei knew that the rightists had to fall into his lap whether they liked it or not, and cultivated the left down to the grassroots level with scrupulous zeal. Teams went out into the slums, the factories, the farms, organizing votes; on election day baby-sitters supplied by the party organization made it easier for mothers to vote.

7. FRAP made enemies by several blunders, including one fierce attack on the church in Congress, when a senator called priests "vampires," something unprecedented. Allende, running for president the third time, was a dull candidate.

8. A peculiar wave of hysteria, the origins of which are unknown, rose as a result of rumors that residents of the *callampas*, or squatter towns, would sweep into Santiago and take over the houses of the bourgeoisie in the event of a FRAP victory.

9. Some citizens even went so far as to fear an armed attack by Argentina if FRAP won, on the assumption that the Argentines would not tolerate a Communist regime on their frontier. There was even wild talk of military intervention by the United States.

One leading Socialist I met adduced another reason, that the general atmosphere of the time was not propitious for the left. He added an astonishing sentence, "Kennedy died, and Goulart lost power in Brazil."

How Leftist Is Frei?

One of the President's best friends answered this question with the words "So much so that he would be a Marxist except for his allegiance to the church." But this is dubious. Frei has no intention of taking over the means of production, abolishing private property, or establishing the dictatorship of the proletariat. He is hammering hard at the copper companies and the landlords, but within a democratic frame. The Christian Democrat motto is "Revolution in Freedom," but the operative word here is freedom, and "revolution" is used in its South American rather than literal sense.

The long and short of it is that Frei is a reformer. His general line is roughly that of the New Deal of Franklin D. Roosevelt or even the British Labour party. The right should, it would seem, logically welcome rather than oppose him because his brand of moderate leftness is an insurance against a movement farther left. But, as a matter of fact, once the elections were over some elements on the right moved into full bitter opposition and even maintain a kind of unstated parliamentary coalition with the Communists.

The Frei government has one of the hardest and touchiest jobs any government can face, that of fighting off a nondemocratic force by democratic means, without sacrifice of freedom. The Christian Democrat ideal and ambition is, one observer puts it, "to reconstruct certain large elements in society without having to fire a shot or touch a hair on a child's head."

Frei is safe, it would seem, so long as the Vatican and the State Department both support him. The United States, after a hesitant start, has become very friendly. What would happen if the moderate non-Communist left were crushed? That is the mortal danger of dictatorships like those of General Onganía in Argentina and the generals in Brazil—they abolish the free alternative. The liberal opposition has nowhere to go *except* Communism. At least Chile gives hope of a sustained and intelligently directed middle course. But what if the moderate left cannot succeed in putting through its reforms without inducing rightist counterrevolution or upsetting the structure of the state to such a degree that chaos—or Communism—is assisted? The answer is that this is not likely to happen if the true basic interests of the people remain the first imperative, as they do with Frei, and if the electorate is given a fair chance.

Men Around Frei

These comprise what has been called the most "brilliant" cabinet in the world. All its members are intellectuals; most were professors, who have known one another for years, and form an integrated team; they still do their homework, and are not unconscious of their own merit. One of them said to me with engaging audacity, "We make a strong group. We have spent our lives preparing for this role, and we will be the government for thirty years."

Second in command after the president is Bernardo Leighton Guzmán, minister of the interior, born in 1909, a graduate of Catholic University in Santiago, and subsequently a lawyer and professor of the philosophy of law. Leighton, a dedicated, earnest, and boyish-looking man, has mixed political plumage. He came out of the right (as did Frei) and was the creator of the Falange, which was a precursor of the Christian Democrats. He was once Frei's boss. He became a cabinet minister—minister of labor under the elder Alessandri—at the astounding age of twenty-five, and resigned office on an issue having to do with free speech and civil liberties, which he defended. He and Frei have been as close as fingers for thirty years or more.

Gabriel Valdés Subercaseaux, the foreign minister, is sometimes called a romantic. He has charm, grace, and good looks. His wife, a professional musician, plays the viola and flute, and is director of a small exquisitely sophisticated orchestra and choir specializing in fourteenth- and fifteenth-century music. The Valdés home, with its atmosphere of civilized living and devotion to the arts, is a Santiago landmark for those cultured without pretense. Valdés himself, a former publisher and owner of the radio station Cruz del Sur, is a lawyer by profession.[3]

Dr. Valdés became a professor of economic policy at Catholic University in 1954, and even today, while he is the third man in the government, he gives an eight-o'clock class at the university every morning. He thinks that it is of the utmost importance to keep abreast of what students are thinking, even if he has to teach them to find out. His wife teaches too. Valdés derives from a long tradition of public service. His great-great-grandfather was a president of the republic, and one of his grandfathers held the post he himself now holds, minister of foreign affairs.

Sergio Molina Silva, the minister of finance, is not yet forty, has a lively mind, and was dean of the faculty of economics at National University in Santiago. A civil engineer, Domingo Santa María Santa Cruz, who was a professor of physics at the School of Engineering at Catholic University, is minister of economy. And so it goes. Juan Gómez Millas, minister of education, is a professor of the history of geography and a former rector of the University of Chile; the minister of justice, Pedro J. Rodríguez González, one of the founders of the party, is a professor of civil law; Hugo Trivelli Franzolini, another young man who is a political veteran, is minister of agriculture. Men are given posts consonant with their academic or other training. The minister of public works, Modesto Collados Nuñez, is a civil engineer; the minister of health, Dr. Ramón Valdivieso Delauney, is a physician; the minister of mining, Eduardo Simián Gallet, is a geologist who played a direct role in the recent discovery of oil in southern Chile.

One powerful and attractive figure is Radomiro Tomic Romero, the Chilean ambassador to Washington, the leading theoretician in the party. He was a founder of the old Falange, its president twice, one of Frei's closest associates, and the president's chief brain truster for many years. Of Yugoslav

[3] The first time we saw Minister Valdés he took us to a pleasant informal back room in his suite in the Moneda, where we began to talk over cups of coffee. A pearl-gray telephone rang; it was the president, summoning him, and that ended our interview—before it could begin. Later, given another appointment, we sat down at the same table in the same positions and had coffee again and once more the same telephone rang—again the president! But this time Valdés did not have to go to see him, and we talked for an hour.

origin, Dr. Tomic was a professor of social legislation at Catholic University, then a senator, and has always been a man of the left.

Two men of consequence outside the cabinet are Jorge Ahumada and Raúl Sáez, the planners—Ahumada mostly on the agricultural side, Sáez on industry. Both are technicians, "laboratory men," and apolitical; Sáez, an engineer, has been largely in charge of the recent negotiations over copper, and was one of the "Nine Wise Men" on the Alianza. Another stimulating person is Dr. José Mayobre, secretary-general of ECLA, which has its headquarters in Santiago. Dr. Mayobre is a Venezuelan, not Chilean, and he is an international civil servant, but his local influence is wide.

Two Notable Churchmen

Raúl Cardinal Silva Henríquez, primate of Chile, is sometimes called "the instant cardinal," not in disrespect but as an affectionate sobriquet, because his rise in the hierarchy was so unprecedentedly swift. He was elevated from monsignor to bishop to cardinal within five years during the papacy of John XXIII. Next to Dom Helder Câmara in Brazil, he is probably the most conspicuous liberal in the upper hierarchy of the church throughout the whole of South America. He has been a friend of Frei's for twenty years.

The cardinal, in his late fifties, is stocky, with a big head, bushy black eyebrows, and luminous dark eyes. Although courteous he seemed ill at ease, even tense, at the beginning of our interview; he does not see foreign journalists often. Later, talking about himself rather than politics, he became more relaxed. His father, of modest means, managed agricultural properties, and he was the sixteenth child of his family. The cardinal went to the public schools, and did not prepare himself for holy orders until after getting a degree in law at Santiago University. As a priest he edited a church newspaper in Chile, headed a Catholic relief organization, and organized a low-cost housing project for the poor. Again we see the Chileno instinct to reform.

Cardinal Silva became a public figure overnight in 1961, a year after he received the red hat, when he issued a nine-thousand-word pastoral letter urging social change. To add deed to word he donated some fifty thousand acres of farmland owned by the Santiago church to impoverished tenants, who are now operating this—through cooperatives—as a kind of pilot project for Frei's land reform. A further gift of thirteen thousand acres came in 1965. The cardinal was photographed at the plow—he had learned how to use one during his boyhood. He has made other headlines—without in any way opening himself to the charge of being a sensationalist—by speaking on racial and religious tolerance in a synagogue, urging that "excessive veneration" of and "sentimental devotion" to the cult of the Virgin Mary was a danger to Catholic institutions, and, in general, as a warm supporter of the second Ecumenical Congress held at the Vatican under Pope Paul VI.

The Cardinal's 1961 pastoral letter aroused pointed interest all over South America, because, better than any other document, it reflected the view of the reformist or "revolutionary" wing of South American Catholicism. Silva stated that, in his view, social reform is the only answer to Communism, and that, although he passionately deplored Communism and ruled out any association with it, cooperation between the church and the Communist-Socialist Front should be possible within certain limits. This pastoral letter was read out to every Catholic congregation in Chile, and 200,000 copies of its text were distributed. It called for land reform, punishment for tax evaders, the "curbing of the big monopolies," and a vastly extended program of education. The cardinal criticized "those wealthy Chileans who deposited their money abroad while millions were in misery at home." "One tenth of the Chilean population receives almost half the national income. This bad distribution of Chile's riches is paid for in malnutrition of the people. . . . Social injustice and poverty foster Communism. We must not be reactionaries. We are on the brink."

*

When I asked people in Chile a standard question, "Who runs this place?," I heard some standard answers—Frei, copper, Congress, women, the United States, "a gang of do-gooders," the fire department, and "the people." Then came one unexpected, "The University of Louvain." This was a reference to the wide local prestige of Father Roger Vekemans, a Belgian Jesuit who was educated at Louvain. He came to Chile ten years ago, and is an indissoluble part of its intellectual community. It is not correct, however, to call him "the" *éminence grise* behind the Frei government, as is sometimes said. Nobody is that. Nor is he a Jesuit secret agent, except in the sense that all Jesuits are, in a way, secret agents. Father Vekemans had, and has, no official position whatever. He was a professor of sociology at Catholic University, nothing else. Now he operates a foundation for sociological research on his own, nothing more, but his influence is pervasive on the highest level. Time and again we heard ideas formulated by him repeated by others, even if they did not fully appreciate where the ideas had come from.

This is a most remarkable man, one of the most exciting I met in South America. Monsignor Vekemans is tall, lean, craggy, with pale spellbinding eyes. He has logic, drive, and determination. He asked us to lunch, and, since he is a true Belgian, this was a stupendous affair, beginning with *erizos* (sea urchins), pâté de foie gras, and mussels as big as your fist. It was also modest, served in his office (which had recently been damaged by an earthquake), and with nobody else present except a secretary. Vekemans talked with sophisticated eloquence and intensity for three and a half hours. First, about South America in general. This is, contrary to general thought, already a middle-class continent, and it is *western*. "We are not Pakistan." "You cannot build a housing program here as you would in Iran." And it is all the same continent, even though Chile differs from Paraguay more than Sweden from Greece. Politics? The Christian Democrats won here because of fear of Communism. The right had, under Alessandri, a last chance to do something for the people; it did not do so, and "buried itself." "We" filled the vacuum. The right will not dare to attack Frei in the last analysis, no matter how strenuously it opposes him now, because he is their insurance against further revolution from the left. "The secret of Christian Democracy is that it gives an alternative." It combines democracy, faith, and ideals.

The Communists have lost charisma, he went on. They are dated, out of style. The hard core of the movement is still hard, but "the clientele" is playboy. The Socialists, not the Communists, are those who have turned to Peking, to get away from the stultifying hand of Moscow. Revolution, if it comes, will come from the military technocrats, not the Communists. *"Power rests on the myth of power,"* and Communists have lost the myth.

Finally, Father Vekemans talked about the people. "They, not copper, are the essential raw material!" It is the people who make the basis wealth. But Chile is a "marginal" country; that is, the people are not "on the ladder." Even if voting is obligatory and they vote intelligently, they do not otherwise partake of the benefits of society. Thirty percent of the population are peasants, starving on huge feudal properties; 30 percent are "subproletarians" in the squatter towns. They don't go to movies enough, read newspapers enough, play games enough. Out on the *fundos*, big estates, they are still no more than "dust on the land." And the people must be brought into the fabric of society, given focus and human dignity through reform. "If we fail, the game's up."

The Frei Program

President Frei had moved slowly, partly out of his natural habit of caution and temperateness, partly because of political necessity. His majority in the house of representatives has been secure since March, 1965, but, as we know, he does not command the senate. Major elements in his program include the Chileanization (partial nationalization) of copper, to be described in the next chapter, land reform (which may cost as much as half a billion dollars in the next six years), tax reform, already being steadily applied, and the extension of primary education. New schools are to be built under a program designed to make free compulsory school attendance effective throughout the whole nation within the next six years. Seventy-five thousand more children are in school this year than last. As to taxes, collections rose 67 percent in 1965 over 1964.

A new labor code is being written, which will include the unionization of rural workers. The housing program envisages sixty thousand new homes per year, and a concept known as Promoción Popular is being vigorously pushed. This began as a kind of self-help project for slum dwellers, but has now gone beyond this, and is an attempt to confront the major problem alluded to by Father Vekemans, namely the desperate necessity to incorporate the under-possessed further into the fabric of society, so that they will "belong." The twin reasons for not belonging are lack of education and poverty. So there has to be a double effort—not merely to build new schools but to increase national income and give economic opportunity. But reform on the scale envisaged by the Frei planners is fantastically expensive, and it may be a long time before it pays off and the "economic potential" is sufficient to support Promoción Popular. Meantime, the inflation has to be controlled.

Men have had easier jobs than Frei's.

The Opposition—FRAP

The picture here, like almost everything in Chile, is moderately complicated. FRAP, as already noted, consists of two main constituents, Socialists and Communists, and, uniquely in the world, the former are more leftist, more radically inclined and extremist, than the latter. Socialists here are not moderate Fabians, not Social Democrats in the European sense; one must forget all about analogies to men like Willi Brandt, Harold Wilson, or the Scandinavian labor leaders. They are outright Marxist revolutionaries, much more so than the Kremlin Communists.[4]

Relations between the Socialists and Communists within FRAP are fluid. The Communists dominate it, but the titular leader is Dr. Salvador Allende, a Socialist. This came about partly because the Communists thought—rightly—that he would be a more effective presidential candidate in 1964

[4] Ernest Halperin, *Sino-Cuban Trends: The Case of Chile*, p. 5. This pamphlet is a major source for material on FRAP and the Chilean left.

than any of their own men, and he was the only Socialist they would accept.

Senator Allende is a Freemason, which also lent power to his position, since Masonry is an important local force. Born of the upper classes in 1908, Allende is a doctor of medicine; he made his first political speech at the funeral of his father, who was a well-known nonconformist professional man, when he was seventeen. Dr. Allende is a vigorous and magnetic personality, and has a nice bourgeois exterior. But he is often called "cynical," which puts him at a disadvantage vis-à-vis Frei, an unashamed idealist, in the eyes of many voters, particularly women. He joined the Socialist party early in the 1930's, rose rapidly, and has been a senator since 1945.[5] He was close to Castro for some years, and attended the Tri-Continental Congress of Revolutionary Movements held in Havana in 1966.

Castro himself has, however, lost much face in Chile, and FRAP carefully avoided any mention of him in the 1964 campaign. Allende does not want a Communist dictatorship in Chile, and thinks that he can "manage" the Communists, his colleagues say. But he represents the pro-Communist wing of the Socialist party and stands for full collaboration with the Communists.

Raúl Ampuero Díaz leads the anti-Communist wing of the Socialists within FRAP. An islander, born in 1907 in Chiloé off the southern coast, Ampuero is the son of a schoolteacher. He studied law and medicine; then politics seized him, and he rose to be secretary general of the socialist party in 1946 and a senator in 1953. He has been called a Titoist, and is accused of having split the party. Ampuero is a brilliant dialectician. One point he stressed when we met was that the Frei reforms could not possibly work because, to be effective, they would have to be operated in a full revolutionary context, which the Christian Democrats could not tolerate because they are still essentially a capitalist party. We asked him to outline the differences between the Socialists and Communists, and why he, for instance, is not a Communist although he takes pride in being a Marxist and a revolutionary. First, he said, the Communists have become dead in the head, standpat. They are no longer a true revolutionary force, as the Socialists are. Second, they do not represent any essential *national* interest. Third, they zigzag. Elaborating on this Ampuero went all the way back to the Soviet purges in the 1930's and the Stalin-Hitler pact, which, he averred, his own party had opposed vigorously at the time.

Another figure on the left bears the remarkable name Clotario Blest; he is

---

[5] Back in 1941, when Allende was minister of health, I wrote that he was "obviously a man marked to rise." At that time one wing of his Socialists had their own paramilitary organization known as the "steel shirts."

the former head of the CUT, the Confederation of Trade Unions, which has 600,000 members. Aging now, Blest is both a Trotskyist and a fervent Roman Catholic; his emblem was a combination of crucifix, hammer, and sickle.[6] He was the man chiefly responsible for the organization and growth to political influence of Chilean labor, which is now one of the principal power factors in the country. Of an altogether different stamp is the youthful Senator Carlos Altamirano, generally thought to be the coming man of the Socialist party, a man well-born, agreeable, and intensely bright. He has passionate convictions, which he expresses with dedicated force. Sometimes he takes a line articulately anti-American.

Leader of the Communists is Luis Corvalán Lepez, a journalist and schoolteacher, born in 1916, who became a senator in 1961 and who is secretary general of the party and an editor of *El Siglo*, its mouthpiece. Corvalán gives the impression of a man irremediably marked by dogma, Moscow dogma, and he takes the current "soft" party line, or *vía pacífica*, without divagation, as against the Chinese wing of the party. Recently he talked on the same platform with the chairman of the Christian Democratic party, and said that the Communists believed in "some degree of participation with the government," because cooperation might ensure more progress in social reform.

But the PCCh (Communist Party Chile) is, it should never be forgotten, a *real* Communist party. We have come a long way now from the dreamer-dilettantes in Brazil, or those who, as in Argentina, merely hope for change. The Chilean Communists are well defined, well disciplined, and by far the best organized in South America; they have a long record of participation in political affairs, and derive strength from both the industrial proletariat and the intellectuals. The party dates from 1912, and, as I mentioned long ago in Chapter 8, calls itself the oldest Communist party in the world, predating the Russian; it was admitted into the Comintern as far back as 1921. Card-carrying membership is, however, only about twenty-five thousand.

The official Kremlin line, as reflected in Chile, is to play down the prospect of immediate violent revolution on the ground that this is "unnecessary"; the present structure will disintegrate of itself, the leaders assume, whereupon they can take full advantage of the ensuing situation. Meantime, as just mentioned, they are prepared to cooperate with the bourgeoisie to an extent, and might even take part again in a Popular Front government. Policy on the international side is based on anti-imperialism, which means anti-Americanism. In every way possible they seek to discredit the United States, the basic aim being to demonstrate that we are unable to maintain

[6] Halperin, *op. cit.*

cordial relations even with our closest neighbors. Castro is, on the other hand, disliked. The PCCh has had no official relations with Havana since early 1962.

Whereas the Frei regime is content with its plan for the "Chileanization" or partial nationalization of the copper industry, the Communists go much farther (as do the Socialists) and demand immediate complete nationalization. Other American interests in Chile to be nationalized are Ford (an assembly plant), General Electric (lightbulbs), Abbott (pharmaceuticals), American Screw (a nut and bolt factory), Singer (sewing machines), J. Walter Thompson (advertising), International Telephone & Telegraph, American and Foreign Power (electricity), and several other companies. Chilean banks, insurance companies, and other elements in big business will be absorbed later.[7]

Since FRAP is composed of Socialists, Communists, a minor group named PADENA, and a fourth splinter association (National Vanguard of the People), the impact made by the split between Moscow and Peking was complicated. It led first to widespread defections from the Moscow branch of the Communists, which was a bitter blow to Corvalán and the orthodox Kremlin leaders. Khrushchev's fall provoked another split. The Peking wing in Chile is known as the Spartacus movement. The Socialists split too, and many Socialists joined Spartacus. In general the trade union element in FRAP as a whole remained loyal to Moscow, whereas Peking drew off rural workers, students, and intellectuals.

Nine senators out of 45 belong to FRAP, 19 congressmen out of 147. This gives the left in Chile a far greater parliamentary strength than in any other South American republic, particularly in the senate, which is what counts. An interesting by-election occurred in Valparaíso in March, 1966. The Christian Democrats won, but dropped two percentage points from their figure in 1964; FRAP rose from 20 percent of the total vote to 28 percent.

Here too Frei has his problems.

[7] Henry Gemmill in the *Wall Street Journal*, November 20, 1963.

CHAPTER 15

More Complexities in Chile

Chile is God's mechanism for keeping Argentina
from the Pacific.
—SANTIAGO SAYING

In Chile now, cherries are dancing,
The dark mysterious girls are singing,
and in guitars, water is shining.
The sun is touching every door
and making wonder of the wheat.
—PABLO NERUDA[1]

As EVERYBODY knows Chile is one of the most oddly shaped of nations,
hanging down the west coast of South America like a bell rope full of knots
and kinks. Twenty-six hundred miles long, it has a longer Pacific coastline
than the United States, and is never broader than 220 miles; the average
width is only about 125 miles, and yet it covers a total area as big as Texas.
The land is a kind of narrow shelf between the Andes and the Pacific, a
balcony. As somebody said to me in Santiago, "You have to be thin to be a
Chileno. Otherwise you fall off!"

Lord Bryce noted many years ago that "the Long Land" resembles
Norway, and is the only South American country with a taste for the sea.
The Chileans are a maritime people. They are also mountain people, because
the country is unique not merely for its shape, but for the fact that the
Andes are its spinal column. Now for the first time in this book we come to a
west coast Andine country, and the Andes will be with us solidly to the end.
Chile has not quite so many spectacular single peaks as Argentina—six
higher than twenty thousand feet, however—but the Andes are all over the

---

[1] From "A Visit to Neruda," by Alastair Reid, *Encounter*, September, 1965.

place, covering a third of the total area, and making a dramatic and formidable curtain only a few miles from the sea.

Moreover, these stupendous mountains twitch and tremble, and, as a result, Chile is chronically afflicted with earthquakes, some of them savage. One, which is still sorely remembered, killed 25,000 people and obliterated 50 towns in January, 1939. The great earthquake and tidal wave of May, 1960, which almost tore the country apart near Valdivia, a southerly port, caused damage estimated at $400 million, left 350,000 citizens homeless in midwinter, and was responsible for more than 5,000 deaths. Another big one (there are small tremors all the time) struck in the Valparaíso area early in 1965. Then there have been countless avalanches, floods, volcanic eruptions, landslides, and damaging storms. The Chileans are, like Japanese, intensely earthquake-conscious. I was told that, if you cannot get out into the street when the floor starts shaking, the thing to do is stand beneath the heaviest doorway available or lie flat under a big table. Earthquakes make the people somewhat inert. They feel that there is little point to building a dam or factory if nature is going to destroy their work at any moment. They are convinced that a serious quake is inevitable every five years or so; in between they tend to be fatalistic.

Comment about earthquake relief can be sardonic. This is from a Santiago newspaper in 1965:

> Until the close of this edition, the following foreign aid had been received (for the earthquake victims): *Estados Unidos*—35 tons of yo-yo's; 35 promises of loans from the Inter-American Development Bank, 6 more from the International Monetary Fund, and 139 notices of loans overdue for previous earthquakes, plus an autographed photo of President Johnson 18 x 24 cms. *Soviet Union*—25 radio-controlled rockets; 15 agitators; 32 bazookas; 5 cases of vodka, and one spy with camera. *Cuba*—5,000 copies of "Guerrilla Warfare" by Che Guevara; 72 tons of extracts from the speech made by Fidel Castro on the inauguration of children's games at El Guajarito. *Argentina*—Their deepest sympathy; a long-play (*sic*) record of the latest creations of Alfredo de Angelis; and an autographed letter from Foreign Minister Miguel Angel Zavala Ortiz, stating that "the earthquake is one proof more of unbreakable Argentine-Chilean friendship."

Earthquakes may serve to make citizens inert, but they cause unease as well. I have heard three reasons adduced for the nervousness and dislocation conspicuous in the national character. (1) Earthquakes. (2) Too much fish in the diet, which leads to surplus iodine and hyper thyroidism, as in Japan. (3) Not enough sleep. Chilenos are notorious for liking to stay up all night, and this is indeed an attractive characteristic if not overdone. Chile is the one country in the world where it is impossible to be late for anything. Dinner is difficult to procure in a hotel before 10 P.M. or later, which can also happen in Spain, Russia, and eastern Europe, but not with quite the Chilean nonchalance. My wife and I dined out five nights in a row in Santiago in embassies or private houses; we sat down at 11:15, 10:45, 11:20, 10:15, and 11:45 respectively. I would ask desperately, as we headed home at 2 A.M. or later in each case, "When do Chileans *sleep?*" Answer: "Sundays."

But the blunt fact is most Chileans have been accustomed for years to a sound siesta in the afternoons, after a two-to-three-hour lunch. President Frei, a bold man, made this illegal for government workers in 1966, and the new rules, which provide for a lunch period limited to half an hour, will be applied to private business soon. Office hours were set from 8:30 to 4:30, instead of the former 9:30 to 1:30 and 4 till 7:30. The president ordered all bars closed between 4 and 7. The reasons for all this were that lack of sleep at night and prolonged siestas by day were causing "disorganization," and that the load on the city's transportation system needed lightening. Most residents of Santiago go home for lunch, which means four rush hours a day. Mr. Frei then proceeded to take a whack at prostitution, night life, and the like. Chile is one of the few countries where girls in the strip-tease shows appear stark naked, and subterranean vice is floriferous.

*

From top to bottom Chile has three main divisions. The professional geographers spoil this simple picture by pedantic splits and subdivisions, but three are enough for the layman. In the north, bordering on Peru and Bolivia, is the Atacama Desert, one of the most arid regions in the world. There are spots where no rain has fallen in four hundred years; a visitor can fly over this area for hour after hour, and never, in hundreds of square miles, see a single house, fence, road, human being, or tree. In opulent contrast is Central Valley south of the desert, the saddle of the country, which strikingly resembles Central Valley in California; washed by Andine water, it is magically fertile; here three-quarters of all Chileans live. Then, as we shall see in the next chapter, comes archipelagic Chile, with its profuse forests, gleaming mountain lakes, promontories, fjords, secluded velvety glens and valleys, and alleyways of water; there are places here where it rains almost every day of the year. Altogether, only about 5 percent of the land is arable and the country has to import roughly $140 million worth of food a year to live. (But this is caused by agricultural imbalance, mismanagement, and erosion as well as the poor quality of the soil.)

Chile lays claim to part of Antarctica, and possesses Easter Island (Rapa Nui) 2,400 miles out in the Pacific, famous for its mysterious stone monuments. Closer are the Juan Fernández Islands about 400 miles off Valparaíso, where Alexander Selkirk, the original of Robinson Crusoe, was shipwrecked. The voting population of the Juan Fernández group (three islands in all) is 106, and the islands have been used on occasion to house political prisoners. A special succulent type of lobster caught here is a standard delicacy throughout Chile.

The origin of the name "Chile" is in dispute. It has nothing to do with Mexican peppers. One theory is that it comes from *chiri*, a word in a Peruvian Indian language meaning cold; the Incas found it cold when they got here. Another is that it is a corruption of an Aymará word for "land's end," and still another is that it derives from the cry of a small sea bird, the *triles*, which sounds like "Cheele-Cheele."

Pedro de Valdivia, one of the boldest of Pizzarro's captains, marching down from Peru, brought most of Chile into the Spanish domain beginning in 1540. A previous expedition had failed because of fierce, stubborn, and skillful resistance by the Araucanian and other Indians who inhabited the land. These had even resisted penetration by the Incas before the white man came. The Araucanians were the toughest warriors ever known among Indians in South America. The Spaniards lost more men trying to subdue them than in *all* their campaigns elsewhere on the continent. But Valdivia, a man of rude and heroic parts, succeeded in establishing a foothold in central Chile, founded Santiago and Concepción (as well as the seaport Valdivia named for him), and set up Spanish rule. Seeking to press into the south in 1553, he was captured by the Araucanians and executed by being made to swallow molten gold. The legend has it that the Indians said, "You come for gold—here it is."

Chile's national hero is Bernardo O'Higgins, who, together with the Argentine General San Martín, delivered the country from Spain in the early 1800's. His name is on countless boulevards, monuments, parks and the like throughout Chile. It was spelled at one time or other Higgnes, Higgns, Higgnis, Ignes, Igsegns, Ihiggyns, Egis, and Hexis.[2] O'Higgins was born in Chile, but was as Irish as St. Patrick or a shillelah. His father, Ambrose Higgins, came out of Ballinary, Ireland, moved to Spain, emigrated to South America, and, astoundingly enough, rose to be governor of a Chilean province and then viceroy of Peru, no less, under the name Ambrosio O'Higgins. Bernardo's mother, Isabel Riquelme, was Chilean, and he was born in the town of Chillán on August 20, 1778; he was illegitimate.

[2] *O'Higgins*, a pamphlet in the Pan American Union Series for Young Americans.

Young Bernardo was cast off by his father, and went by the name Riquelme until Ambrosio died. But the father arranged for him to get a good education abroad, and he studied in Cádiz and London, coming under the influence of Francisco Miranda, the great Venezuelan revolutionary who lived in exile at the time. Bernardo was apprenticed to a London firm of watchmakers, but this occupation did not hold him long. Returning to Spain, he became acquainted with San Martín, who was a student there, and, a young man all smoke, smiles, and flame, decided to devote his life to the cause of Chilean independence. He managed to return to South America, take part in the Argentine revolution, and cross the Andes with San Martín. They won a decisive battle against the Spanish loyalists at Maipú on April 5, 1818, a historic date for Chile. His alert blue eyes flashing, O'Higgins led his troops in person even though he was suffering from fever and had a badly broken arm.

San Martín did not want political power and he presently stepped aside for O'Higgins, who became "Supreme Director" of the new nation. But O'Higgins was accused of "arrogance, irresponsibility, and undemocratic methods" by the rich Creoles, seemingly because he believed in "adorable equality" and took the side of the poor.[3] Also, like the generals in Argentina, he gave vast quantities of land to the army officers who served under him, and thus unwittingly helped create the imbalance in landownership that has been the curse of Chile ever since.

When O'Higgins was forced to resign office in 1822, he told the national assembly, "If my faults have caused misfortunes that can only be purged by blood, take such vengeance on me as you wish! Here is my breast!" The reply was, "Long live O'Higgins!" Retiring to Peru he never saw Chile again, and died in Lima in 1842, aged sixty-four. Like San Martín and so many other South American patriot-revolutionaries, he never enjoyed the fruits of the independence he helped to win.

O'Higgins spoke Araucanian, and liked to have Indians around him. The intractable Araucanians did not cease to be a problem till long after his death. They were not, as a matter of fact, finally subdued in the Chilean south until 1883, and their claim is that they are the only South American Indians who never surrendered; they simply decided to stop fighting.[4]

*

Chile has 8,460,000 people, about the same number as Greece. Sixty percent are urban, a large proportion for South America, and half are under

---

[3] The phrase "adorable equality" is from Pendle, *op. cit.*, p. 145.

[4] The last major battle against Indians in North America took place in 1890, the Battle of Wounded Knee against the Sioux in South Dakota.

the age of twenty-one. The literacy rate is 84 percent, which is high, and the growth rate 2.3 percent, or average for the continent. But, even in such a civilized and comparatively well-developed country as this, the life expectancy at birth is low, only about forty years in many areas, and one out of every five Chilean students is being fed by the USAID school-feeding program.

Chileans are very touchy on the subject of racial mixture, and claim to be largely white. Yet, with the exception of a handful of Creole-descended pure whites, almost everybody with roots in the country has a touch at least of Indian blood. This is a *mestizo* nation par excellence, with the white strain predominating, and integration has become virtually complete. There are no Negroes and only about 200,000 surviving Araucanian or other Indians.

Large numbers of Europeans entered Chile in the last century, in particular Germans, Basques, and Yugoslavs. The landed oligarchs are mostly of Basque descent, and the Valdivia–Puerto Montt area is almost solidly German. I mentioned in the preceding chapter names which give some indication of the variety of European components in the population—Leighton, Thayer, Ross, Subercaseaux, Alessandri, Tomic. The leading patrician family in Santiago, by name Edwards, has a remote Jewish origin. Then—merely picking among metronymics of public figures—we have Doolan, Gossens, Ward, Newman, Frödden, Etienne, Lane, Schmidt, Eschaurren, Guissen.

The national character is difficult to assess, partly because so many elements contribute to it. One quality is a passionate love for Europe, and another is intellectual weight and love of the arts. Still another is the cultivation of superiority without any suppressed feeling of inferiority—a balance difficult to attain. "We have gone downhill quite happily for the past fifty years," one eminent Chilean told me urbanely. There is little false pride or xenophobia, but one thing that seems to strike a spark is dislike of Argentina. Finally one must mention a factor which no anthropologist or sociologist has ever been able to explain satisfactorily—that Chilean women are just about the prettiest in the world.

A Word About Santiago

> They have talked to me of Venezuelas,
> Of Paraguays and Chiles.
> I don't know what they say.
> I only know the skin of earth
> And that it has no name.
>   —PABLO NERUDA[5]

[5] From "A Day with Pablo Neruda," by Selden Rodman, *Saturday Review,* June 9, 1966.

Santiago, the fourth-largest city in South America,[6] is pressing close to having a population of 2,500,000—which means than it is bigger than any city in the United States except New York, Chicago, and Los Angeles. Lying about seventy miles from the Pacific at an altitude of some seventeen hundred feet, it is ringed by superb mountains, which are snow-capped most of the year; there are peaks almost four miles high within fifty miles, and one of the best skiing resorts in the world, Portillo, is only a few hours away. This is one of the few great capitals (Vienna and Beirut are others) with first-class skiing in their outskirts.

Santiago itself is, however, its miraculous view aside, a somewhat dingy city. The paper currency is almost as filthy as in Brazil. There are no new glass skyscrapers, and the principal street, the Boulevard O'Higgins or Alameda, seems shabby compared to the glossy, sumptuous avenues of Buenos Aires. People dress drably—mostly in black. There are appalling queues almost everywhere, particularly at the bus stops. Citizens scratch and scramble to get on the buses, which are inhumanely crowded; the small buses are called *liebres*, hares, and are packed like cans of worms. Traffic is, however, not nearly as anarchic as in Rio de Janeiro or Buenos Aires; drivers even obey red lights, and do not chase pedestrians down the streets. It is even possible to park.

Almost all Chilenos are proud of Santiago, and tend to say that they were born here even if they were not. There are all manner of contrasts and curiosities. A large illuminated figure of the Virgin Mary stands on the crest of San Cristobal, on the edge of the city, and is a characteristic symbol. Another in a different dimension is the Union Club, which represents the established intelligentsia much in the manner of the Atheneum in London, and is one of the most distinguished clubs in the world. In the suburbs a *huaso*, cowboy, complete with poncho, lariat, and flat hat, may be seen lounging on a horse outside the premises of a *gasfiter*, plumber. The postman expects a tip on the delivery of a letter, because he gets virtually no salary, and if you want real coffee in a restaurant or bar you say "café-café." To ask just for "coffee" in the singular will bring you the powdered kind.

Summing up Santiago I would say that it is an extremely civilized city, but physically somewhat down at the heel. Knowledgeable North Americans, like itinerant foreign correspondents who know South America well as a whole, almost universally call it their favorite capital in the hemisphere, because it reminds them of London or New York, with a high intellectual content, fondness for culture and the arts, particularly ballet, and a modern, congenial atmosphere. Men of talent are conspicuous on every side, and carry substance.

[6] After São Paulo, Buenos Aires, and Rio de Janeiro.

Another distinction is that Chile, although small, has made striking contributions to intellectual and professional life abroad by providing international civil servants for the UN, like Hernán Santa Cruz of the Food and Agricultural Organization among many others. "Santa Cruz" is, incidentally, a name almost as common as our "Smith" or "Jones."

Still another uniqueness is the quality of the police. There is only one uniformed police force in Chile, the Cuerpo de Carabineros; the commanding officer is an army general, and the service is totally outside politics and supposedly incorruptible. Nowhere else in South America are the police so respected and esteemed. The Carabineros not only maintain public order, handle traffic, and perform the normal police duties all over the nation, but engage in civic action; they teach school in the outlying areas, work on rehabilitation programs, and, in general, are on call for everything from earthquake relief to social service. Many a peasant woman has had her child in a police station. The corps has about 25,000 men led by 1,200 officers. The Carabineros have a splendidly martial band, and are famous for their horsemanship; they put on an equestrian show every year which rivals that of the Spanish Riding School in Austria.

Santiagueños, as residents of the city are called, are extraordinarily hospitable, and love gossip. Even the tallest, tightest walls have ears. The director of public relations of an airline knew about our appointment with President Frei before we did. Families are apt to be large; at one dinner party I met two diplomats about to leave for posts in Europe; one had eight young children, the other six. A vast web of cousinly relations seems to make everybody related to everybody else. But society is not nearly so closed as it is in Argentina; the aristocracy is much more fluid, more alive.

The well-to-do talk about taxes and the high cost of living, as who does not. They complain bitterly about taxes, but are not likely to mention that, until recently, in a country nicely sprinkled with millionaires, only 11,000 people declared their income to be higher than $5,000 a year. They say that what the country needs is "development of the internal market," but resist to the uttermost the one thing that would expedite this, land reform. They say that there is too much bureaucracy, and indeed the public services are overstaffed. They discuss the merits and demerits of CORFO, the government planning and development agency, established in 1938, and mention a bewildering lot of institutions known by acronyms, most of which I never was able to identify securely, like INDAP, ENAMI, CORA, CONSFA, and SNA.

Concentration of moneyed power reaches a point in Santiago unmatched elsewhere in the continent. Recently I read a paper by the writer Osvaldo

Sunkel, prepared for delivery before the Royal Institute of International Affairs, London. Mr. Sunkel points out that economic power in the hands of the elite "permeates all activities of social life, and has led to the growth of a system of control of government, press, finance, and middle class employment." For instance one percent of shareholders of banks and insurance companies hold 35 percent of the total value of all shares on the Santiago stock exchange. Five percent of families earn 40 percent of the national income.

Social security, which is almost as advanced and comprehensive as in Uruguay, is an acutely controversial subject. Several employers told me that they pay up to 43 percent to the insurance funds, whereas the workman contributes only 8.25 to 10 percent. Above all, people on every level complain about the inflation—and with justification. The price of bread has jumped 300 percent in five years, and mortgage loans cost 20 percent interest. There is little incentive to save. A manufacturer said to me indignantly, "You ask me to invest in *this* country?—when I don't know what value the currency will have three weeks from now!"

I met a well-known actress, who told me that she got the equivalent of $8 for a morning's work on TV. A first-class bilingual secretary will earn about $37.50 a month, and a university professor about $200. A popsicle costs 8 cents, and an average automobile $9,000. Beef is $1.75 a pound, and Scotch $23 a bottle. A shot of imported Bourbon in a bar costs $3.50.

The national drink of Chile is, of course, wine, and this is superlative, probably better than any except French. And here we enter the kingdom of the pisco sour, which will stay with us into Peru and beyond; this is eau de vie from a local grape, beaten into froth with lemon juice, white of egg, and a touch of sugar, and served as a cocktail. Or you can have your pisco straight; it tastes faintly like slivovitz. Tea is another national institution; a snack taken at teatime bears the curious name *once*, reminiscent of the British "elevenses," because *once* means "eleven." Probably the best-known Chilean dish is *pastel de choclos*, a stew containing beef, chicken, corn, raisins, and onions, with a variety of herbs; and Santiago *empanadas* are famous—hot turnovers filled with anything from cheese to edible seaweed. I had once a memorable hot soup made of beef blood. A kind of sugar, seared with a hot iron so that it becomes syrup, is delicious in your coffee. Chilean fruit is glorious, and the seafood little short of spectacular. The best-known fish is the *congrio*, a kind of eel; a local bass known as *corvina* is, I think, the best whitefish I ever tasted. *Locos* (abalones) are often served, as are *choros* (big mussels) and *picorocos*, an elongated crustacean which is pulled out of its spiky shell and eaten alive, although it wriggles like a thumb.

There is no commercial TV in Chile. The only authorized outlets are the University of Chile, Catholic University in Santiago, and Catholic University in Valparaíso—three channels only. Of the hundred-odd radio stations, all but one are, however, privately owned. The principal Santiago newspaper is *El Mercurio,* which appears in Valparaíso as well; founded in 1827, this is the oldest newspaper in Chile still being published, and, local informants say, the oldest daily newspaper in the Spanish-speaking world. People call it the "Dean." I asked what it stood for in the way of policy, and received the answer "Tutankhamen." But as a matter of fact *El Mercurio* is more modern-minded than that; it came out for Frei in 1964. The *South Pacific Mail,* which appears weekly in English, is the oldest English-language newspaper in Latin America. The Spanish edition of *Reader's Digest* is, following the usual pattern, the biggest-selling magazine.

Cultural realms are broad. The first—and only—South American writer ever to win a Nobel prize, the poetess Gabriela Mistral (real name Lucila Godoy y Alcayaga) was a schoolteacher in northern Chile. There are any number of interesting writers today, such as the veteran novelist Manuel Rojas, author of *The Son of a Thief* and *A Glass of Milk,* who married a youthful American student whom he met while teaching in the United States, and younger men like Enrique Lafourcade, whose *King Ahab's Feast* was recently translated into English. Well known are Benjamín Subercaseaux, author of *Chile, a Geographical Extravaganza,* and, in a different category, the vigorous radical poet Nicanor Parrá.

Roberto Matta, the surrealist, is one of the foremost living painters, and Claudio Arrau is, as everybody knows, a distinguished pianist. A well-regarded musician and cultural figure at large is Domingo Santa Cruz, a former chairman of the UNESCO Commission on Music and dean of the Faculty of Musical Arts at Santiago University. He has been vitally responsible for the extension of musical studies and performance throughout the country. Ballet is, as noted above, wildly popular—almost on the level of football! There should also be a word about the revival of folk music; its leading proponent is Isabel Barra, and its spiritual home the island of Chiloé. The national dance, which arose out of folklore ballads, is the *cueca.* A guitar, short harp, and tambourine are the instruments, and it much resembles dancing I saw in Paraguay. In Santiago we went to one *boîte* specializing in folk music; it resembled Montmartre, but with a more stirring atmosphere. The singing seemed to come out of the very entrails of the nation.

Pablo Neruda, Chile's best-known poet, was born sixty-two years ago, the son of a railway worker; his real name is Neftalí Reyes Basoalto. At twenty he wrote a book, *Twenty Love Poems and a Desperate Song*, which sold more than a million copies all over the world and is still selling. For a time Neruda served in the Chilean diplomatic service abroad. He was strongly influenced by the Spanish Civil War, and became a Communist. Returning to Chile, he settled in Isla Negra, a village on the Pacific near Valparaíso, and, with interruptions, one of them caused by political exile, has lived there ever since. Neruda is a capacious person, colorful, solid, rugged, and possessed of a fierce joy in life. Jean-Paul Sartre refused the Nobel prize some years ago because, among other reasons, he felt that Neruda should have had it instead, and Harold Macmillan, in his capacity as chancellor of Oxford University, bestowed on him the degree of Doctor Honoris Causa of Oxford —the only South American ever to be so honored.

This is a fragment of a Neruda lyric:

> This night is the same night; it whitens
> The same trees; casts similar shadows;
> It is as dark, as long, as deep, and as endurable
> As any other night. It is true: I do not want her.[7]

Neruda threw himself into Chilean politics on his return from Europe, and became a senator in 1945. He is still a member of the Politburo of the Communist party; he issued an energetic polemic against Peking recently, and is a frequent speaker at FRAP rallies. But it is as a poet that he will be remembered; a British critic has called him "a one-man Renaissance." For many years Neruda was denied entrance to the United States because of his Communist allegiance; this is the kind of thing that really does make sophisticated men and women all over the world, let alone South America, snicker at the State Department.

. . . And Other Cities

The seaport ANTOFAGASTA (pop. 110,000) in northern Chile is a thriving city even though its hinterland is the bleakest of deserts, because copper and nitrates flow through here to ships carrying them to world markets. A large illuminated anchor is set into a hill near the town. A local guide, *Chile*, says that the Antofagasta desert "ranks as thirteenth in world orden" [*sic*], and that "the natives living in mid-desert are ideal food for study owing to their remarkable arqueologic background." The region is, the booklet continues, marked by a decided "solar intensity." The local seafood is luxurious, includ-

---

[7] From "Neruda," an unsigned article in the *New Statesman*, London, June, 1965.

ing "soused fish," "octopus chowder," and "Abolony turnovers." Antofagasta also has importance as a railhead, with stertorous Trans-Andine trains
chugging off to La Paz and Buenos Aires—when weather permits.

VALPARAÍSO, the "Pearl of the Pacific," has forty-one hills, cable cars like
San Francisco, and squatter towns in the hills, as in Rio. This is Chile's most
important port, with a population of around 260,000; here a fifth of Chilean
industry is clustered. One of its historic sights is Mirador O'Higgins, where
the Supreme Director watched the Chilean fleet (under a British admiral)
set out to attack the Spanish in Peru in the 1820's. Five miles north of
Valparaíso is VIÑA DEL MAR, the seaside resort which equates with Punta del
Este in Uruguay or Mar del Plata in the Argentine. It is not merely a holiday
town, but has large industrial installations.

The River Bío-Bío separates central Chile from the forested south, and
marks the old Indian frontier. Here is CONCEPCIÓN, the country's third city
(pop. about 195,000), a fast-growing metropolis with a stubborn spirit; it
has taken frightful blows from earthquakes and tidal waves, and has several
times had to be rebuilt. One uniqueness is that the local university is
financed by the municipal lotteries, a sensible procedure. Nearby are Tal-
cahuana on the Pacific, an important naval base, and the massive Huachi-
pato ("duck trap") steel plant, the largest on the continent except Volta
Redonda in Brazil. A Chilean corporation, the Compañía de Acero del
Pacífico, S.A., known universally as CAP, operates this plant, and is doing
well; it feeds on coal fields fifteen hundred feet underwater in the Pacific.
Here, as in much else, Chile is tackling the onerous problem of combining
public nationalist interests with private foreign investment by a carefully
worked-out compromise. CAP is held 25 percent by the Chilean government,
18 percent by foreign investors; the rest is in the hands of 7,000 small individual shareholders, 2,600 of whom are employees of the company.

Further south is VALDIVIA (pop. around 100,000), which has a strong
and pervasive German texture, dating from immigrants who fled Europe in
1848. Here is Austral University, built by Pedro de Valdivia soon after he
founded the city in the 1540's, and numerous industrial establishments.
Dairy products and foodstuffs are produced by a solid community of small
farmers, like those in the German areas in Brazil. Again I quote Chile, if
only for its delightful use of the English language: "Valdivian Week is
celebrated in February of every year and most events are held on the
waterfront, such as: regattas, fluvial firemen's exercises, processions of gaily
adorned embarkations and euforic [sic] boweries where music and song
prevail."

Visiting the University

As is the case with the universities in Buenos Aires and Lima, this is scattered over a wide area; there is no central campus. One afternoon we visited the School of Journalism as a guest of its dean, the well-known journalist Mario Planet; we were told that to do so would be a risky adventure, because students were on strike—this had nothing to do with the university, but was provoked by a rise in bus fares. We emerged unscathed. The University of Chile, sometimes known as Santiago or National University, has around thirteen thousand students in Santiago, three thousand more in branches at Valparaíso, Antofagasta, and Arica, a dreary town in the extreme north. The School of Public Health is the best in Latin America, and medicine is better practiced in Chile than in any hemisphere republic except the United States.

Each faculty elects its own dean every three years, and the faculty as a whole elects the rector every five years, an unusual system. The students have nothing to do with faculty appointments, as they do in some South American universities.

Tuition is free, or virtually so, at Santiago, and competition to enter the university is keen. The curriculum is curious. There is, for instance, no provision for specialized study in the liberal arts; every student has to belong to a professional school of one type or other. To study Keats you have to enroll in the Pedagogic Institute. What the university wants above all to turn out is a cadre of professional technical men—engineers, agronomists, architects. But there is little private opportunity for these, and so most graduates are compelled to enter government service and become bureaucrats; the government is the only sure source of jobs. The dropout rate is startling. One dean told me that, in a faculty (= school) with 200 students, only three pushed through to graduation last year.

Catholic University, with four thousand students, is another important institution; it is, as we have seen, the hearth of the Frei government and is probably a better school than National. Another Catholic University is in Valparaíso.

Christian Democrat influence is gaining in the student bodies of the state universities, which is a source of distinct satisfaction to the regime. But an estimated 35 percent of students, 25 percent of faculty, which numbers eight hundred at Santiago, are Communist inclined.

We spent some hours with a roundtable of students, but this lacked the spark of a similar occasion in Buenos Aires; I felt not so much an atmosphere of yearning, of eagerness to get out into the world, of intellectual passion, scope, and curiosity, as of negative frustration (or perhaps shyness) and apprehension about talking freely. Two of our group were Communists, four were Christian Democrats. The first questions asked us were, "Did the United States foment the Castelo Branco revolution in Brazil?" and "How much influence do the copper companies have on United States foreign policy?" So the familiar images arose of wicked old Uncle Sam upsetting South American applecarts and being the prisoner of private interests. We asked each student in turn why they had backed Frei or FRAP. The Frei supporters said (a) Communism had no real roots in South America, (b) Frei was in a better position to give Chile development, (c) he was finding his way toward a "third solution," something between Communism and unlimited private enterprise, as witness his copper policy, (d) Chileans did not want to move into "a new orbit," i.e., the Soviet world. The Communists said, (a) Frei was a prisoner of the right, and the right would get him in the end if he persisted in being independent; (b) no liberal democratic system, even if semi-socialist, could solve the fundamental problems of the country, like land reform; (c) people lived in "subhuman" conditions. I went around the table asking what Chile needed most, and the most interesting answer was "Action." Then talk returned to the United States. "We cannot go against you," one of the Christian Democrat boys said, "but we want to be equal partners. You take everything out of us—we lose our identity."

*

Primary education is free and, in theory, compulsory for all children between seven and fifteen, but not all children actually go to school because of lack of facilities. Chile was "the first country in Latin America to establish a system of public education," and the national government has supervised education throughout the nation since 1842, says a local guide. About 1,400,000 children are enrolled in the public schools, with 30,000 teachers; some schools work double shifts, and an essential point in the Frei program is that every child in the country shall at least be able to register at a school by 1968. Even the *carabinero* stations are being used to register and enroll students at present. But, although education is supposed to be compulsory for eight years for those who attend, it seems (statistics are confusing) that the average period of actual attendance today is only 2.4 years. Out of a hundred children in first grade only 30 percent reach secondary school, and of these only 9 percent reach a university. But these figures are better than the average for South America, and they will improve.

Birth Control and Abortion

As might well be expected, Chile, with its tradition of responsible citizenry, has the most advanced program in South America in response to the population explosion. Even though this is an overwhelmingly Catholic country the government permits the operation of a body known as the Asociación Chilena de Protección á la Familia, the first organization of its kind in South America devoted to family planning. Its president is a pediatrician and former officer in the National Health Service, Dr. Luisa Pfau David; the vice president, Dr. Onofre Avendaño, is a professor of obstetrics and gynecology and an official of the World Health Organization. Both have studied at North American universities. Intensely high-minded citizens, they came to see us one morning and discussed their problems.

Their association is not a government body, but came into existence (in 1963) through the initiative of professors of medicine and public health at both the Santiago universities, national and Catholic, mainly because of worry about the steeply rising abortion rate. It must observe certain taboos, and proceed cautiously; such terms as "birth control" and even "planned parenthood" are not publicly used, for fear of the reaction this might provoke in reactionary Catholic circles. But the government allows its committee to operate, if quietly, and even encourages it. The main work of the association is provision of birth-control services and the dissemination of information, which it does in sixty-four free clinics in Santiago and elsewhere in the country. These are indirectly financed by the government, directly by foreign grants.

Members of the committee I met do not think that Chile has a serious population problem in itself. The country could support many more people, although the annual population growth is around 2.3 percent, whereas the rate of increase in food production is only 1.9 percent. The heart of the issue is the uneven distribution of population. Santiago has doubled its number of people in twenty years, and urbanization has brought gripping problems. Other factors are involved as well. Upper-income families average 2.7 children; those lower have twice this number, 5.5. Mothers with none but rudimentary education have 4.4 children; women on the university level have 2.4.

Abortion is illegal in Chile, but occurs at a fantastic rate, if only because of ignorance or lack of opportunity to acquire contraceptive means. There are estimated to be 140,000 abortions a year as against 240,000 live births, a proportion above one in two. An abortion costs from 50 escudos ($15) up, and can be had virtually at any street corner; many are botched, with the results that no fewer than 40 percent of women aborted require hospitalization; two-fifths of "maternal deaths" in Santiago are due to abortions. This places an enormous strain on the medical structure, to say nothing of its cost in human values. Hospital beds, nurses, blood banks, and the like are all in desperately short supply.

It is perfectly legal for a Chilean woman to go to a doctor to request advice on contraception or get birth control apparatus, and many do. But more do not, because of poverty, religion, fear, or ignorance. Besides there are not enough private physicians available, and *public* clinics throughout the country do not provide this advisory service. The government, severely worried by the abortion crisis, finds itself in a dilemma. It does not wish to check population growth completely, but it does want to do away with the evils of criminal abortion. So the proposal is being advanced that the Public Health Service be empowered to supply contraceptives and give advice, thus supplementing the work of the association. Recently the ministry of health set up important instrumentations to this end, which are a large step forward.

Catholic opinion on all this is fairly liberal—compared to what it is in Brazil or Argentina—and public discussion of the problem takes place freely. The principal point at issue is method. Catholic doctors, even communicants, will now prescribe contraceptive pills in certain circumstances, something unheard of in most of South America, but they will not countenance the use of the intra-uterine device—the ring or coil. Thousands of Chilean women do, however, use the I.U.D., which is prescribed and fitted by "nonreligious" doctors, even if they are nominally Catholic. Pills cost 6–8 escudos a month ($1.80 to $2.40); the average fee (in private practice) for fitting the I.U.D. is 15–30 escudos ($4.50 to $9.00).

Certainly the attitude of the Frei government, Catholic as it is, is more liberal on this topic than that of any other government Chile has ever had, if only because it is genuinely interested in popular needs. President Frei plans to open the eighth world conference of the International Planned Parenthood Federation in Santiago in 1967.

Notes on Copper and the Land

Chile is the third greatest copper producer in the world, after the United States and the Soviet Union. Copper provides roughly two-thirds of all its foreign exchange, and up to 70 percent of its national revenue. Without the production and export of copper Chile could not, in a word, survive. The

United States is the biggest customer. If you want to give a Chileno a headache tell him that the alchemists may concoct synthetic copper some fine day. Before copper the Chilean economy depended largely on nitrates, and Chile had a world monopoly on this substance, which was (and still is) indispensable for the production of fertilizers and explosives, for many years. When a German chemist invented a process for the "fixation" of nitrogen, that is, taking it out of the air, so that nitrates could be synthesized, the Chilean nitrate industry never recovered from the blow, although it still contributes to the national economy.

But as to copper. The first point to state is that roughly 85 percent of the immense Chilean copper production is in the hands of three American corporations—Kennecott, Anaconda, and the Cerro Corporation, smaller and a newcomer to Chile. Anaconda and Kennecott purchased their copper properties back in the 1900's from local interests. Kennecott operates through the Braden Copper Company, a subsidiary. Its great mine El Teniente, eight thousand feet up in the Andes near Santiago, is one of the richest mineral deposits on earth, and accounts for 40 percent of all Chilean copper production. Chile, in turn, provides Kennecott with 25 percent of its total world production of copper. Anaconda's total world production comes 65 percent from Chile.

Anaconda has three subsidiaries in Chile. Its principal mine, Chuquicamata in the nitrate country up north, is said to hold a quarter of all the copper in the world; here ore is dug from a huge open pit, in contrast to El Teniente, a mountain being chipped out from the inside. Near Chuquicamata, which is a name almost as legendary for copper as Kimberley is for gold, lies a new ore body, Exotica, which is also being worked by Anaconda. This company also has a large underground operation at El Salvador, down the coast, and a smaller mine, La Africana, near Santiago. Cerro's mine, Río Blanco in the Andes, is operated by a subsidiary, Compañía Minera Andina.

The stake of the American companies in their properties in Chile is, as must be obvious, prodigious. The companies pay no royalty, but are steeply taxed; taxes are, indeed, the highest mining taxes in the world, ranging from 67 percent of gross taxable income to not less than 83 percent. The mines pay into the Chilean treasury every year more than all other tax collections in the country combined. The present rates represent a rise from 33 percent a quarter of a century ago—a tidy index to the way the world has changed and, incidentally, to the power of Chilean nationalism.

But the companies still make a handsome profit on their investment. This is what has made copper such a sore point in Chile over the years. The mines are, after all, part of the Chilean national domain on Chilean soil;

why, the nationalists ask, should they not be taken over outright by the Chilean government, and put to the service of the people. Copper touches a particularly sensitive spot, in consonance with developments all over South America, because it is an "extractive" industry; foreigners, no matter what taxes they pay, are held to be shameless exploiters because they drain out of the country an essential national resource, to say nothing of the profit they derive. Chile wants its copper to be its own, and a spirited, sometimes abusive campaign against the American companies has gone on for a generation.

But Chile could not pitch out the companies overnight; its economy would crack. President Frei, on assuming office in 1964, rejected the FRAP concept of nationalization and worked out a compromise arrangement with the owners for "Chileanization" of the mines. Negotiations were prolonged and difficult. But the companies had to come to heel, because in the long run, this being the modern world, their position was untenable; and after all Frei was better for them than Allende and the Communists. Most people think that, all things considered, the companies got a pretty good deal. Frei had a desperately hard time getting his copper bill through his own congress; it passed the house easily enough, but not the senate, where, as we know, the Christian Democrats do not have a clear majority. Not only did FRAP oppose the president; so did the right-wing Radicals. ("Radicals" in Chile are not radical at all.)

These difficulties were further compounded when, in January, 1966, workers at Kennecott's El Teniente went on strike although Chilean miners are by far the best-paid labor in the country. But they demanded higher wages to compensate for the 25.9 percent rise in the cost of living last year, caused by inflation, and the strike was legal; it was followed, however, by wildcat strikes on various Anaconda properties, including El Salvador, where riots took place and a number of strikers were killed by police, much to the country's shame. President Frei in a nationwide speech said in March that strikes, led by extreme leftists seeking to embarrass his regime, had cost the country $57 million—"enough to build 500 schools."

The government's copper bill envisages first a doubling of copper production from the present 620,000 tons a year to 1,200,000 tons, which will make Chile the largest copper producer in the world. Next, the agreement calls for partial nationalization. The Chilean government is to take over 51 percent of Braden, the Kennecott subsidiary, 25 percent of Cerro, 25 percent of one Anaconda subsidiary, and 49 percent in an important exploration company, thus becoming part owner of the industry. Payment to the companies is to be spread over twenty years in a complicated arrangement.

Moreover, the three companies pledge themselves to invest very large sums in an immediate five-year expansion program—Braden $200 million, Anaconda $150 million, Cerro about $80 million—to assist development in cooperation with the Chilean government. The companies in return will have their taxes reduced, and are to be guaranteed against expropriation.

The net result is what one Chilean observer calls "painless nationalization." The essence of the settlement is cooperative investment and control between the Chilean government and American private enterprise. No pressure was put on Chile by the United States government. Both sides are satisfied largely because the arrangement is directly hinged on the hope of vastly increased production, which should bring augmented revenue to all.

*

If copper is the first problem in Chile, land is the second; perhaps land should be put first. The two are closely intermeshed, because Frei's projected land reform, which may cost as much as $500 million, cannot easily succeed without the revenue that copper provides.

There are 150,000 landowners in Chile, of whom between 2,600 and 3,000 own 60 percent of the cultivable land. "Irrigated land is what counts, it's the only land we'd bother to expropriate," a Communist expert told me. Other estimates on tenure vary depending on the definition and quality of the land involved. Seventy-five percent of arable land is owned by 5 percent of the people, according to one American authority; another says 2.2 percent.[8] By terms of another estimate two-thirds of all arable land is divided into 4.4 percent of total holdings; multitudinous very small owners, about half the total number, hold 1.6 percent. Compare such figures to those in the United States!

The net result is, of course, not merely backward agriculture but outright feudalism, particularly in Central Valley, the heart of the country. Huge *fundos* cover hundreds of square miles, and are operated by individual or family owners like medieval serfdoms. Bryce wrote fifty years ago that Chile was the prisoner of a hundred families, and circumstances have changed little since. Some *pelicones*, feudal owners, even resist the use of modern agricultural machinery. The *rotos*, peasants, are largely sharecroppers, and live out their lives mostly in circumstances of degrading squalor, but Chile—something very unusual for South America—has a minimum wage for agricultural workers, the equivalent of 53 cents a day. Not all *rotos* get this princely sum, however. Small owners have a difficult time as well, because many do not have access to water, and their minifundia may be laid out in

8 Dr. Milton S. Eisenhower and Professor John J. Johnson respectively.

such a way as to make productive agriculture impossible. A family farm may, for instance, be five miles long and ten feet wide.

Another deleterious factor is underuse. Twenty-one percent of all the irrigated land in Chile still lies fallow, hard to believe as this fact may be. The rich landowners leave much of their huge properties idle because land does not, as it does in the United States or France, mean predominantly a method of subsistence through agriculture, but a variety of other things. Land is (a) a status symbol; (b) something that gives you a nice place for the weekend; (c) a hedge against inflation; (d) collateral for investment. Then, too, land is only lightly taxed.

One result is that Chile cannot feed itself. This was not true thirty years ago, but it is true today. The country once exported onions to France, fruit to Texas, carnations to Miami, but not now. Chile grows only about 30 percent of the agricultural products it needs, and actually has to import $140 million worth of food a year.[9]

Another consideration is that agricultural interests in Chile tie in closely with big business interests, which tend to be commercial rather than industrial. Investment does not take place in production, which should be the kernel of the economy in an inflationary era, as much as in banking, insurance, maritime interests, and trading companies. A web of interlocking directorates, in which the landowners are dominant, confirms this pattern, with the result that the whole moneyed class concentrates on resisting land reform. One reason why Frei has had such difficulty with his land bill is that practically all Conservative and Liberal members of congress, half the Radicals, and, more important, some fifty out of his own Christian Democrats, are landowners.

Other obstacles in the way of effective land reform, which seem all but insuperable, are technical. For one thing, titles to land have come to be nearly impossible to prove, and the judicial system is appallingly slow. Water rights play a large role. In one recent case eleven years passed before a court settlement was reached on a contested line of property. So landowners do business with a handshake, and nobody knows what's what.

President Frei has, however, worked out a concrete, drastic reform program, which at the moment of writing is being fought out in Congress clause by clause. Thirty thousand words long, his bill is by far the most adult, serious, and far-reaching attempt at land reform in the history of South America. Fighting it bitterly (the situation is analogous to that concerning copper) are the oligarchs on one side and the extreme left,

[9] This figure went up last year to $157 million, according to a recent letter by Ambassador Tomic in the *New York Times*. The strain on the national economy is obviously severe, and could be ruinous.

represented by the National Peasant Federation, on the other. The bill provides for the immediate expropriation of all privately owned farm properties bigger than two hundred acres, together with any farmland judged to be "poorly cultivated or entirely neglected." This, it is estimated, will give land to 100,000 peasants within five years—indeed an ambitious program. Farmers whose plots are too small to be economically productive are to be "regrouped" in cooperatives. About four thousand large estates will be broken up first. Compensation is to be in the form of an immediate 10 percent cash payment, the rest in bonds maturing over twenty-five years.

*

To sum up, Chile is the principal country in South America which, from the people's point of view, is really doing something about it—"it" being the morass of bad housing, tax evasion, lack of education, disorganization, exploitation, lack of social coherence, inequitable ownership of land, disparity between rich and poor, that are so characteristic of the continent. This is what makes Chile such a vital, glowing beacon for the future. From this over-all point of view it is the most important country in South America, and Eduardo Frei is its most important man.

USAID and the Alianza

When I asked United States authorities in Santiago what Alianza projects I might visit in town or the immediate neighborhood I had no idea that the choice would be so rich. I was offered Boys High School No. 7, Girls Experimental School No. 3, a waterworks system, La Platina Crop Experimental Station, a social center, a child care center, a playground, a CORVI (municipal housing administration) project, the Manuel de Salas-João Goulart apartment building, and the José Joaquín Prieto–Santiago Society Primary School. All this was near enough to be done in a day.

Girls School No. 3 is a smart new building in white and blue, with six hundred students and devoted to teacher training; one of seven hundred new schools in Chile, half its cost is being paid by USAID. The loan is to be repaid in forty years, with a ten-year grace period in the event that the school should be destroyed by an earthquake. Building operations in Chile are always vulnerable from this point of view. The school, which is bright as a smile, takes girls from the fifth grade to the twelfth; the minimum age is ten, and most students are boarders from various sections of the country, a significant development. It is part of an effort to give teachers' education a broader urban basis. The girls wear a special blue-and-white uniform, which means "Hands off!" to eager and pertinacious boys who might try to flirt with them on the streets or grab at them at bus stops. Seven hours a day go to study, with one hour devoted to religious instruction between the fifth and eighth grades. I asked a teacher if foreign languages were included in the curriculum. *Claro que sí!* English is obligatory from the seventh to the twelfth grade, French from the eighth. I tried to talk to some of the girls. They were too shy.

The Platina agricultural station, a research establishment, covers 750 acres and has a staff of 150 technicians. Here work proceeds on peaches, apples, grapes, hybrid corn, and forage. The locale, a few miles out of Santiago, is spectacular beyond belief, with the great serrated wall of the Andes on three sides; some plaster had flaked off the brand-new buildings because of a recent earthquake. AID financed construction of the plant, and the Rockefellers have made provision for scholarships and equipment; the University of Minnesota, through the Ford Foundation, is working on a program of technical assistance. The central impulse is to improve agricultural production. One technician told me, "Anything that California has, we have!" But Chile does not produce an agricultural yield even remotely comparable to that of California, as we know. What is necessary is a major lift to production, which research and technical aid will assist. Help from the Alianza is appreciated at Platina in several fields that may seem minor, but are important. For instance, the library is enabled to maintain subscriptions to agricultural journals from all over the world, which it could not otherwise afford because of the shortage of foreign currency.

American cooperation helps Chile in diverse ways. The Food for Peace program, operating out of U.S. Public Law 480, helps to feed no fewer than 1,900,000 Chileans, according to official American statistics. One enlivening factor in cultural activity is the work of the Institutos Chileno-Norte Americanos de Cultura, or bi-national centers, of which there are no fewer than fourteen in Chile. These institutes are autonomous, privately financed, nonpolitical, and nonsectarian. One in Santiago has a library of twelve thousand books in English, six thousand in Spanish, and teaches everything from languages to the Chilean form of tap dancing.

I heard the Alianza attacked by conservative Chileans on four different counts: (1) It is a mistake, because it leads citizens to false hopes of prosperity. (2) "We do not like such attempts to *buy* our allegiance." (3) Too much time and effort are wasted on questions of technical feasibility, that is, elaborate research, before a project is set up. If Isabella had asked Christopher Columbus for a feasibility report America would never have been discovered. (4) American technicians monopolize jobs, and are too expensive. On the other side I heard a left-wing man say that the trouble is that Alianza money only reaches the rich.

The Communist line is, of course, to reject the Alianza wholesale on the ground that it is "neo-colonial." Senator Altamirano told me, "You put $150 million into Chile every year, but you take $350 million out."

Work of the Peace Corps in the Shanty Towns

The shanty towns here are called *poblaciones callampas,* meaning mushroom settlements. Almost a quarter of the population of Santiago lives in these savagely grim locations; the first one we visited, José María Caro, lies near the airport, and holds no fewer than 130,000 people; if it were separated from Santiago proper, to which it is attached like some monstrous burr, it would be the fourth-biggest city in the country.

This is not the worst of the *callampas* by any means. Many of its citizens have actual houses, provided by CORVI, the municipal housing authority which is helped by Alliance funds; some are not squatters in the true sense at all, but pay a modest rent, say 3 escudos a month, or 90 cents, for a kind of pre-fab shelter. But, looking down the wide dreary streets of this enormous settlement, I saw squalor enough. Huts built of tin cans and cardboard have old newspapers in place of curtains over empty window spaces. Wild dogs bark in pitted alleys. Miserably clad children, their noses running, bellies naked, sit in pools of slime boiling with flies, or pluck bits of refuse out of garbage heaps.

Residents of the shanty towns are not vagrants, but men and women who have uprooted themselves to find a new way of life in the cities. It is a very serious matter for an agricultural worker to pull up stakes and set out for the metropolis. As a rule the head of the family takes an exploratory trip, often for hundreds of miles on foot, and returns later to pick up his family; a group of villagers may make the hegira together. Then they build their huts on whatever ground may be available, and here they squat.

Why, I asked, do the hillsmen, the peasants, the peons, descend on Rio and Caracas, Lima and Santiago, in such locust-like swarms? The answer is the same that I gave in discussion of the *favelas* in Brazil. The *campesinos* swarm into the towns because conditions of life in the countryside have become intolerable. It is a ghastly fact that conditions in the slums, hideous as these are, may be *better* than in the *campo,* countryside, where men are serfs. Once in the towns, no matter how grisly the slums may be, the peons have at least a chance of getting some kind of job and thus entering a money economy, instead of being sharecroppers or landless *campesinos.* They can see movies, look at newspapers, and perhaps enjoy other metropolitan satisfactions. Of course this does not excuse the municipality for not giving them better services, amenities, and opportunities.

My escorts to the Santiago shanty towns were American Peace Corps volunteers, and I began to hear something about this remarkable organization. Its members now work in 50 countries all over the world; some 4,600 are stationed in Latin America, and of these about 250 live in Chile. They teach in fields as various as anesthesia, bee-keeping, vocational education, and credit unions,[10] and, most interesting, work at an activity hard to define called "community development." This means—in Santiago as in other South American cities—that the Peace Corps volunteer moves into a specific neighborhood, like a shantytown, finds quarters there, and sets up a life as a member of the community in circumstances identical with those of his neighbors.

If there is no electricity the Peace Corps boy (or girl) has no electricity. If there are no flush toilets, he has no flush toilet. If he has to walk half a mile to bring water in a pail, he has to walk the half a mile. His wages are small—$100 a month in most of the places we visited—and he could not splurge even if he wanted to. He takes the bus, not a taxi; eats local food; suffers insect bites or dysentery; and seeks to live twenty-four hours a day in as nearly as possible the same physical conditions as the squatters.

I asked one volunteer how he could possibly live on $100 a month. His answer was that if the squatter next door, who has a job as a night watchman and has five children, has to manage on half that, it should not be too difficult for a bachelor like himself to get along on $100. As a matter of fact, every volunteer is somewhat better off than he seems, because he gets an additional $75 a month deposited in an American bank at home; this assures him of a nest egg of $1,800 after two years of service, which is usually the limit. Moreover, he has access to free medical care from a Peace Corps doctor while he is on the job, and, in an emergency, he can always get out. All this being said, Peace Corps work in a *callampa* is most certainly not a joyride.

One rule among the volunteers is never to obtrude on their neighbors. They do not force anything down anybody's throat. They may give counsel, but not unless this is asked. What, then, do they actually *do*? The gist of the answer to this is "Give an example." They try to show that decent appearances can be maintained in spite of poverty, to raise neighborhood standards, and to assist people to grasp new opportunities. In a modest way the Peace Corps men and women are "social engineers." The idea, in a word, is to teach the people to live better, to educate and elevate, and to get community action on their "felt needs"—even to play soccer and baby-sit.

[10] To say nothing of accounting, swimming, audio-visual techniques, bricklaying, drama, dental hygiene, and astronomy.

Nine American volunteers are stationed in José María Caro, and I visited the place where David and Charlotte St. John live. David, twenty-four, comes from Florida, and his wife, Charlotte, a year younger, was a schoolteacher in Georgia. They both seemed to represent all that is best in American youth, competent and cheerful, with a nice scrubbed look, lean cheeks, very white teeth, level eyes. Other volunteers from the neighborhood gathered to join us, including Floyd Wilson, a Negro from Chicago, and boys from Milwaukee, San Francisco, New York, and Indianapolis—a typical American cross-section—and we spent the morning talking.

The St. Johns' house, a kind of shed or hut, is clean, simply furnished and adequate, but I was startled by its sheer primitiveness, its pioneer quality of sparseness. Yet, compared to their neighbors, the St. Johns are lucky; they have an actual stove, whereas most of their neighbors are limited to a primitive charcoal burner, to say nothing of two whole (but extremely small) rooms to live in, just for themselves, whereas there are bedrooms down the street where eleven people sleep. And they have the standard CORVI unit, which is a flush toilet, shower, and kitchen sink. What makes life bearable is that water is available.

Nobody in the neighborhood, the St. Johns said, has TV, but almost everybody has a transistor radio, which is a large status symbol. There are no refrigerators, which means that shopping, a laborious process, has to be done almost every day. The St. Johns go to a cooperative called Unicoop, built by the Alliance, the only shop of this kind in any low-income area in Santiago, or the Feria, a traveling market; merchants wander through José María Caro with horse carts twice a week. Few of the houses are screened, although flies are thick, but almost all have walls or fences. The first thing a new arrival builds is a wall to keep the dogs out. There are about one hundred dog bites a week in the immediate vicinity.

The St. Johns and their companions were objects of lively curiosity when they moved in, they told us. Most people in the neighborhood had never seen a foreigner before, and had never heard English spoken. They still call Charlotte "the Argentine," because Argentina is about as far away as the local imagination can readily go. They were particularly interested in Floyd Wilson, because they thought that all Negroes came from Brazil—and promptly nicknamed him "Pele," after the celebrated Brazilian football star.

Among the neighbors are a carpenter, a loom mechanic, an accountant, a builder, and a taxi driver. Their average earning is $30 a month, sometimes $20. A loaf of bread costs 50 cents, and kerosene comes to about 25 cents a gallon. Kerosene is essential for light because there is, of course, no electricity. Local fruit is cheap (the peaches are marvelous, almost as big as grapefruit) but anything imported, like a banana, is expensive. Wine is inexpensive ($1 will buy about 5 litres) and beer is cheaper than a Coke; a bottle of beer costs 7 cents, which happens to be the same price as a quart of milk.

When they first made contact with their neighbors the St. Johns found that three questions were universal:

1. How much did this cost? (Pointing to a suit of clothes or a watch.)

2. Who killed John F. Kennedy? (Most Chileans cannot believe that the assassination was not a plot.)

3. Do people in the United States think that we are Indians? (A great many Chileans have Indian blood, as we know, but nothing upsets them more than to be called Indian.)

The Peace Corps volunteers minimize the "uplift" aspect of their work, and stress self-help. They work closely with Promoción Popular, which aims at social improvement through the initiative of the people themselves, and meet with their neighbors in organized groups, discussing problems all the way from the transportation system, which is miserable, to the work of the new community center, built by the Alliance, and trying to break down the isolation of the community. Well-to-do Chileans practically never visit the *callampas*, which are a kind of no-man's-land; taxi drivers usually refuse to take fares there. One of the boys told me that par for the course into the center of the city, about nine miles away, was three hours on a chain of buses.

Another element in the work of the volunteers in this community has to do with, of all things, rabbits. Chile has an annual demand for about 100,000 pounds of rabbit fur, which can be spun into yarn and made into sweaters and the like, but it only produces a tenth of this amount. So the volunteers, noticing that many squatters raise ducks and chickens, thought that they might go in for rabbits too. They set out to provide an example, and the result is that one male and two impregnated female rabbits are now being made available to residents of the community on request, with the further result that breeding and shearing have become a lively enterprise.

*

Returning to the city over spiny cobbles, I asked about the political complexion of the *callampas*. I had assumed, if only because of their poverty, that most residents stood with FRAP. But no. President Frei and the Christian Democrats carried the shanty town in the last election by a substantial margin. Here above anywhere citizens recognized that Frei is doing something about *it*.

CHAPTER 16

Bottom of the World

The sense of sublimity, which the great deserts of Patagonia and the forest-clad mountains of Tierra del Fuego excited in me . . . has left an indelible impression on my mind.
—CHARLES DARWIN, *Voyage of the Beagle*

SOUTHERN Chile, a unique and stormy region, is the bottom of the inhabited world. Of course Antarctica lies farther south, but it is not inhabited in the normal sense of the term. But Chile has cities and settlements below the 53rd parallel of latitude, far to the south of the Cape of Good Hope in Africa or the southern tip of Australia, as may be seen clearly on any Mercator map.

I had the exceptional good luck of visiting this magnificent, inaccessible, and little-known area through the courtesy of Ralph A. Dungan, the American ambassador to Chile. Mr. Dungan, who was a leading member of the White House secretariat under John F. Kennedy, was setting out on an expedition to southern Chile to donate books to workers' libraries in several remote towns and villages. Mrs. Dungan and their youthful son Peter came along, together with other journalists, Chilean officials, and naval officers.

The ambassadorial plane was an ancient DC-3 stripped to the bone like transport planes during the war; half the seats had been removed to make way for gear. This was going to be a rough trip, and the aircraft had the look of one deliberately toughened up so it could the more easily beat off any possible assault from wind and water. Commander William E. Behringer, one of our pilots, wore a leather battle jacket studded with exotic flashes from combat days in the Pacific, together with an incongruous pair of orange-colored slacks. Most passengers carried stout sweaters and the like; I was unprepared enough to have come without boots or an overcoat.

306

The area we were about to visit, with its forlorn and frigid wastes, contains natural wonders without end. Andean peaks rise four miles off the earth's floor in the wildly beautiful and unspoiled Chilean lake country and shimmer through cushions of silver mist. The lakes themselves look like solid blue sapphires set in green rock. Farther south are the Straits of Magellan, the twisting slaty waterway which connects Atlantic and Pacific, and the island of Tierra del Fuego, split between Chile and Argentina and seldom seen by any traveler. Still farther south in a shambles of broken reefs, crooked promontories, and ice-blue glaciers is Cape Horn, the extreme southerly tip of the American continent, which we duly rounded from the air, next to its forgotten brother, False Cape Horn.

About 550 miles below Santiago the Chilean bell rope begins to fray. The coastline, comparatively smooth above, breaks up into a jagged mélange of inlets, bays, fjords; the region has been aptly called a "topographical hysteria." The lakes, crowded with improbable-looking islands, crouch smoothly under the overwhelming cordillera of the Andes. In one small sector there are seven peaks higher than any mountain in the United States.

Fishermen, hikers, skiers, mountain climbers find this countryside a paradise, but nature has been known to submit it to explosions of the most berserk violence. The ravages of the 1960 earthquake, which tore the whole region apart, are not yet effaced. At one point near Valdivia the spine of rock under the earth's surface actually broke; pockets of land subsided, farms became lakes never seen before, and the level of the land rose perceptibly some miles away like skin over a savagely broken bone.

Chile's area of interlocked waterways stretches roughly nine hundred miles from Puerto Montt, the chief town of the lake region, to the end of the line where the continent expires at Cape Horn. At Puerto Montt the Atlantic and Pacific stand roughly four hundred miles apart, separated not merely by the Andean cordillera but by the broad pastures of Patagonia in the Argentine. Then the continent gradually becomes narrower, tapering off, as the two oceans approach each other. Our trip led us steadily southward over the diminishing haunch of land until the oceans met.

We skidded out of Santiago on a greasy morning and reached Puerto Montt, which is named for an old-time president of Chile, Manuel Montt, around noon. Weather—a howling wind—stopped us here for a night. It was too dangerous to fly. A sturdy little town, PUERTO MONTT (population 65,000) is the capital of Llanquihue Province, and the *intendente*, or governor, is thirty-two-year-old Sergio M. Elliot G., an enthusiastic Frei supporter. The strongest foreign influence in the community is, however, not British, as the governor's name suggests, but German. Germans and Austrians began to colonize this area, with its ruggedly romantic scenery, in the 1850's, as mentioned in a previous chapter. But Puerto Montt did not remind me so much of Bavaria or the Salzkammergut as it did of small American cities in Appalachia. Old frame houses have big dilapidated porches and steep roofs, resembling photographs of towns in West Virginia by Walker Evans.

The main thing to say about this city is that it is the beginning of the end of the world, even though it has such amenities as a good hotel and even a well-trained symphony orchestra. The railway from Santiago ends here, and so does the Pan-American Highway. Roads are scant below this point, and you travel best by air, boat, or your feet. The atmosphere is one of eerie remoteness. The Alliance for Progress is working on several projects, but I did not feel that I was in the environment of the Americas I know. A sniff of the baleful, of the deceptive, a piercing aroma of unknown horizons, are discernible. Here the frontier begins.

Punta Arenas and the Straits

We reached PUNTA ARENAS, the southernmost city in the world, the next day. There are a few "communities" even more southerly, like Puerto Williams, which we also visited, but Punta Arenas, with fifty-five thousand people, is the most southerly place in the world that can fairly be called a city. Ushuaia, on the Argentine side of Tierra del Fuego, lies further south but its population is only about three thousand.

The flight took us over broad-backed scenery, but clouds made it hard to see anything except the more conspicuous icy peaks, which look like sharp vanilla sundaes. The most difficult mountains to climb are not, however, the really big ones, but a spiny mass at the southern end of the range called the Torre de Paine. Not till the 1960's were these conquered. Underneath us the lakes and waterways spread and interlocked. Not only are land and water inextricably mixed up; so are countries. At one town the republic of Argentina reaches a point only twelve miles from the Pacific, if you consider the adjacent waterways to be Pacific water.

First, let me place Punta Arenas geographically. It lies on the extreme southern edge of the South American continent, which is to say that it is on the northern shore of the Straits of Magellan, midway between Atlantic and Pacific. The gap between the two oceans has now narrowed to three hundred miles. Facing Punta Arenas across the straits is Tierra del Fuego, eleven miles away. At this point southern Chile looks like a thigh becoming a calf, and Tierra del Fuego is a sharply turned right foot.

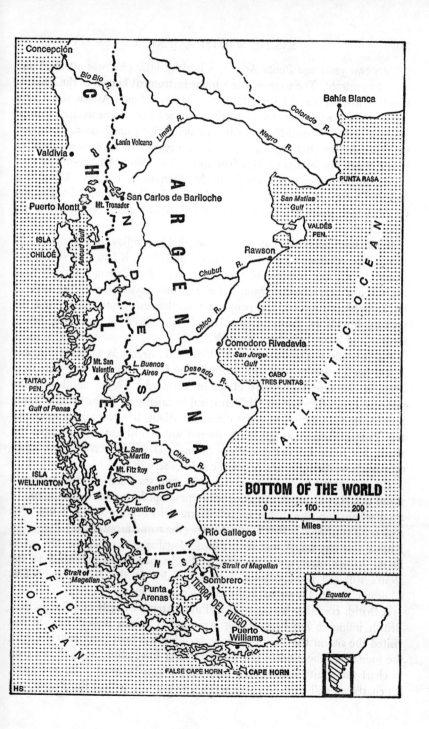

BOTTOM OF THE WORLD

0   100   200
Miles

Fifty-two years ago Punta Arenas, a healthy little city, was attacked and almost murdered. The weapon was a blunt instrument known as the Panama Canal. Until the canal opened for traffic in 1914, Punta Arenas was a vital coaling and provisioning station on the main sea route from western Europe and the eastern United States to the Pacific. Ships from Boston, Liverpool, or Marseilles, en route to Lima or San Francisco, had no option except to pass through the Straits of Magellan and call at Punta Arenas—unless they took a much longer way through the Mediterranean, the Suez Canal, the Indian Ocean, and the breadth of the Pacific. Then came the Panama Canal, which shortened the route by thousands of miles. So Punta Arenas suffered.

It did not quite die, but another severe blow followed—the decline of sheep. The economy of the Punta Arenas hinterland is based on sheep, but sheep are not the commodity they once were. First, natural sheep's wool has taken a heavy beating from nylon and other synthetics as the basis of textile products; second, few people eat mutton any more. As a result the packing houses in Punta Arenas, which specialized in exporting frozen mutton and lamb, have been hard hit.

But it would not be correct to think of Punta Arenas as a ghost town, and it still has a refreshing pioneer quality. One factor contributing to its well-being is the recent discovery of oil in Tierra del Fuego; another is the presence here of important Chilean naval installations. Tourist traffic, made possible by the advance in aerial communications, has potential importance too. Twenty years or so ago Punta Arenas was almost unreachable from the north, but today LAN, the Chilean airline, has a daily service from Santiago—when weather permits. Argentine airlines serve it too.

Even so, this city is still *terra incognita*, and standard works of reference make mistakes about it. An American encyclopedia noted for its normally good scholarship says that it is "in" Tierra del Fuego, which it is not. One reason for confusion is that Punta Arenas (the name means Sandy Point, but I never saw any sand) was once called Magallanes. In fact the change to Punta Arenas came quite recently, and reference books published in the 1930's still call it Magallanes. It was founded in the 1850's to confirm Chilean claims to the straits, and used as a penal colony.

A British consulate was opened in Punta Arenas as early as 1875. In fact, British influence has been strong ever since Captain Robert Fitzroy first visited the site in the 1820's. Fitzroy, an adventurer-navigator-meteorologist, the founder of the modern science of weather forecasting, was the first man to chart the straits and, though they were drawn between 1828 and 1835, his charts are still used. His ship was a 240-ton brig named the *Beagle*, and his official naturalist, who rode with him from December, 1831, to October, 1836, and wrote a celebrated book about the voyage, was none other than Charles Darwin, then in his early twenties.

Darwin's words are stirring. Indians saw the *Beagle* as it entered the straits, and lit signal fires. The sea was violently rough. The ship anchored in the Bay of Good Success, which had also been used by the illustrious Pacific explorer Captain Cook. "A party of Fuegians were watching us," Darwin writes. "They were perched on a wild peak overhanging the sea and surrounded by wood. As we passed by they all sprang up and waving their cloaks of skins sent forth a loud sonorous shout." Then a landing party visits the shore. "It was without exception the most curious and interesting spectacle I ever beheld. I would not have believed how entire the difference between savage and civilized man is." Darwin approaches an old man, whose only garment was "a large guanaco skin with the hair outside." The British visitors bestow bits of red cloth as gifts, whereupon the natives become friendly. "This was shown by the old man patting our breasts and making something like the same noise which people do when feeding chickens. . . . At last he gave me three hard slaps on the breast and back at the same time, and making most curious noises. He then bared his bosom from me to return the compliment."

More than a hundred years after Darwin British place names still illuminate the maps of all this stormy region—Mount Wharton, Cockburn Canal, Hardy Peninsula, Otway Bay, Skyring Sound, and islands named Stewart, Gilbert, Londonderry, Waterman, Morton, Hanover and Clarence. Other picturesque place names are Bahía Inútil (Useless Bay), so called because its waters are permanently choppy, Seno Ultima Esperanza (Last Hope Inlet), Fiordo Obstrucción, and Desolation Island.

Next to British the chief foreign influence today is Yugoslav. Many people whom I met, including the *intendente* and the local archbishop, bear Yugoslav names, and the town of Porvenir (population 3,300), a few miles away on Tierra del Fuego, is almost solidly Yugoslav in origin. The colony dates from days before World War I, when hundreds of stout Serbs, Croats, and Slovenes, particularly those with a maritime background along the Dalmatian coast, migrated to Chile in order to avoid military service under the old Austro-Hungarian monarchy. The countryside resembled home.

Punta Arenas may be forlorn, it may seem derelict, and it certainly is off the beaten track, but it has all the familiar characteristics of the typical South American city, from the inevitable public square, on which the governor's palace abuts, in the center of town, with its trees and flowers, to the shanty towns on the outskirts, where squatters have moved in. Everything is on a minor scale, but the note is metropolitan. Streets are laid out in neat rectangles; thirty-five run north and south, twenty-five go east and west. The leading hotel, called the Cabo de Hornos, is—no exaggeration—one of the two or three best I found in all South America: brightly decorated, sensitive to the needs of travelers, with an unexpectedly good restaurant and a bar which not only produces a decent pisco sour but a decent dry martini.

But the Cabo de Hornos is like a cut gem set in a quarry. The roughest thing about archipelagic Chile is the weather. There are storms of unimaginable ferocity, and sometimes the winds blow eighty miles an hour. Even on a so-called "moderate" day it may be impossible for a man to walk against the wind. November, the equivalent of our May, is the windiest month. Winters (our summers) would be unendurable if the winds did not die down for several months after April. The days are agonizingly long in summer, when the sun rises at three-thirty and sets at ten at night, if only because the wind never stops. It may seem odd, but the winters, even though the days are short, are easier to bear.

For all its meteorological violence, Punta Arenas has pretty flowers, shrubs, and gardens. Of course everything has to be screened and sheltered. In one British garden I saw raspberries shielded by clumps of willow, which, incidentally, had been imported from another rough maritime location, St. Helena.

Sheep entered the economy here in about 1865, brought from the Falkland Islands by a Briton and a Scot. A group of forty Scottish pioneers, who are known to this day as the "forty shepherds," are the foundation of the local aristocracy. Sheepholdings have to be large since it takes roughly one hectare to support a single animal. One dominant company, the Ganadera Tierra del Fuego, S.A., owns roughly 900,000 sheep out of the total of 3.2 million in the area, has property covering several million acres, and is said to be the largest enterprise of its kind in the world.

The local sheepmen are extremely proud of the quality of their white wool. On a big farm seventeen to twenty shearers, mostly Chileans of Yugoslav origin, are able to shear two thousand sheep a day, and a good dual-purpose animal gives eleven pounds of wool at a shearing and will be useful for meat as well. Large fortunes were made in the Punta Arenas neighborhood in the early days. A renowned character was Mauricio Braun, of Lithuanian extraction, who married the daughter of a Spanish-descended shopkeeper named Menéndez. They had a large family. For many years Braun said to anybody who would listen that his ambition was to have fifty-three grandchildren—why he chose this particular number is unknown; on the anniversary of his golden wedding he counted up to forty-seven and conceded that this was enough. He was the founder of the Ganadera company. Two Braun-Menéndez houses, monstrously Victorian in architecture, are among the proudest relics Punta Arenas has; one has quarters for fifty people. It is seldom used today, however, because most members of the family live in Buenos Aires or elsewhere abroad. Even now the Braun-Menéndez holdings are so big, particularly in Argentina, that, according to local legend, a traveler can drive all the way from Punta Arenas to Buenos Aires, some thirteen hundred miles (the trip takes a hard five to seven days) and sleep every night on a different Braun-Menéndez property. These properties are not, of course, contiguous, but are conveniently—if accidentally—placed like giant stepping stones.

The great local landowners are less powerful these days than formerly, because many of the big "stations" have been split up by inheritance, and the country's ambitious land-reform program is beginning to take effect. The state buys land as it becomes available and then sells, auctions, or leases it to small holders; about two-thirds of the total pasture area of the region has been subdivided in this manner. Politics here are strongly Socialist.

Sven B. Robson, who came out to Punta Arenas forty years ago from London to work in a packing factory and who is now the town's leading citizen and serves as the honorary British consul, took me around. Sights? Punta Arenas has a ski tow, the most southerly in the world, and one of the few covered tennis courts in South America—covered, because the wind makes outdoor play impossible most of the year. The city has a British school, a tiny British church, and a British club, which, except for the fact that it is not tropical, might have come straight out of Somerset Maugham. Three billiard tables that seem too large to be real dominate one of the rooms, and the library, with huge, worn buff-colored leather chairs, looks like "a stage set from a Victorian melodrama," and was, from internal evidence, well maintained till the middle 1930's.[1] Then book buying must have faltered. I peeked at shelves loaded with books I had known quite well in my youth and that seemed inexpressibly dated now, like early novels by Michael Arlen and A. S. M. Hutchinson.

Mr. Robson showed me a bound newspaper file, dated 1926, of the *Magellan Times*, which carried the motto "the furthest south British newspaper," and which stopped publication long ago. The copy I saw had passages about the social life of such local celebrities as the Mauricio Brauns, and advertisements for hardware, rope, and sheep dip.

But the chief sights in Punta Arenas are, as is natural, maritime. We

[1] *South American Handbook*, p. 250.

drove near the naval station and saw, among other relics, the scarred, rusty prow of a Chilean cutter called *Yelcho*, which rescued the British explorer Sir Ernest Shackleton in 1917. Shackleton was returning from a gallant but unsuccessful try for the South Pole on his celebrated ship *Endurance*. Then, in cold sunshine, we climbed a hill and caught a full view of what we had come so far to see, the Straits of Magellan. Two or three wrecks lay half submerged, and small boats danced back and forth carrying firewood and onions. To the left lies Magdalena Island, full of penguins; to the right, we looked toward Dawson on the Pacific side. At Point Dungeness the tides have been known to rise 46 feet, higher than any in the world except in the Bay of Fundy, and capable of lifting a ship up out of the water, careening it, and sliding it off again. The straits, full of crooked intersections, are 330 miles long, 2½ to 15 miles wide. A bit of mist cleared, and we saw suddenly one of the least-known sights on earth—the somber blue coastline of Tierra del Fuego on the other side, corroded, mysterious, and sinister.

The Isle of Fire

We continued to have good luck with weather, even though this was April, the equivalent of October in the north. The next day was reasonably clear, and the winds mild. Ambassador Dungan shepherded us into the DC-3. I had not noticed before that each passenger had a pack, attached to the next seat, marked "Exposure Suit," and containing brilliant orange-yellow gear. Presumably we would put these suits on, like a man dressing correctly for dinner, if we had trouble and were forced to ditch. But nobody could survive long in water as cold as it is in these frigid wastes, no matter what he wore. I asked Captain W. J. Rush, the American naval attaché to Chile, who was with us, what would happen in the event of a forced landing; his reply was brief and cheerful, "Don't think about it."

We crossed the Straits of Magellan at 1,500 feet, aiming east in a long slant, and took 7½ minutes to reach Tierra del Fuego. The island has a burnt look, but still retains traces of green—brownish green, olive green, and the green of lima beans. The land is flat for the most part (but the Andes give a last flick of their stupendous tail near the southern edge), and there are few trees, because they cannot survive the wind.

I saw a few farmhouses with roofs painted the variety of pink known as "shocking," a road or two, and mile upon mile of pasture. The name Tierra del Fuego (Land of Fire) probably comes from the explosive sunsets characteristic of this part of the world or from the flares lit by primitive

Indians when mariners passed down the straits long ago. We began to descend and I was startled to see thin plumes of flame burning on the dull terrain; these, which can be seen day and night, come from the petroleum fields. Gas is burned off at intersections in the pipelines. Four hundred years ago Tierra del Fuego was lit by exotic fires, and so it still is today.

Strictly speaking, Tierra del Fuego is not an island at all but an archipelago, with thousands of small islands. As an indication of the lack of accurate information I might mention that one well-known encyclopedia gives the total area as 18,500 square miles, another as 28,000. The main island is penetrated by Useless Bay, Whiteside Channel, and Almirantazgo (Admiralty) Sound. About two-thirds of the total area is Chilean; the rest, a triangular chunk to the east, belongs to the Argentine. The boundary was drawn by a commission appointed by King Edward VII of England in the early years of the twentieth century, at the request of the Chilean and Argentine governments, and has never been contested. Perhaps this is the reason—such is the prestige of the British royal house—that both Argentines and Chileans have recently sought the intercession of Queen Elizabeth II in settling a contemporary boundary dispute.

We landed at a Fuegian town, if you could call it a town, with the remarkable name Sombrero, population six hundred. Atlantic and Pacific have now come closer; the huge South American continent, in its final downward thrust, has narrowed to a spiny arrowhead. This is all sheep country—immense tracts of land are used for pasture. But I saw only two sheep the whole day. Both were lawn mowers in Sombrero, cropping the grass.

Oil was discovered in Tierra del Fuego in 1945, and Sombrero was built as a by-product of the petroleum rush. Dating from 1957–60, it is among the newest communities in the world; it is the "capital" of the oil fields, and a model town has been set up. Here are housing units for technicians and workers, several schools (but the high school has only two students), a nicely equipped hospital, and a fascinatingly ambitious community center, which includes a bowling alley, a swimming pool, a tropical garden under a glass roof, a solarium and a large basketball court, also used for what South Americans call "voleibol." I noticed the church too, built in the most modern style, colored blue, ochre, and white with a roof in the shape of a steep tent. Everything is clean, because the wind blows it so.

We talked to teachers who gave out a healthy pioneer note, and to technicians who have surrendered good jobs elsewhere to give a lift to this newly developed region. Most are employees of the government, since ENAP (Empresa Nacional del Petróleo), which owns and operates the oil fields, is a state enterprise. Foreign concessions for petroleum are not permitted in Chile, although ENAP may make contracts with American and other foreign companies for specific tasks on a contract basis.

Magellan discovered Tierra del Fuego in 1520, and it was visited by Sir Francis Drake in 1578. The former entered the straits from the Atlantic at a point called the Cape of Eleven Thousand Virgins; it took him thirty-eight days to traverse the passage, after subduing a mutiny. It was Magellan who gave the name Tierra del Fuego to the archipelago (he also invented the names "Patagonia" and "Pacific"), and he described it as a country "stark with eternal cold."

Drake lost two ships traversing the straits, and, when he had finished the passage in sixteen days, he renamed his own ship the *Golden Hind*—apparently by way of celebration. These are passages from the account of Francis Pretty, gentleman at arms, one of Drake's companions:

> The 17th day of August we departed the port of St. Julian, and the 20th day we fell with the Strait of Magellan, going into the South Sea; at the cape or headland whereof we found the body of a dead man, whose flesh was clean consumed. The 21st day we entered the Strait, which we found to have many turnings, and as it were shuttings-up, as if there were no passage at all. . . . The land on both sides is very huge and mountainous; the lower mountains whereof, although they be monstrous and wonderful to look upon for their height, yet there are others which in height exceed them in a strange manner, reaching themselves above their fellows so high, that between them did appear three regions of clouds. . . . This Strait is extreme cold, with frost and snow continually; the trees seem to stoop with the burden of the weather, and yet are green continually, and many good and sweet herbs do very plentifully grow and increase under them. . . .
>
> The 24th of August we arrived at an island in the Straits, where we found great store of fowl which could not fly, of the bigness of geese; whereof we killed in less than one day 3,000, and victualled ourselves thoroughly therewith. . . . The 7th day we were driven by a great storm from the entering into the South Sea. . . .
>
> Not far from hence we entered another bay, where we found people, both men and women, in their canoes naked, and ranging from one island to another to seek their meat. . . [2]

Today there are three surviving aboriginal Indian groups, the Onas, Yahgans, and Alakalufs, but their total number is probably no more than a few thousand. One story is that there are only fifteen genuine Onas left. All three have considerable anthropological interest; they are primitive in the extreme (but the Yahgan language has thirty-two thousand words), with a

---

[2] "We Took the Silver and Left the Man," by Francis Pretty, reprinted in *Impressions of Latin America*, edited by Frank MacShane.

complex family structure. One island tribe has, incredibly enough, a taboo against crossing water. More than a century ago missionaries came into Tierra del Fuego representing the Church Missionary Society of England. They had marked success. Four young Yahgans, three youths and a girl, were brought back to England by Captain Fitzroy; their names were York Minster, Boat Memory, Jimmy Button, and Fuegia Basket. They were duly installed in a villa at Walthamstow, which a great many years later became Clement Attlee's constituency, and were ceremoniously presented to King William IV and Queen Adelaide to show how satisfactorily the heathen had become adjusted to puritan, western standards. "The queen placed her own little lace cap on Fuegia Basket's head."[3] The Indians were shipped back to Tierra del Fuego on Fitzroy's next voyage, and took up residence on Navarino Island. York Minster and Miss Basket married and became respectable members of the community. But Jimmy Button reverted to savagery and years later instigated a massacre in which a missionary station was wiped out.

Late in the nineteenth century Tierra del Fuego was invaded by a remarkable man named Popper. He was a Rumanian engineer resident in China who heard that gold had been discovered in Tierra del Fuego, as indeed it had been. He managed to get there and procured a concession. Some authorities think that he was in reality the Archduke Johann Orth, of the imperial Habsburg family, who disappeared en route from Salzburg to South America in the 1880's, after a shipwreck, and whose fate has never been satisfactorily determined. The world lost all trace of him, and a persistent legend has it that, for reasons unknown, he transformed himself into Popper. Be this as it may be, Popper built up an army of fifty men, dressed them in gaudy Hungarian uniforms, found gold, and made war against other prospectors. He wrote reports for newspapers in Buenos Aires from time to time, and these stress some of the obstacles he faced. One enemy was a bird which fed on the eyes of live sheep. Indians were so troublesome that a bounty was paid for their ears. Popper and the Braun-Menéndez interests, which were also beginning to penetrate Tierra del Fuego at the time, fought bitterly. Popper died in the Argentine in 1889; one story is that he was poisoned.

Cape Horn and Back

From Sombrero, with its brusque, empty terrain connoting loneliness and danger, we flew dead south, skirting the Argentine frontier, toward Cape Horn. Fresh snow lay like powdered sugar on the bleak hills, and there were

[3] *Uttermost Part of the Earth*, by E. Lucas Bridges, p. 31, an enthralling book about early missionary days in Tierra del Fuego.

also agglutinated masses of older snow—slimy, yellowish, shiny, and faintly phosphorescent like mounds of a million fish eyes. We passed over one marvelous lake, and I thought it was the loveliest thing I had ever seen. Presently we came out over the open sea dotted with islands like the Wollastons, and then, as we descended abruptly to fifteen hundred feet, a thirty-knot tail wind helped blow us around Cape Horn. Not many men alive have seen it or, as the old word is, rounded or "doubled" it. Cape Horn is as a matter of fact not a true cape at all, but the southernmost small island of an island group. We passed over these islets swiftly from the Atlantic side to the Pacific. There is very little to see except mountain ridges, ragged valleys, and a deeply indented shoreline, cut into by giant scallops of ocean. But we knew that we had come to the end of the road. Here Atlantic and Pacific meet at last and the western hemisphere reaches its extreme southerly tip. Only once before have I ever seen two great oceans meet and merge in this way, off the Cape of Good Hope in South Africa. Here as there no line marks the merger.

Our plane turned north and the pilot called out, "Beg pardon, may I have that map back? It's the only one we have and we're navigating with it."

Cape Horn was discovered in 1616 by a Dutchman who named it for Hoorn, a village in his native Holland. It has never been inhabited, except perhaps by a few stray Indians. Sometimes whalers still round it. Otherwise nobody but a madman would take a ship here, since the Straits of Magellan provide a quicker, less agitated passage. These are among the most dangerous waters in the world.

Next we stopped at a community called Puerto Williams, which, Antarctica excepted, is the most southerly inhabited place in the world. Actually at this point we were not very far from the northern tip of Chilean Antarctica, but too far for a DC-3's fuel capacity. Puerto Williams lies on Beagle Channel just underneath Tierra del Fuego, and is probably the most isolated community on earth. The flight here from Cape Horn was the most spectacular I have ever had. We took a mildly indirect route in order to see the glaciers near Nassau Bay. Our pilots brought us down to eight hundred feet and we twisted through a long, sinuous line of glaciers, so close that it seemed that we could scrape snow off them. The pilots kidded about putting some ice in the ambassador's lap. The glaciers take the form of immense apron-shaped chutes of ice, a vivid luminous blue in color, and are cut off at the corners like chunks of rock crystal.

Puerto Williams, the population of which is about three hundred, is a Chilean naval and meteorological station. No doubt it was set up partly as a bit of flag waving vis-à-vis the Argentines across Beagle Channel. It was named, oddly enough, not for an Englishman but for a Chilean admiral whose name was Williams and who first claimed the Magellan territory for Chile. Even more oddly, *another* Chilean named Williams, also an admiral, is a hero in this region, and a statue to his memory was recently put up in Punta Arenas. The original name of Puerto Williams was Puerto Luisa. I do not know who Luisa was. Puerto Williams is inexpressibly remote and forlorn. We hiked from the airstrip to a shaky dock and, going down an even shakier gangplank, boarded a "papa" boat, or LCVP, a small landing craft used by the U.S. Navy during World War II. No object whatever was to be seen except another landing craft marooned nearby. We crossed an estuary, and on the mainland—or was it the mainland?—we strode up a steep muddy path toward the commandant's house. The automobile population of Puerto Williams is exactly three: a school bus, a Land-Rover, and an ancient jeep. There are no roads; no streets; no shops; no money (everything is paid for by scrip); no playing field or community center; no newspaper; no outdoor lights at night; no TV or movie; no anything. Planes fly in with supplies for the naval officers stationed here, but bad weather may cut Puerto Williams off from the mainland for months at a time; officers and personnel assigned here must take special psychological tests to determine whether they can survive the remote and frigid loneliness.

A few Indians still live in the brush near the solitary school. One, a renowned local character, is named Cristina Hirsch de Chacun, and, since she is reputedly 120 years old, she has every right to her nickname, which is Grandma. Her tribe is the Yahgan, and she lives in a hut built for her by the government; she was taught English by the missionaries a century ago, if the legend is to be believed, and still speaks it. We went to call on her and her words to me were, "Get on with you, fellow."

Now I have to report that, after slogging across muddy fields, we had lunch at the home of Captain Pedro Jorquera, the commandant of the post, and his Santiago-born wife; like so many Chilean women, she is tall, beautiful, and chic. And here in this community beyond the beyond, stranded in a limitless bleak vacuum we were served a lunch consisting of a superb king crab, long strips of filet mignon that might have come from a good restaurant in New York, French cheese ripened to the precisely correct pitch, and a complicated fantasy for dessert. While we enjoyed this feast we looked at pleasant pictures on the walls, listened to Beethoven on records, exchanged gossip about Santiago, and discussed Pablo Neruda, J. B. Priestley, Elvis Presley, and the vagaries of American foreign policy.

I do not know what is the lesson of this except that a good lunch is always enjoyable, especially if it takes place at the bottom of the world, but the experience seemed to prove that it is possible to maintain civilized values even in an outpost as incalculably distant and primitive as this, if you have enough good taste, courage, and imagination. And of course Chile is one of the most civilized countries in the world.

CHAPTER 17

El Señor Presidente de Perú

Peru . . . the forgotten antecedent.
—FERNANDO BELAÚNDE TERRY

O Peru! Land of metal and melancholy!
—FEDERICO GARCÍA LORCA

FERNANDO BELAÚNDE TERRY, the president of Peru, one of the most stirring as well as attractive men of the Americas, is an architect by profession. Educated partly in the United States, he has scope, charm, and passion—in a country which has substantial need for reformist passion. Politically his line is liberal–progressive, slightly to the left of center, and his tasks are, to understate the situation, manifold.

Belaúnde has been called "an architect of hope." Several of his close associates are architects, and Peru is, the mild joke has it, run by an "architectocracy." A good architect must, of course, be both an artist and a builder—a dreamer who gives form to a conception; architects are planners, men with a sense of structure. But some of Belaúnde's critics think that he is bound too much to the thesis that he can enact profound changes in the order of society by mere physical alterations. Sometimes he is called "a physical resources man." But in the president's own mind it is the vision that counts, and this is radiant.

Peru, Bolivia, Ecuador, the three Andean countries on the West Coast, are altogether different from any we have encounted thus far. To put it in the crudest terms, they are distinguished by (1) top-of-the-world geography, (2) Indians, (3) the bleakest poverty, (4) feudalism, (5) colonial economy, and (6) a predisposition to raw violence, but this last characteristic is less conspicuous in Peru than in Bolivia.

Peru itself, probably the most colorful nation in South America after

321

Brazil, gives the figurative impression of being an island—proud, dense, and closed. Uniquely among all the countries we have visited, it had an Indian *civilization* long before the Spaniards came, which gives it some cryptic characteristics. Today the most ingrown and tightly knit of American oligarchies holds it thumb-bound, and there are phenomena in social content still darker than almost anything in Darkest Africa. This explains Belaúnde's addiction to what he calls "Peruvianism" and the necessity for "the conquest of Peru by its own people."

Chile, which may have seemed complicated enough, is easy-pie compared to Peru. A thoroughly integrated state, Chile has no language or racial barriers, an advanced metropolitan elite, and an educated and responsible electorate. Peru is chaotic by comparison. Overwhelmingly the principal problem of Peru is to bring the submerged, shattered mass of illiterate Indians, who number 50 percent of the population and who are for the most part utterly excluded from national life, into the body of contemporary society. Many still live on a starvation plane.

Belaúnde comes out of the aristocracy, but he is not a true oligarch in the Limeño meaning of the term. His background is intellectual, not plutocratic. His family probably cannot be easily traced back more than six or seven generations, whereas to be a Peruvian lord in the fully starched sense means having antecedents who go all the way back to Pizarro, ten or eleven generations. Moreover, although he was born in Lima, Belaúnde has a strong association with Arequipa, a provincial town which, to the Peruvian nobility, is Oshkosh. Then too, even though his ties to the upper level are close, the president is full of imagination and has always been a rebel; he has, in fact, been characterized as an extremely nice man who desperately wants to be a true reformer but, in the last analysis, is prevented from this by being bound by unbreakable ties with his own class. The analogy to Franklin D. Roosevelt should not be stressed too much, but is suggestive.

The president, who was born in 1912, is, like Roosevelt, controversial as well as beguiling. His father, Rafael Belaúnde Díez Canseco, was a teacher who also had a vivid political life, and served two terms as prime minister; his grandfather was a minister of finance, and one of his great grandfathers a president of the republic. Belaúnde *père* fell into disfavor, spent a period in jail, as do practically all South American politicians with brains, and moved to Paris in 1924, in voluntary exile, with his family. Later he became a professor of Latin American studies at the University of Miami, Florida, where his son continued his education. Changes brought the father back to political life in 1933, and he served in a diplomatic post in Mexico for a

period, during which Fernando studied architecture at the University of Texas. He received a degree there in 1935.

Returning home, young Belaúnde set out to practice architecture in Lima; he was more interested in municipal projects, laying out suburban developments and the like, than in domestic architecture. He became fascinated by satellite cities and public housing, and rose in 1950 to be dean of the National School of Architecture. Meantime, following his family's example, he immersed himself in politics. He was strongly influenced by one of his uncles, Víctor Andrés Belaúnde, who was variously ambassador to the United States, representative of Peru at the UN, and chairman of the UN General Assembly. He himself served as a federal deputy from 1940 to 1946, and made his first run for the presidency in 1956. He became president after a third try in 1963.

Fernando Belaúnde is a well-built smallish man, compact and graceful, with a wide eager smile. He wears his hair *en brosse*, and has large sparkling eyes. His manner is boyish, candid, charming. Belaúnde has found time to learn to fly, and, three or four years ago, fought a duel with a deputy who had made scurrilous remarks about him; this was not a comedy duel, and both men were slightly wounded. In 1962 he defied an order prohibiting political rallies, and was packed off to jail. He made a daring attempt to escape from the prison where he was confined—on an offshore Pacific island. Eluding his guards he jumped into the chill water and swam toward a launch where a group of rescuers, his friends, had arranged to pick him up. Belaúnde is a powerful swimmer, but, because of what a biographer calls a "coordinational error" in planning, the attempt failed. He was released from confinement some time later.

The president's chief quality, aside from those obvious like courage, earnestness, and vision, is probably his sense of public trust, although he does not have the usual stigmata of the do-gooder. He has confidence, likes new ideas, and takes opposition in his stride. His first campaigns electrified the nation. Here was something new—an intellectual of good birth running against the oligarchy as a people's man. Normally the populace is wary of intellectuals, because they have so often proved to be no more than the chorus for a dictator. When Belaúnde finally won his way to the presidency—by a 39 percent vote—he formed the first middle-class civilian government in Peruvian history.

Belaúnde stalks ideas like a panther and, clever, always leaves room for a second look at anything. His love affair with Peru is like that for a woman. His approach is generous. His defects, on the other hand, have worried his supporters. People say that he acts too much on impulse, cares little for economic realities, and is an indifferent administrator. But he has made a magnificent record so far against all manner of obstacles, even though the wisecrack is that his policy seems to consist of little beyond the concept "Back to the Incas." Personal contact sometimes leaves him seemingly preoccupied. He can mount the back of a truck and make a terrific speech, but he is likely to be immersed in his own thoughts at the dinner table—a man who can establish relationships with many more easily than with one. But what a charmer he is when he wants to be!

Meeting the President

Real laws do not have texts.
—FERNANDO BELAÚNDE TERRY

My wife and I arrived in Lima from Santiago at the grimmest of all hours in airplane travel—around 2 A.M. We were courteously met at the airport, but the passage through customs and the trip into town were interminable, and we were not settled in our hotel until 4 o'clock or later. Exhausted from the rigors of Chile, we thought we would take the morning off. The phone rang at 9:30. One of the president's aides was talking, and he told us that Señor Belaúnde would see us at 11. So we had little time to check our Peruvian files, compose questions, and otherwise prepare ourselves for the interview. Excited and alarmed, we took a taxi to the palace—keeping in mind that the president, without any word from us, had got in touch with us before we fairly had our feet on the ground. Obviously he has efficient sources of information.

The presidential palace, fronting the Plaza de Armas, is a grand affair. The presidential guard, in gaudy uniforms, was changing and—as in Paraguay—it did the goose-step, armed with sabers. Once inside, though, we saw that the guards wore plain service uniforms, and carried efficient-looking tommy-guns. The president speaks perfect English. No man could have been more eloquently agreeable. His eyes shine. He is obviously an idealist. He started to talk about Peru in general. He wanted extremely to have us see things outside Lima, and in particular to make contact with one of his principal babies, Cooperación Popular, a kind of local Peace Corps. He started talking about archaeology, and mentioned the analogies between Peru, Egypt, and Mesopotamia. I tried to ask him about the origins of his own career and his political beliefs, but he would not get off the subject of Peru itself, except for a moment or two. He did mention that his father, still active at seventy-five, influenced him profoundly, and that, loving to travel inch by inch all over Peru, had taught him to do the same thing; this was the origin of his own prodigious local travels and his feeling of kinship for the Indians out on the hills. He mentioned then that his father had never cared anything at all about money, which was true of himself as well—but he laughed, adding that it was always easy not to care about money if you have some.

On being asked if he had been much influenced by architects like Frank Lloyd Wright, Mies van der Rohe, or the contemporary Brazilians, the president replied, "There can be hero worship, but I have no heroes." Trying to draw him out, I said with no originality whatever that there must be some connection in his life between building houses and building a nation, and this caught his interest. He fished in his desk for a piece of paper, repeated the word, "Building . . . building," and told us a little story. Back in 1956, he recounted, he had taken four architectural students on a trip through the remote backlands of Peru, traveling on foot, muleback, and canoe. Once he waded "up to his knees in mud" for four days. One night he and his companions came to an inaccessible distant village. Its citizens, greeting him, said that he must pause to see their community; he replied that he couldn't do so because he had to make a speech in a village further on that night. But they prevailed upon him to have a look, because, they said, they were so proud of what they had built, and Belaúnde saw to his astonishment that here was a new church, a new school. He asked, "Who built this school?" and they replied, "We built it." He said, "Who built this road?" and they replied, "We built it." Now, pausing dramatically as we sat with him, the president read from the page he had taken from his desk. This was an English translation of the speech he had made in the second village that night, stimulated by what he had seen in the first. It was on the theme of "the people built it," and this has dominated part of his public thinking ever since.[1]

Now Belaúnde rose from his desk abruptly, and took us for a tour within the palace, a glossy and sumptuous sight. I will not say that the palace is as magnificently appointed as the Elysée in Paris, but almost. It even reminded me of the Escorial near Madrid, with its enormous rooms with marble pillars reaching to high ceilings, fluted ornamentation in gold, glistening stone floors, tapestried walls, and furniture of extreme sober dignity and elegance. We reached the state dining room, a chamber that seemed to be almost as big as Westminster Hall, with wooden choirs at each end, jigsawed into intricately scrolled designs. Belaúnde said he had used this room only twice in the course of his presidency—one time was for General de Gaulle. The room easily seats three hundred people sitting down to table. What has Belaúnde done with it? Made it into a studio! From one end to the other are

---

[1] The president was so eager to have us seize the full significance of this experience that he insisted that we read the speech aloud back to him, which made an engaging episode.

architectural frames, charts, designs—some of them not merely large but fully worked-out relief models of irrigation projects, roads, and the like.

The president led us presently into a patio, where we saw a fig tree planted by Pizarro, which still bears fruit. Then, in another patio, came a prize display—the Sayhuiti stone. This is a replica of a large rock, fourteen feet high, five wide, found recently in the department of Apurimac, near Cuzco where the original still is. Belaúnde had it copied. This fabulous rock, a bas-relief which gives the contours of a whole society, is, he said, comparable historically to the Rosetta Stone. Its tunnels, walls, channels, terraces, granaries, cisterns reproduce exactly the patterns of life in a pre-Inca community a thousand years ago, and reveal with precise detail the technological capacity of the earliest Indians. Belaúnde has had a hose attached to the stone, and he turned the water on. This flowed through the model in the way it did in the original a thousand years ago, and shows us today the intricate skill the Indians had in hydraulic engineering. This stone is, the president went on, pointing proudly, "encyclopedic." It gives a three-dimensional vision of a reality that predates the celebrated ruin at Machu Picchu; engraved on it are the faces of men, women, children, and the figures of monkeys, birds, and insects; this is a true "funeral monument" to a mighty past.

The chief executive asked us to lunch later in the week. Apparently it had not occurred to him that we had managed to reach the palace this morning without guidance, and he explained, "Come in by the entrance near the railway station. You won't get lost, because there are lots of palaces in Lima, but only one railway station." He looked wistful.

*

For lunch, seeking to give us a cross section of political and cultural affairs in Lima, Mr. Belaúnde gathered about twenty people. The guests included Felipe Benavides, a man of affairs who took us to Iquitos later; an American graduate student from Harvard working on Cooperación Popular; and Peru's most distinguished man of letters of the old school, Ciro Alegría. Belaúnde was at once nervous, gracious, appealing, sensitive, and slightly abstracted. He drew charts and maps on my wife's menu card to illustrate things he wanted us to see in Iquitos, and talked about the new fishmeal industry which has made Peru the biggest fishing nation in the world. He told us what to look for while flying over the Andes, and mentioned some of the exploits of Henry Meiggs, "the American Pizarro," who built the first railway across the Andes.

I sat next to Señora Schwalb, the wife of Dr. Fernando Schwalb López Aldana, then prime minister and minister of foreign relations, one of Belaúnde's closest associates. A librarian by profession, she has been working on the records of the old Lima *cabildo* (town hall) which have never been made available to scholars before, and is a member of today's Lima Municipal Council—an activity characteristic of Peru's "new women." I asked her what was the greatest change in the country in the past decade or so, and she replied that people thought more nowadays in terms of the nation as a whole, not just Lima. The gravest problem of the country, she believes, is population pressure. Then too she thought that there were too many transistor radios out in the countryside. Señora Schwalb is certainly not against progress by radio or in any other way, but she gave it as her opinion that thousands of Indian listeners were not educated enough to assimilate what they heard. More than fifty thousand cheap transistors, mostly Japanese, were sold in Peru last year.

After lunch the president wandered back and forth among his guests almost aimlessly. He showed us some books (including one on ancient Peru by a professor at Long Island University), and talked about the Forest Road and Cooperación Popular, the two concepts closest to his heart.

The Forest Road

Peru . . . like a man looking for glasses he is wearing . . . disoriented.
—PARAPHRASED FROM FERNANDO BELAÚNDE TERRY

Few, if any, Peruvian presidents have ever traveled so widely in the country as Belaúnde, and his profound and intimate knowledge of Peru is one of his most considerable sources of power. He has visited hundreds of villages and knows them down to the names of the daughters of the mayor. He has seen sheep, "like balls of yarn," tumble down precipices, and watched peasants bent double under burdens of a hundred pounds of coca leaf, from which cocaine is derived and which is almost universally chewed by the upland Indians. The president likes to use his legs. "Step by step they give you hard reality," something quite different from the "visual panoramic sensation" to be had on helicopters.[2] The waterways fascinated him in particular. He had not realized that Peru has five thousand miles of navigable rivers, more than three times the length of its Pacific coast, and that the canoeist in the jungle is "what the gondolier is to Venice."

[2] *Peru's Own Conquest*, by Fernando Belaúnde Terry, translated by David A. Robinson, Lima, 1965. I am much indebted to this small but intensely revealing book. Most of the quotations from Belaúnde which follow in this and subsequent chapters come from its illuminating pages.

Of sixteen hundred towns in Peru, President Belaúnde discovered, twelve hundred lacked potable water, sewage, and an electric power system; *half* had no access to roads. The unity of the highlands has been lost, and he became convinced that one reason for this was that the old Inca Road stretching north from Cuzco to Quito and south into Chile had never been replaced. "A road creates as it is being created, revealing the country to itself." Villagers asked him why he exhausted himself trying to reach them, saying, "There are few votes here." Belaúnde replied that he was not asking for their votes, but searching for their ideas. A civilization once existed here equivalent to that of the Nile, and so it is necessary to "study our own secrets."

Out of all this—and much else—came the Belaúnde concept of the marginal "Forest Road." The basic idea is to develop and tap the *selva*, the forested area, much of which is cut off from the rest of the country for want of communication. It is difficult to get the wealth of the country out westward across the Andes, and, moreover, the Pacific ports are indifferent. Belaúnde's idea is to augment the westward flow by making it possible for the incalculable riches of the land to go eastward as well—down the rivers to Atlantic ports. The great river systems of South America all start here; the headwaters of the Amazon, Orinoco, and La Plata are scarcely a hundred miles apart. In a word the president is seeking not merely to recreate the old Inca highway, but to build a new frontier, create a new economy.

Work has already begun on this vast project, in cooperation with Colombia, Ecuador, Chile, and Bolivia. As envisaged the road will touch on or traverse all these countries; it will be twenty-five hundred miles long, not including the numerous access roads which will be its lights and liver. Nor will the Forest Road be hit-or-miss; it is to be an integrated effort to capture and make use of the internal resources of all five nations, particularly those inaccessible at present. For every mile built, the experts say, thirty-five hundred acres of land will be made accessible, so that measures for land reform can be expedited. Altogether, Belaúnde says, this will be a project comparable to building the Panama Canal, and should have just as beneficent an effect. It will cost no more than $400,000,000, he thinks, and ought to be completed within twenty years.

Cooperación Popular, several times mentioned above, is the second principal Belaúnde contribution. It resembles Promoción Popular in Chile but is more ambitious, and derives from the Inca concept of community service. The president wants to revive the Inca "law of brotherhood" by "popular cooperative methods." There is an element of the grandiose in this, as there is in the concept of the Forest Road; Belaúnde *is* a visionary. He says, "Human resources are raw material too—leaders have to be built," and adds, "How can I ever go back to these people—after having given them hope—if we do not do these things?" About two million people are involved in Cooperación Popular, and some fifteen hundred projects have been completed so far. The basic concept is that the villagers themselves make their own decision as to what they need most—road, school, or dam—and then proceed to build it. The community works as a whole to give the concept eyes, hands, and feet. Labor and material come from the people themselves, and the government—in many cases assisted by the Alianza—seeks to provide the tools and technical assistance.

Politics, Politics, Politics

The political situation today is somewhat peculiar in Peru. Four principal parties exist, but none of these has a majority in parliament; hence two rival and bitterly hostile coalitions have developed. Some fancy politics attends this, but I will try to keep this description brief.

On the Belaúnde (government) side we have:

1. Belaúnde's own party, known as Acción Popular, standing on the democratic left. It has 14 out of 45 senators, 38 out of 140 representatives, and is thus distinctly a minority party. Composed largely of the president's own personal following, its frontiers are somewhat fluid. The leadership is young and technical-minded. Its secretary general, a civil engineer, is only thirty-three; the minister of agriculture, a professional agronomist, only twenty-nine. Its main strength, aside from Belaúnde's leadership, is support from the army, particularly younger officers. The army's role is vital. The army was largely instrumental in the process by which the president reached office, and helps keep him there.

Acción Popular is a kind of left-wing hold-all but contains few—if any—admitted Communists. Its extreme left split off last year. Belaúnde was frequently described as being "Communist-inclined" during the election campaigns of 1962 and 1963, and there is no doubt that he accepted Communist support during both. He has never made any move to pay the Communists off, however. One of the reasons that he is so devoted to Cooperación Popular is that, he thinks, this organization is a kind of insurance against the "psychological discontent" the Communists represent.

Another word on this and on his general political-philosophical position. Though he accepted Communist votes he is vividly anti-Marxist, and has written that Peru will unfortunately commit the last-ditch "sin" of denying its "Andean reality" if it ever adopts a regime based on Communist principles. Belaúnde's ideal is "British or Scandinavian cooperativism," in order to give the country the advantage of a capitalist structure without being laid open to exploitation or abuse. What he admires most in the Communists is their capacity for planning, and, like Frei in Chile, their discipline.

Sub-leaders of Acción Popular are Dr. Schwalb, mentioned above, and former prime minister J. Oscar Trelles, a neurosurgeon who is supposed to be considerably more to the left than Belaúnde. Dr. Trelles was accused of a "soft" response to guerrilla uprisings in the hills in 1965, and was forced to resign, whereupon Belaúnde made him ambassador to Paris.[3] Also the government came under severe criticism at the time because of an extraordinary tragic accident—for which it was in no way responsible—when more than three hundred people were crushed to death in a riot during a football game.

2. The Christian Democrats, with two senators, eleven representatives, are the second element in the Belaúnde coalition. They began to grow in the late 1950's, probably reflecting the rise toward power of President Frei in Chile. Like the Freístas, the Christian Democrats are intellectual, reformist, somewhat stuffy, and dedicated to large government participation in economic matters. Their leader is Héctor Cornejo Chávez, and they stand to the left of center, but not as far left as Belaúnde.

The opposition is a welding of two fantastically different groups. An analogy might be an alliance between Senator Goldwater and Norman Thomas.

3. The National Odreísta Union, with six senators and twenty-four deputies. This received about a quarter of the popular vote in the last elections. General Odría, its leader, is a fascinating character; although he is a full-dress military man, he does not represent the army as such, because the Peruvian army has its own special orientation. His basic support comes from the big cotton and sugar interests and the upper middle class. Odría, who looks Indian, has been president of the republic twice—as a result of a coup d'état from 1948 to 1950, and then as a regularly elected candidate between 1950 and 1956. He was in those days considered to be a representative of the extreme right, and hackles were raised in liberal circles over the whole continent when President Eisenhower decorated him with the Legion of Merit, as he similarly decorated Peréz Jiménez, the Venezuelan dictator.

4. The Apristas, under their legendary leader, Haya de la Torre. These make the biggest party in the country, with twenty-five senators, fifty-seven representatives. APRA (American Popular Revolutionary Alliance) has vaguely Marxist roots and was often called "Communist" in the old days,

---

[3] Cf. Richard W. Patch, *A Note on Bolivia and Peru,* American Universities Field Staff, 1965, p. 22, a useful source for both countries.

but it has swung markedly to the right in recent years, and is now considered —by the American authorities in Lima—to be a "democratic" party. This is an interesting development, inasmuch as Haya de la Torre, thought of proverbially as a dangerous and inflammatory radical, was forbidden entrance into the United States for many years. General Odría and Haya have been bitter enemies. It was Odría who, seeking to destroy Haya, hounded him into taking refuge in the Colombian embassy in Lima, where he was forced to remain incommunicado for more than five years. Similarly Haya detested Odría. But now they work together against Belaúnde. More on Haya later. I asked a leading Aprista how such a combination as Odría-Haya could possibly have been put together, to say nothing of why, and received the suggestive dry reply, "Ever heard of the Hitler-Stalin pact?"

Still another party is coming up, the Social Progressives, but they have little concrete importance at present. They think—with a certain amount of justification—that Belaúnde is steadily moving rightward and, being leftist radicals, have risen to oppose him.

All this makes for shattering complications. Not only is Belaúnde a minority president, but he will continue to be confronted with a congressional opposition stronger than his own coalition for several years to come, because presidential and congressional elections occur at the same time in Peru, and these are not scheduled to take place till 1969. He cannot have the good luck that came to Frei in Chile, who, by winning a mid-term election, became assured of a parliamentary majority for the rest of his term. Belaúnde is saddled with an unbeatable parliamentary opposition for the duration of his presidency. Moreover Peruvian presidents are, in the familiar South American way, forbidden to succeed themselves, and so he cannot run for a second term until another intervenes.

How, then, do laws get passed at present? First, by making compromises. Belaúnde usually gets his way on major measures, although this serves to force him to the right. Second, the opposition hesitates to be too obstructionist out of fear that it will damage its own position in the country. Third, in the event of a real crisis—for instance in connection with the budget— everybody wants to be on the bandwagon. One ameliatory factor is that both government and opposition compete vigorously for the middle-class vote, promising citizens everything but the moon, with the result that, in spite of much conniving and confusion, social services continue to advance. Even Odría now stands for land reform and social betterment.

*

To make this background clearer a few dates should be kept in mind. Peru entered the modern period in 1930 after the downfall of a miserable little dictator named Leguía, and, with the exception of one tempestuous period in which five presidents served in eighteen months, has had a fairly orderly development ever since. There were several somewhat dull but worthy presidents, like General Oscar Benavides (1933–39), and Dr. Manuel Prado y Ugarteche, who had two terms (1939–45 and 1956–62). In between came Odría. Belaúnde ran for the first time, as stated above, in 1956. The key to this race was the position of the Apristas, who, outlawed at that period, could not run a candidate themselves, although, then as now, they were the strongest party in the country. Belaúnde lost this election largely because he did not have APRA support. Haya de la Torre, the Aprista leader, was the key to everything.

Came new elections on June 10, 1962. Nobody won. That is, Haya, legalized at last, received the largest number of votes by a narrow margin, but no candidate polled a full third of the electorate, which, by Peruvian law, is necessary for the election of a president. Much unpleasant intrigue attended this election. Belaúnde, supported by the army, struggled by every possible means to keep the Apristas out, whereupon the election was put into the hands of congress. A complete and confused impasse followed.

On July 18, 1962, a few weeks later, a junta forcibly overthrew the incumbent president, Dr. Prado, who was filling out the last days of his second term. A Sherman tank—among those furnished Peru by the American military aid program—butted its way noisily through the palace gates, after an ultimatum, and a group of seemingly leftist generals seized power.[4] The United States, under the Kennedy administration, took a grave view of such a glaringly anti-constitutional procedure, and at once severed diplomatic relations with Peru, cutting off both economic and military aid, which stunned the junta. As a result it promised to constitutionalize itself.

This story was further complicated by the role played just before the election by the American ambassador at the time, James I. Loeb, who, in the campaign, took a fervent pro-Aprista line. In plain fact American policy was completely muddled. We reversed ourselves on non-recognition of the junta within a month.

On June 9, 1963, to almost everybody's bewildered surprise, the junta restored constitutional government, and new elections took place. Belaúnde ran again, won, and has been president ever since.

Army and Church

The army could probably throw out President Belaúnde at any moment it chose. But it is not likely to do so in the normal course of events, not merely

[4] One nice euphemism for this event was "institutional turnover."

because it regards Belaúnde highly, but, in the usual South American manner, because it considers itself to be an instrument of order and "constitutional" continuity. On his side the president cultivates the army assiduously, and maintains close relations with its leading officers. The chief political significance of the army is its bitter and historic hatred of the Apristas, which derives from events many years ago. Probably the army would not have made its coup in 1962 had it not felt that nothing but force could keep Haya de la Torre from attaining power. The Apristas, on their side, call the army a creature of the Communists—also of the Pentagon, on the theory that American military assistance is what gives the army power—which is certainly a case of accusing an adversary of accepting two widely different sources of support.

Actually the army has somewhat marked Nasserist-neutralist tendencies, although Belaúnde himself is firmly pro-American. Officers are generally of European descent; the rank and file is Indian. But, as time goes on, the armed forces continue to take on more and more the coloration of the nation; one Limeño told me that he had attended the graduation ceremony for military cadets year after year, and that the young graduates become darker skinned each year. The navy, as in most of South America, is much more aristocratic and conservative; the air force traditionally scorns politics. The air force has performed a very large service in helping to open up the country. Working in close harmony with the civilian companies, like the admirable Faucett, it helped to pioneer civil aviation, laying airstrips in the *selva*, which became known as "eyebrows of the jungle." There are some eighty to eighty-five of these in the back country now, and whole valleys have been brought to life by aviation transport.

One Peruvian department, San Martín in the northeast, even today does not have a *single* road, although it covers 17,100 square miles and has a population of 154,000. At least thirty sizable towns throughout the country have no communications at all, not even by river, unbelievable as this fact may seem. What comes out—cotton, tobacco—must go by air. San Martín and similar provinces now being developed are called proudly "the new Peru."

The most notable thing about Peru's army is its addiction to Civic Action, which means vocational training. About twenty-five thousand conscripts enter the service every year; most are illiterate, and efforts are made to teach them to read and write. Then during the last three months of his two-year term, the conscript goes to a kind of trade school where he is taught a skill—like carpentry, metal work, or building. The advantages of this process are for the most part eagerly seized, since no other vocational training is available in Peru. What it means in essence is that almost any Indian boy, getting out of the army, can find a job.

Belaúnde has been notably skillful in his handling of the army; his own faith and vision have made it become interested in social welfare almost in spite of itself. Also, by cooperating in his projects, the army has taken advantage of a good opportunity for recovering lost prestige. High officers have at their disposal advanced schools which, according to the conservatives, are dominated by left-wing civilian professors, who encourage a strong leftish trend.

*

President Belaúnde is a devout Catholic, and this substantially assists his political position. One of his boyhood friends, still very close, is the youthful Cardinal Archbishop of Lima, a Franciscan. The church hierarchy does its best to keep out of politics in Peru but is, as goes without saying, a strong standpat force. Divisions in it follow the same pattern as in most of the rest of South America.

Many Catholics, particularly the Indians, are only nominally so, and the country has no fewer than ninety-four thousand Protestants. Masonic lodges are supposed to be scattered throughout the army, as in Chile. (Plenty of South American Masons are, however, good Catholics; it is perfectly possible to be Catholic and Mason at the same time.)

Father Salomón Bolo Hidalgo, a priest who is co-president of the National Liberation Front, an extreme leftist group, was arrested in July, 1965, and is still in jail. He had taken a strong pro-Castro line, and is accused of having supported the recent "guerrilla revolt" near Cuzco, the old Inca capital up in the *sierra*. But priests who wander quite so far are rare.

Birth control is, of course, widely practiced in upper circles in Peru, but has not yet become the public issue it is in Chile. Curiously enough—for such a Catholic county as Peru—divorce is not merely legal, but almost as easy as in Mexico.

Haya de la Torre and the Apristas

We must take time out now for a brief disquisition on Haya de la Torre, a man full of magnificent quixoticisms and contradictions but an original just the same, and in his early days a person of defiant, soaring spirit. What he gave was, in a word, hope. APRA, American Popular Revolutionary Alliance, his creation, was the first mass movement ever put together in South America which sought to express the suppressed inchoate dreams of the peasantry, the crushed and destitute, the landless masses and workers of the towns.

It is somewhat difficult to sum up the old Aprista creed. Haya stood for three things—first, the liberation and education of the Indians and their incorporation into the national life not merely in Peru but elsewhere. Second, intra-American unity and the eventual coalescence of the whole of Latin America into a single organism. Third, social progress. Haya was not a Marxist or even a Socialist but he had a passionate fixed belief in emancipation and reform. Above everything he stood against feudalism, serfdom, and colonial exploitation.

A good many other South Americans have had these concepts and ideas, but none ever got to the point reached by Haya whereby he built a powerful national party to give concrete expression to his program, and almost—not quite—succeeded in reaching power. And even today, with Haya aging and in decline, APRA is still the best-run party in Peru, the most faithful to a coherent ideology, the most numerous, and the strongest. It has a totalitarian organization, and is extraordinarily well-disciplined.

Haya de la Torre, whom I met three times on a previous visit to Peru, looks exactly what he is, a lineal descendant of the *conquistadores*. Some have thought that he was an Indian or *cholo* (half caste) rising out of the masses. But the contrary is true. He came out of the Spanish provincial aristocracy, and went *to* the masses. He was in those days tallow-skinned, medium in height, with heavy shoulders. His shiny black hair swept into a flying wedge over each ear. He had a powerful eagle's nose, bright olive-brown eyes, and a splendid voice. Víctor Raúl Haya de la Torre was born on February 22, 1896, in northern Peru. It pleases him that his birthday is the same as George Washington's, and also that his mother's name was Cárdenas, since he has profound admiration for ex-President Cárdenas of Mexico, a revolutionary like himself. His father was a journalist; one of his uncles was a priest. He grew up in a perfectly respectable, intensely Catholic atmosphere. Three things happened to Haya in his youth. First he visited Cuzco, the ancient capital of the Incas. There he became transfixed—as Belaúnde was transfixed years later—but not only by the ruins; he saw not merely the dead splendors of the Inca civilization but the intolerable poverty of the contemporary descendants of the Incas. Second, Haya went to the University of Córdoba in the Argentine, and became a part of the sociopolitical fermentation, the intense "spiritual revolution" as he calls it, then going on among the students there. Third, he became saliently influenced by the great Mexican revolution. "I was sure of only two things in those days," he told me. "First, that Córdoba was my mother, and Mexico my father. Second, that all the Americas must stand together, and that we must all be different from Europe."

Haya returned to Lima, busied himself in student politics, came into conflict with the authorities, and was promptly exiled. There followed eight years of travel—in Panama, Cuba, Western Europe, the United States, Soviet Russia—during which Aprismo was born. This was the happiest period of his life, he says. He made a living as a journalist, lectured at Harvard and other schools, and kept in contact with what was going on in Peru.

Again he returned to Peru in 1930, seeking to put the APRA program, which was now fully developed, into operation. He was called a "Communist" and a crackpot. His program inflamed the masses. The army opposed him with vehement determination, and an explosion came. Twenty-seven Aprista deputies who had been elected to Congress were arrested in 1932 by the military, and Haya's men in Trujillo, his home city, rioted in protest. They attacked the barracks there, and killed twenty-six soldiers. In retaliation, the army rounded up six *thousand* Apristas, mostly young men, and shot them on the spot.[5] Haya himself became a refugee.

Thereafter his vicissitudes made history. He spent fifteen months in jail in the 1930's, and APRA, although it was officially suppressed, continued to have a vigorous life underground. He came close to reaching power again in 1948, but General Odría forestalled him. To escape Odría's police, he took refuge in the Colombian Embassy in Lima on January 3, 1949, and remained sequestered there until April 6, 1954. During all this time he never left the building, which was surrounded by armed police. Why did he choose the Colombian Embassy? Because Colombia has both a juridical and long-entrenched democratic tradition, and it is ruled by a "gentleman" class.

At last, in 1954, General Odría gave Haya a safe conduct whereby he was enabled to leave the country, and he spent a year or two abroad. Then in 1956, when President Prado took office, APRA was legalized and Haya was enabled to come home again. I have already touched briefly on what happened to him in the election of 1962, when, his supporters insist, he was counted out by fraud. Haya, to sum up, tried to make the Indians his base—what Belaúnde seeks today. This did not work out, and he veered gradually to the right. Embittered, he chose to make an alliance with his old enemy, General Odría, and lost a good deal of prestige by doing so. He has

[5] *Time*, March 12, 1965, an admirable cover story on Peru.

become a confused reactionary. But he created the first genuine people's movement in contemporary South America and will not be easily forgotten.

*

Nowadays Belaúnde rides in Haya's tracks. Haya is probably too old now—seventy—ever to reach the presidency, and Belaúnde's vision is sharper, more realistic and focused to a more practical objective. Haya wanted to create "inter-America." Belaúnde wants to recreate Peru.

CHAPTER 18

Peruvian Medley

I look with contempt on the missiles of misfortune. The sole master of my heart is my conscience.
                                        —SIMÓN BOLÍVAR

A much greater danger [to the United States] than Communism would be the emergence of a continent that wants to be for itself.
                                        —CARLOS GRIFFIN

Rich men talk about basic reforms, and then brand as Communists those who make them real.
                                        —DOM HELDER CÂMARA OF BRAZIL

PERU, the third-biggest South American republic, more than three times the size of California, is magnificently triune. Seen from left to right this triple entity consists of a narrow strip of stark desert stretching for fourteen hundred miles along the Pacific coast, then the overpowering Andean *sierra*, then the *montaña*, the jungle lowlands which comprise half the country. What makes this physical structure the more remarkable is its concentration. Where else can a visitor, if he uses an airplane, go from the Sahara to the Himalayas to the Congo in a day? Even in an automobile the visitor can bathe in the surf near Lima at ten in the morning and straddle a pass higher than the Jungfrau by noon.

Indeed the mountains are spectacular. The *cordillera* has three main ranges, and Huascarán (22,200 feet) is the highest peak. An apt description is that the country is "a platform of rocks." Earthquakes are frequent, but less so than in Chile. The rivers have interest too; some 60 trickle down the Andean slopes and make sharp green valleys in the ochre desert. Incredibly enough, only 86 miles separate the Pacific and Atlantic drainage basins. Peru faces east as well as west, and, as we know, the mighty Amazon is born in the

339

uplands here, and Iquitos, fifteen hundred miles downstream, is served by ships that ply directly to and from Europe. The Amazon country is vital to Peru because its lush tropical quality compensates for the sterility of the coastal plain.

I know few flights more revealing than the long run from Chile up to Ecuador over Peru. For hundreds of miles on end there is no single road, house, or human being, as is the case over the jungles of Brazil. But here the pattern is of limitless rugged emptiness, as if you were flying over some monstrous rusty moon.

Then the trip from Lima "up the hill" by car or train is dramatic. You climb the gray ribbon of road through tunnels and chasms of savage, aggressive rock colored everything from amber to magenta. The automobile road is the only one in the world whereon you rise from sea level to almost sixteen thousand feet in eighty-five miles. Get out at the crest of the pass, try to walk a step and, like as not, you come close to collapsing with an exploding roar in your ears from the assault of that incredible suddenly achieved altitude.

Here too is the steep zigzagging path of the Central Railroad, one of the most remarkable on the globe, which taps the rich mining country near Cerro de Pasco and La Oroya. Its American builder, Henry Meiggs, said, "Where the llama can climb, I can lay rail." This sensational railway reaches the greatest height ever attained by a standard-gauge line, and one of its stations near the mines is the highest in the world. South American statistics are notably chaotic, and three different reference books give the attitude of this variously as 15,807 feet, 15,693 feet and 15,865 feet. Perhaps the platform slants.

The Peruvian uplands not only have a profusion of llamas but four other species of cameloid. Choice llamas are affectionately called "*guapallamas*" and have tassels put in their ears, although they are ill-tempered creatures as a rule. How grazing animals related to the camel ever reached these remote American stations is unknown. The llama is not strong, and can carry only about fifty pounds; it has, however, been used as a beast of burden since ancient times. The alpaca is a small llama, more or less. The other varieties are the guanaco, which apparently came originally from the Argentine pampa; the huarizo, a llama-alpaca cross; and the vicuña with its special brand of luxurious fawn-colored wool. Vicuñas are still found wild, as are guanacos, and are hard to tame.

Perhaps a fourth Peruvian geographical division—if it can be called such—is the Pacific. This has inestimable importance to the nation, mainly because of a phenomenon known as the Humboldt Current, named for the great German naturalist. A flow of frigid water, this current hugs the shore and produces peculiar meteorological conditions, which in turn have created the Peruvian coastal desert. Moreover, it foams with fish, and these profoundly benefit the local economy in several ways. There is, first of all, the normal fish catch. Then, in older days, the fish attracted enormous quantities of birds which, following the Humboldt Current as it flows north, ate fish and dropped their dung on islands off the coast; this provided Peru with its celebrated guano, which makes fertilizer. Peru, it may be fairly said, is the only nation in the world which lived basically for a long period on bird manure. Recently a third element entered the picture—fishmeal. This is a ground-up protein made out of anchovies, and is used for poultry feed and other purposes. The fishmeal industry has been fantastically successful, and the quantities of anchovies and other small fish caught have been sufficient to enable Peru to pass Japan, as President Belaúnde pointed out to us, to become the first fishing nation in the world. But as more fish are taken the production of guano (by the birds) decreases, which causes alarm to some Peruvian economists. The fishmeal business was helped substantially by American investment. There are no fewer than 155 fishmeal factories, and one fishmeal town, Chimbote, has grown from a population of 5,000 to 150,000 almost overnight, according to local estimates.

The Humboldt Current has, finally, striking repercussions on climate. For reasons difficult for a layman (this layman, anyway) to understand, its icy water inhibits rain along the coast; it hasn't rained in Lima for twenty years or more. Instead a light fog bank rises to hover over the city for six or seven months a year; out of this squirts a mist which is close to being rain, but isn't. Known as the *garúa*, it strongly influences the Limeño character.

Are Indians People?

Peru has a population of about 12 million, only a little more than Pennsylvania; the rate of growth is very high—more than 3 percent—with an annual surplus of births over deaths of 100,000 a year. The racial mix is 49.5 percent Indian, about 40 percent *cholo* (the local term for *mestizo*) and 10 percent white and miscellaneous—also a handful of Negroes, mostly descended from slaves who worked on the cotton plantations or who were house servants of the old families. Crosses between Indians, *cholos* and Negroes are called *sambos* or, less derisively, *morenos*, the word "*moreno*" meaning brunette. There are some 90,000 Chinese, whose forefathers came in as railway labor (as they did in California in the early days), and a substantial Japanese community.

Some statistics are typically South American—in other words lugubrious. The country lacks at least a million housing units, and in some Andean villages only one out of 325 citizens can read or write. The average annual income ranges from $80 or less in the high *sierra* and *montaña* to $155 along the coast. Tuberculosis takes a large toll in the highlands, infant mortality is appalling, and medical services short. On the average, a woman has to bear eight to ten children to have three survive to adolescence. The potato is the staple foodstuff. These are consumed in large quantities because, dug out of the soil by the peasants, they cost virtually nothing. I heard a cynical remark from a Lima aristocrat, "We're the best-nourished undernourished country in the world." There are approximately six million Indians in Peru; those worst off live on what is called the *puna*, the intermontane plateau below Cuzco. A watchword is, "No one has ever seen poverty who has not been on the *puna*." Plenty of peons live near the town of Puno who do not make a cash wage of two cents a day.

There are two principal Indian tribes, the Quechua and Aymará, many thousands of whom cling to their own languages and are not merely illiterate but do not speak or understand Spanish. This creates an immense gulf in the nation. Few Spaniards on their side ever bother to learn Quechua or Aymará, except specialists and those in the mountain regions who must learn at least a few words of an Indian language in order to talk to their workmen, servants, and the like. The situation is quite different from that in Paraguay, where almost all Spanish-speaking citizens learn Guaraní.

One index of the importance of the Peruvian Indians is that they are essential to the national economy, since they can work more easily at high altitudes than the white man. They do not get much reward. They live in adobe or straw huts, on feudal properties or splinter freeholds, scraping a bare living out of rock.[1] Called "Indios," their status is even lower than that of *campesinos* in other South American republics. Most live outside the money economy altogether, and have no participation in the national life; only about 200,000 vote. Not only do they have little if any scholastic education, but they are not taught to do anything with their hands, except till the soil in a grotesquely primitive manner. An Indian boy escaping from the hills and coming down to Lima will not know how to screw in a light bulb or tie a shoe. The peons work in the fields and pastures twelve, fourteen, sixteen hours a day, are stunted in growth, and numbed by the altitude. They drink *chicha*, a fermented corn beer, and chew coca leaves. To release the narcotic in coca it is necessary to make the raw leaf alkaline, so the leaves are usually mixed with ashes or a powder made of calcium rock.

[1] Patch, *op. cit.,* p. 21.

Relationships between white master and Indian serf can be archaic. Recently nine peasants were found poisoned near Puno. Bland announcement came from the local authorities that they had died of a "collective heart attack."

Indians were never outright slaves in Peru; the law forbade this. Negroes were slaves, but not the Quechuas or Aymarás, who still have a dark, secretive streak of pride and independence, no matter how grueling their lot is. Perhaps curiously, the great mass tends by and large to be conservative, not radical; apathy is a more pronounced characteristic than a will to revolutionary change. These are a patient people, inscrutable too—like "blanket" Indians in the United States in former days. One force making for modernization and change is, as noted in the preceding chapter, the transistor radio.

"Indian" can be a fighting word in Lima. People are sensitive about their Indian heritage. I asked a bronze-skinned university professor, clearly of Indian blood, if he were proud of his "Inca descent"; his reply was extremely hesitant. Many people partly Indian are reluctant to admit this, although they comprise two-fifths of the population. When I asked innocently enough how the problem was being tackled of bringing the Indian division of the nation into the body of the state, people commented with exasperation that I should not put the cleavage on a racial basis, and that I should use words like "poor" or "underdeveloped" instead of "Indian." Then too I met worthy citizens who denied that the gulf existed. One cabinet minister—who also had obvious Indian blood—burst out, "How can anybody say fairly that the Indians are excluded from society? Come with me to the senate. You will see that two-thirds of its members are of Indian descent!" But when I asked if enough had been done for the Indians in the course of the past twenty-five years almost everybody conceded that it had not.

Perhaps curiously the two men who stand most clearly for "Indianization," Haya de la Torre and Fernando Belaúnde, are both whitest of white. Belaúnde's attitude is thoroughly modern. He believes in what he calls "cultural hybridization," and says that Peru must face frankly and accept the fact that it is the product of *mestizaje*, or a fusion of peoples. "We cannot evade history," Belaúnde adds. "Our hybrid blood is fertile." Such candor on the racial issue is unusual in Peru, not merely for reasons of social taboo but because of politics. A serious obstacle in the path of a progressive leader is that, if he gives sympathy or support to the Indian position, he will run the risk of being denounced by the lily-white plutocrats as a "radical" or "Communist."

Economics on a Postcard

Vale un Perú—it's worth a Peru.
—OLD PROVERB

All things told, the Peruvian economy, despite plenty of difficulties, is on the rise. New industries, not only fishmeal, have push and energy, and 430 new firms have set up businesses here since 1963, an impressive number. The gross national product shows an increase of 29 percent between 1960 and 1964,[2] and tax collections have improved by three-fifths in the last few years. The United States is by far the most important element in Peruvian trade; we take 31 percent of the country's exports, and provide 41 percent of its imports. The next biggest customers are West Germany and Japan; the next biggest suppliers, West Germany and the Argentine. Ranked by value the principal exports are nonferrous metals, fodder, petroleum, and fish. An element in the exotic is that the country exports some 50,000 monkeys a year, and an equal number of multicolored tropical birds.

Wages are medium, averaging around 41 cents an hour for industrial employees; this is a small figure by world standards—comparable sums for the United States, Sweden and West Germany are $2.64, $1.51, and $1.04—but not bad for South America. The social security system is comprehensive, elaborate, and advanced—at least in theory—on the general hemisphere model. A government hospital in Lima designed by Edward Durell Stone, the American architect, is, I thought, the best-looking modern building in the city. Citizens of every grade are zealous about their rights under social security and otherwise. A strike of *doctors* took place while we were in the city and I would have hated to be ill at that time, much as I admired Mr. Stone's hospital.

Sugar is the biggest "political" industry, and the sugar properties on the northern coast near Trujillo comprise the largest concentration of sugar cultivation in the world. Their owners are among the most conservative elements in the country, and form an effective pressure group; I even heard it said, on the highest of authorities, "Sugar runs this country." There are only about twenty really big sugar producers, among which the great Gildemeister family, of German descent, is the most prominent. Cotton follows sugar as a "political" industry. Guano is nationalized.

[2] As against 16 percent for Brazil, 14 percent for Chile, 17 percent for Venezuela, 4 percent for Argentina. *Time,* August 27, 1965.

The Peruvian economy is probably the most diversified in South America, and foreign interests are conspicuous, as we shall see below.

History—A Word About the Incas

The Incas, who rose in the *sierra* eight or nine centuries ago, were among the most fascinating people who ever lived. But much about their way of life, no matter how dogmatic some contemporary experts are, must necessarily be a matter of conjecture, since they had no written language and left no written record. They had llamas, dogs, and guinea pigs, as we know from their sculpture, but no draft animals, no iron, and they apparently did not know the use of the wheel. Yet they spanned thousands of square miles with paved trails, like the great Inca Road, and built monuments such as Machu Picchu, comparable to the Pyramids of Egypt. How they possibly performed such prodigious engineering feats is unknown, but it is a safe guess that plenty of human muscle was involved.

The Incas were also superlative artists and craftsmen in gold, as were several of the great Indian tribes preceding them, like the Chavins, Mochicas, and Chimus. These also left imperishably beautiful textiles and ceramics.

At its largest extent the Tawantinsuyo, or Inca Empire, covered 1,200,000 square miles, one-third the size of the United States, and held 6,000,000 people, which happens to be approximately the number of Indians who live in Peru today. The most distinctive characteristic of Inca rule was its combination of autocratic headship and communal development. The Incas were among the first—and most successful—planners in history. Their method of social organization was original. One-third of the crops went to God, one-third to the state, one-third to the producer. Poverty was rare, and destitution unknown. Society was collectivist under a benevolent personalist authority considered to be divine. Food was stored in special depositories as a defense against lean seasons; an obligatory labor system called *mita* was the basis of production, and was self-serving. Social life was built on the family, not the individual; clans were bound into *ayllus* or "village communities," which allotted tasks, shared rewards, and administered punishments.

What, among other things, fascinates President Belaúnde today is that, under the Incas, the domains of religion, state, and community were merged. There was no profit system, and no money; labor was provided by cooperation. Ownership of the land was communal, but families had their own houses, which were private property. The socialist and free enterprise systems merged.

The Incas, who were not so cruel as the Aztecs or the Indians in the United States, and did not practice human sacrifice or burn victims at the stake, arose from the Sun God, Inti, who appeared mystically from the waters of Lake Titicaca, and then moved on to Cuzco. The reigning Inca was always considered to be a son of the Sun, like the emperors of Japan. Lake Titicaca was called "the womb of mankind," and Cuzco the "navel of the universe." Manco Capac was the first Inca; his queen bore the remarkable name Mamma Occllo. Their dynasty did not last long—only till the middle of the sixteenth century. But its flowering was brilliant.

The empire was called colloquially the Land of the Four Sections, and the last Inca was Atahualpa. A civil war was unhappily taking place between Atahualpa and one of his brothers at the time of the arrival of the first Spanish *conquistadores*, under Pizarro, in 1533. As everybody who has read Prescott[3] knows, the Spaniards captured Atahualpa after a ferocious wholesale killing of Indians and then promised him his freedom if he would fill a large room with gold. Dutifully he did so, whereupon Pizarro double-crossed and murdered him.

History: Oddments Across the Years

Francisco Pizarro, a dingy little marauder and despoiler, came from Extramadura in Spain, as did both Cortez and Valdivia. He was an illegitimate peasant boy, a swineherd, who could not write his name—treacherous, a lone wolf, greedy, and vindictive. His feat in conquering Peru was, however, as extraordinary as any military campaign in history; he did it with 37 horses, 183 men. Of course his Indian opponents had neither horses nor firearms. His years of glory were short, since he was murdered in 1541 over an issue having to do with Chile. More than two centuries later, in 1780–81, Indians who still execrated his name attempted to rise against the Spanish dominion, under a revolutionary leader named José Gabriel Tupac-Amarú II. The insurrection was beaten down, and Tupac-Amarú was executed in circumstances of the most revolting barbarity in a Lima public square. His tongue was torn out, and then he was pulled apart by horses, until he "looked like a spider"; this did not kill him, and his hands and feet were then cut off, after which the various elements remaining of his body were put to the flames.[4]

Colonial Peru was cock of the walk. Founded by Pizarro in 1535, Lima

---

[3] Or saw *The Royal Hunt of the Sun* by Peter Shaffer, a play which ran successfully in New York and London in 1965.

[4] *The Green Continent, op. cit.*, quoting a contemporary account.

became the greatest, most resplendent capital in the new world; it ruled the entire continent (under Madrid of course) except for Brazil and Venezuela; even Argentina was a Peruvian "colony" until 1776. Wealth, splendor, ostentation, corruption, decadence—these were keynotes. Forty viceroys ruled between 1542 and 1824, and scarcely a single one is worth a line. At the end, as we know, came liberation under San Martín and Bolívar. Imperial Peru, rich, powerful, brazen, church-laden, and impure, became a republic on its own.

One significant event in the nineteenth century was the War of the Pacific (1879–83), already mentioned in connection with Chile. This is sometimes known as the "fertilizer war," since possession of the great nitrate deposits in the desert between Peru and Chile was at stake. This war, which was prolonged and bloody, had disastrous consequences for Peru. Its best youth were killed off, and the Chileños, who held Lima for two years, devastated large areas of the country. A Peruvian put it to me, "We did not recover for forty years. We were gone with the wind, like your southern states after your civil war."

Half a century later, in the 1930's, as if in compensation for its losses to Chile, Peru took a whack at Ecuador—a weak country unable to resist. Of course Ecuador had had nothing to do with the old quarrel between Peru and Chile. The Peruvians, following a frontier dispute with Ecuador, pinched off large amounts of its territory; this had repercussions which continue to this day. Ecuador still refuses to accept the boundaries which were worked out at the time by an international commission, and resembles Hungary with its *Nem Nem Soha* ("No No Never") slogan when it was ruthlessly cut apart by the great powers after World War I.

Meantime the process had begun whereby Peru became the prime example in South America of colonial economy. Foreign capital bought widely into Peruvian resources to help develop the country and, of course, make money. This is a vital element in Peru's story. By the 1920's half a dozen important American companies were operating in Peru. The Cerro de Pasco Copper Corporation, now known as Cerro Corporation, went to work on immense mineral deposits on the "hill" above Lima, and reached a point at one time of exporting 95 percent of Peruvian copper, 75 percent of its silver, 50 percent of gold. The International Petroleum Corporation, which became a subsidiary of Standard Oil of New Jersey, dominated Peruvian oil, and the I.T.&T. established ownership of Lima's telephones. Above all, W. R. Grace & Company bought into sugar, textiles, and much else. It grew to have very large trade and shipping interests, and became—and still is—half owner of Panagra—Pan American—Grace Airways. William Russel Grace was an extraordinary personage. An immigrant boy from Ireland, he got a job as a ship's chandler in Callao, rose to be a merchant, and entered the guano trade. He married the daughter of a United States ship captain, became an American citizen, and founded W. R. Grace & Company. The business spread over much of the west coast of South America, and by 1935 Grace controlled forty-three different companies. One of its sugar mills is the second largest in Peru, and it controls five-eighths of the cotton output, says one authority. Grace himself settled in New York after many years in Peru, and was twice elected mayor of New York City in the last century.[5]

But to proceed. Americans were not the only ones to dip into the Peruvian pot. The British were represented by large investments in railways, cotton, oil, beer, and flour. An Italian company gave Lima electricity, light and power, and Italians ran Peru's biggest bank. Japanese money went into cotton, and one Japanese company became the single biggest cotton producer in the country. All told, 83.4 percent of Peru's total exports were made up by sugar, cotton, copper, and petroleum, most of which were owned by non-Peruvians.[6]

President of Peru from 1908 to 1912 and again from 1919 to 1930 was Augusto de Leguía. He was a dictator of the old school, and had a lively interest in finance. A small man physically, he weighed less than one hundred pounds; one well-known American journalist of the period, Irvin S. Cobb, described him as being "all whip cord and drawn steel," like "a dynamo packed inside a wristwatch."[7] During the second Leguía presidency American banks lent enormous sums to Peru, more than $90 million in all. Bonds were nicely buttered in those days, and it was revealed after the Wall Street crash that one New York banking house had paid Juan Leguía, a son of the president, $415,000 for helping to "arrange" three bond issues. Revolution came in 1930, and Leguía was forced to flee; captured, he died in prison. Soon most of the bonds began to be defaulted, and by 1931 they had fallen catastrophically from their par value. Thousands of small investors lost their stake.

United States loan makers had such a stranglehold on Peru for a period that, as an example, an American citizen was made the administrator of Peruvian customs with almost complete authority over local finance, something reminiscent of antique days along the China coast. Munition makers had a holiday in Peru, too, in the grand old manner. Peru became entangled with Chile over a frontier dispute involving Tacna-Arica. The Electric

[5] *Peru* in the Pan American Union series of pamphlets on South America, p. 8, and James C. Carey, *Peru and the United States*, a useful book, p. 60.
[6] Carey, *ibid.*, p. 60.
[7] *Ibid.*, p. 32.

Boat Company, an American producer of naval armaments, seeking to take advantage of the nationalist ferment caused by this, sold four submarines to the Leguía government. The State Department, trying earnestly to patch up a peace settlement, aroused the anger of the armaments company, and a letter is on record from one of Electric Boat's officials saying, "It is too bad the pernicious activities of our State Department have put a brake on armament orders from Peru."[8]

This kind of thing did not go on without protests in Peru. One statesman who sought to oppose the Leguía policy of "selling the nation's resources to the highest bidder" was Víctor Andrés Belaúnde, the uncle of today's president. Others were Haya de la Torre, the Aprista leader, and two of his staunchest associates, the distinguished veteran Luis Alberto Sánchez and Manuel Seoane, the present leader of the party. In any case the Leguía era ended in 1930. A new world beckoned, and Peru began to seek a different road.

Foreign Interests Today

Little good have these bounties of nature [in the mines] done to the people of Peru, whether Spanish or Indian.

—LORD BRYCE IN 1912

Nothing like what went on in the lush, depraved 1920's occurs today, but Peru is still strongly colored by foreign industrial and commercial interests. Cerro de Pasco, Grace, and International Petroleum are still dominating factors in the national economy. British, Canadian, Italian, Swiss, and Japanese companies have large entrenched interests. The most important electrical enterprise in the country is Swiss. The Germans and Swiss have a big stake in communications, the French in cement, and the Italians and Swiss in petrochemicals. Swedish and Turkish capital are also involved in several enterprises. As to the United States, American Smelting and Refining came into the country recently, and developed the largest copper mine opened in the world in the past two decades, at Toquepala, with the assistance of the United States government and in conjunction with other companies, such as Newmont, Phelps Dodge, and Cerro. In regard to other metals the Vanadium Corporation of America for many years supplied half the world's production of this critical material from its great vanadium mine in Peru.[9]

[8] *Ibid*, p. 94.
[9] *Ibid*, pp. 170–71.

The Belaúnde government welcomes foreign investment, and advertisements have appeared in the New York press recently pointing out the advantages Peru offers to new capital. American companies doing handsomely in Peru at present include John Deere, Dow Chemical, Du Pont, International Harvester, Johns Manville, Meade Johnson, and the General Milk Company of Los Angeles. General Motors is building a new large assembly plant near Lima, and twelve other automobile companies, including Ford and Chrysler, are following suit.

Nobody in Peru seems to be much interested in such problems as expropriation and nationalization of the mines, in strict contrast to Chile, but the example of Chile is closely watched. There has been no "Peruvianization" of the mining operations, although the foreign mining interests do not even pay an export tax on the minerals they ship out. Instead they are taxed locally like any other corporation; the rates are about the same as in the United States. Cerro de Pasco, representing an immense American investment in dollar terms, has several Peruvian directors, but it is American-run. The Cerro mine above Lima is, incidentally, the world's largest open-pit lead and zinc mine, and has ore reserves estimated at more than fifty million tons. It was originally put together mainly by the giant hands of J. P. Morgan and the Hearst interests.

The Fight Over International Petroleum

But if mining is not a big political issue in Peru, petroleum is. To tell this story fully would take many pages, and I must condense it drastically. Its gist is a quarrel between the Peruvian government and the International Petroleum Corporation, a subsidiary of Standard Oil of New Jersey, which controls 80 to 90 percent of all Peruvian oil production.

The case goes far back. The IPC bought oil properties at La Brea–Pariñas near Talara in northern Peru from a British company, London and Pacific Petroleum, back in 1924. The area covers 643 square miles, and the company town is now a model of its kind. Production has averaged 23,000 barrels a day for some years, and the total IPC investment is put at $190 million. The company is Peru's largest taxpayer, and contributes about $25 million a year to the national revenue; its workers are the best paid in the country.

But go back further. A century ago the La Brea region was known for its tar pits, long before oil was discovered. A tiny parcel of the area, a hundred acres, was bought by British owners, and the area involved grew to more than 400,000 acres.[10] But, it seems, owners in those days paid taxes only on the original 100-acre parcel, which was indeed a lucrative arrangement. Moreover, the British were not concessionaires, but actually owned the land, including the subsoil and what was in it.

Nationalist Peruvians naturally resented this abnormal situation, and began to fight it many years ago. The terms were held to be iniquitous and unjust. Finally in 1922 the case went to arbitration before a Swiss tribunal. This confirmed the British company's ownership of the land, but moved to put taxes on a more equitable basis. Then London and Pacific sold out to IPC.

We move on to the 1950's and 60's. The Peruvian government wrote a new petroleum code. Resentment at the position held by IPC boiled up. The company was willing to accept a change to concessionary status, but hot politics made further agreements difficult to reach. The Peruvians said that the original concession had been fraudulently obtained, and that the old owners had, as was only too obvious, never paid fair taxes. The IPC contended that it was a "good faith holder in due course," and should not be considered to be an entity with the former owners. Then Belaúnde in his 1963 election campaign promised a "settlement" of the dispute within ninety days. This was interpreted widely as a threat of confiscation or expropriation, but no such act has taken place. But the Peruvian congress unilaterally nullified the 1922 arbitration award, and the Senate voted to nationalize the company if it did not accept new terms.

Reaching the presidency, Belaúnde found himself in much the same position as former President Illía of Argentina, who, as we have seen, also promised to move against the oil interests. But, whereas Illía carried out his pledges, Belaúnde did not—preferring instead to open negotiations. Roughly —very roughly—the Peruvians want a sixty-forty split, a royalty agreement, reduction in the length of time IPC can stay in the country, and a fee or bonus of $50 million to cover old tax losses. Such terms, the company contends in rebuttal, are so "confiscatory" as to be unacceptable.

No nationalization, confiscation, or expropriation took place—an important point to remember in regard to what followed, which was that the United States government began to put pressure on Peru. The Hickenlooper Amendment did not come into play. It could not. The dispute centered on the terms of a "projected contract," nothing else. This was sheer power politics. Without making the facts known, the United States began to withdraw financial aid from Peru—obviously blackmail on the part of the State Department in the interests of a private company. About $20 million

[10] *Time*, November 8, 1963.

in so-called soft loans to Peru were held up, and when Belaúnde asked for $16 million to continue the work of Cooperación Popular, through the Alianza, he was rebuffed. It is only fair to state, however, that the Export-Import Bank and the Inter-American Development Bank continued to make advances to Peru.

Withdrawal of Alianza aid was greeted by most Peruvians not merely as a wanton example of bad manners and "crude and archaic" political tactics by the United States, but as a social disaster of the first magnitude for the country. Work was canceled at airports which desperately needed physical improvement, and the building of penetration roads, to feed the new Forest Road, had to be stopped; activity was called off even on such a level as building urgently needed water towers in the shanty towns, all of which produced profound resentment in Peru. I met a cabinet minister who said bitterly, "What do you Americans value most?—a few more dollars in dividends for Esso stockholders at home, or the friendship of a great nation?"

Suddenly in February, 1966, the United States government receded from its hard position, and our policy was dramatically reversed. Long-term development aid to Peru would, it was announced, be resumed. The *New York Times* wrote: "The [former] policy, which froze seven projects worth twenty-four million dollars, and discouraged the drawing up of other projects, was developed two years ago by Thomas C. Mann, then assistant Secretary of State for Inter-American Affairs. Mr. Mann had hoped the policy would persuade the [Peruvian] government to come to terms with the International Petroleum Corporation."[11] Then Senator Robert F. Kennedy revealed that, while American economic assistance to Peru had been held up, American *military* aid doubled in the same year—from $5.2 million to $10 million. Mr. Kennedy's words were, "I am sure our policy makers did not intend this result: but I am equally sure that many Peruvians thought we favored arms over social reform." But it should be pointed out that these funds may have been earmarked for the army's Civic Action program, which has considerable social value.

One remarkable fact is that the principal *right*-wing newspaper in Lima, *El Comercio*, stridently called *for* nationalization of the IPC, not the reverse, during all this controversy. It took a line inflammatorily anti-American. Such is the power of South American nationalism these days. Negotiations between the principals are still continuing. Why did Belaúnde, after having been given a completely free hand by congress, hesitate to push

11 February 10, 1966. Also see William McGaffin, Chicago *Daily News*, December 2, 1965.

through his campaign pledge to act against IPC? Probably the answer is that he felt that, in the event of nationalization, American aid would have been fully cut off for an indefinite period, in retaliation, and he desperately needs continuing Alianza help.

The Alianza and ADELA

USAID is a comprehensive operation in Peru, although the sums involved are not particularly large. Our assistance program—twice interrupted—has amounted roughly to $218.5 million in the past four years, much less than that in Brazil as an example. The Peru program ranges from the Southern Peru Regional Development project in the Indian highlands, our largest operation in South America of this kind except that in the Brazilian northeast, to modest "seed capital" housing loans in the cities. AID is actively involved in land distribution on the *sierra*, tax-enforcement teams, iron ore and fishmeal development, national planning, industrialization projects outside Lima, and the opening up of new lands in the high rain forests of the east.

In a country like Peru aid has ramifications few Americans ever dream of. For instance the American AID mission in Lima is drawing on the services of at least five universities,[12] the New York Institute of Public Administration, the AFL-CIO, the National League of Insured Savings Associations, the Foundation for Cooperative Housing, and the Credit Union National Association—quite aside from such federal agencies as the Bureau of Public Roads, the Federal Aviation Agency, and the U.S. Geological Survey.

Aid comes from other countries too. Since 1960 there have been English, French, Swiss, West German, Italian, and Japanese loans for public projects estimated to exceed $260 million.

Here—just for the record—are some specific Peruvian institutions which are receiving help from the United States.

> Engineering University, Lima ($2,500,000).
> San Marcos University for construction and equipment as a center for science education ($1,500,000 from the Social Progress Trust Fund of the Inter-American Development Bank).
> National Agrarian University.
> Peruvian Institute for Educational Development (scholarships worth $270,000).
> Army vocational training centers ($400,000 from USAID for tools and equipment).

[12] North Carolina State, Iowa State, Stanford, Michigan, and Columbia.

National Junta for Housing and the National Housing Bank ($34.3 million from the Social Progress Trust Fund).

Water system projects ($15,100,000 from AID and the Export-Import Bank).

National Planning Institute ($3,000,000 from AID to finance feasibility studies).

National Office of Agrarian Reform ($16,300,000 from AID; $1,700,000 from the Export-Import Bank).

Hydro-Electric Power Projects at Cañón del Pato and Pativilca ($4,200,000 from AID).

Peruvian Labor Studies Center (highway to develop San Martín department and other road projects).

Forestation projects.

Credit unions.

Research and Extension Service of the Ministry of Agriculture.

El Peru Savings and Loan Association, Lima (financing of home building—$1,100,000 from AID and Public Law 480).

Lima Water and Sewerage Corporation ($8,600,000 from AID, $6,500,000 from Export-Import Bank).

Arequipa Water and Sewage Corporation ($3,700,000 from IDB).

Peru has one of the largest Peace Corps programs in the world, with about four hundred volunteers at work. The Vatican Peace Corps (PAVLA) is also active here, as are volunteers from Britain, Israel, and Sweden.

*

Despite oscillations and recurrent crises, relations between the United States and Peru are good. Student rioters made unpleasant demonstrations against Vice President Richard M. Nixon in 1958, but the incident was not as serious as the one which followed in Caracas. Peru, under Belaúnde, was one of the five countries which refused to vote with the United States at the onset of the Dominican crisis in 1965, but this was probably because the president did not wish to take a course that might have led to trouble with his own left wing. It is important, as always, to distinguish between government and people, difficult as this distinction may be to make in working out public policy. The Peruvian government is, with certain reservations, pro-American by sentiment and conviction; the people are less so, and many feel that the regime is pro-United States only because it has to be. I heard the familiar remark in regard to aid: "The United States is not helping to build *us* up, but is merely protecting itself," and even, "You deal with us as if we were puppies in a kennel." The truism that by and large people hate to be told that they need help applies to Peru as much as it does to Afghanistan or Yonkers. In particular, aid is resented when it has political strings attached and when citizens feel that it will be forthcoming only if the recipient acts as we wish.

*

ADELA, the Atlantic Community Development Group for Latin America, a private, multinational investment company founded largely through the initiative of Senator Jacob K. Javits of New York, is an innovation. Its origins go back to 1961. At that time Mr. Javits, who has a powerful mind, grip, and a forward look in relation to South America as well as to much else, was chairman of the Economic Committee of the NATO parliamentary conference, which brought him indirectly to a study of hemisphere affairs. Javits thought that the situation on the continent was deteriorating politically, economically, and socially at an alarming rate, and sought to do something about it. One phenomenon that disturbed him was the flight of South American capital from its own home, which has been mentioned several times in these pages. The rise of Castro worried him as well.

In a sense, ADELA seeks to counteract the exodus of capital by seeking to draw private capital *into* South America. ADELA is an investment company, not a financing institution. Senator Hubert Humphrey, before he became vice president, joined Javits as a sponsor, and the Ford Foundation and a number of leading American and European private investors—as well as political leaders—worked on the enterprise. Twelve European countries are involved with ADELA, as well as the United States, Canada, and Japan. The company was incorporated in Luxembourg, and an operating office set up in Lima.[13]

So far ADELA has committed $22 million to enterprises in thirteen Latin American republics. In Peru it has gone into fisheries, steel, and heavy industrial machinery.

Two other South American conceptions are occupying Mr. Javits at the moment. One, which has Jules Vernesque possibilities, is to put a new satellite in space to transmit television programs between North and South America. The other is a program for continuing encouragement to LAFTA, the Latin American Free Trade Association, which, in its brief life, has already increased trade 85 percent among its nine member states, mostly by reducing tariffs. But it has not done as well as the Central American Common Market, which preceded it, and on which it was closely modeled. What the senator hopes for eventually is a free-trade zone stretching all the way from Mexico to the Straits of Magellan with more than 200 million

[13] *Time*, April 8, 1966, is authority for this and the following paragraphs.

people and a gross national product of $80 billion, which will be a worthy associate of the European Economic Community or Common Market, and which the United States, in his opinion, should welcome heartily.

The Forty Families and the Land

I have mentioned the army, the church, and foreign interests as power factors in Peru; another is, as goes without saying, the landed oligarchy, which is supposed to be dominated by forty families. These comprise one of the most closely knit, impenetrable and reactionary groups of landed aristocrats in the world. Their heritage goes far back. I heard it said that Peru was not merely run by an oligarchy, but by a "viceregal" oligarchy. One house near the Plaza de Armas in Lima is still owned by the same family that built it in the time of "Don Francisco," as Pizarro is still sometimes familiarly called. There are several great mansions where families have lived uninterruptedly for four hundred years.

Of course the families have ramified out and have become thinned down. Probably there are five hundred leaders of the elite, not merely forty—or forty-two, or forty-five, as the figure is sometimes given. The fact remains that social organization in Peru is still largely feudal at the top.

Two powerful pressure groups exist within the landed class, the SNA (Sociedad Nacional Agraria), and the Asociación de Creadores de Lanares de Perú (Association of Breeders of Wool-Bearing Animals).[14] The commercial interests of the great landowners spread out and interlock in several directions, as in Chile. Seventy-five percent of SNA members are owners of urban building and real-estate companies, 50 percent are substantial stockholders in banks and financial companies, 53 percent stockholders in insurance companies, and 32 percent stockholders in mining companies or petroleum. About two-thirds have substantial holdings in general industry. Figures in relation to the land are close to being unbelievable. They are by far the most extreme in South America. Authority for them is American. More than a million Peruvian farmers do not own any land at all; *82.6 percent of land is owned by 7,266 owners, or only 0.8 percent of the total number of landowners;* the remaining 17.4 percent of land is owned by 871,401 holders, all of whose properties are smaller than 200 hectares; 33.65 percent of all landowners own properties of less than 5 hectares. Breaking down the 0.8 percent of owners who have more than 82 percent of the land, these favored few hold more than 35 percent of tillable land, 30 percent of per-

[14] See *Los Dueños del Peru,* by Carlos Malpica, Lima, 1965. The author is a deputy in congress very far to the left.

manent crops, 93 percent of natural pastures, 74 percent of forests, and 90 percent of unproductive land. One family has an estate as big as Rhode Island, and one *hacienda* is a third of the size of Cuba.[15]

According to Malpica, cited above, disproportion of ownership along the coast, which produces sugar and cotton, is even more acute than in the highlands. One hundred ninety families own 53.6 percent of the arable land in the coastal region. The thirty largest owners possess 28.7 percent. One of the biggest landowners is the church.

President Belaúnde came into office pledged to make a land reform, and at once set about doing so. As a matter of fact all parties contesting the 1963 election promised a land reform; otherwise they would have had no chance of winning. The president's bill, passed after inflamed and prolonged argument, hopes to settle first a million landless (or almost landless) peasants on absentee-held land in plots averaging fifty acres. Marginal land will be taken over before well-managed land. Sugar cannot easily be touched, because the land here is highly mechanized, its owners have overbearing political power, and loss of sugar revenue would cripple the country in regard to foreign exchange. Eventually the Belaúnde government aims to expropriate "all properties over 3,000 hectares that do not pay their way." Expropriated land is paid for partly in cash, partly by eighteen-to-twenty-two-year tax-free bonds; these are negotiable and the theory is that, as they are turned in, they will be used to finance industry. When we talked to him Belaúnde pulled samples of these out of a drawer to show us that they were "real." He mentioned too that in Inca times it took half an acre to support a man; now, an acre or more. It is far too early to say whether or not the Belaúnde scheme will be successful. To date a little more than half a million acres have been turned over to seventeen thousand families.[16]

*

Comments from the aristocracy have been acrid. They say that the Indians will "engulf them," and that to cry for land reform is "communistic." Actually, as Senator Wayne Morse once pointed out, oligarchs of this type do not care much "whether the threat is genuinely communist, or comes from democratic reform elements"; to many there is no difference between these two forces, since they stand to lose either way. The Peruvian elite does not, as a general rule, like to play politics directly. One well-known oligarch became bitterly annoyed some years ago when it seemed that one of his cousins might run for president. "It will prejudice the people against us," he

15 *Invisible Latin America*, by Samuel Schapiro, p. 43.
16 *Time*, July 3, 1964, and December 31, 1965.

said solemnly. Most members of the elite have a curious double-edged attitude toward Frei's land reform in Chile next door. They hate and fear Frei but they say, "He is a good omen for us here, because when he fails it will reduce the pressure to duplicate his experiment in Peru."

But a question remains: if the oligarchy is so all-powerful, why then does it permit the rise to power of moderate or leftist parties like Belaúnde's Acción Popular and the Christian Democrats? One reason is probably pusillanimity. The oligarchy lies low for fear of losing its wealth, even though the lower it lies now the more certain it will be to lose more in the future.

*

After visiting Peru Senator Robert F. Kennedy of New York spoke as follows in the Senate:

> In Peru, outside Cuzco, we met men working their landlord's fields for 45 cents a day, a good wage in an area where others must work 3 days with no pay beyond the right to cultivate a small mountainside plot for themselves. They had never heard of President Kennedy or President Johnson; they had never heard of the United States; they did not know the name of the President of Peru; and they spoke no Spanish, only the Quechua tongue of their Indian ancestors. . . .
>
> The basic problem is that we here in the United States must realize that there is a revolution now going on down there and we must identify ourselves with that revolution. . . . We have preached to them the dignity of the individual, the fact that we want to help them lead their own lives. . . .
>
> However, that does not mean very much to a father who must work on a farm for 12 hours a day 6 days a week for only $1.50, or a man who sees half his children die before they reach the age of one.
>
> We must recognize these facts. . . . We must put ourselves in their shoes. We would not accept such conditions in this country . . . no matter how many persons came to us and preached about free institutions and democracy and how awful communism is.
>
> We can say that communism does terrible things, that there are no free institutions under communism. But how can it be any worse there, where men and women and their children are mostly illiterate, and they can not vote in an election, because there are no schools and there is no way to receive an education?
>
> But we go down there and tell them about the dangers of communism, that they must be for democracy because communism is so dangerous. What does that mean to them? . . .
>
> We must identify ourselves and relate ourselves to the fact that a revolution in Latin America is coming, and will come, either with free institutions, or with extremism on the left or right—which will eventu-

ally end in extremism on the left which, in my judgment, will be communism.[17]

These remarks did not make Senator Kennedy particularly popular either in Washington or Lima, but they show that he has a sharp eye for what is going on.

Communism and the Guerrillas

In the summer of 1965 guerrilla bands began to attack *hacendado* properties in the Cuzco uplands. This followed some years of disaffection, rioting, and bloodshed in the area. Peasants made trouble, and the Guardia Civil, which is generally detested in Peru, shot some demonstrators down. A neighborhood leader, Hugo Blanco, rose in the Convención Valley. An avowed Communist, he had been trained in Cuba in guerrilla tactics. The Convención region was ideal for such activities, because the land tenure system there is one of the most complicated in the world; the peasants were mobile, which is not generally the case in Peru, and Blanco had a comparatively easy time organizing them.

But Blanco was captured after a year and a half, and was put in jail in Arequipa. He has still never been brought to trial. Outrages continued as the countryside became more roused; federal troops had to be brought in, and martial law was temporarily declared.

Things became quieter for a time, largely as a result of news of the impending land reform—which relieved the peasantry. But then the struggle resumed in earnest in June, 1965. Guerrilla bands made raids into valleys, and sought to occupy the big estates. President Belaúnde, trying to minimize what was going on, insisted for a substantial time that this was not a "revolt" at all, but mere brigandage and hooliganism. Indeed, the guerrilla forces never numbered more than about 140 hard-core fighters. But it took seven months to put them down. Many are believed to have been trained in Cuba, and they were strongly under the influence of MIR, the Peruvian leftist revolutionary movement, which contains pro-Chinese, Fidelista, and Trotskyist elements. Following a severe political crisis, Belaúnde was forced to acknowledge the urgency of the situation, and to order military action to be taken on a serious level. United States helicopters helped the government by ferrying Peruvian officers from place to place, but no Americans took part in the actual fighting.

*

Moscow broadcasts regularly to Peru in the Quechua language, as does Peking. The United States—for reasons not readily understandable—has

[17] *Congressional Record*, May 9, 1966.

been slow to do the same thing. The excuse that few Quechua-speaking broadcasters are available does not hold water. Broadcasting can, obviously, be a substantial element in propaganda on the Peruvian *sierra*; almost every family has a transistor radio and, even if the great majority of people cannot read or write, they are quite capable of listening. Cuzco is the political "Moscow" of Peru.

Technically the Communist party is illegal in Peru, but it functions openly. It publishes newspapers and holds meetings. Two Communists, although they hold their seats under another label, sit in the house of representatives. The PCP, the orthodox Communist party (membership around nine thousand), stood openly for Belaúnde in the 1963 election—partly because of its violent antipathy to both his opponents, General Odría and the Apristas. Belaúnde, as noted above, did not refuse their help, but he carefully avoids open association with them now.

Most Peruvian Communists, no matter of what brand, have meantime become united on one fundamental concept, namely that the Belaúnde—or any similar—reforms are useless, and that Peru can be "saved" only by outright, thoroughgoing revolution. Once more we have the long-run picture familiar almost everywhere in South America. The future is a toss-up between Communism, arbitrary military rule, and the forces represented by liberal democracy.

Three Questions à la Mode

What runs Peru?
1. Foreign capital, represented chiefly by the International Petroleum Company, Cerro, Grace, and the Swiss electrical interests.
2. A small pool of the educated class, crisscrossed by family relationships.
3. The army.
4. Belaúnde, Congress, and the parties.
5. Fish.

What ails Peru?
1. Red tape and bureaucratic inefficiency.
2. The sixteenth century.

What does Peru need most?
1. Better government on the middle level.
2. Development, communications, and education.
3. To learn how to stand in line.
4. "A civil war." (I am quoting a planner from Venezuela.)

CHAPTER 19

City of Kings

For many Limeños the great unknown is Peru.
—FERNANDO BELAÚNDE TERRY

In Lima . . . the people have a tendency to stay put.
—NICOLE MAXWELL

LIMA, a stately city, grave and dignified, was named the "City of Kings" in honor of Charles V. "Lima" is a corruption of Rímac, the name of the river which bisects it; Rímac means "River that Speaks" in Quechua. It speaks with a rush, too, since it descends twelve thousand feet in eighty miles. Another nickname for Lima is "Jewel of the Andes," and indeed, although it lies close to the sea at an altitude of only a few hundred feet, it gives something of the atmosphere of a mountain capital, also of a city deeply involved with archaeology. There are numerous shops selling blankets, fur, and silverware from the mountains, and several conspicuous galleries full of pre-Hispanic antiques—both fraudulent and real.

But the main thing to say about Lima, even today, is that it was the dominant Spanish city in South America for three hundred years. It still has the overtones of an imperial metropolis, and it still utterly dominates Peru, so much so that it is sometimes ironically called "a city searching for a country."

Contrasts are, as usual in South America, sharp. The aristocratic quarters of Lima have a sleek detachment and are coated with a fine gloss, but the Jirón de la Unión, the main shopping street, bustles like a narrow Broadway. The Torre Tagle Palace is an early eighteenth-century masterpiece of exquisite carved wood with a tranquil patio and a latticed mirador, but harsh illuminated signs flash nearby—Goodrich, Olivetti, Manhattan Shirts, Suzuki (motorbikes), Volvo, Lufthansa, and Pepsi-Cola. This city has a drowsy past, but is full of contemporary momentum.

361

The population is usually given as 1,700,000, and this represents a quadruple lift in twenty years—a stupendous rise. As a matter of fact nobody knows exactly what the number of people is because of that familiar South American phenomenon, the population explosion. Some estimates put the total at 1,900,000, and, if you include Callao, the seaport, in the metropolitan area it may reach two million. And it is closed in on three sides by the foulest shanty towns on the continent, which grow outward day by day.

The climate, which is mild, together with the *garúa* (mist), make for laziness; people still do take siestas here. There are 156 holidays a year, including Sundays, and in summer shops are tightly closed for three and a half hours at noon—two and a half hours in winter. The fashionable suburbs like Miraflores, on the sea twenty minutes by car from the center of town, and San Isidro, which is built in olive groves, carry a glorious plumage—every variety of tropical bush and flower blooms with vivid color. Tall lanes of royal palms lead to secluded arbors, and I visited at least one house where monkeys climb in the trees and fantastically large and richly colored macaws patrol the garden.

The greatest sight in the conventional sense is the Plaza de Armas, which has the reputation of being the finest public square in the Americas. I thought it somewhat grubby. But few squares can have more compelling historic associations; here *autos-da-fé*, superintended by the Inquisition, brutally took the lives of thousands in colonial times. Four renowned buildings dominate the scene—the cathedral, the archbishop's palace, with its magnificently carved mahogany balconies, the city hall, and the presidential palace, where we met Belaúnde. Sometimes this is known as Don Francisco's house, meaning Pizarro's. I have already mentioned Pizarro's mummified corpse which lies on view in the cathedral, but some experts contend that this Pizarro may not be the real Pizarro. A thighbone sticks out of the shrunken skin, there is a glimpse of a white shoulder bone, the jaw is held to the rest of the face by bits of wire, and blobs of cotton cover some previously vital centers. Nearby is a bridge built in 1610 still known as the Bridge of Eggs. The legend is that the mortar supporting it was made partly with the whites of hundreds of thousands of eggs, to give it a better binding.[1] This leads to a romantic house, once lived in by a lady named La Perrichola, a naughty eighteenth-century beauty who was the mistress of a notable viceroy of the period and is still the source of legend. Her real name was Miquita Villegas, and she is supposed to have been the original of one of the characters in Thornton Wilder's *The Bridge of San Luis Rey*. Offenbach wrote an opera about her.

For my part the greatest sight in Lima is something quite else—the

[1] *South American Handbook*, p. 371.

carcochas. These are unique—like nothing else on earth. They are old wrecks of cars, which still somehow run, and clog the streets. Their state of dilapidation must be seen to be believed. Cars, as they break down, are cannibalized and rebuilt, piece by piece, and become *carcochas,* if only because new cars are so expensive. Often they have no back, sides, or front; one friend of mine swears that he saw one without an engine, though it moved. There are *carcochas* with only three wheels, made into tricycles, and few have lights. Driving at night is a fancy business in Peru. There are *carcochas* every square inch of which is crushed like dirty tinfoil; there are *carcochas* held together by glue, wire, and string. Some *carcochas* are so well known that they have acquired a local identity. One is constructed on the rump of a Rolls built in 1914; another is famous for having parts from seventeen other different makes of car built into it. *Carcochas* are illegal, but nobody pays attention. Because their behavior is unreliable in the extreme, they are dangerous. An official in the American Embassy, looking out of his window, saw four *carcocha* crashes during one morning. If they damage a new car badly, the way is made clear for the eventual appearance of a new *carcocha.*

Urchins at the airport take your picture with Polaroid cameras, a startling contemporary development. Streetcar rails are shiny, indicating that the trams actually run. The city has supermarkets, microbuses, good bookshops, and the inevitable H. Stern jewelry store. The National Club, a patrician organization, has a billiard room so big that, I heard, caddies were used to handle the balls. Not far away I saw a beggar thumbing through a pile of garbage on the open street—a sight which, to be sure, may also be seen in Naples, Cairo, or New York. Police outside the embassies carry tommy-guns, and the whistles of traffic cops give forth a feeble little chirp—bird calls. License plates for automobiles are a year old, because the authorities haven't got around to issuing new ones.

Lima's bull ring is the oldest in South America, the fourth oldest in the world; its first fight took place on February 22, 1566. Bullfighting is a favorite sport, as is cockfighting, though neither rival *fútbol.* One morning we saw the celebrated Caballos de Paso, horses used on some of the big *haciendas* which can do fifty miles in two hours, and which are characterized by their pacing gait; they do not gallop, or even run, but move swiftly with no roughness, no bouncing, no joggling of the riders, who wear ponchos and wide flat straw hats; their bridles are of silver and they carry abnormally large spurs and stirrups shaped like pyramids.[2]

[2] These pace horses are descended from Andalusian, that is Arab, stock, and are carefully trained almost from the moment of birth. Our nearest approximation is the Tennessee walking horse. For an illustration see Kenneth F. Weaver, "The Five Worlds of Peru," *National Geographic,* February, 1964, p. 216.

There are minor signs of political agitation almost everywhere, and I saw scrawlings on walls ranging all the way from "Castro—Traitor and Assassin!" to "Vote Communist" and, of course, "Yankees—Get Out of Vietnam!"

One curiosity—on a small level—is that the concierges in hotels do not sell postage stamps, as is the normal practice abroad, but use a franking machine. Peru, like all countries, has its petty corruptions, and I thought that this was to prevent bellboys from following a habit known to bellboys all over the world—unsticking stamps from letters while taking them to the post office, appropriating them, and throwing the letters away. But I was told that in Lima the franking machines were to keep employees in the actual post office from doing the same thing. Peru is, however, less corrupt in general than some other countries we have visited.

Society is, I heard, "breaking down"; Lima churns. The great families, as already mentioned, have become diffused; I counted forty-one Miró Quesadas in the telephone book, seventy-four Benavideses. Frontiers are melting in several senses of the word. The *cholos*, representing the new middle class, have totally changed the face of the city. There are, however, still surviving a few playboys, gigolos, absolutely classic in type. One exhilarating change has to do with the status of women, particularly youngish girls. Twenty-five years ago—as in Brazil—it would have been unthinkable for a girl of good family to set out to have her own life, or earn a living as a secretary or salesgirl; today this is a commonplace. One Limeño lamented, "Twenty years ago if you went to a dinner party you would know exactly who would be there. Now nobody knows anybody. Ten years ago if you went to a neighborhood movie everybody was a friend. Now nobody knows you."

Among newspapers in Lima the largest is *El Comercio*, run by members of the Miró Quesada family. Its principal political characteristic for a long period has been a passionate hatred of Haya de la Torre and the Apristas; this dates back to May, 1935, when Antonio Miró Quesada, the head of the family and owner of *El Comercio* at the time, was assassinated, together with his wife, by an Aprista desperado. This double murder had political repercussions which survived for many years; the newspaper never mentioned Haya's name. One hundred and twenty-seven years old, *El Comercio* stands on the right—"as closed as Islam," I heard it put—not that Islam is necessarily closed. Yet, rightist as it is, it has taken an inflammatory line, as noted above, against the International Petroleum Company, probably out of sheer excessive nationalism; had it not kept the fires burning on the oil issue this quarrel would probably never have reached the public dimension it attained. *El Comercio's* circulation is about eighty thousand.

La Prensa, not to be confused with the great Argentine newspaper of this same name, has less circulation than *El Comercio*, but a broader influence. One of the half-dozen leading newspapers on the continent, it stands firmly for private enterprise and has, on occasion, looked on Belaúnde with suspicious apprehension. Popular papers are *La Crónica, Expreso,* and *Correo;* the former editor of *Expreso*, the Harvard-trained Antonio Encinas, is one of the foremost journalists in Peru. *La Tribuna*, the APRA paper, has scarcely ten thousand circulation. Mr. Belaúnde has no paper at all, although *Expreso* came close to being so for a time. One interesting survival is the *Andean Air Mail and Peruvian Times*, an English weekly.

Pedro Beltrán, the director of *La Prensa*, is probably Lima's most distinguished citizen. His wife, an American, nicely enhances his activities. Whereas *El Comercio* represents what has been called "repentant Peru," *La Prensa* looks forward. Astute, gracious, and impeccably civilized, Dr. Beltrán has had a full career in politics and business as well as journalism. His conservatism is expressed more in economic terms than political; his thinking is independent, and he wants development. He attended the London School of Economics, became a cotton planter in Peru, went into banking, and served as Peruvian ambassador to Washington. He attacked the Odría dictatorship, and in 1956 went to jail for his pains. Several years later he became prime minister, under President Prado, but his tenure was brief and beset with savage difficulties.

Lima has no contemporary writers of the rank of Borges or Neruda, no musicians comparable to Villa Lobos. However, it has an exceptionally distinguished painter in Fernando de Szyszlo, a stimulating human being as well, whose wife is a poet. He is of Polish origin, and has exhibited widely in the United States and elsewhere abroad; he leads a school characteristic of Peru's awakening to modern art, and works in a style sometimes called "Indo-Cubism." His studio is a mecca for Peruvian artists and intellectuals, and we had some vivid conversation there—insight into Peru as well.

Lima calls itself "the gastronomic capital of the world," which is something of an overstatement, but restaurants exist here representing almost every nationality, and several of these are excellent; one or two are as sophisticated and almost as expensive as the Pavillon in New York, although Lima in general is not a particularly expensive city. Las Trece Monedas has an urbane atmosphere, and the Granja Azul, seventeen kilometers out of town, is worth crossing half a continent to visit. It specializes in chickens roasted on the spit—as much as you can eat—and fabulously original mixed drinks like the Gentle Thunderer (orange juice, cointreau, kirsch, gin) and the Chinese Itch (pisco, Grand Marnier, Scotch).

One typical Peruvian *plat* is *sopa de choros*, a chowder; another, *cabrito al pastor*, is described in a local guide as "kidling with vegetables casserole." *Mazamora morada* is a "pap" made of flour from purple Indian corn, fruit, and sugar. A standard delicacy is *anticucho*, grilled beef's heart. Chunks of this are skewered on bamboo twigs and served everywhere as an hors d'oeuvre; they can be bought on the streets like chestnuts in Paris or Eskimo pies in Brooklyn. Peruvian wine is excellent, particularly a rosé called Tacana. The pisco sours are said by connoisseurs to be less "throttling" than in Chile, because more Angostura is added; the trick to making a perfect pisco sour is to squeeze fresh lemon juice into the mixture at the last possible moment. Another drink, disconcertingly purple in color, is called *chicha morada*, made of mulberry corn, and still another is Inca Kola, "the beverage of national taste," which is colored yellowish green and served everywhere.

The Great Collections

Gold [to the Incas] was the symbol of superiority and preeminence ordered by the celestial will. . . . The Incas made gold a religious symbol, a mark of power, and a badge of nobility.
—RAÚL PORRAS BARRENECHEA

By legend, gold is called "sweat of the sun" in Peru; silver is "tears of the moon." To see antique gold in Lima is an unparalleled experience. We were lucky enough to arrive when, it happened, a comprehensive exhibition of pre-Hispanic art had been gathered at the National Museum of Art; here were not merely golden objects in profusion but potteries of every description, *mantos* or large textile pieces, and smaller fabrics made of toucan feathers and colored in characteristic shades of salmon pink and azure, still softly luminous after a thousand years. Pottery is not merely pottery here, but portraiture—since startling caricatures are often etched into the earthenware in a remarkably contemporary manner. But gold is what is most exciting.

Lima has several museums and private collections of the first class, including the Archaeological and Anthropological Museum, the director of which, Dr. Jorge Muelle, is one of the leading men of his field in the world, and the Pedro de Osma collection devoted to colonial works of art. One institution not to be missed is the Rafael Larco Herrera Museum, with its extraordinary ceramics of the Mochican and other periods. This collection, put together by a wealthy Limeño, has sixty thousand pieces. Some Mochican pottery, dating from A.D. 600, was designed with great practicality as well as beauty; some vessels have a handle like that on a contemporary woman's handbag, contrived so that the water within was neither spilled nor evaporated, and could be drunk easily. Moreover the vessel could be hung on a belt, and did not have to be carried in the hands. These potteries are unglazed; glazing did not come until centuries later, with the Spaniards. If nothing else, the fabulous objects in the Larco museum would seem—to a lay observer—to demonstrate nicely the universality of culture. Obelisks look Egyptian, sculptured heads look Chinese, and the fabrics resemble those of Central Asia, but are finer; one strip we saw has 398 strands to the inch, and is the finest material ever woven.

Most of the human representations here, as is the case with a good deal of ancient Peruvian art, carry a note of menace. These are sinister, baleful, and frightened faces. We saw a line of skulls trepanned by surgeons a thousand years ago. How did they do it? Why? Then too a particular attraction at the Larco, of high interest to sophisticates, is the collection of *huacos eróticos*, which would have made the late Dr. Kinsey blush. These are supposed to be in a "secret" division of the museum, but a small tip (or a smile) will get you in.

An enthralling collection in Lima is that of Miguel Mujica Gallo, a fantastically rich landowner, connoisseur, and author of a resplendent book, *The Gold of Peru*. The Mujica collection, which is private, is situated on a property in the outskirts of Lima, and is, I think, literally the most awe-inspiring private assembly of works of art and curiosities I have ever seen. One room, the size of a tennis court, consists of a horde of animals shot by Mr. Mujica, a keen huntsman, and realistically stuffed and posed. A tiger lies coiled on a sofa, as if ready to pounce. Another gallery houses what experts say is the most complete as well as splendid collection of arms and armor known in the western world. Then in a kind of vault built underground like an air defense shelter, but otherwise only casually guarded, or so it seemed, are gold objects, textiles, and other artifacts and works of art. Here in particular are radiant examples of the Chimu period (A.D. 1100–1300), which represents goldsmithery at its most advanced, complex, and glorious. I never knew before that depilatory tweezers had been made of gold almost ten centuries ago, as well as gloves, humming birds, and replicas of human eyes. Objects range from tiny intricately carved gold ornaments to massive golden figures a foot high, including cuirasses made of golden sheets, as thin as Kleenex. I am barely mentioning the profusion of *tumis* (ceremonial knives), awesome funeral masks heavily set with jewels, beads, repoussé vases, and ornate tall vessels decorated with impassively saturnine or scowling faces. These were the types of incomparable works of art which Pizarro, having acquired them by treachery, boiled down in a pot and, cut into ingots, distributed as vulgar loot.

The Barriadas—Slum Towns

The squatter towns in Lima are called *barriadas,* and are noisome. They form a scabrous crust around two-thirds of the city, expand steadily, and already contain between a quarter and a third of the population—perhaps 500,000 miserable persons. There are at least 150 specific different *barriada* areas. Lima has done very little to come to grips with the ugly problems these represent, although smaller cities, like Piura in the north, have faced the situation squarely, and are trying to clean up.

Here, as in Chile, the main factor driving squatters in droves into the city is unproductiveness on the land; the shanty towns proliferate because agriculture is so backward. A truly comprehensive land reform would, most people say, modify this condition. A peasant coming into Lima usually, again as in Chile, takes an exploratory trip to look the ground over, particularly if he is a migrant worker who has slack time; then after some weeks—or even months—he returns to the hills, organizes a group, and, with his own family and others, works his way on foot back to the city, and moves in on squatter land at night. Why do the authorities not throw the squatters out? They cannot—without risking revolution.

Grim as circumstances are in the Lima *barriadas,* many peasants find themselves better off here than in their original homes on the *sierra,* as is true of the squatters in other South American cities. The determining factor is that, dreadful as life in the *barriadas* may be, conditions are probably better than in the hills if only because opportunities are greater. Men and women are moving up in the social scale, not down, when they come here, because they were virtual slaves before. Here in Lima they can establish neighborhood relationships, earn money, and, with luck, make a place of their own in society—free of feudalism and with a brighter hope for the future of their children. It would be a mistake to assume that *barriada* dwellers have no sophistication. They seek a *solid* way into a new life.

First in Lima we visited a small *barriada* in the Chorrillos district. Here huts are built of adobe, cardboard, tin cans, hunks of rock, and *estera,* a matting made of reeds. The two chief agonies are lack of drinking water and sewage disposal. There are no amenities at all—no assistance from the government, no school, no transportation. Those who live here are mechanics, taxi drivers, masons, barbers, and market workers. A primitive kind of social organization has been built up. Peace Corps volunteers took us in to see the "mayor." He works as a park watchman, and has lived in this *barriada* for three years. I asked him if he had ever been tempted to return to the *sierra,* and his answer was "No, except on holidays." His hut had three luxuries—a kerosene stove, a clay floor, and even a roof. Most of the Lima slum dwellings are not roofed, but this is not so much a deprivation as may be thought, because it never rains. We happened to visit this particular district on what was a triumphant day for the community. By their own labor four hundred people working together for thirty hours had laid a kilometer of pipe, illegally tapping a main water line, and installed four outdoor spigots.

We went then to Pampa de Comas, which has a population of 200,000, that of a good-sized city, and which is probably the most notorious of the Lima squatter towns. On the way we passed the most fetid slum I have ever seen. A stench spreads out from this area that can be sniffed for miles. Savage dogs snapped in alleys crammed with moist filth. In Pampa de Comas itself there is no running water, not even from a spigot, and a barrel of water—bought off a cart—costs sixteen cents—half a day's average wage. Here we met some Peace Corps girls; they lived in the heart of the *barriada,* and only seldom ventured into the center of Lima, a few miles away; first the transportation system is miserable beyond belief, and second they were apt to be molested on the streets or even in the buses. The girls took us to a kind of school where they were teaching women to knit woolens, make sweaters, and the like. One index to the amenities of the community is that, for 200,000 people, exactly one restaurant exists.

"Are you shocked by conditions here?" a pretty twenty-four-year-old volunteer from Ohio asked us.

"Yes."

I had a feeling that she had a certain contempt for our softness.

"It isn't too bad," she went on. "You get nowhere if you let yourself be sorry for the people."

A Glimpse of the University

The University of San Marcos, founded by the Dominicans in 1551, is the oldest in the Americas. It has buildings scattered over a large area; there are five, widely separated, for chemistry alone. We spent one morning at University City, the main campus, which was built in the 1940's; then too we visited the downtown headquarters in a narrow business street near the middle of the city. Part of the main building here faces a square where students often gather to make demonstrations; police break these up by using firemen's hoses, and the water is sometimes dyed bright blue with adhesive ink. In a pale blue wall just below the rector's office is a door artfully concealed, built so that its outlines are barely discernible and painted so that, except on the closest examination, it is invisible. This makes it easy for the rector to get in and out without being observed in case of trouble. Several in recent years have had to get out—in a hurry.

Efforts have been made to concentrate all the ten San Marcos faculties, or schools, in University City, but these have been resisted by the senior professors, among others. Teachers hate to make the trip to this campus, although it is no great distance, because this serves to take them away from other jobs they may have in town. One of the tragedies of education here, as elsewhere in South America, is that nobody can make a living wage just by teaching. A lecturer at San Marcos begins on a salary of around $70 a month; a full professor gets $280. I heard of one teacher who sells electrical appliances at night; one acts on TV.

University City has no dormitories, and little campus life, in our sense of the term, exists, although I saw youngsters sitting around on the grass much as they would at a North American university, glancing at texts, flirting with girls, or loafing. On the whole campus, which holds fifteen thousand people, I saw no more than a dozen automobiles, haphazardly parked; several were *carcochas* falling apart. Interest in collegiate sport is at the minimum.

Tuition is normally free; it takes five years to win what corresponds to our bachelor's degree, six for a doctorate. The libraries are inadequate, and texts inferior; as a rule the professor sells his own mimeographed notes as a text. The campus is immune from search or seizure, in the familiar South American manner, even though it is supported by the government, and strikes are frequent and can be prolonged. As a rule these have nothing to do with the university itself, but may be set off by labor troubles in, say, the sugar properties near Trujillo—sympathy strikes.

The students do, however, impose a certain amount of discipline on themselves. Nobody is allowed to take examinations who cuts more than 70 percent of his classes, an unusual rule for South America. But there are a good many "professional" or "career" students who amount to nothing more or less than agitators and who stay on at the university for year after year until they reach forty or beyond. Students have a 35 percent share in the ruling body of San Marcos, and are thus deeply involved in university organization and management, sharing responsibility with the deans and faculty. They have a one-third say in the choice of a new rector, and in the selection and promotion of professors.

Above all, as is the case everywhere in Latin America, students are inveterately political. By the mere fact of having been admitted to the university they consider themselves to be leaders. All the national parties have campus affiliates, and the National Student Federation is an important pressure group. This was run by the Apristas from 1930 to 1959, then by the Communists (in alliance with Belaúnde and the Christian Democrats) until 1964, now by the Apristas once again. I asked if the students represented a "class." No, because most of them are moving up from class to class.

As in Brazil, Argentina, and Chile we had some vivid hours with a students' round table. I felt again the passionate yearning of these youths, their frustrated will to get ahead, their confused longings to break through the walls of their environment and make their mark in the new world. They gave a sense of young men with a perfervid sense of mission, who were nevertheless pessimistic. One boy was a Communist. I asked him how he stood vis-à-vis Moscow, Peking, and Cuba. Answer: "We were with Castro until we heard the balalaika."

Up the Coast, Down the Coast

Twice we had glimpses of the coastal desert. "Desert" is not an overstatement. Although narrow and penetrated by watercourses, it is as genuine a desert as the Sahara. Winds blow from the sea, and so the sand does not, as might be expected, fall from the top of the bare hills, but is blown upward into topheavy dunes and confused shifting patterns. The wind claws at the dunes, and sand spills down over the roads, which have to be brushed clean every day. Slices of irrigated areas cross like green knives and drop down high precipitous cliffs to the Pacific. The Humboldt Current, making a pure white streak jutting out into the blue ocean, is as visible as a bridle path cutting through a meadow.

Traveling north from Lima on the Pan American Highway we passed a slum town at San Martín de Toros which looked unsavory, and then Ancón, a chic seaside resort with a cliff of tall apartment buildings lining a scallop of water, famous for its deep-sea fishing. Then came a fishmeal factory, which smelt, near the town of Chancay. Shrines along the roads mark places where people—there must be a great many—are killed in automobile accidents; each spot is marked, apparently as a warning. Along the shore we saw the guano islands off broad beaches. We turned inland at last and reached a *tambo*, or countryside shop, selling goods like kerosene, salt, and soap. All this area is an archaeological paradise. For a time bulldozers attached to the *haciendas* or working on the roads were permitted to run carelessly, crushing pottery that has lain under the shallow soil for generations; procedures are more careful now. The dryness of the earth keeps objects in an almost perfect state of preservation, like mummies, and new discoveries occur regularly. If, digging, you chance to hit a graveyard, the chances are that it has lain untouched for hundreds of years, and may give forth immeasurable treasure. Routine finds of beads, pots, and ancient jewelry occur all the time.

A few days later we drove south in the opposite direction along the same road to Kilometer Post Number 148, where we turned off to visit the model *hacienda* operated by Dr. Beltrán, the former premier. A pearly fog played over the dunes, making iridescent patterns in the sand. The irrigated areas are rich enough here to grow three cotton crops a year. Trucks are picturesquely named, like those in Africa; "Untouchables" passed us, and so did "Such Is Life." Traffic accidents take a frightful toll. The trucks go mostly without lights at night, and Indian drivers brought up on burros cannot grasp the speed of the *other* car. The Beltráns shared their wisdom with us during an amiable and informative afternoon. One thing good about the present administration, they think, is that there have been no suppressions of civil liberties whatever under Belaúnde, no political strong-arm tactics, no confiscations or concentration camps.

The White or "Sunshine" City

Peru's second city, AREQUIPA (population around 100,000) lies in a voluptuous valley at 7,500 feet in the shadow of El Misti, an extinct (everybody hopes) volcano 19,200 feet high. The city was taken over by the Spaniards in 1540, and many of its buildings were composed of a white volcanic material; hence the nickname "White City."[3] The climate is exemplary, sunshiny but cooled by an ocean breeze. Lord Bryce many years ago found Arequipa to be "steeped in ecclesiasticism," and it has always been a somewhat recherché cultural center. It is also a main focus of Belaúnde's political strength, also Odría's, and is the seat of the contemporary Trotskyist movement as well—not that Belaúnde, Odría, and the Trotskyists have anything in common.

I quote from *This is Peru*, a local pamphlet published by a travel agency, in description of this "capital of southern Peru":

> One of the Departments with many "touristic attractives." Its climate is dry and it always looks as spring. SOCOSAN, 34 km from the city and at 2.345 m. S.N.M. of altitude with its sources of bicarbonate and ferruginous waters, that have a great medicine power. All these places have good hotels and are connected to the city by sidewalks.
>
> You have to know "AREQUIPA PORTICOS," that are located in the Plaza de Armas, square of the city, and are the most beautiful of

[3] *South American Handbook*, p. 392.

America because of its architecture and symmetry and were reconstructed in 1874. Its famous "SOCIETY TEMPLE" of barroco style starting its construction in 1595, and was finished in 1698, that primitive temple was destrtoyed [sic] by an earthquake in 1582 and it's very important to know that in the "SELICS ALTARS" there is one spine from the SPINE CROWN OF CHRIST.

Indians in Arequipa wear marvelously colorful costumes, and sit in the sun selling alpaca rugs in spacious squares. This was a considerable city long before the Spaniards came.

CHAPTER 20

Jungle, Amazon, and the Inca Highlands

> The three fixed pivots of Peru are God, land, master.
> —ANONYMOUS

> We come upon permanence: the rock that abides and the word:
> the city upraised like a cup in our fingers,
> all hands together, the quick and the dead and the
>   quietened; death's
> plenitude holding us here, a bastion, the fullness
> of life like a blow falling, petals of flint
> and the perduring rose, abodes for the sojourner.
> a glacier for multitudes, breakwater in Andes.
> —PABLO NERUDA ON MACHU PICCHU
>   (translated by Ben Belitt)

> Peru is an extensive cemetery of dead cities, which, like men,
> are born, mature, age, and die.
> —FERNANDO BELAÚNDE TERRY

OUR HOST Felipe Benavides, my wife, and I tramped through the mist to the neat line of Faucett planes waiting on the apron of the Lima airport, and found ours. An enterprising airline, Faucett was once jokingly called "the Atlas Tunnelling Corporation," but as a matter of fact it has an almost perfect safety record. The flight from Lima to Iquitos on the Amazon is a dizzying experience, one of the great flights of the world. We crossed swiftly the lane of desert along the coast, and then soared high over sharp black peaks, like enormously magnified shiny chunks of coal; the mountains rose all around us, some capped with smears of marshmallow—snow. I have crossed the Andes by air six or seven times, and have never ceased finding this to be a spectacular adventure. We climbed twisting between the unending black-white crags to nineteen thousand feet—in a plane smallish and nonpressurized. A stewardess gave us purple *chicha morada* to drink with one hand, and adjusted oxygen tubes with the other. The descent began; ears split. As we dipped and rocked, I saw a tranquil rug of green, which seemed to be smooth grass. No—trees. We approached Iquitos, and there was the oily green snake of the Amazon.

IQUITOS (population around 60,000) is called "Peru's Atlantic Port," although it lies 2,300 miles from the sea, and already the majestic river has descended almost 1,500 miles from its point of origin in the Andine hills. Large freighters carry their wares regularly between Iquitos, Liverpool and Antwerp; the journey to Europe takes thirty-six to thirty-eight days. In the other direction, there was no communication between Lima and Iquitos at all except on foot, an arduous journey which could take some months, or by water, until recent times. To get from Lima, the capital of the country, to Iquitos, the principal city of eastern Peru, it was necessary to travel circuitously by sea through the Straits of Magellan or the Panama Canal, then all the way around the continent and up the Amazon from the Brazilian port of Belém. Today the trip takes two hours by air.

Despite the speed of contemporary air travel, Iquitos seems to exist in a world totally different from that of Lima. Lima, we heard, does "nothing" for it. Here we stand within a stone's throw of Ecuador, Colombia, and Brazil. This is a territory all its own—Amazonian. There was, as a matter of fact, a separatist movement in Iquitos at one time, designed to make Loreto, the department of which it is the capital and which covers almost a third of Peru, a separate nation. Iquitos lived mainly on rubber before the turn of the century. A settlement near the Putumayo River was the scene of unspeakable atrocities committed against the Indian rubber workers, the investigation of which brought Sir Roger Casement, the Irish patriot, to fame in 1911.[1] The rubber boom collapsed in Peru as it did in Manaus, the Brazilian city further down the Amazon. Then came a boom in timber—particularly mahogany and other tropical hardwoods. But stupid owners cut the big mahogany out, and planted nothing in its place; the forests died and Iquitos shriveled.

Today Iquitos is suffused with an atmosphere that might have been dreamed up in a collaboration between Graham Greene and Evelyn Waugh at their most tropical—moist at the edges, limp with heat, romantic, sapped of moral energy, full of odd characters, exhausted, and inexpressibly remote. Yet it is a clean city, and it does not give a derelict impression. There are, of course, startling contrasts. The hotel has outlandish aspects, including

---

[1] Casement was sent to the jungle by the British government after his successful similar investigation in the Congo.

mahogany-colored drinking water, but in our room stood a Japanese-made noiseless electric fan, more modern than any I have ever seen in the United States. Vultures, which look like turkeys, stroll on the Malecón, the soggy promenade facing the Amazon, but you can buy imported British ice cream in a shop known familiarly as Lyons' Corner House. The heat can be fantastically severe for a day or two—up to 110 degrees—whereupon savage rains cool the city off. One local peculiarity is that there are no stones. If you want to throw a rock you have to make it out of cement.

Iquitos was built out of a strange assortment of European remnants—scrolled steel balconies from France, tile from Portugal; the first traders were French Jews. Today the population includes a handful of Europeans, about twenty Americans (mostly Peace Corps and missionaries) and exactly three Negroes. Most other residents are Indian. Indian women walk under black umbrellas, and some have bands depressed into their foreheads, like Kikuyu women in Kenya, made by the pressure of harnesses anchored on the head—necessary so that they can carry huge loads. We saw aged porters bent and staggering under fantastic burdens—as much as 150 pounds of jute. They climb straight up the slippery Amazonian banks bearing weights like this, and get a wage of ninety cents a day for doing so. Children have old, old Indian faces, but are clean; I never saw a beggar. They carry everything from bowls of fruit to sewing machines on their heads, like youngsters in Africa. The dogs look healthy so that, as one local observer put it, "You know that the people have enough food."

When the Booth Line ships come in they take ten days to unload, since no mechanical contrivances are available. Everything has to be hauled by hand. I asked why people did not revolt against their poverty and misery, and received one answer, "They don't know yet that they are miserable." There is no need for shelter against cold, and food is plentiful. On an island we saw some very tall trees rising like sentinels along the shore—Brazil nut trees. The nuts are seeds, filling a pod the size of a coconut. Enough to eat in the way of fruit can be plucked off trees everywhere. But that the people have enough to eat does not mean that they are well nourished.

The days pass pleasantly at Iquitos. The day usually began when we were awakened by the shriek of parrots outside our room, a brass band playing the Peruvian national anthem, which is endless, or the grunt of an old Constellation flying freight down the river. The hotel is comfortable in a true Gauguinesque style, and the town has, believe it or not, no fewer than six radio stations. Large quantities of beer are drunk at the bar, and one enticing hors d'oeuvre is a preparation of marinated piranha, the man-eating fish. But here along the Amazon human beings feed on the piranha, not vice versa. Tall tales are told of local personalities, like the old-time marksman who, somewhat demented, goes out alone in the jungle and shoots at Indians for fun. When everything else fails one can sit on the terrace and watch detached fragments of island, which can reach a large size, float imperturbably down the Amazon.

One morning, riding in a seashell of a boat, we turned off the river into a tributary known as the Itaya, and visited Belén,[2] the floating village which is the Iquitos *barriada*, but more than that—a market too. Here houses—not houseboats, but actual houses—lie placidly in the swift river. Moored to the shore, they undulate with the Amazon flow, which can rise sixty-five feet; some seem to be on dry (or rather moist) land, but they will be in the water again as soon as the river rises. Why don't the houses sink? Wood floats. Moreover, the logs are heavily greased with water-resistant oils. Sometimes, however, a house breaks off and starts careering down the river on its own, as if gone berserk, whereupon it must be retrieved, a wild scene. We passed one "island"—a barge filled with gasoline drums—obviously the town's filling station. Other barges dipped past us with cargoes of bananas, propelled by Indians with arrow-shaped paddles. Women on the banks washing their clothes turned their backs modestly, covering their breasts, as we progressed. Dugout canoes moved incessantly from house to house—floating shops. "Nomads of the river" passed by on rafts and in rough canoes.

The scene is much like that along the river in Bangkok, Thailand, but the surroundings are cleaner here. Squatters pay no rent. They have no light, and sleep in hammocks suspended on the open floors, or decks. Most of the houses carry names proudly; one we saw was "Paris." President Belaúnde calls Belén a "Venice without palaces," and says that it represents "one of the most genial human condensations in Peru."

Patrick Nichols, the honorary British consul, who also represents the Booth Line, Faucett, and several other enterprises, took us around. A vigorous young man, Mr. Nichols has two pets, both named Charlie—a furry little marmoset which practically never leaves his shoulder, and an eleven-foot boa constrictor, which lives under his house; this is haunted, and has a man-sized indoor swimming pool as a bath, containing large bizarre roaches and other insects, which Mr. Nichols collects. Charlie, the boa constrictor, is only dangerous if he succeeds in wrapping his tail around a stout support and is thus anchored to produce leverage when he squeezes. Mr. Nichols took us to see some local industry. Aside from more ordinary crops, Iquitos lives on *leche caspi*, a form of chicle from which chewing gum is made, and heavy, hollow rosewood logs, which provide essences for per-

[2] Of course not to be confused with Belém, the Amazonian port on the Atlantic.

fume. Several American chewing-gum factories have installations here. We watched Indian workers pick at piles of *leche caspi,* plucking out impurities. A mile or so away, it occurred to me, we could drop in at the local drug store and buy imported chewing gum of any of the well-known brands. In between the gum has traveled to the United States and back, and has undergone remarkable transformations. Similarly rosewood oil leaves Iquitos, and after complicated processes in France and elsewhere, comes back to be sold in the local perfume shop. Another export is *oje,* a powder which goes into laxative drugs; *balata,* a gum used in transmission belting; and *barbasco,* an insecticide.

But, as we soon learned, the prize exports of Iquitos are live—orchids, birds, and animals. We visited a trapping establishment where maned lizards, tiny blue-eyed ocelots, and tropical fish in profusion were assembled for sale to the world outside, also monkeys and a tapir. There are monkeys all over the place. Iquitos sells about fifty thousand a year, and the first monkey to ride in an American space ship came from here. The city is also the site of an interesting and colorful orchid farm, run by a youthful American, Lee Moore. He exports hundreds of varieties of orchid, and has discovered several new species himself, some of which are named for him, on orchid hunts through the jungle. Like the monkeys and parrots, they go out by air—mostly to Miami.

One day we visited what was called an agricultural station at Quista Choca, but it wasn't much of a station. Scarlet macaws and yellow parrots shrieked around us, and, near a translucent lake, we marveled at orchids with straight crimson petals eight inches long, great glowing clumps of golden flowers on the tops of trees, and an astounding plant known as the emperor's stick, heavy as lead and straight as a baton, with a foamy rosy head. You could break a branch with it. Half the jungle seemed dead, however. Huge stalks of trees were etiolated, having been strangled by creepers or eaten alive by termites. Huts of the villagers, with sharply peaked roofs of matting to shed the rain, looked like the shambas in Uganda. They rise on stilts because of fear of animals at night. The Indians here seemed to be totally inert—unlike Africans with their upswinging zest and zip.

Mrs. Nicole Maxwell, author of *The Witchdoctor's Apprentice,* has lived in Iquitos off and on for long periods, and she shared with us some jungle lore during several vivid, rewarding meetings. Several times she has gone out into the fierce bush alone on expeditions in search of pharmaceuticals, having heard that tribesmen deep in the interior make use of drugs with mysterious properties still unknown to western science. In particular she sought an arcane substance said to be capable of inhibiting conception in a

woman, and another which could make her fertile again. Hallucinatory
drinks are made of bark, and a little-known variety of yam produces
cortisone. Mrs. Maxwell told us that the jungle was not as dangerous as it is
supposed to be, but that the natives in some districts are apt to be distrustful
of foreigners because of the legend that they are searching for human fat, an
essential ingredient in atomic bombs! As a modern variant of the traditional
beads to give as tokens to savages, Mrs. Maxwell carried glass eyes, a gift
which made a spectacular impression on witchdoctors and the like. Many
Indians near Iquitos are still altogether primitive; they wear lip plates, and
file their teeth. But others, Mrs. Maxwell told us, greet the wayfarer wearing sunglasses and smoking filter cigarettes.

Consul Nicholas lent us his scarlet speedboat one afternoon, and we set
out to have a look at the Amazon together with two of its tributaries, the
Nanay and the Monen. The splendid river is seventy-six feet deep here, and
a mile or more wide, the current is vigorous, six knots or more, and the water
is foul with logs. Even so, we did sixty knots or better, skimming the
water with its iridescent pools of scum. This is a very dangerous river.
"The Amazon is flat only on top," one of our guides told us, and no attempt
is made to rescue a man who is so unfortunate as to fall overboard from a
steamer—the current is too swift. The waters are full of electric eels, alligators, and other unpleasant phenomena. Islands continually shift, break
apart, and float downstream sliding this way and that, which makes navigation hazardous. The big ships coming upriver from Belém are obliged to
carry two experienced pilots, not merely one.

We skipped round and about in a vibrating green gloom. The water leads
everywhere and nowhere, between somber lanes of dripping vegetation. On
the glistening, fawn-colored river, in giant scrolls, lie promontories shaped
like hearts. Not for miles did we see a house, a road, or a human being. The
prevailing impression was of land and water becoming one as in the days
before the world was born. A greenish dusk fell, and the jungle banks
became indistinguishable from their absolutely still reflections in the water.
We were shooting forward on a wet green mirror. Islands thrust themselves
forward in the deep shadows, but we could not tell if they were islands or
phantoms. We stopped at one greasy, grassy bit of shore in search of a
trapper's house. It was deserted. The loneliness closed in on us. Our
boatman couldn't get the motor started again, and we fussed with it
nervously. Disaster! This was no place to spend the night, and we didn't
have so much as a match with us. To add to the confusion I slipped down
the bank and found myself sitting in the water. Then, with motor repaired,
sliding swiftly home at sixty knots, through the dank emerald mist, we

scraped an alligator. I would not have been surprised if it had been a brontosaurus.

Next, through the courtesy of President Belaúnde, we spent a day as guests of the Peruvian navy on the gunboat *Amazonas*. The surroundings continued to be picturesque. At a river intersection the Amazon mingled with a tributary; the line of demarcation between green and brown water was as clear as that between grass and a dirt road. Thatched boats like floating huts passed by, and Indians in heavy dugouts paddled against the stern current. After several hours we reached Indiana, a Canadian missionary station. Man is fairly leashed to the river here; the water controls all movement. We learned that it is an unwritten law that any steamer, passing a person stranded on its banks who wants a lift, must stop and serve.

Our gunboat, which was very martial but somewhat down-at-the-heel, with guns pointing upward that are occasionally fired in practice rounds, is one of five engaged in the Fluvial Civil Service. Belaúnde founded this organization, and is justifiably proud of it. The idea is to bring rudiments of administration and technical help to the spongy, isolated river villages. Once a week gunboats carrying doctors, nurses, teachers, administrators, glide slowly up and down the Amazon bywaters, feeling their way along the shifting shoals to remote forlorn settlements. Technicians set up radio sets as part of an educational program, and doctors and dentists operate. The ill are carried out. These boats are, in effect, floating civic centers.

Our expedition took place on a Sunday, however, and so it had some properly convivial holiday aspects. Our escorting officers were at play, not work. Lunch was stupendous, and lasted almost four hours. Hors d'oeuvres were yucca and various species of exotic pickled fish, and seven stout courses followed. To drink we had pisco sours, whiskey, *cocona* (a delicious and unusual soft fruit drink), beer, Inca Kola, red wine, and crème de menthe—more or less in that order. It was 105 in the shade.

Up in the Sierra

Peru—a receptacle into which eons of meaning have been poured.
—FERNANDO BELAÚNDE TERRY

The ancient Inca capital CUZCO, called the "navel" of their universe, lies in an intermontane valley, at 11,480 feet, and has some 80,000 people, mostly Indians. It differs from Iquitos as much as Boulder, Colorado, from Savannah, Georgia—more. We spent several days here under the able, earnest, and discriminating tutelage of Earl E. Smith, who was head of the USAID establishment in Cuzco at the time.

The altitude made me gasp and puff from the moment we arrived on a Faucett plane from Lima, and I do not know what to thank Mr. Smith for most—the amiable stimulus of his conversation, the amenities of his house, or the oxygen which he siphoned into me at intervals.

Cuzco has been called the archaeological capital of South America. No president of Peru, however, ever bothered to visit it until 1940. Remnants of Inca walls are to be seen on every hand, and La Compañía de Jesús, the great cathedral built by the Jesuits in 1668, rises on the site of what was once the Inca Palace of Serpents. Most of the early colonial churches were made of Inca stones. There are several commanding Inca sites, but any attempt to find out much about them is frustrating; nobody knows what the true Inca story is, because, as mentioned previously, these extraordinary and mysterious Indians had no writing. The Incas were Quechuas, but "Inca" means correctly a ruling class, not a tribe or race.

The Incas may not have left written records, but they certainly left stone. This has large archaeological interest today, and a city ordinance forbids any tampering with—much less demolishing of—an Inca wall; you have to build around it or incorporate it into the modern structure. The Incas joined their immense stone blocks without the use of any mortar, or, so far as we know, any other adhesive; the stones in their massive walls are so perfectly joined that, even today, you cannot slip a knife blade between them, as practically every visitor to Cuzco is told at once. We marveled at Kenko, an amphitheater made of curved stone, and Tambomachay, which was apparently a bathhouse in an imperial reserve; its fountain still gives water. The principal ruin is the great fortress of Sacsahuaman, an L-shaped redoubt commanding the site of the ancient city.[3]

Cuzco maintains continuity with its rich past, but it is a modern city as well. Spanish families—which flow uninterruptedly from colonial times—are still prominent today. We met one landowner, of impecabbly Castilian origins, whose house is a baroque dream, and who spent many years trying to perfect an invention which, he says, will enable a person to attach wings to himself, and fly like a bird.

The first thing we saw in Cuzco was a large ugly sign scraped out of rock on a hillside carrying the legend "Viva El Peru," made by the military. The second was a dead dog in the middle of a narrow sharply cobbled street. I

---

[3] A good many contradictory spellings exist for these names and many others in the highlands because Quechua was not a written language at that time.

asked how long it would be before the sanitary department got around to removing it. Our guide replied, "Quite a while."

Cuzco's airstrip looks like the extension of a dilapidated boulevard, and is surrounded by public buildings—a hospital, a seminary, and the university. The town has a nice cohesive look, because the law is that all buildings must have tile roofs, so that it will seem uniform. Eucalyptus groves surround the city. The biggest local enterprise is a brewery, but a textile plant employs more people. There are three local radio stations, and one TV channel which operates part of the day.

The Cuzqueño Indians, with their staring flat eyes, go mostly barefoot, and wear saucer-shaped hats, often colored red. Men in white panama hats are usually *cholos*, not Indians. Most women seem to have children on their backs—or even a pig or small lamb—held in a kind of sack, which is tied around the body and bound with a long pin, sometimes made of silver. The skirts are often colorful. Indians here are not so clean as the jungle Indians. They are isolated, somewhat rude, and mortally suspicious of outsiders. If a Spanish-speaking visitor approaches a village, they assume that he is either a tax collector, a military man looking for boys to draft, or a recruiting officer for the *haciendas*, who will take their children into slavery. And indeed he may be one of these three.

"They hate us, and sooner or later they will swallow us up," a white man said. "It's the Indians or us." Most Indians have strong religious impulses; nominally Catholic, they still pursue pagan gods for the most part, and many worship their ancestors. In fact their spiritual life resembles that of Africa, where, as is well known, Bantu communities may be composed of two divisions, the living and the dead. Most Indians in the hills over Cuzco grow potatoes, and there is no cash crop. They drink no milk, and perhaps kill a llama for meat once a year or so. But a llama, which can cost $7, is a big investment. "The Indians here live on a lower level than the burros," a Peace Corps boy told me. Malnutrition, caused by lack of protein, is a major problem; primary schooling, free, is compulsory in theory, but many parents cannot afford to send their children to school, or the schools may be physically impossible to reach. Buses don't exist, and the parents need the child's labor at home. Those who do go to school learn a bit of Spanish and then, by the time they are adolescent, are apt to drift back to illiteracy again, speaking Quechua. The language barrier makes for difficulty. Roughly the situation would be the same if in New York City every school child spoke nothing but German, but was taught in English.

Eighty percent of students in the university are Communists—no wonder. Educated Cuzqueños veer strongly to the left; several prominent professors, civic leaders, and lawyers are active Communists.

Land is, of course, the most agonizing of all local problems—moreover, what the land will support. All this area is heavily overpopulated in relation to what it grows. Of course if modern methods of cultivation were in use the land could be made more productive, although the problem is complicated by climate, lack of water, and bad soil. The universal farming implement is still a primitive stick armed with a small blade, and having a crossbar foot-rest. There are varying systems of land tenure, which are much too complicated to describe in detail in this space, and three main categories of Indian worker. First are those who have no legal title to any land, but have a small plot on the owner's *hacienda* considered to be theirs, with a mud hut and a few animals. They get little, if any, cash wage, but the owner gives them free a glass of *chicha* twice a day, and perhaps a few kilos of squash two or three times a year. The treatment depends on the individual *hacendado*. Second, there is a large group of Indians who live in legally recognized "communities" broken into minifundia. The average individual holding is little more than an acre. There is no *hacendado*, but an overseer appointed by the Indians themselves. These are "fixed" on their tiny plots and cannot be ejected, unlike the peasants on the *haciendas*. The extreme fragmentation of land makes mechanical equipment impossible, and most community holders live on a subsistence level. Third, migrant labor. Indians who hire themselves out during the harvest have no homes, and live in temporary bivouacs made of corn shocks or cactus leaves. Their wages range *up* to the equivalent of eight cents a day.

USAID does a big job in Cuzco. This, as already mentioned, is head-quarters for our large and ambitious Southern Peru Regional Development Project. The AID domain covers the eighteen southern departments of Peru. roughly one-third of the country, mostly in the mountains and on the *selva*, their forested slopes. For some time it was hard to explain to the Peruvians just what the Alianza was, that it had no president, did not give orders, and was a concept going far beyond that of merely doling out American dollars to hemisphere republics. One large segment of USAID here is concerned with agriculture—cooperatives, irrigation, credit, and reform in general. Progress is slow. For one thing a great many Indians, accustomed for years to nothing but exploitation, stubbornly resist suggestions for improvement. Our agronomists could teach them quickly how to grow much better varieties of potatoes, but they won't listen. "Our kind tastes better," they insist. Second, AID operations are closely associated with the Forest Road, particularly in helping to build access roads. The United States contribution to this Belaúnde concept is expected to reach $40 million in all, and plans are complete for building at least a thousand miles of road on a schedule that extends to 1979. One morning we visited a school where army conscripts do their last three months of service learning a trade. We watched boys hard at work making rugs out of hides, learning to work with tin, laying bricks, and being taught how to plumb and solder. The boys looked cheerful. USAID is involved in this program by way of technical assistance and providing tools.

Peace Corps boys and girls are conspicuous near Cuzco, and we heard several of their stories. One bright American girl stationed at Chincheros, thirty kilometers from Cuzco, learned that a sergeant in the local Guardia Civil, a *cholo*, was shaking peasants down for 30 percent of their crops; he worked in collusion with a corrupt judge in Urubamba, the local county seat, who was his cousin. If the peasant didn't pay up, he would be arrested on fabricated charges, "tried," and pitched into jail. The Peace Corps volunteer, revolted by this state of affairs, went to the Guardia Civil, got nowhere, heard the stories of several Indians who had been victimized, visited the jail, and still got nowhere. At last she went all the way up to the prefect for the Cuzco district, an appointee of the federal government. He acted at once. The Guardia Civil officer was moved out of the district, the judge rebuked, and the prisoners released.

Not only do Peace Corps volunteers improve neighborhood relationships in Cuzco, but they try to bridge the human gap. Their own horizons are, I found, much expanded by this process. Involved is a quality of heart. These American boys and girls will, most people assured me, be much better American citizens when they return home, if only because they have learned something about foreign affairs on an intimate eye-to-eye level. They may even fruitfully influence United States foreign policy in the future. Not only is the Peace Corps doing something to South America, but South America is doing something to the Peace Corps.

*

Seventy miles north of Cuzco is the great ruin Machu Picchu, one of the greatest—and most mysterious—sights of the world. You get there by a phantasmagorical railway carved out of the rock along the valley of the Vilcanota, a sacred river to the Incas; flowing into the Urubamba, this joins other rivers which, mingling their fast waters, eventually form the Amazon. The "train" is not, I imagine, sacred to anybody; it consists of a double car, and was originally Japanese, used on the subways there. Seats are narrow, and legroom scant. This train, or car, proceeds by way of a terrifying series of switchbacks, chugging alternately forward and backward. When a breakdown occurs the driver climbs out, clips open a line of telephone wire, and inserts an instrument in the gap which, with luck, gives him communication to the nearest station. This happened to us once. Hilarity in the car was febrile, as we waited to see if the call would get through. Along the roadbed, up and down, down and up, are blue lupin, scarlet bells, and copses full of small yellow daisies. Indians gather at the stations; their babies wear hats. To every side is the profile of formidable mountains. At the end of the line the traveler, somewhat breathless, takes a bus on a road which seems to be almost diabolically set with precipitous zigzag turns, each sharper than the last. One bridge is so narrow that the story is that the bus has to be newly polished every other day; otherwise it wouldn't get through. As if to show the visitor that he is in the modern world after all, and may even survive, a neat new power station built by the Alianza may be seen near the entrance of this. Not far away is a spiderweb bridge supposed to be on the site made famous by *The Bridge of San Luis Rey.*

Machu Picchu, the "Lost City of the Incas," was discovered in 1911 by Hiram Bingham, a youthful Yale professor who later became a Connecticut senator and governor. It lies between two towering sugarloafs of mountain, one taller than the other, on the edge of the only abyss I have seen that truly deserves the appellation "abyss." It goes straight down clean, sharp, and menacing. The ruin, seen from the terrace of a comfortable inn, where the dry martinis are good, lies shelf on shelf melting into the shaggy blue-gray mountains. "The builder does not destroy the topography, but seems to caress it," are words President Belaúnde used to describe this majestic—but extremely neat—terraced stone ruin commanding imperiously the emerald valley.

Nobody knows the precise origin or purpose of Machu Picchu; it may have been a summer capital for Inca rulers, a fortress, or perhaps a retreat for youthful virgins dedicated to the sun. Out of 173 skeletons discovered, 150 are of women, an unusual proportion. Machu Picchu contains palaces, aqueducts, observation towers, dwellings, and no fewer than 100 stairways, containing 3,000 perfectly fitting stone steps. How men managed to build all this by hand is a mystery. This imperishable structure dates from the 11th century A.D., and is, in a literal sense, one of the wonders of the world. Here—to quote the president once more—"a work of art surges from the harmonic unity of architecture and the earth." But tramping through it is an onerous experience if the visitor is not acclimated to the altitude.

*

From Cuzco to the town of PUNO, a hundred miles south in the other direction, takes a hard day's travel by road. The road is like a frayed rope stretched taut. A balloon of our own dust followed us. The immense altitude crushes the lungs. Indians along the roads wear stovepipe hats; when you wave they do not wave back. One village had a long windowless wall intersected by narrow dark doors facing the road; I thought that this must be a stable, but it was a kind of dormitory for the workers. We saw small squalid huts decorated with green leaves or a basket, or made conspicuous by a pole carrying a torn red flag; the basket means that bread is available here, and the red flag says that there is something to drink, probably *chicha*. These shops sell small cones of ash as well, which are bought by the coca chewers.

We stopped briefly at a village with a charming old Spanish church on a pretty square with bells in the tower and a wooden balcony. Here the people walk on pebbles sharp as thumbtacks on their bare feet, and beggars wear thin multicolored rags. Men ran past us bent over double with shocks of corn, which made a peculiar swishing noise as they moved. The men do not walk, but *run*, in unison, to their chores, in spite of the altitude. Broken earthenware pots sit on the adobe roofs, and have a symbolic voodoo significance.

We saw two owls, one bicycle, a man threshing with a flail, and a bulldozer. Drunken Indians sat by the roadside; they are bad drunks. Women lean over to pick something up without bending their knees, a phenomenon which, at one spot on the road, we watched with interest while a blue heron soared suddenly across a waterhole with black-white hawks circling below. Further on we ran into a fiesta; Indians gathered into a big loose circle, and, almost expressionless, danced with gloomy determination. Two wore masks, which seemed to twitch, as drums and pipes made barbaric music. Two dancers were drunk, and fell down with a crash—no one paid attention.

We turned off the road near Pucará to visit a Peace Corps installation where the volunteers operate a handicraft cooperative. We almost crashed into the leader of the group—on a narrow gutted road. Two bulls precious to the community had escaped, and he was trying to track them down. This is all cattle country.

Puno, the capital of the *puna*, on Lake Titicaca, sits at 12,650 feet (I was busy inhaling oxygen, which we had brought with us), and has 20,000 people and a chilly atmosphere; the round-season temperature is about 45. Some streets are so savagely jagged, full of enormous holes, that even a jeep cannot pass. Cuzco has tiled roofs, but here roofs are made of tin; Cuzco is pure Quechua, but Puno is both Quechua and Aymará. Indeed Puno's main street, running from the Plaza de Armas to the docks, is supposed to be the dividing line between the Quechua and Aymará "nations." Puno lies not in a valley but on a high, barren plateau. Here there are seas of *ichu* grass; very little else will grow, and stock breeding is the foundation of the economy. Some of the nearby ranches are extensive, but 80 percent of all the people in the Puno area are totally landless. Only about 60,000 citizens out of 800,000 in the area have the right to vote, because of literacy restrictions.

Stanford, North Carolina, and Iowa State participate in development projects here, and AID is assisting the local university. We talked to the rector of this struggling but worthy institution, through the courtesy of Earl Smith, who was still our host. The rector, a forester by profession, told us that he had three faculties: veterinary science, agronomy, and economics, and two "schools"—livestock management and nursing. There are 372 students and 40 teachers. Students are co-governors at the university, and are powerful enough to break the career of any teacher. The president of the students' organization is a Communist, along with 30–40 percent of the student body.

Puno and JULIACA, a neighboring town lying at 12,551 feet, one of the highest communities in the world, have strong missionary elements. The Seventh-Day Adventists are active here, and so are the Maryknoll Fathers, who have worked out a technique for teaching in Quechua and Aymará by radio; this is one of the most fruitful centers of educational radio in the hemisphere. The Reverend Daniel McLellan, a Maryknoll missionary born in Denver, has done monumental work for the community, in particular by the creation of credit unions. These are functioning now all over Peru, and have become a lively business.

*

Puno stands on the western edge of Lake Titicaca, which, connecting Peru with Bolivia, is the highest navigable lake in the world, more than two miles above sea level (12,506 feet). Near it are brown shiny peaks rising two miles higher. The water is very deep, more than 1,400 feet, and the lake is big enough to take nine hours to cross by steamer. Floating islands, made of a local reed, are conspicuous, and canoes put together out of this same rush-like material ply back and forth, almost indistinguishable from the islands and bits of bank.

Travel across Lake Titicaca is a vivid experience. The service is maintained by a fleet run by the Southern Railway to the Bolivian port Guaqui 127 miles away. Our ship seemed not only to be a haven comparable for comfort to the *Queen Mary*, considering its surroundings, but it conveyed an enticing atmosphere composed equally of British spit-and-polish and Peruvian charm. The first boat operated by this line, which is now run in as routine a manner as the London Underground, was bought in England in the 1860's, hacked apart at Mollendo, a port near Arequipa, hauled across the Andes in pieces by burro, and then reassembled on the lake. The Titicaca waters are not merely icy cold, exposed as they are to the prodigious altitude, but treacherous. Pilots have to train for five years, and there are twenty changes of course in the overnight trip, plus others which may have to be made to avoid collisions with floating islands.

Peruvian Miscellany

Peruvian intellectuals still write anguished essays on such themes as "Does Latin America Exist?" and a peculiar small round yellow potato (not sweet), standard fare in Lima, is the best potato I ever ate. Peru has 150,000 TV sets, and its best-quality vicuña sells for $88 a yard. Some words derived from Quechua are *condor*, *coca*, *guano*, and *alpaca*.

Peru is the world's greatest supplier of bismuth, and the world's largest whaling stations lie in offshore waters. Twenty-pound trout may be found in Lake Titicaca by sticking your finger in the water, and a black marlin weighing 1,560 pounds was taken recently off Cabo Blanco, the world's record catch of this variety of fish.

Vicos, up in the Andes, is a model Indian village created largely by United States stimulus, and is an experiment that has been well worthwhile. The American hospital ship *Hope*, another worthy experiment, often visits Peruvian harbors. Peru has an odd variety of upland sheep, with four horns, and a thousand rabid dogs were caught in Lima in nine months during 1964. A Peruvian made the first solo flight across the Alps in 1910, and Peru was the first Latin American country (1961) to receive radio signals bounced off the moon.

*

So now we reach Bolivia, which is Peru exploded.

CHAPTER 21

Men and Events in Bolivia

Whatever the Bolivian armed forces want, the country wants.
—LOCAL ADAGE

THE president of Bolivia is a remarkably picturesque and successful air force general named René Barrientos Ortuño, full of spice, confidence, and dash. He carries with him a cops-and-robbers atmosphere, and has been called "a wild man of the air," but he has plenty of non-wild attributes. The president won his wings at Enid, Oklahoma, and trained at Randolph Field, Texas. Bolivia plus Texas makes an interesting combination, and Barrientos partakes of the nature of both these entities with their broad opportunities and sense of the frontier.

Bolivia is probably less well known than any other hemisphere republic except Paraguay, and it may be useful to post a word of foreground:

1. The *altiplano* near La Paz, the co-capital, lies at a staggering altitude, even higher than the Inca highlands in Peru. This is veritably a top of the world, and it seems to be the end of the world as well. La Paz itself, the highest capital on the globe, has an airport situated at 13,358 feet, more than two and a half miles above sea level. Its vicinity resembles a moon crater—remote, unreal, and almost magically isolated.

2. Bolivia is the most melodramatic country on the continent. An old wisecrack is that this is the nation where almost anything can happen and everything does.

3. It is also miserably, desperately poor, with an average per capita income around $100 a year, one of the lowest in the world. A large percentage of the population lives at a starvation level.

4. Like Paraguay, it is landlocked. Chile took its Pacific seacoast in 1883, which is still a sore point with the Bolivians.

389

5. Much of it looks like an extension of Peru, and, even more than in Peru, the population is preponderantly Indian—as much as 70 percent—which helps give it its special quality of aridity, stillness, strangeness. But it is an extremely agreeable country as well.

6. Politics are explosive, and violence—sometimes of the most bizarre variety—is frequent. A major struggle for power has been that between the government and labor forces in the mines, which maintain their own armed militia.

7. The economy depends on tin.

General Barrientos, about forty-five, has plenty of bravado as well as color. Several years ago, having risen fast to become chief of the Bolivian air force, he faced an ugly scandal when three recruits were killed in a parachute drop near La Paz. The opposition charged that the reason was inferior equipment—the chutes were defective, and would not open. Barrientos went straight to the air force barracks, and asked a startled newspaperman to pick out any chute from the stack the others had come from; he put it on, ordered an officer to fly him over the La Paz airport, and bailed out. (He had only parachuted once before, he told me.)

He has a fresh, engaging quality, and is something of a scamp—or perhaps just a wily and effective politician. He conducts politics with as much drama as flying, and is equally daring at both. At the time I visited Bolivia he faced a critical decision—whether or not to run for president in the next elections. He was already the "provisional" president of the country, but, leading an army–air force junta, he had reached this post by means of a coup d'état. Now he wanted to constitutionalize himself, that is, be formally elected to the presidency in an ostensibly democratic manner, by popular vote. He was not sure, however, of the support he could muster. Announcement came suddenly that he had decided *not* to run. At once "revolutionary disturbances" erupted in various key spots throughout the country. Airports were closed, and barricades went up along the roads. Then it became dramatically known that these demonstrations were not against Barrientos, as had been assumed, but, on the contrary, were *for* him—staged to persuade him to reconsider his decision and be a presidential candidate after all! Nobody seemed to express much surprise or objection when, a little later, the news leaked out that agents of Barrientos himself had just "happened" to be visiting the places where the "disturbances" took place at exactly the time they occurred, and presumably set them off.

Barrientos was not, as a matter of fact, formally inaugurated as president of Bolivia until August, 1966, a year and a half after this playful episode. The fabulous vicissitudes in between are too complicated to go into in this space. For a period General Alfredo Ovando Candia, the commander in chief of the armed forces, a master manipulator, a veritable Richelieu, with whom Barrientos has an exceedingly complex relationship, was co-president. The country had two chief executives. Ovando had been co-president once before—for an hour!

General Barrientos loves to fly and has his own old DC-3 which he uses constantly, piloting it himself. New military planes sometimes arrive in Bolivia and he checks these out as a hobby; he has set records in several. Sometimes he schedules cabinet meetings for 5 A.M., so he can use the rest of the morning for inspection trips by air. Back in 1952, when he was a youthful air force lieutenant, he played an interesting minor role in the celebrated revolution of that year—soon to be described—the revolution which is still the alpha and omega of political life in the country. He flew to Cocha-bamba, the provincial town which was his home, and raised several fellow officers to the side of the rebels. Then it was he who was chosen to dart down to the Argentine by air and fetch Víctor Paz Estenssoro, the exiled revolu-tionary leader, and bring him triumphantly back to the country to become president. A truce was supposed to be in force when, with Señor Paz as his passenger, the daring young lieutenant reached the capital, but his plane was fired on and only his skill as a pilot saved the two men from being shot down.

The president says that he has had four miraculous escapes from disasters in the air. Once he crash-landed a non-amphibian plane in a river. He told me with a careful grin, "I do not think I am going to die easily."

There have been eight attempts to assassinate Barrientos, and he has survived them all. Several of these were genuine enough, but rumors that two may have been somewhat spurious (Bolivians are a suspicious people) will not die down. In 1964 a gunman approached him and, at close range, shot at his chest; the bullet bounced off his United States pilot wings, which he always wears. Bits of metal from these were embedded in his skin, and he had to go to Panama for medical treatment—American authorities flew him there. This incident occurred at a time when Paz Estenssoro, head of the MNR or National Revolutionary Movement, the dominant political force in the country, had expressed unwillingness to accept Barrientos as a running mate for the presidency. He was fed up with Barrientos, who had intrigued against him. But the shooting turned Barrientos into a martyred hero, and Paz could not resist the newly mounting pressure to accept him. No assailant was ever caught—or even named. In time Barrientos brutally deposed Paz by means of a *coup de main*, and succeeded him as president.

Some months after this *attentat* another gunman opened fire on Barri-entos's automobile on a lonely road and the general was slightly wounded.

Again he became a hero to the populace and once more this pointedly served his political convenience. Arrests were made in this case, but nobody was ever tried or convicted. So a certain amount of mystery still attends both these affairs.

Barrientos was born on May 30, 1919, in a small town near Cochabamba. His father was of Spanish descent, his mother an Indian. He learned to speak Quechua before Spanish, loves it, and is a terrific orator in this Indian tongue, much more effective than in Spanish. One of his principal sources of power has been his close association with the poverty-blanched, coca-chewing Indians living their frigid and exiguous existence up in the hills. He has always played on the *campesino* side.

Indeed this is no son of the rich, no oligarch. He was for many years a conspicuous figure in leftish revolutionary circles. He still thinks of himself as a man of the moderate left. His childhood was hard. His father died, and he lived in a Franciscan orphanage from seven to twelve. His first thought was to become a priest. Managing to reach La Paz he worked his way through high school and entered the military academy. He had a part-time job as a night watchman, and he sometimes passes today buildings where he worked, surveying them with appropriate emotion. Barrientos joined the MNR, the Paz revolutionary party, when he was about eighteen. The academy expelled him for revolutionary activity, and he spent three months as a fugitive out on the *altiplano*, hidden by friendly peasants. He returned to La Paz, organized a so-called Congress of Campesinos, and was arrested and jailed three times—for most of 1946, six months in 1949, and two months in 1950. During one of these periods in prison he was savagely beaten, so much so that, he told me, he almost lost the use of a leg.

The revolutionary forces won the presidency in 1952, and Barrientos, having taken up aviation, was sent to the United States for training. His entrance into Bolivian politics on a serious level came on his return.

The president is of medium height, good-looking, muscular, with intensely black hair cut in a longish crew cut—a porcupine cut. He has large bright eyes and a florid skin. His English is excellent, his sense of humor lively, and his spirit eager. His wife is an extraordinarily pretty girl from Cochabamba, and they have five children. The general's vitality is inexhaustible. Campaigning through the countryside he makes eight, ten, twelve speeches a day, piloting his own plane between encampments, and then likes nothing better than to gather friends around him and dance most of the night. He knows hundreds of peasants all over the country by face and name.

We met President Barrientos twice; each time the circumstances were intriguing. When we arrived in La Paz the altitude troubled me even more than it had in Cuzco and Puno. I turned as blue as ink. I thought that an hour or two of rest might help, but, before we could even unpack, there came a complicated summons apparently giving us appointments practically at once with both the American ambassador and the president. The ambassador, Douglas Henderson, a veteran career officer, is, incidentally, one of the two or three best ambassadors we have in all Latin America, and I thought he ran the best embassy we visited.

Still blue in the face, we set out by taxi for the palace, not having the faintest idea where it was in relation to the hotel, and, arriving there, laboriously climbed what seemed to me to be just about the highest and steepest staircase I had ever seen. Puffing, gasping, I managed somehow to reach the top. Then before I could catch even the slightest breath we were seized and hurled peremptorily through a large doorway—where Barrientos was having a conference with Mr. Henderson and members of his cabinet!

So we became part of a cabinet meeting, the first time this has ever happened to me. Six or seven officers in air force and army uniforms sat around a large table. Hovering close was the celebrated General Ovando, who looked the perfect picture of a shadowy, somewhat enigmatic *éminence grise*. At once an interchange took place between Barrientos and the canny Ovando. Still struggling for breath, I mentioned that the last time I had been in Bolivia the country was a kind of company town in the hands of the tin merchants, and asked if this was still the case. General Ovando replied amiably, "No, it is now a country in the hands of the tin unions." Barrientos quickly interceded with a laugh, saying, "No, not in the hands of the unions, but we do have difficulty with troublemakers in the unions." General Ovando was then equally quick to interject, saying the unctuous words, "We are not against unions, there should be unions, but we are against having the unions used for political purposes and making trouble for everybody by means of trickery."

I was invited to ask other questions, and, with the cabinet ministers standing by with amused but slightly bewildered curiosity, I could think of nothing but to inquire of the president what he thought of the Forest Road project of President Belaúnde, his counterpart in Peru; he jumped up with excitement and produced from another table the massive book Belaúnde had shown us in Peru and which had been prepared in New York, outlining specific engineering plans for the project in vast technical detail. Patting it with a smile, Barrientos said, "This book is my bible." Presently he added that the real value of the road would be that the *people* will have built it themselves. A road merely given to a community means nothing, he said, but if the local citizenry builds it with their own hands, against almost insurmountable obstacles, it can mean a lot. "If the *campesinos* build it they will not allow it to fall to pieces, because it is theirs and they *care*."

This broke the ice and—the cabinet still attentive—we approached other topics. Barrientos said that Communism in Bolivia was not, to his mind, a serious problem. The party was legal, but many of its members were not hard-line at all, but "Marxist thinkers." That Communism existed in Bolivia was, he continued, perfectly understandable; it grew naturally out of the misery under which people lived. "They are Communists because of their stomachs, not their heads." Land reform was important, the president went on, but the actual *division* of property was not the most important thing about it, because the mere giving of land to peasants meant little if they did not have machinery, credit, access roads, seed, fertilizer, and cooperatives. "The mere division of land has become old-fashioned." Then the general began to talk about the army, which, he insisted, was not a political force in itself, but protected and served "all" the people. After half an hour I asked a final question—what had started him on his career? Enigmatically he pointed to two large portraits of military officers at each end of the room. He did not explain, and General Ovando took us courteously—but still with a faintly ominous air—to the door.

A day or two later we were asked to lunch at the president's villa. A modest California-style bungalow in a residential community, it lies a thousand feet or so below the palace in the center of the town. La Paz is built in tiers. There was no pomp or show. I never saw a photograph of Barrientos on public display in La Paz. A boy with a hose watered the road to keep the dust down. It happened to be Señora Barrientos's birthday, and the house was stacked with flowers, most of them gladioli of impressive dimensions. We had lunch out in the garden. Men and women were, as is often the case at official lunches in South America, segregated at different tables. Lunch started with champagne, and was copious. I had never before tasted *chirimoyas*—custard apples.

Several cabinet ministers were present, and the general, wearing a simple blue air force uniform, introduced them jovially as "my minister of money" and "my minister of teeth"—in this latter case the minister of health, who happens to be a dentist. All are youngish men who, clearly, regarded an invitation to lunch with the president as a serious matter, and behaved accordingly. Members of the junta, I learned, take the salary or income that they had in nongovernment life. Barrientos is, for instance, paid what his rank as a three-star general calls for, a modest sum. All ministers play football, but I did not find out whether this was obligatory or not. I was much impressed by the quality of these men, particularly of the minister of planning, and again by the president himself. He talked about his own career, his love for flying, the inordinate complexities of the political situation, and his dreams for the future. His last words, defending the military nature of the government, were, "We have offered the politicians everything. They will not respond, and we have a long, hard way still to go." But Barrientos is accused by many oppositionists of having "betrayed" the MNR and the great 1952 revolution.

Heritage

My curiosity remained high about the two portraits in the cabinet room in the palace which the president had pointed to when we saw him there. A friend enlightened me. Both are of former presidents of Bolivia who gained power by revolution, who were both youthful military men and idealists in terms of their own reckoning, who stood against feudal privilege and foreign exploitation, and who were both probably a little crazy and met violent deaths.

The first was Germán Busch, president from 1937 to 1939. Had he lived he might have been one of the most interesting men of the Americas. His father was a German doctor, his mother an Indian. Born out in the jungle, with an uncanny instinct for jungle sights and sounds, he was very athletic and good-looking—except for some bright gold teeth—with glittering blue eyes. He was neurotic, ambitious, brutal, and naïve; he had never seen a city until, late in boyhood, he came to Santa Cruz, and he thought that La Paz was the greatest metropolis in the world. He drank like a fish.

Busch carved out a political life for himself after the Chaco War against Paraguay, in which he was a hero, rising to be president. Early in his term he suddenly abolished congress and set up the first avowedly totalitarian dictatorship in the modern style in the Americas. His motto was Bolivia for the Bolivians. He hated foreigners. His predecessor had confiscated the $17 million Standard Oil investment in the country, which pleased him, and he continued to harry the oil interests. Busch hated the big tin merchants as well and was, all in all, a people's man. He gave the country its first labor code, encouraged unionization of the tin miners, and had both Marxist and Nazi advisers.

Lieutenant Colonel Busch shot himself in August 1939, after a night of drinking, apparently as a result of hysterical disillusion at the corruption he found on every side. A good many people still think that he was murdered, but the circumstances of his death almost surely rule this out.

The second portrait showed Major Gualberto Villarroel (1943–1946), another radical young military president. He rose to power after the Catavi massacre (1942) on the *altiplano*, when government troops indiscriminately shot down striking miners with their wives and children. He was one of the early leaders of MNR, the revolutionary party, and Dr. Paz Estenssoro, its chief in later years, served as his minister of finance. He was an extremely unstable man, who was strongly under Peronist influence for a time. Seriously he set out to do something in Bolivia for the Indians and *cholos*, half castes, on the bleak, forbidding hills. Rightist elements in the army and a mob at large then made a *Putsch* against Villarroel. He was shot down in the palace—the same palace where Barrientos works today—and pitched out of a window. Then, when he was still alive, he was hanged on a lamppost on the Plaza Murillo, which the palace faces. This lamppost is known to almost every Bolivian today. It has been converted into a shrine, and is attended day and night by a detail of the presidential guard.

These, then, are the two men whose influence set René Barrientos off on his career. The President is not an easy person to sum up. An American in La Paz said of Barrientos, "Perhaps not a big man in the world sense, but a wonderfully nice guy. He's a patriot, not a crook. He's pulling this country out of a hole, and his ideology doesn't matter."

CHAPTER 22

Bolivian Baedeker

It is harmful to our own country and devastatingly hurtful throughout Latin America for us carelessly or maliciously to label as "communist" any internal efforts to achieve changes for the benefit of the mass of the people. . . . We should not make the mistake of issuing wholesale, unintelligent charges that provide a verbal smoke screen for the Communists. . . . We should not confuse each move toward socialization with Marxism, land reform with Communism, or even anti-yankeeism with pro-sovietism.
— MILTON S. EISENHOWER

If Bolivia ever has a Communist revolution it will make China look like Vassar.
— ANONYMOUS

WHAT I have indicated about Bolivian characteristics needs extension. The country is the fifth largest in South America in area, about twice the size of France. One cliché is that if it did not exist it would be necessary to invent it because it fulfills a historical necessity as a buffer state keeping Peru, Chile, Brazil, and Argentina from having a common frontier. It has had four capitals in its history—Sucre, Cochabamba, Oruro, and La Paz—and, like the Union of South Africa, has two now. La Paz is the de facto capital but the official capital is still the old colonial city Sucre, with its Spanish veneer, which houses the Supreme Court. The executive branch of the government and the legislature sit in La Paz.

Probably—to go into deplorable superlatives—Bolivia is the most politically unstable nation in the world. One reckoning gives it 175 "revolutions" since independence in the 1820's; anoter says 179 "changes of government" have taken place in 126 years, better by a good deal than one a year.

397

Comparatively few visitors to Bolivia go anywhere except La Paz, and the altitude inevitably makes a dominant impression. But in fact the *altiplano*, with its prodigious heights, covers only a third of the country. Two-thirds of the total population live on this lofty intermontane plateau, however. Steady brutal winds sweep the land almost bare, and even the llamas and alpacas look skinny and forlorn. The altitude takes a savage toll of the Indians, who are the only people capable of surviving the rigors of the habitat at all; life expectancy on the *altiplano* is thirty-two years, and women of twenty-five, their faces lined and ravaged, look seventy. A friend told me, driving near La Paz, "You can live here three months without ever seeing a person smile."

Corn is one crop; potatoes another. There are no fewer than 112 different varieties of potato, all cultivated by scratching a few inches of barren soil with wooden tools. The so-called "Irish" potato had its origin here. People eat and drink potatoes. They are variously roasted, stewed, ground to powder, or made into a mash, fermented, and distilled.

Bolivia has two large geographical divisions aside from the *altiplano*—the eastward *yungas* or mountain slopes, and, farther east, the *llanos* or lowlands, which are still a true frontier, with lonely swamp and jungle partly unexplored. This is an Indian country par excellence, and Indians comprise at least 70 percent of the total population; they are divided mostly into two great tribes whom we have already met in Peru, the Quechua and Aymará. The former, of Inca descent, conquered the Aymarás in pre-Colombian days, but the latter, living mostly on the *altiplano*, are supposed to be tougher now. "You can't dent an Aymará with an iron pipe," I heard it said. Another sardonic remark was, "Germ warfare would not work here." But, as a matter of fact, Bolivian Indians are extremely susceptible to disease, particularly tuberculosis, when they come down from the mountains; in some parts of the country two-thirds of the children die before the age of two.

In general, both Quechuas and Aymarás are among the most obdurate, inert, and unassimilable people in the world. At least a third of the total population of Bolivia does not even speak Spanish. The Indians scrape a miserable pittance out of crusty soil, live totally outside a money economy (i.e., they haven't any money), drink an explosive local spirit made of fermented corn, like *chicha* in Peru, and chew coca interminably—sometimes mixed with ashes—to numb their misery.

Bolivia has very little manufacturing industry, and has to import more than half the food it consumes. This is, in fact, a beggar nation—but how violently the proud, patriotic Bolivians will hate this being said! One modernizing factor is the movement of peasants into the towns: some 400,000 Indians have descended from the hills in the past few years. Another is the army. Theoretically every conscript has a three months' period of vocational training after his military service, in a Civic Action program like that in Peru, but this is continually frustrated because of lack of money. Army privates have to be fed on 16 cents a day. They get only two meals, bread and coffee in the morning, a bowl of soup in the afternoon. But when a boy finishes his army training and, in consequence, receives his identity card which he will hold throughout life, this confirms his citizenship and, in a phrase with grim connotations, he "becomes a human being."

*

Bolivian history goes far back into the foam of time. The country was part of the Inca empire, and Pizarro sent his captains here in the 1530's, seeking gold. What they discovered was not gold, but silver. Potosí, south of La Paz, had the richest silver deposits ever known, and presently, as the silver seekers swarmed over what was called its "rich hill," it became the biggest city in South America. The *conquistador* Pedro de Anzúrez founded a capital at La Plata, which was later successively renamed Charcas, Chuquisaca, and finally Sucre, which it is today. Bolivia became known as the Audiencia of Charcas, or Upper Peru, under the Peruvian viceroyalty, and was enormous, comprising parts of what are now Argentina, Brazil, Chile, Uruguay, and Paraguay. Independence came in 1825, following the campaigns of the youthful General Sucre, for whom the capital was named, and the country was called "República Bolívar," in honor of the Liberator. Later this was shortened to Bolivia.

History during the nineteenth century was fantastically convulsive. One improbable dictator, by name Mariano Melgarejo, known as the "Scourge of God," a *cholo* who had touches of megalomania and was a wholesale murderer as well, may live in footnotes to history because he publicly insulted the British minister to Bolivia of the day, tore off his clothes, sat him naked on a donkey, and drove him out of town. News of this unfortunate episode eventually reached Queen Victoria and, in consequence, she ordered Bolivia to be erased from all official British maps. Those were the good old days.

In 1932–35 came the Chaco War with Paraguay, a root source of much subsequent Bolivian development. Not only did the war bleed both countries dry economically and otherwise; it caused profound political—even spiritual—outrage in Bolivia, the loser. It made men seek new values. The old ruling class became discredited. There developed a fierce discontent with "the power of the mine owners and the archaic political system dominating the country."[1] Moreover, defeat led to vehement xenophobia. This was one reason why Standard Oil of New Jersey was expropriated in 1937, the first such expropriation in the history of South America. Standard was accused of impeding the Bolivian war effort. President Roosevelt took the shock calmly, and did not send in the marines. Much later Standard obtained a settlement.

More important were direct political developments. In revolt against decades of fantastically unstable, corrupt, and inefficient government, the citizenry, crushed and inert as most of it was, began to stir. Sheer revulsion at what went on gave impetus to a revolutionary movement, led by bitterly disillusioned young army officers who allied themselves with a group of left-wing intellectuals, mostly exiles. Another factor was that pronounced Nazi elements existed in Bolivia at this time. German influence was probably more conspicuous here than in any South American republic except Chile and Ecuador. The Germans controlled LAB, the local airline, which had a good deal of strategic importance,[2] and—something that not one reader in a million will know or remember—one of the German officers training the Bolivian army was none other than Captain Ernst Roehm, who later became Hitler's closest friend and leader of the SS in Germany, and whom Hitler killed.

The MNR (Movimiento Nacionalista Revolucionario), which ruled Bolivia for twelve years from 1952 to 1964, was founded in 1941. Its three leaders were Paz Estenssoro, a lawyer and intellectual of Indian blood, a *cholo* of great quality named Hernán Siles Zuazo, and Juan Lechín, the slick, resourceful boss of the miners, of whom more later. The MNR was a witches' pot at the beginning. It included Peronist, pro-Nazi, democratic, pro-ally, Communist, Fascist, anti-Semitic, Trotskyist, and other weirdly varied elements.[3] It drew on RADEPA, a secret society representing the disaffected and reformist military, and (for a time) on a left-wing agglutination known as PIR, led by a remarkable man José Antonio Arze. Basically it was nationalist, bourgeois, anti-plutocratic, and, as I heard it sardonically put, "against starvation."

[1] From an American fact sheet published in La Paz.

[2] Allen W. Dulles, who many years later became head of the CIA, was the principal United States negotiator in arrangements with the Bolivian government whereby LAB was reorganized and the Germans squeezed out.

[3] Cf. *The Bolivian National Revolution*, by Robert J. Alexander, also Hubert Herring, *op. cit.*

The MNR grew even while most of its guiding spirits were in exile. In 1951 came elections the results of which were contested. Seemingly Paz and the MNR won hands down, but conservative elements in the army prevented Paz from assuming power. A military junta ruled the country for a year; then came the revolution of April 9, 1952, made by the MNR—the landmark from which all subsequent Bolivian history extends. Paz Estenssoro, recalled from exile (in Barrientos's plane), became president of an MNR government, and the earth shook. This set out to be a *real* revolution, and Bolivia has never been the same since.

Víctor Paz Estenssoro, a small slight man wearing spectacles and with a face curiously oblong in shape, had a middle-class background and was a professor of economics as well as a lawyer. In the early days his enemies, of whom there were plenty, denounced him as both a Nazi and a Communist. He was neither. Born in 1907 in a small town in the remote southeast of Bolivia, he studied at the University of San Andrés in La Paz. During the Chaco War against Paraguay he was decorated for bravery, and rose to the rank of captain. He studied in Germany for a period, and was once arrested on the charge of being a German agent. Found innocent, he was released.

The MNR–Paz revolution in 1952 sought not merely to end abuses in the country but to effect, if possible, a genuine transformation of society. It set itself against various outrages—such as that the big landowners could sell their peons—like livestock—as part of their property. It was the nearest to being a true revolution of any in Latin America in the past half century, excepting those in Mexico and Cuba, and aimed at a drastic change in economic as well as political power. Paz, this seemingly frail man, struck equally against agrarian feudalism and the domination of the country by the tin merchants who, although mostly absentees, had utterly controlled local politics. He instituted universal suffrage; he made a substantial land reform; he nationalized the railways and, above all, the mines.

What is most important, Paz put force behind his nationalization of the mines. As a counterpoise to the army he created a workers' militia, and gave the miners arms. The unions were given a veto over management decisions. One curiosity is that, during this period, Paz Estenssoro received substantial financial support from the Eisenhower administration in Washington, largely because the State Department thought that, if he fell, the alternative was bound to be chaos or, worse, Communism. It took Washington about three months to get around to recognizing him, but then it backed him steadily to the end. It had taken the United States much longer to get around to recognizing Villarroel because we thought that he was a Peronist, hence pro-Nazi.

Paz Estenssoro had plenty of defects. He was too cold, people said, too calculating. He ruled by division. He was fanatically ambitious. He thought that nobody but himself could run the country. There was a certain amount of terror by the police in the style of totalitarian regimes in Europe. I had drinks with a man who had spent seven years in a concentration camp; his back had been broken under torture, and his brother had been blinded. Several opponents of the administration mysteriously disappeared. One distinguished political leader of today—whom I also met and talked to—was picked up by the police one morning, and thrown into an unlit, unheated cell which he shared with sixty others for a period. The prisoners were given no food and, if food was brought in from outside, the jailers fouled it.

Abrasive difficulties presently came to Paz Estenssoro. His first term lasted from 1952 to 1956 and, in the usual South American manner, the constitution forbade him to succeed himself. The man closest to him at this time was Hernán Siles Zuazo, whose father had been a president of the republic. Playing a leapfrog game, Paz arranged for Siles to succeed him from 1956 to 1960; Paz himself spent this period as ambassador to London. Then, returning to Bolivia, he took over from Siles in turn and became president again from 1960 to 1964. He and Siles made a team. Many in Bolivia think that Siles, an able man, deserves more credit for the early program and success of the revolution than Paz himself. He led the actual fighting in 1952, which was savage, and once, while he was president, went on a hunger strike to end a labor dispute.

Troubles on the economic side became almost insuperable during the twelve years the MNR held power. The revolution failed to achieve its full aims. One fault was corruption. The railways went to pieces under government rule, and the former British owners had to be called back—not as owners, however, but as managers under contract. The land reform, which had begun well, with property distributed to 150,000 Indian families, slowed down. Most importantly there came trouble in the mines. Labor relations were chaotic, and production slipped. Payrolls were swollen, and featherbedding rife. The militia took hostages (a group of Americans on one occasion) and became a law unto itself. There were riots, strikes, outrages.

I am trying to compress here a story of fabulous complexity. Paz began to lose grip, and the triumvirate—Paz, Siles, and Lechín—broke up. So far the MNR had ruled virtually without any interference by the army, but now the military became restive. The revolution was, in a word, becoming de-revolutionized. Time came for the 1964 elections. Determined to stay in power alone, Paz Estenssoro rigged the constitution so that, against all precedent, he could succeed himself, which he proceeded to do. He won, but the victory was empty, since the opposition boycotted the elections. Then in October, 1964, soon after he began his new term, the climax came. Paz had been obliged to accept General Barrientos as his vice president under pressure from the regular armed forces; they resented the growing power of the militia, which had become, in effect, the Paz private army. The two men had been close for years, but now Barrientos sulked and plotted. Confused internecine struggles for power led to rioting and bloodshed. The country came near exploding. Then Barrientos organized a *Putsch* to throw Paz out, and, on November 4, 1964, he took over the presidency as head of a "provisional" military junta.

The enigmatic General Ovando, who seemingly took a position against Barrientos for a time, but who was patriot enough not to want a civil war, told Paz Estenssoro that he was being flown into exile. Paz protested violently. Ovando paid no attention, saying merely, "I am going to take you to the cemetery or the airport, whichever you prefer." Ever since Paz has lived in Lima.

*

Theoretically at least the Barrientos government is not a dictatorship, and political activity, although subdued, continues. The MNR, no longer the party that it was, is split. The Barrientos wing is now called the Bolivian Revolutionary Front, and is composed of elements like the Popular Christians, who organized the general's campaign in the countryside, and the Social Democrats. One interesting man is Señor Sanjinés, a West Point graduate who has held a number of public posts and who may be a consequential figure in the future.

Outside the Barrientos coalition are the Bolivian Socialist Falange (FSB), a moderate right center group, and the Authentic Revolutionary Party (PRA), slightly left of center. The extreme left, headed by Juan Lechín, since his break with Paz, is now called PRIN, the Partido Revolucionario de Izquierda Nacionalista. The Communists have several parties, and a splinter Nazi party, called the Organización Nacional Socialista Americana (ONSA), still exists. Its members are mostly Bolivians of German descent, and it has no serious influence. The respectable right has disappeared as a parliamentary force, as it has in several South American countries, like Venezuela. A friend in La Paz told me, "To destroy a person here just say that he's on the right."

Exactly what Barrientos himself stands for is not easy to determine. A man of action, he is not much given to abstract thought. His enemies say that he has destroyed the revolution, but this is not quite the case. He did destroy Paz, but Bolivia will never revert to the days of feudal rule by the tin merchants and landed gentry.

Tin

Bolivia depends on tin even more than Chile does on copper. Other minerals are important too, but tin is king, supplying 80 percent of the country's budget and more than two-thirds of its export earnings. Bolivia's twenty thousand tin miners produce around 25 percent of the total world supply of tin.

For many years Bolivian tin was controlled by three huge companies, and these in turn dominated the entire nation: (1) The Hochschild interests, which produced roughly a quarter of its yield of tin. Mauricio Hochschild was a German Jew of Argentine nationality, whose company had large ramifications, particularly in Chile. (2) The Compagnie Aramayo des Mines en Bolivie, a Swiss corporation owned by the Aramayo family, which was Bolivian, but with strong British interests. (3) The Patiño organization which accounted for almost half of production, and was headed by Simón I. Patiño, an almost mythical character who amassed a fortune estimated at $500 million in the 1920's, and was supposed to have been the seventh-richest man alive.

Patiño, the foremost tin merchant in the world, was three-quarters Indian; nobody knows his exact origins. As a youth he ran mule and llama trains up into the hills, and, by accident, became the owner of a small tin property. Before long Patiño had, at Catavi, the largest tin deposits on earth. Then, as the ubiquitous tin can spread over the world, his wealth increased. He knew that Bolivian tin was of poorer quality than that in Malaya, and that local production and freight costs were too high because Bolivia was so inaccessible to world markets. So he capitalized his companies abroad, bought into the Liverpool tin smelters, and then invested heavily in the properties of his chief competitors, the producers of Malaya. So eventually he became the tin king of the world.[4]

Patiño left Bolivia in 1922. Only rarely did he return to his native land—he did not visit it once during a period of nineteen years—but he became Bolivian minister to Spain and then France, which served his interests, to

[4] Paraphrased from *Inside Latin America.*

put it mildly, by giving him diplomatic immunity and a tax-free status. According to one authority his annual income was greater than the national budget. There is no record of his having ever contributed anything substantial to the country whose mineral resources rewarded him so stupendously.

The miners who produced unprecedented fortunes for the Patiños, the Aramayos, the Hochschilds, often came close to starving. Next to the serfs of the Brazilian northeast, they were the poorest community in the western world. There was little social legislation to protect them—in those days—and tuberculosis, silicosis, and other diseases ravaged them. Life expectancy for a boy in the mines was thirty. The miners were "trapped in the 16th century." They had to work by literally "tearing the metal from the walls of the deep caverns with their fingers."[5]

Came the great 1952 revolution. Paz Estenssoro expropriated the three companies forthwith, and nationalized the mining industry. A government organization, Corporación Minera de Bolivia, known universally as COMIBOL, was set up to run the mines, including tin. Paz gave the tin workers arms, and, as we have seen, organized them into a militia in order to protect the revolution. The unions, rising in power, became a state within a state—underground in the literal as well as figurative sense. But nationalization did not work out as the MNR had hoped. It never achieved the ends envisioned. There were several adverse factors, including a slump in the world price of tin. As always, countries with one-crop economies are at the mercy of forces beyond their control. The mines became almost totally disorganized, and Communist influence grew steeply. Mismanagement in COMIBOL was scandalous. Another factor was that the mines were, in plain fact, wearing out. Equipment was antiquated, and the tin became more and more difficult to reach. The top—the cream—was gone.

As a result the mines showed a 40 percent decrease in yield over a period of ten years, although the working force rose from 18,000 to 26,000 miners. Administration became insufferably bad, with politics intermixed with almost every decision, and COMIBOL lost money at an alarming rate.

Reform began in 1961 with the creation of what is known locally as "Operation Triangle," a $50 million rehabilitation project financed by the United States, West Germany, and the Inter-American Development Bank, which once again proved itself to be as useful an institution as any in the Americas. But the central issue remained—who was to control the mines, the government or the unions. After a series of bloody strikes and other

[5] Washington *Post*, November 22, 1964.

disorders Barrientos cracked down on the miners' militia in 1965. He exiled Lechín and Siles, restored order of a sort, and sharply cut down on the number of mine workers, operating under a state of siege.

Most wiseacres in La Paz had said that he would never dare do this, partly because he still considered himself to be a people's man and the inheritor of the MNR tradition, partly because he could not risk a flat show of force vis-à-vis the unions. But he took the chance, and one result is that the mines showed a $2 million profit last year, their first since 1953. If necessary, he will use the army to run the mines.

Portrait of a Labor Leader

Juan Lechín Oquendo is a tall, slim, silver-haired man with a silver mustache, low-voiced, grave in manner, and deliberate in speech. We met in the headquarters of the miners' union in La Paz; the building was unheated, and the weather chilly; Lechín wore an overcoat. Our talk took place before Barrientos exiled him. He has been vice president of the republic (under Paz during one term), a senator, president of the senate, minister of mines, and ambassador to Italy. What counted, though, was his position in the labor movement. As executive secretary of the Bolivian Labor Federation he dominated the miners and their unions for many years.

Lechín is, or was, a national hero for quite another reason—as a football star in his youth. He still walks with the grace and power of a jaguar. Born in 1915 in a remote village, he was the son of a Lebanese trader; his mother was Indian. He went to school in Oruro, an important mining town, and then to the American Institute, which is supported by missionaries, in La Paz. At sixteen he left school because of poverty, and went into the mines near his birthplace, working as a driller. He has recorded that the temperature in the pits was 120 degrees while he worked his shift, but below freezing at night in the stone hut where he slept. Lechín rose fast and, while still in his teens, became a union organizer, taking time out for football. He became head of the local miners' syndicate in 1944 at twenty-nine, and was made secretary of the national federation eight years later, thus coming into close contact with the MNR.

Whereas Paz and Siles lived mostly in exile in the early days, Lechín stuck it out in Bolivia, and was sent to jail several times. His relations with Paz were correct for a long period, and he remained loyal to him until 1960, although he had become bitterly disillusioned. Paz was magnificent in the early days, he told us. He recounted some of the achievements of the revolution. Before 1952, 70 percent of citizens who would normally have been eligible were not permitted to vote; the total vote in one presidential race was 45,000—in a country of 3½ million. Paz vastly widened the electorate, and brought schools—at least in theory—to the Indian illiterates. But, because of his greed for power, he betrayed the revolution later, repudiated his glowing vision of social reform, and deprived the country of what it needed most, liberty. The MNR became a shadow. Lechín continued to talk about the 1952 revolution, which he helped to make, and which still—obviously—haunts his dreams. It was not only a genuine revolution, he told us, but "pure." There was nothing vengeful about it. It was not directed against private property. There was no Communist influence whatever at that time. It was not confiscatory. It was a genuine people's movement, nationalist in essence, which sought to get rid of the exploiters, bring land and education to the people, and end discrimination against the Indians.

Mr. Lechín was guarded about Barrientos. He said that it would be a mistake to think that military rule was "bad" just because it was military. Bolivia, he went on with a dry laugh, is not the United States. Stability should never be stressed to the point where it impedes development, but there come times when a government has the duty to maintain itself by force, if necessary. I asked him if he, the leader of the non-Communist left, had any Communists in PRIN, his new party, and he responded, "No." But a good many persons, including several in the American colony in La Paz, call him a "Communist," which he decidedly is not.

Lechín feels that he should rightfully have been Paz's successor as president in 1964, and that he was double-crossed. Whether he will ever return to a consequential position cannot be known.

Portrait of a Communist

Simón Reyes is a serious young man, but when he smiles the smile fairly explodes, lighting up his strong Indian face. Reyes is tall, with a jet-black pompadour and a high aquiline nose; with deeply etched lines in his face; he has the look of a man who has known plenty of suffering, despite his youth. His father was a tailor, his mother a cook. Born in the Chaco near the Argentine frontier, Reyes is thirty-two.

Reyes is a Communist, the third or fourth man in the hierarchy of the PCB, Communist party of Bolivia. We met him in the same building, the headquarters of the miners' union, where we had seen Lechín, and the older man happened to drop in as we talked. He put a hand on Reyes's shoulder and said cozily, "You're a good boy, very bright, but young. When you grow up you will be with us and join PRIN." Mr. Reyes smiled agreeably and replied, "Never!"

This was one of the most interesting men I met in South America. His impact was like that of Father Vekemans, the Jesuit intellectual in Chile, though no two men could be more different in background, training, or political ideas. But Reyes has a compelling quality, like Vekemans. We talked for almost three hours, and from first to last he was reasonable, logical, earnest, and full of conviction and spark.

Reyes gave us a sketch of his career. He went to primary school in his home town and then, while going to night school, worked as a shoemaker, construction worker, and typographer. Partly under the influence of his father, a radical, he became a Communist at eighteen. He was jailed several times for disseminating political pamphlets and attempting to organize the local workers. Moving into the mining country, he got work near Potosí, the old silver capital, and rose in the labor movement, similarly in the party. Between jobs he has visited Moscow four times.

We asked him why, in view of the unutterably miserable circumstances of the *campesinos*, the Communist party was not stronger than it is. The *campesinos* were, he replied frankly, hard to reach. Their hunger is not the only factor; they need leadership. "Peasants alone do not make a revolution; they have to be taught how to make it." We asked him what he thought of foreign aid—whether he resented USAID and whether he would accept Moscow aid, if proffered. He replied that the Bolivian Communists were not against foreign aid as such because the country so desperately needed development, but that the Bolivians must remain "masters" in their own house—a sentiment vociferously widespread on the continent, and not just on the part of Communists.

His chief grievance against the United States seemed to be that we were, he said, "dumping" cheap consumer goods into Bolivia—powdered milk, inexpensive clothes, small mechanical gadgets. These, in his view, could be produced just as well in Bolivia and would be much less expensive. My wife then put a forthright question, "If you were the American secretary of state with the true interests of Bolivia at heart what would you do?" Mr. Reyes replied, very seriously: (1) Make more money available to us for new small industry. (2) Give technical assistance for the mechanization of agriculture, particularly corn. (3) Reduce American export trade in order to give the Bolivian balance of payments a chance to improve. (4) Cut off arms and military assistance.

We asked then how Mr. Reyes proposed to make the Bolivian mines more productive without reducing the labor force or lowering wages, a key question. This was a large and intricate problem, he conceded. He did not, however, think that wages were the linchpin of the difficulty. First, the mines are physically difficult to operate. Ore has to be extracted from sources eight hundred meters below the surface, whereas in Malaya it lies on top of the earth. Here it costs $1.65 to produce a pound of tin, as against 70 cents in more favored terrain. Second, "faulty administration" has severely hurt production. Third, Bolivian tin is still at the mercy of foreign smelters, particularly in England, since it has no major smelters of its own. Smelting is the basic trouble, not production, and foreign smelting diminishes national profits.

It happened that the trade union federation had set up a demonstration against the American Embassy for this day, in protest against United States intervention in the Dominican Republic. As we talked we could hear bands play martial music on the streets outside, as a parade was formed. With extreme politeness, Mr. Reyes said that we would have to excuse him because he was scheduled to make a speech at the demonstration. He proceeded to fish a paper from his pocket, read to us the last paragraph of the speech, which was vigorous and had a nice ironic touch—and then invited us to be his guests for the show! We said that we could not quite see our way to doing this, and that, as a matter of fact, we knew that the embassy was tight shut, fearing an assault. Graciously Mr. Reyes then told us to inform the ambassador that he would not dream of attacking the building but would just march past, which is what happened.

As we left, Reyes mentioned the splinter or "telephone booth" parties within the general Communist frame. As in Chile, there are several of these, including a group known as POR, not to be confused with PIR (just another Bolivian complication), and no fewer than *four* different Trotskyist parties, two of which have newspapers with the same name! He said that the local split between Kremlinists and Pekingists had been caused more by conflicts in personality than ideology, and that the Chinese wing did not carry much weight or point. All told there are probably not more than ten thousand regular party members in Bolivia.

*

That evening I met a distinguished former cabinet minister, who said, "Yes, we are the hemisphere country nearest to anarchy and chaos, but the Communist party is not strong enough in itself to make an overturn." This I am sure is true at present, but it may not always be true.

A stimulating book by François Houtart and Emile Pin, *The Church and the Latin American Revolution*, has a passage[6] outlining the following conditions as being necessary before a revolution can succeed in South

[6] Quoted from the sociologist Harry M. Johnson.

America. I. A pronounced rupture within the social order. This has already occurred in several hemisphere republics. II. An alerted public opinion. III. A leader. IV. Behind the leader a revolutionary group, whether "a political party, a secret society, or a guerrilla band." The existence of the groups "is very important, for it provides the masses with a concrete reality with which they can identify themselves." V. A revolutionary ideology. VI. A weak government. VII. "Idealization of the future."

Several of these conditions exist in Bolivia now, several obviously do not. The Barrientos regime's principal claim to merit is that it wards off further instability.

Hemisphere Affairs

The United States has not always done well by Bolivia in financial realms. Like Chile, this country was an early target for "sucker loans." Small American investors lent their money to Wall Street in the 1920's; Wall Street lent it to Bolivia; soon Bolivia was forced to default on roughly $57 million of its obligations. Loans had jumped from $6 million to $60 million in a brief period, obviously a sum greater than the country could afford.

Many years later American aid to Bolivia was sadly botched. The following is from the *Hispanic American Report*, published at Stanford University, California, April, 1960. It refers to pre-Alianza days:

> It was discovered that no accurate financial records of [United States] expenditures or losses were kept until 1957, and that more than a million dollars were unaccounted for. Between 1954 and 1957 more than $2,000,000 in food and fiber gifts were lost through overcrowding of ports serving Bolivia and theft of material in transit. . . . A million dollars were wasted on a discontinued irrigation project in . . . eastern Bolivia, which was so remote from populous areas that it could not be used. Two plants costing $225,000 to produce yucca flour will probably never be used, since there is no market in Bolivia for yucca flour. An agricultural vocational training center costing $160,000 was abandoned because it was too far in advance of Bolivia's needs. Agricultural equipment worth $500,000 was lost . . . because, again, it was unsuited to Bolivian agriculture. . . . One confidential source pointed out that a sizeable percentage of aid had been diverted to the repayment of Export-Import Bank Loans so that the bank could maintain its record of no defaults. Another portion allegedly went for repayment of defaulted foreign loans which were contracted in the early part of the century under such scandalous terms that many do not think repayment should be resumed.[7]

This kind of thing has, it should be pointed out emphatically, altogether ceased today. The USAID mission in La Paz is one of the most competently

[7] Quoted in *Invisible Latin America*, by Samuel Schapiro, pp. 131–32.

run on the continent. One detail is that United States funds provide daily meals for more than 340,000 people—nearly 10 percent of the nation. American aid to Bolivia is, indeed, substantial; altogether our aid program here is the highest per capita of any country in the world, although it was suspended briefly after the Barrientos coup. We give a special accent to road construction and the building of a modern communications network in collaboration with the Bolivian self-help program, which resembles Cooperación Popular in Peru. All told the American contribution to Bolivia has come close to $400,000,000 in the past decade, and, in an average year, equals about 30 percent of the total national budget, a startling proportion.

As a result, charges are heard locally from both left and right that Bolivia has become no more or less than a United States colony. A friendly person in La Paz—not at all anti-American—asked me quizzically, "Are you sure that you do all this for *us*?" Once more the familiar picture arises, that of the Colossus of the North trying in a somewhat fumbling way to come to grips with a forlorn hemisphere republic, embracing it with loans, grants, and gifts, showering it with affection (if it will only be so obliging as to maintain the status quo), while the smaller country, bewildered, sensitive and wary, accepts this charity out of the simple necessity to keep alive but is suspicious of our motives and often hates doing so.

*

The principal private American investment in Bolivia is Gulf Oil, although W. R. Grace (merchandising, cement, flour) is important too. Gulf began Bolivian operations in 1956, and has spent $98 million so far in exploration and development. This came about after the Paz government reversed its old confiscatory policy in regard to petroleum, but local distribution is a monopoly in the hands of a government agency, Yacimientos Petrolíferos Fiscales Bolivianos (YPFB). The Gulf fields lie near Santa Cruz in the east; 55 out of 101 wells drilled to date have produced oil, and potential resources are believed to be enormous. A 360-mile pipeline is being built from Santa Cruz to the highlands which will join another, owned by YPFB, going down to Arica, Chile, on the sea. Production is modest so far, but export of about 25,000 barrels a day is expected to begin soon. Companies other than Gulf are at work as well.

*

The Soviet Union is probably more interested in Bolivia than in any other hemisphere republic with the possible exception of Uruguay, because of its geographical position and vulnerability, but its advances have amounted to little so far. Some years ago Mr. Khrushchev offered Paz Estenssoro a credit of $150 million to build a smelting mill, but the project did not materialize partly because of opposition from our State Department. Later Czechoslovakia won a smaller contract for an antimony plant.

Bolivia broke off diplomatic relations with Chile in 1962, charging it with "aggression" after a highly complicated dispute over water rights on the Lauca River, which flows through both countries. Bolivia even went so far as to withdraw temporarily from the OAS, as an indication of the seriousness with which it viewed this matter, and sporadic gunfire has taken place between Bolivian and Chilean frontier guards. But Bolivia could not survive without commercial relations with Chile, which are unimpaired in spite of the diplomatic break, because its lifeline is the railway from La Paz across the Andes to Arica, where the Bolivians have their own free port. Chilean capital, incidentally, played a very large role in the early development of Bolivia, and Chile was the biggest economic factor in the country, just as Argentina was the biggest political factor, until the full entrance of the United States into the Bolivian arena.

Venezuela broke off diplomatic relations with Bolivia in 1964 after the Barrientos coup, much to Bolivian resentment. Venezuela is, as has been noted, a spunky country with convictions. It adheres to the so-called Betancourt doctrine, whereby it refuses to recognize nations where military governments have taken power by force, and at present has no diplomatic relations with six or seven Latin American countries, including Argentina, Brazil, and Ecuador. Bolivians call this policy "unreal."

La Paz, the Co-Capital

This city has a quality like none other in the world largely because of its altitude. The airport bears a sign, "Highest Commerical Airport in the World—13,358 feet—Not Open at Night." A well-kept new highway, financed by the Alianza, leads into the town itself, which lies in a bowl like a terraced open-mine pit. There can be a thousand-foot difference in altitude between lunch and dinner, since buildings stand at anything between 11,000 and 12,500 feet. Then too one can reach La Paz by rail or road from Lake Titicaca. On this trip we came by road, passing the impressive Inca ruins at Tiahuanaco. By and large Bolivian roads are better than Peruvian roads, but dustier. At one intersection we saw the mangled wreck of a smashed red automobile stuck on a post, as a warning to motorists, like the roadside shrines in Peru. But La Paz has no fantastically decrepit *carcochas* like Lima.

Another word about the airport, which is remarkable. It is almost four miles long, which it has to be on account of the altitude—planes take longer to land in thin air—and is ninety feet higher at one end than at the other, which makes a 2 percent grade. Pilots do not appreciate this unique characteristic. Jets could not land here—because of the altitude—until quite recently when the airport was extended, but now Panagra (Pan American Grace Airways) and other lines fly in on routine schedules. Sometimes llamas and baffled-looking sheep have to be chased off the far end of the runway before a plane can land. I have never seen an airport so exotic except perhaps that on Ascension Island in the South Atlantic, where the landing strip has a curve in the middle.

LA PAZ, correct name Nuestra Señora de la Paz, had 78,000 people half a century ago, 325,000 today. Visitors are apt to feel that they are at the end of the world—in an eyrie Shangri-La unbelievably remote. One thing striking is that La Paz gives the impression of being an extremely silent city. Close by are peaks, snow-clad most of the year, which rise to a height of almost four miles, and which provide a spectacular *mise en scène* as well as contributing to the atmosphere of lonely, cloud-wrapped isolation. Soaring up to these are barren, tawny hills and ranges of lower mountains which cover two-thirds of the horizon.

I saw signs, "Yankees—Get Out of Vietnam," on several street corners, where squat Indian women wearing bowler hats and braids sit stolidly in the thin sunshine, selling oranges arranged in triangles and pyramids. The traffic cops are well trained, and taxis will take a passenger any distance for the equivalent of 8 cents. The leading hotel is comfortable, and its room service was swifter, it seemed, than any other we encountered on the continent. The registration card says that the "Donning Room" is on the eighth floor and, four lines below, "Coat and Tie for the Dinning Room." The roof garden has telephone service at your table, just as in the smartest of smart restaurants in New York. The local beer is formidably good and the local brand of imitation American cigarettes, known as Pacific, seemed to me a cut above Jockey Clubs in Argentina, Hiltons in Chile, or Ministers in Brazil.

Power failures occur frequently, and make life exciting—especially when you are caught in an elevator between floors. The power company, which is Canadian, says that its rates are the lowest in the world. "Out of 53,000 subscribers, 20,000 pay less than 50¢ a month for service and 8500 pay less than 4¢."[8]

Smuggling, as in Paraguay, is vivaciously widespread. Goods come up from

[8] "A Never-Never Land High Above the Sea," by Hunter S. Thompson, *Christian Science Monitor*, April 15, 1963.

the Arica railway and find their way to a place which, with engaging candor, calls itself the Black Market Shop. It sells dynamite by the stick, among other things. This is a country very dynamite-conscious. Indians fish in the lakes by tossing dynamite in the water, which blows the fish out, and a game not for the timid, sometimes played by the local beatniks, resembles Russian roulette: competing youngsters hurl sticks of dynamite at a wall, and the winner is the one who waits until his wick is shortest. Another distinction is that, until recently, La Paz was one of the few cities in the world with no fire department. One exists now, but it is rudimentary, consisting of a solitary wagon which deals with such freak fires as those caused by faulty wiring. Real fires cannot easily take place, because there isn't enough oxygen in the atmosphere to support them. Paceño housewives cook by electricity or kerosene.

One renowned local character is Monsignor Andrew Kennedy, a Catholic from St. Louis who has lived in Bolivia for some years, and who has been acting vicar general of the La Paz archdiocese. He has a large and deserved reputation as a social worker, and it was he who, singlehanded, settled a dangerous students' strike in 1964 just before the Barrientos coup, and then negotiated a truce between the government and the rioters that brought a stop to serious bloodshed. Another American, Mrs. Ann Wasson, has labored devotedly to create a rehabilitation establishment for handicapped children. She told us, "The only way to get anything done in this country is to wear out the patience of the other person."[9] But she said this with affection, not resentment.

The altitude in La Paz afflicts some people (like my friend Sacheverell Sitwell), and mysteriously leaves others untouched. The embassies and hotels have cylinders of oxygen ready for the comfort or resuscitation of unacclimated visitors. Local aeronautical experts became worried when it was discovered a year or two ago that American astronauts who frequently soar over Bolivia in outer space have parachutes set to open automatically at 10,000 feet above sea level. Here a flier would be buried deep in the earth before the chute could open. I heard one little joke, "What this country needs most is less altitude." *Soroche*, or altitude sickness, is attracting considerable study by research scientists; its principal effects are, aside from

---

[9] Then she recounted a story of an Indian woman who bought fifty ears of corn at a local market, whereupon she confessed that she did not have any money. A child was strapped to her back. The Indian woman said, "I will leave the child as security and get the money." She took the corn—and never came back for the baby.

shortness of breath and giddiness, pulmonary edema and a change in the constitution of the blood and in the thickness of the heart wall if a person sensitive to altitude is exposed for a longish period. Oxygen usually brings quick relief, and "Soroche pills" are available; these reduce the faintness, loss of appetite, and insomnia characteristic of this peculiar ailment. Most people in good health, however, adjust quickly. They play football and tennis, and Chacaltaya, an hour from La Paz, has a ski run at seventeen thousand feet.

*

Other cities on the *altiplano* are SUCRE (altitude 10,300 feet), the official capital, which still holds splendid colonial traces and has a university, San Francisco Xavier, founded in 1624; the old silver hill POTOSÍ (13,340 feet) which produced $600 million worth of silver in the course of its turbulent history; and ORURO (12,160 feet), the contemporary mining center, famous too for its incandescent devil dances held during carnival. Oruro, a railway center, also commands the road into La Paz, and this gives it a considerable strategic importance; anybody in power here can cut the capital off from the rest of the country.

COCHABAMBA (population around 80,000, altitude 8,570 feet) lies on the edge of the great Andean *yungas*, and is called "the garden city." A "cultural fortress" like Córdoba in Argentina or Arequipa in Peru, it has an effervescent political life as well. This was Barrientos's redoubt during his vice-presidency under Paz. Its citizens are mostly Europeans or *cholos*, who enjoy their luxuriant semitropical surroundings, and tend to look down snobbishly on the rest of the country. Cochabamba is as different from La Paz as a town in the Vale of Kashmir is from an outpost in the high Himalayas. Here among other sights is the huge palace which belonged to Señor Patiño, the tin king, and which is now a museum. The Maryknoll Fathers have their South American headquarters in Cochabamba.

Eastward in SANTA CRUZ, the principal city of the *llanos*, lowlands, Founded in 1595, it existed in utter isolation for century after century, and is still largely a Spanish enclave with a hinterland producing rice, cotton, sugar. The town has risen from fifteen thousand people to sixty thousand in a little more than a decade. What helped end its isolation was an all-weather road, financed by the United States, connecting it with Cochabamba. Curiously enough Franklin D. Roosevelt, who had a great eye for geography, first suggested this road. Santa Cruz is linked by rail to both Argentina and Brazil, but not to the rest of Bolivia. Many Japanese live here.

Hostage to Fortune

"How can a country whose only source of foreign exchange is a single unprofitable industry possibly maintain itself without depending entirely upon external systems?" This question, posed by a La Paz economist recently, is indeed the rack-and-pinion of the Bolivian problem. Foreign aid is indispensable to the well-being of the country, perhaps even its survival. Meantime political development proceeds slowly, but this is still a nation sharply divided between two forces only—government and governed.

CHAPTER 23

The Curious Entity of Ecuador

The beautiful madness of this lovely land . . .

—LUDWIG BEMELMANS

ECUADOR, a highly unstable small country, was once formally consecrated to the Sacred Heart of Jesus, and gives a strong religious flavor. Travelers in older days report that Protestants were sometimes stoned on the streets of Quito, but I am not sure that this can be true, because I do not know where the Protestants could have come from. This is one of the most solidly Catholic nations in the world, although a large proportion of the population today is Catholic in name only (many Catholics are not "practicing") and the country has had long periods of decidedly anticlerical rule—a familiar South American contradiction. The other principal things to say are that Ecuador has a romantic, doll's-house quality, and supports itself largely by the export of bananas.

There are other sharp dichotomies. Quito has fabulously ornate churches, almost buried under centuries of gilt, but peasants lounging on their steps are among the poorest on the continent, lucky to earn 10 cents a day. The military do not form an elite class, but the armed forces manage to hold for themselves more than 30 percent of the national budget. Only 40 percent of tax collections reach their proper destination, the treasury, but the currency is sound. The atmosphere in general is chaste, even sanctified, but Quito has what is reputed to be one of the fanciest small bawdy houses in the world.

Ecuador means "equator." The country, about the size of Arizona, with 5,200,000 people, is bisected by two lines, one invisible, one visible—the equator from east to west, and the Pan-American Highway from north to south. A few miles north of Quito, a delightful small city, stands a monument bearing the magic ciphers 0° 00' 00" to denote the latitude; standing

417

there (huddled in a raincoat like as not, because the altitude makes it cold),
you comprehend that the earth's stout waistline, the equator, is, even if not
visible, real. You stand "with one foot in the northern hemisphere, one in
the southern."

This is a modest decent country, with a countryside so clean that it looks
combed. A major problem is, as in Peru, incorporation of the crushed, destitute Indian masses into the body of the state. The racial composition is
40 percent pure Indian, 10 percent white, 40 percent *mestizo*, and 10 percent
Negro-mulatto. The large *hacendados*, landowners, associated with business
interests in the towns, live in uneasy—but not readily admitted—fear that the
Indians, if educated and developed, will take over political and economic
power. So, as in Peru again, the tendency is to deny them education and
other opportunity in order to keep them submerged.

Ownership of land shows the usual South American imbalance. The
church is still by far the biggest landlord. As to private holdings, 300 large
estates occupy 65 percent of the total arable land of the country; 14,000
small holdings occupy 3 percent. Put in another way, less than one percent
of the population owns more than half the land. The peons who actually
work on the soil lived for many years on the *huasipungo* system, which
means that they were given a small plot by the landowner in exchange for
their labor, plus a minute cash wage. Usually the *huasipunguero* was in debt
to the landlord all his life, and could not move. As recently as ten years ago
properties were sold with Indian workers included in the price, as if they
were bushels of wheat or cattle. The junta[1] did away with *huasipungo*, and
the peasants are now entitled to own their own land—if they can afford to
buy any.

Ecuador's principal curse, which derives in part from economic maladjustment, is a fantastic degree of political instability, as in Bolivia. There have
been 16 constitutions in 115 years and, in one recent 23-year period, the country had 22 different presidents, dictators, or ruling juntas. No president in the
twentieth century filled out his four-year term till Galo Plaza Lasso (1948–
52), an able and attractive man whom I shall mention later.

Why is Ecuador so extraordinarily poor as well as unstable? Why does it
not, like Peru, make use of the fish swimming in its waters? One answer I
received to this question was hard to take seriously: "Our sardines are too
big; they do not make the right kind of fishmeal." I asked why Ecuador,
although it is traversed by the same majestic mountains, had comparatively
little wealth in minerals, although Peru is rich. Again the answer, although it

---

[1] A junta, to be described below, was the ruling body of Ecuador from 1963–66.

came from a responsible person, was unsatisfactory and defeatist: "Our mountains are volcanoes; all they produce is ash."

Ecuador has three distinct areas: a coastal strip, hot and gummy; the Andean highlands; and the Oriente, or jungle region in the east. Whereas the Peruvian coast is a sterile desert, Ecuador's is as green as beans; apparently the reason for this is that the cold Humboldt current changes course, shoots out into the Pacific, and does not inhibit coastal vegetation here. As to the Andes, the Ecuadorian peaks are positively Himalayan in their grandeur. There are two ranges, with a long sleeve between; the country has no fewer than twenty-two mountains between two and a half and four miles high, several of which are so steep and rough as to be virtually unclimbable. Two celebrated volcanoes are Cotopaxi (19,344 feet), the highest active volcano in the world, and Chimborazo (20,577 feet), which, like Fuji, has a perfect snowcapped cone. Both are far loftier than Mount Whitney or Mont Blanc, the tallest peaks in the continental United States and Europe respectively.

The three regions of the country do not have a high opinion of one another. The coast is white, mulatto, Negro; the Andean hills mostly *mestizo*; the Oriente, which comprises half the area of the country, mostly Indian. A great many Indians still do not speak or understand Spanish; one remote tribe has a language which, oddly enough, is said to resemble Korean. Most Indians are as placid as milkmaids in Normandy, but there are genuine savages too, some of the fiercest and last to survive in the Americas, who sew boars' teeth into their lips, wear paint, and use blowguns with poisoned darts. The Jívaros are an inclement people; the Aucas too. When, in the old days, they killed their enemies, they decapitated them and shrank their heads, which became a fast-moving article in illicit trade, because of their picturesque appeal as souvenirs.

The two chief cities, Quito and Guayaquil, are jealous competitors; a major element in the national struggle for power for many years has, in fact, been the rivalry between Quito, with its lights blinking high in the wings of the Andes, and Guayaquil, the crowded commercial port on the Pacific.

Along with Colombia and Venezuela, Ecuador is commonly known as one of the three "Bolívar countries." All three lay close to the liberator's heart, and formed a single country (Gran Colombia) under his rule until 1830. But Ecuador is much more closely linked today with Peru, because of their related geography, Indians, and historical development. Peru is, however, a dirty word in Ecuador. The two countries had a bitter frontier dispute over territory near the Amazon in the early 1940's, which erupted into open warfare; Ecuador lost. A settlement, guaranteed by the United States, gave Peru 71,000 square miles of Ecuador, more than half its present area, which

Ecuadorians have vehemently resented ever since. They continue to regard themselves as an Amazonian nation, even claiming Iquitos, and their official maps still include the lost territories as theirs. Ecuador has been cut into by other neighbors as well—Colombia and Brazil. But it is the Peruvian "steal" that hurts most, and it still plays an international political role today. I asked a member of the ruling junta which ran the country when I was there why Ecuador had refused to go along with the United States in April, 1965, on the issue of sending troops to the Dominican Republic; one element in a frank reply was that Ecuador still feared aggression by Peru and resented our "pro-Peru" line in 1942.

This is, indeed, a sensitive and prickly country. When General Charles de Gaulle visited Quito in 1964 he gave the same decoration, the Officer's Cross of the Legion of Honor, to all four members of the junta. A former Ecuadorian cabinet minister, disgruntled by having been exiled to Colombia, wrote an article about the De Gaulle visit which mentioned snidely that the general had given a superior decoration, the *Grand* Cross of the Legion of Honor, to the presidents everywhere else in South America; reaching Ecuador, this article made a scandal. The four junta members, humiliated, protested to the French ambassador and asked for Grand Crosses. The reply came that the Grand Cross is given only to a single head of state, and that the French would be delighted to bestow it on Admiral Castro Jijón, the chairman of the junta, but the other three members would have to content themselves with the lesser decoration. The Ecuadorians replied stiffly that their junta members were equal in status, and that, if the French would not promote all four equally, they would send the original decorations back. Paris was adamant. So the decorations were returned to France, whereupon, the story goes, General de Gaulle sent back to Quito the Ecuadorian decoration that had been given *him*.

Quito and Guayaquil

The dogs go to church here, they wander in and out, and during the midday heat they lie on the cool floors and sleep in the confessionals.

—LUDWIG BEMELMANS

People make mild fun of QUITO (9,375 feet, population 380,000) on occasion; it has been called the city of "a thousand churches and one bathtub." In fact the number of churches is only fifty-seven, and the dashing new Hotel Quito, one of the smartest on the continent, has perfectly good plumbing, as have countless other buildings. Another legend is that a young woman may go to the five o'clock show at the movies with a boy friend, but not the seven; after sundown, which comes at six every day of the year, chaperonage is essential. Then too the story is heard that a prisoner of extraordinary agility may escape from the town jail by climbing over a wall and jumping to a projecting ledge of the next building; if he succeeds the police and onlookers do not chase him, but clap and cheer. If he doesn't succeed he is dead. It's a long fall.

Jewel-like, suffused with charm, the center of the *sierra*, Quito is romantic, aristocratic (as compared to Guayaquil), and, except for politics, tranquil. Even though it is the second-highest capital in the world[2] it has little of the sense of strain that lack of oxygen brings to Cuzco or La Paz. Its site is, of course, magnificent. Quito lies in a cupped palm of the Andes, with Mount Sangay, a volcano still defiantly active, close by, and others clearly visible on a good day. The weather is, however, often cloudy. Airplanes, unable to penetrate the overcast into the elegant little airport, which closes at night, may have to overfly it, and stories are heard of the weary traveler who, returning to his home in Quito from a visit to Lima, is flown willy-nilly on to Bogotá, then back to Lima from Bogotá the next day, still with no chance to land. Five unsuccessful passes at Quito in five days is a record for this course.

The main dining room of the Hotel Quito is on an upper floor; here hundreds of lights are visible at night, up and down the steep hills, but no signs. I was reminded of a remark by G. K. Chesterton to the effect that Times Square in New York would be doubly impressive to a man who could see but not read. The visitor to Quito is not disturbed by advertisements. The Indian waitresses here wear an enchanting costume—blouses embroidered at the top with puffed-out sleeves, wide multicolored skirts, and gold beads circling the throat from chin to chest; their hair is arranged in long black braids caught by strips of colored ribbon halfway down, below which it spreads out loose. (Indians on Ecuadorian football teams sometimes wear their hair long, or play with it braided.) I do not want to give too sentimental a picture of the ravishingly costumed Quito waitresses. There are stern realities in the life of servants here. I gave a bowl of fruit to the girl who took care of our room; she became inarticulate with thanks, and then made me sign a chit saying that I had *given* it to her; otherwise she might have been accused of theft. This was one of the few times in my life when I had to sign for giving something away.

There are no shantytowns in Quito, no *favelas* or *barriadas*, because people could not survive in them—it's too cold. The new town has, for the relatively prosperous, residential blocks of pretty, small villas with paved

2 The highest is La Paz.

streets, lawns, and even sidewalks, separated from the streets by grassy strips—something novel in South America. A peculiar scent seems to settle over the city at night—eucalyptus burning in the fireplaces. The groves around Quito contain no fewer than four hundred different varieties of this quick-growing tree, which was imported in the first instance from Australia. Another tropical city up in the sky has this same fragrant aroma of eucalyptus—Addis Ababa in Ethiopia. One element in the city's charm is remoteness; to get an airmail letter from Lima can take a fortnight, although it is only two hours away by air, and there is no long-distance telephone service at all.

Scrawlings on walls are not permitted in Quito; if a person is caught daubing political signs on a building the punishment fits the crime—he is made to scrub them off. One curiosity is that Quito, for all its poverty, is the only city on the continent with pasteurized, bottled, sealed, and *dated* milk. The hotel has a smart, lively casino. There are two universities—national and Catholic—with good academic standards, and a well-known American school founded by Galo Plaza. Both universities have aid-financed contracts with American universities in the manner familiar all over South America. A favorite dish is roast guinea pig; another a mélange of cheese and fried mashed potato called *llapingachos*. Restaurant and bar bills are numbered so that they can be used in the national lotteries, a mechanism which also enables the government to keep watch on tax returns.

Ludwig Bemelmans, the artist and writer, who spent a happy long holiday in Ecuador some years ago, made a record of three items he saw on a menu:

> HAYS KRIMM (ice cream)
> AIRISTIU (Irish stew)
> WIDE NAVEL WISKY (White Label Whiskey)[3]

One morning we visited the social security installations. The director, Dr. Carlos Andrade Marín, is a former mayor of Quito, minister of health, and speaker of the House of Representatives; his father, whom I met a quarter of a century ago, was a well-known physician, rector of the Colegio Nacional Mejía, and minister of social prevision. South America is a great continent for sons following fathers. The present Dr. Andrade told us about his work. Social security is advanced in Ecuador. Its administration is not part of the government, but autonomous, and it is the biggest financial institution in the country; it owns large properties (including the Hotel Quito) and has a tidy revenue from investments in sugar, cement, and housing. The social

---

[3] *The Donkey Inside*, by Ludwig Bemelmans. Viking Press, New York, 1941.

security system here, one of the oldest on the continent, provides a basic old-age pension, health insurance, medical care, and both accident and unemployment insurance; to support it the employee pays 5 percent of wages, the employer 5 percent, and the state 15. All workers are covered, including professional men, artisans, and domestic labor, except—the usual catch in South America—peons on the land. A man in the towns retires at fifty-five with a pension of 75 percent of his wages for life; a woman gets seven weeks off at 75 percent of her salary when delivering a child.

The great shining sights of Quito are the churches. The cathedral, on Plaza Independencia, a formidable structure with large green domes, contains the tomb of General Sucre, the superlative soldier who was Bolívar's advance man, and the monastery of La Merced nearby has a replica of Big Ben, built by an English bell maker in 1817. One stunning church-plus-monastery is San Francisco, which, my guidebook tells me, is "the earliest religious foundation in South America," built in 1535 by a Flemish Franciscan who was the first man to plant wheat in the country. The prize church is La Compañía, the interior of which is almost solidly covered with gold and which has intricately carved balconies, an impressive gold-leaf high altar, and a golden sheen between ornate walls. I have never seen a church to match it except perhaps São Francisco in Bahia.

The Plaza Independencia resembles the central squares in other South American cities, but has a picturesqueness all its own; here are dignity, a touch of melodrama, and elements of musical comedy as well. It reminded me of the piazza in Capri, except that the narrow shops look like caves, and Indians, stolid as they may be, emerge from them fluttering in their ponchos like bats.

Here stand the cathedral, the archbishop's gaunt palace, the town hall, and, above all, the presidential palace, a building full of wonders. In one room, large enough for sixty-four guests at a single table, a frieze of portraits of all the presidents of Ecuador stretches under a heavy gold-ornamented ceiling. A balcony, from which dictators were wont to harangue the mobs, looks conveniently over the square, in the very best South American tradition. I thought that this was the most attractive palace of its kind on the whole continent.

The entrance hall is decorated solidly with large mosaic panels by the country's best-known artist, Oswaldo Guayasamín. These, radiantly powerful, depict the discovery of the Amazon in 1541 by Francisco de Orellana, the head of an expedition sent out from Quito. "Origin of our Destiny" portrays the beginnings of this epic; knights in armor, led by a magnificent orange-colored horse, leave Quito; the conquerors pole themselves down the river, and the sacrificial death of an Indian maiden is shown. "The Path Is Marked by Their Blood and Our Spirit" shows the sacrifice of three thousand aborigines who are "glorified"—by being slaughtered to celebrate the taking of the Amazon.

These murals represent Guayasamín, a Marxist, in his most patriotic historical mood. When he tackles modern themes he is a fighting radical, who has gone to jail for his convictions; he is at work now on a vast panorama of the miseries of modern man. The name Guayasamín means "White Bird in Flight." He is so well known and respected as an artist that, in spite of his political beliefs, he was given the commission to do the palace murals. Besides, like Jorge Amado in Brazil, Guayasamín is fun—bursting with ardor and *joie de vivre*, also a stubborn man, with the reticences of the true artist, and full of force. A pure Indian, with the blackest of black hair, powerful shoulders, and tenacious quickness of eye and appreciation, he sings, sighs, and groans aloud as he paints, crouched like a bull; his wife is a Belgian poetess of distinction.

*

Three hundred miles away from Quito on the coast, GUAYAQUIL (population 550,000) is as different from the capital as can be imagined—tropical, commercial, turbulent, aggressive. Guayaquil, as I heard it put, is "open at the bottom"; society is fluid, unlike that in Quito. One leader of the community is Luis Noboa, who made a fortune in rice, flour mills, bananas, banking: he came from humble beginnings. Guayaquil is well known for, among other things, its manufacture of "Panama" hats, which are made of a straw called *toquilla* and do not come from Panama at all. Its chief sight, after the throbbing waterfront, is the "White Cemetery," a burial ground locally famous, and, like many coastal cities, it contains a heterogeneous population; less Catholic than Quito, it has seven Masonic lodges. Lord Bryce described it as being a "pest-house" fifty years ago, because it was subject to the ravages of yellow fever. About half the people today live in shantytowns.

Guayaquil is not as attractive as Quito, but is more important in that it is the financial, commercial, and economic pivot of the country. After bananas, the principal export, Ecuador lives on cacao, shipping, coffee, rice, balsa wood, sugar, and mercantile interests generally. The merchants, particularly the importers, not only largely control the economy, but have marked political power. Ecuador has little industrialization because the importers prefer to buy manufactured goods abroad, then sell them to the local market, and are in a position to enforce their will. Cacao was the country's chief product until the 1950's. But a blight known as the witchbroom disease descended on cacao, and, largely under the stimulus of Galo Plaza, a systematic effort was made to build up bananas as a substitute, with the result that Ecuador became presently the world's largest exporter of bananas. The banana business has, however, suffered recently, to Guayaquil's dismay. Several American companies have a stake in bananas, including United Fruit. But the holdings and influence of this colossus are minor here, and it does not remotely have in Ecuador the position it holds in the banana republics of Central America. Incidentally, bananas are the biggest fruit industry in the world.

A Packet of Personalities

Galo Plaza, president from 1948 to 1952, ran again in 1960, but was beaten; his prestige is such, however, that he remains a consequential figure in the life of the country. Plaza is in his late fifties. He has devoted much of his time recently to the UN, which he has served both in the Lebanon and the Congo; he put in a hard spell in Cyprus as well, as special representative of the secretary general. Vigorous, cheerful, magnetic, proud of his country, Galo Plaza went to Georgetown University in Washington, D.C., played star football at the University of California, did a bit of amateur bullfighting, and, in Ecuadorian politics, has always been a force for decency and moderation. His father, Leónidas Plaza Gutiérrez, was also a president of the republic, and served for a time as Ecuadorian ambassador to Washington; Galo was born in the United States. The father-to-son tradition, so widespread on the continent, illustrates the narrowness of the arc in which good men are to be found.

I met Galo Plaza in Quito for the first time in 1940, and, although he was not particularly well known at that time, I made a somewhat casual prediction that he would be president of the country someday. He made it eight years later. I thought then as now that he was one of the ablest as well as most attractive men of the Americas.

The venerable Dr. José María Velasco Ibarra, a man of the old school, has returned recently to Ecuador after years of exile. He has been president of Ecuador no fewer than four times; his followers are known as the "Velasquistas," and he himself has been called the "great absentee" and even the "National Personification."[4] Some fifteen thousand of his inflamed followers greeted him tumultuously at the airport when he came back for the last time, but most left-wingers detest him, and have called him "a pilferer of

[4] Herring, op. cit., p. 534.

public funds."[5] His regimes were always personalist, and his record mixed. He has taken an outspoken anti-American line on occasion. His oratory, although old-fashioned, is supposed to be like oil on a fire, and one of his remarks is often quoted: "Give me a balcony, and I will govern." But the balcony on the presidential palace is still there, and Dr. Velasco is not on it.

The leader of the orthodox Conservatives, Camilo Ponce Enríquez, another former president (1956–60, between two Velasco terms), was imprisoned briefly by the junta. A landowner who comes from a well-entrenched oligarchical family, Dr. Ponce has been a lawyer, diplomat, and university president. He told us that what the country needed most was political stability, and that the possibility of Communist penetration was not to be ignored. But the Communists are difficult to deal with, he says, because if the government cracks down on them too hard they gain by establishing the "mystique" that they are being persecuted.

Aurelio Dávila Cajas, a young conservative leader, able and alert, Jesuit-trained, an engineer by profession who is professor of mechanics at the Catholic university, is still wondering what happened to him on the night of June 29, 1965. He was suddenly picked up by the police, arrested, and confined to a cell without light, heat, a bed, or a window, for four days; he was held incommunicado, was not allowed to read, and was never even interrogated. There was no explanation whatever when he was released as suddenly as he had been arrested. Mr. Dávila thinks that the junta associated him by mistake with student demonstrators who had recently stoned the palace. But he is conservative, not a radical. Many left-wingers went to jail as well.

A fabulous and engaging character was Carlos Julio Arosemena, who rose to the presidency after Velasco's last ouster. It was he who was deposed by the junta in July, 1963. A rich man's son, born of the elite (his father was also a president of the republic), he had strong left-wing tendencies; he visited Moscow, expressed sympathy for Castro, and advocated a neutralist position. The armed forces determined to get rid of him, and did so. The excuse was easy, because Arosemena, an extremely complex person, liked alcohol. He got drunk in public, even at elaborate official ceremonies, in circumstances that would have been hilarious if they had not been tragic as well. The fabric of the country was disintegrating, even beyond its normal state of slaphappiness; the situation seemed comparable to that of Brazil in the last days of Goulart. The government scarcely functioned. I asked one participant in the coup what had caused it. His reply was sardonic

---

[5] Reuters dispatch to the *New York Times*, May 25, 1966.

"Drinking [by Arosemena] and chaos around the corner." On the other hand Arosemena's thirst may well have been exaggerated by enemies who wanted to smear him.

Glimpses Backward and Ahead

Ecuadorian history goes far back, and Quito, originally Quitu, was the seat of a pre-Inca Indian hegemony well before A.D. 1000. Ranging north from Lima, the Incas conquered the country in the fifteenth century, and made Quito their northern capital; then civil war between the two Inca brothers, Atahualpa and Huáscar, split the Indian domains. Came the Spaniards, and Pizarro betrayed and executed Atahualpa in 1533, as we know. Sebastián de Belalcázar, one of Pizarro's captains, established San Francisco de Quito as the Spanish capital of Ecuador the next year.

Under colonial rule Ecuador was a combination of proud, aloof citadel and sleepy backwater. Negro slaves were brought in during the eighteenth century to work the plantations along the coast, and the stamp of the landowning oligarchy, backed by the church, became fixed in the pattern which exists to this day. Nationalist pressure against Spain could not be contained after a time, and the country won its independence following a great battle on the flanks of Mt. Pichincha, sloping into Quito, in May, 1822, when General Sucre wiped out the loyalist Spaniards. Bolívar subsequently met General San Martín, who had just finished liberating Peru, at their famous—but enigmatic—conference at Guayaquil. Ecuadorian history from 1830, when the country split off from Bolívar's Gran Colombia to become a republic on its own, has formidable ups and downs. One leading figure for many years was President Gabriel García Moreno, a fanatic Catholic reactionary who, "with bowed back," bore the cross himself in public processions, followed by penitents flagellating themselves; he abolished citizenship for non-Catholics, modernized the country in other respects, and was beaten to death by an assailant in 1875. Twenty years later Eloy Alfaro, a Liberal, became president, took a strong anticlerical line, instituted germinal reforms, and ruled till 1912, when he too met a violent and unexpected death—he was torn to pieces by a mob. Ecuador has had, with one exception, nominally Liberal, i.e., anticlerical, governments ever since.

A military junta deposed President Arosemena on July 11, 1963. Its members were:

Admiral Ramón Castro Jijón, president. Navy. About fifty, of middle-class stock. Educated partly in Chile. The "weakest" member. A liberal.

General Luis Cabrera Sevilla. Army. Born in 1915, had a conventional service career—the "strongest" member.

General Marcos Gándara Enriquez. Army. A technician, who has been a professor of both hydraulics and cartography. About forty-five. The most "intellectual" member.

Colonel Guillermo Freile Posso, chief of staff of the air force. Fortyish, trained in the United States. The liveliest and most aggressive member. Deposed after a period for being too "ambitious."

Of these four I had talks with three. They impressed me as being desperately earnest men, patriots, who were confused and baffled, except Gándara; not really up to their jobs, but doing their best to arrest a deep inner decay in government. They seemed to regard themselves primarily as technicians, reformers, without regard to the usual political labels, as indeed do most military Putschists in South America. Gándara, who derived from a rich landowning family and went to school in Spain and Italy, talked vividly in terms of advanced social reform, with Fascist touches. But none was an outright reactionary. All stood for civic responsibility as they saw it, even though Freile proved to be an adventurer and overreached himself.

The junta came into being spontaneously, its members told us, by a snap-of-the-finger decision; there was no prolonged conspiracy. Its membership was fortuitous, created by rank, not personality: the three service chiefs simply agreed that something drastic had to be done, and then brought in Gándara for his brains. The dominating motive was certainly fear of Communism. Communists had filtered into several key positions, and General Gándara told us, with clearly apparent horror and indignation, that a Communist had occupied the very chair he was now sitting in as Supervisor of Public Action. But again this must be seen in its local context; considering what was going on in Ecuador it is a miracle that there were no more Communists than there were.

*

The junta repeatedly promised to return to constitutional government, but never quite had the grip or sufficient desire to do so. There came serious strikes in Guayaquil in 1965, promoted in the first instance not by left wingers (who however helped to spread the disorders) but by the conservative mercantile community. The junta had passed a decree raising import duties to encourage local industry, and the powerful Guayaquil merchants who live by trade, bitterly resented this.[6] Meantime the junta alienated

6 They were also responsible—for the same reason—for one of Velasco's tumbles from power.

other conservative elements in the community by sketching out a land reform and inaugurating a new tax program. But it was gradually being forced into a defensive position, which hurt its prestige, and the left continued to be hostile. Strangely enough public opinion still counts in Ecuador.

After another year of turbulence, strikes, and riots the junta was cast out in March, 1966, flat on its collective face. The major force throwing it out was the army, from which it had sprung. Conservative non-junta officers felt that the time had come for change once more. Citizens who had accepted the junta, even if reluctantly—because it seemed to be the ultimate in last resorts—despaired. The army decided to take a chance on civilian government if only because other alternatives had given out, and Clemente Yerovi Indaburu became provisional president under a pledge to hold elections within six months. A Galo Plaza man, he accepted the post with reservations. Nonpolitical, a businessman, he had been minister of agriculture under Mr. Plaza, and as such superintended the policy of building up the banana industry to replace cacao as the major instrument in the national economy. Yerovi was born of a prosperous family in Guayaquil in 1904. His personality is somewhat dim. He worked as a river pilot for a time, became a ship's captain on one of his father's fleet of boats, and went into commerce, becoming a prosperous importer. He was president of the National Planning Council, Ecuadorian ambassador to UNESCO, and Ecuadorian representative to the European Economic Community. Radical students call him a "servant of the oligarchs."

*

One word on the Communist position. The junta outlawed the party and exiled its principal leaders. Probably the rank-and-file membership (underground) is no more than two or three thousand. Strongly under Communist influence were FEUE (the National University Students' Organization, now dissolved), and CTE, the principal trade union organization. If you ask a reasonable observer in Quito the most serious of all questions in this connection—what is the Communist *potential* here?—the answer is likely to be that it is considerable. This country is as shaky as its own volcanic terrain. Some fear exists of the possibility of an incursion of Communist guerrillas from Colombia next door, across a frontier impossible to control. Two associated statements I heard are relevant. One is that "negative anti-Communism" is as dangerous as Communism itself, because the oligarchs "magnify" Communist power through their fear of it but at the same time are too sterile to introduce the kind of reform which might cause its influence to diminish. The other is in a familiar vein, "If we don't straighten things out here somebody else will." Both remarks came from conservatives.

The Colón Archipelago, or the Galápagos

These islets out in the Pacific, made of volcanic lava, belong to Ecuador. The United States was permitted to make use of them in World War II, but Ecuador is zealous in its protection of their status. The Galápagos, which resemble no other islands in the world, number about sixty and are sparsely inhabited; some of their names are—or were—nicely British (Indefatigable, Albemarle). What keeps them in the news from time to time is the exoticism of their wild life, which has fascinated naturalists from Darwin, who stopped off here after seeing what he thought might be the "missing link" between ape and man in Tierra del Fuego, to William Beebe and his bathysphere. Here are tortoises which live for several hundred years and weigh a quarter of a ton, monster lizards, and marine creatures of bizarre variety. One astonishing statistic, which is duplicated in several standard works of reference, is that 37 percent of all the species of shore fish, 47 percent of the plants, and 96 percent of the reptiles in the Galápagos, are found nowhere else in the world. Bird life is remarkable as well. No wonder Darwin called the islands "a living laboratory of evolution."

Political prisoners are regularly shipped out to the Galápagos by the Ecuadorian authorities. Their lot is rough, and torture is not unknown.

CHAPTER 24

Colombia: The Background of the *Violencia*

> *Under the sky the pampas,*
> *Upon the pampas my horse,*
> *Upon my horse me,*
> *Upon me my hat.*
> —LLANERO SONG QUOTED BY GERMÁN ARCINIEGAS

COLOMBIA IS probably the most baffling of all the South American republics. Potentially rich beyond measure, it has recently been the nearest to bankruptcy of any country on the continent. A nation intensely proud of its intellectual tradition, it has been grossly dominated by long periods of violence, known as the *violencia*, right to today. Colombia is withdrawn in character, complicated to grasp, and rent by paradox. Also important is the fact that, here in Colombia, we enter the Caribbean sector, which means among other things that the United States watches it with particular attention. The fact may be denied, but the Caribbean is still, in the old-fashioned phrase, an American "sphere of influence," where military intervention took place a good many times earlier in the century—even recently, as in the case of the Dominican Republic in 1965.

Colombia depends to a large extent on coffee for its livelihood, has a weirdly intricate political system, and holds seventeen million people, who live on a rain-soaked terrain that is partly a spiny pincushion, partly a moist flat plain. Bogotá, the aloof capital, perched 8,660 feet up in the Andes, is nicknamed "the Athens of Latin America" because of its devotion to culture, but lawlessness invades its streets. The country club is almost startlingly luxurious, but there are workers in its industrial suburbs who are lucky to

431

earn $5 a week. The old folklore says that it is so sophisticated that even the bootblacks read Proust, but spectators are apt to be frisked before being admitted to a football game.

No Colombian president has ever been assassinated, but the country has survived at least thirty revolutions in the past 150 years. It is the third or fourth most industrialized country in South America, but, although almost three times bigger than California, it has only 1,800 miles of railroad, hardly more than in the outskirts of Chicago. It is the largest producer of gold on the continent and the third petroleum producer, and has set up an important steel industry at Paz del Río, but is broke.

Both prosaic and colorful, it partakes equally of Europe and America. Bullfighting and baseball are both favorite sports—basketball as well. It considers itself to be extremely civilized, but the death rate is one of the highest on the continent, and life expectancy is only 44.2 years.[1] It has Avianca, one of the best airlines in the world, but illiteracy above the age of 15 is 37 percent, and 90 percent of primary students drop out of school before the fifth grade.

Colombia is the third-largest country in South America by population, the fourth by area. It has coastlines on both Atlantic and Pacific, the only South American country that has, and stretches far enough south to have seventy-three miles of frontier on the Amazon. On the banks of the great river here is an uncomely outpost named Leticia. Back in 1930 a silly little war broke out between Colombia and Peru over this stretch of Amazonian wilderness, which was settled by the old League of Nations, one of the few international rents the League ever did patch up.

The western sector of Colombia is completely dominated by the Andes; their majestic cordillera splits into three ranges, which fan out like fingers and divide the country into wild isolated fragments. Between the giant ranges lie sinuous slow rivers like the Magdalena, and astoundingly fertile valleys like the Cauca. East of the Andes is a vast stretch of flatland, largely uninhabited, known as the *llanos*, together with moist jungle regions. "Less than two percent of the population is spread out over half the total area."[2]

Climate in Colombia is, as has been aptly said, "vertical." There are no seasons, since it is bisected by the equator, and the weather depends on the altitude. The upper tier is coldish all the year around, the lower hot. This makes for a large diversity in agriculture, and Colombia produces everything

[1] Life expectancy in the United States is 69.4 years.
[2] *Colombia Today—and Tomorrow,* by Pat M. Holt, a brilliant account of con temporary Colombia. See also the *South American Handbook,* indispensable as always.

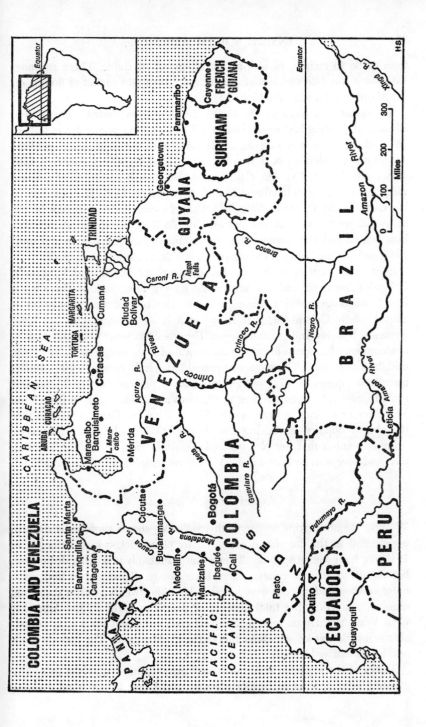

COLOMBIA AND VENEZUELA

from cattle to orchids, as well as the all-important coffee. There are more than seven hundred varieties of orchid, more than *all* varieties of flowers on the Atlantic seaboard of the United States.

The remarkable physiognomy of the country has promoted acute sectionalism, thus assisting backwoods violence. The mountain people live in walled-off pockets, have a strong local identity, and maintain fierce political partisanship. Colombia is, I heard it put, "ideal bloodfeud country" with village pitted against village, clan against clan, family against family. Rural gangs descend on remote villages to raid crops and get food. The processes of law enforcement are made difficult by lack of communication except by air; many villages can only be reached on foot. As for cities the great metropolises Bogotá and Barranquilla were not connected all the way by rail until 1961, and the trip between them took sixteen *days* before the age of air.

In strict contrast to such countries as Argentina, Brazil, and Venezuela, Colombia has never had any substantial foreign immigration. There are a few German-descended communities, but the rest of the population is almost solidly Colombian, that is to say it is an amalgam of three basic elements, Spanish, Indian, and Negro. The stock has never been enriched by contemporary European blood, by the arrival of large numbers of, let us say, middle-class Italians. The racial compound today is 20 percent white (almost exclusively Spanish), 47.8 percent *mestizo*, 6 percent Negro, 24 percent mulatto, and 2.2 percent Indian; the Indians are divided into no fewer than 398 different tribes. One reason why immigration has been so scant is that the church opposed it, fearing that immigration would dilute its power. Another point is that the Negroes and mulattoes are a law-abiding community, and have scarcely been involved in the contemporary *violencia* at all.

Aspects of the Violencia

We must come to grips now with this *violencia*, such a profoundly disturbing element in the life of this extraordinary cloud-cuckoo land. It began in 1948 and has gone on sporadically ever since. Probably it is dying down now, but its effects on the country have been savage. Between two and three *hundred thousand* citizens were killed in less than twenty years, a staggering number, more than the total number of deaths in battle in the American Civil War. What was, indeed, a virtual civil war raged for a long period, although little was known about this in the world outside. The episode was a murderous national tragedy.

Traces of the *violencia* atmosphere still exist—to understate the case. The morning after arriving in Bogotá my wife and I met in our hotel a young

American woman whom we had known in New York and who now lives in Colombia. My wife was wearing some modest jewels—a gold bracelet and a jeweled wrist watch. "Take those off," our friend said. "Don't go out on the streets with any jewelry that can be snatched. The thugs will tear them off you in broad daylight."

We did not follow her advice and nothing happened to us, but we heard several first-hand stories about thuggery and robbery in the best quarters of town. We were warned emphatically not to walk on the streets after dark, and never to take any taxi not directly provided by the hotel. An epidemic of kidnapings was going on. All this might have been dismissed as little more than something vaguely menacing and disagreeable in personal terms, but it added up to something more. Uneasiness, apprehension blanketed the city. Men and money were skipping from the country, the government was floundering, and political morale was low.

Householders in fashionable neighborhoods, we discovered, had their own guards—vigilantes. Owners wired their properties with electric alarm systems, if they could afford them, and prominent citizens hired bodyguards or carried guns. Pistols were actually put on sale at the Ministry of War, and, if a person had a certificate of good character, he could obtain one subject to three conditions: (a) he must not carry it when drunk; (b) he must not load it in public; (c) he must surrender it on demand. Classes to teach housewives how to shoot in order to protect themselves were set up by the authorities.

Lawlessness is certainly not a monopoly of Bogotá, and thousands of men and women never get into trouble. Some areas may be unsafe at night, but this is also true of New York City. Years ago Chicago lived through a virtual reign of terror, but few citizens ever actually saw a murder. But the atmosphere of Bogotá and other cities in Colombia, to say nothing of the countryside, is peculiarly sinister. One night my wife and I dined alone in a restaurant in a district like the East Sixties in New York and took a taxi back to our hotel, situated in a location comparable to the Waldorf's. In a ten-block ride at 11:30 P.M. we did not see a single pedestrian on the streets or pass a single automobile. At night this capital goes under wraps. People are afraid.

This is all particularly surprising in view of the Colombian tradition, which is based on constitutionalism, law, and justice. Colombian leaders are mostly high-minded, humane, and temperate—perhaps somewhat arid and doctrinaire as well—in addition to being intellectually sophisticated. How then explain the *violencia* which has disfigured the country in recent years? This is the most perplexing of all the Colombian paradoxes. To answer we must go far back.

Groundwork

The original El Dorado of the *conquistadores,* Colombia was discovered in 1500 by Alonso de Ojeda, a shipmate of Columbus, and has a confused and romantic history. One objective was the whereabouts of an Indian king who was reputed to gild himself once a year as part of a sacred ceremony, shower himself with gold dust, and offer emeralds (for which Colombia is still famous) to the gods. And gold was, indeed, found by the *conquistadores,* although not in such quantity as in Peru.

In 1538 a poet-adventurer named Jiménez de Quesada marched from the coast to the site of what is now Bogotá, named it Santa Fé de Bogotá, and established an outpost there. The Indians in the neighborhood, the Chibchas, so primitive in some respects that they did not even know the use of draft animals, offered little resistance. Although they had no civilization to rank with that of their neighbors, the Incas to the south, they had managed to develop a communal system of landownership and they were capable of producing marvelously effective works of ornamentation in gold. Meantime a German adventurer named Nikolaus de Federmann, representing the German banking house of Welser but carrying authority from the King of Spain, also sought to stake out a claim in the country, as did another *conquistador,* Sebastián de Belalcázar, one of Pizarro's captains, who was working his way up toward Bogotá from Ecuador. He founded the cities of Cali and Popayán.

The three adventurers met at Bogotá and made a pact, dividing their authority. Thereupon the development of Colombia (which was named Nueva Granada) began, and the colonial period got under way. The country covered an immense territory, since it included what is now Venezuela, Ecuador, and Panama as well as Colombia itself. Part of the Viceroyalty of Peru until 1718, it eventually reached a viceregal status of its own. Spain largely neglected it, and a century passed without much incident. Then came the rash of Creole nationalist revolts all over South America in the early years of the nineteenth century. The Colombian upheaval (1813–19) was made by Simón Bolívar himself, assisted by Francisco de Paula Santander, an intellectual who became a stirring military leader and politician. At last the rebels won, and the independence of the country (now called Gran Colombia) was proclaimed on December 17, 1819.

Ecuador and Venezuela split off from Colombia almost at once, becoming republics on their own. Bitter political strife afflicted Colombia, which now reverted to the name New Granada. Two parties arose, Conservative and

Liberal, which is the origin of the two-party system that has distinguished the country ever since. Bolívar, no democrat, was father of the Conservatives, Santander of the Liberals. The Conservatives wanted a unitary state under a strong central government and were fanatically pro-Church; the Liberals wanted a federal system, with the provinces holding a commensurate share of power, and were fanatically anticlerical, even though they might be good Catholics. After half a century of struggle, the Conservatives won a short-term victory and in 1886 promulgated a new constitution, which is still the basic law of the land although it has been amended several times. Colombia became a unitary state under a strong central government with powerful church influence.

But partisan feeling between Conservatives and Liberals remained furious. The two-party system, as in Uruguay, excluded everybody else. This was not a case of Whig against Tory or Republican versus Democrat; it was Lancaster against York, or Montague versus Capulet. Probably no country except Ireland has ever had such internecine politics. The two parties alternated in power till 1899, when the Liberals revolted against a Conservative regime, and a bloody civil war, known as the "War of a Thousand Days," broke out and lasted till 1902. The dead numbered not less than a hundred thousand.

In 1903 came the great fracas over Panama and the canal. President Theodore Roosevelt, as he boasted later, "took the canal." The gist of this story, if I may repeat a word from Chapter 8, is that the United States became determined to build a canal on Panamanian territory, which belonged to Colombia, but the Colombian government did not agree to the projected terms. So Panama suddenly had a "revolution," and we "intervened" promptly on the revolutionary side, thus making the new Panama our puppet and enabling work on the canal to begin. Colombia was paid off with $25 million. The Colombians were so humiliated that they did not acknowledge the loss of Panama for almost twenty years. But the War of a Thousand Days had so weakened the country that it could do nothing to resist Roosevelt's maneuver.

Colombia was more or less tranquil from 1903 to 1948 under both Conservative and Liberal governments. But sullen fires burned under the surface. Then came an extraordinary event which is basic to an understanding of almost everything that has happened since—the assassination of a man named Jorge Eliécer Gaitán.

Aftermath of a Murder

People in Bogotá still talk about this murder as if it happened yesterday. An aura of mystery, sacrifice, and legend has grown up around it, and it still calls forth conjecture and expostulation. Gaitán, a left-wing Liberal, was mayor of Bogotá; the national government was, however, Conservative at the time, which made for strain and conflict. A man of the people, Gaitán had introduced important reforms as minister of education in a previous Liberal government, and was probably the best mayor Bogotá ever had. He shook things up. He defied stagnation and convention. He was windbaggy and immoderate—a demagogue. To a degree he resembled Fiorello H. LaGuardia in New York. His magnetism was compelling. The political situation in Bogotá became chafing, and on April 9, 1948, Gaitán was shot and killed by a nondescript character named Roa Sierra, who was lynched at once by an inflamed mob. But some people, right down to this day, do not believe that Sierra was the real assassin, or, if he was, know whether he acted out of private impulse or was put up to the job by someone else, possibly the diehard Conservatives, who had become more and more outraged by what they called Gaitán's inflammatory leftness. There is no evidence of Liberal or Communist complicity.

The best supposition is that the murder was not a political plot, but merely an incident that reflected the hysterical mood of the community at the time, like the assassination of John F. Kennedy in Dallas. It seems clear that Sierra, the killer—if he was the killer—had a disturbed personality and was in the midst of a severe emotional crisis. One story is to the effect that he was the lover of a woman who, he happened to find out, was also the mistress of their postman. They had a violent quarrel, and the woman screamed insults at Sierra, sneering at him for being "a poor devil." He shouted at her, "You will find out someday whether I am a poor devil or not," ran into Gaitán on a downtown street, and forthwith shot him in order to become famous and redeem himself in the eyes of his young lady.[3]

One peculiarity is that the assassination and its aftermath took place while Colombia was supposed to be on its best behavior, because Bogotá was host that week to the ninth meeting of the Inter-American Congress, the one that

[3] Fidel Castro, a youthful student, happened to be in Bogotá at the time and is supposed to have been an eye-witness to the killing, but there is no evidence whatever associating him with it. Castro was only twenty-two in 1948, and a totally unknown figure. I have met several eye-witnesses to the murder, including a British diplomat who happened to be standing a few feet from Gaitán.

created the Organization of American States. The distinguished guests, both North and South American, then had to face three days of terror on the streets, because Gaitán's death was immediately followed by what is now called the *bogotazo*, a bloody blowup. Indignant Gaitán supporters ran wild, and became a mob. The police, inert, did little to stop them, because most were Gaitán sympathizers. The rioting became uncontrollable and, at the end of three days, when order was restored, a large part of downtown Bogotá had gone up in flames and no fewer than two to three thousand citizens had been killed. The whole city might have been burned out except for a sudden severe providential rain. Incidentally the commander of the emergency airlift which flew stranded Americans out of the town was none other than General Matthew B. Ridgeway, later to become the American commander-in-chief in Korea and chief of staff.

The *violencia* then broke out as a series of minor incidents which developed into a kind of "undeclared civil war," distinguished not merely for its appalling number of casualties for the next nine years but for its ferocious brutality. Children were spitted on pitchforks; citizens had their lips, noses, or ears cut off. The focus of this phase of the *violencia* was not Bogotá, but the inaccessible mountainous countryside. A crazy search for vengeance, long pent up, increased its horrors. Conservatives sought to revenge themselves for their men killed in the *bogotazo*; Liberals for the death of the martyred Gaitán. A characteristic of Colombia is the way fiercely partisan groups tend to cling together geographically; for a hundred years the hinterland has been dotted with Conservative or Liberal villages, often close together, which hated each other. So when the *violencia* increased, mountaineers of one complexion would descend on those of the other, raid their villages, set them on fire, and maim or kill their citizens. Then the next village would retaliate. It was as much as an outsider's life was worth to wear innocently a red necktie in Conservative territory (red being the Liberal color), or a blue tie (blue = Conservative) in Liberal domains.

Economic factors entered into this. Liberals could not get jobs, particularly government jobs, on which subsistence might depend, in Conservative territory; Conservatives could not get jobs in Liberal territory. Unless a man followed a given political line he could not find work. Then rural juntas arose trying to organize the countryside; to this day, about 8,500 of these survive.

Sectionalism, political partisanship, addiction to blood feuds, and poverty do not go the whole way in explaining the *violencia*. Plenty of countries have backwoods mountaineers and intricate or unwieldy political systems without being afflicted by prolonged terrorism and violence. Colombians like to say that some mysterious "x" factor may be involved. For instance it is suggestive that the *violencia* was most rabid in communities where the suicide rate is high.

Horrified by the carnage, sensible men in Bogotá sought to stop it. The only way to do so was to establish a political truce on the highest level, since politics was the dividing line. More than two hundred thousand people had been killed. This was war. The survival of the country was at stake. The government at this time, 1957, was in the hands of a stopgap military junta, following four years of arbitrary rule by an enterprising and ambitious dictator, Gustavo Rojas Pinilla. The junta pitched Rojas out, and then announced, in the best South American tradition, that it would run the country only until constitutional rule was re-established under a freely elected civilian president.

Thus the way toward a truce was assisted. The story is extremely convoluted. The Liberal leader, Alberto Lleras Camargo, a former president of the country and one of its most civilized citizens, took the initiative. Leader of the Conservatives was the mastodonic Laureano Gómez, also an ex-president and an extreme reactionary, who was living in exile in Spain. Lleras visited him twice, and after thorny negotiations they succeeded in patching up an agreement for a coalition government to be called the Frente Nacional. This was made effective in 1958, and has ruled Colombia ever since. And, for the time being, the *violencia* stopped. But the National Front itself **has** produced bewildering severe problems.

How the National Front Works

The National Front, as worked out by Lleras Camargo and Laureano Gómez, had three main planks which were written into the constitution. Any attempt to change them thus becomes a constitutional issue, and makes modification difficult. The main provisions were:

1. For sixteen years (from 1958 to 1974), spanning four presidential terms of four years each, the presidency was to alternate between the two chief parties, with no other allowed to run. First Liberal, then Conservative, then Liberal, then Conservative again, was the presumptive sequence.

2. "Millimetric" parity was established throughout the entire government and bureaucracy. The apparatus of government was to operate on the basis of halves.[4] If the top man in a government office was a Liberal, the man below him had to be a Conservative, and so on alternately down the line.

---

[4] With certain exceptions. The foreign minister has to be of the same party as the president. The minister of the interior must be of the other party.

This resembles the "Proporz" system in Austria, which was similarly installed to remedy a seemingly irreparable feud between the leading parties.

3. A two-thirds vote was required to pass legislation in Congress, instead of a simple majority.

Elections were held, and Lleras Camargo, the Liberal, who had been president briefly before, became president again—the first under this new and unprecedented system. He served from 1958 to 1962, and was duly succeeded by a Conservative, Guillermo León Valencia, who held office from 1962 to 1966. Gómez was titular leader of the Conservative party, but he did not run because he was too old and reactionary to be an acceptable candidate.

Both the Liberal and Conservative parties are "vertical" in structure. Even before the National Front they necessarily represented every color in the spectrum, containing wings from extreme right to moderate left, because no other effective parties existed. The two-party system knocked all the others out. Another point is that, with the passage of time, the differences between the two parties had begun to narrow. Federalism is no longer a live issue, and neither is clericalism and the position of the church. The adage began to be heard, "The only difference between Liberals and Conservatives nowadays is that the Liberals go to mass at 8 A.M., the Conservatives at 10."

The *violencia* died down temporarily when the National Front became established, and this much must be said for it. Politically, however, it has not been working well and few Colombians think that it will live out its full span till 1974. In fact the biggest political issue in the country today, next to inflation, is how the National Front is to survive. Not many people like it, but nobody has been able to work out a substitute. The principal objections seem to be the following:

First, government no longer represents the will of the voters, at least on the presidential level, since the next president *must* belong to a stipulated party whether this is what the people want or not.

Second, the system induces apathy, also restlessness. There have been large abstentions of voting in recent elections. Who cares about voting, since it is known beforehand which party will win?

Third, the government of the day is not on its toes, since it knows that it cannot succeed itself. There is little incentive to push a program through. What would the administration of Lyndon B. Johnson be like if it were absolutely established that his successor in 1968 *had* to be a Republican?

Fourth, Conservatives tend to vote for the most conservative of the Liberal candidates, Liberals tend to vote for the most liberal Conservatives. This makes it extremely difficult to define issues. Political confusion is the rule, because every politician is dependent on the *other* party for electoral support.

Fifth, it is almost impossible to get legislation through Congress efficiently, since this is divided half and half between Liberals and Conservatives. Each party has 50 percent of the membership, but it takes a two-thirds vote to pass a law. So votes have to be traded and manipulated.[5]

Sixth, Liberals outnumber Conservatives by a 60–40 ratio in the country at large, and so the parity system is unfair. What will happen in 1970? Why should the Liberals, now in power, voluntarily give it up since they could continue in office indefinitely if elections were unfettered and the National Front did not impose the alternation system?

Enter More Guerrillas

To make confusion worse the *violencia* cropped up again in the early 1960's, and, although it never reached the pitch of 1948–57, it is still a vexing headache. There are several differences between the early violence and that of today. For one thing the first phase was largely rural, but now it has penetrated into the towns; for another kidnaping has become a new and sinister weapon in the hands of thugs and terrorists; for still another, Communism entered the picture as a serious factor. Finally, the texture of the *violencia* itself has changed.

In its first phase it was mostly a matter of Conservatives murdering Liberals and vice versa; then it became a struggle between bandits-at-large versus government-at-large, something quite different. Some terrorists today are not merely desperadoes, but rebels. Disturbances are no longer largely a business of blood feud and vendetta, but of revolt against national law, although this is not necessarily motivated by ideology. "Bandit kingdoms" arose in several provinces, which were difficult to wipe out. A situation arose almost like that in Kenya during the Mau Mau terror. Revolt and banditry became combined, and then kidnaping entered the picture.

Probably the territorists discovered the value of this by accident; clearly it was a good way to finance their activity. The first conspicuous victim was a wealthy businessman and former cabinet minister named Harold Eder, a person of top importance, who was kidnaped in March, 1965. The bandits killed him at once, but, not revealing this, asked $250,000 ransom for him. They did not get it. Five weeks later came the case of Oliverio Lara, a man

---

[5] Holt, *op. cit.*, has a full, acute treatment of all this.

almost equally well known. He was seized on April 27, and, as of the moment of writing, is believed to be still alive. Medicine has been delivered to him, but the kidnapers will not let him go. Altogether about two hundred kidnapings classified as major occurred during 1965, along with countless minor cases. A foreman in a factory can be captured, salted away, and held for $40.

The government, as former President Valencia told me, will not assist in the payment of any ransom, and it seeks to keep families from doing so. The theory is that ransom payments will make matters worse, and even "put the government on the side of the kidnapers." Victims and their relatives or friends must simply sweat it out.

One notorious desperado carries the nickname Tiro Fijo, or Sure Shot.[6] His real name is Pedro Antonio Marín; he is thirty-four, commands about a thousand guerrillas, and is said to have been responsible for at least two hundred murders. His inaccessible domain is in the high Andes near Bogotá, where he set up what he called the "Independent Republic of Marquetalia." Here, in an area covering fourteen hundred square miles, he has made his own law for years and has been impossible to capture. Recently his men waylaid a bus, killed thirteen of its passengers (including two nuns), and then raided the town of Inzá, where they executed the mayor and chief of police and made speeches to the populace urging revolution. With Tiro Fijo on this foray was a Cuban agitator, who also spoke. Army units have taken several of Tiro Fijo's outposts, and found in them Castro leaflets and other Communist propaganda; it seems clear that he maintains close touch with Cuba, although he is probably more an apolitical bandit than a Communist himself.

The Communist party is perfectly legal in Colombia, in spite of the two-party system. The secretary general of its official (Moscow) wing, Gilberto Vieira, has held this position for twenty years or more, and is an old-line figure on the Thorez-Togliatti model. The party has a freely circulated newspaper, but its membership is small, probably about thirteen thousand. Peking influence has risen sharply in recent years. The Communists run for office quite as a matter of course, but they have *to mask themselves as Liberals* or *Conservatives* to do so—another National Front absurdity. The House of Representatives in Bogotá has five members believed to be Communist, and the Senate one. On the other hand, Colombia does not maintain diplomatic relations with the Soviet Union, China, or the Com-

---

[6] Most of the guerrilla leaders and bandits bear "romantic" nicknames, like "Revenge," "Black Blood," "The Claw," "Sparks," and, oddly enough, "B.B.C."

munist satellites, except Czechoslovakia; East Germany has, however, a trade mission resident in Bogotá.

Out in the hills a terrorist may not be a Communist at all, but he is almost certain to have picked up elements of Communist theory and teaching on the principles of guerrilla warfare, as embodied in books by Mao Tse-tung and Che Guevera. Naturally he listens to the Havana radio. Who in his position would not? Naturally too the guerrillas take gladly any support and encouragement given them by the real Communists. The official Communist *party* in Colombia is, however, careful not to participate directly in terrorism and accepts no money from the kidnapings, for obvious reasons, but it hopes in good time to inherit the whole guerrilla apparatus. The official Communists dissociate themselves from terrorism altogether. I asked a dozen well-informed Colombians, as well as a number of foreign diplomats, whether they thought that today's banditry was nonpolitical from a general ideological point of view or Communist-inspired— indigenous or supported from abroad. The consensus was that the movement was still largely nonpolitical and indigenous, but that Communist influence was growing steadily. But President Valencia, when I talked to him, firmly took the line that the guerrilla movement *was* Communist-inspired and led, although this was not true in the early days of the *violencia*. He added that the bandits could not exist except for support from outside (e.g., Cuba), that Colombia along with Venezuela had been chosen as a test case to see what damage guerrilla activity could do, and that he himself has been marked for assassination, along with President Leoni of Venezuela. I asked where the guerrillas got their arms from, and he replied somewhat surprisingly, "The United States." Doubtless they are old arms smuggled in by way of Cuba.

Meanwhile, mopping-up operations by the government are proceeding with some measure of success. United States helicopters have assisted the government forces. For the past three or four years the guerrillas have been killing between 3,000 and 4,000 citizens a year, but in 1965 this figure dropped to 1,284. Substantial areas in the Caldas, Valle, and Tolima districts were virtually under the control of the terrorists until recently, but now they have been cleaned up except for a few isolated strongholds.

CHAPTER 25

Colombia: People, Issues, Problems

The Caribbean was the ear in which all the first sounds of
our history echoed. Crime and glory were born there together.
—GERMÁN ARCINIEGAS

THE PRESIDENT of Colombia from 1962 to 1966 was León Valencia, a
Conservative operating under the National Front. Even though he is no
longer chief executive a word about him may be useful, to illustrate aspects
of the national character and scene.

The Palace of San Carlos, the official residence of Colombian presidents,
stands somewhat inconspicuously on a narrow, dingy street, Carrera 16, next
to the Colón theater. State theaters in South America often bear the name
Colón (= Columbus). Contrary to the general practice on the continent,
the palace does not face the main square of the city, which is called the
Plaza Bolívar in Bogotá, but is a block or two away. It looks unimpressive
from outside—partly because it is difficult to get a view of the structure as a
whole—but it has a splendid grace, style, and charm within. I thought that
it was the finest presidential palace I saw anywhere on our trip, although it
is not so outwardly regal as those in Lima or Buenos Aires and not so intimately charming as the one in Quito. The entrance leads to a broad shallow
staircase the width of the entire hall, and is divided into three parallel sections; at the top of each stands a guard on a low pedestal, stiff as a statue and
wearing a brilliant uniform in scarlet, white, and azure. These guards carry
fixed bayonets, if only for show, and on the day of our visit two of the three
were Negroes. We followed our escort through a series of reception rooms,
which flow magnificently into one another through tall open doors, and which
are hung with glittering chandeliers (one I think was the largest I have ever
seen) and filled with French period and antique Spanish gold-painted furni-

445

ture. The rooms carry a note of exquisite delicacy as well as ornateness. The taste is as perfect as at the Elysée in Paris. Downstairs we peeked into a small bedroom—Bolívar's. Here his life was saved by one of the most renowned of his mistresses, Manuela Sáenz (Mrs. Thorne), who hustled him out of a window into the patio below when plotters made an attempt on his life in 1828. The patio still holds a large walnut tree which Bolívar himself planted there as a symbol of his deliverance.

There are no photographers, no TV, no radio interviewers, as is common elsewhere in South America when a visitor is received, and no publicity attends a presidential audience. Such displays are considered vulgar in Colombia.

President Valencia greeted us in a large room dominated by a portrait of Bolívar which, he explained, presented the Liberator as a man, not merely as a soldier. Strange as it may seem, the room contained books. It was the only presidential palace in South America where I ever saw a book. We had two interpreters. One was our own. The other was one of the president's sons, a member of the Colombian diplomatic service who was acting as his father's secretary. Our man offered to withdraw. The president's son protested (in perfect English), "Oh, no, *my* English is quite imperfect, and you had better stay with us and help." It was all very cozy, but formal underneath.

The president, a gentleman, talked and acted like one. Physically he resembled a typical French politician of the old school; he might have been a prewar mayor of Toulouse or a deputy from Nantes, with thinning hair cut straight across in back, red-rimmed eyes, a broken prow of a nose, and a jutting jaw. He wore beautifully cut clothes, as did his son. He was alert, aware, and somewhat cautious. When we were presented I said that I must apologize for my ignorance about Colombia, since we had only arrived the afternoon before. His reply was, "If you have been here twenty-four hours you already know more than most Colombians do."

Valencia's father was a well-known romantic poet who ran for the presidency twice but lost each time. The familiar Colombian fixation on culture may be appreciated by a little story to the effect that Valencia's son is accustomed to identify himself with the words, "I am the grandson of the poet," not "I am the son of the president," when he meets people. Valencia himself is a stickler for family unity and honor. A widower, he has two sons and two daughters, and he startled his audience in a recent campaign speech by saying that, if any of the four children ever disobeyed him or dishonored the family name, he would shoot them all.

Colombians are apt to be pronounced individualists no matter what their family relationships are, and one of the president's brothers, Alvaro Pio

Valencia, is an extreme left-winger—in fact leader of the Communist party in the Cauca Valley. And I heard one of his nephews make an impassioned anti-American speech at an open forum of students in Bogotá which was called to discuss United States intervention in the Dominican Republic.[1] The president himself is vigorously pro-American. He has every right to be, since his country, beset by grave inflationary and other financial problems, could not easily survive without American aid, which has amounted to the tidy sum of $368 million in the past three years.

Guillermo León Valencia was born in the pleasant old colonial town of Popayán in 1909. He started professional life as a journalist, and entered politics in 1935, when he became a state assemblyman, the lowest rung in the ladder, in the Cauca district. His life has been unadventurous, but no South American politician escapes some touch of melodrama. Back in 1957 President Rojas Pinilla ordered Valencia's arrest. Valencia took refuge in the house of a friend, defied Rojas, stood off a cordon of troops with a pistol, and, after much perilous by-play, was finally rescued by the local Catholic bishop.[2] Valencia's relations with the church are not, incidentally, particularly close, even if this anecdote seems to indicate the contrary. Early in 1965 he caused a sensation by declaring publicly that the Catholic church, like so much else in Colombia, had been infiltrated by the Communists. This made the local hierarchy furious, and it demanded proof and an apology, whereupon Valencia withdrew his accusation.

Valencia is an absolutely honest man. Gone here are the familiar corruptions of most of the rest of South America. Convivial, a *bon vivant*, he likes parties, food, and talk. His chief defects are lack of grip, lack of interest in administration, quixoticism, and a tendency to make *faux pas*. During the de Gaulle visit, after an interminable public dinner, he apparently forgot himself and, finishing a resonant speech, ended with the words "Viva España" instead of toasting France, much to the consternation of the guests.

The New President, Carlos Lleras Restrepo

This is an able, tough-minded, and forward-looking man. Lleras was elected president in May, 1966, by a vote of around 1,700,000 to 700,000, but only a third of the electorate voted. Thus, succeeding Señor Valencia, whose administration had gradually become more feeble and inept, he

---

[1] Under the auspices of the Centro Colombo-Americano, the bi-national center operated by the United States in Bogotá. American authorities here have the intelligence and vision to allow meetings to be held at which every variety of opinion can be expressed.

[2] Holt, *op. cit.*, pp. 42–43.

became the third president under the National Front coalition system. He is a distant cousin of Alberto Lleras Camargo, the first president under the National Front. A Liberal, as explained above, had to be elected in 1966—this was obligatory under the constitution. Lleras Restrepo's opponent was José Jaramillo Giraldo, an unknown, who described himself as an "opposition" Liberal, but who was the handpicked candidate of the noisy General Rojas Pinilla, the former dictator who will not stay down. The essential fact is that Dr. Lleras was opposed by both extreme left and extreme right, and, a man of the center, won.

Complicated politics preceded the Lleras victory. He was the obvious Liberal choice, but, early in 1965, he resigned from the race on grounds that have never been altogether explained, and took a holiday in Europe. This is a favorite device among Colombian politicians. Men of affairs take refuge in Europe and use it as a convenient perch as Roman men of affairs used Cisalpine Gaul. Lleras perhaps left the country as a method of attracting more attention to his person, and make it appear that, if he changed his mind and did run after all, he would be responding to a draft. Plenty of United States politicians use similar devices. In any case he soon returned to Colombia, mended his difficulties with both Liberals and Conservatives, and resumed his candidacy.

Dr. Lleras has been in the heart of the Colombian power structure for many years. His background is intellectual, and his father was a well-known professor of medicine and scientist. He has been called a typical "oligarch," but this hardly fits the case. It remains to be seen, however, whether he will be pronouncedly liberal as well as Liberal.

The new president is fifty-eight. He is bald, glossy-looking, bespectacled, and somewhat stocky. He became a doctor of law in 1930, and was elected to the House of Representatives three years later. Almost at once he became interested in land reform, the *sine qua non* of almost everything in Colombia, and by 1938 was minister of finance and public credit. Meantime he became a professor of public finance at the law school, where he taught for thirteen years, while serving at the same time as managing editor of *El Tiempo*—an exhausting double harness. He rose to be president of the Liberal party by 1941, when he was still only thirty-three, and was elected to the senate two years later. It was he who initiated the legalization which made INCORA, the land reform organization, possible, and he introduced as well the bill setting up a Land Credit Institute, which launched a nationwide low-cost housing program. He became anathema to the orthodox Conservatives. Nor did others spare him—his house was burned down in the *violencia* in 1948.

Meantime, the industrious Dr. Lleras found time to be active in big business as a consultant and otherwise. He was president for a time of the National Committee of Coffee Growers, one of the key positions in the country, and he has had close associations with several American companies in Colombia, like Celanese Colombiana, S.A., of which he was president. He is firmly pro-American, and has any number of North American friends and admirers, like David E. Lilienthal, who has worked closely with him for a number of years.

The Lleras government will be honest, middle-of-the-road, and reformist to the extent that this is possible. Most members of his cabinet, as in Chile, are intellectuals or technical specialists, like Bernardo Garcés Córdoba, minister of public works, and Gabriel Betancur Mejía, minister of education, and they make up the strongest government Colombia has had in years. The cardinal difficulty is that a two-thirds majority is necessary to pass legislation, and the Lleras forces do not command so large a vote.

Who's Who

Colombian politics are such a formidable maze that the easiest approach is to list a few personalities. We begin with the Liberals, who are split. The official leader is of course President Dr. Carlos Lleras Restrepo.

Leader of the dissident wing, known as the MRL (Movimiento Revolucionario Liberal) is a vivid character, Alfonso López Michelsen—pronounced Mi-*kell*-sen. His position is left center. But the MRL is also split, and its two divisions oppose each other almost as vehemently as the party as a whole opposes both the orthodox Liberals and Conservatives. One group, which takes the *Línea Dura* (Hard Line), has an outspoken Communist following, approves of Castro, dislikes the United States, and seeks revolutionary changes in Colombia at once. Michelsen's own wing (*Línea Blanda* or Soft Line) is more moderate, though radical enough.

An intellectual, about fifty-three, distinguished, wealthy, López Michelsen is the son of a former president of the republic, Alfonso López Pumarejo, and seeks to carry on his father's tradition. The father, who greatly admired Franklin D. Roosevelt and wanted to emulate the New Deal, although he came out of a prominent mercantile family, was president from 1934–38 and again in 1942–45. He sought to grab Colombia by the neck and bring it to modern times. He set up a social security system that is still one of the best on the continent, encouraged labor to organize, and did more for education than any Colombian in a generation, although this is not to say very much.

Alfonso López Michelsen, the son, who has been a professor of law, partakes of several of his father's characteristics. He is tall, lean, perhaps spoiled, sensitive, and complicated. I asked him where he was educated, and his reply was, "Everywhere!" He went to a Jesuit school in Belgium, a lycée in France, another school in England, and to Georgetown University in Washington, D.C. He talked to us with frankness and precision. One reason, he said, why politics is so difficult in Colombia is that, in spite of its civilized tradition, dissent is still considered to be heresy—a hangover from Jesuit days. A grave disadvantage is lack of good men. "Those who are strong have no brains, those who have brains are not strong."

What López Michelsen stands for most is opposition to the absurdities of the National Front; he thinks that it stifles leadership, makes it impossible to have a genuine opposition, and creates a system in which "nobody can be either winner or loser." It worries him extremely that the *violencia* has spread from rural areas to the towns, because this proves that "authority" is gone. In one election López Michelsen received 23 percent of the total vote. He must be taken seriously if only because he is "respectable" and yet has wide left-wing support.

The Conservative position is more complex. The Conservatives have split, rejoined, and split again. They are like a swarm of fireflies. One wing, that of the Laureanistas, derives from the antique reactionary leader Laureano Gómez, and is led by his son, Alvaro Gómez Hurtado. Again, as in the case of the Lópezes, we glimpse the fibrous power of the father-to-son relationship. Politics are extremely fluid in Colombia, within a rigid frame, and personal leadership plays a pointed role in all these variations. Another Conservative grouping is that of the Ospinistas, who derive from Dr. Mariano Ospina Pérez, a former president of the republic, and who control about 35 percent of the Conservative strength in parliament. But when I was in Bogotá the Ospinistas were supporting the *Liberal* leader, Lleras Restrepo, because of convolutions within the National Front. To the wonders of public affairs in Colombia there is no end.

We approach now several military figures. General Gustavo Rojas Pinilla, sixty-six, who was dictator of the country from 1953 to 1957, still yearns to return to power. His group is the ANP, or National Popular Alliance. One of his chief collaborators is his 29-year-old daughter María Eugenia Rojas de Moreno Díaz, a striking character and a senator; women play more of a role in politics in Colombia than in any other South American country except Chile. It is difficult to determine just what Rojas stands for, or who supports him, but his strength revived sharply during the Valencia period. Mostly he appeals to the lower middle class, unemployed workers, and the disorganized poor—both rural and urban—also to a few intellectuals fed up with the stifling confusions of the political situation, weak government, and stalemate.

General Rojas was unseated in 1957 mostly because moderate elements in the army thought that he was becoming dangerous, and the church came out openly against him. This is a case where both army and church, supposed to be on the conservative side, ousted a conservative. On being driven out of office he was charged with corruption, deprived of his civil rights, and forbidden to enter politics. Nevertheless, returning to Colombia after a period of exile, he imperturbably entered the presidential race in 1962 apparently without objection from anybody. In 1963 he was exiled again to a remote village near the Ecuadorian frontier, but even so contested in the 1964 election as a "bipartisan" and "deliverer." He was not allowed to participate directly in 1966, but the strength of his supporters grew importantly and his movement has become the largest opposition bloc in the country.

One animated Rojista congressman introduced a bill in parliament recently for "Shooting Colombian Presidents." This advocated capital punishment for any head of state found guilty of "irresponsibility" or graft after trial by Congress and approval of the verdict by the Supreme Court. The firing squad, according to terms of the projected bill, would consist of a group of the most eminent citizens of the nation, all of whom would be declared "national heroes," and who would carry out the sentence publicly in the Plaza Bolívar. The bill did not pass.

General Rojas himself, effervescent as always, declared during the 1966 campaign that one item in his program was to discourage marriages between Colombian women and "gringos," and another to stop "the sale of Colombian blood to the United States." This last remark was apparently a reference to the fact that the Colombian Red Cross maintains a blood bank, paying peasants a dollar or two for a pint of blood; the general charged that this went to the United States, where it brought $50–60. The Red Cross denied the story as "silly politics." Rojas was asked at one meeting what he would do to control the Colombian inflation. His reply was, "That's simple. We would lock up all Colombians with money outside the country and not let them go until they paid back the three billion dollars they have hidden abroad."[3]

Another conspicuous military man, but of an altogether different stamp, is Major General Alberto Ruiz Novoa, a tall, attractive, bespectacled officer

[3] However, it appears that General Rojas is not a poor man himself. The government recently took over property of his valued at $370,000 for distribution to peasant families as part of the land reform. Rojas' daughter charged that the seizure "of papa's farm" was "just one more act of persecution." Apparently the Rojas property was valued less highly than neighboring land when the government expropriated it. H. J. Maidenberg and Juan de Onis in the New York Times, March 18 and September 1, 1966.

born in 1917, who was minister of war until he was forced to resign in January, 1965. He was thought to be too visionary, too left wing, and too ambitious. After quitting office it was discovered that he was a subscriber to the *New Statesman* of London; prudently his successor at once canceled the subscription! Ruiz has had an interesting career. He rose by merit. He led the Colombian battalion which fought in the Korean War. He is studious and modern-minded. Some people say he has been "built up" to more than his correct stature by too much publicity in the United States.

Be this as it may, General Ruiz, as minister of war, did more to beat down the bandits in the hills than any other man. First, he set up a political "reclamation" program and put the army to work on civil action projects, as in Peru. He was convinced that arms alone could not solve the guerrilla problem, and that it was necessary to reach the peasants somehow with concrete demonstrations of good will and cooperation. Second, strictly in the military realm, he organized the small picked combat teams known as *lanceros* (lancers) which gave a new technique and impetus to attacking the guerrilla bands.

General Ruiz was asked recently what, in his opinion, was the root cause of guerrilla activity. His answer surprised many—"enslavement of the Indians by the Spaniards centuries ago."

A brilliant young journalist, Alberto Zalamea, is one of the leaders of the National Democratic Movement, a kind of hold-all containing many elements. It is left wing, but vehemently anti-Communist; at the same time it hates the oligarchy and the banks, and seems to reflect Peronism to a degree. Its support seems to come mostly from the upper middle classes and professional men, particularly in Medellín, also from dissident church leaders and off-beat military men. Zalamea's enemies say that he wants a "military solution," and General Ruiz was associated with his group for a time.

Zalamea's wife is the well-known art critic and teacher Marta Traba, the organizer of Bogotá's Museum of Modern Art. The Zalameas represent the liveliest of contemporary tendencies and are as fresh as most of Bogotá is staid. Zalamea is a passionately articulate reformer. He feels that Columbia is run deviously by "go-betweens," which makes for anarchic irresponsibility. Voting is honest in the actual elections, but in the rural areas the *caciques* "own" the votes. Anybody can become a deputy for 50,000 pesos. Communism, he thinks, is certain to rule the country in the end—which would be a tragedy if only because the Communist party is so small numerically—if the moderate, anti-Communist left does not manage to create a regime that will give authority combined with justice, and *do* something for the people.

Indeed economic inequality in Colombia is an "iniquity," and this may be the real, the bedrock reason for the *violencia*. "Colombia is a country where roughly 350,000 people out of 17,000,000 have everything, and the rest nothing."[4]

Two Veterans

Alberto Lleras Camargo (not to be confused with Carlos Lleras Restrepo, the new president) has retired from politics now, but is still a consequential figure because of his large prestige as a former president and his personal qualities. A cosmopolitan, Dr. Lleras is almost as well known in Washington, New York, and western Europe as in Colombia. I talked to him in New York last year when he was acting as editor of *Visión*; the two things he stressed were the danger of Communist penetration by "hit and run" methods and the population increase. He said that Castro still hoped to make Colombia the "Vietnam of South America."

Urbane, immaculate, adroit, Lleras Camargo was born on July 5, 1906. He worked in journalism before entering politics. He became ambassador to Washington at the early age of thirty-six, and has represented his country in a wide variety of posts, for instance as foreign minister and Colombian delegate to the San Francisco conference which gave birth to the UN. From 1948 to 1954 he was secretary general of the Organization of American States, and was president of the republic twice, for a year in 1945–46 and for a full term 1958–62. Later he became president of the University of the Andes in Bogotá, a vigorous new institution.

Laureano Gómez, the veteran Conservative leader, was elected president in 1950, but was ousted by Rojas Pinilla in 1953. In strict contrast to Lleras, Gómez is a deadweight reactionary. He was an engineer by profession, born in 1883 in a town with a strong German background; vehemently religious and pro-church, he had the reputation of being pro-Axis before World War II, possibly because he had served for a time as Colombian ambassador to Germany. Again in contrast to Lleras, who has always been a spirited friend of the United States, he has often taken an anti-American line. But when I met him in Bogotá years ago and asked him whom he would prefer to have at the Panama Canal, Roosevelt or Hitler, he answered Roosevelt. His newspaper, *El Siglo*, which he founded in 1936, is still the fountainhead of conservative thought in Colombia, and he continues to be a formidable extremist.

[4] Rowland Evans and Robert Novak in the New York *Herald Tribune*.

What Runs Colombia?

The answer could not be simpler—the Establishment, known locally as the *sistema*. But this, as in Britain where the term "Establishment" originated, is a somewhat elusive concept to define. Some typical Colombian subtleties are involved, even though a local cliché is, "There is no government here, only a ruling clique."

Essentially the Establishment consists of the propertied class, the business community, the church, and those who have *arrived*. The oligarchy seeks to replenish itself, and social rank and money are not the only criteria. As a matter of fact there are few really big fortunes in Colombia, few *very* rich men, and no hereditary aristocracy of consequence. The basis of reputation is accomplishment. One demonstration of arrival is membership in the Jockey Club, and, after that, the Gun Club. It would be an oversimplification to say that the Jockey Club actually runs Colombia, but it comes close to doing so.

A semi-secret society known as the Mano Negro, or Black Hand, also plays a role. This is a kind of McCarthy organization supported by the big banks and financial interests to oppose Communism.

Elements in the Power Pattern

We should attempt to break down elements in the Colombian power pattern in more detail. First are army and church. Then:

1. The coffee growers. After Brazil, Colombia is the biggest coffee producer in the world, exporting one-sixth of the world's supply. Colombian coffee, mild, is of high quality, and about half the total crop goes to the United States. Since coffee provides between 65 and 70 percent of *all* Colombian foreign exchange, its export is vital; several observers have pointed out that, if coffee goes down a cent a pound in New York, the country loses $8 million. And coffee dropped from 80 cents a pound to 48 cents in the ten years between 1954 and 1964. Most Colombian coffee is grown on small properties (the average *finca* covers less than five acres) by independent small farmers. Almost all of these are banded together in the National Federation of Coffee Growers; this, founded in 1927, is the largest cooperative in South America, and naturally forms a powerful pressure group.

2. The banks, big business, and big agriculture. *Three percent of the*

population own not less than 60 percent of the entire agricultural area of the country, even though ownership of the coffee properties is widely distributed. Large proportions of the big estates lie idle, as in Chile.

3. Students, to be discussed in the next chapter.

4. The political parties.

5. *El Tiempo*, the great Liberal newspaper.

6. Labor. There are two principal trade union federations in Colombia—the Union of Colombian Workers (UTC), strong in textiles, steel, and shipping; and the Confederation of Colombian Workers or CTC (sugar, transport)—but only a comparatively small percentage of the total labor force is organized. A Communist labor organization, COMSICOL, which rose in 1964, has concentrated on workers in petroleum, the country's second industry, and is often accused of supporting guerrilla terrorism. The UTC has been traditionally Conservative, the CTC Liberal. The church has close links with the UTC through worker priests known as "moral advisors." Labor is forbidden by terms of the constitution to play any role in politics, but strikes are frequent.

7. The United States. The direct American investment in Colombia is substantial—$465 million at the moment—with powerful interests in petroleum, cattle, mining, sugar, and bananas, although the United Fruit Company is less active here than elsewhere. No American corporation is, however, any longer in a position to exert *active* pressure on the Colombian government, or to influence legislation directly. Those days are over. Relations between Colombia and the United States are excellent on the governmental level, even though American aid was withdrawn temporarily in December, 1964, because of the financial crisis in Bogotá. We did not wish to advance further loans until the Colombians put their house in order. For a considerable time Colombia was known as the "showcase of the Alianza," and it was the first Latin American country to accept the Peace Corps; probably, after Brazil, it has the most genuinely pro-American government on the continent. The old scars over Panama were healed long ago. All this being said, many Colombians disapproved strongly of American intervention in the Dominican Republic in April, 1965. One statesman told us that he would have liked to vote against the United States request for OAS support (as did Mexico, Ecuador, Peru, Chile, and Uruguay) but that the government did not do so because, he thought, to "go along with the U.S." was better than "breaking the solidarity of the continent." Fear of reprisal also probably played a role. To sum up, American influence and power on an over-all basis are overwhelming, if only because of coffee. By withholding

coffee purchases the United States could, if it wanted to, strangle Colombia in a day.

*

The army presents a peculiar situation. It certainly does not run Colombia exclusively, and it probably does not even have the political veto power of the military establishments in Venezuela and Peru. The army was, it is true, the main force in deposing General Rojas Pinilla, and army elements forced General Ruiz out of his job as minister of war. But the real significance of these episodes is to indicate that the army takes more than a narrow military view. General Rojas was one of its own, but out he went. Its basic inclination is to support civilian government, and to stand by to protect the nation. There is little tendency to make adventures for their own sake or interfere with politics on a day-to-day basis on the part of senior officers. A demonstration of all this came in the summer of 1965 when the minister of war and all five service chiefs (commander-in-chief, army, navy, air force, and national police) joined to issue a manifesto affirming their support of the Valencia government, which at that moment seemed to be on the point of collapse, and declaring that "solution for the nation's economic and political difficulties lay in democratic processes."[5]

Still it would be rash to assume that a military *Putsch* in Colombia is out of the question. After all it is the army itself which decides when it should or should not move.

*

Probably the hierarchy of the Roman Catholic Church has more influence here than in any other South American country. Generally it takes a line conservative in the extreme, following its well-entrenched tradition, and the Conservative party was its handmaiden for many years; the story is, in fact, that the Archbishop of Bogotá "named" every president from 1886 to 1930 during this long period of Conservative rule. Then the Liberals came in and the church has held itself somewhat aloof from political interference ever since, and, like the army, prefers to stay on the sidelines except in circumstances of acute emergency. The late imposing Cardinal Luque went on the radio to appeal for the dismissal of Dictator Rojas Pinilla in 1957.

There have always been strong anticlerical elements in Colombia in spite

[5] H. J. Maidenberg in the *New York Times*, July 11, 1965. Luis Cardinal Concha Cordoba, the head of the church, made a similar appeal.

of—or perhaps because of—the special position of the church. President Alfonso López went so far as to disestablish it, and church and state were separated. This made little difference in its position, however. The church continues to wield so pervasive an influence mostly as the result of three factors: first, church property is still not taxed, and its wealth continues to be enormous; second, it plays a top-heavy role in education, and, third, it maintains an effective organization in the countryside. The local priest is, in rural neighborhoods, usually more influential than the mayor; villages exist where peasants stand in line to get into church on Sundays or, if they cannot gain entrance, listen to the services by a loudspeaker in the courtyard.

Divorce is a somewhat complex issue. The Catholic concept of the indissolubility of marriage is still the accepted rule, and divorce is illegal. Even citizens who marry under civilian law (this is possible if both parties make a public declaration of apostasy, whereupon they are excommunicated) may not get a divorce. But something known as "*divorcio imperfecto*" exists, which makes a legal separation possible—even with alimony. Neither party to a *divorcio imperfecto* may, however, remarry. Much agitation goes on in the Colombian legislature and elsewhere to liberalize the divorce laws, but this cannot be done without modification of the country's concordat with the Vatican. Meantime Colombia recognizes the legality of divorces granted in other states, which makes it more progressive than Argentina.

The standpat hierarchy has been much disturbed by some recent developments. The case of Father Camilo Torres Restrepo is to the point. Torres, thirty-six, who came of a distinguished elite family, was a brilliant firebrand; he was chaplain of the National University for a time and then became too hot for the university to hold. Traveling over the countryside by chartered plane and addressing large audiences, he opened a vehement campaign for social and economic reform advocating "revolutionary changes": this brought him into open conflict with the church elders, and he voluntarily asked to be relieved of his holy orders, saying that it was "impossible for him to exercise his sacred duties as a priest under the present structure of the church." The cardinal archbishop promptly obliged him. Torres attended Communist meetings, attacked the United States, joined FLN (the National Liberation Front, the guerrilla political organization), and eventually went out into the hills himself as a guerrilla fighter. He was killed in February, 1966, when he and a twenty-five-man guerrilla group were ambushed by an army patrol. So the official story goes. But allegations are rife that he was trapped and murdered in cold blood.[6]

[6] FLN is not to be confused with the equivalent organization in Venezuela, known as FALN.

Another outspoken and rebellious young priest is Father Martin Amaya Martínez of Tunja, who also asked to be separated from the church. He said to a group of women students recently that divorce is "more Christian" than the "living hell of an unhappy marriage," and that the Catholic church must "rout out the misery, hunger, and superstitious ignorance of our people" if it is not to "become more of a business corporation than a messenger of our Lord Jesus Christ."

*

A different order of churchman is Monsignor José Joaquin Salcedo G., head of the Acción Cultural Popular, with whom my wife and I spent a vividly remembered afternoon. He has church backing, operates tax-free, and is supported in part by the Colombian government. His importance derives from the fact that he invented a technique, which has gained wide attention elsewhere, for teaching illiterates to read by radio.

Salcedo, who is forty-three, has a grandee's face—elevated, tortured, cold. Born near Bogotá, he derives from British Protestant grandparents on his mother's side. He commands one of the largest, best organized, and most successful communications centers in the hemisphere, and his radio station at Sutatenza, in the hills near Bogotá, reaches some 2,500,000 listeners. He likes to say that even if the Communists take Bogotá someday, his "fortress" at Sutatenza will remain impregnable.

Salcedo has been called a Fascist, if only because his anti-Communism is so intense. He is, or was, close to General Ruiz. He conceives of his mission as one of education, education, education. "The *campesinos* can't go to school, so our school goes to them." Programs are disseminated from Sutatenza on several wave lengths to a multitude of villages, where volunteers assemble children at some convenient point, and, as the radio gives the lesson, explain it on a blackboard. The Salcedo organization has no fewer than 27,000 of these volunteers, covering the whole country. Then too this gaunt, craggy monsignor has built up an extensive publication program, which, he told us, consumes 135 tons of newsprint a month; his principal magazine, the *Campesino*, reaches 750,000 families, and he distributes schoolbooks, pamphlets, action strips, homilies, and guides as well. The texts carry simple messages like "A House Without Hygienic Services Does Not Correspond with Human Dignity" and "Erosion Is the Mortal Enemy of the Soil." Finally, the Salcedo organization has sent out 186,000 vegetable seed packets to the peasantry, and distributes 330,000 free notebooks and pencils to students every year.

Monsignor Salcedo led us out of his office (he has his own well-equipped eleven-story office building, part of which he rents) to a room containing an immense table, one of the largest I have ever seen. Here he has spread out and piled up a mass of Communist pamphlets, books, and newspapers which circulate in Latin America—1,850 titles in all, he told us. This exhibit is designed as a warning. Forty-nine percent of Colombians (Salcedo's figure) are in their teens or younger, and are more than "normally susceptible" to Communist influence "in a period when proper leadership is lacking." The rise of Chinese Communism is particularly dangerous because, he thinks, the Chinese and South American "mentalities" are so similar. About 850 youthful Colombians are studying in Peking or Moscow today, he said. He made another point that I had previously heard expressed elsewhere, that the Communist party has never given a bottle of milk to a South American or built a mile of road, but that its influence widens steadily and it gains adherents day by day, whereas the United States, despite all the aid we give, remains unpopular. This is mainly, in his opinion, because Communism provides a fixed simple goal which an uneducated person can at once grasp and understand, whereas we, the Americans, do little to convey the *idea* of democracy, which is a harder concept to define. Nor, one might add, do the Communists exploit anybody at present or siphon money out of the country; they do not own oil or mines or control utilities or take profits out of local merchandising.

On the wall of this room Monsignor Salcedo showed us a series of charts he had designed. These do not attack Communism *per se*, but, on the contrary, illustrate how feudalism and reaction may encourage Communism. One chart is in the form of a large triangle representing the population of Latin America, 226 million by Salcedo's estimate. At the apex is a small layer, 3 percent of the whole, symbolizing those who have advanced education; next, a slightly larger layer represents the 7 percent who have had what corresponds to high school education in the United States. Below this come the 37 percent (81,300,000) who have been to primary school for at least a year, and at the bottom are the 120 million who have never had any education at all—the illiterates. So far so good, Salcedo says. The educated 3 percent, the elite, the privileged, assume that their position is secure, because they lie at the top of the triangle. But if you invert the triangle they lie at the bottom. The peak on which they sit is extremely narrow, and is vulnerable to pressure. With the triangle turned upside down, the minuscule privileged class lies *beneath* the immense mass of undereducated and underprivileged. "Rich Colombians think that they're on the top, but in reality they're on the bottom." Salcedo concluded his exposition with the dry comment, "South America is an underdeveloped continent, yes, but it is the stupid oligarch, the stupid *estanciero*, who is less developed than the peasant, or he would realize the frailty of his position."

Monsignor Salcedo's opinion of the Alianza does not appear to be high. His own organization, he thinks, has done more for Colombia than the whole apparatus of USAID without spending a single American dollar. "American aid can turn us into beggars," he said, echoing a comment we heard from other South Americans. His final words returned to the theme of education. "Give a *campesino* a house and he still does not have a house, because he is not yet *capable* of operating a house. Education and land reform must come first. This seems to be something that the Americans do not understand." The monsignor has, incidentally, visited the United States no fewer than twenty-seven times. This is one of the most powerful—and somewhat frightening—personalities I met in South America.

Three Overriding Problems

Inflation and a Trembling Economy. When, cashing a check the afternoon I arrived in Bogotá, I asked what the exchange rate was, the girl at the counter replied, "14.30 pesos to the dollar now, but heaven knows what it will be an hour from now." She was exaggerating. The Colombian inflation was not galloping to that extent. Nevertheless the value of the local currency has dropped by half since 1962, and the inflation rate is about 18 percent a year; the cost of living has gone up steadily, and the budget is far off balance. The foreign debt rose from $548 million in 1959 to $956 million last year, and the trade deficit has doubled to reach $750 million, a large sum for a country the dimensions of Colombia.

In fact the country was in such desperate financial straits that national bankruptcy seemed imminent in the summer of 1965. A severe political crisis in August did not help matters, nor did an angry rash of strikes. The country appeared to be disintegrating. High personages in the government and army were caught out in weird scandals. Behind all this lay the invisible but steadily mounting specter of the population problem. The Colombian population rises by 500,000 a year, which means—hour by hour—more mouths to feed.

In September the Valencia government pulled itself together to put through some austerity measures, such as a restriction on imports (in order to save foreign exchange) and a stabilization and development program, although nobody knew quite what it was to "stabilize" or "develop." It became known that thousands of businesses in Bogotá had not even bothered to register with the tax authorities and that businessmen were making pots of money by buying pesos at one rate and selling them at another, since two rates of exchange were in force. One remedial suggestion was to tax steeply Colombians traveling abroad, again to save the peso. Colombians like to travel, which steadily takes money out of the country; believe it or not, Colombians outnumbered all foreign visitors (except Canadians and West Germans) to the New York World's Fair in 1964.

What made the situation all but unbearable, as responsible Colombians saw it, was that the crisis was "so unnecessary." The country is fundamentally sound, with an excellent economic base and vast untapped sources of wealth, but inefficient government, the paralyzingly obtuse selfishness of the propertied class, and plain criminality were wrecking it. There was no real reason for a flight of capital except fear. Colombia has (now I am paraphrasing a leading Bogotá businessman) a dozen major cities, a well-distributed population, a "magnificent" peasantry, a large public domain, a nice balance between rural and urban elements, a good status in industry, unity in language, racial harmony, a civilian-minded army, and the best democratic tradition in South America. Yet it was in acute danger of slipping down the drain. Its basic natural resources were enormous, but it was going broke on account of "structural erosion." Lauchlin Currie, the American economist who is now a Colombian citizen, told us, "The wealth is here—let's get at it!"

There came improvement late in 1965, and, in effect, the United States bailed the country out. Aid was resumed, after having been cut off for a year, by means of a new $65 million loan. Other American assistance included a new Public Law 480 agreement, a treasury loan, and a credit from the Export Import Bank. International credits came from the World Bank and the International Monetary Fund, totaling more than a hundred million dollars.

Land Reform. The situation on the land is improving, and this is one of the few countries in South America where serious land reform is under way. It is certainly needed. I have already mentioned some inequalities in ownership, and there are some 750,000 *campesinos* without any land at all. But the main problem is not merely to break up the *latifundio* and distribute land—actually there are only about fifteen properties bigger than 100,000 hectares—but to make agriculture as a whole more productive, as is the case

almost everywhere in South America. About one-half of the large holdings
are put to no use. As to the small holdings there are 325,000 *minifundio*
averaging less than an acre each, which would gain by being consolidated.
About 70 percent of the total population of Colombia lives on agriculture,
and it is calculated that the number of persons on the land will *double* by
the end of the century. How feed the country then, since it has to import
food now?

A land reform act was passed in 1961 under President Alberto Lleras
Camargo; though mild, it caused such furious Conservative opposition that
gunplay took place actually in the parliament. An Agrarian Reform Institute,
known as INCORA, was set up. One of its presumptive functions was to buy
parts of large holdings not under cultivation, at a fair price, and redistribute
these to fifty thousand peasant families. As a result a new verb promptly
entered the local language—*incorar*, to expropriate. INCORA has made
progress slowly against severe obstacles. It has been helped substantially by
the Alianza. Its director, Dr. Enrique Peñalosa Camargo, is one of the ablest
and most devoted public servants in the nation; he works sixteen hours a day
for little thanks. He has brains, dignity, and vision. What he seeks above all
is to create the kind of technical and administrative machinery that can
operate soundly in the future. "The important thing is not to pass a law, but
to make it work." Meantime, INCORA has given land titles to more than
10,000 settlers on 528,000 hectares, built 1,697 kilometers of road bene-
fitting 128 municipalities, and started development of some 286,000 hectares of a total of 610,000 so far expropriated.

Population Pressure. Colombia had roughly 11 million people in 1950, has
17 million today, and, as I have just mentioned, increases at the unbelievable
rate of half a million a year. The percentage rise is 3.2 percent a year, which
means doubling the population in twenty-three years. Director Peñalosa of
INCORA gave us some startling figures. I cited these in Chapter 7, and they
tell us that if the present rate keeps up the population of Colombia, a relatively small country today, will be 55 million by the year 2000, 325 million
a hundred years from now, and 6 *billion* a hundred years after that.

Not only does the birth rate produce an unprecedented number of new
children; the death rate goes steadily down, through the development of new
drugs, sanitary improvements, and the like. Moreover, the death rate,
between 14 and 17 per thousand today (9.6 in the United States), is bound
to drop still further soon. Another factor is that 42 percent of the Colombian population is fifteen years of age or younger, which magnifies the issue.
These youngsters are not yet full wage earners, and lie outside the organized
labor force; they have to be supported by the adult population to an extent

at least; and they urgently need more education. Finally about half of all Colombian births are illegitimate; one reason for this is that a wedding is so expensive.

Enlightened Colombians have lately become increasingly aware of the gravity of its population problem, and, in spite of the country's Roman Catholic saturation, are beginning to face up to facts. The government, however, maintains no more than a polite academic interest, and has not taken any positive action as yet. Gynecological clinics to give advice to women on contraceptive methods are not permitted, and family planning is not held to be within the governmental realm. Politics as well as religious influences play a role in this. The extreme right uses all the familiar clichés, mainly to the effect that birth control is contrary to tradition and that any interference with "natural processes" is immoral. The extreme left takes the line that decrease in the population will weaken the nation and thus play into the hands of American "imperialism," which wants Colombia to be weak and at its mercy.

Even so, the population explosion is being attacked from several angles. Dr. Hérnan Mendoza, an endocrinologist trained in Montreal, is head of a newly formed Division of Population Studies of the Asociación Colombiana de Facultades de Medicina, which is beginning to do research work of considerable value. A significant fact is that three prominent Catholics are on Dr. Mendoza's board—two Jesuit professors and a priest. Nor has there been difficulty in getting other Catholic supporters, particularly from the University of the Andes and even the Ministry of Health.

Dr. Mendoza showed us some tables prepared by his organization:

PERCENTAGE OF WOMEN IN LEGAL OR COMMON-LAW MARRIAGE WHO HAVE STATED THAT THEY HAVE USED CONTRACEPTIVES, CLASSIFIED BY ORDER OF PREGNANCY AFTER WHICH THE USE WAS STARTED

| | Cumulative percentages in | | |
Order of pregnancy	Bogotá	Caracas	Mexico
Before first pregnancy	7.5	16.1	9.4
Before second pregnancy	29.2	47.6	31.3
Before third pregnancy	50.3	65.5	48.9
Before fourth pregnancy	66.5	75.3	66.0
Before fifth pregnancy	80.0	82.6	75.1
Before sixth pregnancy	85.9	86.1	81.9
Before seventh pregnancy	90.8	90.0	87.3
Before eighth pregnancy	93.9	92.3	88.9
Before ninth pregnancy	94.7	93.7	89.8
After ninth pregnancy	96.5	96.3	93.4

PERCENTAGE OF WOMEN IN LEGAL OR COMMON-LAW MARRIAGE WHO HAVE
STATED THAT THEY HAVE USED CONTRACEPTIVES, CLASSIFIED BY LEVEL OF
EDUCATION

| Level of education | *Percentage who ever used contraceptives* | | |
	Bogotá	Caracas	Mexico
Women in legal or common-law marriage	39.5	59.4	37.5
With no education	14.5	35.7	11.2
Some primary education	28.5	52.8	28.0
Complete primary education	39.8	70.1	43.9
Some secondary education	58.9	76.6	56.8
Complete secondary education	74.5	66.0	64.2
Some university education	73.9	76.0	55.2

A Colombian woman seeking advice on contraception must go to her own doctor, since public clinics are not available; whether or not the doctor will help her depends on how religious he is. A considerable number of women do use the contraceptive pill regularly—about 250,000, or 5 percent of all women in the country. Some 70 million pesos a year are spent on pills, which may be bought without a prescription. Since they are expensive, they are used more in the upper income groups than the lower. But many Colombian women do not use the pill correctly through ignorance or carelessness, and often no medical advice is available to put them right. Use of the uterine coil is just beginning, but there are probably between 5,000 and 10,000 women already equipped with the coil. The church has come to the point of countenancing use of the pill in certain circumstances (disease, menstrual irregularity), though not publicly, but the coil is strictly taboo on the ground that it is "mechanical."

Condoms are illegal; no official ban on their manufacture is admitted to exist, but they are not produced locally and their import is forbidden. So, being contraband, they are expensive and hard to get.

The main long-range hope for a solution of the population problem is, obviously, education and economic advance. Meantime, experts in the field talk about indirect methods of attack. One suggestion is a propaganda campaign to urge young people to delay marriages; if a girl marries in her early twenties instead of at fifteen to eighteen, the birth rate is bound to drop, and the delay gives more opportunity for education. More TV may conceivably keep births down—even the increasing use of twin beds in middle-class families.

The struggle to get church approval for planned parenthood is not yet won by any means, but at least it is out in the open. The wraps are off. The church is no longer "monolithic" on the issue. I had a talk with a Jesuit teacher about niceties in birth control which would have been inconceivable a decade ago. Some profoundly subtle and difficult elements in the problem were raised and freely discussed. One point has to do with the precise instant that conception takes place. Does the coil reject fertile eggs, or does it prevent the egg from being fertilized? What the church seeks is protection of the *soul*, my Jesuit friend went on. But when is the "soul" actually "born"? The church knows, of course, that large numbers of Catholic women are practicing contraception in one way or another, if only by the rhythm method, which I heard called "Vatican roulette"; it is alarmed, too, by the soaring abortion rate. Yet the fundamental objection to modern methods of birth control like the coil remains at the moment what it has always been, that no mechanical device may be permitted to contravene "natural law." The pill is being winked at, but not the coil.

In August, 1965, came something altogether unprecedented. Colombia stood host to the first Pan-American Assembly on Population, which met in Cali under the sponsorship of the Universidad del Valle, the Colombian Association of Medical Schools, and several North American groups. Former President Lleras Camargo made the opening address, and seventy-five delegates, including Catholic priests from several countries, sat for four days listening to discussions on planned parenthood and related topics. Lleras Camargo came out "clearly and forcefully for measures to control population," and *El Tiempo* of Bogotá went so far as to print a diagram illustrating use of the coil, while other newspapers gave the conference extended and explicit coverage. Some members of the Catholic hierarchy protested, but without effect.

CHAPTER 26

More About Colombia

Ecuador is a monastery, Venezuela is a barracks, Colombia is a university.
    —REMARK ATTRIBUTED TO SIMÓN BOLÍVAR

BOGOTÁ, "the Gray City," lies in a steep uneven bowl of mountains. These are magnificently picturesque, but unfortunately they can seldom be fully seen because of the perpetual screen of clouds and foamy mist. Atop four nearby peaks—in the familiar South American manner—stand four religious monuments illuminated at night, including a celebrated church (Monserrate), a cross, and a figure of Christ somewhat like the one in Rio. The countryside nearby is fresh-looking and moistly green. The temperature seldom varies from fifty-eight degrees the year around, and the altitude, about a mile and a half, which is higher than Mexico City or Addis Ababa, bothers some visitors and, combined with the prevailing dampness, is an enervating influence on Bogotá itself.

This is a drab-looking city, in spite of its vivid environs, if only because most citizens wear dark clothes and carry raincoats. A man who leaves his house in the morning without a raincoat is thought to be mad. Clothes have little dash or style, and the crowds in the streets reminded me of those in, of all places, Moscow—with its similar accent on uniformity, utilitarianism, and lack of color. But even if Bogotá seems listless and apathetic it has grown with astounding speed in recent years. Partly this is, of course, due to the influx of *campesinos* from the countryside, as is true in so many South American capitals. Bogotá has come near to quadrupling in population in a quarter of a century, having risen from 450,000 in 1940 to more than 1,700,000 in 1965. Back in 1930 the population was only 235,000, so the increase since that date is sevenfold.

One curiosity is the way streets and houses are numbered. The long avenues, called *carreras*, are intersected by the *calles*, or cross streets, in a gridiron pattern; house numbers are a combination of two pairs of digits, for instance 82–14. If your address is Carrera 17, 82–14, this means that you live on Carrera 17, near the corner of Calle 14, and that your house is the eighty-second building on the block. A similar system exists in Queens, New York. Another demonstration of the prodigious growth of the city recently is the fact that the country club has had to move three different times, farther into the outskirts each time in order to avoid the relentless pursuit of the metropolis, and to have enough room for its golf course and facilities. This club is, incidentally, one of the most expensive in the world; to become a member costs $7,000 for what is known as a "share," plus dues and initiation fees.

Bogotá has a moderately rich social-mercantile-financial core, and its members, whether Liberal or Conservative, tend to stick together. The biggest local business is a brewery, by name Bavaria, the ownership of which is widely diffused. Colombia is reputed to have the largest beer consumption per head of any country in the world except Belgium. Businessmen are, in general, alert and modern minded, and do their best to overcome the musty tradition of the old Bogotá, its lack of vivacity, and the general air of dislocation and disorganization which, to North American eyes, seems to attend so many business enterprises in South America. They are waging a kind of professional revolt against inefficiency, and admire above all what they call the "M.I.T. mind." Salaries are high. A youngster with managerial training can start at $6,000–$7,000 per year.

Despite its intellectualism, Bogotá is sports crazy, and its picturesque old bull ring near the center of town is as well patronized as the *fútbol* stadium.[1] Baseball is beginning to give football a run for its money, and so is *basquetbol*. Children, playing catch or waiting in line to get into a western at the movies, chew *boobly goom*. Many are waifs—they sleep under newspapers on the streets—and shoe shining is a brisk trade. I mentioned in *Inside Latin America* a quarter of a century ago that the *Bogotano* boys finish a shine by smearing the shoes with orange peel, which they still do, and I read not long ago that another favorite smear, supposed to give a splendid shine, is tomato skin. Older youngsters look somewhat like Greenwich Villagers; beatniks are called *nadistas*—nothingists.

The national drink, beer excluded, is a species of spirit called *aguardiente*, which, if taken in substantial quantities, produces sensational results.

---

[1] The star in one game we saw bore the nice name Supercrack.

Food in Bogotá is rich. One specialty is a local fruit, *curubo*, which comes from a vine and tastes like a delicious sweet grapefruit but isn't; its juice is brick-colored. Another is a hot soup called *ajiaco*, which contains potatoes, chicken, capers and a chunk of corn on the cob, to which you add, on being served, a slice of cold avocado. Colombia has a fantastically sweet tooth; its consumption of sugar is said to be the highest in the world, about 40 percent higher per capita than in the United States. Partly this is caused by the enormous popularity of a sugar-water concoction known as *agua de panela*, which many citizens drink as a kind of nostrum. Hotels and restaurants in Bogotá do not add a service charge to the bill, not even a modest 10 percent. Tips are up to you. Taxi drivers do not expect tips as a rule, although rates in Bogotá are among the cheapest in the hemisphere—another Colombian contradiction, in view of the high prices of most commodities and services.

Bogotá has admirable bookshops, but I did not think that they were as good as in Buenos Aires or Santiago. Booksellers operate at a heavy disadvantage because currency regulations (put into force recently as a check against inflation) make it impossible to import new *foreign* books, which have always had a wide audience. Lines of second-hand bookstalls, like those along the quais in Paris, are well attended. There is no single outstanding Colombian writer of the rank of Pablo Neruda in Chile or Jorge Luis Borges in the Argentine; the man who comes closest is probably Germán Arciniegas, an essayist of originality, grace, and power who has also had a distinguished career in diplomacy. Several artists of quality are at work, like Edgar Negret, a sculptor in metal whose work is well known in New York, and the painter Fernando Botelo. The quality of the local TV is fairly high, if only because the upper level of the population demands the best. But only about 150,000 families in the whole of Colombia (population 17 million) have TV.

The Bogotá press is vigorous, and, to an astonishing extent, free. Early in 1965 Jean-Paul Sartre and Simone de Beauvoir published a manifesto in Paris fiercely attacking the Colombian government and army for what they called wanton unnecessary cruelty in cleaning up a guerrilla area. *El Tiempo*, the leading Bogotá daily, had the courage and independence of mind to print every word of this, even though it supports the government, and was bitterly attacked for so doing, particularly by the army. But nobody contested *El Tiempo's* right to give voice to these charges of atrocities committed by the military. The principal Liberal organ in the country, *El Tiempo* is fifty years old, has a daily circulation of some 200,000 (400,000 Sunday) and is one of the great traditional newspapers of the continent, like *El Mercurio* in Santiago. Its ownership rests in the Santos family, and an esteemed former president of the republic, Dr. Eduardo Santos, was its publisher for many years. In 1952 an inflamed Conservative mob sacked the *El Tiempo* building, and subsequently General Rojas Pinilla, the ex-dictator, closed it down for several years, even as Perón closed down *La Prensa* in Argentina. Promptly and with imperturbable spirit the Santos family put out a substitute paper nicely named *Intermedio*.[2]

The principal Conservative paper, *El Siglo*, has little of the prestige of *El Tiempo*, and its circulation is much smaller. *Its* building was also sacked and burned by a mob several years ago—a Liberal mob. One peculiarity of Colombian journalism is the plenitude and detail of its political reporting. Endless pages go to the intricate and fastidious analysis of speeches, maneuvers, and crossplay in the parliament, by experts who are as erudite in their field, with as voluminous and discriminating a command of precedent. as, say, a first-rate baseball reporter covering the World Series in the United States.

Colombians, in particular the intelligentsia of Bogotá, are probably the least nationalist of any people in South America; they have little propensity to exaggerated patriotism, and political xenophobia is not pronounced. They feel themselves to be an extremely superior people, as indeed many are, and they have little of the sensitiveness and inferiority complex of, let us say, the Argentines. Many Colombian aristocrats pattern themselves on the British, and their highest ambition is to be thought of as resembling English gentlemen. Family connections are important, as in Britain, and sharp political enemies can be close personal friends. The people are not outgoing and are reluctant to use thee-and-thou terms until a long relationship has been established (in sharp contrast to Venezuela), and most businessmen, no matter how strong their Liberal or Conservative tradition may be, tend to stay out of politics.

Bogotanos—to proceed with generalizations somewhat risky—are proud of their intellectual tradition, free press, and liberal attitudes. The power of the church is often privately—or even publicly—deplored. Nor do Colombians have much addiction to the cult of *machismo*, the expression of masculine virility: to be exaggeratedly self-conscious about *macho* is thought to be vulgar.

At a party one night I heard a guest explode with passionate indignation at what he called "major" Colombian failures. There is no law in this country worth the name, he said; the judicial system is abominable, and public administration is a disgrace. The upper classes—snobbish, parochial, and insufferably pompous—have no social vision whatever, but they compose

[2] James Nelson Goodsell, *Christian Science Monitor*, March 31, 1961.

the Establishment and run the country. Their minds are closed, and they have no sense of humor. Bogotá may, as is true, have eleven universities, but it is a city utterly devoid of charm.

On the other hand I myself found Bogotá fascinating if only because it was so full of total strangers eager to be of service or indulge their curiosity. Never, except possibly in Japan, have I ever encountered anything like the stream of letters, telegrams, telephone calls, and unscheduled visits that greeted us. The telephone never stopped ringing. I should add too that this increased the atmosphere of confusion that characterizes Colombia, because everybody told us something different. This is indeed one of the most difficult, complex, and contradictory countries in the world.

One sight in Bogotá is the Museo del Oro, or gold collection, housed in the vaults of the Bank of the Republic. (Incidentally this bank sells emeralds across the counter, like a jewelry store, but by appointment only.) Not even in Peru or in the great museums of Egypt and the Soviet Union have I ever seen such a glorious collection of gold objects. It includes no fewer than 8,000 pieces of pre-Hispanic gold weighing 150,000 grams, five times the weight of all similar gold ornaments in other museums throughout the world. The types represented, in full variety, include Quimbaya (from Antioquia), Calima (in the valleys west of the Cordillera Occidental), and Muisca, near present-day Bogotá. Not without reason was Colombia celebrated as the original El Dorado. Antique Colombian gold ornaments are strikingly different from those in Peru or Central America—lighter, more fanciful. The Indians who made these exquisite works of art reached the height of their skill as far back as the fourth century A.D., but many objects might well be the product of the imagination of a contemporary goldsmith. One thing impressive to the untutored visitor is the wide range of composition. I looked at ornaments that resembled top hats, bibs, and egg cups; toadstools, bookmarks, shells, and piano keys; falsies, chaff, spoons, penises, and lizards; pumpkins, antlers, hourglasses, dump wagons, crowns, and pelicans.

Bogotá is the home base of Avianca (Aerovías Nacionales de Colombia), founded in 1919 and the second oldest commercial airline in the world (KLM was first), as well as the oldest on the continent. In its first year, using Junkers F-13's, it flew 12 passengers and carried 1,817 pounds of cargo; in 1964 it operated more than 50,000 flights, and carried 1,750,000 passengers. It covers Colombia like a skein, maintaining the country's postal delivery and serving the most remote communities against almost insurmountable obstacles in weather and terrain, and is an international carrier as well, with jet services to North America and Europe. Its safety record is excellent, it serves some of the best food and drink I have ever had on an airline, and its hostesses are distinguished by the smartest of smart scarlet cloaks, deriving from a traditional shepherd's costume.

Avianca's early history is curious. Originally called Scadta, it was a German company, operated by German pilots. In the late 1930's when the possibility of war between the United States and Nazi Germany became acute, American authorities became worried about what role Scadta might play; it had excellent planes and experienced German pilots who knew the whole Caribbean area well and who flew daily near the Panama Canal. A surprise bombing by Nazi agents was not impossible. Difficult negotiations took place which led, first, to a rule laid down by the Colombian government (then, as now, very friendly to the United States), that a Colombian pilot must always accompany a German pilot in flights near the Canal; second, to the eventual breakup of the Scadta organization. The German pilots were dismissed and the company was taken over partly by Pan American Airways and by the Colombian government, under the new name Avianca. Pan American is still a substantial shareholder, but control, operation, and management are Colombian.

Where's Where

Colombia is rich in cities and has no fewer than ten, besides Bogotá, with populations over 100,000. Communications between them are difficult except by Avianca; each is an isolated entity in its own domain. Several off-the-beaten-track departments have very little urban development; Quibdó, the capital of Chocó department on the Pacific, and the center of the country's platinum deposits, is the only city in the department, and the *llanos* in eastern Colombia are virtually uninhabited. Vaupés, a department on the southern Venezuelan border, is bigger than many American states, but has only 10,100 people; the population of its capital, Mitú, is 840.

After Bogotá the largest city in the country is CALI (population 693,000), the capital of Valle del Cauca, which lies between the Western and Central Cordillera. It *doubled* its population in the decade 1951–61. To reach Cali from Bogotá by rail and road (the trains don't go all the way through) takes 11¼ hours; by Avianca, about an hour. A sinuous and precipitate railway connects it with the Pacific 105 miles away, and it taps a region rich in sugar, cotton, and other agricultural products. Cali is heavily industrialized, and has disgraceful shanty towns; people pour in from the hinterland partly to escape banditry, partly to earn cash wages in the new expanding factories. Unemployment is, however, high. Colombian contrasts are dramatic as always. A statue of Christ on a hill dominating the town is so large that it can be seen for thirty miles (in good weather). A correspondent of the *New York Times*[3] mentions that *half* the children in a shanty town known as Siloé, with a population of 22,000, die before they reach the age of five. This is known as the "hotel slum" because "thirty percent of its residents move out each year and are replaced by new migrants from the countryside." Yet Cali has a marked tradition of civic responsibility, and it possesses what is probably the best medical school in South America, attached to the Universidad del Valle and supported in part by the Rockefeller Foundation and other American benefactors. The Ford Foundation contributes to other divisions of this university.

Cali is also headquarters for the CVC or Cauca Valley Corporation, one of the most hopeful projects in South America. Sometimes this is familiarly called "El Lilienthal," because its founder and moving spirit was David E. Lilienthal, former head of both the Tennessee Valley Authority and the Atomic Energy Commission and presently chairman of the Development and Resources Corporation of New York. Even license plates on automobiles used by the authority bear his name. The Colombian goverment was prevailed upon to invite him to initiate a scheme for the Cauca Valley, similar to TVA, in 1954. The basic concept was to set up a public regional body like TVA, hinging on unified development, so that the resources of the valley—hitherto scarcely scratched—could be put to fruitful use. The World Bank and other agencies lent assistance and so did the Colombian government, although the president at the time, Rojas Pinilla, did not seem to understand the project fully, to put it mildly, and difficulties over taxes were vexing. Work, however, did go forward. Flood control, irrigation, new techniques in agriculture, the full use of human resources are all part of the program, as well as the copious production of electric power. The city of Cali has triple the amount of power it had eight years ago. Operation of the CVC is exclusively Colombian. One of its merits is, as Lilienthal says, the way it has attracted youthful citizens to public service.

Six hours south of Cali by train, 40 minutes by air, is the charming old city of POPAYÁN, population 63,000. "Popayán is to Colombia what Weimar is to Germany, or Burgos to Spain," says one authority. One of its hotels is named, oddly enough, the Lindbergh; another the Roosevelt. Popayán has numerous churches and monasteries, a good small university founded in 1827, a Holy Week celebration that brings in many visitors, and a patrician atmosphere. No fewer than seven presidents of Colombia, including Señor Valencia, were born here.

[3] Richard Eder, February 23, 1964.

MEDELLÍN, capital of Antioquia and the third-biggest city in Colombia (population 691,000, altitude 5,046 feet), lies 12½ hours overland from Cali by car and train, an hour by air; it compares to Bogotá roughly as São Paulo, Brazil, compares to Rio. Medellín is, as its inhabitants proudly point out, a commercial dynamo, the industrial heart of the country. It differs sharply from Bogotá or the lazy coastal cities. It is full of bounce and tang. It has animation and ambition. Once again we must note Colombian sectionalism and the strength and tenacity of local characteristics. The Antioqueños look down on Bogotá as being dead in the head, while they make the money that keeps the country going. The population here is largely white, in contrast to Cali, which is predominantly *mestizo*, and the coast, which has a strong Negro substratum. Men from Medellín do business not only in Medellín, but, like Scots, spread out to do work elsewhere; all over Colombia they run banks, insurance companies, and business enterprises. What made Medellín important in the first instance was its textile industry; the first looms were set up in 1902, and textile manufacture has been so successful that the city is sometimes called the "Manchester of Colombia." Medellín is also well known for its flowers, and has a pleasant annual flower festival, and, in another direction, for the work of the Whirlpool Foundation in sponsoring a technical institute for training students in industrial management.

Medellín has responded to the *violencia* with more resolution than other cities. Vigilante groups have been organized, and children of the well-to-do go to school by armored car. When a special siren is heard every automobile in the streets has to stop until it is searched for weapons or even for guerrillas hidden in the trunk.

BARRANQUILLA (population 523,348), CARTAGENA (185,000) and SANTA MARTA (57,000) lie close to one another on the steaming Caribbean coast, which is cotton, cocoa, and banana country. The *costeños* are much more relaxed, more easygoing, than residents of the uplands, and the *violencia* scarcely exists in these amiable cities. Barranquilla, a busy commercial port, has little historical interest, but Cartagena is soaked with color and a romantic tradition. Founded in 1533, it was a prime target for British and other buccaneers in the good old days of the Spanish Main; it was a key post not merely for itself and the rich trade it controlled but because it commanded entrance to the rest of the country. The Spaniards, seeking to make it impregnable, surrounded it with sixteen miles of wall, forty feet high and fifty feet thick, which still stand, and fortified it with impressive bastions. "There were six gates, shut at ten each evening and the keys handed to the governor." But, despite all this, Cartagena was taken and sacked by several invaders, including Sir Francis Drake in 1586 and the pirate Henry Morgan in 1697. Some forty years later came another assault against the Spaniards led by the British sailor Sir Edward Vernon, but it failed. One of George Washington's brothers accompanied Vernon on this expedition, and Mount Vernon was later named for him.[4] Cartagena has been called the most beautiful city in the Americas.

Cartagena was given the official name "Ciudad Heroica" by Simón Bolívar during the revolutionary wars, when the Liberator was based there and the city stood up valiantly against investment by the loyalist Spanish forces. Not for 120 years was the appellation "Hero City" similarly used again, when the Russians gave this name to Leningrad, Odessa, and other Soviet cities which had successfully withstood prolonged German siege.

Santa Marta, the "Pearl of the Americas" and the capital of Magdalena department, was founded by the *conquistadores* as far back as 1525, and is still a fascinating little city—one of the oldest in the Americas. Sir Francis Drake once took it in a famous raid, and Bolívar died here at the age of forty-seven.

We Visit the University

The National University in Bogotá, the largest and most important in the country, looks more like a university in the United States than do most in South America, with a leafy well-kept campus. It is less diffuse than San Marcos in Lima, and it is not as much a radical hotbed or fortress as some of the newer university "cities," as in Caracas. The rector, Dr. José Félix Patiño, a prominent surgeon, attended Yale; his second in command, Dr. Rafael Casas, also a surgeon, went to Harvard. Both were professors of surgery before becoming administrators, and both are thirty-eight.

During a crowded morning Rector Dr. Patiño sketched some of his problems. He told us about the background of the autonomy issue—the university is theoretically immune from interference by the army or police in the familiar South American pattern—and discussed the university's relation to the government, which helps support it. Also it has received financial aid from the Development Programme of the United Nations, the Rockefeller Foundation, and the Alianza.[5] The National University has eight to nine

---

[4] Defender of Cartagena on this occasion was a rip-roaring hero named Blas de Lezo who was one-eyed, one-armed, and lame. He withstood Vernon's attack for 56 days although the Englishman had 27,000 men, 3,000 guns. *South American Handbook*, p. 271.

[5] Other American and international institutions which contribute to the National University or cooperate with it are the Ford Foundation, the University of Wisconsin, Yale, the Inter-American Development Bank, and UNESCO.

thousand students, who are a fair sampling of the country at large. Eighty-five percent of all come from the lower income groups, and boys outnumber girls in a ratio of six to one. Only about one percent of Colombian youth, Dr. Patiño told us, ever get to any university at all. A child is often considered to be a source of income for his family from about the age of twelve; not only are parents hesitant to support a child's further education, but they expect the child's active help in supporting them.

Tuition at Bogotá ranges from 100 pesos a year ($7 at the present rate of exchange) to 6,000, depending on the income of the family. Most students pay the lowest rate. A room in a dormitory can be had for $1.50 a year, and meals are served at one-third of cost. The faculty numbers 1,300, but only 400 of these are "exclusive"; professors are obliged usually to have other jobs and some even hold teaching positions at several different rival universities at the same time, as is the case all over South America, in order to earn an adequate living—a scandalous system. The highest salary paid a professor is the same as that of the highest grade of the civil service, 6,600 pesos a month or $461.50. This comes after ten years' service; the starting salary is 3,800 pesos, which makes it difficult to recruit good men.

Most students at Bogotá follow roughly the same intellectual pattern, Dr. Patiño, an exceptionally talented and attractive man, continued. They are apt to have a sense of guilt at the hardship they may be inflicting on their parents by continuing their studies, and many have as well a sharp conviction of social responsibility, arising out of the miseries around them. Then as a rule comes a period of disillusion, when they abruptly discover that the university is not all that they hoped for, and that many teachers are not socially motivated at all. This produces frustration, noncooperation, acute political partisanship, and a drift to Communism. Student strikes, usually on issues not connected with the university at all, occur intermittently, and the institution is struck—shut down—for about 15 percent of the school year.

On the other hand, direct Communist influence is less conspicuous here than in other national universities on the continent, for instance those in Chile and Venezuela. Dr. Patiño thinks that his faculty of thirteen hundred does not contain more than twenty actual Communists, and that there are only about three hundred in the student body. Students actively assist in running the university. Two of the nine members of the executive council, the highest administrative body, are students; each of these must be among the top eight in his class.

Universities in the United States have three main functions: research, the transmission of culture, and the teaching of professions. The National University and other universities in Colombia have to do more than this, because they are considered to be sociological tools as well, instruments of national development. Dr. Patiño and his associates are fully conscious of this, and at the same time are hard at work on plans for academic renovation. The various "faculties" (schools in our sense) are being consolidated, from twenty-six to eight, according to a new pattern; large attention is being paid to students' social needs; library facilities are to be made better; and the old curricula are being reorganized.

*

Another university among those in Bogotá (there are twenty-five in the country as a whole) is the University of the Andes, a new institution. This has a modern outlook, seeks to build up its own well-trained staff (eighty percent of its professors are now full-time), uses advanced teaching methods, and hopes to give attention to experimentation and research like universities in the north; it has exchange arrangements with Cornell and M.I.T. which promise much, and is "private, nonpolitical, and nondenominational." Its chief difficulties are financial, and research is impeded for lack of funds. Another interesting school is Incca University, under the articulate leadership of Dr. Jaime Quijano C. A famous older institution is Javeriana University, operated by the Jesuits.

Statistics about education in general in Colombia are not quite what one would expect from a country so proud of its intellectual distinction. At least five million adults are still illiterate, and 38 percent of children of school age do not go to any school at all. Only 12 percent of primary school students go on to secondary schools, and, as Dr. Patiño told us, only about one percent of the latter proceed to a university. Most teaching in the lower schools is abominably inadequate, and the curriculum is old-fashioned in the extreme. There has never been a John Dewey here.

Anybody tempted to minimize the role played by students in the political life of Colombia has only to glance at events in the summer of 1965. Student riots led to the virtual paralysis of the country, came near to causing the downfall of the Valencia government, and provoked the imposition of a state of siege in Bogotá—which, incidentally, is still in force.

The root cause of this fierce outburst was United States intervention in the Dominican Republic, of which rebellious students made an issue. The immediate cause was a contretemps at the University of Antioquia in Medellín, where the police, in defiance of the long-established autonomy principle, invaded the campus to apprehend student rioters. The students said that the rector of the university, Dr. Ignacio Velez Escobar, contrary to all precedent, was responsible for this and had invited the police to intervene, and they promptly demanded his head. Riots flared up all over the country. Señor Valencia, who was still president at the time, submitted to the student demands and forced the rector to resign, but then the minister of foreign affairs, a loyal Antioquian, resigned from the government in protest at the rector's dismissal. Ten other cabinet ministers likewise resigned, and the country seethed.[6]

We Visit Kennedy City

Ciudad Kennedy, or Kennedy City, a huge residential building project on the outskirts of Bogotá, is the principal demonstration of American aid in Colombia, and one of the proudest monuments of the Alianza. We drove there one slimy morning passing on the way a graceful twin obelisk memorial to Ferdinand and Isabella and, equally a parent to Colombia, the monolithic representation of a Chibcha head. The city becomes frayed and dingy at the edges, but, as in the outskirts of Lima, there are impressive evidences of industrialization—small factories sprouting everywhere. I saw Bayer, Agfa, Philips, among foreign firms. Posters proclaimed the virtues of the JCC (Communist Youth Party) and the *Línea Dura* (the Hard Line of the MRL). I saw no "Yanqui Go Home!" signs, but scribbles saying "Down with the Oligarchy" were abundant.

We reached SENA, one of the most talked-of institutions in Colombia, an industrial school devoted to vocational apprenticeship. Run by an autonomous agency of the government, it trains twenty thousand young workers a year, and is paid for by a payroll tax on private companies, an interesting experiment. Next we came to something as negative as SENA is positive, a hideous little shanty town called Barrio Tres Equinas. Squatters,

---

[6] One of the few men who have had an encounter with angry students recently and who came out the winner is Covey T. Oliver, the American ambassador, a quick-witted and energetic man. The American Embassy in Bogotá is perched high in an office building and, like most of our embassies in South America at present, is closely guarded and full of iron grills, locked passages, barred gates and doors, and other protective paraphernalia, as well as marines equipped with tear gas and firearms. Even so, a group of about forty students managed to gain entrance recently by the device of going up in the elevator one or two at a time during the lunch hour. Ambassador Oliver came back from lunch to find his quarters overrun by these youngsters shouting protests about American policy. Keeping his head he invited leaders of the group into his private office to talk things over, and asked them why Santo Domingo aroused them so vehemently. "Because you invaded it!" one boy said. "But you are invading my embassy," replied the ambassador. He asked each boy what he was studying and one responded, "International law." The ambassador replied, "Then surely you must know that you are breaking the law here by trespassing on diplomatic territory." Gradually the discussion became friendly and after an hour the students left.

driven desperate by privation, descended on this site some time ago and took over part of a housing development in the course of construction, and nobody has been able to get them out. Anybody who suggests their removal is called an "oligarchical assassin" by the leftist press, and the government does not want to risk a showdown on the issue.

So we reached Ciudad Kennedy. The hope is that projects like this will, in time, replace the squatter communities, which are called *tugurios* in Colombia. The country lacks 279,000 housing units today—in other words more than a quarter million families do not have housing. Built in a sprawling series of open lots, Ciudad Kennedy will, when complete, take care of 100,000 people in 14,000 dwelling units; of the total investment, more than 200 million pesos, about half comes from the United States. The project was jointly inaugurated by President Kennedy and former President Lleras Camargo on December 17, 1961.

Kennedy was not, I learned, the original name of this development. It was first called Ciudad Techo; *techo* means roof. The change to Kennedy came after his assassination, and was the result of the intense and altogether spontaneous emotion caused locally by this event. The night of Mr. Kennedy's funeral more than twenty thousand candles burned in the windows of the new houses, and the residents themselves took the initiative in naming it for his memory.

"Nearly all the major social activities supported by the United States under the Alianza are represented at City Kennedy," says an official pamphlet. It has (or will have when completed) fourteen schools, educational TV, three health centers, market areas, civic centers, a theater, a hospital, churches, parks, playgrounds and nurseries—a very large and ambitious concentration of services. The idea is not merely to provide amenities but to follow through on the principle that, in a developing society, the introduction of one improvement will lead dynamically to an impatient demand for others.[7]

Sprawled against a gray horizon like blotting paper, City Kennedy has the somewhat desolate look of most housing projects, but is not so depersonalized. It contains a number of small owner-built individual dwellings where families live on incomes ranging from 280 to 1,000 pesos a month ($19.60 to $70). The head of the family takes out a loan averaging 6,850 pesos ($480) in order to buy a lot priced at 5,000 pesos, which leaves him 1,850 pesos—not much—for cement, building blocks, roofing, furniture (if he has none), and fixtures. Usually a new tenant moves in as soon as the walls and roof are in place, and completes the work when he can. Carrying charges on the loans

[7] *The Alliance for Progress in Colombia*, Bogotá, 1964.

run from 60 to 140 pesos a month over twelve to fifteen years and the interest works out to an average of 6 percent, very low for South America. These figures are important, because they put decent housing within the reach of almost anybody with a job—anybody who can get in, that is. The waiting list is long.

Here in Ciudad Kennedy we encountered Peace Corps workers for the last time on our trip—two determined, competent, and very pretty American girls, who, like the volunteers we met in Lima and Santiago, worked on community development and, doing so, lived exactly on the level of their neighbors. They had a small house, hardly more than a shed, but it was neat, making a bright enlivening spot in a dreary cityscape. The girls' activity included such projects as coaching a boys' football team, demonstrating food supplements to housewives, and teaching mothers to make inexpensive Christmas gifts for children who had never had any. They had staggered boys of the neighborhood by showing that they knew how to build fireplaces (which are thought to be unhealthy in Colombia) and do metalwork and carpentry. But the boys don't take them out. They are too shy, too poor, or already married.

During our visit one man sauntered in without warning and floriferously asked us to transmit his thanks for his home here to Jacqueline Kennedy. Then we met two Colombian women with whom the girls had a close neighborly relationship, and I gained a bit of insight into local realities by talking to them, hard as it was to draw them out. The American girls are "co-godmothers" of their most recent children. One, thirty-four, had her first child on her fifteenth birthday, and her latest is her sixth. Her husband, an upholsterer, seldom earns more than 500 pesos a month ($35) and he is lucky to have a home in Ciudad Kennedy. The other, also thirty-four, has had twelve children, of whom ten are living, and is married to a bus driver who earns on the average 320 pesos a month ($22.40); bus drivers on private lines in Bogotá are paid according to the number of passengers they carry, and they split the fares with the owner of the bus, the owner taking the bigger share. The bus operated by this man was in bad repair and continually broke down, which automatically reduced his income. The upshot is that he had $22.40 a month, less than a dollar a day, for the support of himself, his wife, and ten children.

*

To list all the Alianza projects in Colombia is impossible in this space. There are hundreds and they run from electric power development to road construction. Similarly one must omit any mention here of the work done by the Development Programme of the UN, which has twelve projects under way, eight of them in training programs. Nor have we room for any but the barest mention of another phase of Peace Corps activity—its elaborate, ambitious, and highly successful work in educational TV. More than 300,000 Colombian children in primary schools, 30 percent of those in the nation, are now receiving part of their education by means of this new process sponsored by USAID and the Colombian government and operated by Peace Corps volunteers.

. . . And to Conclude

Colombia is, then, a country both splendid and squalid, both forward-looking and standpat, both fair and foul. It boils with ferment, and its contradictions are, to say the least, remarkable. Respect for the intellect is at one pole, predisposition to violence at the other; and this dichotomy seems to be irreconcilable. The country is a mélange of Socrates and Jack the Ripper. An explanation may be that, for unknown reasons, but of which geography is certainly one, Colombia still represents the fundamental atavistic conflict, not yet resolved, between Spaniard and Indian, which is characteristic of much of the west coast of South America. Here, in a manner of speaking, the wars of the *conquistadores* are still being fought. In any case the example of Colombia indicates that intellectuals, who tend to look inward, are likely to be poor rulers or administrators in communities where the ruled are not given adequate opportunity for advance.

CHAPTER 27

Visiting Venezuela

> What kind of manhood will they [the South American republics] develop? What place in the world will they ultimately hold?
>
> —LORD BRYCE IN 1912

Now at last we reach Venezuela, the tenth and final country on this long continental journey. It bears close resemblances to several other republics we have visited, and is one of the most provocative of them all. Several patterns we have seen elsewhere will reappear in Venezuela, where a moderate reformist government holds power and strongly resists extremist influence. Here too we will encounter once more such phenomena as restive students, a rapidly expanding population, slum towns, a prodigious industrial development, efforts to reform agriculture, the problem of military influence, and a shocking disparity between social classes, between rich and poor.

But four large factors make Venezuela different—unique. This sparkling and vigorous nation lies in a category all its own. First, it is rich. Some three and a quarter million dollars drop into the national till every day of the year, without work, because of its wealth in oil. Second, geographically close to Cuba, it has been involved in much of recent Cuban history; it has had a bristly recent experience with terrorism, and is supposed to be Castro's first objective in South America, his first target, if he has exterior objectives left. Third, Venezuela is not only a democracy, but an *effective* democracy, one that works. Fourth, it has more social vision than any mainland republic except Chile, plus social conscience, the knowledge that getting ahead entails development and reform; here—even more than in Chile—are zip, push, and élan, as well as money enough to pay the bills.

481

Among Venezuelan characteristics are vehemence, gustiness, and a tendency to roughhouse. There is no creeping terror in Caracas to compare with that in Bogotá and nothing has ever happened to match the murderous civil war that disfigured Colombia for twenty years, but, on various levels, Venezuela presents a somewhat rowdy—even trigger-happy—atmosphere. On the first night of Carnival I went to a dance in the leading hotel in Caracas, something equivalent for respectability and chic to the St. Regis in New York. Two tough little cops with ugly small submachine guns blocked the stairs leading to the dance floor, and searched every man who entered— mostly opulent citizens of the upper class. This was one of the few times in my life I have been frisked. I asked the hotel manager how many guns had been taken from guests—twelve. The guns are checked at the cloakroom in a perfectly routine manner, impounded in a closet, and returned in a matter-of-fact way to their owners when they go home.

Not too much should be made of this. It is simply a convention in Venezuela to carry arms. As they do in Mexico, fathers often give their sons their first revolvers as an eighteenth birthday present.

A few days later, sitting on my hotel terrace, I saw dark smudges rising against the sky and then became aware of an intensely acrid smell—burning rubber. Students were stopping taxis, turning them over, and setting them on fire, in order to keep them off the streets. This was part of a demonstration to support a transportation strike. I went to keep an appointment at the university, and was told that this was a somewhat risky adventure, because the university is a hotbed of radical discontent. My chauffeur, Rudy, although bold as a lion, didn't like the idea of entering the premises; he thought that we ran a grave risk of being pitched out on the street and having our car burned. We went in anyway. At the entrance to the campus were two large fire engines. Apparently students have these ready for *putting out* fires after they start them if they get out of control.

Nothing untoward happened to us at the university, but two students were killed and ten wounded by police elsewhere in the city that day. There are four different police forces in Caracas—the regular police, National Guardsmen, Technical Police (PTJ), and National Police or DIGEPOL.[1] As to the university it is one of the best in South America, with a magnificent $300 million campus, 22,000 students, and an autonomous status since 1784—also this is an armed citadel. About 30 percent of the students, 20 percent of the faculty, are supposed to be Communists, and my quarry that morning was a well-known Communist professor. His office was locked, and he did not show up. Then I met him accidentally at a fashionable lunch that same day—which was mildly embarrassing because he had either been avoid-

[1] Washington, D. C., has five.

ing me or had forgotten the appointment. But I had "risked my life" (so my chauffeur said) to call on him.

I had an appointment at the American Embassy the same afternoon but it was difficult to get there because the place was being surrounded by youngsters demonstrating against American policy in Vietnam. Police dispersed them by shots fired over their heads; nobody was hurt, but the episode was unpleasant. Before they were chased away several students managed to hurl ink against the embassy walls, splotching them. Considerable refinement attends the use of ink in Venezuela in these circumstances. Ink *bottles* are never thrown because these will not break when they hit a wall, unless the thrower is close up and has an arm like Sandy Koufax. Instead the demonstrators use electric light bulbs; they saw off the ends of these, fill them with ink, cork them and let fly. They are easy to throw and burst at the lightest contact. The ink is indelible and hard to get off. The next day I saw embassy workmen wearily scrubbing the disfigured walls.

I do not mean to make light of this episode or have it appear as nothing but a noisy lark. The students felt that they had a legitimate grievance, and acted in deadly earnest, attempting to register protest by the only means at their disposal. Nor should I neglect to mention genuine tragedies which come out of trigger-happiness in Caracas. That same week two American Peace Corps boys were shot by police; one was killed, one severely wounded. Driving into Caracas from the airport they inadvertently passed a PTJ checkpoint, which was not marked or otherwise identifiable. Police followed their car and brought it to a halt two blocks away, then shot the two boys pointblank as they emerged from the car even though they had their hands up.

*

The general situation *in re* violence in Venezuela differs from that in Bolivia, say, or Colombia. There is little possibility of breakdown or civil war. Venezuela has a robust government and, thanks largely to its inherent wealth and the legacy of its last president, Rómulo Betancourt, one of the great men of contemporary South America, its position is relatively secure. Troubles may be afoot, but there is little danger of disintegration or collapse.

Another Word About Students

Student agitation in Venezuela is no new thing. Listen to the following:

The morals of the University are taken very seriously by the people of Caracas as are all boys in that country where a child is listened to, if he be a male child, with as much grave politeness as though it were a veteran who was speaking. The effect is not good, and the boys, especially in the University, grow to believe that they are very important factors in the affairs of the state, when, as a matter of fact, they are only the cat's paws of clever politicians, who use them whenever they want a demonstration and do not wish to appear in it themselves. So these boys are sent forth shouting into the streets, and half the people cheer them on. . . .

I obtained a rather low opinion of them because they stoned an unfortunate American photographer who was taking pictures in the quadrangle, and because I was so far interested as to get a friend to translate for me the sentences and verses they had written over the walls of their college. The verses were of a political character but so indecent that the interpreter was much embarrassed. . . . As the students of the University of Venezuela step directly from college life into public life, their training is of some interest and importance. And I am sure that the Venezuelan fathers would do much better by their sons if they would cease to speak of the University in awe-stricken tones, but would rather take away the boys' revolvers, teach them football, and thrash them soundly whenever they caught them soiling the walls of their alma mater with nasty verses.

This was written 70 years ago in 1896 by the well-known foreign correspondent Richard Harding Davis.[2] *Plus ça change, plus c'est la même chose.*

Venezuela: Some Introductory Aspects

Although Venezuela is only the sixth-largest country by area in South America, it is bigger than Texas by a third and bigger than any European country except Soviet Russia. The Orinoco, sixteen hundred miles long, one of the master rivers of the continent, bisects it, and there are four distinct regions—the hot, dripping coastal zone adjoining the Caribbean; the mountainous area near the Colombian frontier; the interior plains or *llanos* characterized by cattle; and the jungles of Guayana (= Guiana in our spelling). The Andean highlanders are often called the "best" people in the country, and Venezuela has always been marked by a struggle for power between the tough mountaineers and the lazier population along the coast. The last four presidents before Betancourt were all born within twenty miles of one another in the Andean province of Táchira.

There are no more than 7,200 miles of paved highway in the whole country—less than in Connecticut! But such is the underdevelopment of South America as a whole in terms of roads that this minuscle figure gives

[2] *Three Gringos in Venezuela and Central America*, by Richard Harding Davis. Harper & Brothers, pp. 265–66.

Venezuela the most extensive highway network on the continent. The country pullulates with automobiles. One out of every four families in Caracas has a car, an almost unbelievable figure for South America. Importation of foreign cars is, incidentally, forbidden, but they are assembled here; thirteen United States and European manufacturers have assembly plants in the country, and production in 1965 reached the respectable total of 65,000 units—cars, jeeps, taxis, buses, trucks. Similarly the importation of American cigarettes is forbidden, but American companies produce them locally.[3]

Railways never got a start at all partly because of the difficulties of terrain, partly because the Venezuelans were too busy fighting interminable civil wars when the railway age began. The country—three times the size of Italy—*has only 220 miles of railroad*. Communications by air, as in Colombia, have however advanced tremendously; there are no fewer than 171 airports and airstrips. An old timetable tells me that it took Pan American Airways from 7:15 A.M. on Saturday to 11:30 A.M. Sunday to fly from Miami to La Guaira, the airport for Caracas at that time, with an overnight stop at Maracaibo, the oil city, in the early 1940's. There were two flights a week. Today New York and Caracas are only four and a half hours apart by jet, and several airlines fly the route with comfortable regularity.

Venezuela has about eight and a half million people today, fewer than the city of Tokyo. But the rate of increase is very high, 3.4 percent, and the population will probably double by 1985, in the familiar pattern. Roughly 54 percent of the people today are under the age of nineteen, and two-thirds are either children or very old, which means that every Venezuelan has to work for two others. About half of all births are illegitimate, and no fewer than 176,000 children were abandoned in 1962 and became either homeless waifs or wards of the state. Conditions of those on the streets are pitiable. Some do not know their last names or how old they are. They roam the gutters, sleep on the streets, and often become criminals at an early age. A recent story[4] says that a Nazi surgeon, who fled to Venezuela and changed his name, has been hired to mutilate and disfigure children when they still live with their parents so that they will be more effective beggars later. In poor countries a beggar can be an asset to a family. The same kind of thing happens in Egypt.

One perhaps fanciful reason given for Venezuela's extraordinary population growth is the automobile. As I heard it put, "A car is a bed, and this country has become a gigantic garage." Another remark in levity is that most

[3] The automobile industry began in Venezuela with the construction of a General Motors assembly plant in 1948.

[4] Reprinted from the Buenos Aires *Herald*.

children are born in November, because the festivities of Carnival take place in February. Figures are, in any case, startling. MARACAIBO, the oil center, has climbed from 18,000 in 1918 to 475,000 today. Caracas had 80,000 people in 1925, 275,000 in 1941, and has grown to 1,500,000 or more today.

The racial picture is inevitably mixed, with *mestizos* and mulattoes comprising about 65 percent of the population; among these are a number of *zambos*, an Indian-Negro cross. As to the rest, roughly 20 percent are white, 8 percent Indian, mostly in the jungle, and 7 percent Negro, mostly along the coast. Immigration has played a substantial role until recently, and close to a million Italians, Spanish, Portuguese, and Germans, as well as representatives of no fewer than thirty-two other nationalities, came into the country after World War II. Some curious economic patterns have been produced by this. Often a man's national origin can be told by his job. Italians have gone largely into the building trades, and work as barbers, bakers, waiters. Most taxi drivers in Caracas are Spaniards or Canary Islanders, and the Spaniards have also concentrated on domestic service. Shopkeepers are often Italians, Portuguese, and Lebanese (loosely called "Turcos" or "Arabes") and there are about 15,000 Cuban exiles mostly in white collar jobs. Some 17,000 United States citizens live in the country.[5]

Social fluidity is marked, and a middle class, which will in time join the upper class, is rising strongly. The desideratum is to make the middle class bigger. A good many rich families are still conspicuous, and, since this is South America, an "upper crust" certainly exists, but there is no hierarchically entrenched feudal class like that in Peru or Argentina. A small percentage of landowners owns a disproportionate share of the land, but they do not exert direct political power as a class. Many big landowners and cattle ranchers in the *llanos* killed each other off in the so-called federal wars with the result that the old-time aristocracy was much thinned down; most of today's big fortunes have been made in the past thirty years or so, and rose out of industrialization rather than agriculture. As the local *mot* has it, "We dropped right out of the trees into our Cadillacs."

The richest man in Venezuela, an industrialist-philanthropist named Eugenio Mendoza, started life as an office boy, and a deputy foreign minister was once a minor clerk in an oil company. This is a country where, as in the United States, people work their way up. There are some marvelously complicated personal connections; everybody knows everybody. I met a venerable doctor who has served one family and its offshoots for three generations. Manuel Mantilla, the executive secretary to the president, is the

[5] Compared to some 480 Americans in Paraguay as an example.

brother-in-law of Domingo Alberto Rangel, the inflammatory leader of MIR, a revolutionary party. Jóvito Villalba, the veteran head of one of the parties in the government coalition, has a former wife who is married to Gustavo Machado, the Communist party leader now in prison. This same lady has a brother who is prominent in Acción Democrática, the leading government party. Members of the elite have been known to pay Christmas calls on Communists in jail. Such vagaries are, of course, typical not merely of Venezuela but of most of the rest of South America.

Prices are high, if only because the economy is booming. From 1961 to 1963 the average annual growth rate was 6.4 percent, and the gross national product rose 8 percent in 1965 as against the preceding year. As to cost of living Caracas is the most expensive city in the world. A recent UN survey, putting New York at 100, rated Caracas at 150. The ranking of some other cities was Santiago 95, Montreal 92, Paris 90, Lima 84, Buenos Aires 82, Istanbul 76, Rio de Janeiro 71, and Cairo 60.

The Capital—Caracas

This is one of the most astonishing cities I have ever seen. Lying at an altitude of 3,136 feet in a narrow, long trough made by the Avila Mountains, founded in 1667 and once called Santiago de León de Caracas, it does not seem to be an integrated city at all, but a series of separate communities eccentrically linked together. It looks as Manhattan might look if bits of suburban White Plains, N.Y., or fields near Greenwich, Connecticut, lay between Forty-second Street and the Battery. The city does not have a center or focal point. It expands like a hand with fingers constantly stretching out and grabbing bits of hill or valley. The American Embassy and the Hotel Tamanaco stand today on what was a sugar plantation only a quarter of a century ago, and tall apartment buildings look down on the golf course of the country club. (The club did not progressively move as did that in Bogotá.)

The architecture of Caracas (pronounced Car-*ahk*-as) is defiantly modern, and what was once a sleepy Spanish village with ambling streets has lost most of its old touches of white plaster and red tile. Large tenements called *bloques* or *superbloques* rise with window panels painted orange, sea green, mauve, and pink in the manner of Le Corbusier, and look like canvases by Mondrian or a swarm of oblong butterflies.

I went to bed one night with automobile horns and the sound of screeching tires in my ears, and was wakened by cocks crowing.[6] Directly facing the Shell Building, in one of the new centers of town, is Carlota Airport, which is as if London had an airport just off Piccadilly Circus. Nowadays it is used mostly for helicopters and small military and private planes, but it can also serve in an emergency as a convenient escape hatch for people in a hurry to leave the country. The former dictator, Colonel Marcos Pérez Jiménez, known universally as P.J., escaped in this manner at dawn on January 23, 1958.

The commercial airport nowadays is Maiquetía, twelve miles away near the sea. A splendid four-lane motor highway, known as the Autopista, connects it with Caracas, and this, built by Pérez Jiménez, cost $70 million and, mile for mile, is said to be the most expensive road in the world. Similarly a hotel near the airport, also built by P.J., who had a madness for construction, cost an estimated $30 to $45 million and is supposed to have been the most expensive hotel of its size ever built. Pérez Jiménez spent vast sums on Central University as well, and was also responsible for much of the city's sensational housing development. He sacrificed the country for the city. The *campo* was abandoned. No rural schools were built, no roads, no hospitals, no water lines. A pudgy little profiteer, P.J. was a city man. To say that he took a cut on his various projects is an understatement, like saying that the Emperor Nero maintained pet lions for fun. P.J. was in the *business* of making money.

Traffic congestion in Caracas today is so spectacular that it makes even Rio seem sedate. The city has more than 160,000 automobiles, including 12,228 taxis,[7] and distances are formidably long: four rush hours occur every day (because most office workers go home for lunch) and traffic jams can be impenetrable. Accidents occur frequently but they are seldom serious—nothing more than a scraping of fenders. The altercations between citizens that are apt to follow can, however, be acrimonious; drivers have been known to pull out pistols and start shooting. If somebody is badly hurt it is considered to be much more important to call a priest than a doctor or ambulance. Curiously enough, the city has no public transportation in the form of trams or a subway; *Caraqueños* who do not have their own cars travel by bus, ordinary taxi, or by the omnipresent, agile *por puestos*, which are cheap taxis taking several passengers by the seat, like a miniature bus.

One-third of the Caracas population, about half a million people, lives in

[6] A writer in *The New Yorker* records a similar experience. He was awakened in a downtown hotel by the bray of burros. Cf. "Letter from Caracas," by Bernard Taper, *The New Yorker*, March 6, 1965, a first-rate article.
[7] More than in New York City, which has 11,772.

ranchos, the name Venezuelans give to their squatter towns. These perch on the hills like the *favelas* in Brazil, but the standard of living is somewhat higher. A good many of the Caracas huts and sheds have TV aerials protruding from roofs which are made of flattened tin cans, packing cases and cardboard held down by loose chunks of tile. My chauffeur, Rudy, who was once a night-club performer in New York, took me to visit his own *ranchito,* where, in two rooms, he and his wife, two or three adult relatives, and his nine children live in a hut made of rough cement blocks put together by his own hands. The neighborhood is almost intolerably squalid, but Rudy, a man of enterprise, has a small icebox and TV. Water comes from a spigot in a nearby alley. The water is what makes him lucky: more than 40 percent of all dwellings in Caracas, this "rich" city, do not have any immediate access to water at all.

Caracas is devoted to the pocket more than to elevation of the spirit, and banks are more to be seen at street corners than bookshops. The newsstand at the Tamanaco has *Playboy, Elegante Welt* and *Paris Match* well displayed, but close by are pamphlets with titles like *Venezuela 1959 Income Tax Law, Organic Statutes of the Obligatory Social Security Regulations,* and even *Navigation Law of 1944.* Near the thirty-story twin towers of Centro Simón Bolívar, where the principal government offices are housed and which has an eight-lane avenue passing through it, I saw publications like *Literatura Soviética* and *Pekín Informa* prominently available at newsstands—together with baby alligators called *babas.* This, like most South American capitals, is a very mixed-up city.

The press is outspoken and articulate. The leading independent newspaper *El Nacional* (circulation around ninety thousand) is run by the Otero Silva family. One of its proprietors is a distinguished left-wing poet. The tabloid *Daily Journal* resembles the English-speaking dailies in Rio and Buenos Aires, but has a more professional tang. One dominating personality in local journalism is Miguel Angel Capriles, the local Beaverbrook. I heard him called both a left-winger and a Fascist; he owns three powerful dailies, *Ultimas Noticias, El Mundo,* and *La Esfera,* as well as several magazines, and vigorously attacks the government on several planes. The principal literary figure in the city in the older generation is still the venerable Rómulo Gallegos, the author of well-known novels like *Doña Bárbara,* who was once president of the Republic. The late Mariano Picón-Salas, author of *The Ignoble Savages,* was a man of letters of exceptional distinction, who also served in the diplomatic service (to combine literature with diplomacy is a healthy tradition in South America) and had enlightening influence as president of the National Institute of Culture.

Most businessmen and officials work hard in Caracas. The day begins at eight; this is not a "*mañana*" city, and the siesta is largely gone. One *Caraqueño* told me, perhaps not altogether seriously, that a prime cause of anti-Americanism was that "the oil companies had abolished the siesta." Businessmen are vociferous in their self-criticism and complaints. "We have never had a market economy here, because no South American can tolerate competition." "Companies fix the price, and then share the market." "The trouble with Venezuela is that nobody will risk capital on anything that does not guarantee a return of 100 percent." "Yes, yes, we take in a billion dollars a year from the oil companies, and don't manage to waste more than a third of it."

Secretaries and office girls are, I heard, fantastically unreliable; they work hard for a time, then collapse or disappear. Often a girl, going home to lunch, will reappear for the afternoon in a different costume. A soft job is called a *cambur*, a local word for cooking banana, and these are zealously sought out and retained, particularly in the lower civil service. Many public services are sloppily run—and no wonder, considering the salaries paid. An American businessman recently wrote a letter to the governor of an important state; it came back three weeks later with the notation "Addressee Unknown." There are several curiosities in the realm of social mores. It is technically forbidden in Caracas to walk *behind* a statue of Bolívar because this shows disrespect, and for a woman to wear shorts on the public street is considered indecent—indeed she may be subject to arrest.[8] Native Venezuelans are not allowed in the leading bordello known as the Penthouse, which is reserved exclusively for foreigners.

Annals at a Glance

Venezuela was discovered by Christopher Columbus in 1498, and penetration by the Spaniards began the next year. The name is a distortion of "Little Venice"; the country was so called because Indians of the day lived in huts built on stilts in shallow lagoons near the sea. Development in Venezuela pursued roughly the same path as in Colombia, but it was more of a backwater and the substratum of Spanish culture never became so deep. Charles V of Spain farmed the country out to a German banking company, run by the Welser family, for a time; pearls and salt became large items in trade, and slaves poured in. Venezuela was so little developed under the Spanish hegemony that it did not even have a newspaper or printing press till 1808.

[8] *South American Handbook*, pp. 450 and 467.

Liberation came in 1811. One of its architects was a picturesque adventurer, Francisco de Miranda, the most attractive of all the revolutionaries of the era; he fought in the French Revolution, and had friendships with Catherine the Great, Pitt, and Washington. He is called the "Precursor," because his campaigns preceded those of Bolívar, who, as we know, was born in Caracas (in 1783). The two leaders quarreled, and Bolívar, according to one version of the story, betrayed Miranda to the Spaniards. Venezuela remained part of the amalgam known as Gran Colombia until 1830, then struck out on its own. Twenty-two of its first thirty presidents were generals, and the period of incessant civil war began. The country had no fewer than twenty-four constitutions and more than one hundred changes of government after Bolívar.[9]

In 1908 began the dictatorship of Juan Vicente Gómez, nicknamed the Sorcerer or the Catfish; it lasted until his death in 1935, or twenty-seven years. Gómez was a murderous blackguard. It is impossible to understand the realities of Venezuela today without reference to Gómez. He ran the country like a huge private estate, and built up a fortune estimated at $200 million. Oil was discovered during the Gómez regime and he imposed political stability of a sort on the country, which it badly needed. The cost of this advance was, however, large. Gómez was a *mestizo* from the Andes, and never altogether learned to read and write; he never married, and had between eighty and ninety bastard children. "He made use of tortures of inconceivable brutality; political prisoners, of whom there were thousands, dragged out their lives bearing leg irons (*grillos*) that made them permanent cripples, if they were not hung upside down till they died." He was quite capable of hanging victims by meathooks through their throats, having chosen them by lot.

Raúl Leoni, the president of the republic today, wrote a recent article[10] in which he says that "Venezuela did not enter the 20th century until the death of Gómez. Until then ours was a semi-feudal, semi-colonial state still living in the 19th century."

After Gómez came a period of breakout, liberation and confusion. The bung had been pulled from the cask. Political parties, after having been suppressed for almost thirty years, began to sprout again; the jails were

[9] Bernard Taper in *The New Yorker, op. cit.* Another authority, David Holden in the *Manchester Guardian Weekly*, reprinted in *Atlas*, August, 1963, mentions that there were at least fifty "major" rebellions between 1830 and 1900, and that the government was violently overthrown thirteen times. He puts the total number of constitutions at twenty-six.

[10] *Foreign Affairs*, July, 1965. The passage quoted above is from *Inside Latin America*.

emptied, freedom of speech was guaranteed, and women got the vote. But political coherence was lacking; two weak military governments made a mess of government. After some ten years of effervescent transition Rómulo Betancourt, leader of the Acción Democrática, which still runs the country, became provisional president in 1945, and proceeded to give it the best administration it had ever had, under democratic leadership. Acción Democrática, which I shall allude to again below, was a left-wing reformist party, but not Marxist as its enemies often said. Betancourt decided after a time to step down from office himself. A completely free and honest election was held in December, 1947, which was won triumphantly by the A.D. candidate, the novelist and man of letters Rómulo Gallegos. He was handpicked to run by Betancourt.

In his first term of office Betancourt raised taxes, set up a government-controlled development corporation, worked to improve public health, forced higher royalties out of the oil companies, sought to reform education, and felt his way toward making a land reform. But the A.D. went too far too fast. It alienated the conservative community and mortally affronted the army by a plan to build up a civilian militia as a counterpoise to the regular armed forces. So the army struck against the Gallegos regime, ousting it by a coup d'état in November, 1948. Betancourt had no position in the Gallegos government, but he was exiled. Power was taken over by Colonel (later General) Marcos Pérez Jiménez, whose dictatorship in one form or other lasted for ten years, from 1948 to 1958. Some knowledge of the P.J. period, like that of Gómez, is indispensable to an understanding of Venezuela today. P.J. did a great deal of public building, as has been noted above. He also revoked most of the reforms of the Betancourt period, imposed a strict censorship on the press, attacked labor, outlawed the A.D., and threw political opponents into jail. P.J. was so lurid a figure that, even at the risk of interrupting this brief narrative, we should have another word about him. He came from humble beginnings in the Andes, as did Gómez, adopted a military career, and became president before he was forty. One of his major sources of power was that "he managed to create the impression that anybody who opposed him was a Communist," and reactionaries in the American colony in Caracas adored him for the simplest of reasons—he kept the left down.[11]

Down? This is to put it somewhat mildly. The following is not from any left-wing organ but from Time, August 23, 1963. "In P.J.'s torture chambers, prisoners were slashed with razors, burned with cigarettes, forced to si

[11] Cf. Adolf A. Berle, Jr., "Latin America: the Hidden Revolution," Reporter May 28, 1959, a prescient article.

for hours on blocks of ice. Some prisoners were force-fed harsh laxatives and then, in a chamber of horrors awash with blood, excrement and vomit, they were forced to walk naked around a razor-sharp wheel rim. . . . P.J. operated a corrupt police state with lush graft for insiders and imprisonment and torture for opponents."

As stupid a small blunder as any that the United States has made recently in South American policy came, as noted in Chapter 8, under the Eisenhower-Dulles administration when P.J. was called to Washington and given one of the highest American decorations, the Order of Merit. This created resentment—even outrage—almost everywhere in South America. The decoration did not, however, do P.J. much good in his native land. The army had become convinced that he had outlived his usefulness, and, like a jackal, he was ousted by a coup d'état in 1958.

P.J. fled to Miami and set up residence there in a $300,000 house, with five automobiles, a yacht, and a team of bodyguards, to say nothing of a fortune estimated at anywhere from $250 million to $700 million.[12] The Venezuelan government, charging that he had misappropriated $13.4 million from the treasury during his tenure in office, opened proceedings for his extradition so that he might be returned to Caracas and put on trial. The legal proceedings in America dragged out interminably but in the end P.J. lost his case; he was the first deposed chief of state ever to be extradited from the United States. Taken back to Venezuela, he was imprisoned in a four-room suite in the Model Prison, which had been built by his administration, and was treated well, given a TV, and allowed to see friends.

When he was brought to trial the prosecution contented itself with asking for a 13½-year sentence, presumably one year for each million dollars he was supposed to have embezzled; there were several murder charges against him, but these had been dropped since the United States would presumably not have permitted his extradition if this had meant exposing him to a capital sentence. The deciding vote on the American Supreme Court by which his extradition was insured was cast by Arthur Goldberg, now the American ambassador to the United Nations.

P.J.'s trial ended in October, 1965, but at the moment of writing the case has not yet been decided. His last appeal to the court included a furious denunciation of Senator Robert F. Kennedy, who was attorney general of the United States when he was extradited, and whom he recklessly accused of "framing" him. There was, of course, no evidence for this wanton charge.

[12] This last figure is on the authority of the *New York Times*, August 17, 1963, quoting court proceedings in Miami.

After the downfall of P.J., Betancourt became president again, stayed in office for five uninterrupted years (1958–63), and inaugurated the "modern" period of Venezuelan history. Betancourt was, and is, an astounding phenomenon. His basic contribution was himself. He was the first chief executive in the country's history who came to office by free elections, who served out his full term as constitutional president, and who then turned over the office to a freely elected successor. He proved that political stability, even in a country as turbulent as Venezuela, was possible under democracy.

Still under sixty, Betancourt has spent a total of twenty-one years in jail, exile, or hiding. A short, bristly, somewhat rotund man with heavy glasses, he has magnetism, burning energy, and a rebellious spirit. Whenever I asked anybody to characterize him the first adjectives I heard were "impetuous" and "pugnacious," and nobody has ever doubted the genuineness of his fervor for reform.

This dynamic personality was born in 1908 in a village near Caracas, the son of a poet who earned a living as a cashier in a grocery. He started to work for a living at twelve, and managed later to enter the law school of Central University; he worked part time as a bill collector for a tobacco company, and one of his early teachers was Rómulo Gallegos, the writer whom he helped make president years later. At the university he organized a students' movement and, following a strike which he led, he was jailed by the Gómez dictatorship; he records that the leg irons clamping him to a dungeon wall weighed ninety-six pounds. By some miracle he was released after a few weeks, and fled the country. Arriving in Costa Rica he resumed his studies, married a schoolteacher, and became a Communist. He did not, however, stay with Communism long, and in later years described the episode as "a youthful attack of smallpox that left me immune from the disease."

A number of Betancourt's classmates went to jail with him and shared his exile, and these are known collectively today as "the Generation of 1928." Among them a half dozen leaders are still prominent, including Jóvito Villalba, the head of one of the parties in today's coalition, and Raúl Leoni, Betancourt's successor as president—also Gustavo Machado, the Communist leader. It is important to make note of this "Generation of 1928," still united by the badge of jail and exile, because its members—Machado excepted—are still the alpha and omega of the ruling clique in Venezula today. Such political continuity is rare in South America. The group resembles Pilsudski's colonels in Poland between the wars or the hard-core inner circle of resistance fighters in postwar France.

In the middle 1930's Betancourt, who now called himself a socialist, organized a social democratic party originally named Organización Venezolana, which developed into the Acción Democrática. It contained at the beginning lively Marxist elements, but nowadays it has become heavily bureaucratized and has lost most of its revolutionary zeal. Its basic tenets were—and are—social progress, planning, and economic reform. It grew up in the days of the "Popular" parties led by José Figueres in Costa Rica and Luis Muñoz Marín in Puerto Rico, and strongly resembled them—also, in spirit, the Roosevelt New Deal and John F. Kennedy's New Frontier.

Having become president again in 1958, Betancourt set a record on his first anniversary of office by becoming the first constitutionally elected chief executive in the history of Venezuela to hold office for 365 days.[13] He did not forget that the army had ousted him in 1948 and he carefully worked for good relations with the military; he also came to appreciate the importance of good relations with the United States and cultivated these with attention, but it was he who first put serious pressure on the oil companies to raise their royalties to Venezuela. He has also been described as having been "dangerously lenient to communism," but this did not keep him from suspending the Communist party in 1962 and putting its leaders into jail. The Communists detest him. Actually his general course was middle left, and he was continually harassed by extremists on the left.

There were certainly obstacles. Six military or semi-military uprisings took place, as well as a steady series of terrorist outbursts from the left. In June, 1960, he narrowly escaped assassination when a bomb exploded near his automobile; two of his aides were killed, and he himself was wounded. This attack was organized by Dictator Trujillo of the Dominican Republic, who hated Betancourt with passion. Considering the difficulties involved, Betancourt's concrete achievements were considerable. His public health program was emphatic, as it had been in his first term, and the death rate fell. He continued to push for land reform, and did more for education than any president in Venezuelan history; elementary school enrollment jumped to 80 percent during his term of office, and Venezuela now has the lowest illiteracy rate in the western hemisphere after the United States, Canada, Cuba, the Argentine, and Uruguay. Industrialization went on vigorously with the result that two-thirds of the country's consumer goods are now manufactured at home in Venezuela, as against one-third ten years ago.[14] Above and beyond

[13] *Time,* February 8, 1960. Another president also reached this mark but he was not "constitutional" strictly speaking.
[14] *Christian Science Monitor,* March 2, 1964.

all this he gave the country a sense of pride, achievement, and political stability.

*

The Venezuelan constitution not only forbids a president to succeed himself but does not allow him to run again for ten years, until two terms have passed. Betancourt had to hold elections in 1963 to make way for a successor, Sr. Leoni. He has made no attempt whatever to interfere with politics since that time, has always disclaimed any wish to be a power behind the scenes, and tends to stay out of the country. But the personality of this gritty little infighter is such that, despite his manifest defects, he is still inextricably bound up with the atmosphere of contemporary Venezuela, and we shall mention him several times again.

CHAPTER 28

Venezuela, Its Leadership and Politics

*The first question we should ask ourselves is: What is Latin
America? . . . What are we? . . . Never before has a society had, to such a degree, this tragic obsession, which might
be called "the ontological anguish of the Latin American."
. . . The Latin American has always, somewhat like Hamlet,
pondered his real nature, asking himself, "What am I: white,
Negro, Indian, mestizo, European, something that partakes of
all this, or something distinct? . . . The deep concern for
knowing what we are, what I have called "the anguish of
being," has existed since the Conquest.*
—ARTURO USLAR PIETRI

RAÚL LEONI, is a labor lawyer by profession, about sixty. It is nicely significant that Betancourt, the first constitutionally elected chief of state in
Venezuelan history ever to serve out his full term, should be succeeded by
Sr. Leoni, another constitutional president chosen by free elections, making
two in succession. Now if Leoni is able to maintain office for his full five
years another signal precedent will have been established—ten uninterrupted
years of democratic rule. As a Caracas citizen told me, "If Leoni sticks it out
we will have passed the hump."

President Leoni, a big solid man with smooth jowls and bulging mouth,
has luminous hazel eyes behind Goldwater-like spectacles, finely manicured
nails, and, like most South American presidents, beautifully cut clothes. The
president, born of a Corsican immigrant family in the Guayana country,
managed to get to Caracas at fourteen to make his way in life. He rose high
in the labor movement, worked for a time with the International Labor
Office, and served as minister of labor in the first Betancourt government (1945–48). Labor is more important in the political life of Venezuela

497

than in any other country in South America except possibly Argentina and Bolivia. Trade union membership is around 1,500,000 and there are 4,000 different unions, including strong peasant unions; labor is by far the biggest element in the Acción Democrática, the Betancourt-Leoni party.

When Leoni took over from Betancourt, the scene was dramatic. The new president ceremoniously took from the old the three traditional symbols of presidential power—a tricolor sash, the key to a cabinet which contains the first constitution of the country, and—inevitably—an urn containing the ashes of Simón Bolívar. The city was tense, because of the threat of terrorism, but nothing untoward occurred. Of course Leoni and Betancourt had been associates for many years; Leoni too was a member of the "Generation of 1928" which fled the country under the Gómez tyranny. Many years ago both were penniless exiles in Colombia, where they ran a fruit stand together; Leoni told me that they never made a profit because they gave most of their stock away to fellow exiles. Later they established a printing press and published a revolutionary newspaper, which still exists, in Barranquilla, Colombia. But nowadays there is scarely a hint of the revolutionary in Leoni. He spent nineteen years in exile, jail or hiding, but he acts, talks and looks today like a highly polished and prosperous member of the upper bourgeoisie.[1]

Betancourt did not particularly favor Leoni as the candidate of Acción Democrática in the 1963 elections but Leoni's political prestige in the labor movement was such that he could not be passed over. A favorite game in Caracas today is to compare the two leaders. Betancourt is more a firebrand, more brilliant and assertive, also possessed of a lively and responsive sense of humor; Leoni is solider, more contemplative, and more difficult to fathom. A good politician, he has little of the restless vehemence that marks Betancourt. Betancourt seldom gave orders. He acted on impulse, but Leoni tells people what to do. He is probably a better administrator and the atmosphere of government is smoother. On the other hand he lacks his predecessor's fierce inner fire, and inspires respect rather than passionate adulation. The opposition doesn't hate him as it hated Betancourt.

Person of the President

President Leoni asked me to lunch at Miraflores, the presidential palace in old Caracas. I admired its sense of polished luxury—also the smart atten-

---

[1] Congressman John H. Rousselot of California attacked him as an ex-Communist in a speech in the House of Representatives, September 23, 1961. Rousselot was defending Pérez Jiménez and vitriolically denouncing Betancourt.

tiveness of guards (no spiked helmets here but businesslike service uniforms) with their Sten guns held close to their bellies. Assembled was an imposing constellation of public men and women—the head of the trade unions, the chief of staff of the army, and several cabinet ministers, all waiting for the president. I thought that this would be a splendid occasion for general talk. It did not turn out that way. I got something better. After a drink or two I was suddenly marched into an adjoining room, where, without warning, I found myself thrown together with the president as lights flashed and TV cameras turned. Dr. Manuel Pérez Guerrero, the minister of mines and hydrocarbons, served as interpreter. Then abruptly we left the palace. I had no idea what was happening or where we were going. A military band gave the presidential salute outside Miraflores and I was deposited into a large black motorcar. The president, Dr. Pérez, and I sat in the back as a guard tucked himself into place next to the chauffeur. Apparently Mr. Leoni had decided to have me to lunch at his home, about half an hour away in the residential quarter known as Altamira, instead of at the palace. The eighteen or twenty guests at the palace were left stranded there to have lunch alone. I hope they got a good lunch. Immediately preceding us was an open car with its exposed seats facing backwards; on these sat army guards with machine guns across their knees. This seemed to me to be an adroit and efficient way to insure the president's safety. The guards do not have to stand up, lean out of automobile windows, or crane this way and that. They not only covered us directly but also could automatically watch other automobiles as well as people on the streets through the device of the backward-facing open seats. Then I saw another novelty—three motorcycle policemen who incessantly swooped in broad circles around and around our car. First one would shoot ahead, make a wide turn, and be replaced by another so that one motorcycle was always immediately ahead of us, one abreast, and one behind, with each constantly changing position as we proceeded. This was probably the most exhilarating automobile ride I ever had. Yet, incredibly enough, there was nothing ostentatious about it, and I don't think that many onlookers even knew that the president was passing by.

The president's house is known as Los Núñez, and is a modest Beverly Hills–type villa which the government rents and puts at the disposal of the chief executive. Betancourt lived here for some years, and President Kennedy was his guest here when he visited Caracas in December, 1961; Betancourt moved out of his own room to give it to J.F.K., whom he admired extravagantly. The Leonis are leaving Los Núñez soon because it isn't big enough—they have five children—and are moving into a district called La Carlota near the airport, which has more style.

Leoni works a fifteen-hour day, like Betancourt, and seldom has time for relaxation, but I noticed a big open-air movie screen in the garden. Sometimes late at night he plays dominoes with his wife. He told me that he had sometimes made as many as eighteen speeches a day in the last election campaign, and spoke altogether in four hundred different townships. He never carries arms, as his predecessor always did.

Doña Menca Fernández de Leoni, a youthful pretty woman, sat with us at lunch. She comes of a well-to-do rancher's family, and is an ardent Catholic. She took little part in the conversation, as is the custom with wives in South America, although she was both amiable and spirited. We had a typical Venezuelan meal—*paticas de cochino*, spiced pigs' feet with a rich peppery sauce, and a vegetable dish made with manioc, together with a bit of sherry and red wine. The desserts were sumptuous. This is sweet tooth country, like Colombia. The president's talk covered a broad arc, and lunch lasted till 4:30 P.M. One of Mr. Leoni's preoccupations is, naturally enough, Communism, and he talked about guerrilla activity in Venezuela, which, till recently, seriously disrupted parts of the country. He thinks that Castro's influence has waned perceptibly everywhere in South America, but that the Cubans are still capable of making local trouble. There are, however, no more than five hundred guerrillas still active in the mountains, he thinks, and the Communist movement in the towns is weak and divided. Mr. Leoni progressed to an associated topic, civil liberties, which has been a pointed issue since the government cracked down on the Communist party in Congress, and sent several leaders to prison without trial—seven deputies, two senators.[2] The president insisted that the total number of political prisoners in the country does not exceed nine hundred, and all of these will be duly tried in time, he said. "They are not in jail because they are Communists, but because they were terrorists who broke the law. Citizens must respect the privileges of the state if the state is to respect the privileges of citizens."

Along with labor the chief force behind Leoni—at the moment of writing at least—is the army, and he is sensible enough to cultivate it. Without army support he could be ejected in a minute. But he does not overtly kowtow to the military, and they have respected him so far. Every time the president gives an officer a commission he ceremoniously presents him with a copy of the constitution, and his relations with the army command have been good. There have been no attempts at coup d'état like those which occurred under Betancourt.

[2] Several of these have subsequently been released.

More About Politics and Politicians

Politics in Venezuela are complicated, but not quite so much so as in Chile, say, or Colombia. The Leoni coalition, called the *Ancha Base* (broad base), has three principal constituents.

1. The A.D., Acción Democrática, founded by Betancourt, is still the biggest party in the country, with almost a million well-organized members, but it does not command a majority in parliament, and Leoni, like Betancourt, rules by coalition, although it is a different coalition. Some of its vigor and idealism have diminished with success, and the party seems somewhat dated; it had to bear most of the brunt of the early struggle to establish democracy in Venezuela, and this produced deep scars and fissures. Somewhat oddly, it appears to have greater strength in the rural areas nowadays than in Caracas and the towns. The party has always been marked by scrupulously honest leadership. Next to Leoni its most powerful member today is probably Dr. Gonzalo Barrios, the minister of the interior, a man full of pith and bounce and another veteran from the days of 1928.[3]

2. The Unión República Democrática, or URD. This important group, led by Jóvito Villalba, is a moderate Social Democratic party. Dr. Villalba was another original member of the Generation of 1928. He spent many years in exile abroad. Returning to Venezuela and running for president in 1952, he legally won the election, but Pérez Jiménez, whose word was law, "voided the elections" and pitched him out of the country; he then became "president in exile" in Panama. Villalba flirted for a time with Castro and the Communists but his movement, like Acción Democrática, has steadily become less radical. He is accomplished, civilized, and articulate. A bust of Lincoln stands on his bookshelf next to the Great Books series. He feels that the basic Venezuelan problem is what to do with power. In the United States, he put it, the main task of a president in normal times is merely "to keep things going," whereas in Venezuela, still a developing country, political power must be an instrument for direct social and economic liberation. Is the government doing enough for the people? Certainly not. No government does. The great tasks are to make democracy workable, give greater opportunities, and distribute income better.

The principal obstacles to progress, Villalba thinks, are these: (a) The

---

[3] Two other A.D. leaders of consequence, who lead what are called the pro- and anti-Betancourt wings of the party respectively, are Carlos Andrés Pérez, the anti-left former minister of the interior, and Jesús Angel Paz Galarraga, the secretary general, who represents younger, more radical elements.

government still has to operate in a kind of vacuum, caused in part by the fact that Venezuela for more than thirty years, under Gómez, had no free press, no congress, no political parties, no municipal councils, and no judicial system or process of law. (b) Lack of education. (c) Betancourt, Leoni, and the rest are oldish men and youthful leaders have not yet come up. (d) Castro and the Communists are a constant danger; Castro's revolution "stunned" Venezuela and forced Betancourt to the right.

3. The Frente Nacional Democrática (FND), founded in 1964 and led by Arturo Uslar Pietri, sixty, a distinguished man of letters; Uslar has such intellectual prestige that the word "Uslarismo" is sometimes used in definition of his views. The FND is a center party, not leftist like its two partners. Uslar says that he entered the present coalition mostly to be a stabilizing influence. He did not take part in government under Betancourt. His father was a German immigrant, and he looks a bit like Dean Rusk, with a massive dome of forehead. Dr. Uslar represents an archetypical South American species at its best—the combined philosopher-poet, patriarch, and politician. I asked him why so many South American intellectuals were both politicians and men of letters. First, Latin America carries on the tradition of the European Renaissance, and is the natural home of the "universal man." Second, politics in South America have always had a strong ideological base, and therefore men of politics must be well grounded in philosophy. He thought, too, that intellect is more respected in the southern hemisphere than in the United States.

Dr. Uslar originated the phrase, "Sow the oil," heard on every side in Venezuela, and which I will explain below. He is a strong individualist, and, although a man of the center, refuses to be called an "*anti*-Communist." One of his novels, *Red Lances*, has been translated into several languages. Well known in the United States, Uslar taught Latin American literature at Columbia University for a time.[4]

*

Turn now to the opposition. Its principal element is the Partido Social Cristiano, called COPEI for short. This is the Christian Democratic party, directly analogous to the one in Chile, and its leader, Dr. Rafael Caldera, fifty, is probably the most influential Christian Democrat in South America after President Frei. A worthy, modest, and attractive man, who has a lively sense of decency and humor, Caldera has run for president three times, in

[4] The Uslar party pulled out of the Leoni coalition early in 1966, partly because it felt that it was not being given enough representation in the government.

1947, 1958, and 1963, winning 22 percent, 16 percent, and 20 percent of the vote respectively. He and his party were members of the Betancourt coalition, but dropped out under Leoni because Caldera felt that Acción Democrática was moving too slowly, and that the people, ahead of the government, should be given a real alternative. "This country is *moving*," he told me earnestly. He is, of course, a strong Catholic and COPEI is the middle-class Catholic party, but it has marked left-wing tinges. Caldera has served four jail terms for political activity, and once spent a period of exile in New York. A lawyer by profession, he is a leading member of the world committee of Christian Democratic parties.

MIR (Movimiento Revolucionario Izquierdo or Revolutionary Left Movement) was founded in 1960 by radicals expelled from Acción Democrática and has an extreme left-wing—even Fidelista—texture. Its polemics are vociferous, and its leader, Domingo Alberto Rangel, was arrested recently for alleged terrorist conspiracy. As to the official Communist party, led by the brothers Gustavo and Eduardo Machado, it got 6 percent of the presidential vote in 1958. Neither MIR nor the Communists are officially suppressed, but they are not allowed to run candidates in national elections or hold public meetings: hence it is difficult to gauge their putative strength. Probably the total Communist party membership is 30,000.

Among minor opposition parties the most interesting is the FDP, Fuerza Democrática Popular, a group on the non-Communist left which has 12 seats out of 179 in the Chamber. Its leader, Wolfgang Larrazábal, is a vivid personality. He too was a member of the Generation of 1928, who, on his return from exile, entered the navy and rose to be a vice admiral. He was head of the military junta which ruled the country briefly after the downfall of Pérez Jiménez, and ran against Betancourt for president in 1958, coming out second. It is difficult, however, to take Admiral Larrazábal altogether seriously nowadays, if only because of his impetuous playboy tendencies. A celebrated ladies' man, renowned for his good looks, he attracts supporters by singing in night clubs and playing the guitar.

*

One striking point is that there is no rightist party in Venezuela. "Reactionary" is a dirty word, and for a man even to be called a "conservative" is a political kiss of death.

Another is that graft and corruption are at a minimum. Venezuela has probably the most honest government and public administration in Latin America next to Chile.

Who and What Run Venezuela?

1. The army.
2. Labor and the trade unions.
3. Oil.
4. Political parties and leaders, particularly those of the Generation of 1928.

As to the army, what runs *it?* The answer isn't easy. There is no fixed military caste in Venezuela, no elite clique of officers. The army is a national army, raised by selective conscription, and officers are chosen by competitive examination in the military schools. An interesting point is that Venezuela has no noncommissioned officers, since these are supposed to represent a type (like Batista in Cuba) too easily tempted to making *golpes* or coups d'état.

Most officers come from the Andes and rise from humble beginnings; they tend to keep to themselves and, in Caracas, seldom conspicuously leave the magnificent officers' club built for them by P.J. In the familiar South American pattern, the army seems to consider itself to be the servant of continuity and constitutionalism, the arbiter between "government and chaos." There are, however, irresponsible elements, and these can be dangerous. In May, 1962, came an uprising of a marine battalion at Carúpano, and in the following month the garrison at Puerto Cabello similarly rose. Both coups were quickly put down by loyalist forces. What was most interesting about these affairs was that the rebels worked with leftist—not rightist—civilian elements, which may mean that Communists had filtered into the military units involved.

The Venezuelan army has, incidentally, never fought a foreign war. It gets less than 10 percent of the national budget—the smallest percentage of any country in South America except Uruguay. To sum up, the top leadership of the army, if it chose to make a coup, could certainly upset any government, and is meantime in a position to exert substantial veto power, but it is unlikely to assert itself except in the event of an extreme national emergency.

What about the church? Church and state are still united in Venezuela, and the church still receives a subsidy from the government. But the Roman Catholic hierarchy does not have anything like the influence on political affairs that it has in Colombia, as an example, or Ecuador. People are, as I heard it put, "Catholic but not church-going," as indeed many are all over South America; probably not more than 10 percent of the male citizenry goes to mass. "The nearer to church, the further from God," is a local saying. Church influence is expressed mostly in education, particularly secondary education, and in opposition to birth control.[5] Divorce is legal.

Sowing the Oil

Here in Venezuela oil and water do mix. The richest petroleum deposits ever known to man until recent discoveries in the Middle East lie northwest of Caracas in Lake Maracaibo, adjoining the Caribbean. Derricks rise directly out of the water as they do at Baku on the Caspian. Venezuela is the third-biggest producer of oil in the world, after the United States and the Soviet Union, and the biggest exporter. Once more we must grapple with a few figures. The Venezuelan proved reserves comprise about 7 percent of the total known world reserves, and production, more than 3.2 million barrels a day, is about 12.5 percent of total world production. Oil provides no less than 65 percent of the country's national revenue, and gives the government an income of roughly $1.1 billion a year.

"This country is an oil factory," is the way President Leoni expressed it to me. Oil has been known here since the 1870's, but the first large well did not come in till 1914, and the industry did not become commercial on a serious scale until the 1920's. Then oil poured out so abundantly and was so handsomely salable that Venezuela presently became the only country in the world without a cent of foreign or domestic debt. Three foreign companies gained concessions which dominated production, and they still do—the Creole Petroleum Corporation, a subsidiary of Standard Oil of New Jersey, Royal Dutch Shell, and Gulf. Creole, a brilliantly operated organization, is said to be the largest petroleum-producing company in the world, and is probably the most profitable.[6] Mobil, Sinclair, Texaco, and other American companies have a smaller percentage of production, and the Venezuelan government is represented by a public company, the CVP or Corporación Venezolana del Petróleo, but this produces little.

When I first visited Caracas twenty-five years ago the foreign companies took for themselves roughly 80 percent of petroleum revenues; the country only retained 20 percent. Action by Venezuela gradually changed this percentage to the 50-50 ratio common in the Middle East, and at present the country gets approximately 66 percent, the companies 34 percent. Both

---

[5] But the investigation of population dynamics and growth as it affects economic planning is beginning, and the government has established an office for population studies in the Ministry of Health.

[6] It has not had a strike of its labor force for seven years. Several of its directors are Venezuelan. Its payments to the Venezuelan government amounted to $475 million in 1963 but even so its net income reached $254 million.

sides seem reasonably well satisfied with this proportion. All the foreign concessions have terminal dates, and most expire in about eighteen years; the last will go in 1997. It is almost certain that these will not be renewed and that no future concessions will be granted; future production will be solely on a contract basis. "Concession," like "reactionary," is a dirty word in Venezuela. However, the problem is somewhat abstract in that the oil reserves are expected to give out in about 1988 and so the future of the industry is uncertain in any case. Meantime there is surprisingly little agitation for further change in royalty and tax payments now, and no situation exists to compare with that in Peru, where expropriation is a public cry. Nor do the oil companies seem to be personally hated like the copper companies in Chile.

But it cannot be denied that substantial public sentiment in Venezuela resents the basic and underlying situation, namely that oil produced largely by foreign concessionaires still utterly dominates the country. Attitudes in this area cannot be measured by percentages. Nobody wants his homeland to be a colony. A great national resource largely in the hands of non-nationals strikes at the very root of national pride. Adolf A. Berle wrote recently, "The inhabitants of these [Latin American] countries feel that they are not really masters in their own houses. . . . Citizens react much as Americans would if, let us say, a German company were to emerge as owner of the entire steel or electronics industry in the United States."[7]

One exacerbating factor is that the exploiting companies, gaining wealth from a Venezuelan national resource, might well have been more generous when the industry was expanding and they could easily have afforded bigger royalties. Advances had to be forced out of them bit by bit.

On the other hand, it is conceded by almost everybody that it is the oil revenues from foreign concessionaires today which make possible the country's program of social reform, and it is indeed an irony often mentioned in Caracas that private petroleum interests in the United States and elsewhere abroad should be paying for a large share of Venezuela's experiments in planned economy.[8] Capitalist oil is thus contributing to social revolution.

Why is the impulse to go the whole hog, expropriate, and thus obtain 100 percent of all oil revenues instead of 66 percent not more strongly expressed among Venezuelans? The fundamental answer is that this process would probably in the end cost more than it would gain, both politically and economically. Venezuela might find its markets suddenly cut off. Meantime the government keeps a wary eye on the companies, and, as the somewhat

[7] *New York Times Magazine,* January 26, 1964.
[8] *The New Yorker, op. cit.,* p. 108.

ominous phrase has it, steadily "refines its accounting procedures." There are several points at issue, like price. World petroleum prices have slumped, partly because of overproduction in the Middle East and because oil is produced more cheaply there. Oil brings in more than a cool billion dollars a year to Venezuela now, but it will not do so much longer if prices continue to fall. Foreseeing this, the Venezuelans took the lead in 1960 in establishing the Organization of Petroleum Exporting Countries (OPEC), a kind of international marketing agency with eleven nations represented, in an attempt to regulate production and achieve enough strength ultimately to face the importing nations on better terms. Its headquarters are in Vienna.

In spite of its stupendous wealth in oil, Venezuela has few oil millionaires like those in Texas. Several local citizens became rich through the sale or exchange of oil leases some thirty years ago, but no millionaire *class* has ever risen. The country is the millionaire. Another curiosity is that, although oil provides 90 percent of the country's foreign exchange and more than two-thirds of its total revenue, the industry employs no more than 2 percent of the nation's workers, a situation making for imbalance.

The petroleum companies on their side play a careful game today and do everything possible to stay out of politics and controversy. There is no oil lobby as such. The operators want to let well enough alone, and at all costs to avoid ostentation or contention. Oil executives in the top echelons are men of considerable sophistication, who know the underlying realities of the situation, and are punctiliously correct in their dealings with Venezuelans. But in the medium and lower ranks of oil men—and their wives—I encountered characters as monstrous as exploiters along the China coast in older days. They were true equivalents of the "old China hands," and I would not have been surprised to see some such sign as "Dogs and Venezuelans not allowed" outside their bailiwicks in Caracas.[9] They hold Venezuelans in utter contempt, have only the minimum of contact with them, and think that Betancourt was a cross between Mephistopheles and a gorilla. "What this country needs is a strong *hand*," they hiss darkly, meaning a strong hand like that of P.J. They even tend to snub the American Embassy because this maintains harmonious and correct relations with the Venezuelan government.

*

Before setting out for South America my wife and I called on Dr. Enrique Tejera-París, the Venezuelan ambassador in Washington. He exclaimed

[9] "Dogs and Chinese Not Allowed" was a notorious sign outside a British club in prewar Shanghai.

proudly, "In our country we build whole new cities!" What he was referring to was SANTO TOMÉ DE GUAYANA, which lies out in the wild pristine bush near the confluence of the Orinoco and Caroní rivers. Here is the nucleus of a new and important industrial development. Santo Tomé (or Ciudad Guayana, as it is sometimes called) is only 350 miles away from Caracas, but it cannot be reached directly by road and no railroad exists; if you do not fly you must travel by foot and canoe. But the export of industrial goods is possible because these can be shipped out to the Atlantic via the Orinoco, which has seven "inland ports" and is navigable to freighter traffic.

W. H. Hudson's classic *Green Mansions* was written about this florid and almost impenetrable country; so was *The Lost World* by Sir Arthur Conan Doyle. The capital of the region is CIUDAD BOLÍVAR, a city of sixty thousand people which was originally called Angostura; the flavoring material known as Angostura bitters first came from here. Nearby are aborigines, and the *South American Handbook* says—perhaps not altogether seriously—that if you visit Indian villages "you naturally buy yourself a blow gun" to shoot poison arrows with. In a nearby wilderness called the Gran Sábana is Angel Falls, the highest (3,212 feet) uninterrupted waterfall in the world, 2½ times the height of the Empire State Building. I had always assumed that Angel Falls was named because of its resemblance to some celestial phenomenon, but in fact the name comes from the man who discovered it in 1937—Jimmy Angel, an American bush pilot who crash landed here.[10]

The origin of the Santo Tomé industrial development is the concept "Sow the Oil," that is, the use of oil revenues for diversification of the national economy now, so that when petroleum runs out in eighteen or twenty years the country will have a wider industrial base and be permanently viable. This concept, promoted largely by Betancourt, is basic to all contemporary Venezuelan thinking. Oil is perishable, and therefore must be replaced by *renewable* forms of wealth—this is the idea. Hence the Guayana experiment began, and an organization known as the Corporación Venezolana de Guayana (CVG) was set up and the building of Santo Tomé got under way. Venezuelans like to say that no cities in the world have ever similarly been built from scratch in such difficult territory except Brasília and Chandigarh in India. Santo Tomé was chosen as the site partly because the Caroní, a tributary of the Orinoco, can produce practically unlimited amounts of water power, and the area is fantastically rich in iron, bauxite, and other minerals. You can pick iron ore right off the ground, and the reserves are believed to

[10] In August, 1965, Rolan Angel, the seventeen-year-old son of Jimmy Angel, led an expedition to the wreck of his father's plane still lying near the top of the falls.

amount to no less than four million tons of exceptionally pure ore, one of the largest and richest deposits in the world.

Santo Tomé's population, about 80,000 today, is expected to triple in ten years. But lack of know-how and the shortage of skilled labor have slowed up development. An imposing $360 million steel plant, opened in 1963, is government-owned and operated by the CVG with outside cooperation; it has lifted steel production from 70,000 tons to 300,000 tons, but is not working at full capacity. Another development is a 330-foot dam nearby on the Caroní, which will be the biggest dam in the world after Krasnoyarsk and Aswan, and which is being built with the assistance of Kaiser Industries; the World Bank has lent this huge enterprise $85 million, and it is scheduled to be completed in 1967. Still another project is an aluminum reduction plant owned jointly by the CVG and Reynolds International. By 1975 the Guayana complex will, it is hoped, produce 21 percent of Venezuela's total industrial output, 19 percent of all its goods and services. And this was untracked territory twenty years ago—the sheerest jungle wilderness.

Two large American mining companies have, however, been active in the area for a good many years, long before the Venezuelan planners got busy. Bethlehem discovered iron at a location called El Pao in 1941 and has been extracting substantial quantities of ore since 1951. In 1947 geologists for U.S. Steel located another extraordinary deposit, a mountain composed almost solidly of ore, at Cerro Bolívar, and have been working it successfully. Bethlehem operates through the Iron Mines Investment Company of Venezuela, U.S. Steel through the Orinoco Mining Company. Both pay taxes and royalties which amount to 51 percent of earnings. Exports of iron ore over the past several years have exceeded $100 million a year.

*

Dr. Manuel Pérez Guerrero has been minister of mines and hydrocarbons since 1963, and much of the above is his domain. He is brilliantly typical of the new Venezuelan type of public servant. Expert, correct, urbane, he was born in Caracas in 1911, received most of his education in France, speaks perfect English, and became an official of the League of Nations in the 1930's. Later he worked in several African countries as a director of technical assistance for the UN. His language is often eloquent, and he speaks about oil almost as if it were rare old wine, "useless as long as it remains in its natural cask, the earth." He is an ardent nationalist within an intelligent international frame.

Dr. Pérez Guerrero previously served in Venezuela as minister of finance and director of CORDIPLAN, the national planning agency set up by Betancourt; now, as minister of mines, he has one of the most trying jobs in the country. The foreign concessionaires like and respect Dr. Pérez, even though he keeps them under tight rein. A man whom the oil people do not like is his predecessor, Juan Pablo Pérez Alfonzo, who is sometimes thought to be an *éminence grise* behind Pérez Guerrero. It was Pérez Alfonzo who implemented Betancourt's "contracts-instead-of-concessions" policy, and I heard one foreign entrepreneur call him "the number two screwball in the country," presumably because he took steps to keep Venezuela's future oil resources in Venezuelan hands. (Of course No. 1 was Betancourt.)

Another personage typical of the new Venezuela is Dr. Héctor Hurtado Navarro, forty-six, the present head of CORDIPLAN. He has bright blue eyes, an upturned nose, courage, brains, and vision. Hurtado is a dreamer, but he knows hard facts. The son of a coal miner, he started work in a printing shop at the age of twelve, and as a youth came strongly under the influence of Haya de la Torre in Peru, and later of the Communists. But Hurtado could not endure Communist dogmatism and intolerance; he joined the Acción Democrática, becoming a government servant and technician. I dined with him twice in circumstances of the utmost informality. One evening Dr. Hurtado had as guests an Argentine, a Chilean, a Peruvian, and a Bolivian—all economic planners—so that I could get some idea of the way the planning concept has seized imaginations over all of South America. The Venezuelan national plan is staked out for four years, but Hurtado says that planning should be "part and parcel of our dreams," hence perpetual. On the other hand he feels that excessively long-range-planning "is consolation for what you know you cannot do," and consequently he seeks to emphasize the immediate, the practical. What he wants above all is to train, train, train people for technical responsibility.

Drama enters into this, Hurtado says—poetry enters into it. The challenge is, as in Chile, to reach the masses and achieve a full process of social transposition without altering the basic existing order. The most pressing difficulty of the democratic left is to present a program simple enough for the people to grasp and comprehend. "One of my tasks is to convince the leadership of the party that the problem is so complex."

*

If the question "How socialist is Venezuela?" is asked the answer is apt to be mixed. Nobody in power wants to interfere with the private sector, and this is a country where, as a glance at Caracas amply shows, free enterprise is still heartily entrenched. But the Venezuelan state owns the petrochemical industry, natural gas, the largest housing agency in the nation, a hotel network, and the railways. It controls salt, matches, one steel company, one oil company, and one coal mining company. It plays a role in cigarette paper, fisheries, pearls, and sugar processing, and it fixes the prices of pharmaceuticals, milk, and meat. One recent law establishes that one-third of all petroleum and gasoline products on the retail market must be sold through the CVP.[11] It believes devoutly in the planning process, and is responsible for the large developments in the Guayana region.

What Venezuela Needs Most

When I put this question to leading citizens I liked best the reply of Dr. Uslar, the philosopher-politician: "A little sense." A leading literary figure, Miguel Otero Silva, answered with the single word "Enlightenment!" One prominent attorney replied, "To observe the rules of the game. Anybody who reaches power here thinks that he has the right to make new rules of his own." President Leoni said, "Political agreement and cohesion, in order to activate a full program of social reform and development."

Castro, Communists, and the FALN

Venezuelan-Cuban relationships have almost the character of love-hate, and Venezuela is often called a "Cuba-on-the-mainland." Powerful forces in Venezuela helped Castro when he was still fighting in the Sierra Maestra, and took a strong line "in faithful support of the Cuban Revolution." Castro made a triumphant trip to Caracas immediately upon gaining power in Havana in 1959, and, after broadcasting to the citizens from his airplane, received a vociferous welcome, being identified with such concepts as "redemption" and "social justice." He had kicked out the hated Batista just as Venezuela had got rid of Pérez Jiménez, and cocked a big snook at the United States to boot.

But then the favorable attitude to Cuba cooled sharply because most Venezuelans viewed with distaste Castro's subsequent evolution. Betancourt in particular became furiously anti-Castro. A contributing element to this was probably the fact that Betancourt himself had once been a Communist, although briefly; Communist apostates hate Communists almost as vehe-

---

[11] This does not, however, hurt the foreign oil companies much because they sell only about 5 percent of their total production locally, but it is thought to be a somewhat uncomfortable augury for the future.

mently as Communists hate apostates. The Cubans proceeded to launch a severe propaganda campaign against the Caracas government; the watchword was, "Turn the Andes into the Sierra Maestra." Venezuela replied by breaking off relations with Cuba in November, 1961; later came episodes having to do with Cuban arms smuggled into Venezuela by Communist agitators, and as a result Venezuela requested a meeting of the Organization of American States, asking for sanctions against Cuba, in December, 1963. The ferocious hatred of Communists all over the world for Betancourt dates from this, and relations between Venezuela and Cuba have never been resumed.

Meantime FALN emerged—Fuerzas Armadas de Liberación Nacional—composed mostly of Venezuelan Communists trained and armed in Cuba, many of them students, writers, artists. Probably FALN never had a hard core of more than five hundred members, but its activity ravaged parts of the country. Forty-seven police were murdered in Caracas during the course of 1962 by FALN agents; banks were robbed and newspaper offices invaded by bold and skillful saboteurs. FALN succeeded in hijacking a government freighter, dynamiting oil lines, bombing the leading hotel, burning a Sears, Roebuck warehouse, making off with a well-known Spanish bullfighter, kidnaping two different American officers who were deputy commanders of the United States military mission, attacking the American Embassy, and even stealing five French paintings, worth $500,000, which had been lent to Venezuela for an exhibition.[12] All this had direct political motivation—to keep the country jumping and embarrass Betancourt, which it did.

Betancourt's reform program was seriously held up. He retaliated by police and military measures and by suspending the activity of the Communist party in parliament. The disturbances became dangerous in at least eight provinces, particularly Falcón, near the sea, and guerrilla warfare got under way almost on the scale of that in Colombia. The government put nine thousand troops, led by officers trained in the United States Army's counter-guerrilla school in Panama, into the field. But the uprising never reached a critical point mainly because the peasantry as a whole remained loyal. The guerrillas never succeeded in investing and holding any actual territory as they did in Colombia, and raids were mostly of a hit-and-run variety.

Many FALN fighters were not Communists at all from a serious ideological point of view. The story that Castro sent out into the Venezuelan countryside teams which brainwashed villages wholesale is an exaggeration. What did happen was that destitute young Venezuelan intellectuals, aim-

---

[12] The five artists were well chosen—Cézanne, Van Gogh, Picasso, Braque and Gauguin.

less, disillusioned, and driven to the breaking point by misery, joined the movement spontaneously, although listening in to the Cuban radio probably gave them a nudge. This was also true in the towns. A kind of lost generation of frustrated zealots sought to express itself. On the other hand a number of Venezuelan émigrés certainly did receive training in Cuba as terrorists and saboteurs, and a good deal of foreign money was available, including one big shipment of cash from Italy, which the Venezuelan government dramatically intercepted.

The basic FALN objective in Caracas was to influence voters to boycott the December, 1963, elections, which put Leoni into power, because this would discredit the government. Two symbols appeared everywhere—a beard to symbolize Castro, a pipe for Betancourt. (The president was an inveterate pipe smoker.) This effort failed ignominiously because 90 percent of the eligible voters did actually vote, saying, "Pipe yes, beard no," and the transition from Betancourt to Leoni proceeded without interruption.

Acts of violence still occur widely in Venezula, but they are not so serious as before. Urban disorder has greatly diminished from the pitch it reached during "the extremism" four years ago, and the hinterland is steadily being brought to order. The only thing that could have brought the government down was continuing, direct, and massive support of the guerrillas by Cuba, and for a good many reasons Castro has been unable or unwilling to involve himself to any such degree.

*

Probably the total number of avowed Communists in Venezuela does not amount to more than 30,000, which is a considerable decline from membership at its peak ten years ago. Leadership is lacking. The party has a stronger basis among intellectuals than in the working class, a phenomenon common to almost all South American countries except Bolivia, and its main object nowadays is to infiltrate the armed forces.

El Siglo, the Communist daily in Caracas, is a full-size newspaper with a better professional touch than most party organs on the continent, and is published without censorship or interference. The party also circulates a sixteen-page weekly, Las Masas a la Ofensiva, but its circulation is insignificant. Seemingly the government does not wish to suppress these organs because to do so would invalidate the emphatic stand it takes for free speech.

However, about 1,200 Communists were arrested and jailed in 1963 of whom 916 still await trial; 217 have been freed, according to a statement to me by Dr. Barrios, the minister of the interior. That these 916 have not yet been tried is, of course, an outrageous violation of civil liberties in the North American context, and most Venezuelans are acutely sensitive on the subject, which is a sign of advance. In January, 1965, a curious new law came into effect whereby terrorists who give themselves up are granted the choice of being tried and serving a jail term, deportation into exile, or confinement to their home areas without other punishment. The object is to encourage the guerrillas to surrender. Also Communists at present being held under terrorist charges may be allowed to go into "voluntary" exile without trial if they so opt—a novel experiment in penology.

To sum up, Castro and Communism are still a vivid preoccupation in Venezuela, but the possibility of any actual seizure of power or revolution is remote.

Affairs Abroad, Aims at Home

Venezuela, a peppery as well as strident small nation, has always taken a sharply independent line in foreign policy, and is somewhat choosy about its relationships. It refused to recognize the coup made by the Argentine army to depose Frondizi, although the United States did, and it severed relations with Brazil when Castelo Branco replaced Goulart as president in the turnover of April, 1964, although the United States strongly supported this change. The reason in both cases is that Venezuela, which has not forgotten Gómez and P.J., does not approve of military regimes installed by force. Meantime Venezuela was until recently the only South American republic engaged in an overt quarrel with a European power.[13] The country adjoins Guyana, the former British Guiana, on the east and claims some sixty thousand square miles of territory in a dispute dating back to 1899. Until Guyana became independent in 1966 students occasionally demonstrated in front of the British Embassay in Caracas, brandishing signs saying "England Go Home."

Venezuelan relations with the United States are cordial, and were certified by a visit made by Betancourt to President Kennedy in 1961. Betancourt was vastly popular in Washington in New Frontier circles, as was JFK in Caracas. The United States accounts for about 65 percent of all foreign investments in Venezuela, and this American involvement, estimated at something like 2.8 billion dollars, represents a large share of our total investment in South America. Nor should it be forgotten that the United

[13] Except Argentina which has the long-standing dispute with the British over the Falkland Islands.

States takes about 40 percent of Venezuela's exports of petroleum, which gives us a virtual stranglehold on the country if we should ever choose to exert it. The United States is not always popular in Caracas, nor are some of its representatives. Vice President Nixon was mobbed here in 1958, and was lucky to escape with his life. In 1965 the Venezuelan parliament voted unanimously to condemn the unilateral intervention of the United States in the Dominican crisis—"one of the very few times in history when there was such a vote"[14]—and abstained in the critical resolution sponsored by the United States asking for OAS support in the Dominican operation, although Venezuela had asked *us* for help in imposing hemisphere sanctions on Fidel Castro two years before.

United States aid to Venezuela through the Alianza is comparatively light, about $60 million in the first year and tapering off ever since. AID has made no loans to the country since 1962, but supports technical assistance in various fields—housing, secondary education, public safety, agricultural credit—on a modest scale, about $1.6 million a year. The Inter-American Development Bank has made two $10 million loans under the Social Progress Trust Fund, one for a low-cost rural housing project, one for rural water supply. The Export-Import Bank lent $31.5 million to Venezuela in 1964 to assist development in steel and aluminum, and for industrial equipment, a bridge on the Orinoco, and the purchase of aircraft for VIASA, the national airline. Food for Peace contributed $10.3 million in 1964.

*

Among private American financial institutions at work the most interesting is IBEC, the International Basic Economy Corporation. This, a Rockefeller organization, undertakes activity in a good many developing countries, all the way from Thailand to Zambia, and is particularly conspicuous in South America—Argentina, Brazil, Chile, Colombia, Peru, Uruguay, above all Venezuela. IBEC was established by Nelson Rockefeller, who had been Co-ordinator of Inter-American Affairs in Washington during the war and had a lively interest in South America, together with his brothers, in 1947. The idea was to set up businesses on a profit-making basis that would at the same time assist local development. It sought to concentrate on projects closest to the people, like those involved with food and shelter. Its main fields today are poultry breeding, low-cost housing, mutual funds, and food production, processing, and distribution, and it has become a flourishing multi-million-dollar enterprise.

[14] Marquis Childs, New York *Post*, July 8, 1965.

IBEC has in Venezuela a chain of twenty-four supermarkets which have considerably aided the local economy aside from bringing retail food prices down by about 15 percent. When IBEC opened its first store in Venezuela in 1949, some 80 percent of the foodstuffs it sold had to be imported. Now most of these items are locally produced, with consequent stimulus to the economy. Milk was another big operation. The story that the Rockefellers actually "introduced" pasteurized milk into the country is not quite correct, but they advanced its use by modern methods—for instance by selling milk in paraffinated cartons and by home delivery. Then too IBEC has created shopping centers, gone in for soluble coffee production, and manufactures household wares. Milk and bread are, incidentally, both subsidized by the Venezuelan government in order to keep prices within limits—about 25 cents for a quart of milk or loaf of bread today.

Another Rockefeller organization is AIA, the American International Association, founded by Nelson in 1946. This is a non-profit organization devoted to rural development, communication, and education in association with government.

The Country in Summary

Venezuela presents on the whole what is probably the brightest economic and political picture in South America. Here, at the end of this long multifaceted book, we reach a natural climax. Venezuela abounds with energy, push, and social vision. There are plenty of opportunities still to be seized, but here is a community on the move—perhaps rough and bristly, but getting somewhere fast.

1. As to matters of public health, the life expectancy of a Venezuelan was 59.6 years five years ago, 65.2 years today. Malaria was eliminated in a spectacular three-year campaign from 1945 to 1948, and, partly as the result of a sound program of sanitation improvement, the country has the lowest mortality rate in South America, 10-15 per thousand.

2. Advance is lively in education too. Government figures say that illiteracy has dropped from 53 percent at the end of the Pérez Jiménez dictatorship in 1958 to 20.3 percent in 1964. Facilities have been given to 930,000 new students in the past few years, and five out of every six children now receive at least a modicum of primary schooling. Venezuela is putting a higher proportion of funds into education than any country in South America, 13 percent of the budget. Education gets more from the budget than defense.

3. An effective land reform program is getting under way, the most am-

bitious on the continent next to that in Chile. The planners think not only in terms of splitting up big properties but of road construction, waterway development, marketing assistance, and fundamental research in agronomy. Some 85,000 *campesino* families have been settled on productive land so far, and 200,000 more families, about a million people, are to be settled by 1970.

4. Industrial advance has, as we know, been spectacular. The economy is booming, an $850 million public works program is in being, and the gross national product, around $6 billion in 1962, rises impressively year by year. The average per capita income is above $800, very large for South America. The country bursts with economic challenge, and it is on the threshold of becoming a genuine industrial state under national planning. Unemployment is, however, severe, and some 250,000 peasants are still landless.

5. Venezuela has the strongest labor movement in South America, except possibly Argentina, and the middle class is probably developing more rapidly than in any other country. The gap between rich and poor, the worst of all headaches in the hemisphere, is narrowing, but this is not to say that a large number of citizens are not still very poor.

6. Democratic procedures are working well by South American standards, and the concept of constitutionalism has taken a new firm root, if only because more people steadily attain a bigger vested interest in political stability. Governments may fall, but they are not so likely as before to be succeeded by capriciously imposed antisocial dictatorships. Citizens have discovered how powerful the free voice can be. An astute foreign diplomat told me, "The greatest change here in ten years is the acceptance of democratic concepts. The government has proved that stability, progress and reform are possible without dictatorship."

Venezuelan Miscellany

The discoverer of the drug chloromycetin is a Venezuelan, and the country has thirty-two different species of eagle. Foreign residents in Caracas often have difficulty in remembering recent dates because, they say, the climate is always the same, as a result of proximity to the equator, and this makes it difficult to relate memory of events to the weather. The local equivalent of gyppy tummy is called *mayo* because it seems to occur most often in the month of May, and the prevailing local winds are given picturesque names like hurricanes in the United States. Eighty percent of the goods sold by the Sears, Roebuck stores are now Venezuelan-made. Venezuelans are baseball-mad, and Luis Aparicio, one of the first local men to win a place on a United States major league team, is a hero. A gambling game played by almost everybody is Cinco y Seis, based on horseracing. Venezuelans drink vast quantities of Scotch, and as good a restaurant as any I know in South America is Hector's in Caracas. The American oil men comfort themselves by saying that Venezuela is "a Pentagon place, not a State Department place," and foreigners are called *musius*, from "monsieur." The local unit of currency is colloquially known as the "B" (Bolívar), and the country has no death penalty.

CHAPTER 29

Summary to Conclude

> *If we cannot help the many who are poor,*
> *we cannot save the few who are rich.*
> —JOHN F. KENNEDY

> *The threat from communism . . . cannot be met merely*
> *by force.*
> —LYNDON B. JOHNSON

So NOW we conclude this long and convoluted trek through a continent stuffed with imponderables. It remains to survey the scene as a whole, but South America is difficult to generalize about. It lacks focus, and themes are interwoven and confused. When I went to Africa in preparation for *Inside Africa* in 1952–53 the central issue was identical and outstanding in nearly every country—nationalism. This was a continent stirring, throbbing, to be free. Similarly when I wrote *Inside Russia Today* the central theme was unmistakable and unavoidable—de-Stalinization. I could go all the way back to illustrate my point further. The first *Inside Europe* (1936) dealt in large part with Hitler, Stalin, Mussolini, because it was impossible to describe Europe without taking note of the consequences of their rise, although many people did not see this at the time. *Inside Asia* (1939) concentrated necessarily on imperialism and the brutal thrust of expansionist Japan.

The great continent to the south of us is mixed up, a grab bag of contrasts and conflicting tendencies, but nobody can miss four elemental points.

First, South America on our doorstep is much bigger than the United States. Consider again merely one fact, such as that Brazil alone has three states bigger than Texas. Its physical splendors are magnificent.

Second, the continent contains peoples of fantastic, illimitable variety at

519

several different but concurrent stages of development. Many still live in a semicolonial status under feudalism.

Third, poverty in South America reaches a pitch almost beyond the comprehension of the average North American. Literally millions of citizens exist desperately or numbly on the edge of starvation a few hours by jet from New York.

Fourth, people at large are coming to the point of actively wanting to do something about their destitution, their virtual exclusion from the decencies of society, which makes a blowup inevitable.

For this indeed is a continent on the brink of revolution. A genuine prerevolutionary pattern has been reached. Future revolutions may not necessarily be Communist, but radical reformist movements partaking of both left and right on the Perón model, possibly led by technocrat military juntas. People are so desperate for change and improvement that they will take almost anything. If revolutions fail or are aborted, then there is the possibility of disintegration into unresolved chaos and scramble.

The three main causes of potential revolutionary expression and possible turmoil are clear. First, the people will not continue to tolerate their present miseries and deprivations. Education, even if scant, is bound to unleash intensified revolutionary forces. Second, the oligarchs and propertied classes will not presumably give up their privileges without a fight. Third, reformist governments of the day, taking the liberal line, like those of Frei in Chile, Belaúnde in Peru, and Lleras Restrepo in Colombia, may turn out to be too slow, too "nice." The reactionaries may pull their teeth, or they may be unable to pay the cost of their reforms.

Forces that tend to stifle revolution are several too. People lack leadership, and are inert. Conditions of life are, despite everything, gradually becoming more tolerable in several countries, which serves to soften revolutionary tendencies. The population explosion, instead of causing tumult, may so exhaust the social and political energy of nations in process of development that they will stay put. On the other hand, to produce more people is not exactly the best assurance of keeping them down.

Then too there is the large anti-revolutionary force represented by the United States, exerted in any number of fields from price support to military aid. How to strike a balance in establishing serious domestic reforms without affronting elements in the United States has been an arduous problem in several countries; more than one president walks this tightrope. One development is almost certain—the new revolutionary regimes, if they materialize, will almost surely carry a decisive anti-American note, if only because we in the United States have been so long and intimately associated with the *ancien régime.*

Now as to individual countries one might say the following—

Argentina, the most advanced nation of our ten, the most developed, is derelict, frustrated, and divided—a shadow state gripped by psychoses because the world has passed it by. The struggle between Peronists and non-Peronists still splits the country, in spite of the new military government. Perón may have been a looter and destroyer but he brought the working class into the fabric of society for the first time, and was thus a seminal provocative force. The present dictatorship is full of troubles.

Sprouting out from Argentina, like lumps on a potato, are *Paraguay* and *Uruguay*. A musical comedy nation in some respects, *Paraguay* is nevertheless proud, passionate, and unexpectedly full of stirrings in spite of the fact that it is an outright military dictatorship. *Uruguay*, its neighbor, in strict contrast, is one of the purest democracies and welfare states known to man, but steaming with troubles because its exercises in social reform cost too much for it to maintain. Like you and me, it cannot quite manage to make both ends meet.

Chile swims valiantly in a sea of difficulties. Its president, Eduardo Frei, is probably the ablest chief executive in South America, as cool and balanced as a Swiss watch, grave, kindly, a leftist Catholic intellectual pledged to a resolute program of reform, but obstacles of almost insurmountable difficulty confront him. Yet Chile presents an encouraging spectacle and may well be called the most important republic in the hemisphere because of its effort to steer a decent middle way.

Bolivia is magnificently aloof, unpredictable, anarchic, and divided by a perennial conflict between the government, under a dashing picture-book general, and the left-wing miners. This is the only country on the continent which has had a genuine modernizing revolution in recent years, and it contains the most militant labor movement in the Americas. Communist influence is strong.

As to *Peru* it is a unique entity, one of the most fascinating nations in the world, if only because of its triple quality—composed as it is of desert, jungle, and mountains that make the Alps look like divots. Its president, Fernando Belaúnde, is an architect—that is, a creator, an artist, but also a man of action, who wants to make dreams come true. The major problem is how to incorporate the great mass of impoverished Indians into the body of the state. Building of the new great "Forest Road" may help.

Ecuador is both wild and comely. It is a delightfully likable small country. In transition from rule by a military *junta*, it faces harassing difficulties. Then to the north we enter the world of Mare Nostrum, the Caribbean. *Colombia* for years has been standpat, dominated by violence, and riven by politics both abrasive and abstruse; but it seems to be coming out into a smoother fairway at last. *Venezuela* has more social vision, more reformist energy, than any country on the continent except Chile; it is a better democracy than most, has a responsible electorate, gives forth ideas as well as petroleum, and likes to think that its long-time instability is no more.

Finally, *Brazil*. This behemoth, comprising half of all South America, is a whole great world in itself—at once sumptuous and eaten up by execrable poverty, both backward and enlightened—also brilliant, variegated, and temperate in its attitude to the racial problem. Its chief preoccupation is, or should be, internal development and integration—extension inward of its own frontiers—with democratization to be hoped for in the future. Today's government is a military regime which seems to be putting the clock steadily back out of fear of chaos and Communism.

Some Generalizations Recapitulated[1]

Now as to conclusions—

1. The great South American continent, so often ignored, sometimes scorned, of such profound and manifest importance to the United States, so crossed and seared by competing influences, is in a state of flux. Change means modernization and reform, which means in turn that it is often passionately opposed by the elder vested interests. Change cannot take place without sacrifice and struggle, and is slower than it should be. The ancient crust is hard to break.

Even so, a yeastiness is apparent almost everywhere, country by country, and in almost every strata of society. An extraordinary evolution is taking place within the church. The armies, even the oligarchy, feel the impingement and pressure of new ideas. Industrialization has transformed the towns, and the beginnings of land reform have come. There have been enormous improvements in communications, and modest improvements in education and public health. But what about the masses? Millions still live like submen, like animals, but here too change is coming; now many are becoming aware of their miseries and the fact that something can be done to improve their state. The "revolution of rising expectations" is no longer a mere phrase; it can be felt. In the shanty towns, the worst sight on the continent, in hovels out in the cane country in Brazil, in the stark and shriveled Bolivian uplands, men and women hitherto obliterated by poverty are coming to demand a fair share in the fruits of society.

2. Among specific issues the most important in the long run is population

[1] A reader who happens to pick up this book at this point is urged to glance at Chapter 7 above for a similar list of generalizations from a somewhat different point of view.

pressure. The average annual percent of increase of population is, as has several times been pointed out, around 3.5 percent which means doubling of the number of people in twenty years. By 2000 Latin America is expected to have between 600 and 700 million people as against 300 million in the United States. Let's hope they'll be friendly. Nor should it be forgotten that, in South America itself, the problem of feeding this unprecedented vast accumulation of peoples is bound to produce grave political risks. The less people have, the less have they to lose by revolution.

3. There are centripetal forces at work like the Common Market and the growth of the Christian Democratic parties; also centrifugal forces like nationalism. South America is a continent, yes, but it is also ten different countries, several of which have exaggerated—even ferocious—nationalist impulses. Nationalism is important because (a) it gives demagogues a rallying point; (b) it encourages military expenditure, since the army is the national badge.

4. South America needs above everything education, development, and political stability. It is difficult to establish a priority among these factors because they interlock. You cannot extend education without the financing that will come from development; but development is similarly impossible without an educated cadre. And neither education nor development is possible without some measure of political stability—stability of the right kind. Anything is better than old-style dictatorship.

5. On the whole the last two years have been encouraging from the United States point of view. Democratic processes have been strengthened in several countries. Free elections in both Venezuela and Chile have been won by the moderate, pro-American left, and a civilian president has replaced the military junta in Ecuador. Terrorism in Colombia and Venezuela has been largely liquidated, and a guerrilla outburst in Peru has been put down. Brazil is very much on the American side under its present regime, as is Bolivia. Argentina under its new military government is a question mark. On the other hand, the United States intervention in the Dominican Republic hurt American prestige almost everywhere.

6. American aid under the Alianza continues to be life blood to large areas of the continent. Several countries might collapse without it.

7. Politics are still predominantly personal—one reason why they are so astoundingly fluid and changeable in so many countries. Since I began work on this book twenty-one months ago five countries out of ten have had changes in the presidency. The ordinary labels and classifications do not apply, even in such broad terms as left and right.

The decline of the conventional right as a *parliamentary* force is marked.

Rightist interests still exist of course, but their direct political power is seemingly on the decline, unless expressed through the army. In Bolivia the parties officially classified as "conservative" have only 4 deputies out of 105 in the chamber; in Peru, 3 out of 140; in Venezuela, 12 out of 158. The future struggle for power in most of South America will probably lie between two varieties of left, the moderates like the Christian Democrats in Chile and the Acción Democrática in Venezuela, against those more extreme. From one point of view the non-Communist left carries more hope for the future than any other group or faction on the continent. It takes the left these days to beat the left.

8. The principal economic preoccupation—at least in the three "ABC" countries, Brazil, Argentina, and Chile—is inflation, which arises from bad economics and lack of confidence. The best answer to inflation is industrialization, but this is not an easy process, and deflationary measures can be extremely painful. One may also mention again that it will continue to be difficult to achieve viable economies in South America until the citizenry at large learns to pay taxes, and until wealthy plutocrats are forced to give up their cozy habit of exporting capital out of the country into the haven of Swiss and other foreign banks. Land reform is of course another essential.

9. Every country pays lip service at least to the principles of the welfare state, and social security systems are, in theory, advanced, even in a dictatorship like Paraguay. No politician could dare nowadays to come out against such basic elements of paternalism as old-age pensions, medical benefits, and so on for urban citizens. (Rural citizens are another matter.) The *principle* of welfare statism or modified collectivism within the shell of free (= licensed) enterprise is accepted everywhere, although its application may be dishonest, chaotic, or abused.

10. Among the best people in South America today are the technicians, the elite volunteers, the intellectualized upper bureaucrats who "look to collectivist planning as a short cut to development," and "place heavy reliance on the state as a direct entrepreneur," in the words of Roberto Campos, the Brazilian minister of national planning. Among the planners are men like Campos himself, Héctor Hurtado in Venezuela, Enrique Peñalosa Camargo in Colombia, and a group which has devoted itself with selfless diligence to international exercises, such as Raúl Prebitsch (Argentina), the father of the LAFTA concept for free trade within the hemisphere, Felipe Herrera (Chile), director of the Inter-American Development Bank; Carlos Sanz de Santamaría (Colombia), a lynchpin of the Alliance for Progress; and José Antonio Mayobre (Venezuela), former head of ECLA, the UN Economic Commission for Latin America.

11. But men like these face appalling problems. This continent, we must

say once more, is shamefully underdeveloped; it is where 15 million children have no schools, where the life expectancy rate is about forty, where adult illiteracy exceeds 50 percent, where countless towns and villages still lack even such a primitive commodity as water, and where peasants ground down to torpor have to live for a day on what a North American spends for a shoeshine or a cigar.

12. A tendency is apparent to combine public and private money, both domestic and foreign, in new investment and development of industrial resources, thus "reconciling the profits of capitalism and the public services of socialism."[2] Examples are steel in Chile and Brazil and several large enterprises in Venezuela.

13. When I first visited South America a quarter of a century ago one country (Brazil) could fairly be listed as an outright dictatorship, four (Argentina, Bolivia, Paraguay, Venezuela) as "army-dominated," three (Chile, Uruguay, Colombia) as democracies, and two as being in transition from dictatorship to democracy (Peru and Ecuador). Today the score, by most reasonable judgment, would be two outright dictatorships (Paraguay and Argentina), five democracies (Uruguay, Chile, Peru, Venezuela, and Colombia), two semi-dictatorships altogether dominated by the army (Brazil, Bolivia), and one tossup (Ecuador) where military influence is strong but where civilians rule. Perhaps a summing-up of the picture is that every country deserves a better government than what it has.

14. We must square up finally to the question of democracy. It may pain the idealists to hear it said, but a great many South Americans are not yet up to the full practice of the democratic system. They don't have the education necessary. Moreover, democracy has been discredited because it has been so often weak, diffuse, and corrupt, and also because, as pointed out earlier, it has been the traditional handmaiden of the oligarchy which, by manipulating elections and controlling parliaments, has managed to retain its feudal privileges while ruling within an ostensibly democratic frame.

Democracy in itself, a difficult and expensive form of government, does not necessarily mean progress in Latin America, as the example of several countries shows. But dictatorship does not bring progress either, even if it imposes temporary stability. Plenty of people will remember the pregnant words of John Stuart Mill, that even a good dictator is bad, because he compromises the future; Augustus gave way to Tiberius. The fact remains that the essence of democracy is the sharing of power, and a comparatively small percentage of South Americans are willing to accept the full subtle implications of this definition.

One solution might be to follow the Mexican example. The president of

[2] James Reston in the *New York Times*, September 11, 1966.

Mexico, representing the broadest possible political arc, is elected under a one-party system, and then proceeds to rule like a virtual dictator for six years, whereupon he is *out*. He cannot be president ever again. He can do practically anything he wants during his term, but the people know that this is limited. The catch is "one-party system." For other Latin American countries limit their presidents to a single term. What makes the Mexican system workable is the evolution whereby a single large hold-all party contains all the principal ingredients of the state. Several of the new African countries have sought recently to copy this development as a compromise between democracy and dictatorship. Its major drawback is that a one-party system almost inevitably leads to corruption—the stability of the bad with the good.

Another device sometimes suggested to make governmental procedures easier is a partial shift from the American presidential to the British parliamentary system. Several countries, like Brazil and Peru, have created the post of prime minister under the president at one time or other to effect this end. It didn't work.

15. South American relations with the United States are fair enough, but could be better. I have gone into this subject in some detail in Chapter 8 above. The main factors provoking anti-Americanism are psychological elements, like jealousy and an atavistic resentment at exploitation and fear of intervention, i.e., the old big stick. Many South Americans deplore North American aid, even though they accept it.

16. No communist coup d'état or revolution is likely at the moment in any South American country although there are several vulnerable spots like Bolivia and Uruguay, and although many South Americans, particularly students, intellectuals, and the radical labor class, have articulate Communist sympathies. Ecuador is violently unstable, and Chile, with a 39 percent Marxist vote, came close to voting itself Communist in 1964. There are several reasons for the present Communist position, including fragmentation of the local parties, the feeling that international Communism has passed its peak, the power and vigilance of the United States, the fact that China plays little direct role, and the circumstance that Soviet Russia gives a low priority at present to disturbances in South America and the underdeveloped world. The Russians seem, in fact, to be more interested in improving their relations with the Latin American republics than in subverting them; their trade is increasing, and, as has been noted, the Soviet Union and several satellites have even extended financial aid to nations like Argentina and Brazil, thus serving to buttress their present governments. But of course Soviet policy in the large *is* subversive. Infiltration, agitation, and propaganda proceed dis-

creetly, and the Kremlin will pick up any plums it can get in Latin America, a splendid plum yard. And of course in the long run Communism—or chaos— is absolutely inevitable in South America through revolution or otherwise if the continent is not educated, democratized, and developed. The price of freedom is modernization and reform.

As to Castro, an armed invasion of any South American republic by Cuba is almost inconceivable. His prestige has sagged badly since the Kennedy-Khrushchev confrontation, when it became clear that he had no free will of his own. Training of terrorists, emission of propaganda, and support to an extent of guerrilla movements in the Caribbean (now largely beaten down) mark his present limits. On the other hand Castro still holds an interesting symbolic position. He commands a small Latin American nation that thumbed its nose at the mighty United States and, despite every impediment including political and economic boycott, has got away with it for the time being.

And So to End

What South Americans want most is a better standard of living and to be treated as equals. They want their politics and their economics to be their own. They do not see life in our terms, and we must attempt at all costs to think of them in their own South American context, not ours. They resent what they call their loss of pride, their loss of dignity, vis-à-vis the American Goliath; they feel used. One reason why President Kennedy left such an ineffaceable impression is that he recognized realities and gave hope. He spoke in such terms as "the right to social justice, land for the landless, education for those who are denied education, and the end of ancient institutions which perpetuate privilege." The United States should vigorously and comprehensively take the side of the *people*, even if a consequence of this is radical social change. South America needs us, but the whole great quivering bunch of grapes of a continent is determined to establish its own destiny. South Americans are, in fact, just like us—they want to be for themselves.

Country	Area (square miles)	Capital	Population (latest estimate)	Rate of Population Increase (percentage)	Racial Composition
Argentina	1,079,965	Buenos Aires	22,250,000	1.8	98% white
Bolivia	419,470	La Paz (technically Sucre)	4,285,000	1.4	70% Indian; 25% mestizo; 5% white
Brazil	3,287,199	Brasília (formerly Rio de Janeiro)	82,125,000	3.4	Highly complicated, 60% officially "white," but white is a term difficult to define; 25% mixed; 15% Negro
Chile	296,717	Santiago	8,460,000	2.3	Technically white, but with large Indian admixtures: some surviving pure India
Colombia	447,536	Bogotá	17,020,000	3.2	47.8% mestizo; 24% mula 20% white; 6% Negro; 2. Indian
Ecuador	116,270	Quito	5,200,000	3.2	40% Indian; 40% mestizo; 10% white; 10% Negro or mulatto
Paraguay	157,000	Asunción	1,995,000	2.4	97% mestizo; 3% white; handful of pure Indians
Peru	496,496	Lima	11,625,000	2.6	88% Indian and mestizo; 12% white
Uruguay	72,153	Montevideo	2,800,000	1.4	White
Venezuela	352,051	Caracas	8,550,000	3.4	65% mestizo; 20% white; 8% Indian; 7% Negro

Date discovery by Europeans (approx.)	Date Independence	Brief Description
1516	(1810)-1816	Best-developed state in South America, but a sad country, crippled by spiritual malaise. Superb grasslands, mountains, lakes; Buenos Aires is one of the great capitals of the world. One half of population Italian born or of Italian descent
1532	1825	Mostly a lofty isolated plateau, with no access to sea. Has been called "a project, not a nation," and has come close to chaos because of unresolved political and labor conflicts. Had a real revolution
1500	1822	Glorious beaches, carnival, voodoo; wild opulence side by side with savage poverty, although the country is potentially rich enough to provide comfortably for all; brilliant, variegated, profuse. Good race relations
1533	(1810)-1818	Oddly shaped like a bell rope; scenery of unparalleled grandeur. Hot for progress and reform under a liberal Catholic regime. Pretty women, dinner at midnight, highly civilized
1509	1818-1819	Bleak, damp, mountainous; the only country which faces both the Caribbean and the Pacific. Seems steadier now after years of ferocious internecine politics. High intellectual standards but banditry endemic
1526	1822	Bolívar called it a "monastery." Lives mostly on bananas. Alpine capital like a gilt toy, full of charm. Until recently ruled by a junta of four military "presidents." Unstable
1537	1811	A picturesque remote station in the wilderness, landlocked, forlorn, but with new quickening elements. The one country where the Indian has absorbed the Spainard, instead of vice versa
1531	(1821)-1824	Magnificent combination of desert, jungle, precipitous Andean peaks, inaccessible rolling uplands. Derives from Inca culture in part, and seems to be almost as Indian as Bolivia. Progressive government
1516	1811	Welfare state par excellence, with advanced democratic practices; run by a panel of nine civilian "presidents." Cowboys, beaches, beefsteak. Could be vulnerable to Communist penetration
1498	1811	Rich through petroleum; vast social energy combined with planning concept; a vibrant, hardboiled, and purposeful country under democratic leadership. Location makes it Castro's theoretical first target

Country	Principal Problems	Character of Government
Argentina	Inflation and other economic troubles; resolution of conflict between present government and adherents of exiled ex-dictator Perón; struggle between entrenched landed interests and powerful labor forces in towns	Military dictatorship
Bolivia	Army squabbles; end of political anarchy; poverty; how to sell its tin; how to improve status of Indians; Communism	Dominated by military
Brazil	Development of the interior; uneven distribution of wealth; corruption; inflation; how to return to constitutional government; feudalism in northeast; Communist stirrings	Dominated by military
Chile	Land reform; inflation; copper; strengthening of democratic processes vis-à-vis oligarchy, also extreme left, which commands 39% of electorate. Really attacking its social problems	Democracy
Colombia	Inflation; political instability and healing of old wounds of violenzia; population pressure; development at large	Democracy
Ecuador	How to make government work; rivalry between Quito and Guayaquil; land reform; Communism	In transition from military rule
Paraguay	Poverty	Dictatorship, but with vestigial political activity permitted
Peru	Incorporation of the great mass of submerged Indians into the body of the state; political stability; land reform; communications; recent guerrilla uprising	Democracy
Uruguay	Heavy cost of paternalistic system; unwieldiness of bureaucracy; mismanagement	Democracy
Venezuela	Education; development of industrial resources; land reform; what to do when oil gives out; guerrilla troubles	Democracy

Leading Political Personalities	Per Capita Income	Principal Exports
...neral Juan Carlos Onganía, president ...der junta; ex-president Juan Domingo ...rón (exiled); former president Arturo ...ondizi	$508	Meat, wheat, wool
...neral René Barrientos, president; ...neral Alfredo Ovando, former co-president	$158	Tin, lead
...arshal Humberto Castelo Branco ...resident); General Artur da Costa e ...lva (presumptive successor); Carlos ...cerda, ex-governor of Guanabara; ...berto Campos, Minister of National ...anning	$172	Coffee, cotton, iron, cocoa, sugar, lumber, tobacco, sisal
...uardo Frei Montalva (president); ...lvador Allende, leader of FRAP ...ftist coalition in opposition); Raúl ...npuero (socialist)	$457	Copper, nitrates
...rlos Lleras Restrepo (president); ...berto Lleras Camargo (ex-president); ...neral Rojas Pinilla (former dictator); ...onso López Michelsen (left-wing liberal)	$298	Coffee, petroleum
...emente Yerovi Indaburu, in succession ...military junta	$200	Bananas, coffee
...neral Alfredo Stroessner (president ...d dictator) head of Colorado party	$201	Meat, wood
...rnando Belaúnde Terry (president); ...ctor Raúl Haya de la Torre (Aprista)	$244	Nonferrous metals, sugar, cotton
...shington Beltrán (Blanco) ex-chairman ...tional Council; Jorge Batlle Ibañez ...lorado); Alberto Heber, present chief executive	$550	Wool, meat
...úl Leoni (president); Rómulo Betancourt ...-president, leading spirit of A.D. party); ...ito Villalba; Arturo Uslar Pietri; Rafael ...dera (Christian Democrat)	$851	Petroleum, iron ore

Country	Budget (last available figures in millions of dollars)		Trade Balance (millions of dollars)	U.S. Direct Investment (millions of dollars)	U.S. Aid under Alianza Program, 1961-1965, incl. Grants Loans, Technical Aid, Food for Peace, etc. (millions of dollars)
	Receipts	Expenditures			
Argentina	$931	$1,065	$384 (deficit)	$828	$271.8
Bolivia	$48	$53	$43 (deficit)	$32	$194.4
Brazil	$722	$1,002	$81 (deficit)	$1,128	$960.8
Chile	$417	$614	$95 (deficit)	$768	$560.9
Colombia	$297	$291	$21 (deficit)	$465	$368.0
Ecuador	$116	$109	$19	$51	$120.1
Paraguay	$27	$28	$2	?	$37.3
Peru	$332	$312	$16 (deficit)	$448	$218.5
Uruguay	?	?	$12 (deficit)	$65	$38
Venezuela	$1,344	$1,239	$1,649	$2,807	$188.9

Literacy (percentage)	Life Expectancy (percentage)	Position of Communist Party	Diplomatic Relations with Soviet Union
1	59	Technically legal, but operates with difficulty. 60,000 to 70,000 members	Yes (also with 5 satellites including trade missions)
1	50	Legality uncertain; operates through other groups. Membership about 6,500, badly split. No seats in chamber	Yes (trade missions from Hungary and Czechoslovakia)
0	53	Outlawed but active. Moscow group has probably 30,000 members underground	Yes (also with 6 satellites including trade missions)
4	57	Legal. Received 157,000 votes last election, has 10.5% of congress	Yes (also trade mission from China)
4	46.3	Legal. Membership about 13,000; several seats in congress	No (but diplomatic relations are in effect with Czechoslovakia and East Germany)
0	52	Outlawed in 1963. Underground membership 2,000 to 3,000	No
8	45	Outlawed since 1936	No
1	46	Participates in elections but without party affiliations; several deputies in parliament	No
4	64	Legal. Won 3.52% of vote in last election	Yes (also with 6 satellites including trade missions)
	65.2	"Suspended," but votes through left-wing allies. Party split, with probably 30,000 members in all	Yes (also Poland and trade mission from Czechoslovakia)

ces: Overseas Business Reports, U.S. Chamber of Commerce, June 1965; The Gallatin Annual of International Business, 1965; American Handbook 1965; Atlas of Latin American Affairs (Praeger); World Strength of the Communist Party Organizations; cal Handbook of the World (Council on Foreign Relations, 1964); Columbia Encyclopedia; Worldmark Encyclopedia; New York s, Dec. 5, 1965

Acknowledgments and Bibliography

THERE ARE so many people to thank for their generous help on this long book that I scarcely know how to list them. First should come Hobart Lewis, president and executive editor of *Reader's Digest*, who suggested the project in the first place and then supported it amply and with discriminating good will through twenty-one months of what I think is the hardest work I have ever done. To this acknowledgment to Mr. Lewis I would like to add similar acknowledgments to a round dozen of his able and discerning colleagues on *Reader's Digest*. Moreover, the *Digest* printed several chapters of *Inside South America* in abbreviated form while I was writing it, for which my thanks again.

Second, Cass Canfield of Harper & Row, my publisher. This makes the sixteenth or seventeenth book we have worked on together over the years, and all I can say is that they would have been impossible to write without his patient (sometimes impatient) encouragement, advice, and stimulus. Mr. Canfield is not only a publisher, but an editor in the true sense of that overworked word. I want also to express my profound thanks to Mrs. Beulah Hagen, his associate, a stout supporter in this as in other voluminous campaigns. This book would never have got to press without her. Several other friends at Harper & Row propped me up when I needed help, which was often, and my debt to Miss Marguerite Hoyle, among others, is substantial.

Among those who have read the entire work in manuscript or proof, and from whose advice I greatly benefited, are Donald Lubin, executive director of the Western Hemisphere Region of Planned Parenthood, and Alexander Lindey, attorney-at-law.

My wife, Jane Perry Gunther, accompanied me on all but a fraction of the trip, and did much of the work involved, as she has done on all the recent Inside books and others I have written since 1948. I cannot convey adequately how much I owe to her durability, vision, editorial skill, political savvy, and élan. She was unsuccessful, however, in trying to help me master the arcane mysteries of a tape recorder. I still continue to take notes by hand, as I have been doing for the past forty years or so.

535

Then too I must mention my friend and secretary Alice Furlaud, who deserves copious and earnest thanks. She typed my disorderly manuscript in several drafts, patiently continued to try to teach me to spell, and went through tedious hours checking files, doing research, and putting errant chapters together. The work could not have been done without her help, particularly in the last desperate moments. (I was late as usual.)

I am not listing here the names of all those who helped my wife and me, with amiable hospitality and otherwise, during the course of our trip, which was strenuous. I flirted with the idea of printing a complete list like those in *Inside U.S.A.* and *Taken at the Flood*, but such a procedure seemed pretentious and of little interest to the general reader. Besides I did not want to get any of my South American friends into trouble. My ideal day was to spend the morning with the government and the afternoon with the revolutionaries, or vice versa. I have already mentioned that I saw the ten presidents of the ten countries we visited—rather, I saw thirteen out of the ten, because Ecuador had four at the time of our visit there. American officials put themselves at our disposal almost everywhere with the utmost cordiality. We met the ambassador or head of mission in every country. Similarly we benefited substantially from talks with admirably informed British officials in every capital.

The late Adlai Ewing Stevenson gave us introductions to two presidents, the cardinal archbishop of Santiago, Chile, and half a dozen other eminent personages, including Dr. Pedro Beltrán in Peru, Dr. Gainza Paz in Buenos Aires, and three Chilean cabinet ministers. All his letters bore fruit. Robert M. McClintock, a former American ambassador to Argentina, gave us introductions to both President Illía and General Onganía, his successor, as well as to other high-ranking Argentines. Carlton Sprague Smith, the well-known specialist in Brazilian studies and musicologist, contributed manfully a great sheaf of invaluable introductions, together with much other material, to say nothing of illuminating conversation.

William Benton of the Encyclopaedia Britannica procured for us lists of names from two knowledgeable experts, Professor Kalman Silvert of Dartmouth and Luis Baralt, formerly Cuban ambassador to Canada. Among others who helped us with introductions were Stanley de J. Osborne, partner in the banking house of Lazard Frères; Alfred A. Knopf, publisher, whose hospitality to South American writers is legendary, and who put us onto Jorge Amado in Salvador, Bahia, among others; Mrs. Edwin M. M. Warburg; Mrs. Norris Darrell; Fleur Cowles; Eustace Seligman, partner in Sullivan and Cromwell, attorneys-at-law; Philip W. Quigg, managing editor of *Foreign Affairs*; Dr. Pedro Zuloaga of the Venezuelan Embassy to the UN; Leland S. Brown, vice president of the First National City Bank, New York; Paul G. Hoffman, who sent us to repesentatives of the Special Fund of the UN (now known as the Development Programme) everywhere in South America; Roberto M. Heurtematte, associate director of The Special Fund; Clayton Fritchie, former assistant to Ambassador Stevenson; John Paton Davies, Jr., author of *Foreign and Other Affairs*, who has had long experience of Peru; and above all Carl T. Rowan, the columnist, who was at that time director of the United States Information Agency, and who alerted his staff to our arrival everywhere on the continent. Our best thanks go to the able USIA men everywhere.

Paul H. G. Wright, director of British Information Services in New York, paved the way for us in British circles. Nina Georges-Picot of *Reader's Digest* did some useful research. I want to thank too Miss Jean Gunther and Miss Janet Rigney of the Council on Foreign Relations, New York, for their help. Various officials of Pan

American World Airways, in particular Mrs. Julie Smith Sewell, rendered us stout and cordial service. I want to thank the representatives of Panagra and Avianca too —their men on the spot gave us much-appreciated help when we needed it. Miss Sally Belfrage, author of *A Room in Moscow* and *Freedom Summer*, read large portions of the manuscript and brought to this task her expert, sensitive, and sympathetic understanding and knowledge of the third world.

Following at random are the names of some who gave us guidance in New York, by talk or briefings before we set out, or amplifications on our return—Senator Robert F. Kennedy; Senator Jacob K. Javits; Mr. and Mrs. William Van den Heuvel; Barbara Ward (Lady Jackson); Walter Lippmann; Alfred H. Barr, Jr., Director of Collections of the Museum of Modern Art; Gavin Scott, head of the Time-Life Bureau in Madrid; Henry Raymont and Harrison Salisbury of the *New York Times*; John M. Cates, Jr., Latin American specialist on the staff of the American delegation to the UN; Henry Labouisse, former American ambassador to Greece; James Vincent Sheean; Mrs. Muriel Murphy; Hamilton Fish Armstrong, editor of *Foreign Affairs*; David E. Lilienthal, former head of the Tennessee Valley Authority and the Atomic Energy Commission (who also gave us several introductions); Gavin Young of the London *Observer*; our good friend Felipe Benavides, O.B.E., of Lima, who was our host on the trip to Iquitos never to be forgotten; Mr. and Mrs. Gardner Cowles; Dr. William Griffith, director of the Center of Soviet Studies, M.I.T.; Dr. Alberto Lleras Camargo, former president of Colombia; Joseph Farland, former American ambassador to Panama; Tito Leite of *Reader's Digest* in Brazil; the late Dr. Alfred Frankfurter, editor and publisher of *Art News*; George G. Daniels, a *Time* senior editor in charge of Latin America at that time; and, in a category all his own, Ernst Halperin, author and Latin American specialist, member of the Institute of International Studies, M.I.T., who has had long experience of Chile and is now resident in Brazil.

And in Washington—Arthur Schlesinger, Jr., author of *A Thousand Days* and much else; Thomas C. Mann, former assistant secretary of state for Inter-American Affairs, who gave us official introductions all along the line; various State Department officials who I imagine will not want to be mentioned by name; Tad Szulc, now the Madrid correspondent of the *New York Times*; Richard Goodwin, who was at that time a member of the White House secretariat; William D. Rogers, the brightest spirit on the Alianza program, who gave us particularly valuable hints and leads as well as introductions; Dr. Arturo Morales Carrión of the Pan American Union; Walt W. Rostow, presidential adviser; Enrique Tejera-París, ambassador from Venezuela; and Senator Wayne Morse.

Finally let me convey warm appreciation to the distinguished artist Oswaldo Guayasamin, of Quito, Ecuador, who painted a portrait of me in record time—to be seen on the back of the jacket of this book.

BIBLIOGRAPHY

ABEL, ELIE. *The Missile Crisis*. J. B. Lippincott Company, Philadelphia, 1966.
ABELL, MAC. *Buenos Aires Through Bifocals*. Guillermo Kraft, Buenos Aires, 1961.
ADAMS, MILDRED, editor. *Latin America: Evolution or Explosion?* Dodd, Mead & Company, New York, 1963.

ALEXANDER, ROBERT J. *The Bolivian National Revolution*. Rutgers University Press, New Brunswick, New Jersey, 1958.
————. *Prophets of the Revolution*. The Macmillan Company, New York, 1964.
————. *Today's Latin America*. Doubleday & Company, Garden City, New York, 1962.
————. *The Venezuelan Democratic Revolution*. Rutgers University Press, New Brunswick, New Jersey, 1964.
AMERICAN UNIVERSITIES' FIELD STAFF, K. H. Silvert, editor. *Expectant Peoples: Nationalism and Development*. Random House, New York, 1963.
ANTON, FERDINAND. *Peru*. R. Piper & Company, Munich, 1959.
ARCINIEGAS, GERMÁN, editor. *The Green Continent*. Alfred A. Knopf, New York, 1944.
Argentina *Contemporánea*. Museu de Arte Moderna do Rio de Janeiro.
At Home in Uruguay. Montevideo, 1961.
BAUMANN, HANS. *Gold and Gods of Peru*. Oxford University Press, London, 1963.
BEALS, CARLETON. *Eagles of the Andes*. Chilton Company, Philadelphia, 1965.
BELAÚNDE TERRY, FERNANDO. *Peru's Own Conquest*. American Studies Press, S. A., Lima, 1965.
BELFRAGE, CEDRIC. *The Man at the Door with the Gun*. Monthly Review Press, New York, 1963.
BENTON, WILLIAM. *The Voice of Latin America*. Harper & Brothers, New York, 1961.
BERLE, ADOLF A. *Latin America—Diplomacy and Reality*. Harper & Row, New York, 1964.
BERNSTEIN, MARVIN D., editor. *Foreign Investment in Latin America*. Alfred A. Knopf, New York, 1966.
BINGHAM, HIRAM. *Lost City of the Incas*. Atheneum, New York, 1963.
BISHOP, ELIZABETH and THE EDITORS OF LIFE. *Brazil*. Time, Inc., 1962.
BLANKSTEN, GEORGE I. *The United States' Role in Latin America*. Laidlaw Brothers, River Forest, Illinois, 1963.
BORGES, JORGE LUIS. *Dreamtigers*. University of Texas Press, Austin, 1964.
————. *Fictions*. John Calder, London, 1965.
————. *Labyrinths*. New Directions, New York, 1964.
————. *Other Inquisitions 1937–1952*. University of Texas Press, Austin, 1964.
BOXER, C. R. *The Golden Age of Brazil 1695–1750*. University of California Press, Berkeley and Los Angeles, 1964.
Brazil in a Nutshell. Brazilian Government Trade Bureau.
Brésil 1964. Ministère des Relations Extérieures, Rio de Janeiro, 1964.
BRIDGES, ESTEBAN LUCAS. *Uttermost Part of the Earth*. E. P. Dutton and Company, New York, 1949.
BRYCE, JAMES. *South America: Observations and Impressions*. The Macmillan Company, New York, 1912.
BUSHNELL, G. H. S. *Peru*. Thames and Hudson, London, 1963.
CAREY, JAMES C. *Peru and the United States, 1900–1962*. University of Notre Dame Press, 1964.
Chile, Guida Turistica 1965. Departamento de Transporte, Santiago, 1965.
Chile Is Like This. Instituto Chileno-Norteamericano Cultura and The Association of American Women of Chile, Santiago.

CLARK, GERALD. *The Coming Explosion in Latin America.* David McKay Company, New York, 1963.

COWLES, FLEUR. *Bloody Precedent.* Random House, New York, 1952.

DAVIES, JOHN PATON, JR. *Foreign and Other Affairs.* W. W. Norton, New York, 1964.

DEAN, VERA MICHELES. *Builders of Emerging Nations.* Holt, Rinehart and Winston, New York, 1961.

DE IMAZ, JOSÉ LUIS. *Los Que Mandan.* Editorial Universitaria de Buenos Aires, Buenos Aires, 1964.

DE LA VEGA, GARCILASO (Alain Gheerbrant, editor). *The Incas.* Avon Books, New York, 1961.

DE MADARIAGA, SALVADOR. *Latin America Between the Eagle and the Bear.* Frederick A. Praeger, New York, 1963.

DOS PASSOS, JOHN. *Brazil on the Move.* Doubleday & Company, Garden City, New York, 1963.

DRAPER, THEODORE. *Castro's Revolution: Myths and Realities.* Frederick A. Praeger, New York, 1964.

The Economic Development of Latin America in the Post-War Period. United Nations, New York, 1964.

EISENHOWER, MILTON. *The Wine Is Bitter.* Doubleday & Company, Garden City, New York, 1963.

FANON, FRANTZ. *The Wretched of the Earth.* Grove Press, New York, 1963.

FLEMING, PETER. *Brazilian Adventure.* Grosset & Dunlap, New York, 1933.

FODOR, EUGENE, editor. *Fodor's Guide to South America.* David McKay Company, New York, 1966.

FORBES, ROSITA. *Eight Republics in Search of a Future.* Frederick A. Stokes Company, New York, 1933.

FREYRE, GILBERTO. *Americanism and Latinity in Latin America.*

———. *Brazil.* Pan American Union, Washington, D.C., 1963.

———. *The Mansions and the Shanties.* Alfred A. Knopf, New York, 1963.

———. *The Masters and the Slaves.* Alfred A. Knopf, New York, 1964.

FURTADO, CELSO. *Diagnosis of the Brazilian Crisis.* University of California Press, Berkeley and Los Angeles, 1965.

Gallatin Annual of International Business. American Heritage Publishing Company, New York, 1965.

GALLO, MIGUEL MUJICA. *The Gold of Peru.* Aurel Bongers Recklinghausen, Hattingen, Germany, 1959.

GEORGE, MARY. *A Is for Abrazo.* Venezuelan-American Association of University Women, Caracas, 1961.

GERASSI, JOHN. *The Great Fear.* The Macmillan Company, New York, 1963.

GORDON, LINCOLN. *A New Deal for Latin America.* Harvard University Press, Cambridge, Massachusetts, 1963.

HALPERIN, ERNST. *The Chilean Presidential Election of 1964.* Massachusetts Institute of Technology Center for International Studies, Cambridge, Massachusetts, 1964.

———. *Sino-Cuban Trends: the Case of Chile.* Massachusetts Institute of Technology Center for International Studies, Cambridge, Massachusetts, 1964.

HANKE, LEWIS, editor. *Do the Americas Have a Common History?* Alfred A. Knopf, New York, 1964.

HERRING, HUBERT. *A History of Latin America.* Alfred A. Knopf, New York, 1965.

HIRSCHMAN, ALBERT O. *Journeys Toward Progress.* The Twentieth Century Fund, New York, 1963.

———, editor. *Latin American Issues.* The Twentieth Century Fund, New York, 1961.

HOFFMAN, PAUL G. *World Without Want.* Harper & Row, New York, 1962.

HOLMES, OLIVE. *Latin America: Land of a Golden Legend.* Foreign Policy Association, 1947.

HOLT, PAT M. *Colombia Today—and Tomorrow.* Frederick A. Praeger, New York, 1964.

HOUTART, FRANÇOIS, and PIN, EMILE. *The Church and the Latin American Revolution.* Sheed and Ward, New York, 1965.

HOYLE, RAFAEL LARCO. *Las Epocas Peruanas.* Lima, 1963.

It's Proper in Peru. The Comité Norteamericano Pro-Peru, Lima, 1961.

JOFFROY, PIERRE. *Brazil.* Studio Vista, London, 1965.

JOHNSON, JOHN J., editor. *Continuity and Change in Latin America.* Stanford University Press, Stanford, California, 1964.

———. *Political Change in Latin America.* Stanford University Press, Stanford, California, 1965.

———, editor. *The Role of the Military in Underdeveloped Countries.* Princeton University Press, Princeton, New Jersey, 1962.

KEEN, BENJAMIN, editor. *Americans All: the Story of Our Latin American Neighbors.* Dell Publishing Company, New York, 1966.

KROPP, MIRIAM. *Cuzco, Window on Peru.* The Studio Publications, Inc., in association with Thomas Y. Crowell Co., New York, 1956.

La Responsabilidad Empresarial en el Progreso Social de Venezuela. Maracay, Estado Aragua, Venezuela, 1963.

Land of Lace and Legend. La Colmena, S.A., Asunción, 1965.

LANGER, WILLIAM L., editor. *Encyclopedia of World History.* Houghton Mifflin Company, Boston, 1948.

Latin America (bibliography). The Royal Institute of International Affairs, 1941.

LEVI-STRAUSS, CLAUDE. *Tristes Tropiques.* Atheneum, New York, 1964.

LEWIS, OSCAR. *The Children of Sanchez.* Random House, New York, 1961.

LIEUWEN, EDWIN. *Arms and Politics in Latin America.* Frederick A. Praeger, New York, 1965.

———. *Generals vs. Presidents.* Frederick A. Praeger, New York, 1964.

———. *U.S. Policy in Latin America.* Frederick A. Praeger, New York, 1965.

MACSHANE, FRANK. *Impressions of Latin America.* William Morrow and Company, New York, 1963.

MAIER, JOSEPH, and WEATHERHEAD, RICHARD W. *Politics of Change in Latin America.* Frederick A. Praeger, New York, 1964.

MALPICA, CARLOS. *Los Dueños del Peru.* Fondo de Cultura Popular, Lima.

MARCENAC, JEAN. *Pablo Neruda.* Pierre Seghers, Editeur, Poitiers, 1963.

MATTHEWS, HERBERT L., editor. *The United States and Latin America.* Prentice-Hall, Englewood Cliffs, New Jersey, 1965.

MAXWELL, NICOLE. *Witch Doctor's Apprentice*. Houghton Mifflin Company, Boston, 1961.

MORRIS, JAMES. *Cities*. Harcourt, Brace & World, New York, 1964.

———. *South America*. Manchester Guardian and Evening News Ltd., Manchester.

NEHEMKIS, PETER. *Latin America, Myth and Reality*. Alfred A. Knopf, New York, 1964.

PENDLE, GEORGE. *A History of Latin America*. Penguin Books, Baltimore, 1963.

———. *Argentina*. Oxford University Press, London, 1965.

PHELPS, KATHLEEN DEERY. *Birds of Venezuela*. Editorial Lectura, Caracas, 1963.

PICON-SALAS, MARIANO. *A Cultural History of Spanish America*. University of California Press, Berkeley and Los Angeles, 1965.

PIKE, FREDERICK B., editor. *The Conflict Between Church and State in Latin America*. Alfred A. Knopf, New York, 1964.

———, and D'ANTONIO, WILLIAM V., editors. *Religion, Revolution and Reform*. Frederick A. Praeger, New York, 1964.

PRESCOTT, WILLIAM H. *The Conquest of Peru*. Doubleday & Company.

ROBERTS, EDWIN A., JR. *Latin America*. The National Observer, Silver Spring, Maryland, 1964.

ROBERTSON, WILLIAM SPENCE. *Rise of the Spanish-American Republics*. The Free Press, New York, 1965.

ROOSEVELT, NICHOLAS. *Venezuela's Place in the Sun*. Round Table Press, New York, 1940.

SCHLESINGER, ARTHUR M., JR. *A Thousand Days*. Houghton Mifflin Company, Boston, 1965.

SCHMITT, Karl M. and BURKS, DAVID D. *Evolution or Chaos*. Frederick A. Praeger, New York, 1963.

SCHNEIDER, RONALD M., and KINGSBURY, ROBERT C. *Atlas of Latin American Affairs*. Frederick A. Praeger, New York, 1965.

SCHURZ, WILLIAM LYTLE. *Brazil, the Infinite Country*. Robert Hale, Limited, London, 1962.

———. *This New World*. E. P. Dutton & Company, New York, 1964.

SCOTT, JOHN. *How Much Progress?* Time, Inc., 1963.

SHAPIRO, SAMUEL. *Invisible Latin America*. Beacon Press, Boston, 1964.

SITWELL, SACHEVERELL. *Golden Wall and Mirador*. World Publishing Company, Cleveland and New York, 1961.

SMITH, T. LYNN. *Brazil: People and Institutions*. Louisiana State University Press, Baton Rouge, Louisiana, 1963.

Social Aspects of Economic Development in Latin America. 2 volumes. UNESCO, Paris, 1963.

Social Change in Latin America Today (introduction by Lyman Bryson). Random House, New York, 1960.

South American Handbook 1965. Trade and Travel Publications Ltd., London, 1965.

SPENCE, EILEEN, and LÓPEZ, ANNA. *Feira Fare*. Rio de Janeiro.

STOETZER, O. C. *The Organization of American States*. Frederick A. Praeger, New York, 1965.

SZULC, TAD. *Dominican Diary*. Delacorte Press, New York, 1965.

———. *Latin America*. Atheneum, New York, 1966.

————. *New Trends in Latin America.* Foreign Policy Association, New York, 1960.

————. *The Winds of Revolution.* Frederick A. Praeger, New York, 1963.

TANNENBAUM, FRANK. *Ten Keys to Latin America.* Alfred A. Knopf, New York, 1964.

This is Peru. Peruvian Government Tourist Corporation, Lima, 1964.

A Tourist's Guide to Colombia. Colombia National Tourist Bureau, Bogotá, 1963.

Towards a Dynamic Development Policy for Latin America. United Nations, New York, 1963.

TREND, J. B. *South America.* Oxford University Press, London, 1941.

URQUIDI, VICTOR L. *The Challenge of Development in Latin America.* Frederick A. Praeger, New York, 1964.

VALCARCEL, LOUIS E. *Cuzco, Archaeological Capital of South America.* Banco Italiano, Lima, 1933.

VANEGAS, CARLOS VARGAS, and FLOREZ, JORGE MATIZ. *La Vaca del Campesino.* Editorial Andes, Bogotá.

VANGER, MILTON I. *José Batlle y Ordóñez of Uruguay.* Harvard University Press, Cambridge, Massachusetts, 1963.

VON HAGEN, VICTOR W. *Realm of the Incas.* New American Library of World Literature, New York, 1961.

WAGLEY, CHARLES. *An Introduction to Brazil.* Columbia University Press, New York, 1963.

————. *Brazil, Crisis and Change.* Foreign Policy Association, 1964.

WARD, BARBARA. *The Rich Nations and the Poor Nations.* W. W. Norton & Company, New York, 1962.

WENDT, HERBERT. *The Red, White, and Black Continent.* Doubleday, New York, 1966.

WHITEFORD, ANDREW HUNTER. *Two Cities of Latin America.* Doubleday & Company, Garden City, New York, 1964.

WILGUS, A. CURTIS, editor. *The Caribbean: Venezuelan Development.* University of Florida Press, Gainesville, Florida, 1963.

WILGUS, A. CURTIS, and D'ECA, RAUL. *Latin American History.* Barnes and Noble, New York, 1964.

World Strength of the Communist Party Organizations, 17th Annual Report. Department of State, Bureau of Intelligence and Research, January, 1965.

Worldmark Encyclopedia of the Nations. Harper & Brothers, New York, 1960.

ZULOAGA, GUILLERMO. *A Geographical Glimpse of Venezuela.* 1965.

*

I should also mention standard works of reference, such as the *Encyclopaedia Britannica,* the *Columbia Encyclopedia, Facts on File,* the *Statesman's Year-Book* (1965–66), *Political Handbook and Atlas of the World* (published by the Council on Foreign Relations, New York), and in particular *The South American Handbook,* 1965, to which I want to make grateful acknowledgment. I have cited references to this indispensable book many times in my text, and it appears often in the source lists below. A model guide, the *Handbook* is not merely a comprehensive and discriminating assembly of contemporary information, but is valuable for its historical material as well. The Fodor *Guide* is also good.

I have been collecting material on South America for many years, and some of my files go back to the 1930's. Most of the periodicals and newspapers I used are familiar, and over the course of several years I have tried to read everything they printed on South America—*Foreign Affairs, Current History, World Today* (published by the Royal Institute of International Affairs, London), the *New York Times,* The New York *Herald Tribune,* and the *Christian Science Monitor.* The *Visión Letter* helped keep me posted after my trip, as did *Time, Newsweek,* the *Guardian* of Manchester, as well as other publications, particularly the *New York Times.* For a time I subscribed to a news report issued by the Maryknoll Fathers in Peru. The *Latin American Times,* a daily published in New York for a brief period, was useful while it lasted. I have glanced at *Latin American Report,* published in New Orleans, from time to time. Unfortunately *Hispanic-American Report,* published by the Institute of Hispanic-American and Luso-Brazilian Studies at Stanford University, under the direction of Ronald Hilton, an invaluable record, stopped publication at about the time I started my book.

Pamphlets I read by the score—also various government bulletins. The fact sheets put out by the National Council of Catholic Women have been useful. The series of pamphlets on countries issued by the Pan American Union in Washington are attractive, and I used them often.

Source Lists and Amplifications

Without being pedantic about it I have sought to use footnotes throughout the text to indicate direct quotations as well as for other obvious reasons, such as citing authority for a fact. The material that follows gives other sources for which I did not use footnotes because of fear of cluttering the body of the book. To keep this within reasonable bounds I have not repeated the full titles mentioned in the bibliography but have usually referred merely to the author. If the author is represented by several titles I have indicated the correct work by an abbreviation which, on reference to the bibliography, ought to be easily understandable. I am also including here a few amplifications of my text. I am not giving sources for material which reached me by word of mouth, although I met and interviewed some seven hundred South Americans, and what they told me represents by far the largest share of my source material. This book is long enough already. So let me content myself with a broad general acknowledgment to those who shared their wisdom and experience with us so generously.

Foreword

The quotation at the head of the chapter is from Milton S. Eisenhower, who indeed entitled his book on Latin America *The Wine Is Bitter*. John P. Gillin, "Some Signposts for Policy," in Bryson, *Social Change*, p. 44, mentions the emotionalism of South Americans. Adolf A. Berle has, as usual, some penetrating things to say on South American isolation in "Are We 'Ignoring' Latin America?," *New York Times Magazine*, November 24, 1963. Edmund Wilson's antipathy to Hispanic studies is mentioned in *Encounter*, September, 1965. That South America "lies on the margin of history" is from Pendle, *History*, p. 16. That 2 percent of the people own 70 percent of the wealth is from a speech delivered in Caracas by Arthur Schlesinger, Jr., on May 11, 1963. David Rockefeller, "A Formula for Prosperity," *Saturday Review*, October 12, 1963, is my source for comparative incomes. Illiteracy figures are from a speech by Averell Harriman, and those on the death rate in Brazil from *Brazil* in the admirable *Vista* series, p. 22. For political stability consult Szulc, *Winds*, p. 78, an extremely useful book. For various revolutions see "Revolution and Stability in Bolivia" by Dwight B. Heath, *Current History*, December, 1965. Herring mentions the number of presidents in Paraguay. Other statistics relating to South American lack of development and education come from Hirschman, *Issues*, p. 163, *Time*, August 16, 1963, and "The New World of Latin America," by Teodoro Moscoso, *Saturday Review*, October 12, 1963, an admirable article. Mr. Moscoso was the first administrator of the Alliance for Progress. Also see Szulc, p. 48, on water. Mr. Szulc makes the astounding statement that "lack or improper use of national resources prevented a supply of water in 1961 from reaching 100 million Latin Americans, or nearly one-half of the population." And Mr. Szulc is never wrong.

I list now some over-all sources from periodicals which I found useful during the whole course of my book—"Rediscovering Latin America," a special issue of *Encounter*, September, 1965; "No Christ on the Andes," an economic survey of Latin America by Norman Macrae in the *Economist*, September 25, 1965; Senator Robert F. Kennedy's two-day speech in the United States Senate, May 9 and 10, 1966, as reported in the *Congressional Record*, which I have cited several times in my text; a variety of valuable articles by Leonard Gross in *Look*; "Why Latin America Is Vital to Us," by Herbert L. Matthews, *New York Times Magazine*, April 26, 1959; "Latin America: a Broad Brush Appraisal," by Philip W. Quigg, in *Foreign Affairs*, April, 1964; "Revolution of Rising Expectations," a useful supplement to the *Economist*, April 22, 1961; "What's Wrong With Latin America," *U.S. News and World Report*, May 24, 1965; "Southward Ho! a Guide to South America and the Caribbean," by Beatrice de Holguin and Judith Friedberg, *Show*, November, 1962; "Focus on Latin America," *Viewpoint Magazine*, No. 2; a group of Latin American articles on the general theme of the search by the continent for its own identity, *Atlas*, August, 1963; "The News From Latin America," *Columbia Journalism Review*, excerpted from a report to the Center for the Study of Democratic Institutions; "The New World of Latin America, a Twentieth Century Adventure in Discovery," a valuable special supplement published by the *Saturday Review*, October 12, 1963; and "A New Look at Latin America," by Charles E. Lindblom, *Atlantic*, October, 1962.

Chapter 1—Brazil, a Piebald Mastodon

Any number of authorities discuss Brazilian temperateness. Fodor, p. 449, mentions that "Brazilians don't like revolutions, wars, or fast deaths." Schurz, p. 210, taking note of the Vargas dictatorship, remarks that it was "a new phenomenon" in Brazilian politics, and Freyre (*Brazil*, p. 53) notes that none of Brazil's "colonial viceroys, kings or presidents was a victim of political assassination." Also see Fodor, p. 430, and Bishop, p. 41. Herring, p. 723, describes homeland and colonies as being "under one geographic roof." See also Pendle, *Latin America*, which I have several times cited in my text, p. 70. For *convivência* see "An Interview with Gilberto Freyre" by Keith Botsford, *Encounter*, November, 1962. Carlos Lacerda mentioned that Brazil was a continent with its colonies inside it in a speech in New York. For statistical matter in general I have relied on the *South American Handbook 1965*, hereafter to be referred to as *Handbook*. Life expectancy figures are from *Time*, June 30, 1966. For the swamp area in Mato Grosso see Wagley, *Introduction*,

p. 88. Schurz, p. 1, mentions that Brazil has three states bigger than Texas. Figures on Maranhão, Amapá and "the world's largest and densest rain forest" are from *Handbook*. Clark, p. 29, is my authority for the statement that there are five different railway gauges, and my figure on paved roads is from Freyre, *Brazil*, p. 92. "Unimproved" roads extend to 289,000 miles. The saying that the Portuguese used white women for marriage, etc., is from Freyre, *Masters*, p. 20. For Aleijadinho see Emily Hahn in *The New Yorker*, November 5, 1960, and the brilliant small *Vista* guide by Pierre Joffroy. Some of my details about race are from Wagley, *Brazil*, a useful pamphlet published by the Foreign Policy Association in its Headline Series. Details about discrimination are from *Newsweek*, September 7, 1964. My authority for the statement that Brazil had no university until 1924 is the *Latin American Times*, August 20, 1965. For relations between Portugal and Africa see "Brazil and Africa: a New Policy?" by James C. Brewer, Institute of Current World Affairs, December 20, 1964, the *New York Times*, August 5, 1965, and the Emily Hahn and *Encounter* articles cited above. Some lines about coffee burning in the old days are paraphrased from my *Inside Latin America*; also see the *Economist*, September 25, 1965. Clark, p. 26, has figures on land reform, as has "The Land Reform Issue in Latin America" by Thomas F. Carroll, printed in Hirschman, *Issues*, p. 163. I have used much material from Juan de Onis of the *New York Times*, an admirable reporter, in this and the following four chapters. For finance see *Time*, July 10, 1964, and the *New York Times*, various dates between 1963 and 1966. Leonard Gross in *Look*, June 2, 1964, mentions that the return of American investors in Brazil is modest. For Petrobras I have followed Gallatin, p. 76. For loans and credits to the Castelo Branco government see the Rundt *Weekly Intelligence Bulletin*, February 1, 1966. New investment associated with ADELA is mentioned in *Time*, October 15, 1965. Brazilian sense of balance and acceptance of reality are from Freyre. The quotation from Barros is from the *New Republic*, October 27, 1962; also see the Wagley pamphlet on Brazil and *Vista*, p. 160. For Kubitschek see Marquis Childs in the *New York Post*, "Brazilian Magic," August 12, 1965. *Time* has several articles about Goulart and corruption, as has *Newsweek*, May 11, 1964; also see the *Wall Street Journal*, May 11, 1964, and *Look*, March 23, 1965.

Chapter 2—From 1500 to 1966 in Twenty-One Pages

Herring, Bishop, Schurz, Pendle, Freyre, and Johnson, have been indispensable on historical matters. The phrase "hot and oleous air," is from Freyre, *Masters*, p. 13, as is the description of King Pedro as "Queen Victoria in breeches." "Father of the poor" as a description of Vargas is from an article in *The Reporter*, July 23, 1959. "Democratic Caesarism" is mentioned in "The Anatomy of Dictatorships," by Otto Maria Carpeaux, in *Civilizaçao Brasileria*, Rio de Janeiro, reprinted by *Atlas*, August, 1965. Doubt has often been cast on the authenticity of the Vargas suicide note. Dos Passos is interesting on the Lacerda-Vargas explosion. For new material on Vargas and others I am indebted to a chapter from a forthcoming book by John Dulles, *Post-Dictatorship Brazil*, which I was privileged to see in manuscript. *Time*, June 12, 1964, has figures on industrial improvements during Kubitschek. Tad Szulc in the *New York Times Magazine*, January 29, 1961, writes vividly about Quadros in "Do Not Despair: Janio Is Coming." Bertram B. Johansson, *Christian Science Monitor*, September 13, 1961, gives an interesting analysis of the Quadros resignation. Quadros as Groucho Marx, not Karl, is from several sources, including *Time*, June 30, 1961, which also mentions his efforts to control extravagance. Other tidbits about Quadros are in Dos Passos, p. 161, and various articles in the *New York Times*. A private memorandum is my source for the remark by Prestes to the effect that a Communist takeover was "unnecessary." Gerassi, p. 77 *et seq.*, is interesting on Brizola. For details of the coup in April, 1964, my sources are, among others, the *New York Times*, April 1, 1964, the *World Today* pamphlet cited in the text, and Allen Young in the *Christian Science Monitor*, September 4, 1964. Emanuel de Kadt, "A Brazilian Impasse," *Encounter*, September, 1965, mentions Goulart as a popular reformer, but the *Economist* (September 25, 1965) calls him "this weak, foolish, and utterly inadequate man." Also see the *New Statesman* (October 18, 1963, and May 8, 1964) and "Brazil in Quandary," by John J. Johnson, *Current History*, January, 1965. "When Executives Turn Revolutionaries," by Philip Siekman, *Fortune*, September, 1964, mentions the number of cabinet changes under Goulart. The Quigg article in *Foreign Affairs* noted above has a word about "superversion." I first heard the word from Lincoln Gordon, the American ambassador in Brazil. My authority for the Petrobras scandal is the Dulles manuscript. "The Coup in Brazil," by Christopher George, *World Today*, May, 1964, is brief but invaluable on the coup itself. "South America's Moment of Truth" in *Look*, March 23, 1965, mentions that successors to Goulart found "far fewer communists than they had expected."

Chapter 3—Brazil: A Sheaf of Personalities

The remark by Castelo Branco that the next time he wears a uniform he will be in his coffin is from *Look* in the article just cited. Boxer mentions an eighteenth-century governor with a name similar to Castelo Branco's. Details of Castelo Branco's fortune are from the *Reader's Digest* article footnoted in the text; also see *Newsweek*, April 27, 1964. "Interim Regime in Brazil," by Ronald M. Schneider, *Current History*, December, 1965, describes the Guanabara election. For the new parties see *Time*, December 31, 1965, and February 1, 1966; *Time* is also my source for the Lacerda-Campos interchange. For Lacerda as a "destroyer of presidents" see Bishop, p. 133, and Dos Passos, p. 168 *et seq.*, who also talks about the Brazilian president whose "foreign interests" were Haig & Haig, Johnny Walker, etc. Belfrage, p. 113, deals with Lacerda critically. That the ruling class seeks to prevent illiterates from voting in order to keep the poll down is mentioned in one of the Robert F. Kennedy speeches in the U.S. Senate. Pendle, *Argentina*, p. 178, raises the question whether or not a tropical country can ever be a great power. That the army is not "monolithic" is mentioned in the *World Today* article already cited.

Chapter 4—Brazil: A Sheaf of Cities

The quotation from Robert Lowell is from "Dropping South: Brazil," *New Statesman*, February 8, 1963. For the early history of Rio see "Romantic Rio," by Alan Rankin, *Reader's Digest*, January, 1965. Bishop, p. 6, is my authority for the definition of Carioca; *Vista*, p. 10, for the derivation of the name Guanabara. I am uncertain of the source of the story that Lúcio Costa designed Brasília on a postcard. Lynn Smith is good on fetichism, voodoo, and the like. The Stevenson quotation is from "Our Plight in Latin America," *Look*, November 22, 1960. Bishop, p. 140, uses the locution "vertical slum." For the *favelas* see Fodor, p. 440. Wagley (*Introduction*), p. 117, and the articles in the *Economist* cited above. A Brazilian Trade Bureau pamphlet, "Brazil in a Nutshell," has interesting facts and figures on São Paulo and other cities. That São Paulo is four times the size of Paris is from *Handbook*, p. 557. I have followed Gallatin closely on the expropriation of American companies. See Scott, p. 69, for automobiles. For Matarazzo I have drawn on the *Vista* book and elsewhere. Fodor, p. 336, mentions that steel and cement went to Brasília by air when the city was being built, and *Time*, April 9, 1965, has details of the contemporary gold rush. Also see Gene Gleason, New York *Herald Tribune*, May 17, 1960, and *Atlas*, July, 1964, for Brasília. My material on the Brasília-Belém road was gathered in Rio by word of mouth, but *Time*, January 17, 1966, has other interesting details. Wagley, p. 72, mentions Novocap. For the Amazon in general I have used the *National Geographic News Bulletin*, September 8, 1964; a brochure issued by the Pan American Union; and "Colossus of Rivers," by David Reed, *Reader's Digest*, September, 1963.

Chapter 5—The Northeast Plus Other Brazilian Headaches

The quotation from Dom Helder Câmara has appeared in both Marquis Childs, "The View From Brazil," New York *Post*, March 11, 1963, and George C. Lodge, "Revolution in Latin America," *Foreign Affairs*, January, 1966. Antonio Callado, one of the most distinguished of present-day Brazilian journalists and the representative of the *Encyclopaedia Britannica* in Rio de Janeiro, was the first writer to expose the contemporary realities of the northeast problem. Ralph Nader, *Christian Science Monitor*, September 30, 1962, is revealing about Recife. That the northeast was expendable is from Hirschman, *Journeys*, pp. 85–87. Landowners are discussed by Tad Szulc, *Revolution*, p. 56. Under the *cambao* system a peasant has to work one day a week without pay. Clark, p. 248 *et seq.*, is informative on Celso Furtado. Figures on aid are from Dom Bonafede, New York *Herald Tribune*, October 28, 1965. Sources for my miscellany include Fodor, p. 509, *Vista*, *Worldmark*, *Brazilian Bulletin*, July, 1965, and Wagley.

I would like to add a word here about Brazilian labor. For considerations of space I did not go into this subject in the dimension it deserves. Labor is a potent and growing force in Brazil, but its official status is difficult to define. I have stated that the great unions are controlled by the government, but, although this is true, they have managed to retain a considerable degree of power and influence. To sum the matter up, the controls over labor established by Vargas still remain in effect. The government, through the Ministry of Labor, has absolute jurisdiction over organized labor; it charters labor unions, supervises their elections, approves (or disqualifies) candidates, and is otherwise empowered to intervene in labor affairs. There is no effective collective bargaining or recourse to other basic rights by workers, as such rights are recognized in the United States. A mandatory provision in union charters pledges the unions' "collaboration with the authorities . . . subordinating economic or professional interests to the national interest." But the army has to listen to labor carefully for fear of alienating it.

Chapter 6—The Spanish-Speaking Half of the Continent

Tannenbaum, p. 98, mentions that half the population of the Andean states do not understand Spanish. The Quigg article in *Foreign Affairs*, already cited, searches out some of the centrifugal and centripetal forces in South America. See also: "Latin America: Myth and Reality," by John M. Cates, Jr., *Foreign Service Journal*, September, 1964. As to nomenclature one authority suggests "Saxo-America" for North America and "Eurindia" for South. Lord Bryce's description of the physical similarities and differences between the North and South American continents has never been excelled. Charles Wagley, "The Peasant," in *Continuity and Change in Latin America*, the anthology edited by John J. Johnson, has some interesting figures on agriculture. Berle, p. 5, and James Morris mention how empty South America is; the latter has some suggestive population figures, and Matthews, pp. 10–11, is good on physical characteristics. I have paraphrased a sentence or two about the Andes, also some historical material, from *Inside Latin America*. Olive Holmes, *Latin America*, a Headline Series pamphlet published by the Foreign Policy Association back in 1947, mentions that South America can be crossed by water. For the land see Hirschman, p. 164, and Johnson, *Continuity*, p. 11. Edwin Lieuwen, *Arms and Politics*, surveys the importance of Latin America to the United States in several spheres. Pendle, p. 86, stresses the point that the founders of South American independence had little education in self-government, and mentions that the Spanish dominions belonged technically to the crown of Castile. For Indians see *Newsweek*, December 6, 1965. The Spaniards killed twenty million Indians in the West Indies alone, according to the missionary-chronicler Fra Bartolomé de Las Casas, quoted by Lewis Hanke, *Encounter*, September, 1965. General sources for my historical section are Herring, Madariaga, Nehemkis, Houtart, Tannenbaum, Robertson, MacShane, and Arciniegas. The phrase "I obey but I do not do it" is from the *Economist*. Also see *Saturday Review*, October 12, 1963. The biographer of Bolívar whom I quote is Carleton Beals, *America South*, p. 201.

Chapter 7—"More Changes, More Chances"

The title of this chapter comes from the old-time British foreign correspondent H. W. Nevinson. Bryson, p. 181, talks about *Mozambismo*, the tendency to look down on anything native. *Colombia Today—and Tomorrow* by Pat M. Holt, an admirable book, p. 181, mentions the economic aspects of *machismo*. For women in industry, etc., see *Time*, January 8, 1965. My authority for the work of American "population attachés" is the *Visión Letter*, January 26, 1966. AID money is now helping—or soon will begin to help—planned parenthood groups in Colombia and Peru. For the fall of the military dictators see Cates, Lieuwen, and Houtart, pp. 107–10. Tannenbaum, p. 184, points out cogently how these were supported by United States big business. See also "Latin America: the Hidden Revolution," by Adolf A. Berle, *Reporter*, May 28, 1959. A memorable statement from this is the following: "They [the dictators] were . . . the worst possible long-range allies of the United States. Help or cordiality extended in their direction merely meant convincing the oppressed peoples of their countries that the United States was their enemy." Lodge alludes to the rise of a managerial elite in the *Foreign Affairs* article cited above. H. J. Maidenberg, *New York Times*, January 28, 1966, has some revealing things to say about taxes. Pendle, *History*, p. 162, states well the connection between tax dodging and dependence on foreign capital. For the flight of South American capital see Shapiro, Benton, Eisenhower, and Robert Coughlan in *Life*, 1964. The quotation about the status quo of misery is from the Szulc pamphlet *Latin America*, p. 41. Clark, p. 91, makes the point that armies in previous days were "protectors of the oligarchy against the people." Lieuwen, *Arms and Politics*, p. 141, mentions the paradox about constitutionalism to which I allude. See also S. E. Finer, "The Argentine Trouble," *Encounter*, September, 1965. Joseph Newman, New York *Herald Tribune*, February 21, 1960, has military budget figures. The Frei quotation is from Pike and D'Antonio, p. 118. For religious matters see *Time*, August 23, 1963; Henry Lee in the New York *Herald Tribune*, December 25, 1963; and Leonard Gross in *Look*, October 9, 1962. Comparative figures for serfs in South America and prewar Russia are from the *Saturday Review*, November 3, 1962. Tannenbaum, *op. cit.*, is superb on the "closed societies" represented by the *hacienda* system. The quotations about capitalism and free enterprise are from Clark, p. 392, and Eisenhower, p. 69. For South Americans as dogmatists see Cates, *op. cit.* For the students' revolt at Córdoba see Barnard L. Collier, New York *Herald Tribune*, June 10, 1963.

There should have been further word in my text about the universities in this connection. The Córdoba revolt came for several reasons. Students sought not only to remedy various grievances but to escape from the general monastic pattern of Catholic instruction and to counteract remnants of the old church doctrine that its only function was to save souls. There was no attempt by the church to transfer the elements of Spanish culture to the surviving Indian population.

Chapter 8—Big Neighbor, Communism, and the Alianza

Some details about Latin American votes in the UN are from an article of mine in *Look*, January 15, 1963. That three countries would not promise to invade Cuba is on the authority of Clark, p. 385. References to making the OAS a more effective body are from Juan de Onis, *New York Times*, March 12, 1966. *Newsweek* (August 9, 1965) is a source for the Camelot fiasco. For Operación Simpático see the *New York Times*, February 4, 1966; for the Selden affair, authorities include *Time*, October 7, 1965, and, for Latin American reactions, *Atlas*, November, 1965. For the OAS I have drawn on *Time*, May 14, 1965, the *New York Times*, December 21, 1965, a Foreign Policy Association pamphlet, and "This League of Nations Actually Keeps the Peace," by Blake Clark, *Reader's Digest*, June, 1958, condensed from *Western World*. "A South American Bloc," by Fernandes Diez de Medina, from *Nova*, La Paz, reprinted in *Atlas*, August, 1963, mentions that the OAS reflects thinking in Washington rather than the hemisphere. For visa denial see Carlos Fuentes in *Book Week*, April 24, 1966. Tannenbaum is revealing on this lamentable topic, and also (p. 177) mentions the South American reaction at North American treatment of Negroes. That seventeen desk officers in the State Department never served in the countries to which they were assigned is stated by A. A. Berle, Jr., "Are We 'Ignoring' Latin America?" *New York Times Magazine*, November 24,

1963. Lodge, *op. cit.*, states that our image "is tarnished by the suspicion that it is committed to the status quo and therefore to passive resistance against change." Lieuwen, *Policy*, p. 119, describes the paradox over U.S. withdrawal of recognition from Peru in 1962, as does Senator Robert F. Kennedy in his Alianza speech. For the Johnson Doctrine see Richard Eder in the *New York Times*, January 19, 1966. Mr. Eder mentions that "the administration's Latin American policy underwent a shift of emphasis from a rigid policy of opposing military coups to a policy of assisting military governments if they showed any signs of working for economic or social betterment." For United States support of dictatorships see Thayer Waldo, "Why Latin America Distrusts Us," *Harper's*, November, 1958. Senator Robert F. Kennedy is authority for the statement that we have intervened twenty-one times in the Caribbean between 1898 and 1924, *Congressional Record*, May 9, 1966. John Plank, "Our Good Neighbors Should Come First," *New York Times Magazine*, June 6, 1965, is eloquent on Caribbean matters. Recent speeches by Senator Wayne Morse deal effectively with the ambiguity of our intervention policy. I am indebted to James Reston, *New York Times*, May 8, 1966, for the amounts of American holdings in Canada. The statement from Dean Rusk is from Scott, *op. cit.* Several passages from my section on the Monroe Doctrine and what followed are paraphrased from *Inside Latin America*. "Defensive imperialism" as a description of the Monroe Doctrine is from Campos, cited in the text. Arthur Schlesinger, Jr., *op. cit.*, pp. 171–72, mentions that FDR made no attempt to extend the New Deal into the hemisphere. Ernest Halperin, "The Decline of Communism in Latin America," *Atlantic*, May, 1965, a revealing article, describes the nationalist component in Communism. Pertinent remarks on Castro's triple threat capacity and much may be found in Robert Coughlan, "The Staggering Problem," *Life*, already cited. For Communism in general see Kennedy, Clark, Adams, and Houtart, p. 118, who points out how Communism exploits the "flagrant structural deficiencies of Latin America." Szulc, *Winds* (pp. 190–91), says that Moscow is quiescent about Latin America because it does not want another major confrontation with the United States, and that the cost on the spot would be too great. An article in *Atlas*, August, 1963, mentions that Latin American Marxism is apt to be more anti-American than pro-Marxist. See also the article by John Paton Davies, Jr., "A Crisis of Casualness in Latin America," *Harper's*, August, 1964; also "A New Look at Latin America," by Charles E. Lindblom, *Atlantic*, October, 1962. Several sources mention that the Alianza has no "structural body." For AID see Lieuwen, *Policy*, p. 115, and Alexander, *Today's Latin America*, pp. 81–82. For "tied" dollar aid consult Marquis Childs, cited above, also Juan de Onis in the *New York Times*, March 30, 1966. That there is too much identification with the United States is mentioned by Moscoso, *op. cit.* Alianza statistics come from *Time* and Barnard L. Collier in the New York *Herald Tribune*. Figures on military assistance are given by Leslie Gould in the New York *Journal American*, April 6, 1966. I have closely followed Lieuwen, *Arms*, pp. 201–7, on arms matters in general; also see Felix Belair in the *New York Times*, June 11, 1966. The tidbit about riot equipment comes from Elie Abel.

Chapter 9—Backdrop to Argentina

Several of the quotations about Argentina are from Arciniegas, and some basic statistics come from *Handbook*, pp. 77–79. The Javits proposal is from the *New*

York Times, July 18, 1966. Estimates of the railway deficit vary widely; *Newsbook*, p. 132, puts the figure at $700 million a year, higher than mine. Authority for water supply figures is Gallatin, p. 421. A penetrating analysis of Argentine character appeared in *Look*, June 2, 1964. Budget figures and gross national product are from *Time*; also see Scott, p. 55. Several writers mention that the *pampa* has no rocks or pebbles, and *Handbook*, p. 50, is authority for the statement that Patagonia means "big feet." For the Welsh communities and Ushuaia see Robert Berrellez in the *Christian Science Monitor*, March 3 and 8, 1965; that a daily Welsh newspaper exists is from Morris, p. 4. Population details are from the Pan American Union booklet on Argentina (revised edition, 1964) and Gallatin, p. 220. *Handbook*, p. 115, and the Pan American pamphlet just cited describe the fishing in Mar del Plata in identical language. I have followed Pendle, *Argentina*, in several historical matters, for instance the item about *La Frigorifique*. See also *Handbook*, indispensable as always, which is my source for the grants of land given to army officers by President Roca. Fodor also mentions this piquant detail. Some details about Irigoyen are paraphrased from *Inside Latin America*, p. 286. That eight out of ten Argentine presidents were army officers between 1930 and 1958 is mentioned by Lieuwen.

Chapter 10—From the Colonel to the General

Fleur Cowles (*Bloody Precedent*, p. 144) mentions that Perón's name may originally have been Peroni. The remarks about Perón by Dr. Eisenhower are from *Wine*, p. 255. Details of Perón's first marriage come from the *New York Times*, December 13, 1963; his remark about not being superstitious is from *Time*, January 3, 1957. Pendle is my main source for Perón's work in social affairs; this book strongly influenced my own thinking. For Perón's industrialization program see Scott, as well as an article by Arthur Hurwich in the New York *Post*, December 6, 1964; for Evita's grave see *Latin American Times*, August 12, 1965. Authority for the statement that forty Peronists were executed in 1956 is *Latin American History*, p. 300. The New York *Herald Tribune*, December 18, 1964, mentions that if Illía served out his full term he would have been the first Argentine president in his generation to do so, but he didn't. For "Peronists without Perón" see Charles Keely, Copley News Service, *Brazil Herald*, March 13, 1965. For anecdotes about Illía I used the *Visión Letter*, September 29, 1965; *New Republic*, March 27, 1965; Rowland Evans and Robert Novak in the New York *Herald Tribune*, December 18, 1964, and Henry Raymont in the *New York Times*, October 24, 1965. Details about Frondizi's tenure at Bariloche are from Edward C. Burks in the *New York Times*, March 29, 1963. That Frondizi survived thirty-five crises in four years is on the authority of Gladys Delmas, *Reporter*, January 3, 1963. *Newsweek*, April 15, 1963, describes the abortive naval coup put down by General Onganía. For details of the Pistarini-Caro encounter, see an Associated Press dispatch to the *New York Times*, June 29, 1966.

Chapter 11—B. A.

The *yeísmo* is mentioned in *Worldmark*, p. 19. Some details about cities appear in a local pamphlet, *Buenos Aires Through Bifocals*. For South American shanty towns in general see Samuel Schapiro, "What the President Won't See," *Reporter*,

March 3, 1960. The *New York Times*, January 17, 1964, is authority for the statement that there are fifty-five different shanty towns. For university dropouts see "A Problem for Cortenos," *Atlas*, November, 1965, reprinted from *Todo*, Buenos Aires. James Barry, New York *Herald Tribune*, August 2, 1964, is an authority for details about Vandor and Framini, as are articles in *Time* and *Newsweek*. For Cardinal Caggione see Arthur J. Olson in the *New York Times*, January 6, 1966. For Borges consult André Maurois, "A Note on Jorge Luis Borges," *Paris Review*, Summer–Fall, 1962. The article in *Holiday*, December, 1965, to which I refer is by Saul Maloff. Gay Talese, *New York Times*, February 5, 1962, has details about the blindness in the Borges family.

For reasons of space I did not include in my text a general statement of labor's attitude toward Peronismo as given me by José Alonso, the former secretary-general of the CGT, and others. The gist of their attitude is that "Peronism is not Perón," although he is part of it. Whether El Líder ever comes back himself or not, is, in the last analysis, irrelevant. He is held to be the author of an idea so germinal, so powerful and all-embracing, that it will continue to exist whether with him or without him. He himself is not interested in returning to Argentina for the sake of power but to "redeem" the historical record; moreover he wants vindication while he is still alive. Perón is accused by his enemies of having supported labor, then of having supported himself *on* labor, but he gave labor more than he took from it. There were three stages in Perón's history. First, as a youthful army officer, he saw at first hand how a reactionary agricultural economy produced evils all the way from an unbalanced economy to malnutrition in children. Second, on reaching power, he gave the worker his proper place in society, stimulated interest in public affairs, and provided not merely social reform but full employment. Third, his reforms alienated the oligarchy, which punished him by arraying both foreign and domestic capital on the side of his opponents. Hence, to preserve himself, he had to curtail civil liberties.

After the expropriation of *La Prensa*, which produced further international reaction, Perón became convinced that he must curb the army, because it was impossible for the country to develop so long as the military forces consumed as large a share of the budget as they did; as a result, the generals turned against him. So did the church, but he never quarreled with the church as such, only with the ecclesiastical hierarchy. As a matter of fact his relations with the church were always quite good till the very end. It was often said that Perón held power by a combination of army support plus labor, but this cannot be true, because it was the armed forces that knocked him down, and labor did not rise in the streets to save him. What, then, *was* his source of power? The answers I got were moral authority, vision, belief in social justice, and the gift of hope. This analysis has a somewhat Marxist tinge, but several labor leaders put it this way with great emphasis, even though Perón is anti-Marxist.

Chapter 12—Uruguay on the Rocks

The quotation at the head of the chapter comes from Vanger. *At Home in Uruguay*, a pamphlet published in Montevideo in 1961, is my source for several bits of local color. Also I have used the Pan American Union brochure on Uruguay, for instance for the detail that Uruguay is the fourth-largest meat consumer per capita in the world. Noñato is mentioned in *Handbook*, p. 437, as is nutria. Herring mentions that Artigas was a cattle rustler and Gerassi, p. 194, notes his title as "Protector of the Free People." The quotation about Uruguay being "ungovernable" is from the Pendle history, p. 188. The duel involving Luis Batlle Berres is mentioned in the *New York Times*, July 16, 1964. For a useful brief summary of social security legislation see the *Times*, January 10, 1962. The item about women getting to work early is from the New York *Herald Tribune*, February 16, 1964. For civil servants see Richard West in the *New Statesman*, October 22, 1965, and for the banking crisis *Time*, January 14, 1965; details on income tax are from the *Christian Science Monitor*, November 8, 1963. Gerassi, p. 199, is revealing on corruption in bureaucracy. *Human Events*, December 14, 1963, discusses critically several aspects of the welfare system.

Chapter 13—A Semi-Affectionate Look at Paraguay

I found the Voltaire quotation in the *Encounter* issue on Latin America. No really good history of Paraguay exists in English, or, scholarly friends tell me, even in Spanish. Figures for road and rail are from *Handbook*, p. 351, and Gallatin, p. 837. Some pro-Paraguayans insist that exiles from the country are not really exiled, and that they should no more be described as such than Greek merchants, let us say, living outside Greece; in other words, they are voluntary expatriates. But I am not sure that the word "voluntary" tells the whole story. Perhaps they were not formally exiled but they fled because life at home was intolerable.

Richard West, "Uncle Fred's Kingdom," *New Statesman*, November 26, 1965, has a fair assessment of this and other issues, and makes a point of Paraguayan charm. The flowering trees in Asunción are mentioned in *Land of Lace and Legend*, published locally. The quotation about the War of the Triple Alliance is from *Handbook*, p. 350. Madariaga, p. 7, mentions the relationship of foreign oil companies to the Chaco War. The phrase "humanize the law" in reference to contraband comes from Pendle. A dispatch in the Chicago *Daily News*, January 6, 1965, by Gerry Robichaud, says that a Paraguayan tradition is to "put the *contrabandistas* under the protection of the military—for a price." Of course elements of the army are deeply involved in the racket.

Chapter 14—A Good Man in Chile

Valuable sources on Chile are the two Halperin pamphlets, an American Embassy fact sheet, and *Chile, Election Fact Book*, prepared by the Institute for the Comparative Study of Political Systems, Washington, D.C., 1964. That Chile has gone thirty-two years without a revolution is from *Time*, November 3, 1964. Statistics on housing, malnutrition, et cetera, are from Halperin, Gallatin, and an admirable report on Chile in the *Atlantic*, June, 1965. This mentions, *inter alia*, that the Chileans are "'the most civic-minded people in Latin America." Frei's "Christian humanism" is mentioned by several writers, including Joseph S. Roucek, "Chile in Geo-politics," *Contemporary Review*, London, March, 1965, an important article from which I have borrowed several items. See Leonard Gross, *Look*, June 2, 1964, for a good account of Frei. Mr. Gross mentions that Pope Paul VI "saved" Frei on one occasion. Henry Raymont, *New York Times*, November 4, 1964, mentions that workers and peasants were welcomed in the Moneda when Frei was inaugurated. The *New York Times* printed a useful sketch of the president on September 7, 1964, as did the *Christian Science Monitor*, September 17, 1964. For Frei's congressional victory in 1965 see *Time*, March 19, 1965, also Herbert L. Matthews in the *New York Times*, July 26, 1965. There are splendid photographs of the city's firemen in "Santiago, Bright Star of Chile," by Richard Llewellyn, *Holiday*, November, 1963. I have followed *Inside Latin America* for events between the wars, also for the career of Marmaduque Grove. Brian Crozier, "Latin American Journey," *Encounter*, December, 1964, is useful on political background. See Rowland Evans and Robert Novak in the New York *Herald Tribune* for Frei's dilemma in trying to make a social revolution "without wrecking the country." For Cardinal Silva see Marquis Childs in the New York *Post*, August 10, 1965. R. Hart Phillips in the *Latin American Times*, September 13, 1965, gives details on Frei's program, as does *Newsweek*, September 21, 1964. Halperin, mentioned above, is very good on Ampuero and Corvalán. Ampuero calls the Spartacus people "soda-fountain guerrillas," according to Halperin. Clark, pp. 236–37, notes that Allende is a 33rd degree Mason.

Chapter 15—More Complexities in Chile

"Change and Frustration in Chile" by Osvaldo Sunkel, a paper which I was privileged to see in manuscript, and which was about to be presented at a conference, "Obstacles to Change in Latin America," at the Royal Institute of International Affairs, London, is a useful source. Several writers have been fascinated by the fact that Chile, in spite of its shape, is bigger than Texas. See Arciniegas, p. 122, for geographical details nicely presented. Divisions of the country are described by Roucek, *op. cit.*, who also gives theories about the origin of the name of the country. Johnson, *Continuity*, is revealing on Santiago University. I did not have room in my text to describe the admirable extension work done by this institution, particularly in the arts. For instance, it supports musical organizations all over the country. See also the Pan American Union pamphlet on Chile. Herring, p. 144, gives one version of the manner of Valdivia's death, Arciniegas another. The latter says that he was eaten alive. For USAID see Martin Arnold in the *New York Times*, December 18, 1965. Verification of several details about Santiago comes from *Chile Is Like This*, published by the Instituto Chileno–Norte Americano de Cultura and the Association of American Women of Chile. That only 11,000 people declared their income at more than $5,000 a year is from the *Atlantic* article of June, 1965, cited above. Senator Kennedy mentioned land reform with bright acumen in the second of his Senate speeches. For Neruda see the *New Statesman* article footnoted in the text, also "Writers in Isolation" by Howard Taubman, *New York Times*. The item about the anchor in Antofagasta is from *Chile Is Like This*. For CAP see James E. Warner, New York *Herald Tribune*, December 18, 1960. *Handbook* is good on cities. Roucek, just cited, has valuable background on copper, as have several articles in *Newsweek*. For Anaconda, Kennecott, etc., see Edward C. Burks in the *New York Times*, June 7, 1964, also Mildred Adams, "President Frei and the Copper Goose," *New Republic*, December 18, 1965. For land reform I have drawn on *Newsweek*, September 21, 1964, and the *New York Times*, March 18, 1966. Elements in the copper settlement are described in the *New York Times*, April 14, 1966, and the Washington *Post*, August 7, 1965. For land figures see Sunkel, Roucek, and *Latin America* in the Foreign Policy Association series. Scott, p. 50, is authority for the statement that minifundia can be five miles long and ten feet wide. Benton, p. 31, states that 21 percent of the land is fallow. For land in general see *Newsweek*, September 21, 1964, and Arthur J. Olsen, *New York Times*, January 8, 1966. An item in the *Latin American Times* demonstrates how close land reform and inflation are to the hearts of the people, as well as their capacity for direct action. A farmer recently pushed his way into a Santiago bank, leading a bull, which he wished to sell then and there as part of a mortgage payment.

Chapter 16—Bottom of the World

Handbook mentions that Punta Arenas is laid out rectangularly with twenty-five streets in one direction, thirty-five in another. Dispatches by Henry Raymont, *New York Times*, April 10, 11, and 13, 1965, describe the trip we took. For petroleum in Tierra del Fuego see Edward C. Burks, *New York Times*, March 6, 1962. James Becket, *Christian Science Monitor*, March 27, 1963, mentions the adventurous Popper, the only reference to him I have ever seen in print. "Tierra del Fuego," by Peter Matthiessen, *Américas*, February, 1964, is an evocative description of this dreary archipelago.

Chapter 17—El Señor Presidente de Perú

Peru's Own Conquest, by Fernando Belaúnde Terry, introduction by David A. Robinson, American Studies Press, S.A., Lima, 1965, has clearly been a major source for this and the following chapters. Also, through the courtesy of President Belaúnde, I was privileged to see the original manuscript of this work. Book and manuscript differ in text, and my debt is large to both. *Time*, March 12, 1965, an interesting cover story on the west coast, is a source for several details in Belaúnde's career as well as other material. An unsigned profile of the president appeared in the *New York Times*, July 29, 1963. A critical view of the Forest Road project, expressing the opinion of several observers in Peru, may be found in Scott, pp. 34–35. For Cooperación Popular see a report in the *Atlantic*, May, 1966. Robert E. Mc-Nicoll, *Recent Political Developments in Peru*, Inter-American Economic Affairs, has useful political background. An invaluable source, which I have dipped into several times, is Richard W. Patch, *A Note on Bolivia and Peru*, American Universities Field Staff, 1965. This is a discerning and articulate report. Footnotes in the text convey my obligation to James R. Carey, *Peru and the United States*, an admirable guide to politics, economics, and finance. See also a report in the *Atlantic*, November, 1962, and the *Latin American Times*, August 20, 1965. Lieuwen, *Arms and Politics*, and Johnson, *Role of the Military*, are useful on military background. Carey, pp. 8–11, is particularly good on Odría, also on the role played in 1962 by Ambassador Loeb, pp. 216–17. Carey also mentions an interesting Peruvian journalist, Eudocio Ravinas, author of *The Yenan Way*. I wish I had had space to write about Mr. Ravinas in my own pages. For Father Hidalgo see the *New York Times*, March, 16, 1966. For Haya de la Torre I have picked up several passages from *Inside Latin America*.

One of the *Atlantic* reports just cited says that when we withdrew recognition from the junta which seized power in 1962, we stopped $81 million in Alianza economic aid, withdrew military assistance of $5 million a year, and threatened "to cut off Peru's privilege of selling $19 million worth of sugar to the United States at preferential prices." Clark, pp. 416–17, mentions that the Kennedy administration reversed itself and recognized the junta after only a month. The *Atlantic* article also describes Belaúnde as being "far-left" in those days, and adds that the junta was also "far to the left."

Chapter 18—Peruvian Medley

Peru in the Pan American Union series is useful on the geographical divisions of the country, and mentions "the Land of the Four Sections." The phrase "platform of rocks" comes from this. Some geographical details are derived from a former work of mine. Some interesting statistics appear in a pamphlet called *Peru*, published by Industrial Development, February, 1965. That only one out of 325 citizens can read and write is from Eisenhower, p. 22; also see Benton, p. 17. *Handbook*, pp. 364–65, is good on Indians and also has an admirably succinct account of Inca characteristics. Wendt, p. 209, mentions that the Inca Empire has been called "the first socialist state in world history." Average wage figures are from *Time*. For *ayllus* and the *mita* see the Pan Amerian pamphlet just cited, also *Life*, September 24, 1945. Bryce, p. 477, mentions that the Incas were less cruel than Aztecs or Red Indians, and did not practice human sacrifice. I have drawn on several authorities for Pizarro. Figures about Leguía come from *Inside Latin America*, as do a line or two about the Incas. Herring, p. 549, points out that Peru has no export tax on minerals. For petroleum see Senator Robert F. Kennedy's speech to the Senate, May 10, 1966, and Marquis Childs, Washington *Post*, July 28, 1965. ADELA is described in "The Fortunes of ADELA" by Senator Jacob K. Javits, *Columbia Journal of World Business*, Spring, 1966, as well as *Time*, April 8, 1966. That one Peruvian department is as big as Rhode Island is from the Kennedy speech. For land in general see Scott, the *Time* cover story, and the *Atlantic*, May, 1966. Juan de Onis, *New York Times*, August 29, 1966, has material on the methods whereby the guerrillas were beaten down, also *Newsweek*, July, 1965. "Yankee Go Home? Stay Home? Intervene?" by John Paton Davies, Jr., *New York Times Magazine*, May 23, 1965, has some stimulating thoughts on the Communists.

Chapter 19—City of Kings

Handbook, p. 369, describes Lima's fog and Scotch mist, and mentions the lady known as La Perricholi, as does Fodor, p. 208. Bryce is, as usual, discriminating in his description of the Plaza de Armas. Herring, p. 550, has a sympathetic account of Dr. Beltrán. Kenneth F. Weaver, "The Five Worlds of Peru," *National*

Geographic, February, 1964, describes the Larco and other museums to the accompaniment of vivid illustations. The quotation at the head of the gold section is from the preface to the Mujica book on gold, a magnificent production. *This is Peru,* quoted on Arequipa in the text, is not to be confused with a more literate pamphlet which bears the same title. Both are published in Lima.

Chapter 20—Jungle, Amazon, and the Inca Highlands

The Neruda quotation is from *Selected Poems of Pablo Neruda,* translated by Ben Belitt, Grove Press, New York. The *Peruvian Times,* January 7, 1966, has interesting material on Iquitos. "Lima, I Love You, Oddly Enough," by Richard Bissell, *Holiday,* June, 1964, is vastly amusing about much in Peru. I have continued in this chapter to draw widely on both the Belaúnde book and manuscript. For the land, see "Revolution of Rising Expectations," *Economist,* April 22, 1961. Sources for the miscellany include Schapiro, *Handbook,* the *Geographic* article, and an American Embassy fact sheet.

Chapter 21—Men and Events in Bolivia

Time, April 2, 1965, has details about Barrientos as an aviator. A brief profile of the president appeared in the *New York Times,* November 10, 1964. Some lines in my description of Busch come from *Inside Latin America.* Busch and Villarroel are well described in Alexander, *Bolivia,* pp. 26–28 and 34–38. "The U.S. in Latin America" by Ronald M. Schneider, *Current History,* January, 1965, is useful for background, as is another *Current History* article, December, 1965, "Revolution and Stability in Bolivia," by Dwight B. Heath. I wish I had been able to write more about General Ovando, an extraordinary character. His relations with Barrientos make a fascinating and cryptic study. Valuable insight on the whole Bolivian picture may be had from "Bolivia: U.S. Assistance in a Revolutionary Setting," by Richard W. Patch, a chapter in Bryson. Another interesting essay by Mr. Patch appears in Silvert. He takes a dim view of Barrientos.

Chapter 22—Bolivian Baedeker

The first quotation at the top of the chapter is from Eisenhower's *Wine,* and was written in particular reference to Bolivia. For potatoes see the Pan American Union pamphlet on Bolivia. Schapiro, p. 126, mentions that two-thirds of Bolivian Indians are not merely illiterate, but cannot even speak Spanish. Carey, *Peru,* uses the phrase "beggar nation," p. 224. I have used *Time* (November 1, 1963; May 29, 1964; and June 14, 1966) for various details, as well as the *New York Times* (April 21, 1959; December 14, 1963; November 2, 1964; June 2, 1965; and July 30, 1966). The Siles hunger strike is mentioned in Wendt, p. 12, and in "Bolivia's Revolution," by Ricardo Ocampo, in *Memento,* Caracas, reprinted in *Atlas,* January, 1965. For details of the coup which displaced Paz see Henry Lee in the New York *Herald Tribune,* November 8, 1964. I have had to foreshorten drastically my treatment of this fantastic episode. Many flamboyant details of the month-by-month violence preceding this event have also had to be omitted for lack of space. Nor do I mention the United States withdrawal of aid from Barrientos except in passing. Herring states that Patiño had an extraterritorial status which assisted his tax situation. Pendle, *op. cit.*, mentions that the United States supported the MNR out of fear of "chaos or communism," and adds the nugget that the Patiños hired Lechín as a boy because they wanted to put him on their football team. Details about Bolivian cities are from *Handbook*, Fodor, and other sources. The question at the conclusion of the chapter was posed by Peter Barnes in the *Christian Science Monitor* quoting an unnamed Bolivian economist, May 6, 1963.

I have had to skip much in this treatment of Bolivia. A wonderful long book could be written about this country, so full of saturnine marvels. I have not mentioned the inflation which drove the exchange rate from 190 bolivianos to the dollar in 1952 to 16,000 four years later. But this disaster made money for some. "A complex system of multiple exchange rates prevailed, whereby some could buy dollars at the old rate of 190 bolivianos, and resell them (or, theoretically, sell goods imported with them) at the prevailing rate, thereby becoming millionaires overnight with a minimal investment and no risk." This is from the Heath article in *Current History* already cited.

Chapter 23—The Curious Entity of Ecuador

The quotations from Bemelmans are from his enchanting *The Donkey Inside* (Viking Press, New York, 1941). Forbes, p. 283, mentions that Protestants have been stoned in the streets. Both Fodor, p. 168, and *Handbook* describe the 0° 00′ 00″ line where a person can stand with one foot in the northern hemisphere, one in the southern. Eisenhower, p. 22, is a source for details on land ownership. Authorities for political instability are Tannenbaum, pp. 147–51, Szulc, p. 78, and an unsigned article in the *Atlantic*, November, 1965; this is also a source for the percentage of tax collections reaching the treasury and details about the *huasipungo* system. Fodor is good on the Oriente and its Indians, pp. 175–77, and *Handbook* is authority for the statement about Masonic lodges, also for details about the churches. The *Economist*, March 26, 1966, describes the relation between restaurants, lotteries, and taxes. The New York *Herald Tribune* (January 3, 1965) quotes a spokesman of the Ecuadorian army as stating that Arosemena was alcoholically inclined; the *New York Times*, March 31, 1966, says that he "was deposed for alcoholism." Arciniegas, p. 357, is a source for details about García Moreno. Material on Yerovi is from the *New York Times*, April 2, 1966, and *Time*, April 8, 1966. For the Galápagos see "Life Stands Still" by Dorothy Dawes, *Latin American Times*, September 10, 1965.

Chapter 24—Colombia: The Background of the Violencia

The quotations at the head of both this and the next chapter are from *The Green Continent*, the Arciniegas anthology. Holt, cited in the bibliography, has supported me several times in these Colombia chapters. That 398 Indian tribes exist in

Colombia is from *Handbook*, as are details about gold in the early days. The *New York Times*, May 31, 1964, mentions the "Independent Republic of Marquetalia." Nicknames of terrorist leaders are from the *Latin American Times*.

Chapter 25—Colombia: People, Issues, Problems

The story about President Valencia and his children is from the *New York Times*, May 8, 1962. For Lleras Restrepo consult a *Times* profile, May 3, 1966. For labor see Richard Eder in the *New York Times*, May 1, 1964, and *Newsweek*, July 20, 1964. The quotations from Torres and Amaya are from H. J. Maidenberg in the *New York Times*. For Salcedo and radio techniques in education see Benton, pp. 114–116, and Holt, p. 180. *U.S. News and World Report*, June 26, 1965, has figures illustrating the extent of Colombia's financial crisis; so has *Time*, December 11, 1964. Clark, always perceptive and informative, is my authority for several statistics on landownership and has the detail (pp. 86 and 92) that the land reform issue provoked gunfire in parliament; he also mentions the expensiveness of weddings. A wedding can cost a peasant a month's wages. Figures on population are from a speech by Dr. Peñalosa at the Alumni Club of the University of the Andes, June 11, 1964. For the Cali conference see the *New York Times*, August 23, 1965. Some of my statistics about education come from Waldemar Bellon, *Washington Post*, a Reuter's dispatch. For political developments following the student riots in 1965 see the *New York Times*, August 21, 1964. This is also my authority for the number of Colombians visiting the New York World's Fair.

I mention in my text the disintegration which occurred in the last unhappy months of the Valencia government. For instance a high officer of the air force had to be dismissed from his post for alleged participation in a scheme to smuggle whiskey into the country. Another scandal had to do with a prominent cabinet minister, who was forced to resign; he had been so indiscreet as to appear publicly at the funeral of a butcher who had been murdered in front of his shop in Bogotá. The butcher, it seems, was none other than a celebrated former bandit who bore the name "Captain Poison"; he had gone into "retirement," but must have left enemies behind. Why the minister went to his funeral is unknown, or who shot the butcher. In any case the gesture cost the minister his job, and further upset the country. The *New York Times* is my source for both these episodes.

Holt, p. 68, has interesting details about an alleged deal between Valencia and Lleras Restrepo for the presidency. For Rojas Pinilla see Szulc, pp. 92–94. The item about the bill to execute unsatisfactory presidents is from the *Latin American Times*, August 13, 1965.

Chapter 26—More About Colombia

For the hills around Bogotá see *Handbook*, p. 285. Richard Eder mentions the influence of climate on Bogotá in the *New York Times*, August 11, 1962. The old *Everyman's Encyclopedia* is my source for Bogotá's population back in 1930. Details about street and house numbers are from a fact sheet put out by the American Embassy. The item about shining shoes with tomato skin is from an Associated Press dispatch, *Christian Science Monitor*, April 5, 1962. Geographical and other details on cities, for instance that the statue of Christ in Cali can be seen for thirty miles, are from *Handbook*; this is also (p. 303) the source of the quotation about Popayán. *Colombia*, published by the Pan American Union in Washington is, like the other booklets in this series, well prepared and useful. The date of the first looms in Medellín is from a local pamphlet. For the Cauca Valley Authority I have used a speech (February 24, 1964) by Dr. Bernardo Garces Córdoba, its managing director, as well as a pamphlet by David E. Lilienthal, *The Road to Change*, adapted from a lecture (1964) given by Mr. Lilienthal at Columbia University in New York. For the basic Colombian dichotomy see an eloquent article by H. A. Murena, "Latin American Culture: To Be or Not To Be," from *Communita*, Milan, reprinted by *Atlas*, 1963. Fodor, p. 143, mentions the story about Cartagena and Mt. Vernon.

Chapter 27—Visiting Venezuela

Authority for the statement that Central University in Caracas cost $300 million (it was built by Pérez Jiménez) is *Newsweek*, June 29, 1964, which also mentions that it has been autonomous since 1784. "Venezuela" in the American Republic series has much useful statistical matter, as have the fact sheets and the background notes put out by the United States Embassy in Caracas, the Venezuelan Embassy in Washington, and the Creole Petroleum Corporation. The origin of the Venezuelan automobile industry is mentioned in the *Latin American Times*, September 28, 1965. Gallatin, p. 1054, is my source for railway mileage and details about water. Details on Maracaibo's population are from *Handbook*, p. 445. Cost of living rates are from *Time*, July 14, 1961. Some elements of the life of Caracas are well described in an unsigned Canadian dispatch to the *New York Times*, August 23, 1964. Horace Sutton, *Saturday Review*, May 11, 1963, mentions the cost of several of P.J.'s grandiose projects. Gerassi, p. 356, has a footnote about Capriles. José A. Valbuena, New York *Herald Tribune*, November 6, 1964, has interesting material on P.J. Also see Szulc, pp. 71–72 and 104, Eisenhower, pp. 190–93, and in particular Barnard L. Collier, New York *Herald Tribune*, August 25, 1963, and other dates. Betancourt's years in jail or exile are mentioned in the London *Times*, April 19, 1960. A bibliography of Betancourt could extend for pages. The *New York Times*, December 16, 1961, has the quotation on the Communist party and smallpox. The *New Yorker* article, p. 141, cited in the text, mentions Betancourt's cultivation of the army, as does A. A. Berle in the *Reporter*. Also see "Venezuela Strives for Democracy," by David Holden, *Manchester Guardian Weekly*, reprinted in *Atlas*, August, 1963. "A Crisis of Casualness in Latin America," by John Paton Davies, Jr., *op. cit.*, says that Betancourt was "dangerously lenient to the communists."

Chapter 28—Venezuela, Its Leadership and Politics

The opening quotation is from *Politics and Change in Latin America*, p. 66. For President Leoni see Bernard Taper in the *New Yorker* article just mentioned, an article in *Time*, August 7, 1964, and Richard Eder in the *New York Times*, March 12, 1964. The Rousselot speech was printed in the *Congressional Record*. *Newsweek*,

March 23, 1964, describes the three symbols of presidential power given ceremoniously by Betancourt to Leoni. The *New Yorker* article mentions that Leoni's father was a Corsican. Lines about other leaders in Acción Democrática are in the *Visión Letter*, September 22, 1965. Good analyses of the political situation in general are by Barnard L. Collier, New York *Herald Tribune*, December 8, 1963, also by Rowland Evans and Robert Novak in the same paper, October 21, 1963; see Collier too for Larrazabal. That Uslar has refused to say that he is "anti-Communist" is on the authority of the New York *Herald Tribune*, November 11, 1963. Religious matters are discussed by John M. Cates, Jr., in his article in the *Foreign Service Journal* already mentioned. For petroleum see Harry B. Ellis, *Christian Science Monitor*, November 3, 1960. I have drawn on *Newsweek*, February 22, 1965, for details about industrial development in the Guayana region, also Gallatin, *Time*, *Visión*, and the *Christian Science Monitor*. The item about Angostura bitters is from *Handbook*, p. 461. Venezuela's support of the early Castro is mentioned in the London *Times*, April 19, 1960. For Castro and FALN see *Newsweek*, February 25, 1963, and July 5, 1965. I regret that I did not have room in my text to report on the exploits of Captain Douglas Bravo, one of the guerrilla leaders. *Time*, March 19, 1965, is my source for the "new experiments in penology." Several items in my miscellany are from *Worldmark*. *A Is for Abrazo*, a local pamphlet, mentions gyppy tummy, the picturesquely named winds, and gambling.

Further details about Central University in Caracas, which I did not include in my text because of shortage of that well-known commodity space, are the following. It shares one difficulty with most other universities in South America in that there is so little "raw material" to draw on, since high school graduates are scant. Another is that the School of Journalism—as an example—graduates thirty or forty students a year, more than can possibly be absorbed into appropriate jobs. The departments in Caracas most thoroughly infiltrated by the Communists are economics, agriculture, journalism, and the humanities. The university receives its funds from the legislature, but this has little control of how they are spent. Discipline is lax on almost every level. No professor would dare defy a student openly. Tuition is free, and the students have, as elsewhere on the continent, an important share in the workings of the executive council of the university. The campus has become both a refuge and a fortress for red-hot left-wingers who cannot easily be arrested while they stay within its area; one Communist deputy is supposed to have lived here for a year, never leaving it. One Communist told me with a kind of detached, amused pride that the university is, in short, a kind of substitute for a Soviet-Chinese-Cuban embassy.

Chapter 29—Summary to Conclude

The quotations from Presidents Kennedy and Johnson are from "The Alliance for Progress: Symbol and Substance," the two-part Senate speech by Robert F. Kennedy already cited. Chester Bowles, quoted by Vera Michaelis Dean, mentions the choice between bloody revolution and long-range democratic planning in *Builders of Emergent Nations*, p. 172. The apparent choice between Communism and rule by military junta is percipiently seen by John Paton Davies, Jr., in his *Harper's Magazine* article cited above. The quotations about collectivism from Dr. Roberto Campos are from "Relations Between the United States and Latin America," an article which I mention in my text and which is included in *Latin America: Evolution or Explosion*, the anthology edited by Mildred Adams. Arthur Schlesinger, Jr., *A Thousand Days*, p. 768, is my source for the quotation from President Kennedy. See also "Our Good Neighbors Should Come First," by John Plank, *New York Times Magazine*, May 6, 1965.

INDEX

Index

Format by Sidney Feinberg
Set in Linotype Electra
Composed, printed and bound by American Book–Stratford Press, Inc.
HARPER & ROW, PUBLISHERS, INCORPORATED